THE FIRST URBAN CHURCHES 7
THESSALONICA

WRITINGS FROM THE GRECO-ROMAN WORLD SUPPLEMENT SERIES

Clare K. Rothschild, General Editor

Number 21

THE FIRST URBAN CHURCHES 7
THESSALONICA

Edited by
James R. Harrison and L. L. Welborn

SBL PRESS

Atlanta

Copyright © 2022 by Society of Biblical Literature

All rights reserved. No part of this work may be reproduced or transmitted in any form or by any means, electronic or mechanical, including photocopying and recording, or by means of any information storage or retrieval system, except as may be expressly permitted by the 1976 Copyright Act or in writing from the publisher. Requests for permission should be addressed in writing to the Rights and Permissions Office, SBL Press, 825 Houston Mill Road, Atlanta, GA 30329 USA.

Library of Congress Cataloging-in-Publication Data

First urban churches / edited by James R. Harrison and L. L. Welborn.
    volumes cm. — (Society of Biblical Literature. Writings from the Greco-Roman world Supplement series ; Number 7)
    Includes bibliographical references.

    ISBN 978-1-62837-102-4 (v. 1 : pbk. : alk. paper) — ISBN 978-1-62837-104-8 (v. 1 : ebook) — ISBN 978-1-62837-103-1 (v. 1 : hardcover : alk. paper)
    ISBN 978-0-88414-111-2 (v. 2 : pbk. : alk. paper) — ISBN 978-0-88414-112-9 (v. 2 : ebook) — ISBN 978-0-88414-113-6 (v. 2 : hardcover : alk. paper)
    ISBN 978-0-88414-234-8 (v. 3 : pbk. : alk. paper) — ISBN 978-0-88414-235-5 (v. 3 : ebook) — ISBN 978-0-88414-236-2 (v. 3 : hardcover : alk. paper)
    ISBN 978-1-62837-226-7 (v. 4 : pbk. : alk. paper) — ISBN 978-0-88414-337-6 (v. 4 : ebook) — ISBN 978-0-88414-336-9 (v. 4 : hardcover : alk. paper)
    ISBN 978-1-62837-261-8 (v. 5 : pbk. : alk. paper) — ISBN 978-0-88414-418-2 (v. 5 : ebook) — ISBN 978-0-88414-419-9 (v. 5 : hardcover : alk. paper)
    ISBN 978-1-62837-400-1 (v. 6 : pbk. : alk. paper) — ISBN 978-0-88414-506-6 (v. 6 : ebook) — ISBN 978-0-88414-505-9 (v. 6 : hardcover : alk. paper)
    ISBN 978-1-62837-443-8 (v. 7 : pbk. : alk. paper) — ISBN 978-1-62837-445-2 (v. 7 : ebook) — ISBN 978-1-62837-444-5 (v. 7 : hardcover : alk. paper)
    1. City churches. 2. Church history—Primitive and early church, ca. 30–600. 3. Cities and towns—Religious aspects—Christianity. I. Harrison, James R., 1952– editor.
    BV637.F57 2015
    270.109173'2—dc23   2015021858

Contents

Abbreviations vii

An Epigraphic Profile of Thessalonica from the
Hellenistic Age to the Roman Empire
    James R. Harrison 1

Imperial Divine Honors in Julio-Claudian
Thessalonica and the Thessalonian Correspondence
    D. Clint Burnett..63

A Return to "Peace and Security": The Parts and the Whole
    Alan H. Cadwallader 93

"Times and Seasons" or "Peace and Security"?
Paul and the Clash of Eschatologies in Thessalonica
    Joel R. White..123

Infants, Orphans, Children, and Siblings:
Strengthening the Familial Bonds of the *Ekklēsia* of the
Thessalonians in God the Father and the Lord Jesus Christ
    Rosemary Canavan 151

The Emergence and Development of Christianity in
Thessalonica in the Postapostolic Age (Second through
Sixth Centuries CE): An Epigraphic and
Archaeological Perspective
    Julien M. Ogereau 175

"Sounding Forth": Reading the Thessalonians as God's
Musical Instrument
    Isaac T. Soon 237

Paul, the Jews, and the Thessalonians: New Observations
on 1 Thessalonians 2:14–16
     Angela Standhartinger 249

Gentle Philosopher, Rhetorician, or Selfless Benefactor?
Paul's Apostolic Image and Ethos in 1 Thessalonians 2:1–12
     James R. Harrison 269

Roman Provincial Coinage and Paul at Thessalonica
     Michael P. Theophilos.. 313

Contributors... 339
Ancient Sources Index.. 343
Modern Authors Index... 369

Abbreviations

Primary Sources

1 Clem.	1 Clement
1 En.	1 Enoch
1 Regn.	Dio Chrysostom, *De regno i* (*Or. 1*)
1 Tars.	Dio Chrysostom, *Tarsica prior* (*Or. 33*)
1QH^a	Hodayot^a *or* Thanksgiving Hymns^a
1QM	Milḥamah *or* War Scroll
1QS	Serek Hayaḥad *or* Rule of the Community
2 Bar.	2 Baruch (Syriac Apocalypse)
2 Tars.	Dio Chrysostom, *Tarsica altera* (*Or. 34*)
4 Regn.	Dio Chrysostom, *De regno iv* (*Or. 4*)
4Q181	Ages of Creation A
4Q390	apocryphon Jeremiah E
11Q13	Melchizedek
Adul. am.	Plutarch, *De adulatore et amico*
Aen.	Virgil, *Aeneid*
A.J.	Josephus, *Antiquitates judaicae*
Alex.	Dio Chrysostom, *Ad Alexandrinos* (*Or. 32*); Plutarch, *Alexander*
All.	Heraclitus, *Allegoriae* (*Quaestiones homericae*)
Amic.	Cicero, *De amicitia*
Ann.	Tacitus, *Annales*
Anth. Gr.	Anthologia Graeca
Ascen. Isa.	Martyrdom and Ascension of Isaiah 6–11
Asin.	Pseudo-Lucian, *Asinus (Lucius)*
Att.	Cicero, *Epistulae ad Atticum*
Aug.	Suetonius, *Divus Augustus*
Aul.	Plautus, *Aulularia*
Barn.	Barnabas

Bell. Cat.	Sallust, *Bellum catalinae*
Bell. civ.	Appian, *Bella civilia*
Bell. Jug.	Sallust, *Bellum jugurthinum*
Bib. hist.	Diodorus, *Bibliotheca historica*
Borysth.	Dio Chrysostom, *Borysthenitica* (*Or.* 36)
Brut.	Plutarch, *Brutus*
Caes.	Plutarch, *Caesar*
Cal.	Suetonius, *Gaius Caligula*
Capt.	Plautus, *Captivi*
Carm.	Horace, *Carmina*
Cat. Min.	Plutarch, *Cato Minor*
Cel. Phryg.	Dio Chrysostom, *Celaenis Phrygiae* (*Or.* 35)
Cic.	Plutarch, *Cicero*
Claud.	Suetonius, *Divus Claudius*
Clem.	Seneca, *De clementia*
Cod. justin.	Codex justinianus
Cod. theod.	Codex theodosianus
Com.	Naevius, *Comedies*
Comm. ser. Matt.	Origen, *Commentarium series in evangelium Matthaei*
Comp. Ages. Pomp.	Plutarch, *Comparatio Agesilai et Pompeii*
Const. ap.	Constitutiones apostolicae
Contempl.	Philo, *De vita contemplativa*
Cor.	Demosthenes, *De corona*
Corp. herm.	Corpus hermeticum
Crit.	Plato, *Critias*
Ctes.	Aeschines, *In Ctesiphonem*
Decal.	Philo, *De decalogo*
Def. orac.	Plutarch, *De defectu oraculorum*
Dem.	Dinarchus, *Contra Demosthenem*
Dial.	Justin, *Dialogus cum Tryphone*
Diatr.	Epictetus, *Diatribai (Dissertationes)*
Dig.	Digesta
Div.	Cicero, *De divinatione*
Dom.	Suetonius, *Domitianus*
Eleg.	Propertius, *Elegiae*
Ench.	Epictetus, *Enchiridion*
Ep.	*Epistula(e)*
Epict. diss.	Arrian, *Epicteti dissertationes*
Epigr.	Martial, *Epigrammata*

Epist.	Pseudo-Libanius, *Epistulae*
Epit.	Florus, *Epitome de T. Livio Bellorum omnium annorum DCC Libri duo*
Exil.	Dio Chrysostom, *De exilio* (*Or.* 13)
Fab. Aes.	Phaedrus, *Fabularum Aesopiarum libri quinque*
Fact. dict.	Valerius Maximus, *Factorum ac dictorum memorabilium libri IX*
Fast.	Ovid, *Fasti*
Fin.	Cicero, *De finibus*
Flacc.	Philo, *In Flaccum*
Frag.	*Fragmenta*
Geogr.	Strabo, *Geographica*
Georg.	Virgil, *Georgica*
Gos. Pet.	Gospel of Peter
Gramm.	Suetonius, *De grammaticis*
Hab.	Dio Chrysostom, *De habitu* (*Or.* 72)
Hell. Per.	Pausanias, *Hellados Periegesis*
Her.	Philo, *Quis rerum divinarum heres sit*
Hipp.	Euripides, *Hippolytus*
Hist.	Cassius Dio, *Historia romana*; Herodotus, *Historiae*; Polybius, *Historiae*; Tacitus, *Historiae*; Thucydides, *History of the Peloponnesian War*
Hist. Aug.	Historia Augusta
Hist. eccl.	*Historia ecclesiastica*
Hist. Rom.	Velleius Paterculus, *Historia romana*
Hom.	*Homiliae*
Hymn. Hom.	Homerici hymni
Ign. *Eph.*	Ignatius, *To the Ephesians*
Ign. *Phld.*	Ignatius, *To the Philadelphians*
Ign. *Rom.*	Ignatius, *To the Romans*
Il.	Homer, *Ilias*
Imag.	Philostratus, *Imagines*
In cont.	Dio Chrysostom, *In contione* (*Or.* 48)
Inst.	Gaius, *Institutiones*; Quintilian, *Institutio oratoria*
Irr. gent. phil.	Hermias, *Irrisio gentilium philosophorum*
Isthm.	Dio Chrysostom, *Isthmiaca* (*Or.* 9)
Jul.	Suetonius, *Divus Julius*
LAB	Liber antiquitatum biblicarum
Leg.	Cicero, *De legibus*; Plato, *Leges*

Leuc. Clit.	Achilles Tatius, *Leucippe et Clitophon*
LXX	Septuagint
Marc.	Tertullian, *Adversus Marcionem*
Mil.	Cicero, *Pro Milone*
Mor.	Plutarch, *Moralia*
Mus.	Pseudo-Plutarch, *De musica*
Nat.	Pliny the Elder, *Naturalis historia*
Nic.	Isocrates, *Nicocles*
Noct. att.	Aulus Gellius, *Noctes atticae*
Nov. const.	Novellae Constitutiones
Od.	Homer, *Odyssea*
Off.	Cicero, *De officiis*
Onom.	Pollox, *Onomasticon*
Parad.	Cicero, *Paradoxa Stoicorum*
Peregr.	Lucian, *De morte Peregrini*
Phaed.	Plato, *Phaedo*
Phaedr.	Plato, *Phaedrus*
Phoc.	Plutarch, *Phocion*
Pis.	Cicero, *In Pisonem*
Pol.	Aristotle, *Politica*
Pol. *Phil.*	Polycarp, *To the Philippians*
Pomp.	Plutarch, *Pompeius*
Praec. ger. rei publ.	Plutarch, *Praecepta gerendae rei publicae*
Ps.-Clem.	Pseudo-Clementines
Pss. Sol.	Psalms of Solomon
Pyth. orac.	Plutarch, *De Pythiae oraculis*
Rab. Post.	Cicero, *Pro Rabirio Postumo*
Rep.	Cicero, *De republica*
Res gest. divi Aug.	Res gestae divi Augusti
Rhet.	Pseudo-Dionysius, *Ars rhetorica*
S. Olam Rab.	Seder Olam Rabbah
Saec.	Horace, *Carmen saeculare*
Sat.	Juvenal, *Satirae*
Saturn.	Macrobius, *Saturnaliorum Libri Septem*
Satyr.	Petronius, *Satyricon*
Sept. sap. conv.	Plutarch, *Septem sapientium convivium*
Serv.	Dio Chrysostom, *De servis (Or. 10)*
Silv.	Statius, *Silvae*
Sol.	Plutarch, *Solon*

Stoic. rep.	Plutarch, *De Stoicorum repugnantiis*
Strat.	Frontinus, *Strategemata*
Strom.	Clement, *Stromateis*
Sull.	Cicero, *Pro Sulla*; Plutarch, *Sulla*
T. Benj.	Testament of Benjamin
T. Levi	Testament of Levi
T. Mos.	Testament of Moses
T. Naph.	Testament of Naphtali
Thes.	Plutarch, *Theseus*
Thuc.	Dionysius of Halicarnassus, *De Thucydide*
Tib.	Suetonius, *Tiberius*
Tim.	Plato, *Timaeus*
Trist.	Ovid, *Tristia*
Tro.	Euripides, *Troades*
Tusc.	Cicero, *Tusculanae disputationes*
Tyr.	Dio Chrysostom, *De tyrannide* (*Or.* 6)
Virt.	Dio Chrysostom, *De virtute* (*Or.* 8)
Vit. Ant.	Plutarch, *Vita Antonii*

Secondary Sources

ΑΘ	Αρχαια Θεατρα
AASS	*Acta Sanctorum Quotquot Toto Orbe Coluntur.* Antwerp, 1643–
AB	Anchor Bible
ABSA	*Annual of the British School at Athens*
AEC	*Archaiologike Ephemeris 1981, Chronika*
AD	*Archaiologikon Deltion*
AEMT	*To archaiologiko ergo ste Makedonia kai ste Thrake*
AF	*Archäologische Forschungen*
AHES	*Archive for History of Exact Sciences*
AJA	*American Journal of Archaeology*
AJEC	Ancient Judaism and Early Christianity
AJP	*American Journal of Philology*
AmJT	*American Journal of Theology*
AMNG	Imhoof-Blumer, Friedrich, ed. *Die antiken Münzen Nord-Griechenlands.* 6 vols. in 4. Berlin: Reimer, 1898–1935.
AMT	Archaeological Museum of Thessaloniki

ANF	*The Ante-Nicene Fathers*. Edited by Alexander Roberts and James Donaldson. 1885–1887. 10 vols. Repr., Peabody, MA: Hendrickson, 1994.
ANRW	Temporini, Hildegard, and Wolfgang Haase, eds. *Aufstieg und Niedergang der r.mischen Welt: Geschichte und Kultur Roms im Spiegel der neueren Forschung*. Part 2, Principat. Berlin: de Gruyter, 1972–.
ANS	American Numismatic Society
ANTF	Arbeiten zur neutestamentlichen Textforschung
ApOTC	Apollos Old Testament Commentary
APR	Ancient Philosophy and Religion
ASAtene	*Annuario della Scuola Archeologica di Atene e delle Missioni Italiane in Oriente*
AT	*Antiquité Tardive*
BCH	*Bulletin de correspondance hellénique*
BCHSup	*Bulletin de correspondance hellénique Supplément*
BDAG	Danker, Frederick W., Walter Bauer, William F. Arndt, and F. Wilbur Gingrich. *Greek-English Lexicon of the New Testament and Other Early Christian Literature*. 3rd ed. Chicago: University of Chicago Press, 2000.
BDF	Blass, Friedrich, Albert Debrunner, and Robert W. Funk. *A Greek Grammar of the New Testament and Other Early Christian Literature*. Chicago: University of Chicago Press, 1961.
BE	*Bulletin épigraphique*
BECNT	Baker Exegetical Commentary on the New Testament
BETL	Bibliotheca Ephemeridum Theologicarum Lovaniensium
BGU	*Aegyptische Urkunden aus den Königlichen (later Staatlichen) Museen zu Berlin, Griechische Urkunden*. Berlin, 1895–.
BHG	Halkin, François, ed. *Bibliotheca Hagiographica Graeca*. 3rd ed. 3 vols. Brussels: Société des Bollandistes, 1986.
Bib	*Biblica*
BibInt	*Biblical Interpretation*
BMC	*British Museum Catalogue*

BMC Macedonia	Head, Barclay V., and Reginald Stuart. *British Museum Catalogue of Greek Coins, Macedonia, etc.* London, 1879.
BNTC	Black's New Testament Commentary
BR	*Biblical Research*
BSac	*Bibliotheca Sacra*
BSGRE	Brill Studies in Greek and Roman Epigraphy
BTB	*Biblical Theology Bulletin*
BWANT	Beiträge zur Wissenschaft vom Alten und Neuen Testament
ByzZ	*Byzantinische Zeitschrift*
BZAW	Beihefte zur Zeitschrift für die alttestamentliche Wissenschaft
BZNW	Beihefte zur Zeitschrift für die neutestamentliche Wissenschaft
CAH	Bury, J. B., et al., eds. *The Cambridge Ancient History*. 12 vols. Cambridge: Cambridge University Press, 1923–1939.
CahA	*Cahiers archéologiques*
CBET	Contributions to Biblical Exegesis and Theology
CBQ	*Catholic Biblical Quarterly*
CCS	Cincinnati Classical Studies
CIG	Boeckh, August, ed. *Corpus Inscriptionum Graecarum*. 4 vols. Berlin, 1828–1877.
CIJ	*Corpus inscriptionum judacarum*. Vatican City: Pontifico Instituto di Archeologia Christiana, 1936–1952.
CIL	*Corpus Inscriptionum Latinarum*. Berlin, 1862–.
CIRB	Struve, Vasilii, ed. *Corpus inscriptionum regni Bosporani*. Moscow, 1965.
ClQ	*Classical Quarterly*
CNG	Classical Numismatic Group
CNT	Commentaire du Nouveau Testament
ConBNT	Coniectanea Biblica: New Testament Series
COQG	Christians Origins and the Question of God
CP	*Classical Philology*
DBAT	Dielheimer Blätter zum Alten Testament und seiner Rezeption in der Alten Kirche
DOP	*Dumbarton Oaks Papers*

DSSSE	García Martínez, Florentino, and Eibert J. C. Tigchelaar, eds. *Dead Sea Scrolls Study Edition*. 2 vols. Leiden: Brill, 1995.
EA	*Epigraphica Anatolica*
EC	*Early Christianity*
ECL	Early Christianity and Its Literature
EKKNT	Evangelisch-katholischer Kommentar zum Neuen Testament
ENTRAMT	Essays on the New Testament and Related Ancient Mediterranean Texts
EO	*Échos d'Orient*
ETL	*Ephemerides Theologicae Lovanienses*
FD	*Fouilles de Delphes. 3. Épigraphie.* Paris, 1929
FRLANT	Forschungen zur Religion und Literatur des Alten und Neuen Testaments
FS	*Foucault Studies*
GNT	Grundrisse zum Neuen Testament
GRBS	*Greek, Roman, and Byzantine Studies*
Hesperia	*Hesperia: Journal of the American School of Classical Studies at Athens*
Historia	*Historia: Zeitschrift für alte Geschichte*
HNT	Handbuch zum Neuen Testament
HSCP	*Harvard Studies in Classical Philology*
HTR	*Harvard Theological Review*
HTS	Harvard Theological Studies
HUT	Hermeneutische Untersuchungen zur Theologie
HvST	*Hervormde Teologiese Studies (HTS Teologiese Studies/HTS Theological Studies)*
IAnkyra	Mitchell, Stephen, and David French, eds. *The Greek and Latin Inscriptions of Ankara (Ancyra)*. 2 vols. München: Beck, 2012–2019.
IAph	Reynolds, Joyce, Charlotte Roueché, and Gabriel Bodard, eds. *Inscriptions of Aphrodisias*. 2007. http://insaph.kcl.ac.uk/iaph2007.
IAssos	Melkelbach, R., ed. *Die Inschriften von Assos*. Bonn, 1976.
IBC	Interpretation: A Bible Commentary for Teaching and Preaching

IBethShe'arim	Schwabe, M., and B. Lifshitz, eds. *Beth She'arim.* Vol. 2, *The Greek Inscriptions.* Jerusalem, 1974.
ICC	International Critical Commentary
ICG	Breytenbach, Cilliers, et al., eds. Inscriptiones Christianae Graecae (ICG): A Digital Collection of Early Christian Greek Inscriptions from Asia Minor and Greece. Berlin: Edition Topoi. http://repository.edition-topoi.org/collection/ICG. doi:10.17171/1-8.
IDelph	Lefévre, François, ed. *Corpus des inscripons de Delphes.* Vol. 4, *Documents Amphictioniques.* Paris, 2002.
IEph	Wankel, Hermann, et al., eds. *Die Inschriften von Ephesos.* 8 vols. Bonn: Habelt, 1979–1984.
IFayum	Bernand, E., ed. *Recueil des inscriptions grecques du Fayoum.* 3 vols. Leiden: Brill, 1975–1981.
IG	*Inscriptiones Graecae.* Editio Minor. Berlin: de Gruyter, 1924–.
IG 10.2.1	Edson, Charles. *Inscriptiones Thessalonicae et viciniae.* Fasc. 1 of *Inscriptiones Macedoniae.* Part 2 of *Inscriptiones Graecae X: Epiri, Macedoniae, Thraciae, Scythiae.* Berlin: de Gruyter, 1972.
IG 10.2.1s	Nigelis, Pantelis M. *Inscriptiones Thessalonicae et viciniae, Supplementum Primum.* Berlin: de Gruyter, 2017.
IGBulg	Mihailov, G., ed. *Inscriptiones Graecae in Bulgaria repertae.* Sofia, 1956–1970.
IIasos	Blümel, W., ed. *Die Inschriften von Iasos.* 2 vols. Bonn, 1985.
IItalia	Degrassi, A., ed. *Inscriptiones Italiae XIII: Fasti et Elogia.* Rome, 1937.
IJO	Noy, David, et al., eds. *Inscriptiones Judaicae Orientis.* 3 vols. TSAJ 99, 101, 102. Tübingen: Mohr Siebeck, 2004.
IKorinthMeritt	Meritt, B. D., ed. *Corinth.* 8.1, *Greek Inscriptions 1896–1927.* Cambridge, MA, 1931.
ILindos	Blinkenberg, C., ed. *Lindos.* Vol. 2, *Inscriptions.* Copenhagen, 1941.
IMagnMai	Kern, O., ed. *Die Inschriften von Magnesia am Maeander.* Berlin, 1900.

IMaked	Rizakis, T., and G. Touratsoglou. Ἐπιγραφὲς Ἄνω Μακεδονίας. Vol. 1, Κατάλογος ἐπιγραφῶν. Athens, 1985.
IMakedChr	Feissel, Denis, ed. *Recueil des inscriptions chrétiennes de Macédoine du IIIe au VIe siècle*. BCHSup 8. Athens: École Française d'Athènes, 1983.
IMylasa	Blümel, W., ed. *Die Inschriften von Mylasa*. I. *Inschriften der Stadt*. Bonn, 1987.
Int	Interpretation
IPriene	Gaertringen, F. Hiller von, ed. *Inschriften von Priene*. Berlin, 1906.
ISBE	*International Standard Bible Encyclopedia*. Edited by Geoffrey W. Bromiley. 4 vols. Grand Rapids: Eerdmans, 1979–1988.
IStratonikeia	Sahin, C., ed. *Die Inschriften von Stratonikeia*. Bonn, 1981–1990.
IT	Edson, C., ed. *Inscriptiones Thessalonicae et viciniae*. 1972.
IThess	Nigdelis, Pantelis M., ed. *Epigraphika Thessalonikeia: Symvole sten politike kai koinonike historia tes archaias Thessalonikes*. Thessalonike: University Studio Press, 2006.
IVPNTC	IVP New Testament Commentary
JACSup	Jahrbuch für Antike und Christentum Ergänzungsband
JBL	*Journal of Biblical Literature*
JdI	*Jahrbuch des Deutschen Archäologischen Instituts*
JECH	*Journal of Early Christian History*
JECS	*Journal of Early Christian Studies*
JEH	*Journal of Ecclesiastical History*
JETS	*Journal of the Evangelical Theological Society*
JHS	*Journal of Hellenic Studies*
JIH	*Journal of Interdisciplinary History*
JÖB	*Jahrbuch der Österreichischen Byzantinistik*
JRA	*Journal of Roman Archaeology*
JRS	*Journal of Roman Studies*
JRSM	Journal of Roman Studies Monographs
JSJ	*Journal for the Study of Judaism in the Persian, Hellenistic, and Roman Periods*

JSJSup	Journal for the Study of Judaism Supplement Series
JSNT	*Journal for the Study of the New Testament*
JSNTSup	Journal for the Study of the New Testament Supplement Series
JSP	*Journal for the Study of the Pseudepigrapha*
JTS	*Journal of Theological Studies*
JTSA	*A Journal of Theology for Southern Africa*
KEK	Kritisch-exegetischer Kommentar über das Neue Testament (Meyer-Kommentar)
KFF	Herzog, Rudolf, ed. *Koische Forschungen und Funde*. Leipzig, 1899.
LCL	Loeb Classical Library
LD	Lectio Divina
LNTS	Library of New Testament Studies
LSJ	Liddell, Henry George, Robert Scott, Henry Stuart Jones. *A Greek-English Lexicon*. 9th ed. with revised supplement. Oxford: Clarendon, 1996.
MA	*Mediterranean Archaeology*
MedMed	The Medieval Mediterranean
MEFR	*Mélanges d'archéologie et d'histoire de l'École française de Rome*
MillSt	Millennium Studies
MJBK	*Münchner Jahrbuch der bildenden Kunst*
MM	Moulton, James H., and George Milligan. *The Vocabulary of the Greek Testament*. London, 1930. Repr., Peabody, MA: Hendrickson, 1997.
MMFEP	*Monuments et mémoires de la Fondation Eugène Piot*
MRR	Broughton, T. R. S. *The Magistrates of the Roman Republic*. 3 vols. Atlanta: Scholars Press, 1951–1986.
MS Vat. lat. 5729	Manuscript Vatican lat. 5729. Vatican, Biblioteca Apostolica Vaticana.
NA[27]	*Novum Testamentum Graece*, Nestle-Aland, 27th ed.
NA[28]	*Novum Testamentum Graece*, Nestle-Aland, 28th ed.
NB	*Niš and Byzantium*
NCB	New Century Bible
NCCS	New Covenant Commentary Series
NedTT	*Nederlands theologische tijdschrift*
NewDocs	*New Documents Illustrating Early Christianity*. Edited by Greg H. R. Horsley and Stephen Llewelyn. North

	Ryde, NSW: The Ancient History Documentary Research Centre, Macquarie University, 1981–.
NIBIJ	*Nāme-ye Irān-e Bāstān: The International Journal of Ancient Iranian Studies*
NICNT	New International Commentary on the New Testament
NIGTC	New International Greek Testament Commentary
NIV	New International Version
NKJV	New King James Version
NovT	*Novum Testamentum*
NovTSup	Supplements to Novum Testamentum
NRSV	New Revised Standard Version
NTD	Das Neue Testament Deutsch
NTOA	Novum Testamentum et Orbis Antiquus
NTS	*New Testament Studies*
O.Claud.	Bingen, J., A. Bülow-Jacobsen, W. E. H. Cockle, H. Cuvigny, L. Rubinstein, and W. Van Rengen, eds. *Mons Claudianus. Ostraca graeca et latina.* Vol. 1. Cairo, 1992.
OGI	Dittenberger, W., ed. *Orientis graeci inscriptiones selectae.* 2 vols. Leipzig, 1903–1905.
ÖTK	Ökumenischer Taschenbuch-Kommentar
PACS	Philo of Alexandria Commentary Series
PCC	Paul in Critical Contexts
PG	Patrologia Graeca [= *Patrologiae Cursus Completus*: Series Graeca]. Edited by Jacques-Paul Migne. 162 vols. Paris, 1857–1886.
PGL	*Patristic Greek Lexicon.* Edited by Geoffrey W. H. Lampe. Oxford: Clarendon, 1961.
PIR[1]	Klebs, Elimar, and Hermann Dessau, eds. *Prosopographia Imperii Romani Saeculi I, II, III.* 3 vols. Berlin: Reimer, 1897–1989.
PIR[2]	Groag, Edmund, et al., eds. *Prosopographia Imperii Romani Saeculi I, II, III.* 2nd ed. Berlin: de Gruyter, 1933–.
PL	Patrologia Latina [= *Patrologiae Cursus Completus*: Series Latina]. Edited by Jacques-Paul Migne. 217 vols. Paris, 1844–1864.
PLB	Papyrologica Lugduno-Batava

PNTC	Pillar New Testament Commentaries
P.Oxy.	Grenfell, Bernard P., et al., eds. *The Oxyrhynchus Papyri*. London: Egypt Exploration Fund, 1898–.
PRSt	*Perspectives in Religious Studies*
PSI	*Papiri greci e latini.* (Pubblicazioni della Società Italiana per la ricerca dei papiri greci e latini in Egitto). Florence.
PSN	Paul's Social Network
PW	*Paulys Real-Encyclop.die der classischen Altertumswissenschaft*. New edition by Georg Wissowa and Wilhelm Kroll. 50 vols. in 84 parts. Stuttgart: Metzler and Druckenmüller, 1894–1980.
PWSup	*Supplement to PW*
RAC	*Reallexikon für Antike und Christentum*. Edited by Theodor Klauser et al. Stuttgart: Hiersemann, 1950–.
RB	*Revue biblique*
RevEB	*Revue des études byzantines*
RevPhil	*Revue de philologie*
RGRW	Religions in the Graeco-Roman World
RHE	*Revue d'histoire ecclésiastique*
RHPR	*Revue d'histoire et de philosophie religieuses*
RIC 1	Sutherland, C. H. V. *Roman Imperial Coinage.* Vol. 1, *31 BC to AD 69, Augustus to Vitellius.* 2nd ed. London: Spink, 1984.
RN	*Revue Numismatique*
RPC	Burnett, Andrew, Michel Amandry, and Ian Carradice. *Roman Provincial Coinage.* Vols. 1–2. London: British Museum, 1992–1999.
SBB	Stuttgarter biblische Beiträge
SBLDS	Society of Biblical Literature Dissertation Series
SBLSBS	Society of Biblical Literature Sources for Biblical Study
SBS	Stuttgarter Bibelstudien
SEG	Supplementum epigraphicum graecum
SH	Subsidia Hagiographica
SHBC	Smyth & Helwys Bible Commentary
SIG	Dittenberger, Wilhelm, ed. *Sylloge inscriptionum graecarum.* 4 vols. 3rd ed. Leipzig: Hirzel, 1915–1924.

SNG Ash	Kraay, C. M. *Sylloge Nummorum Graecorum: Great Britain 5. Ashmolean Museum (Oxford): Pt. 4, Paeonia-Thessaly*. London: Oxford University Press, 1981.
SNG Cop	*Sylloge Nummorum Graecorum, Denmark: The Royal Collection of Coins and Medals, Danish National Museum*. 43 parts. Copenhagen: Munksgaard, 1942–1979.
SNTSMS	Society for New Testament Studies Monograph Series
SP	Sacra Pagina
SR	*Studies in Religion*
STAC	Studien und Texte zu Antike und Christentum
STCP	Studi e testi per il Corpus dei papiri filosofici greci e latini
Syll²	Dittenberger, W., ed. *Sylloge inscriptionum graecarum*. 2nd ed. Leipzig, 1901.
TAM	Kalinka, Ernst, et al., eds. *Tituli Asiae Minoris*. Vienna: Verlag der Österreichischen Akademie der Wissenschaften, 1901–.
TANZ	Texte und Arbeiten zum neutestamentlichen
TBN	Themes in Biblical Narrative
THKNT	Theologischer Handkommentar zum Neuen Testament
TLZ	*Theologische Literaturzeitung*
TM	*Travaux et Mémoires*
TNTC	Tyndale New Testament Commentaries
TSAJ	Texte und Studien zum antiken Judentum
TynBul	*Tyndale Bulletin*
VC	*Vigiliae Christianae*
VCSup	Vigiliae Christianae Supplements
VerbEccl	*Verbum et Ecclesia*
WBC	Word Biblical Commentary
WMANT	Wissenschaftliche Monographien zum Alten und Neuen Testament
WUNT	Wissenschaftliche Untersuchungen zum Neuen Testament
XA	Xenia Antiqua
ZNW	*Zeitschrift für die neutestamentliche Wissenschaft und die Kunde der älteren Kirche*
ZPE	*Zeitschrift für Papyrologie und Epigraphik*

An Epigraphic Profile of Thessalonica from the Hellenistic Age to the Roman Empire

James R. Harrison

Founded by King Cassander of Macedon in 315 BCE and named after his wife, Thessalonike, the half-sister of Alexander the Great, Thessalonica developed into a strong, independent Hellenistic city until Rome's conquest of Macedonia in 168 BCE. Upon the construction of the Via Egnatia between 146 and 120 BCE—the Roman highway stretching from the Adriatic Sea to Thessalonica[1]—the city became a major commercial center and the capital of the Roman imperial province of Macedonia due to its strategic position as the conduit between the East and the West. This was aided by its proximity to the city's harbor on the nearby Aegean Sea, providing direct access to Roman Corinth via its harbor port of Cenchreae. As a result, the city possessed two significant advantages: it was the site of the Roman governor's residence and its security was ensured by the presence of Roman troops therein. A faithful ally to Rome during the civil war, astutely shifting its alliances to the eventual winner during this period,[2] Thessalonica was honored with freedom (*civitas liberae condicionis*) in 42 BCE (Pliny the Elder, *Nat.* 4.36; see *IG* 10.2.1.6). This allowed the city self-governance, the right to mint imperial and autonomous coin issues, and

---

1. On the important discovery of a 70-m section of the Via Egnatia unearthed in a Greek subway dig at Thessalonike in 2012, see "Ancient Road Unearthed in Greek Subway Dig," CBC News, 26 June 2012, https://tinyurl.com/SBL4221a. This essay will not discuss the material evidence of later Christian Thessalonica. See Cilliers Breytenbach and Ingrid Behrmann, *Frühchristliches Thessaloniki*, STAC 44 (Tübingen: Mohr Siebeck, 2007). See also the essay of Julien Ogereau in this volume.

2. On the shifting alliances of Thessalonica, see Callia Rulmu, "Between Ambition and Quietism: The Socio-political Background of 1 Thessalonians 4:9–12," *Bib* 91 (2010): 396–97.

freedom from taxation. In 44 BCE the province was transferred to senatorial status, with the result that the distinctively Macedonian civic officials, the politarchs (see Acts 17:6, 8),[3] became the leading civic officials in Thessalonica, functioning as judges and council members and, in some cases, also as members of the *koinon*, the provincial council of Macedonia.

Few archaeological remains of the first-century CE city that the apostle Paul visited are extant.[4] Long before this, there is evidence of an archaic temple (500 BCE):[5] but by the time of the Hellenistic period, the city was based on orthogonal planning and was protected by a fortification wall. Its public buildings were located around an agora, whose existence is confirmed by a 60 BCE inscription (*IG* 10.2.1.5, ll. 7–9, 19–20).[6] The extant structures included a serapeum, a gymnasium and bathhouse, a *praetorium* belonging to the republican period, and two cemeteries in the northwest region of Neapolis. Toward the end of the first century CE, a new complex of public buildings was established for the city's burgeoning needs: a new forum and row of shops to the southeast and a theater-stadium were undertaken.[7]

---

3. See n. 41 below.

4. On Hellenistic Thessalonica, see Michael Vickers, "Hellenistic Thessaloniki," *JHS* 92 (1972): 156–70. On Hellenistic and Roman Thessalonica, see Christoph vom Brocke, *Thessaloniki – Stadt des Kassander und Gemeinde des Paulus: Ein frühe christliche Gemeinde in ihrer heidnischen Umwelt*, WUNT 2/125 (Tübingen: Mohr Siebeck, 2001), 22–73; Polyxeni Adam-Velini, "Thessalonike: History and Town Planning," in *Roman Thessaloniki*, ed. Dēmētrios V. Gramenos (Thessaloniki: Thessaloniki Archaeological Museum, 2003), 121–76. See also Hëlmut Koester, "Archäologie und Paulus," in *Religious Propaganda and Missionary Competition in the New Testament World*, ed. Lukas Borman, Kelly Del Tredici, and Angela Standhartinger, NovTSup 74 (Leiden: Brill, 1994), 393–404.

5. On the archaic temple, see Christopher Steimle, *Religion im römischen Thessaloniki. Sakraltopographie, Kult und Gesellschaft 168. Chr.–324 n. Chr.*, STAC 47 (Tübingen: Mohr Siebeck, 2008), 28–49.

6. A measure of caution is apposite here. The two occurrences of ἀγορά are either fully or partially restored (*IG* 10.2.1.5, l. 9 [ἀγορᾶς], l. 20 ἀγ[ορᾶς]). The partial restoration of ἀγορά in line 20 makes the full restoration of line 9 more likely, especially given that the same highly formulaic phrase is proposed for the original Greek inscription in each case: "in the most prominent place of the agora."

7. On the theater-stadium, see Michael Vickers, "The Theater-Stadium at Thessaloniki," *Byzantion* 41 (1971): 339–48; Adam-Velini, "Thessalonike: History and Town Planning," 157–59; vom Brocke, *Thessaloniki*, 60–64. Whether the second-century

Recent scholarship on the intersection of the discipline of archaeology with New Testament studies, however, has highlighted some of the inadequate methodological assumptions that have placed in question some of the "assured" results proposed for Paul's letters in their archaeological context.[8] Consequently, we will undertake an epigraphic profile of Hellenistic and Roman Thessalonica and bring in supplementary archaeological and numismatic perspectives where they throw light on the evidence of the inscriptions.[9] From there we will posit how central motifs in the epigraphic evidence intersect with the New Testament documents and the Thessalonian epistles in particular. Hopefully a more cautious approach to assessing the Thessalonian evidence will emerge. We commence with an epigraphic evaluation of Thessalonian honorific culture.

1. Thessalonian Honorific Culture from the Hellenistic Age to the Early Empire

1.1. Hellenistic Thessalonica: Divine and Human Honors

Four inscriptions from the collection of Charles Edson give insight into the honorific culture, human and divine, in Hellenistic Thessalonica. In a fragmentary decree (230 BCE), two individuals, having served as soldiers by the side of King Demetrius II of Macedon (239–229 BCE), are eulogized for their services to the city (*IG* 10.2.1.1). In another fragmentary decree, datable to July 223 BCE in the reign of Antigonus III (229–221 BCE), five Macedonian figures are honored, including a priest (*IG* 10.2.1.2). In the only dedication to royal figures, King Philip and King Demetrius are honored, but with no further clues to context or date (*IG* 10.2.1.25). The most important inscription from this period, an ordinance of King Philip V in the month of May 187 BCE (*IG* 10.2.1.3), touches on the divine honor of

---

CE Odeion was an expansion of a prior first-century CE Odeion is a moot point in modern scholarship.

8. Laura Salah Nasrallah, *Archaeology and the Pauline Letters* (Oxford: Oxford University Press, 2019); Cavan Concannon, "Archaeology and the Pauline Letters," in *The Oxford Handbook of Pauline Studies*, ed. Matthew K. Novenson and R. Barry Matlock (Oxford: Oxford University Press, 2020), 5–7.

9. For the Thessalonian inscriptions, see *IG* 10.2.1; IThess; *IG* 10.2.1s. For a commentary on Edson's volume, see Louis Robert, "Les inscriptions de Thessalonique," *RevPhil* 48 (1974): 180–246.

the property of Egyptian god Serapis, to whom a sanctuary was devoted at Hellenistic Thesssalonica.[10] The ordinance is set out below:

> Ordinance issued by King Philippos (V). And from Serapis' property let no one alienate anything in any manner nor pledge any of the other dedications nor introduce concerning these a decree. But if anyone does any of the things that have been forbidden, [he shall be] subject to the punishment for theft; and after exaction of the (amount) alienated from his property, it shall be restored to the sanctuary. And similarly, the treasuries of the god shall not be opened [without] the (presence of the) *epistates*, and the judges nor the money before them be expended carelessly but [with] their knowledge. And if not, let the person who did any of these things be subject to [the same] penalties.[11]

The mention of the royal official titled *epistates* (ἐπιστάτης) at the treasury of the serapeum, who was based at Thessalonica to oversee the money of the sanctuary,[12] makes it likely that the temple had royal patronage: otherwise, why would the treasury funds be inspected by a royal official? Consequently, Sarah Pomeroy and colleagues propose that "the Hellenistic rulers manipulated religion in their own interests," with the result that, as Edward Pillar concludes, "the ruler's interests are less for the worship of

---

10. For discussion of the Hellenistic serapeum at Thessalonica, see Vickers, "Hellenistic Thessaloniki," 164–65; vom Brocke, *Thessaloniki*, 37–41; Steimle, *Religion im römischen Thessaloniki*, 81–88; Helmut Koester, "Egyptian Religion in Thessalonike: Regulation for the Cult," in *From Roman to Early Christian Thessalonike: Studies in Religion and Archaeology*, ed. Laura Nasrallah, Charalambos Bakirtzis, and Steven J. Friesen, HTS 64 (Cambridge: Harvard University Press, 2010), 134–39; Angeliki Koukouvou, "The Sarapieion: The Sanctuary of the Egyptian Gods Rises from the City's Ashes," in *Archaeology behind Battle Lines in Thessaloniki of the Turbulent Years 1912–1922*, ed. Polyxeni Adam-Veleni and Angeliki Koukouvou, AMT 19 (Thessaloniki: Ministry of Education and Religious Affairs, Culture and Sport, 2012), 104–11; Lindsey A. Mazurek, "Globalizing the Sculptural Landscapes of the Sarapis and Isis Cults in Hellenistic and Roman Greece" (PhD diss., Duke University, 2016), 182–216. On Egyptian deities at Thessalonica, see Rex Witt, "The Egyptian Cults in Ancient Macedonia," in *Ancient Macedonia: Papers Read at the First International Symposium Held in Thessaloniki, 26–29 August 1968*, ed. Basil Laourdas and Ch. Makaronas (Thessaloniki: Institute for Balkan Studies, 1970), 324–33; Steimle, *Religion im römischen Thessaloniki*, 79–132; Koester, "Egyptian Religion in Thessalonike," 133–50.

11. Trans. Stanley M. Burstein, ed. and trans., *The Hellenistic Age from the Battle of Ipsos to the Death of Kleopotra VII* (Cambridge: Cambridge University Press, 1985), §72.

12. LSJ, s.v., "ἐπιστατεία," III: "keeper of treasury or archives."

the gods and more for seeking to pursue political goals."[13] There is little doubt that the Macedonian king acquired the ready cooperation of the Thessalonian elites through his patronage. But simultaneously his regime gained the divine blessing of Serapis, a powerful Egyptian god whose influence throughout Greece was increasingly expanding and whose worship was worth cultivating.[14] However, despite the power and prestige of the serapeum in the ensuing Roman period, evidenced by its large number of worshipers, "its relationship to the authorities of the city is unknown,"[15] in contrast to the Hellenistic era.

Finally, Pomeroy's polarization of religious and political aims misunderstands the intersection of the divine world with the earthly realm of the political ruler, who became a conduit of the gods' blessings within the cities of his empire on behalf of his subjects. There was a mutuality and interdependence in the relationship that must not be minimalized by modern skepticism and our predilection to separate religion from politics. In the Hellenistic age the civic authorities of Thessalonica honored dignitaries on whom the safety of the city depended (e.g., the well-disposed soldiers of the Macedonian king, priests of the local cults) and above all the Macedonian king himself, ensuring that his beneficence was extended to the city in significant ways, especially in the divine realm.

1.2. Republican Luminaries

A surprising amount of republican epigraphy has survived from Thessalonica, but the following epigraphic examples are revealing in regard to (1) the history of the city at various junctures, (2) their focus on Roman honorands, and (3) the motivations of those erecting the inscriptions in

---

13. Sarah B. Pomeroy et al., *Ancient Greece: A Political, Social, and Colonial History* (Oxford: Oxford University Press, 1999), 468; Edward Pillar, *Resurrection as Antiimperial Gospel: 1 Thessalonians 1:9b–10* (Minneapolis: Fortress, 2013), 83.

14. Ludovic Lefebvre writes: "C'est dans ce contexte d'effervescence spirituelle et politique que la diffusion de Sarapis a été possible. Elle a été favorisée par ces «brassages de populations», constituées notamment de voyageurs, de mercenaires, de marchands et d'aventuriers." See Lefebvre, "La diffusion du culte de Sarapis en Grèce continentale et dans les îles de l'Égée au IIIe siècle avant J.-C.," *RHPR* 88 (2008): 464.

15. Katerina Tzanavari, "The Worship of Gods and Heroes in Thessaloniki," in Gramenos, *Roman Thessaloniki*, 246. For a Roman marble head of Serapis (150–200 CE), excavated from the area of the serapeum and copied from a Hellenistic type, see Tzanavari, "Worship of Gods and Heroes," 245, fig. 43.

some instances. First, there is the highly restored Thessalonian decree that honors Metellus "Macedonicus" thus: "The c[ity] (honours) Quintus Caeci[lius son of Quintus Metellus], praetor [of the Romans], its sa[viour and benefactor]" (*IG* 10.2.1.134).[16] The occasion of the honor was Metellus's delivery of Thessalonica from the uprising of Andriscus (Pseudo-Philip VI) in 148 BCE. Andriscus was a powerful pretender to the Macedonian throne, which had been vacated after Rome had defeated Perseus in 168 BCE. Claiming to be Perseus's son in 150 BCE, Andriscus had announced his intention to retake Macedonia from the Romans and then proceeded to conquer Thessaly. But he was thwarted by Macedonicus at the Battle of Pydna, with Macedonia being formally reduced to a Roman province in 146 BCE. In 143 BCE the proconsulship of Metellus Macedonicus was also celebrated by the Macedonian Damon in this dedication to Zeus Olympios because of the continued beneficence of the proconsul to Thessalonica: "to Zeus Olympios on account of his *aretê* and goodwill which he continues to manifest to myself and the home city (i.e., Thessalonica) and the rest of the Macedonians and the other Greeks" (*IG* 10.2.1.1031, ll. 5–7).[17]

In the latter inscription, status and ethnicity move on a descending scale from citizenship in one's home city ("to myself and the home city") to its regional ethnic identity ("the rest of the Macedonians") and then to the wider Greek world ("and the other Greeks"): it reveals how eastern Mediterranean Greeks thought about their identity in antiquity. However, Paul, as Luke renders him in Acts 21:39 (see also Rom 1:16b, 3:1–2, 9:9–5, 11:16–18), prioritizes his covenantal identity as a Jew over that of his citizenship in his home city: "I am a Jew, from Tarsus in Cilicia, a citizen of no mean city" (NKJV). Nevertheless, the apostle is well aware of the status accrued by his citizenship of a prestigious city in the eastern Mediterranean basin. The ancient sources articulate clearly the status required

---

16. For translation and discussion, see Holland Lee Hendrix, "Thessalonicians Honor Romans" (PhD diss., Harvard University, 1984), 19–22. In our epigraphic corpus, however, Roman generals are not the only focus of military praise. Thessalonian soldiers are also regularly honored for their service by other states. At Philippi: IThess T25 (= *IG* 6.1.2646), T44. At Caruntum: IThess T23 (= *IG* 10.2.1.1033). At Acquincum: IThess T31 (= *IG* 10.2.1.1023). At Viminacium: IThess T39 (= *CIL* 3.14507).

17. For translation and discussion, see Hendrix, "Thessalonicians Honor Romans," 22–25.

to be considered a noteworthy city, whether it is the type of buildings required for that classification (Pausanias, *Hell. Per.* 10.4.1) or the rhetorical tropes necessary for establishing personal status should one's city lack sufficient distinction.[18] Additionally, the Greek and Asian cities eagerly vied to outdo one another as the most important metropolis or as the possessors of neokoros status.[19] In the case of Thessalonica in the republican era, we shall see that the status of being free was the prized epigraphic and numismatic boast.[20]

Second, there is an honorific inscription "Cnaeus Servilius son of Cnaeus Caepio quaestor of the Romans," datable by his quaestorship to the year 105 BCE (*MRR* 1.556), and erected by various gymnasiarchs and ephebes for (presumably) unspecified benefactions (oil?) to the gymnasium (*IG* 10.2.1.135).[21]

Third, the highly fragmentary decree of *IG* 10.2.1.6 (42–41 BCE), dealing with civic honors voted by the assembly, refers on three occasions to the free status of the city of Thessalonica (ll. 5: "fr[ee] Thessalonicans"; 6:

---

18. Menander Rhetor writes: "*If the city has no distinction*, you must inquire whether his nation as a whole is considered brave and valiant, or is devoted to literature or the possession of virtues, like the Greek race, or again is distinguished for law, like the Italian, or is courageous, like the Gauls or Paeonians. You must take a few features from the nation … arguing that it is inevitable that a man from such a [city or] nation should have such characteristics, and that he stands out among all his praiseworthy compatriots" (*Treatise* 2.369.17–370.10). For this reference I am indebted to Jerome H. Neyrey, "Luke's Social Location of Paul: Cultural Anthropology and the Status of Paul in Acts," in *Fabrics of Discourse: Essays in Honor of Vernon K. Robbins*, ed. David B. Gowler, L. Gregory Bloomquist, and Duane F. Watson (Harrisburg, PA: Trinity Press International, 2003), 126–64. For discussion of epideictic rhetoric on the issue, see Craig S. Keener, *Acts: An Exegetical Commentary*, 4 vols. (Grand Rapids: Baker Academic, 2012–2015), 3:3182.

19. E.g., IEph 1a 22, ll. 40–42: "the greatest and first metropolis of Asia, and the twice-neokoros-of-the-Augusti city of the great Ephesians." See Pliny the Elder regarding Pergamum: "by far the most distinguished city in Asia" (*Nat.* 5.30). On neokoros status, see Sreven J. Friesen, *Twice Neokoros: Ephesus, Asia and the Cult of the Flavian Imperial Family*, RGRW (Leiden: Brill, 1993). On rivalry among ancient cities, see Keener, *Acts*, 3:3182–83.

20. Neokorate status was only accorded to Thessalonica in the late empire (*IG* 10.2.1.164; 10.2.1s.1074–75), spanning the period from Gordian III to a third neokorate under Gallienus. For the numismatic evidence, see Barbara Burrell, *Neokoroi: Greek Cities and Roman Emperors*, CCS NS 9 (Leiden: Brill, 2004), 198–204.

21. For discussion, see Hendrix, "Thessalonicians Honor Romans," 26–27.

"(they) are [f]ree"; 11: "free"). The much-vaunted celebration of the city's freedom involves the acclamation of M. Antony and C. Caesar (Octavian, the future Augustus) as victors over Brutus and Cassius, evidenced by Antony's decisive defeat of Brutus at Philippi in 42 BCE. This is confirmed by the ΘΕΣΣΑΛΟΝΙΚΕΩΝ ΕΛΕΥΘΕΡΙΑΣ coin issue (*RPC* 1.1.1551), accompanied on the obverse by the bust of Eleutheria ("Freedom"), registering the victory of Antony and C. Caesar. Furthermore, the calendar years of the city were dated for a short time from Antony's victory over Brutus.[22] The depth of gratitude owed by Thessalonica to Antony is better understood when one recalls Brutus's plans for the city, announced as a future reward to his fellow soldiers at Philippi in 42 BCE: "(Brutus) promised to give over to those who fought bravely two cities for plunder and booty, Thessalonica and Lacedaemon" (Plutarch, *Brut.* 46.1).

Fourth, part of a white marble fountain basin is dedicated to "[- - Cornelius] Sulla, s(on) of S(ervius), q(uaestor)" (*IG* 10.2.1.29). This figure, known elsewhere to us as Publius Cornelius Sulla (d. 45 BCE), is the second brother from a republican noble family, whose otherwise unknown father was Servius Cornelius Sulla. But, significantly, Servius was the brother of the famous Roman general, statesman, consul, and dictator Lucius Cornelius Sulla (138–78 BCE), the victor of the Roman civil war won on behalf of the Optimates. In the case of Publius, he was later implicated with the conspiracy of Cataline at Rome (63 BCE: Sallust, *Bell. Cat.* 17.3.47; Cicero, *Sull.* 6). Why such a conspiratorial figure as Publius was honored at Thessalonica is hard to say, apart from the fact that relatives of Sulla highlight their connection with the dictator elsewhere in the eastern Mediterranean basin. Thus Lucius Cornelius Sulla was also honored by his grandson Memmius at Ephesus in the late republican period

---

22. *IG* 10.2.1.109, l. 1: "in year three [of Antony]"; *IG* 10.2.1.124, l. 1: "[in] year [?] of Ant[o]ny"; *IG* 10.2.1.83 l. 1: "in year five [of Antony]." For discussion, see Hendrix, "Thessalonicians Honor Romans," 28–37. In terms of the reckoning of time in the ancient Mediterranean basin, note the portable sundial found at Aphrodisias mentioning Thessalonica, with other cities listed (Crete, Athens, Thessalonica, Cyzicus, Nicomedia, Constantinople) and their latitudes (respectively, 35, 37, 43, 41, 42, 41): IThess T59. For discussion, see Derek J. de Solla Price, "Portable Sundials in Antiquity, Including an Account of a New Example from Aphrodisias," *Centaurus* 14 (1969): 259–63. More generally, Michael T. Wright, "Greek and Roman Portable Sundials: An Ancient Essay in Approximation," *AHES* 55 (2000): 177–87; Richard J. A. Talbert, *Roman Portable Sundials: The Empire in Your Hands* (New York: Oxford University Press, 2017).

(IEph 2.403.1–2). The implicit connection made to Rome's famous dictator, via Publius's father, was probably the real honorific incentive behind this monument: the family of Publius perhaps hoped to acquire deflected family glory by this public dedication of the fountain, as opposed to trying to reestablish Publius's fame via his (now) compromised career.

The late republican evidence reveals the increasing dependence of Thessalonica on Roman benefactors and their generals for the deliverance of the city from an opportunistically staged uprising. The Thessalonian decision to side with Antony and Octavian against the assassins of Julius Caesar was strategic in the long term, ensuring its free status before other Greek city states. Last, even late in the republic the ancestral honor of a great forbear could counterbalance a career that had not progressed very far in the *cursus honorum* or that had been derailed by unwise alliances.

1.3. The Imperial Rulers

Of great importance for the New Testament period is the mention of the temple to the divine Caesar at Thessalonica (*IG* 10.2.1.31, ll. 1–12) from the Augustan era:

> - - - -
> - - - - BOSA - - - - - - - - - - -
> proconsul - - - - - - - -
> of Latomia buil[t the]
>   tem[ple] of Caesar.
> (5) In the time of the priest and agon[othete of Im]-
> perator Caesar
> Augustus son [of god] - - - - - - - - -
> -os son of Neikopol[eos, priest]
> of the gods Do[- - - - - - son of - - - - -]
> (10) -pos and (priest) of Roma a[nd Roman]
> benefactors, Neik[- - - - - - - - son of]
> Paramonos.[23]

The inscription provides strong testimony to the importance of the Thessalonian civic cults of "the gods" and "of Roman benefactors"—discussed below along with their distinctive accompanying officials—as much as the worship of the apotheosized Caesar in the city. Other significant city offi-

---

23. For discussion, see Steimle, *Religion im römischen Thessaloniki*, 49–54.

cials are mentioned later in the inscription, indicating that it is an official decree of the city,[24] or, at the very least, an acknowledgment of the Thessalonian elites who were involved in the oversight and building of the imperial temple. It is curious that Thessalonica was not able to acquire neokorate status until much later in its history, beginning, as noted, under Gordian III (238–44 CE).[25] It is possible that the "proconsul" named in line 3 "may have been a party to the construction or dedication of the building."[26]

This strong attachment to the Julian house and the Julio-Claudian cult is confirmed by the dedication to Livia (post-14 CE: *IG* 10.2.1s.1060), already consecrated as divine in the Greek East before her official senatorial apotheosis in 44 CE in the Latin West under Claudius: "Goddess Julia Augusta ([θεᾷ Ἰουλίᾳ Σεβαστῇ]), wife of god Augustus Caesar and mother of Tiberius Caesar: the city (honors her)." In a fragmentary inscription from 61–62 CE (*IG* 10.2.1.130; see also *IG* 10.2.1.131, l. 3), there is reference to "[[Nero]] [Claudius] Caesar Augustus Germa[nicus]," but significantly the name Nero has been subsequently excised by enemies of his principate in a *damnatio memoriae*.[27] There are fleeting references to Tiberius and Claudius (*IG* 10.2.1.131, ll. 4 and 3, respectively).

In the Flavian era (89 CE: *IG* 10.2.1.34), we read that "[the city of the Thessalonian]s (honors) Imperator Caesa[r Domi]tian Augustus, [son of Vespasian god]." But in terms of honorific inscriptions to the Nerva-Antonine rulers, again there are only fleeting references to Nerva and Trajan (*IG* 10.2.1.138).

Speaking more generally in terms of the epigraphic genres, beyond the New Testament period there is a letter of Antoninus Pius (142–162 CE: *IG* 10.2.1.15) and an honorific inscription to him (145–166 CE: *IG* 10.2.1.36), another letter of an unspecified imperator (second–third centuries CE: *IG*

---

24. Hendrix, "Thessalonicians Honor Romans," 109, 113. *IG* 10.2.1.31, ll. 13–18: "the politarchs"; ll. 19–20: "the superin[tendent] of the work"; l. 20: "trea[surer of the city]"; l. 22: "[the] architect[t]," the commissioner of public works?

25. See n. 20 above. See *IG* 10.2.1.164: ἡ Θεσσαλονικαίων μητρόπολις · καὶ κολωνία καὶ δ · νεωκόρος; see also *IG* 10.2.1.165, 167; 10.2.1s.1073, 1074, 1075. During the reign of Decius in 250 CE, Thessalonica was also made a colony (*IG* 10.2.1.164–65, 167). On Roman *colonia*, see Constantina Katsari and Stephen Mitchell, "The Roman Colonies of Greece and Asia Minor: Questions of State and Civic Identity," *Athenaum* 95 (2008): 219–47.

26. Hendrix, "Thessalonicians Honor Romans," 109.

27. See James R. Harrison, "The Erasure of Distinction: Paul and the Politics of Dishonour," *TynBul* 66 (2016): 161–84.

10.2.1.19), the dedication of a temple and stoa to the divine Augusti and the city (second century CE: *IG* 10.2.1.102), a vow on behalf of Septimius Severus (193 CE: *IG* 10.2.1.138–39) and Severus Alexander (193 CE: *IG* 10.2.1.141), and two decrees of Justinian (*IG* 10.2.1.23–24), to cite a few examples. By contrast, one is struck by the paucity of the extant Julio-Claudian and Flavian honorific epigraphy, with the main extant Neronian inscription having been subjected to retrospective dishonoring.[28]

The thinness of the epigraphic evidence can be supplemented by the iconographic and legend evidence of the Thessalonian coinage, too extensive to cover in depth at this juncture.[29] However, in the case of the Julio-Claudian period, a few pertinent examples will suffice. There is a revealing emphasis on the Julio-Claudian family members as much as on the ruler, including a sharp focus on the females. Livia is assigned a coin issue herself in the Augustan reign, with her bust accompanied by the legend ΘΕΑ ΛΙΒΙΑ ("goddess Livia") or ΘΕΟΥ ΛΙΒΙΑ ("Livia (wife) of the god") on the obverse.[30] Here we see in some of the Thessalonian numismatic issues the divinization of Livia in the Greek East well before her divinization in the Latin West. Again, the head of the young Gaius, the future Julian heir at the time, is placed tellingly on the reverse of a coin

---

28. For Roman magistrates and officials at Thessalonica, including military officers, see *IG* 10.2.1, index, s.v. VI. "Res Romanae Magistratus et Officiales/Res Militares," 308–9.

29. On the Thessalonian coinage, see the essay of Michael Theophilos in this volume.

30. *PIR*[1] 1.1563. Andrew Burnett, Michel Amandry, and Pere Pau Ripollès state: "The issue of Livia (1563) has been included in the lifetime issues of Augustus, despite the honorific ΘΕΑ or ΘΕΟΥ, since it uses the name ΛΙΒΙΑ rather than ΣΕΒΑΣΤΗ, normal after AD 14 … (nevertheless) a parallel exists under the Thessalonian League (1427) where Augustus is called θεός on a coin where Livia is called Livia rather than Sebaste" (*RPC* 1.1:298). Notwithstanding, the ascription of ΘΕΑ to ΛΙΒΙΑ is certainly bold during Augustus's lifetime, presuming that the inscription could be dated to late in his reign: but such overly effusive accolades are not unusual in the Greek East. For example, Emma Stafford writes: "On Thasos between 16 BC and AD 2 honours are recorded for 'Livia Drusilla, wife of Caesar Augustus, goddess benefactor (θεὰν εὐεργέτιν) … while at Corinth around AD 21–3 the programme of Caearean games included performance of a poem 'for the goddess Julia Augusta (εἰς θεὰν Ἰ[ο]υλίαν)." See Stafford, "The People to the Goddess Livia: Attic Nemesis and the Roman Imperial Cult," *Kernos* 26 (2013): 205–38. The two inscriptions referred to are *IG* 12.8.381 B 6–7 (Thasos) and IKorinthMeritt, pp. 28–29, no. 19 (Corinth). More generally, see Gertrude Grether, "Livia and the Roman Imperial Cult," *AJP* 67 (1946): 222–56.

with the laureate head of Augustus on the reverse (1–4 CE).³¹ Upon the death of Gaius (4 CE), a new coin was issued, with the laureate head of Augustus on the obverse and the head of the sole remaining non-Julian heir, the Claudian Tiberius who had been adopted by Augustus in 4 CE, now strategically placed on the reverse (4 CE onward).³² The honorific sensitivities posed for provincial cities by the unfolding saga of the succession crisis in the Augustan principate had to be monitored as much as in their numismatic issues as by face-to-face diplomacy.

Upon the change of Livia's nomenclature to Julia Augusta ('Ιουλία Σεβαστῆ) in 14 CE, other female members acquired the "Augusta" (ΣΕΒΑΣΤΗ) epithet, as was the case with the legends accompanying the busts and seated representations of Livia on the reverses of the Tiberian coinage.³³ The title "Antonia Augusta" is applied to the reverse representations of Octavia the Younger (ΑΝΤΟΝΙΑ ΣΕΒΑΣΤΗ / ΑΝΤΟΝΙΑ ΣΕΒΑΣΤΗ ΘΕΣΣΑΛΟΝΙΚΕΩΝ)—niece of Augustus, sister-in-law of Tiberius, paternal grandmother of Caligula, and mother of Claudius—in the Caligulan issues.³⁴ This is the case despite Antonia's own refusal of the honorific "Augusta" given to her by Caligula upon his succession in 37 CE (Suetonius, *Cal.* 15.3; *Claud.* 11.2). Again we see the keenness of the provincial mints to attribute a more exalted honorific status to Julio-Claudian family members in comparison to the more cautious approach of the mint of Rome in the Latin West.

In the Claudian period, the bust of Antonia features on the obverse,³⁵ whereas, in Neronian reign, the bust of Agrippina II, the mother of Nero, also appears on the obverse and the reverse. Other male relatives appear on the obverse of coin issues: the charismatic and highly popular Germanicus, the father of Caligula, probably issued at Caligula's accession, and also Brittanicus, the son of Claudius.³⁶ Once again, the wide-ranging

---

31. *PIR*¹ 1.1.1564.
32. *PIR*¹ 1.1.1566.
33. ΣΕΒΑΣΤΗ ΘΕΣΣΑΛΟΝΙΚΕΩΝ (*PIR*¹ 1.1.1567–71).
34. *PIR*¹ 1.1.1573–75.
35. Claudian period: ΑΝΤΩΝΙΑ/ΜΑΡΚΙΑ (*PIR*¹ 1.1.1581–85, 1587). Neronian period: obverse, ΣΕΒΑΣΤΗ/ΑΓΡΙΠΠΙΝΑ ΣΕΒΑΣΤΗ (*PIR*¹ 1.1.1604–1606A); reverse, ΘΕΣΣΑΛΟΝΙΚΕΩΝ (*PIR*¹ 1.1.1501). Burnett et al. observe: "The alternative legend ΜΑΡΚΙΑ is puzzling … it is not used elsewhere as a name for Octavia" (*RPC* 1.1, 298).
36. Germanicus: ΓΕΡΜΑΝΙΚΟΣ ΘΕΣΣΑΛΟΝΙΚΕΩΝ (*PIR*¹ 1.1.1572). Brittanicus: ΒΡΕΤΑΝΝΙΚΟΣ ΘΕΣΣΑΛΟΝΙΚΕΩΝ (*PIR*¹ 1.1.1588).

sensitivity of the Thessalonians in honoring a spectrum of Julio-Claudian family figures by means of their coinage is evident.

1.4. Other Honorands and Aspects of Thessalonian Honorific Culture

We commence this section with a September 95 BCE Thessalonian inscription honouring the gymnasiarch Paramanos:

> The Youths [οἱ νέοι]. Athenagoras son of Apollodoros, Pyrros son of Kleitomacho[s], Neikosratos son of N[e]ikomachos, Diogenes son of Epigenos, Straton son of Kenon, N[e]ikeratos son of Androkles made the motion: Whereas Paramanos son of Antigonos, elected gymnasiar[ch] for the year 53, has e[ngag]ed very eagerly in the oversight of the office with g[race], zealously offering himself among those who provide for public expenses and increasing the customary honours G[- - - - -] for the gods and Roman benefactors; (and) being c[on]cerned with good order in the place a[nd gen]erally endeavouring after that which is most proper in all things, he has not neglected t[he] attendant [ex]pense, but rather has [com]pleted his term of office - - - - TÊS - - - - - - - having given the oil; and it is good that those who aspire to public re[cog]nition [φιλοδόχῳ] obtain the appropriate honours so that others also when they consider the honours bestowed by the Youths might strive for similar honours; be it resolved by those from the gymnasium to commend Paramonos for his aspiration (to public recognition) and honour him with a crown of young shoots and a bronze likeness, life-sized and painted, and the (honorific) decree engraved on a stone stele is to be given a conspicuous place in the gymnasium; expenses for the painted likeness and the stele are to be met by the presiding treasurers. Sanctioned (by vote) in the year 3 and 50, on the tenth day from the end of Hyperbrtaios. (*IG* 10.2.1.4)[37]

Although the decree is entirely conventional when compared to other honorific decrees in the eastern Mediterranean basin, it nevertheless provides important insights into the protocols of honor extended to benefactors at Thessalonica, the motivations driving ancient benefactors, and the Thessalonian civic cults of "the gods" and "of Roman benefactors" in the city. At the outset, local benefactors aspired to public recognition (φιλοδόχῳ) by beneficence, bringing honor to themselves and their

---

37. For translation (here slightly adapted) and discussion, see Hendrix, "Thessalonicians Honor Romans," 101–5.

ancestors. However, according to the dynamics of the Greco-Roman reciprocity system, the *neoi* had to reciprocate their benefactor with appropriate honors so that other potential benefactors, seeing commensurate recompense of benefactors publicly registered, would strive to attain similar honors by giving further gifts to the gymnasium. Notably, the emulation on the part of this new generation of benefactors was *not* inspired by the beneficence of the original benefactor himself but rather by the public monuments (stela, painted bronze statue) and honorific recognition ("a conspicuous place") accorded to him by the city or, in this case, by the youth of the gymnasium. An unofficial or invisible contractual relationship exists that had to be scrupulously fulfilled between the benefactor and beneficiary if the reciprocity system was to elicit a new generation of new contributors.

The reference to "the gods and Roman benefactors" must be speaking of the civic cults of "the gods" and "of Roman benefactors" at Thessalonica. Wealthy Roman immigrants to Thessalonica engaged in trade and community development within the city, being incorporated into its civic life by marrying Thessalonian citizens, with the result that they could hold civic offices and act as public benefactors when required. Holland Hendrix correctly notes that here "the decree mentions no other deities consecrated by the gymnasium (Heracles, Apollo, Hermes, etc.)."[38] By the time of this inscription,[39] therefore, honors "for the gods and Roman benefactors" (*IG* 10.2.1.4, l. 11) had been established at Thessalonica, with the result that by the time of Augustus there was specifically "a priest of Roma and Roman benefactors" (*IG* 10.2.1.31, ll. 10–11; 10.2.1.133, l. 7). This individual is regularly mentioned alongside "a priest of the gods" (*IG* 10.2.1.31, ll. 8–9; *IG* 10.2.1.133, l. 6) and "a priest and agonothete of the Imperator Caesar Augustus son of god" (*IG* 10.2.1.31, ll. 5–7; 10.2.1.133, ll. 3–4; 10.2.1.32, ll. 2–4).[40] The blessings of the Roman gods were locally experienced at Thessalonica in the munificence of Roman benefactors, so much so that the local Thessalonican benefactor of the gymnasium made sure that he also

---

38. Hendrix, "Thessalonicians Honor Romans," 104–5.

39. Hendrix makes the following important chronological observation: "The inscription bears a date equivalent to September 95 BCE, requiring a revision of Edson's conclusion that the origin of the Thessalonican cult is to be dated 42–41 BCE" ("Thessalonicians Honor Romans," 103).

40. For full discussion, see Hendrix, "Thessalonicians Honor Romans," 98–139.

increased the customary honors of the cult of the gods and the Roman benefactors by providing for the honorific expenses.

Other elite officials are honored in the Thessalonian inscriptions. The frequency of epigraphic reference to politarchs at Thessalonica, the official being mentioned in Acts 17:6 and 8, has been extensively covered by several scholars and need not detain us.[41] There are twenty-seven inscriptions referring to politarchs in Edson's collection (πολιταρχέω, πολιτάρχης, πολειτάρχικος),[42] with two new occurrences in Pantelis Nigdelis's recent collection (IG 10.2.1s.1047, 1063). Convenors of the city council and the citizen assembly, the politarchs introduced the motions in each civic institution, set their official seal on the papyrus copy in the archives, and acted as judges. They ranged in number between three and seven in the city from the first to second centuries CE (IG 10.2.1.126, 133, 137).

Some of the other important civic officials, professions, and public benefactors who are honored in the Thessalonian inscriptions—additional to those in IG 10.2.1.31 above—are set out below:

- *agoranomos* ("clerk of the market" [= Roman *aedile*]: IG 10.2.1.7)
- *presbeutes* in Alexandria ("ambassador": IG 10.2.1.14)
- *agonothetai* ("president") of the Pythian games of Apollo (IG 10.2.1.38; see also IG 10.2.1.152, 154, 155–56; 10.2.1s.1059, 1074–75)
- *gymnasiarchos* (gymnasium "training-master": IG 10.2.1.126, 135, 160, 162–63; 10.2.1s.1045)
- *ephebiarchos* ("overseer of the youth": IG 10.2.1.163)

---

41. See Ernest DeWitt Burton, "The Politarchs," *AmJT* 2 (1898): 596–632; Carl Schuler, "The Macedonian Politarchs," *CP* 55 (1960): 90–100; Greg H. R. Horsley, "Politarchs," *NewDocs* 2:34–35; Horsley, "Appendix: The Politarchs," in *The Book of Acts in Its Graeco-Roman Setting*, vol. 2 of *The Book of Acts in Its First Century Setting*, ed. David W. J. Gill and Conrad Gempf (Grand Rapids: Eerdmans, 1994), 419–31; Horsley, "The Politarchs in Macedonia," *MA* 7 (1994): 99–126.

42. For the Edson references (i.e., in *IG* 10.2.1), see Horsley, "Politarchs in Macedonia," 106–8. One epigraphic example will suffice (first century BCE–second century CE: *IG* 10.2.1.126): "In the time of the politarchs Sosipatros, son of Cleopatra, and Lucius Pontius Secundus, son of Avius Sabinus, Demetrios son of Faustos, Demetrios of Nikopolis, Zoilos, son of Parmenion and of Meniskos Gaius Agilleius Potitus, treasurer of the city, Tauros son of Ammia and of Reglos, gymnasiarch, Tauros, son of Tauros and Reglos."

- doctor (*IG* 10.2.1s.1042, confirmed by the formula in lines 9–10 found in other inscriptions honoring doctors)
- *grammateus* ("clerk": *IG* 10.2.1s.1363)
- *patronus* ("patron": *IG* 10.2.1s.1255)
- *oikonomos* of the city ("steward," "manager": *IG* 10.2.1s.1472)
- *bouleutes* ("councilor": *IG* 10.2.1s.1472)
- *keryx* ("herald": *IG* 10.2.1s.1579)[43]

We gain little idea about the lower echelons in the Thessalonian society from the honorific inscriptions other than references to slaves (§7 below), whatever clues we may pick up from the association inscriptions (§3 below) and from the celebrity circuit of athletes and gladiators (§4 below), as well as occasional passing references to a "muleteer" (IThess Kephalaio 1.10) and a "sailor" (IThess Kephalaio 3.7). How, then, does this honorific culture intersect with the Thessalonian epistles?

1.5. New Testament Intersections

In the 95 BCE gymnasium decree (*IG* 10.2.1.3) above, benefactors were described as those who aspired to public recognition (lit., "love of glory," line 16: φιλοδόχῳ), adding to their ancestral glory through the contemporary esteem accrued by their civic munificence. In another Thessalonian inscription (30 September 57 BCE: *IG* 10.2.1s.1045), an unknown gymnasium benefactor was similarly praised for his love of glory (ἡ φιλοδοξία) and was honored commensurately by the overseer of the *neoi*. The motivation for this reciprocation of his munificence to the gymnasium was that those in the city responsible for the city's building program might appreciate the significant start made in the gymnasium, being inspired by the vision of great glory embodied in the institution of the gymnasium and in its young charges. The overlap of "glory" terminology in both inscriptions

---

43. For New Testament intersections, see Anthony Bash, *Ambassadors for Christ: An Exploration of Ambassadorial Language in the New Testament*, WUNT 2/92 (Tübingen: Mohr Siebeck, 1997); John K. Goodrich, *Paul as an Administrator of God in 1 Corinthians*, SNTSMS 152 (Cambridge: Cambridge University Press, 2012); James R. Harrison, "Paul and the *agōnothetai* at Corinth: Engaging the Civic Values of Antiquity," in *The First Urban Churches 2: Roman Corinth*, ed. James R. Harrison and Larry L. Welborn, WGRWSup 8 (Atlanta: SBL Press, 2016), 271–326. Néstor O. Míguez translates *agoranomos* as "mayor." See Míguez, *The Practice of Hope: Ideology and the Intention in 1 Thessalonians*, PCC (Minneapolis: Fortress, 2012), 53.

is important in honorific rituals, whether viewed from a Greek or Latin context.[44] The inscription is set out below:

> [Decreed by those from the gy]mna[sium]: that [...]gene be praised for (his) love of glory (τῆι φιλοδοξίαι) and that he be crowned with a c[row[n of young shoots and (honored) with a painted and copper image, in order that each of those urging on (the councillors and the people) towards (the erection and maintenance of) public buildings might be a zealous admirer of the beginning (made) in relation to the gymnasium, beholding the great glory [s]et before (πλίστην θεωρῶν [ὑ] ποκειμήνην δόξαν) those who love goodness for the *neoi*. It was decreed that a decre[e] should be inscribed on a stele and erected in the gym[na] sium by the treasurer of the *ne*[*oi*].

Given that civic esteem (ἡ φιλοδοξία) was the primary motivation of the Thessalonian elites and that the civic glory of each new generation at Thessalonica found its location in the paideia of the gymnasium, what alternate understanding of esteem and glory does Paul set forth?[45]

By contrast, Paul makes it clear that he is not seeking to please people, but, being approved by God in his apostolic ministry, he seeks instead to please God, who tests the heart (1 Thess 2:4; see also 4:1). Consequently, he is not seeking glory from people (1 Thess 2:6a: οὔτε ζητοῦντες ἐξ ἀνθρώπων δόξαν), knowing that the priority for himself and his converts is to live a life worthy of God (1 Thess 2:12a; 2 Thess 1:5, 11a), precisely because God has called believers into his kingdom and glory (1 Thess 2:12b, τὴν ἑαυτοῦ βασιλείαν καὶ δόξαν; 2 Thess 2:14, ἡμῶν εἰς περιποίησιν δόξης τοῦ κυρίου ἡμῶν Ἰησοῦ Χριστοῦ). We observed in regard to *IG* 10.2.1.3 that the civic emulation of each new generation of Thessalonians was not inspired by the benefactions of the original benefactors but rather by the benefactor's public recompense by the Thessalonian civic authorities and by the officials of the gymnasium in this instance. Strikingly, in the case of the

---

44. See James R. Harrison, "The Brothers as the 'Glory of Christ' (2 Cor 8:23): Paul's *Doxa* Terminology in Its Ancient Benefaction Context," *NovT* 52 (2010): 156–88; Harrison, *Paul and the Imperial Authorities at Thessalonica and Rome: A Study in the Conflict of Ideology*, WUNT 273 (Tübingen: Mohr Siebeck, 2011), 201–69.

45. See the helpful discussion of Mikael Tellbe on believers and the "court of reputation" in honorific culture. Tellbe, *Paul between Synagogue and State: Christians, Jews, and Civic Authorities in 1 Thessalonians, Romans, and Philippians*, ConBNT 34 (Stockholm: Almqvist & Wiksell, 2001), 131–37.

Thessalonian believers, imitation is cruciform, being modeled on the sufferings of Christ, the apostle Paul, and Jewish believers in the churches of Judea (1 Thess 1:6–7, 2:14–15a; 2 Thess 1:4–5), as well as on the apostle's own exemplum of hard work in his ministry (2 Thess 3:7, 9). Moreover, the coronal honorific awards of the Greco-Roman reciprocity system are eschatologically postponed in the case of believers, until they glory in their crown before the returned Christ at his parousia (1 Thess 2:19, ἣ στέφανος καυχήσεως; see also 3:13, 5:23; 2 Thess 1:9b–10). Indeed, in the case of Paul himself, the honorific crown itself is refocused: the Thessalonian believers are his crown of glory (1 Thess 2:19b–20: ἐστε ἡ δόξα ἡμῶν καὶ ἡ χαρά).

Nevertheless, despite the apostle's upending of aspects of the Thessalonian honor system, Paul establishes a culture of esteem and honor within the body of Christ. Believers are to honor and love their leaders (1 Thess 5:12–23), live at peace with all the brethren (5:13b), and seek the good of all inside and outside the church (5:15b). Above all, in Paul's redefinition of the honor system at Thessalonica, it is Christ alone who is to be marveled at (2 Thess 1:10). Further, it is Christ alone who is to be glorified in his holy people (2 Thess 1:12: "that the name of our Lord Jesus may be glorified [ἐνδοξασθῇ] in you"), with a view to their own eschatological glorification in him (2 Thess 1:12: "and you in him"; see also 2:14b). All earthly glory pales in comparison to the cruciform and risen glory of Christ, joyfully celebrated in all its fullness at his parousia and experienced by believers themselves in their eschatological transformation into Christ's glorious likeness. Paul's use of *glory* terminology in the Thessalonian epistles, distinctive because of its contrast to the traditional Roman quest for glory, is significant in the honorific context of Roman Thessalonica.

2. Thessalonian Cults

2.1. A World Full of Gods

The religious terrain of Thessalonica was populated by a plethora of gods, Roman, Egyptian, and Greek, according to their origins. In the case of the Roman deities, we have already dealt with most of the epigraphic and numismatic evidence relating to the imperial cult in the Julio-Claudian period at Thessalonica.[46] There is additional numismatic evidence on

---

46. *IG* 10.2.1.31; 10.2.1s.1060; *PIR*[1] 1.1563.

the obverse of leaded bronze coins where the bare or crowned head of Caesar is depicted with the legend ΘΕΟΣ, along with the bare head of Augustus gracing the reverse with the legend ΘΕΣΣΑΛΟΝΙΚΕΩΝ.[47] The epigraphic and numismatic evidence for the imperial cult in the Julio-Claudian age is admittedly not extensive but significant nonetheless.[48] Several imperial Thessalonian statues of Augustus, Claudius, and Hadrian convey effectively the wider ideology of Roman rule in the Greek East, which had been incorporated into local Greek religious practices.[49] Indigenous practices were not supplanted by the imperial cult. Noteworthy in this regard is the revival of the Macedonian cult of Alexander Dios in the third century CE during the Severan dynasty (*IG* 10.2.1.275, 276, 278, 933).[50] Nevertheless, the imperial cult was serviced by prestigious individuals, including the nonresident Thracian prince Gaius Julius Rhoimetalces, who was the "priest and ago[nothete and Impera]tor Caesar Augustus son of god."[51] Last, as we have seen (§1.4 above), at Thessalonica the goddess Roma was also linked to Roman benefactors in divine honors, with the result that a civic priesthood was established for both.

The pervasive presence of Egyptian deities at Thessalonica was also an important feature of the religious life in the city, focused especially on the god Serapis.[52] The third-century BCE serapeum, situated within the city walls near the western city gate and the harbor, is now covered by a street of the modern city of Thessaloniki. Our architectural understanding of the building's design is therefore based on a clay scale model of the remains of the original rectangular building (11 m by 8 m).[53] The small temple of Serapis belonged to a complex of structures

---

47. *PIR*¹ 1.1554–55.

48. On the imperial cult at Thessalonica, see Steimle, *Religion im römischen Thessaloniki*, 132–67.

49. For the statues, see Adam-Velini, "Thessalonike: History and Town Planning," 113, fig. 38; 114, fig. 40; 115, fig. 41, as well as the wider discussion of the imperial cult at 109–19; Hendrix, "Thessalonicians Honor Romans," 45–54.

50. See Adam-Velini, "Thessalonike: History and Town Planning," 107–8.

51. *IG* 10.2.1.133, ll. 3–4 (154 CE); see also "priestess of Augustus" (*IG* 10.2.1.270, second century CE). On Rhoimetalces, see Hendrix, "Thessalonicians Honor Romans," 111; Robert, "Les inscriptions de Thessalonique," 212–15.

52. See n. 10 above.

53. See Tzanavari, "Worship of Gods and Heroes," 240, fig. 37. The scale model is now in the Archaeological Museum of Thessalonica.

that formed the sanctuary of Egyptian gods in the city. The building comprised an anteroom and a large hall with a niche and small step before it (a sacred table for the cultic rituals?). Below the anteroom was a passageway (1 m by 10 m) connected to a crypt, in which was a niche with a small herm of a bearded god standing (possibly a representation of Dionysus).[54] Serapis was a chthonic deity who escorted the deceased souls to the underworld, where they provided an account of their good and bad deeds, whereupon they were assigned their respective places in the afterlife.

Sixty-nine inscriptions have been found in the serapeum, including *IG* 10.2.1.3 (187 BCE), discussed above.[55] Caution is required so that we do overestimate the influence of Egyptian religion at Thessalonica because of the abundance of material evidence extant:[56] this may simply reflect the vagaries of archaeological survival. Among the sanctuary inscriptions, there are diverse epigraphic genres present and various deities honored, including

1. vows (*IG* 10.2.1.73, 97–98, 100, 114);
2. thank offerings (*IG* 10.2.1.67, 85, 87);
3. dedications to Serapis and Isis (*IG* 10.2.1.75–80, 87, 90, 92–93, 99), sometimes accompanied in the dedication by another Egyptian deity (e.g., Anubis: *IG* 10.2.1.77–80; e.g., Horus: *IG* 10.2.1.85; e.g., Harpocrates: *IG* 10.2.1.85, 87);
4. a fragmentary decree (*IG* 10.2.1.19);
5. a reference to a temple dedicated to a hero (*IG* 10.2.1.37; see also nos. 48, 64, 821);
6. a fragmentary aretalogy of Isis (*IG* 10.2.1.254);
7. dream-prompted dedications to Isis (*IG* 10.2.1.82, 88, 99; see §5 below); and

---

54. For these details, see Robyn Walsh and Laura Nasrallah, "Thessaloniki," in *Cities of Paul: Images and Interpretations from the Harvard New Testament and Archaeology Project*, CD-ROM (Minneapolis: Fortress, 2005). For the herm from the serapeum, see Tzanavari, "Worship of Gods and Heroes," 240, fig. 38.

55. *IG* 10.2.1.3, 15, 16, 37, 51, 53, 59, 61, 73, 75–123, 221–22, 244, 254–59. The more recent publication of Dafni Maikidou-Poutrino notes some seventy-eight inscriptions. See Maikidou-Poutrino, "Women and Isis Lochia: Commemorations of Divine Protection in Roman Macedonia," *Arys* 16 (2018): 440.

56. Charles Edson, "Cults of Thessalonica (Macedonia III)," *HTR* 41 (948): 182.

8. dedications to other Egyptian deities such as "Osiris and the other gods" (*IG* 10.2.1.107–109, 111, 254, 971) and Ammon (*IG* 10.2.1.541). [57]

Three inscriptions are especially worth highlighting from the Serapeum corpus, either because of their uniqueness in Thessalonian epigraphy or because of their revealing iconography. First, of considerable interest is the sole inscription (*IG* 10.2.1.97, 22/21 BCE) offered to Isis Lochia, the protector of childbirth: "In the year 126, (when) Diogenes, son of Lysimachos, was priest, Iulia Cleoneike daughter of Philodemos (dedicated) the cella and the altars to Isis Lochia [ex-voto]."[58] Although the reason for Iulia's munificence is not explicitly stated, it is significant that this is the *only* inscription in Thessalonica where Isis is referred to as Lochia. The addition of this epithet to the name of the goddess makes it probable that Iulia's benefaction was prompted either as an expression of her thankfulness to the goddess for her previous safe births or as an offering to the goddess for the protection of herself and the safe arrival of her newborn during future childbirths.

Second, an inscribed votive relief offered by Demetrios in honor of his parents for Osiris, the Egyptian god of the dead and the afterlife, provides keen insight into the initiation ceremonies associated with the deity's worship at Thessalonica. The inscription on the pediment (*IG* 10.2.1.107, post-mid-second century BCE) states: "To the initiate Osiris, Demetrios, for his parents Alexander, son of Demetrios, and Nikaia, daughter of Charixenos."[59] The accompanying relief shows the "initiate Osiris" flanked on the left and right by Nikaia and Alexander, who pours a libation from

---

57. For an impressive relief of the jackal-headed embalmer god, Anubis, see Walsh and Nasrallah, "Thessaloniki," s.v. "Dining Association Stele with Relief of Anubis." For heads and statues of Serapis, Isis, and Harpocrates, see Tzanavari, "Worship of Gods and Heroes," 245–47, figs. 42–45. On hero cults at Thessalonica, see Tzanavari, "Worship of Gods and Heroes," 216–20. In regards to the hero Hippalkmos (Ἱππάκκμ[ι]ωι ἥρωϊ: *IG* 10.2.1.48; third century BCE), see also the Thessalonian relief of him "depicted on horseback, wearing chiton and chlamys, attacking a bull with his spear" (Tzanavari, "Worship of Gods and Heroes," 218, fig. 23). For the hero Aulonitas (ἡ συνήθια Ἡρωνός Αὐλωνίτου), see *IG* 10.2.1s.1368.

58. Trans. Maikidou-Poutrino, "Women and Isis Lochia," 440. For discussion, see Steimle, *Religion im römischen Thessaloniki*, 119–20.

59. Trans. Walsh and Nasrallah, "Thessaloniki," s.v. "Votive Relief of Demetrios for Osiris."

a container over the sacrificial altar. Above the altar, Osiris oversees the sacrificial scene with studied attention, while the pouch of coins hanging from Alexander's left wrist possibly indicates "that he was a benefactor of the sanctuary of the Egyptian gods."[60] Rarely do the iconography and its accompanying epigraphic text mutually interpret each other as revealingly as this Thessalonian votive relief.

Third, in *IG* 10.2.1.100 (second century CE) a female devotee of Isis honors the goddess with these words: "According to a vow [κατ'εὐχήν], Phouphikia to Isis for hearing [ἀκοήν]."[61] The thrust of the inscription is devotee's thankfulness to Isis for hearing her vow (or prayer). Again, the iconography intersects powerfully with the epigraphic text. It shows three ears, one to the left, one in the middle, and another right of the votive relief, each ear listening to the others with undiminished attention, symbolically highlighting the continuous access that Isis provided her worshipers.

The traditional Greek and Roman gods also feature regularly in the Thessalonian epigraphic corpus. They include Hades, Apollo, Aphrodite Homonoia, Artemis, Asclepius, the Dioscouroi, Dike, Dionysus, Dis Manibus, Eros, Zeus (with multiple epithets), demigods such as Heracles/Hercules, Helios, *theos* Hypistos, Hygieia, *theoi* (with multiple epithets), Koure, Meter *theōn*, Mithras, Moira, *nymphai*, Hosion Dikaion, Poseidon, Pythia, Roma, the Charites, Jupiter (with multiple epithets), and the cult of the Thracian horsemen.[62] Since Thessalonica lies within sight of Mount Olympus, the mention of important Greek gods such as Zeus, Asclepius, Aphrodite, and Demeter is not unexpected.[63] Personified abstractions,

---

60. Walsh and Nasrallah, "Thessaloniki," s.v. "Votive Relief of Demetrios for Osiris."

61. Translation and commentary by Walsh and Nasrallah, "Thessaloniki," s.v. "Phouphikia to Isis with Relief of Ears." For the relief, see Tzanavari, "Worship of Gods and Heroes," 249, fig. 47.

62. For epigraphic references, see *IG* 10.2.1.310 ("VII: Res Sacrae"); *IG* 10.2.1s.533 ("VI: Res Sacrae"). There is no epigraphic reference to Mithras. Note the two second- to third-century CE finds of the Mithras cult at cemeteries in Thessalonica: a votive relief and terracotta of the god. See Tzanavari, "Worship of Gods and Heroes," 255–59, figs. 49–50; Panayotis Pachis, "The Cult of Mithras in Thessalonica," in *Studies in Mithraism*, ed. John R. Hinnels (Roma: Erma di Bretscheider, 1994), 229–55; Steimle, *Religion im römischen Thessaloniki*, 63–69. On the cult of the Thracian horseman, see the relief on the purple dyers' association inscription (*IG* 10.2.1.291; see Acts 16:14).

63. Edson, "Cults of Thessalonica," 25. There is no Demeter inscription cited by *IG* 10.2.1 or *IG* 10.2.1s, but there are archaeological remains of the goddess in Thes-

too, appear among the deities, including Tyche (*IG* 10.2.1.257) and Nemesis (*IG* 10.2.1.62).[64]

Finally, there are three epigraphic references to Kabeiros, the god of fire and metallurgy, within the city of Thessalonica:

1. *IG* 10.2.1.199, lines 16–17: "temple servant of the most holy ancestral god of Kabeiros" (mid-third century CE);
2. *IG* 10.2.1s.1075, line 6: "an initiating teaching priest of the most holy ancestral god of Kabeiros" (260 CE); and
3. *IG* 10.2.1s.1217, lines 3–4: "I swear you by Kabeiros, after reading this, to dance a while" (second century CE).[65]

Although there are no archaeological remains of the cult in the city, it is clear from the epigraphy that there was in second- to third-century CE Thessalonica a temple of Kabeiros there, along with his cult officials. The earliest reference to Kabeiros's worship at Thessalonica occurs on two coins of Vespasian, one showing Kabeiros holding a rhyton and a hammer and the other displaying the draped bust of the god.[66] It is beyond the scope of this chapter to explore Robert Jewett's contention that the elites of Thessalonica appropriated the cult of Kabeiros, producing a millenarian response on the part of the city's common citizens, a challenge to which, Jewett proposes, Paul responded eschatologically in his Thessalonian epistles.[67] Suffice it to say, all the evidence for the Kabeiros cult postdates both epistles, and it is unlikely that the cult was present in the city at the time of

---

salonica (see Tzanavari, "Worship of Gods and Heroes," 193–98). Note also the bust of Livia portrayed as Demeter in the Archaeological Museum of Thessalonki; see "Thessaloniki, Portrait of Livia as Demeter," Livius.org, 3 April 2020, https://tinyurl.com/SBL4221b.

64. For discussion, see Tzanavari, "Worship of Gods and Heroes," 233–37.

65. Trans. Eduard Verhoef, "Christians Reacted Differently to Non-Christian Cults," *HvST* 67 (2011), article 84, doi:10.4102/hts.v.6i1.804. Verhoef discusses a fourth Kabeiros inscription on a herm (second century CE) 80 km southeast of Thessalonica ("Christians Reacted Differently," 2). For discussion of the Kabeiros cult, see also vom Brocke, *Thessaloniki*, 116–21.

66. *PIR*² 1.327.

67. Robert Jewett writes: "Paul responded to the crisis of a radicalised and hence vulnerable millenarism by writing 1 Thessalonians." See Jewett, *The Thessalonian Correspondence: Pauline and Millenarian Piety* (Philadelphia: Fortress, 1986), 177.

Paul's visit, even if the cult was known elsewhere in Greece in pre-Christian times.[68]

2.2. New Testament Intersections

New Testament scholars have pointed to various intersections between the religious background of Thessalonica and the concerns of the Thessalonian epistles, including Jewett regarding the Kabeiros cult, noted above. A few examples will suffice. In terms of imperial culture, discussion has concentrated on the echoes of imperial propaganda in 1 Thess 4:13–18 and the (alleged) imperial slogan of "peace" and "safety" in 5:3.[69] Note in this regard the contributions of Clint Burnett, Alan Cadwallader, and Joel White in this volume. John Kloppenborg has pointed to the importance of the Dioscouroi at Thessalonica, evidenced by the second- to third-century CE vow (*IG* 10.2.1.56) highlighting their role as paradigms of φιλαδελφία, including familial solidarity and selfless sharing, in antiquity. He airs the possibility that Paul is rhetorically alluding to their exemplum in 1 Thess 4:9–12 (v. 9: φιλαδελφία; see Rom 12:10), even if the apostle is critical of idolatry elsewhere in the epistle (1 Thess 1:9–10).[70] Christoph vom Brocke has suggested that the Kabeiros cult is the focus of Paul's call to holiness in 1 Thess 4:3 and 5:23.[71] The phallic sexual symbols and revelry of the cult of Dionysus (*IG* 10.2.1.28, 59, 259, 303, 306; 10.2.1s.1058) have been proposed to be the reason behind Paul's summons to sexual purity in 1 Thess 4:3–8.[72]

---

68. For criticism of Jewett's position, see John M. G. Barclay, "Conflict in Thessalonica," *CBQ* 55 (1993): 512–30; Helmut Koester, *Paul and His World: Interpreting the New Testament in Its Context* (Minneapolis: Fortress, 2007), 40–41, 57–58.

69. Karl P. Donfried, "The Cults of Thessalonica and the Thessalonian Correspondence," *NTS* 31 (1985): 336–56; James R. Harrison, "Paul and the Imperial Gospel at Thessaloniki," *JSNT* 25 (2002): 71–96; Jeffrey A. D. Weima, "'Peace and Security' (1 Thess. 5.3): Prophetic Warning or Political Propaganda?," *NTS* 58 (2012): 331–59; Joel R. White, "'Peace' and 'Security' (1 Thess. 5.3): Roman Ideology and Greek Aspiration," *NTS* 60 (2014): 499–510. Contra Najeeb Haddad, "Paul in Context: A Reinterpretation of Paul and Empire" (PhD diss., Loyola University, 2018), passim.

70. John S. Kloppenborg, "ΦΙΛΑΔΕΛΦΙΑ, ΘΕΟΔΙΔΑΚΤΟΣ and the Dioscuri: Rhetorical Engagement in 1 Thessalonians 4:9–12," *NTS* 39 (1993): 265–89.

71. Vom Brocke, *Thessaloniki*, 121.

72. Donfried, "Cults of Thessalonica," 337; see also Tzanavari, "Worship of Gods and Heroes," 205–16.

As helpful as these observations may be, they have to be interpreted within Paul's overall understanding of the pneumatic deliverance of the Thessalonian believers and, concomitantly, their summons to a cruciform imitation of their Lord and apostle (1 Thess 1:5–6). Their vocation, Paul states, was to suffer persecution as Christ's faithful disciples in this idolatrous city, despite the pressure that the Thessalonian cults, their officials, and worshipers brought to bear against believers because of their distinctive ethos (1 Thess 1:6, 2:14b, 3:4; 2 Thess 1:4–5). The spiritual determination of the gentile Thessalonian believers was publicly displayed by their abandonment of the social prestige associated with the city's civic cults and, relatedly, by their refusal to be seduced by the deceitfulness of idolatry. In abandoning these lifeless images for the living God, Thessalonian believers were encouraged to wait for the eschatological return of God's risen Son, who would rescue them from the coming wrath (1 Thess 1:9–10). This rich blend of pneumatology, monotheism, and eschatology, the latter christologically modified, and a commitment to cruciform discipleship allowed the apostle to chart a new form of community and social relations for Thessalonian believers (1 Thess 4:3–12, 5:4–11).[73] This would provide a vastly different historical narrative and future for a world doomed to destruction, filled as it was with lifeless gods at Thessalonica and elsewhere.

3. The Thessalonian Associations and the Social Composition of Paul's Churches

The Thessalonian inscriptions and their relation to the epistles of Paul have been intensively studied by Richard Ascough. He has analyzed the comparanda between the Thessalonian churches and the city's associations regarding leadership, communal relationships, and community structures.[74] What clues do the Thessalonian association inscriptions reveal about the social composition of the Thessalonian house churches?

---

73. On how this works out in the mission context of the Thessalonian associations, see Richard S. Ascough, "Redescribing the Thessalonians' 'Mission' in Light of Graeco-Roman Associations," *NTS* 60 (2014): 61–82.

74. See Richard S. Ascough, "The Thessalonian Christian Community as a Professional Voluntary Association," *JBL* 119 (2000): 311–28; Ascough, *Paul's Macedonian Associations: The Social Context of Philippians and 1 Thessalonians*, WUNT 2/161 (Tübingen: Mohr Siebeck, 2003); Ascough, "Redescribing the Thessalonians' 'Mission.'"

We have to respect the rhetorical context of the thirteen Thessalonian association inscriptions.⁷⁵ They are, with one exception (*IG* 10.2.1.255; see §5 below), all honorific, either eulogizing benefactors or memorializing deceased (SEG 42.625; *IG* 10.2.1.291, 506) and living members (*IG* 10.2.1.68), association officials, and cult personnel. This means that the urban elites would be honored at the expense of the thirty-eight male banqueters named in a dedication to *theos hyphistos* (*IG* 10.2.1.68). We know nothing about them other than their ethnic homogeneity as Macedonians (with two exceptions) and, in six instances, their servile origins.⁷⁶ However, there are significant clues in some inscriptions about the social constituency of the Thessalonian associations. For example, the association decree in honor of a benefactor, graced with a relief of Anubis (*IG* 10.2.1.58), reveals a mixed social constituency: the slave names of freemen banqueters (Felix, Primus, Secundus) occur in an inscription honoring a benefactor who "established the meeting place (*oikos*)."⁷⁷

High-profile benefactors also set up for their fellow banqueters four columns adorned with capitals, bases, and lintels (*IG* 10.2.1.48), bequeathed vineyards located in the village (*asty*) of Perdylia for the association banquets of Zeus Dionysios Gongylos (*IG* 10.2.1.259),⁷⁸ and donated vineyards from which funds the priestess honorand would have sacrifices offered "for (her) eternal memory" (*IG* 10.2.1.260). Other individuals of significant social and economic status in the Thessalonian associations include (1) priests (*IG* 10.2.1.70), (2) a priestess (*IG* 10.2.1.206), (3) a merchant shipper (SEG.625), and (4) a city councilor (*IG* 10.2.1.506).⁷⁹

---

75. Richard S. Ascough, Philip A. Harland, and John S. Kloppenborg, *Associations in the Greco-Roman World: A Sourcebook* (Waco, TX: Baylor University Press, 2012), §§47–59.

76. See the detailed exposition of Craig Steven de Vos, *Church and Community Conflicts: The Relationships of the Thessalonian, Corinthian, and Philippian Churches with Their Wider Civic Communities*, SBLDS 168 (Atlanta: Scholars Press, 1997), 134–35.

77. Walsh and Nasrallah, "Thessaloniki," s.v. "Dining Association Stele with Relief of Anubis." Trans. Ascough, Harland, and Kloppenborg, *Associations in the Greco-Roman World*, §47; see also §53.

78. For further mention of Macedonian villages outside Thessalonica, in addition to ἄστυ mentioned above (*IG* 10.2.1.259: normally translated "city," "town"), see κώμη ("village"): *IG* 10.2.1s.1527, l. 3; *IG* 10.2.1s.1532, l. 4. Also *vicus* ("village"): *IG* 10.2.1s.1516, l. 4.

79. On priests, see *IG* 10.2.1.58: "priest for a second time"; 10.2.1.506: "priest of societies of Dionysious"; Ascough, *Associations in the Greco-Roman World*, §54. The

Individuals from the lower social echelon trades are also mentioned, such as those belonging to an association of transport professionals, visually honored by the relief of a donkey driver on the gravestone.[80] Although there is an honorific bias toward the elites in the Thessalonian association inscriptions, a mixed social constituency nevertheless emerges from the evidence above. Was this spread of social echelons reflected in the Thessalonian house churches?

Several New Testament scholars have argued that the social constituency of the Thessalonian churches belonged to the lower echelon of the trade associations, consisting of a homogenous community of freed/free casual workers living around subsistence level.[81] The gentile craftspeople congregation is encouraged by the apostle to work with their own hands (1 Thess 1:3, 2:9, 4:11), though communal support (4:11–12) is firmly in the apostle's sight as opposed to individual self-sufficiency. Seemingly, the congregation belonged to the urban poor (2 Cor 8:2, "extreme poverty"; 1 Thess 4:11–12), but the members were provided significant opportunities for gospel outreach by virtue of their artisan work on market streets (though note the individual instruction mentioned in 1 Thess 2:11).[82] Significantly, the apostle refuses to place any economic pressure on the Thessalonians, supporting himself by means of his own manual labor (1 Thess 2:9; 2 Thess 3:8). The experience of outside persecution would have compounded their vulnerable situation (1 Thess 1:6, 14–16; 3:3–4; 4:12), as well as the vagaries of employment for manual and casual workers in the Roman Empire.[83] There is no hint in the Thessalonian epistles of wealthy benefactors and civic elites in the Macedonian churches who were comparable in size and status to those at Corinth (e.g., 1 Cor 1:26; 6:1–2,

---

gravestone of a merchant shipper shows a relief of a Thessalonian man steering a boat (Ascough, Harland, and Kloppenborg, *Associations in the Greco-Roman World*, §47, fig. 7).

80. Ascough, Harland, and Kloppenborg, *Associations in the Greco-Roman World*, §54, p. 50, fig. 8.

81. See Míguez, *Practice of Hope*, 56–71; de Vos, *Church and Community Conflicts*, 147–54; UnChan Jung, "Paul's Letter to Free(d) Casual Workers: Profiling the Thessalonians in Light of the Roman Economy," *JSNT* 42 (2020): 472–95. More generally, see Ascough, *Paul's Macedonian Associations*.

82. See the classic work of Ronald F. Hock, *The Social Context of Paul's Ministry: Tentmaking and Apostleship* (Philadelphia: Fortress, 1980); see also the qualifications of de Vos, *Church and Community Conflicts*, 152–54.

83. See Jung, "Paul's Letter to Free(d) Casual Workers," 478–83.

7; 11:17–22; Rom 16:1–2, 23). Consequently, Longenecker concludes that the majority of Thessalonian believers eked out an existence at subsistence level.[84] In contrast to the Thessalonian associations, the Pauline churches in the city could not rely on wealthy individuals to subsidize the activities of the whole group. No one, therefore, could naively afford to be idle in the city, waiting for the arrival of benefactions (2 Thess 3:6–13). Significantly, *all* believers are summoned to "help the weak" (1 Thess 5:14b).

However, Timothy Brookins has recently challenged this construct, noting that the account of Acts provides "no indication of lower-class converts."[85] Rather, Luke highlights the elite membership of the Thessalonian church. Note the conversion of leading women in the city (Acts 17:2) and the financial ability of Jason to exercise hospitality and post bail for arrested believers (17:5, 9). Indeed, Luke himself was dependent on the patronage of "most excellent Theophilus" (Luke 1:4; Acts 1:1) for the production of his double volume on Christian origins. Brookins concludes that Luke's characterization of the early Thessalonian church has veracity because someone must have provided accommodation for the meetings of the house churches in the city ("they rushed to Jason's house in search of Paul and Silas": Acts 15:5b NIV).[86] Furthermore, those who had abandoned work in the congregation (1 Thess 4:11; see also 2 Thess 3:6–13) were likely depending on the beneficence of believing benefactors within the Thessalonian congregation, though, I would add, reliance on the civic benefaction of public feasts periodically at Thessalonica should not be discounted.[87]

Nevertheless, we should not overlook the theological purpose animating Luke's rhetorical interest in elite believers and benefactors in

---

84. Bruce W. Longenecker, "Exposing the Economic Middle: A Revised Economy Scale for the Study of Early Christianity," *JSNT* 31 (2009): 248.

85. Timothy A. Brookins, *First and Second Thessalonians*, Paideia (Grand Rapids: Baker Academic, 2021), 12.

86. Brookins, *First and Second Thessalonians*, 12. Alternatively, assuming that tenements also provided meeting places for Thessalonian believers, these would require the payment of rent by individuals. See Robert Jewett, "Tenement Churches and Communal Meals in the Early Church: The Implications of a Form-Critical Analysis of 2 Thess 3:10," *BR* 38 (1993): 23–43.

87. See Bruce W. Winter, "'If a Man Does Not Wish to Work...': A Cultural and Historical Setting for 2 Thessalonians 3:6–16," *TynBul* 39 (1988): 303–15; Timothy J. Murray, *Restricted Generosity in the New Testament*, WUNT 2/480 (Tübingen: Mohr Siebeck, 2018), 180–86.

the Acts narrative (see Luke 7:1–10).[88] Luke depicts the highly stratified social and economic hierarchy of the acquisitive elites (e.g., Luke 12:13–21, 22:24–25; Acts 24:26–27), with a view to highlighting by comparison God's countercultural kingdom community, whose other-centered values were antithetical to the self-interested elites (Luke 6:30–36, 22:26–28; Acts 20:32–35).[89] In other words, given Luke's strong rhetorical purpose, we should not unduly exaggerate the presence of elite believers at Thessalonica on the basis of Acts 17:1–9. At best we can only posit a very light sprinkling of benefactors in a church consisting of a preponderantly poor and marginalized majority.

4. Thessalonian Entertainment

Thessalonica, like other large eastern Mediterranean cities, had a wide range of entertainment to offer to its citizens through its benefactors: athletic games, spectacles, festivals, and competitions. Consequently, the city had substantial entertainment venues that citizens could attend in order to enjoy these activities: the theater-stadium (last quarter of the first century to early second century CE), the Odeion (second century CE), and the Galerian hippodrome.[90] The greatest concentration of epigraphic evidence relates to gladiatorial spectacles, the theater being the main entertainment venue in Roman Macedonia, but each other category of entertainment is represented in the documents.[91]

---

88. E.g., Sergius Paulus of Cyprus: Acts 13:4–14; Lydia the purple seller at Philippi: 16:14–15; Dionysius the Areopagite at Athens: 17:34; elite Thessalonian women (17:2; see Luke 8:3) and a high status Athenian woman Damaris mentions alongside Dionysius (Acts 17:34). See Alexander Weiß, *Sociale Elite und Christentum: Studien zu ordo-Angehörigen unter den frühen Christen*, MillSt 52 (Berlin: de Gruyter, 2015), 29–105. More generally, see David W. Gill, "Acts and the Urban Elites," in Gill and Gempf, *Graeco-Roman Setting*, 105–18.

89. Jonathan Marshall, *Jesus, Patrons, and Benefactors: Roman Palestine and the Gospel of Luke*, WUNT 2/259 (Tübingen: Mohr Siebeck, 2009); Karl Allen Kuhn, *Luke, the Elite Evangelist*, PSN (Collegeville, MN: Glazier, 2010).

90. For discussion, see Matthew Schueller, "Public Entertainment Venues as Urban Network Actors in Roman Macedonia and Thrace" (PhD diss., University of North Carolina, Chapel Hill, 2020), 221–59.

91. Schueller, "Public Entertainment Venues," 149. Given the lateness of construction of the Galerian hippodrome, we will not discuss the inscription of the charioteer Uranius Porphyris (*IG* 10.2.1.842). For discussion, see Schueller, "Public Entertainment Venues," 240–41.

4.1. The Athletic Games of Thessalonica

Three inscriptions mentioning athletes at Thessalonica are worth highlighting here. In *IG* 10.2.1.541 the athlete Ammonius is honored with a partially damaged six-line inscription on a marble sarcophagus, not able to be dated, the final three lines of which (4–6) sum up his achievements thus:

> Skammatis nourished [θρέψε] me and did not bury (me) without tears / until (I managed) to show virtue [ἀρετήν] of soul and strength [κάρτεα] of hands, / (that) at the end of life, (after) toiling (hard), I have pitiable [οἰκτρά] prizes in the games.

Edson understands Skammatis's nourishment (θρέψε) of Ammonius to be a reference to his rearing as a young man (*IG* 10.2.1.175). Importantly, while our inscription underscores the virtue and strength of Ammonius as an athlete, the result of this grueling process at death is Ammonius's possession of "pitiable prizes" (οἰκτρὰ βραβεῖα). This dismissal of the athletic prizes as not worthy of esteem is surprising in this context. It stands in sharp contrast to the multiple incised crowns, objects of great honor and boasting, found on other Thessalonian gladiator inscriptions.[92] Undoubtedly, the social leveling effects of death and the extinction of accumulated glory by our mortality is the motif being highlighted by the writer of the epitaph. Ancient epitaphs do not gloss over the despoiling and unjust effects of premature death or the ravaging demise of a much-loved honorand at its cruel hands. But there are resonances here with Paul's assessment that earthly athletes strive with great discipline for a "fading" crown (1 Cor 9:25b: φθαρτὸν στέφανον), in contrast to believers, who, by living self-disciplined and other-centered lives, will receive from God the "unfading" eschatological crown (9:25b: ἄφθαρτον; see 1 Thess 2:19: στέφανος καυχήσεως, "crown of boasting").[93] Moreover, the present form

---

92. See n. 91 above.

93. See Oscar Broneer, "The Isthmian Victory Crown," *AJA* 66 (1962): 259–63; Gregory M. Stevenson, "Conceptual Background to Golden Crown Imagery in the Apocalypse of John (4:4, 10; 14:14)," *JBL* 114 (1995): 257–72; James R. Harrison, "The Fading Crown: Divine Honour and the Early Christians," *JTS* 54 (2003): 493–529. On Paul and the culture of ancient athletics, see Victor C. Pfitzner, *Paul and the Agon Motif: Traditional Athletic Imagery in the Pauline Literature* (Leiden: Brill, 1967); Jerry M. Hullinger, "The Historical Background of Paul's Athletic Allusions," *BSac* 161 (2004): 343–59; Martin Brändl, *Der Agon bei Paulus: Herkunft und Profil paulinischer*

of the world, with all its accolades of status and power, is fading away (7:31: παράγει).[94] So the dismissive attitudes of our inscription and the apostle Paul to the honorific rewards of the ancient athletic ideal is intriguing. Our inscription does mention the honorific allocation of crowns to the athlete Ammonius, but unfortunately we cannot retrieve its context due to damage of the sarcophagus.[95] The inscription does not mention the type of athletic contests for which Ammonius was honored, but Edson speculates that they were either wrestling, boxing, or, if a spectacle, the gladiatorial games (*IG* 10.2.1.175). The precision of the phrase "strength of hands" perhaps points to either wrestling or boxing.

Last, in terms of references to games in the Thessalonian epigraphic corpus, there are two lists of those in which athletes competed (e.g., the Aktia, Pythia, Asklepedia, Eusebeia, Sebasta, Eleutheria, Panhellenic, etc.), along with the cities that hosted the competitions (e.g., Olympia, Dephi, Nicopolis, Neapolis, Athens, Eleusis, Miletus, among others). Notably, in both inscriptions the games in Thessalonica are mentioned: Πύθια ἐν Θεσσαλονείκῃ (IThess T50, l. 21; T.51, l. 19). Although Thessalonica did not belong to the famous *periodos* ("circuit") of the games in ancient Greece (i.e., the Pythian, Isthmian, Nemean, and Olympian contests), the city, as the capital of the province of Macedonia from 146 CE onward, was an important participant in ancient athletic culture.

Agonmetaphorik, WUNT 2/222 (Tübingen: Mohr Siebeck, 2006); Alan H. Cadwallader, "Paul and the Games," in *Paul in the Greco-Roman World: A Handbook*, 2nd ed., ed. J. P. Sampley, (London: T&T Clark, 2016), 1:363–90; James R. Harrison, *Paul and the Ancient Celebrity Circuit: The Cross and Moral Transformation*, WUNT 430 (Tübingen: Mohr Siebeck, 2019), 109–34.

94. For popular philosophers' critiques of crowning rituals in antiquity, see Harrison, "Fading Crown," 519.

95. *IG* 10.2.1.541, l. 2, ὃν σ[τ]εφάνοις τὰς ΟΙΔ[...]; see 1 Thess 2:19; 1 Cor 9:25. Note, however, the six crowns incised on a Thessalonian inscription honoring a *retiarius* (literally "net-man," that is, a gladiator who fought with a net, trident, and dagger). See Louis Robert, *Les gladiateurs dans l'orient grec* (Amsterdam: Hakkert, 1971), §13. Additionally, on the memorial monument of a *secutor* ("chaser") gladiator, we see Leukaspis with his crested helmet placed on a rectangular shield to his left and to his right a palm branch and small dog. There are thirteen wreath crowns over his left shoulder set out in three rows, indicating the number of times he was heralded as victor in the theater-stadium (*IG* 10.2.1.739; Schueller, "Public Entertainment Venues," 236).

4.2. Gladiatorial Spectacles of Thessalonica

Turning to the role of the gladiator (*monachos*) and the beast-fighter (*bestiarus*) in the arena at Thessalonica, excavated in the 1990s,[96] Klaudios Rouphrios Menon, high priest of the metropolis and colony of the Thessalonians, is lauded for "making preparations for (animal) hunts and gladiatorial games for one day" (IThess 1.10B, ll. 10–11). On another occasion he performs the same public benefaction for three days (IThess 1.10A, ll. 8–9). The Thessalonian benefactress Hispane also left money in her will to stage gladiatorial battles and animal hunts in honor of Antoninus Pius and Marcus Aurelius (*IG* 10.2.1.137; 141 CE). In a fragmentary inscription honoring a *bestiarus*, restored by Nigdeles (IThess 248), there is this graphic vignette: "pursued by a leopard I escape from (his) bite" (IThess 3.6, ll. 6–7 = *IG* 10.2.1s.1516).

Another inscription of a Thessalonian gladiator, set up at Philippoupolis, shows a loin-clothed gladiator, palm in his left hand and a crown in his right hand. To his left there is a crested helmet with a closed visor, and to his right is a small dog (see the dogs in the gladiator iconography of *IG* 10 2.1.306 and 10.2.1.739).[97] The epitaph highlights the gladiator's demise at the hands of his opponent and his postmortem vindication:

---

96. For details of the part of the curved 100-m wide theater excavated at Thessalonica, which is part of a huge circus building and was used during the first through fourth centuries CE, see Giorgos Velenis and Polyxeni Adam-Veleni, "Theatre – Stadium of Thessaloniki," Diazoma, https://tinyurl.com/SBL4221c; Schueller, "Public Entertainment Venues," 221–23.

97. The iconography of the Thessalonian "gladiator" inscriptions is often as revealing as the inscription itself. For example, on a Thessalonian stela (Robert, *Les gladiateurs*, §12) we see a cavalier in the pediment. Below there is a full frontal bust of a beardless man, who is approached on the right by a left-handed gladiator. He has a crested helmet completely hiding his face and holds a dagger in his left hand and a rectangular shield in his right hand. His legs also have substantial protection (e.g., bands protecting his right knee and a belt guarding his upper thighs). Sometimes the relief has almost totally disappeared from the inscription (Robert, *Les gladiateurs*, §14). On the positive Greco-Roman attitude to dogs, demonstrated by the canine accompaniment of the gladiator above, see James R. Harrison, "'Every Dog Has Its Day,'" *NewDocs* 10:136–45. For inscriptions honoring a *retiarius* with substantial iconography on the stone, see Robert, *Les gladiateurs*, §13; *IG* 10.2.1s.1287. For further gladiator iconography, see *IG* 10.21s.1263. For full discussion of the iconography, see Schueller, "Public Entertainment Venues," 234–37.

I, Biktor, a left-handed man [σκευᾶς],[98] lie here, but Thessalonica (is) my father-land;
Fate stretches me out,[99] not the falsely swearing [ἐπίορκος] Pinnas;
let him boast no longer; I had Polyneikes (as my) fellow armed (gladiator), who, having killed Pinnas, avenged me.
Klaudios Thallos organised (this) memorial from (the funds) which I bequeathed.[100]

The left-handedness of Biktor made him an unusually skilled fighter, presumably difficult to parry because of his distinctive fighting technique. The unspecified but implied connection between Biktor and Polyneikes probably indicates a prior contractual relationship that specified who fought against whom,[101] as well as (I would add) who took retribution against opponents who might violate gladiatorial fighting conventions. Pinnas seems to be an instance of such a duplicitous opponent, who was retrospectively killed for his execution of Biktor in their contest. If we adopt a minimalist understanding of the rhetoric employed against him, then ἐπίορκος simply means "liar" or "perjurer." But one wonders why such a specific charge would be aired against one's opponent on a gladiatorial sepulchral monument, other than it being a contemptuous dismissal of the person. More likely the literal translation, "falsely swearing," is preferable

---

98. Robert disagrees with those scholars (e.g., Zlatozara Goceva) who regard σκευᾶς (line 1) as the second name ("Skeuas") of Biktor. See Robert, *Les gladiateurs*, 72; Zlatozara Goceva, "Gladiatorenkämpfe in Thrakien," *Klio* 63 (1981): 494. Instead, Robert argues that the Greek σκευᾶς is the Latin equivalent of *scaeva* ("left-handed person"), a position I have reflected in my translation. Note, too, that some translators render "Biktor" as "Victor" (Goceva, "Gladiatorenkämpfe in Thrakien," 494). I have kept the original form of the Greek in my translation.

99. IThess T41; Robert, *Les gladiateurs*, §34. See IThess T40, ll. 1–3, a gladiatorial sepulchral stela decorated in bas-relief with a standing figure, for another Thessalonian gladiator who has been subdued by Fate: "Such a one you would see, O stranger, (the) figure modelled with stone, / of such quality in courage (ἐν ἀνδρείᾳ) (that) Moira, (the goddess of Fate), deprived me of life, / (my) name (being) Preimogenes, from the fatherland of Thessalonica." In a 200–250 CE Thessalonian epitaph for Q. Fabius Agathopous, we hear of a cult association (συνηθία) of Nemesis, the goddess of theater, games, and retribution, which undoubtedly comprised gladiators and *bestiarii* members (*IG* 10.2.1s.1192).

100. On the payment of "slave" and "free" gladiators, see Michael Carter, "Gladiatorial Ranking and the 'SC de Pretis Gladiatorum Minuendis' (CIL II 6278 = ILS 5163)," *Phoenix* 57 (2003): 104–6.

101. Goceva, "Gladiatorenkämpfe in Thrakien," 494.

because it should be understood against the backdrop of the *sacramentum gladiatorium*. The gladiator swore an oath to his gladiatorial manager "to be burned, bound, beaten, and slain by the sword" (*uri, vinciri, verberari, ferroque, necari patior*: Petronius, *Satyr.* 117; Seneca, *Ep.* 71.23). Carlin Barton insightfully observes regarding the swearing ceremony: "The gladiator, by his oath, transforms what had originally been an involuntary act to a voluntary one, and so, at the very moment that he becomes a slave condemned to death, he becomes a free agent and a man with honor to uphold."[102] Zlatozara Goceva concludes concerning this inscription that only a free professional gladiator had the right of a free person to set up his own monument, as the Greeks did, decorated with his own image as a triumphant gladiator.[103]

Somehow, in a way not specified in the inscription but the general gist of opprobrium is conveyed by the technical term ἐπίορκος, Pinnas had violated his gladiatorial oath in his contest with Biktor, dishonoring himself and the dead Biktor in the process.[104] This justified not only the charge that he was a false oath-swearer but also his subsequent retributory death at Polyneikes's hands. The inscription raises the issue of the probity of oath taking, the ritual being an indication of honor and *fides* ("trustworthiness"). Both Paul and Jesus also highlight the importance of probity in oath-taking (Matt 5:33-37; 2 Cor 11:31: οὐ ψεύδομαι; 1 Thess 2:5a: "as God is our witness").[105]

Five recent epigraphic finds of importance from Thessalonica are a series of invitations to the gladiatorial games; some are highly fragmentary

---

102. Carlin A. Barton, *The Sorrows of the Ancient Romans: The Gladiator and the Monster* (Princeton: Princeton University Press, 1993), 27. Carter refers to the jurist Gaius, who says that even though gladiators had sold themselves into slavery they still retained their status as free men before the law ("Gladiatorial Ranking," 105; Gaius, *Inst.* 3.199).

103. Goceva, "Gladiatorenkämpfe in Thrakien," 495.

104. For an inscription honoring a deceased referee of gladiatorial contests, the referees themselves being most likely ex-gladiators (*IG* 10.2.1.550).

105. On the Jewish context of oaths and the teaching Jesus, see William D. Davies and Dale C. Allison, *A Critical and Exegetical Commentary on the Gospel according to Saint Matthew*, 3 vols. (Edinburgh: T&T Clark, 1988–1997), 1:532-38. On the Roman military imagery of the *corona muralis* present in the boasting passage of 2 Cor 11:30-33 and the importance of verification (11:31b), see Edwin A. Judge, "The Conflict of Educational Aims in the New Testament," in *The First Christians in the Roman World: Augustan and New Testament Essays*, ed. James R. Harrison, WUNT 229 (Tübingen: Mohr Siebeck, 2008), 707-8, esp. 708 n. 119.

(*IG* 10.2.1s.1072, 1076), but others are highly revealing (*IG* 10.2.1s.1073–75) about gladiatorial culture. Two invitations to the games, which not only announce the future games but also a day of animal hunts and gladiatorial battles, are especially worth highlighting, albeit briefly. Each was found in the pavement of the Odeum's orchestra. The first invitation is the to Actian Kabeiran Pythian games (*IG* 10.2.1s.1074; 259 CE) and has "preserved traces of painted scenes of the hunts and fights that spectators were to expect."[106] It was issued by the provincial governor, Tiberius Claudius Rufrius Meno, a Macedoniarch and high priest of the imperial cult, in conjunction with his wife, Baebia Magna, the high priestess of the imperial cult. The second invitation, this time to the Caesarian Triumphal Kabeiran Pythian games (*IG* 10.2.1s.1075), was issued by the same married couple in the following year (260 CE), Meno in this instance being referred to as high priest of Kabeiros and Baebia as Macedoniarch. The intersection between the international prestige that Thessalonica, as the capital of the Roman capital of Macedonia, acquired through these games and the role of provincial governor, Rome's representative in issuing the invitations, created indissoluble bonds of loyalty to the Roman emperors, Valerian and Gallienus, on the part of both parties. This is underscored in the preface to second invitation, this time to the Caesarian Triumphal Kabeiran Pythian games: "On behalf of the health and safety and victory of the eternal distribution of our greatest and most holy lords" (*IG* 10.2.1s.1075).

4.3. Festivals and Competitions of Thessalonica

Regarding Greek dramatic festivals, an epitaph (*IG* 10.2.1.436) possibly refers to a pantomime, though this is by no means certain.[107] However, the presence of pantomimes in second-century CE Thessalonica has been confirmed by the archaeological find of a stone theater mask in the city, possibly originally located in the theater-stadium or the Odeum. From its distinctive features (furrowed brows, sad eyes, downturned mouth), this is undoubtedly the tragic mask of the pantomimes.[108] Additionally, the grave

---

106. Schueller, "Public Entertainment Venues," 247.

107. Mali A. Skotheim, "Greek Dramatic Festivals under the Roman Empire" (PhD diss., Princeton University, 2016), 1:304 n. 202.

108. Schueller, "Public Entertainment Venues," 231. See Polyxeni Adam-Veleni for two Thessalonian figurines of mime-actors. Adam-Velini, "Entertainment and Arts in Thessaloniki," in Gramenos, *Roman Thessaloniki*, 271, fig. 8.

altar of M. Varinus Areskon (*IG* 10 2.1s.1386; last quarter of the second century CE) identifies him as an actor in traditional tragedies through its iconography, depicting the deceased with a tragic mask to the right side of his head (an old woman with wide-open mouth and pained expression).[109] A votive altar at Thessalonica also lists the results of the various competitions in the Pythian games of 252 CE (*IG* 10 2.1.38), enumerating the types of athletic games (pentathlon, pankration, dolichos, etc.: lines 1–29) and their victors. Most important for our purposes, the festivals' musical and dramatic events are listed on lines 1–15 of an excavated stone to the left side of the altar: a Thessalonian tragedian (line 10), the kithara (lyre) player and the singer who provided accompaniment (lines 11–12), a poet (line 4), a trumpeter (line 1) and a herald (line 2).[110] Last, the Odeum, which was situated in the Roman Forum, initially functioned as a council chamber and later as a site for performances in the third century CE. In the orchestra were found three statues of the muses and the fragments of a fourth, but of which there were originally nine, representing the arts and letters. The three remaining statues are "Erato, the Muse of lyric poetry, with her *kithara*, Klio the Muse of history, holding a writing tablet, and Euterpe, the Muse of flutes and tragic dance."[111]

4.4. New Testament Intersections

In what are deemed the authentic letters of Paul, one is struck by the sparsity of agonistic terminology (ἀγών: Phil 1:30; 1 Thess 2:2; see also Col 2:1; 1 Tim 6:12; 2 Tim 4:7), though, as noted, athletic motifs are more widely used in Paul's letters elsewhere. In the case of 1 Thess 2:2 (ἐν πολλῷ ἀγῶνι: "in great conflict"), Paul outlines his recent sufferings at Philippi and his continued proclamation of the gospel in the face of opposition. Most com-

---

109. Schueller, "Public Entertainment Venues," 232–32, fig. 67 417. For a full description of the relief, with photo, see Adam-Veleni, "Entertainment and Arts," 266, fig. 3. Adam-Veleni interprets the significance of the female mask differently from Schueller: "The female mask next to him probably hints at his acting skills in other roles" ("Entertainment and Arts," 266). However, Schueller's "tragic mask" interpretation is more likely because it works with a known dramatic genre and its stereotypical iconography, as opposed to Adam-Veleni's more speculative proposal.

110. On Thessalonian music and its relevance for that interpretation of 1 Thess 1:8, see the essay of Isaac Soon in this volume.

111. Adam-Veleni, "Entertainment and Arts," 269. For photos of the statues, see 267, fig. 4; 268, fig. 5; 269, fig. 6.

mentators acknowledge the athletic origins of the imagery, emphasizing the dimension of God-given courage (1 Thess 2:2a: ἐπαρρησιασάμεθα ἐν τῷ θεῷ) exhibited at the height of the struggle.[112] Here Paul refers, in my opinion, both to his recent shameful imprisonment at Philippi as an ἀγών (1 Thess 2:2a: προπαθόντες καὶ ὑβρισθέντες ... ἐν Φιλίπποις; see Acts 16:19–39) and to the ensuing opposition at Thessalonica (Acts 17:1–10; see 3:4, 7) as an ἀγών.[113] Nevertheless, other commentators, taking their lead from Abraham Malherbe, interpret the ἀγών image in the context of popular philosophy, where the moral philosophers described "their endeavor as a contest or struggle," often experiencing ridicule in public debate with their audiences.[114] In a public contest for these urban crowds,[115] Paul, therefore, contrasts the immense effort undergirding his preaching ministry at Thessalonica with the powerless speech of the philosophers.

Notably, Paul's accent on boldness and courage (1 Thess 2:2a: ἐπαρρησιασάμεθα) does have general resonances with gladiatorial combat in the arena, as noted above (IThess T40, l. 1: ἐν ἀνδρείᾳ). However, Paul uses instead the language of the popular philosophers (ἐπαρρησιασάμεθα) for courage, avoids entirely in his letters the word ἀνδρεία (courage being one of the four cardinal virtues in antiquity), and, most significantly, qualifies the philosophical terminology by the telling addition of ἐν τῷ θεῷ (1 Thess 2:2a: "in God"). In sum, the apostle redefines both the agonistic contexts of the gladiatorial arena and the preaching of the popular philosophers. Thus it is not wise to polarize both of these interpretations unnecessarily, allowing instead for a polyvalence in Paul's language here, especially given the ubiquitous presence of both the games/spectacles *and* the popular philosophers throughout the eastern Mediterranean city states. This is the case irrespective of whether one considers that Paul, in using ἀγών in 1 Thess 2:2, is refer-

---

112. E.g., Béda Rigaux, *Saint Paul: Les épitres aux Thessaloniciens* (Paris: Librairie Lecoffre/Gabalda, 1956), 404; Charles Masson, *Les deux épitres de Saint Paul aux Thessaloniciens* (Paris: Delachaux & Niestlé, 1957), 26.

113. F. F. Bruce refers to Paul's use of ἀγών in Phil 1:30, positing that it refers to his current imprisonment at Rome. See Bruce, *1 and 2 Thessalonians*, WBS 45 (Waco, TX: Word, 1982), 25.

114. Abraham J. Malherbe, *The Letters to the Thessalonians*, AB 32B (New York: Doubleday, 2000), 138; Beverly Gaventa, *First and Second Thessalonians*, Int (Louisville: John Knox, 1998), 24.

115. Earl J. Richard, *First and Second Thessalonians*, SP 11 (Collegeville, MN: Glazier, 1995), 79.

ring to his recent Philippian imprisonment (1 Thess 2:2a; Acts 16:19–39) and his hasty exit from Thessalonica (1 Thess 2:17a) or to the opposition attending his public proclamation of the gospel in Thessalonica, where he modeled a vastly different pattern of ministry to the peripatetic sophists (Acts 17:1–10; 1 Thess 2:3–12).

Finally, the exposure of Paul to the traveling mime show troupes during his travels throughout the eastern Mediterranean basin in the mid-first century CE—though our Thessalonian evidence postdates Paul by two centuries—alerted the apostle to the rhetorical potential of mime plots and characters in constructing his fool's speech in 2 Cor 11:16–12:10.[116] In a rhetorical tour de force, Paul depicts the foolishness of his apostolic sufferings on behalf of his coverts by assuming the "runaway fool" trope of the mime comedies in order to lampoon the boasting of the intruding false apostles at Corinth (2 Cor 11:30–33).[117] In 1 Cor 1–4 Paul's searing diatribe against human wisdom and boasting in leaders, conducted on the basis of the foolishness of the cross, again draws on many of the motifs found in the traveling mime shows.[118]

5. Dream and Vision Revelations at Thessalonica and Early Christianity

Vision and dream revelations, spanning the Hellenistic and early imperial periods, appear infrequently in the documentary evidence of Thessalonica; nevertheless, they form an important part of the wider religious Greco-Roman background within which the author of Acts and the apostle Paul experienced and assessed God's Spirit-given revelation. Five pieces of evidence will be discussed.

First, the Derveni Papyrus is a carbonized book-roll that was found in the remains of a funeral pyre in a tomb at Derveni in January 1962, 12 km northwest of Thessalonica. The scroll—comprising twenty-six columns, some of which are badly damaged—had been placed on the funeral pyre as an offering and is dated roughly between 340 and 320 BCE.[119] The book-

---

116. Larry L. Welborn, "The Runaway Paul: A Character in the Fool's Speech," *HTR* 92 (1999): 420–35.

117. Welborn, "Runaway Paul," 152–59.

118. Larry L. Welborn, *Paul, the Fool of Christ: A Study of 1 Corinthians 1–4 in the Comic-Philosophic Tradition*, JSNTSup 293 (London: T&T Clark, 2005).

119. For the *editio princeps* of the whole papyrus, see Theokritos Kouremenos, George M. Parássoglou, and Kyriakos Tsantsanoglou, *The Derveni Papyrus: Edited*

roll itself was originally composed in Ionian Greek near the end of the fifth century BCE, though the identity of its author remains a matter of unresolved scholarly debate. Whoever the author might be, he was a rationalist who reinterpreted traditional Greek literature in light of the pre-Socratic molecular physics, belonging to the tradition espoused by thinkers such as Anaxagoras, the Atomists, and Diogenes of Apollonia. The text is a verse-by-verse allegorical commentary on an Orphic cosmogonic poem (cols. VII–XIV, XXI–XXVI), culminating in column XX, where he attacks initiates of the Orphic mysteries as gullible because they do not understand the strange rites and texts associated with the mysteries.[120] Columns I–V deal with the afterlife, with column VI outlining the rites that ensure the passage of the soul to the life beyond earthly existence.[121] The section of the Derveni Papyrus dealing with dream-visions (col. V) is set out below:

> terrors (?) … ask an oracle … they ask an oracle … for them we will enter the prophetic shrine to inquire, with regard to what is prophesied, whether it is permissible to disbelieve in the terrors of Hades. Why do they disbelieve (in them)? Since they do not understand dream-visions or any of the other occurrences, what sort of proofs would induce them to believe? For, since they are overcome by both error and pleasure as well, they do not learn or believe. Disbelief and ignorance are the same thing. For if they did not learn or comprehend, it is impossible for them to believe even when they see dream-visions … disbelief … appears.

The author asks why the initiates of the mysteries, when they enter a prophetic shrine to inquire about the future or the afterlife, either do not believe the oracle given or reject the terrors of Hades. The answer is that they do not understand the dream-vision properly, which, given the wider context of the work, must be interpreted in an allegorical manner.[122] Here disbelief

---

with *Introduction and Commentary*, STCP 13 (Florence: Casa Editrice Leo S. Olschki, 2006). See also Gábor Betegh, *The Derveni Papyrus: Cosmology, Theology, and Interpretation* (Cambridge: Cambridge University Press, 2004); Marco A. Santamaría, ed., *The Derveni Papyrus: Unearthing Ancient Mysteries*, PLB 36 (Leiden: Brill, 2019). In what follows, I am using the translation of Richard Janko, "The Derveni Papyrus ('Diagoras of Melos, Apopyrgizontes Logoi?'): A New Translation," *CP* 96 (2001): 1–32.

120. On the aim of the text, see Janko, "Derveni Papyrus," 2–3.
121. Amir Ahmadi, "The 'Magoi' and 'Daimones' in Column VI of the Derveni Papyrus," *Numen* 61 (2014): 484–508.
122. Janko "Derveni Papyrus," 19 n. 82.

is equated with ignorance in the arts of the proper allegorical interpretation of dream-visions. However, the writer highlights that the potential initiates are not only overcome by conceptual error but also are too devoted to "pleasure": a hedonistic lifestyle prevents the dream-vision recipient from progressing any further in understanding correctly what the horrors of Hades truly signify.[123] In sum, as James Russel observes,[124] Orphism was not incongruous with the beliefs of fourth-century BCE Macedonia: the mother of Alexander the Great, Olympias, engaged with the Macedonian Bacchanalia, which Plutarch styles "Orphic" (*Alex.* 2), and Orphic inscriptions have been found on three fifth-century BCE bone plates at Olbia.

Second, by the time of the first-century BCE through second-century CE epigraphic evidence from Thessalonica, a literalistic emphasis on the content of dream revelation predominated, as was the case with the epigraphic tradition. The thanksgiving (εὐχαριστήριον) of G. Ioulius Orios to the great Saviour Theos Hypistos (*IG* 10.2.1.67; 74/75 CE) was occasioned by a dream experience (κατ' ὄνειρον) in which he was "solemnly warned (χρηματισθείς) and saved (σωθείς) from great danger over the sea." Two further κατ'ὄνειρον ("in answer to a dream") formulae appear: there is a dream-prompted dedication of Parmenion, son of Dionsios, to Isis (κατ'ὄνιρον: *IG* 10.2.1.99; first century BCE/first century CE), while the other revelation-inspired dedication, offered on behalf of the child of Polukleitos, is made to Isis, Serapis, and the temple-sharing gods (*IG* 10.2.1.88; first century CE). A variation on the revelation formula (καθ' ὅραμα: "in answer to a vision," *IG* 10.2.1.82; second–first centuries BCE) occurs in another dedication to Serapis and Isis.[125] Here we see a direct link between dream revelation and cultic responses to the gods, either expressing gratitude for beneficence experienced or exuding praise in response to divinely initiated revelation. Interestingly, in each case the god initiates the dream experience, prompting the human response, rather than vice versa.

---

123. See Betegh, who argues that the theology of the Derveni Papyrus "leaves little room for a direct divine personal intervention," leaning instead more toward a natural theology (*Derveni Papyrus*, 356–57).

124. James R. Russel, "The Magi in the Derveni Papyrus," *NIBIJ* 1 (2001): 50.

125. Another Isis revelation formula (*IG* 10.2.1.120), pertaining to a dream or vision, could be "Venetia Prima (given) according to a command (κατ' ἐπιταγήν)." On the plaque are impressions of the deity's footprints. Trans. Walsh and Nasrallah, "Thessaloniki," s.v. "Votive Inscription with Feet." For the relief, see Tzanavari, "Worship of Gods and Heroes," 250, fig. 48.

Third, there is an extensive dream revelation regarding the foundation of an association of Serapis.[126] There Xenainetos experiences a marvelous dream (θαυμάξαι τε τὸν [ὄ]νειρον, lines 7–8) in which Serapis stood beside him. Xenainetos is ordered, upon his arrival in Opus, to carry a letter, which will be left under his pillow, to his political rival Eurynomos and to ask him "to receive Serapis and his sister Isis." Upon the miraculous receipt of the letter, Xenainetos meets with his rival Eurynomos, and the latter is unexpectedly persuaded to establish Serapis and Isis among the household gods in the household of Sosinike. Consequently, sacrifices are regularly offered by Sosinike. Moreover, Eunosta, granddaughter of Sosibas, continues the administration of the mysteries of the gods among those not initiated in the cult upon the death of Sosinike. In sum, the considerable difficulty of persuading a political rival to establish a household of association of Serapis in Opus—the motivation for which would be initially viewed by the rival with great suspicion and subsequently with envy if the association were successfully established—only serves to underscore the divine legitimation of the Serapis association in the city and the accompanying miraculous power of the god's dream revelation.

How do such dream revelations at Thessalonica intersect with the narrative of the book of Acts? The skepticism of the Derveni Papyrus, where the dream content is allegorized in order to be understood, is not the case in the book of Acts, where "dreams and visions" are included in the prophetic media (καὶ προφεύσουσιν: Acts 2:17b, 18b, "and they shall prophesy").[127] They are clearly foretold by Joel's prophecy (Joel 2:28–32 LXX; Acts 2:16–21) and are fulfilled in the outpouring of the Spirit of the risen and ascended Jesus at Pentecost in the present eschatological age (ἐν ταῖς ἐσχάταις ἡμέραις: Acts 2:17, "in the last days"; see

---

126. *IG* 10.2.1.255 (first–second centuries CE); Ascough, Harland, and Kloppenborg, *Associations in the Greco-Roman World*, §52. See Franciszek Sokolowski, "Propagation of the Cult of Sarapis and Isis in Greece," *GRBS* 15 (1974): 441–48; Sarah E. Rollens, "The God Came to Me in a Dream: Epiphanies in Voluntary Associations as a Context for Paul's Vision of Christ," *HTR* 111 (2018): 41–65.

127. The addition of προφεύσουσιν in Acts 2:18b to the LXX text of Joel, forming an *inclusio* with Acts 2:17b, where προφεύσουσιν is present in the original LXX, shows that Luke understood the *whole* text in that light. As F. F. Bruce states: "The effect of the Spirit's outpouring is the prophetic gift, exercised in visions and dreams and by word of mouth." See Bruce, *Commentary on the Book of Acts: The English Text with Introduction, Exposition and Notes*, NICNT (London: Marshall, Morgan & Scott, 1954), 68–67.

also 2:33). Here we are seeing the pneumatic and christological legitimation of the Christian mission proceeding from Jerusalem to the ends of the earth (Luke 24:47-48; Acts 1:8), though with a universal scope that totally eclipses the localized legitimation of the Serapis association in a household at Opus. Prophecy, therefore, includes all the revelatory phenomena mentioned in verses 17-18, with the twofold καὶ προφεύσουσιν framing *both* verbal and vision/dream revelation under the motif of "prophecy" (vv. 17b, 18b). To be sure, visions in Luke-Acts are never labeled prophecy as such,[128] but on three occasions they are closely linked to the revelatory work of the Spirit (Acts 7:55-56, 10:19, 16:7-9). Thus, as Max Turner has argued, over against Christopher Forbes's constriction of prophecy to verbal inspiration, the Spirit also brings prophetic revelation through visions (Acts 2:17b).[129] There are visions of far-reaching theological and social import (Acts 10:10-23, 11:4-17), personal comfort (7:55-56, 18:9-10), and missionary initiative (Acts 9:10-16, 10:3-6, 16:9-10, 22:12-21, 26:12-23). We might also include under this wider category of "nonverbal" prophecy the various Spirit-inspired revelations in Acts (8:29, 39; 10:19; 11:12; 16:6-7; 20:22-23). Thus prophetic revelation in Luke-Acts is not entirely verbal, but Forbes is entirely correct in saying that *contextually* the prophetic word

---

128. Apart from his one source reference derived from LXX Joel (ἐνύπνια, Acts 2:17), Luke avoids any further usage of "dreams" terminology in Luke-Acts (ἐνύπνια; ὄναρ). Instead he confines himself to "visions" (ὅραμα: Acts 9:10, 12; 10:3, 17, 19; 11:5; 12:9; 16:9-10; 18:9), choosing occasionally synonyms for stylistic variation (ὅρασις: Acts 2:17; ὀπτασία: Luke 1:22, 24:23, 26:19). The sole exception to this is "trance" (ἔκστασις: Acts 10:10, 11:15, 22:17). In restricting himself to a narrow strand of terminology, predominantly ὅραμα, one wonders whether Luke is thereby refusing to enter into the complex debates about dream theory and interpretation in antiquity (*pace IG* 10.2.1.82 above: καθ' ὅραμα), although he adopts some of the Greco-Roman techniques of dream narration in Acts (i.e., the double "dream-vision" report; Peter: Acts 10:9-23, 11:4-17; Paul: 9:3-5, 15-16; 22:6-10, 14-16; 26:12-18). On the latter, see John S. Hanson, "Dreams and Visions in the Graeco-Roman World and Early Christianity," *ANRW* 2.23.2:1395-1427. Additionally, see Keener, *Acts*, 1:911-16. More generally, see Naphtali Lewis, *The Interpretation of Dreams and Portents in Antiquity* (Mundelein, IL: Bolchazy-Carducci, 1997). For helpful comments on ὅραμα and ἐνύπνια in the OT, see Luke T. Johnson, *The Acts of the Apostles*, SP 5 (Collegeville, MN: Glazier, 1992), 49.

129. Max Turner and David Mackinder, "Prophecy and Spiritual Gifts Then and Now," in *Christian Experience in Theology and Life*, ed. I. Howard Marshall (Edinburgh: Rutherford House, 1988), 18-19.

declared at Pentecost was the message about "God's deeds of power" (Acts 2:11; see also 4:31, 10:46, 19:6; Luke 1:41–42, 67; 2:25–32).[130]

Significantly, the geographical move of Paul's missionary efforts from Asia to Europe, instigated by the Spirit-initiated vision of the Macedonian man summoning the apostle over to Macedonia (Acts 16:6–10), is another case of such Spirit-inspired prophetic revelation and would have powerfully resonated with Thessalonian readers familiar with dream media in their own historical context. Indeed, the range of visionary inspiration in early Christianity, with its varied pastoral, social, and evangelistic purposes, exceeds in scope and focus the cultic and association-based forms of dream revelation at Thessalonica, probably provoking interest on the part of some Thessalonians in this new movement in Macedonia.[131]

But what do we make of Paul's "visions and revelations of the Lord" (2 Cor 12:1)? It is surprising how often the apostle and the book of Acts refers to his reception of divinely prompted visions and revelations in shaping his missionary decisions and in pastorally empowering him for the task (Gal 1:16; Acts 9:12, 22:17–23; 2 Cor 12:1–4; Gal 2:2 // Acts 11:28–30; 16:6–8, 9–10; 18:9–19; 21:11; 23:11; 27:23–24).[132] While we must acknowledge the Jewish, pneumatic, and christological understanding underlying Paul's visionary revelations,[133] importing thereby a distinctiveness that differentiated Paul's experience from Greco-Roman oneirology, nevertheless the apostle's strong concentration on dreams and revelations would have caught the attention of the Thessalonians familiar with such experiences.

---

130. Christopher Forbes, *Prophecy and Inspired Speech in Early Christianity and Its Hellenistic Environment* (Peabody, MA: Hendrickson, 1997), 51–52. As Forbes states, "It would seem, in light of Acts chapter 2, that 'prophecy' is the general term under which Luke grouped inspired speech phenomena" (52).

131. For an excellent discussion of the "Macedonian man" vision in its Jewish and Greco-Roman context, see Keener, *Acts*, 3:2342–50.

132. See Paul Barnett, *After Jesus*, vol. 2, *Paul, Missionary of Jesus* (Grand Rapids: Eerdmans, 2008), 211–14. Additionally, James R. Harrison, "In Quest of the Third Heaven: Paul and His Apocalyptic Imitators," *VC* 58 (2004): 24–55; Paula Gooder, *Only The Third Heaven? 2 Corinthians 12:1–10 and Heavenly Ascent* (London: T&T Clark, 2006); Colleen Shantz, *Paul in Ecstasy: The Neurobiology of the Apostle's Life and Thought* (Cambridge: Cambridge, University Press, 2009).

133. E.g., Dale C. Allison Jr., "Acts 9:1–9, 22:6–11, 26:12–18: Paul and Ezekiel," *JBL* 13 (2016): 807–26.

44   James R. Harrison

6. The Jews of Thessalonica

David Noy, Alexander Panayotov, and Hanswulf Bloedhorn have collected the six extant Jewish inscriptions from Thessalonica, setting out the latest recensions of each document, translating them into English, and providing excellent commentaries on their lexical, archaeological, and historical contexts (*IJO* 1.13–18).[134] Therefore an extensive discussion of this material individually is not required here, other than to note below several important sidelights providing insight into the Jewish community from the period spanning the second/third through fourth centuries CE. At the outset, however, we will highlight one additional piece of visual archaeological evidence not associated with the above epigraphic finds. A decorated Jewish tomb from the Byzantine period has emerged from foundation excavations for the new campus of the University of Thessaloniki. The tomb possesses a singular rectangular chamber, with walls that are plastered and white-slipped. Its ceiling is barrel-vaulted, with a circle in the middle perhaps signifying "a stylized and schematic wreath," as well as a *memorah* line-drawing that graces one of the end walls.[135] There is, however, no inscription in the chamber. In the case of our inscriptions, there is also a wreath, with an inscription painted inside (*IJO* 1.Mac13), on a fresco in the fourth-century CE tomb (Tomb B) in the courtyard of the Faculty of Law of the University of Thessaloniki. Further, two *memorahs*

---

134. The commentary on Thessalonica is drawn from the prior doctoral work of Alexander Panayotov, "The Jews in the Balkan Provinces of the Roman Empire: An Epigraphic and Archaeological Survey" (PhD diss., University of St Andrews, 2004), 92–107. See also the earlier collection of Denis Feissel, "Appendice II: Inscriptions juives de Macédoine du IVe au VIe s.," *BCH Supplément* 8 (1983): 240–45, though only five inscriptions are discussed. See the excellent discussion of vom Brocke, *Thessaloniki*, 214–32. Additionally, see Irina Levinskaya, *The Book of Acts in Its First Century Setting*, vol. 5, *Diaspora Setting* (Grand Rapids: Eerdmans, 1996), 154–57; Pantelis M. Nigdelis, "Synagoge(n) und Gemeinde der Juden in Thessaloniki: Fragen aufgrund einer neuen jüdischen Grabinschrift der Kaiserzeit," *ZPE* 102 (1994): 297–306; Ascough, *Paul's Macedonian Associations*, 191–212. On synagogal Judaism in the book of Acts, see Daniel Marguerat, "Le Judaïsme synagogal dans les Actes des Apôtres," in *Les Judaïsmes dans tous leurs états aux Ier–IIIe (Les Judéens des synagogues les Chrétiens et les rabbins): Actes du colloque de Lausanne 12–14 décembre 2012*, ed. Claire Clivaz, Simon C. Mimouni, and Bernard Pouderon (Turnhout: Brepols, 2015), 177–200.

135. Asher Avadiah, "Ancient Jewish Communities in Macedonia, Thrace and Upper Epirus," *Gerión* (2015): 222 and fig. 2.214.

appear at the same site, one in Tomb B (1.Mac13) and the other in Tomb A (1.Mac13), both tombs being just 5 meters apart (*IJO* 1:94). There is no archaeological evidence of a Jewish presence at Thessalonica contemporary with the New Testament documents.

What, then, do we learn about Jewish life at Thessalonica and its environs in late antiquity from the clues found in our six documents? First, the direct citation of the Old Testament Scriptures (*IJO* 1.Mac17: Num 6:22–27) and their intertextual echoes (*IJO* 1.Mac13 [fourth century CE]: see Ps 45:8, 11 LXX [MT Ps 46:8, 11]) remain at the center of the piety of Thessalonian Jews.

Second, the bilingualism of Thessalonian Jews is confirmed in the Samaritan dedicatory inscription, citing Num 6:22–27 and employing the letters of the Samaritan script in lines 1 and 15, with lines 2–14 in Greek (*IJO* 1.Mac17: fourth–sixth centuries CE). Scholars have disagreed on the significance of the thirteen deviations from the LXX text of Numbers in the Samaritan inscription.[136] Baruch Lifschitz and Jean Schiby argue that this demonstrates that there was a lost Samaritan Greek translation of the Pentateuch from which the writer is drawing, whereas Emmanuel Tov argues that the inscription writer is revising the LXX text, rendering more accurately the Hebrew text of the Pentateuch.[137] It is more likely that Tov is correct as opposed to the more speculative proposal of Lifschitz and Schiby, because it reflects the great care that Jews generally took in handling the scriptures and, at a local level, it reveals the strong commitment of Thessalonian Samaritan Jews to a correct rendering of the Hebrew text.

Third, the epitaph of M. Aurelius Jacob and Anna (*IJO* 1.Mac15: third century CE), in outlining the fines to be imposed on those who might inter another corpse in a presently occupied sarcophagus, speaks of the payment of 75,000 drachmai to be made "to the synagogues [ταῖς συναγωγαῖς]." As Irina Levinskaya concludes, "The plural form of the word συναγωγή implies that in the third century there were several Jewish communities in Thessaloniki."[138] Given that the book of Acts only men-

---

136. *IJO* 1:103 conveniently sets out the differences.

137. Baruch Lifshitz and Jean Schiby, "Une synagogue Samaritaine à Thessalonique," *RB* 75 (1968): 368–78. Emmanuel Tov writes: "on peut suggérer que l'inscription samaritaine trouvée à Thessalonique fait partie de la tradition des LXX précisément, qu'elle représente une révision particulière de cette tradition." See Tov, "Une inscription grecque d'origine samaritaine trouvée à Thessalonique," *RB* 81 (1974): 399.

138. Levinskaya, *Diaspora Setting*, 156.

tions one synagogue at Thessalonica (Acts 17:2), we are witnessing here a growth in the Jewish presence at the city. Significantly, only large cities such as Rome, Antioch, and Alexandria had multiple synagogues. So this is certainly unusual and worth pondering as a phenomenon. What brought this increased growth about? As Nigdelis speculates, the immigration of Jews abroad after the catastrophes under Titus (70 CE) and Bar Kokhba (135 CE), who had originally been sold abroad and their descendants subsequently freed, provides one explanation for the expansion of the Jewish presence in Macedonia. However, we can draw no conclusions about the organization of the synagogues at Thessalonica and their interrelation.[139] The title πρεσβύτερος (*IJO* 1.Mac18: second–third centuries CE) most likely points to synagogal structures:[140] but because the inscription under discussion has been thought by some to be Christian, certainty is unachievable (*IJO* 1:105).

Fourth, among the Jews honored are solidly Jewish names (e.g., Benjamin [fourth century CE]], Jacob [*IJO* 1.Mac15], Abraham and Theodote [*IJO* 1.Mac16: fifth–sixth centuries CE]), along with Roman names indicating the universal conferral of Roman citizenship in 212 CE (Marcus Aurelius [*IJO* 1.Mac15; see *IJO* 1:97). The Greek name given Marcus Aurelius Jacob, who was "also called Eutychius" ("Lucky," *IJO* 1.Mac15), is intriguing because of its strong association with good fortune and success. However, in a Jewish context prosperity is attributable entirely to the providential blessing of Yahweh (Prov 16:33) as opposed to the vagaries of Fortuna in the Roman worldview. It shows the relative ease with which Thessalonian Jews had assimilated into Greco-Roman culture, yet without losing their distinctive identity as God's covenantal people. Moreover, in light of the summons of the Babylonian exiles to seek the welfare of the city (Jer 29:7), it is significant that the Thracian city in Macedonia, Neapolis (Acts 16:11), including its inhabitants and patriotic supporters, is accorded this prayer-wish in the Samaritan dedicatory inscription: "Prosper [αὔξι], Neapolis, with those who love you" (*IJO* 1.Mac17). Further, the strong likelihood that Thessalonian Jews opted for a mixed burial with their Christian and Greco-Roman fellow inhabitants of Thessaloniki (*IJO*

---

139. Nigdelis, "Synagoge(n) und Gemeinde der Juden," 306. Note Levinskaya: "It is impossible to say whether the Jewish congregations at Thessalonica had unified organisation or were completely independent of each other" (*Diaspora Setting*, 156).

140. On πρεσβύτερος in the synagogue, see R. Alastair Campbell, *The Elders: Seniority within Earliest Christianity* (Edinburgh: T&T Clark, 1994), 44–54.

1:98), as opposed to a separate cemetery, as Levinskaya posits,[141] underscores the same point at the end of their lives.

Last, Edson's inclusion of the original editor's estimation that the reference to Θεός Ὕψιστος ("the Most High God") in *IG* 10.2.1.72 should be seen as a reference to Yahweh of the Hebrews (see Acts 17:2) is highly questionable. Whether any of these inscriptions are Jewish (*IG* 10.2.1.67–72; see *IG* 10.2.1s.1054) is debatable; they are much more likely to be referring to a Greco-Roman cult in the absence of any accompanying Jewish iconography (e.g., the menorah).[142] In sum, the Thessalonian Jewish synagogal communities from the second through fourth centuries CE flourished in their piety, assimilated well into Thessalonican life, and grew in number beyond the normal single synagogue in diaspora cities. The Samaritan focus of one of our inscriptions is particularly interesting in terms of the diversity of expressions within "orthodox" Judaism and the widespread evidence for the presence of Samaritans elsewhere in the diaspora (Egypt, Delos, Iran, Athens, Rhodes).[143] One wonders, for example, whether the Samaritans at Thessalonica had established their own association within the city, with its honorific culture, as had the Samaritans at Delos in the second century BCE.[144]

Turning briefly to our only account of the first-century Thessalonian Jewish community in Acts 17:1–9, there is reference to the synagogue, its attendees dialoguing about the Scriptures with Paul, as well as the presence of Godfearers and prominent women in the Jewish community. The collision of Paul, Silas, Jason, and his entourage with the local Thessalonian Jews resulted in the believers being arraigned before the city politarchs and being charged with turning the world upside down and opposing the decrees of Caesar (Acts 17:5–10a). Some skepticism has greeted this account of Paul's missionary outreach at Thessalonica, but it is beyond the scope of this chapter to delineate and critique this stream of scholarship.[145] Suffice it to say, Todd Still has challenged many

---

141. Levinskaya, *Diaspora Setting*, 156.

142. For full discussion, see Greg H. R. Horsley, "Dedications to the 'Most High God,'" *NewDocs* 1:25–29; additionally, vom Brocke, *Thessaloniki*, 220–22.

143. Stephen R. Llewelyn, "An Association of Samaritans in Delos," *NewDocs* 8:150.

144. *NewDocs* 8:12.

145. Panayotov concludes: "The reliability of the whole episode is very dubious" (*IJO* 1:92).

of the traditional objections (e.g., Luke's anachronism and anti-Jewish thrust; see 1 Thess 2:15b, 16a, 17a) aired against the account of Acts.[146] Nevertheless, it is important to concede with Still that Luke's account is condensed, simplified, and shaped by his own interests, leading to an incompleteness in presentation (e.g., the muted emphasis on the gentile opposition to the gospel: 1 Thess 1:1–10, 2:14b, "you suffered from your own countrymen"]).[147] Additionally, recent scholarship has extensively explored the nature of the charges brought against the Thessalonian believers, helpfully situating them in their imperial context.[148]

7. Thessalonian Freedmen, Slaves, and *Threptoi*

Reference to slaves and freedmen are not numerous in the Thessalonian epigraphic corpus. In an epitaph, a *libertus* ("freedman") is said to have lived eighteen years (*IG* 10.2.1.701). Epitaphs in the eastern necropolis refer to *liberti* among other lists of names (*IG* 10.2.1.s.1198 [2x], mid-first century BCE; *IG* 10.2.1.s.1206 [2x], first century CE), but on one occasion the wife is also mentioned alongside the *libertus* (*IG* 10.2.1.s.1229, second century CE). The sole New Testament occurrence of the Greek equivalent for *libertus*, ἀπελεύθερος, occurs in 1 Cor 7:22. It articulates a radical inversion of the Greco-Roman social structures of slavery, effected by the believer's incorporation into and union with Christ (7:22a: ἐν κυρίῳ;

---

146. Todd D. Still, *Conflict at Thessalonica: A Pauline Church and Its Neighbours*, JSNTSup 183 (Sheffield: Sheffield Academic, 1999), 61–82. On the reasons for Jewish opposition to Paul, see 150–90. *Pace*, on 1 Thess 2:14–16, see the incisive essay of Angela Standhartinger in this volume, arguing that the text is a later interpolation in the epistle.

147. Still, *Conflict at Thessalonica*, 81. See the discussion of Keener on Luke's presentation of the opposition in Luke 17:1–9 (*Acts*, 3:2544–46).

148. Still, *Conflict at Thessalonica*, 260–66; Jennifer H. Stiefel, "A Rhetorical and Social Reading of Christians, Paul, and the Roman Empire in Acts 16–19" (PhD diss., Union Theological Seminary, New York, 2000); Justin K. Hardin, "Decrees and Drachmas at Thessalonica: An Illegal Assembly in Jason's House (Acts 17.1–10a)," *NTS* 52 (2006): 29–49; Jeremy Punt, "The Accusation of 'World Disturbers' (Acts 17:6) in Socio-political Context," *VerbEccl* 37 (2016): a1595, http://dx.doi.org/10.4102/ve.v37i1.1595; Alan H. Cadwallader, "The Political Charges against Paul and Silas in Acts 17:6–7: Roman Benefaction in Thessalonica," in *Stones, Bones, and the Sacred: Essays on Material Culture and Ancient Religion in Honor of Dennis E. Smith*, ed. Alan H. Cadwallader, ECL 21 (Atlanta: SBL Press, 2016), 241–68.

see Gal 3:28): "For whoever was called [κληθείς] in the Lord as a slave [δοῦλος] is a freedman of the Lord [ἀπελεύθερος κυρίου], just as whoever was free [ἐλεύθερος] when called [κληθείς] is a slave [δοῦλός ἐστιν Χριστοῦ] of Christ" (NCB).

The thinker in antiquity who comes closest to this social formulation is Seneca: "You must think carefully about the fact that the man whom you call your slave [*servum*] is born from the same seed, enjoys the same sky, breathes like you, dies like you! You are able to recognise a free man [*ingenuum*] in you as he to recognise a slave [*servum*] in you" (*Ep* 47.10 [Wiedemann]). For Seneca, this dramatic social inversion is caused by a mutual recognition of the common humanity shared by master and slave. However, Brookins is correct in saying that Seneca is only "asking masters and slaves to empathize from within the existing structures, not to imagine themselves, as it were, outside of them."[149] To be sure, there might be a genuine social reversal due to external events affecting the fortunes of slaves and masters in the future, but in the meantime the social dynamic is Seneca's golden rule (*Ep.* 47.11): "treat those whose status is inferior to your own in the same manner as you would wish your own superior to treat you." In the case of Paul, the calling of Christ (ἐν κυρίῳ κληθείς) and the inversion of status created thereby establishes a new set of social relations, *extrinsic* in its origin to believers: it is not an internal empathetic reimagining of the social order by believers, but rather it is predicated on an *external* social reordering *within the body of Christ*, effected by the calling of Christ, and consonant with God's preference for the "nothings of this world" (1 Cor 1:26–29a) and Christ's own self-emptying as a *doulos* on the cross (Phil 2:7–8: μορφὴν δούλου λαβών).

Turning to slaves, there is a sepulchral dedication to a *servus publicus* (οἰκέτη τῆς πόλεως: *IG* 10.2.1.s.1164; third century CE), the "public slave." The *servi publici*, who were not *liberti*,[150] were owned by the state or the community, not by private masters or the emperor in the *familia Caesaris*. If the *servi publici* lived at Rome, their *dominus* ("master") was the

---

149. Timothy Brookins, "(Dis)correspondence of Paul and Seneca on Slavery," in *Paul and Seneca in Dialogue*, ed. Joseph R. Dodson and David E. Briones, APR 2 (Leiden: Brill, 2017), 184.

150. On the manumission process for the *servus publicus*, see Michael A. Flexsenhar III, "No Longer a Slave: Manumission in the Social World of Paul" (MA thesis, University of Texas at Austin, 2013), 17–18. For literary sources on *servi publici*, see Thomas Wiedeman, *Greek and Roman Slavery* (London: Routledge, 1981), 154–66.

Roman people (*populus Romanus*). But if they lived outside in a province in a municipality (*municipium*) or in a colony (*colonia*), as was the case with Thessalonica (*IG* 10.2.1.165, 167, 177, 231), the citizen body of the municipality (*municipes*) is the *dominus*, rendering the *servi publici* subservient to the *concilium provinciae* ("council of the province").[151] In the inscriptions of Rome and the Latin West, the names of the *servi publici* are accompanied by their occupation, and often the city from which they came was added to the slave's name.[152] As far as *servi publici* living outside Rome, we can say on the basis of the Latin inscriptions that they acted as attendants of magistrates, treasurers (*arcarii*), financial agents (*actores*), archivists (*tabularii*), and land surveyors (*mensores*), as well as managers of markets (*macella*) and granaries as *horearii*.[153] In contrast to these more prestigious posts, there were also menial jobs such as maintaining the public baths, producing lead pipes, and making bricks.[154] In our inscription, none of these occupational details are present, though this οἰκέτῃ

---

151. For the above information, see Franco Luciano, "Public Slaves in Rome and in the Cities of the Latin West: New Additions to the Epigraphic Corpus," in *From Document to History: Epigraphic Insights into the Greco-Roman World*, ed. Carlos Noreña and Nikolaus Papazarkadas, BSGRE (Leiden: Brill, 2019), 279. Additionally, N. Rouland, "A propos des *serui publici populi Romani*," *Chiron* 7 (1977): 261–78; Walter Eder, *Untersuchungen zur Entstehung, Entwicklung und Funktion der öffentlichen Sklaverei in Rom.* (Wiesbaden: Steiner, 1980); Alexander Weiß, *Sklave der Stadt: Untersuchungen zur öffentlichen Sklaverei in den Städten des römischen Reiches* (Stuttgart: Steiner, 2004).

152. Stephen Wilson, *The Means of Naming: A Social and Cultural History of Personal Naming in Western Europe* (London: UCL Press, 1998), 26.

153. For the above information, see Franco Luciano, "The Servi Publici: Everybody's Slaves (SPES) Project," at https://www.academia.edu/34504688/The_Servi_Publici_Everybody_s_Slaves_SPES_Project. Dale B. Martin writes: "But slaves were often employed as state accountants and registrars: they collected fees, wrote receipts, and arranged for the erection of statues and inscriptions and the disbursement of funds." See Martin, *Slavery as Salvation: The Metaphor of Slavery in Pauline Christianity* (New Haven: Yale University Press, 1990), 19. As evidence for state accountants and registrars, Martin cites *IG* 2.1.403, ll. 36–52, and *IG* 2.1.476, ll. 37–49 (*Slavery as Salvation*, 189 n. 95). Note, too, IEph 1a.25, ll. 28–30 (125/126 CE), which speaks of the public slave Saturninus, "who has collected, as you claim, large sums from the debtors of the Senate, although the collection did not come within his duties."

154. Martin mentions menial tasks "such as collecting garbage, keeping the city clean, or building and maintaining roads" (*Slavery as Salvation*, 19). Subsequently he cites Pliny (*Ep.* 10.19), who refers to public slaves serving as prison guards (*Slavery as Salvation*, 186 n. 45).

τῆς πόλεως definitely comes from Thessalonica, even if he is not identified as such. In sum, as Dale Martin correctly concludes, there was "a tiered slave structure," where there were "menial slaves and those in positions of authority."[155] A final observation: the phrase οἰκέτῃ τῆς πόλεως does not appear in the Packard Humanities Greek Epigraphy Programme,[156] so there is no further epigraphic evidence from the Greek East that could act as valuable comparanda.

What, then, can be said about our οἰκέτῃ τῆς πόλεως? He was either employed in the civic administration of Thessalonica or in a menial occupation. We cannot draw any conclusion as to why his occupation is not mentioned in his sepulchral dedication: arguments from silence are risky. There is no explicit mention in the New Testament of a *servus publicus*, though it is possible that such slaves, whether manumitted or servile, may have belonged to the urban house churches Paul established. The tiered slave structure of antiquity, in which there were important civic posts available for *servi publici*, as well as prestigious positions for upwardly mobile slaves in the bureaucracy of the *familia Caesaris*, helps us to understand one intriguing feature of Pauline rhetoric: his positive use of the metaphor of slavery in Rom 6:16b and 18b.[157]

Last, two inscriptions from Thessalonica refer to *threptoi* (ὁ θρεπτός, ἡ θρεπτή: "a slave born in the house" or "an adopted foundling") and their place in familial relationships.[158] On a sepulchral monument (*IG* 10.2.1s.1392) Nikeros and οἱ θρεπτοί ("the house-born slaves") honor Oppia Charition, the deceased wife of Nikeros. Elsewhere Ailia Prokla honors Ailia Theodora, "the sweetest house-born slave" (alternatively, "the sweetest adopted foundling") on another sepulchral monument (*IG* 10.2.1s.1396). Again, there is no mention of *threptoi* in the New Testament, but they may well have belonged to the house churches through

---

155. Martin, *Slavery as Salvation*, 19.

156. The recent publication of *IG* 10.2.1s, in which our inscription appears, has not been incorporated in the PHI database.

157. See Paul R. C. Weaver, *Familia Caesaris: A Social Study of the Emperor's Freedmen and Slaves* (Cambridge: Cambridge University Press, 1972); Michael Flexsenhar III, *Christians in Caesar's Household: The Emperor's Slaves in the Makings of Christianity* (University Park: Pennsylvania State University Press, 2019); James R. Harrison, *Paul's Language of Grace in Its Graeco-Roman Context*, WUNT 2/172 (Tübingen: Mohr Siebeck, 2003), 234–42.

158. On familial relationships in the Thessalonian epistles, see the essay of Rosemary Canavan in this volume.

their personal conversion or because of the conversion of entire households through their master.

8. Conclusion

A strategically placed and wealthy polis, Thessalonica adeptly negotiated the arrival of the Roman hegemony in Macedonia (168 BCE) and the ensuing shifts of political power occurring during the civil war of the late republic, thereby ensuring the city's freedom from the Julio-Claudian principate onward. Although the cult of Roma and the Roman benefactors flourished alongside the imperial cult, this Roman focus in no way diminished the potency of the traditional Greek gods and heroes and the powerful imported Egyptian deities. In a world full of gods, the apostle Paul highlighted for the early Thessalonian believers the social and personal cost involved in turning to the living God and his crucified, risen, and returning Son. Not only did they face persecution, but their social constituency was drawn from lower-echelon trade associations, revealing a homogenous community of freed/free casual workers living close to or at subsistence level, without identifiable benefactors within their community. The commonalities and differences between the Thessalonian association inscriptions and the early Christian churches in the city are invaluable in highlighting the ethos of the communities of the first believers.

In locating Thessalonian believers socially, religiously, and economically, we face the limitations posed by the scarcity of extant archaeological remains contemporary with Paul's Thessalonian epistles. But we have seen that the Thessalonian epigraphic corpus has contributed to our understanding of Paul's correspondence in the areas of honor culture, the Thessalonian cults, dream and vision revelation, and slavery, to cite a few examples. The fruitfulness of further areas of research in this regard is demonstrated by the other essays in this volume. Indeed, even in the case where there is no Jewish epigraphic evidence contemporary with the New Testament, the inscriptions and archaeology have revealed a fascinating picture of the vibrancy of the Jewish community in late antiquity at Thessalonica. The writings on the ancient stones in the Macedonian city testify powerfully across the centuries about the life of the Thessalonian citizens and noncitizens, helping New Testament exegetes and social historians to speak more confidently about the life of the first believers residing there.

Bibliography

Adam-Veleni, Polyxeni. "Entertainment and Arts in Thessaloniki." Pages 2262–81 in *Roman Thessaloniki*. Edited by Dēmētrios V. Gramenos. Thessaloniki: Thessaloniki Archaeological Museum, 2003.

———. "Thessalonike: History and Town Planning." Pages 121–76 in *Roman Thessaloniki*. Edited by Dēmētrios V. Gramenos. Thessaloniki: Thessaloniki Archaeological Museum, 2003.

Ahmadi, Amir. "The 'Magoi' and 'Daimones' in Column VI of the Derveni Papyrus." *Numen* 61 (2014): 484–508.

Allison, Dale C., Jr. "Acts 9:1–9, 22:6–11, 26:12–18: Paul and Ezekiel." *JBL* 13 (2016): 807–26.

"Ancient Road Unearthed in Greek Subway Dig." CBC News, 26 June 2012. https://tinyurl.com/SBL4221a.

Ascough, Richard S. *Paul's Macedonian Associations: The Social Context of Philippians and 1 Thessalonians*. WUNT 2/161. Tübingen: Mohr Siebeck, 2003.

———. "Redescribing the Thessalonians' 'Mission' in Light of Graeco-Roman Associations." *NTS* 60 (2014): 61–82.

———. "The Thessalonian Christian Community as a Professional Voluntary Association." *JBL* 119 (2000): 311–28.

Ascough, Richard S., Philip A. Harland, and John S. Kloppenborg. *Associations in the Greco-Roman World: A Sourcebook*. Waco, TX: Baylor University Press, 2012.

Avadiah, Asher. "Ancient Jewish Communities in Macedonia, Thrace and Upper Epirus." *Gerión* (2015): 211–27.

Barclay, John M. G. "Conflict in Thessalonica." *CBQ* 55 (1993): 512–30.

Barnett, Paul. *After Jesus*. Vol. 2, *Paul, Missionary of Jesus*. Grand Rapids: Eerdmans, 2008.

Barton, Carlin A. *The Sorrows of the Ancient Romans: The Gladiator and the Monster*. Princeton: Princeton University Press, 1993.

Bash, Anthony. *Ambassadors for Christ: An Exploration of Ambassadorial Language in the New Testament*. WUNT 2/92. Tübingen: Mohr Siebeck, 1997.

Betegh, Gábor. *The Derveni Papyrus: Cosmology, Theology, and Interpretation*. Cambridge: Cambridge University Press, 2004.

Brändl, Martin. *Der Agon bei Paulus: Herkunft und Profil paulinischer Agonmetaphorik*. WUNT 2/222. Tübingen: Mohr Siebeck, 2006.

Breytenbach, Cilliers, and Ingrid Behrmann. *Frühchristliches Thessaloniki.* STAC 44. Tübingen: Mohr Siebeck, 2007.

Brocke, Christoph vom. *Thessaloniki – Stadt des Kassander und Gemeinde des Paulus: Ein frühe christliche Gemeinde in ihrer heidnischen Umwelt.* WUNT 2/125. Tübingen: Mohr Siebeck, 2001.

Broneer, Oscar. "The Isthmian Victory Crown." *AJA* 66 (1962): 259–63.

Brookins, Timothy A. "(Dis)correspondence of Paul and Seneca on Slavery." Pages 179–207 in *Paul and Seneca in Dialogue*. Edited by Joseph R. Dodson and David E. Briones. APR 2. Leiden: Brill, 2017.

———. *First and Second Thessalonians*. Paideia. Grand Rapids: Baker Academic, 2021.

Bruce, F. F. *1 and 2 Thessalonians.* WBC 45. Waco, TX: Word, 1982.

———. *Commentary on the Book of Acts: The English Text with Introduction, Exposition and Notes*. NICNT. London: Marshall, Morgan & Scott, 1954.

Burrell, Barbara. *Neokoroi: Greek Cities and Roman Emperors.* CCS NS 9. Leiden: Brill, 2004.

Burstein, Stanley M., ed. and trans. *The Hellenistic Age from the Battle of Ipsos to the Death of Kleopotra VII.* Cambridge: Cambridge University Press, 1985.

Burton, Ernest DeWitt. "The Politarchs." *AmJT* 2 (1898): 596–632.

Cadwallader, Alan H. "Paul and the Games." Pages 363–90 in *Paul in the Greco-Roman World: A Handbook*. Vol. 1. 2nd ed. Edited by J. Paul Sampley. London: T&T Clark, 2016.

———. "The Political Charges against Paul and Silas in Acts 17:6–7: Roman Benefaction in Thessalonica." Pages 241–68 in *Stones, Bones, and the Sacred: Essays on Material Culture and Ancient Religion in Honor of Dennis E. Smith*. Edited by Alan H. Cadwallader. ECL 21. Atlanta: SBL Press, 2016.

Campbell, R. Alastair. *The Elders: Seniority within Earliest Christianity.* Edinburgh: T&T Clark, 1994.

Carter, Michael. "Gladiatorial Ranking and the 'SC de Pretis Gladiatorum Minuendis' (CIL II 6278 = ILS 5163)." *Phoenix* 57 (2003): 83–113.

Concannon, Cavan. "Archaeology and the Pauline Letters." Pages 1–18 in *The Oxford Handbook of Pauline Studies*. Edited by Matthew K. Novenson and R. Barry Matlock. Oxford: Oxford University Press, 2020.

Davies, William D., and Dale C. Allison. *A Critical and Exegetical Commentary on the Gospel according to Saint Matthew*. 3 vols. Edinburgh: T&T Clark, 1988–1997.

Donfried, Karl P. "The Cults of Thessalonica and the Thessalonian Correspondence." *NTS* 31 (1985): 336–56.
Eder, Walter. *Untersuchungen zur Entstehung, Entwicklung und Funktion der öffentlichen Sklaverei in Rom*. Wiesbaden: Steiner, 1980.
Edson, Charles. "Cults of Thessalonica (Macedonia III)." *HTR* 41 (1948): 153–204.
Feissel, Denis. "Appendice II: Inscriptions juives de Macédoine du IVe au Vie s." *BCH Supplément* 8 (1983): 240–45.
Flexsenhar, Michael, III. *Christians in Caesar's Household: The Emperor's Slaves in the Makings of Christianity*. University Park: Pennsylvania State University Press, 2019.
———. "No Longer a Slave: Manumission in the Social World of Paul." MA thesis, University of Texas at Austin, 2013.
Forbes, Christopher. *Prophecy and Inspired Speech in Early Christianity and Its Hellenistic Environment*. Peabody, MA: Hendrickson, 1997.
Friesen, Steven J. *Twice Neokoros: Ephesus, Asia and the Cult of the Flavian Imperial Family*. RGRW. Leiden: Brill, 1993.
Gaventa, Beverly. *First and Second Thessalonians*. Int. Louisville: John Knox, 1998.
Gill, David W. J. "Acts and the Urban Elites." Pages 105–18 in *The Book of Acts in Its First Century Setting*. Vol. 2, *Graeco-Roman Setting*. Edited by David W. J. Gill and Conrad Gempf. Grand Rapids: Eerdmans, 1994.
Goceva, Zlatozara. "Gladiatorenkämpfe in Thrakien." *Klio* 63 (1981): 493–501.
Gooder, Paula. *Only The Third Heaven? 2 Corinthians 12:1–10 and Heavenly Ascent*. London: T&T Clark, 2006.
Goodrich, John K. *Paul as an Administrator of God in 1 Corinthians*. SNTSMS 152. Cambridge: Cambridge University Press, 2012.
Grether, Gertrude. "Livia and the Roman Imperial Cult." *AJP* 67 (1946): 222–56.
Haddad, Najeeb. "Paul in Context: A Reinterpretation of Paul and Empire." PhD diss., Loyola University, 2018.
Hanson, John S. "Dreams and Visions in the Graeco-Roman World and Early Christianity." *ANRW* 23.2:1395–1427.
Hardin, Justin K. "Decrees and Drachmas at Thessalonica: An Illegal Assembly in Jason's House (Acts 17.1–10a)." *NTS* 52 (2006): 29–49.
Harrison, James R. "The Brothers as the 'Glory of Christ' (2 Cor 8:23):

———. "Paul's *Doxa* Terminology in Its Ancient Benefaction Context." *NovT* 52 (2010): 156–88.

———. "The Erasure of Distinction: Paul and the Politics of Dishonour." *TynBul* 66 (2016): 161–84.

———. "'Every Dog Has Its Day.'" *NewDocs* 10:136–45.

———. "The Fading Crown: Divine Honour and the Early Christians." *JTS* 54 (2003): 493–529.

———. "In Quest of the Third Heaven: Paul and His Apocalyptic Imitators." *VC* 58 (2004): 24–55.

———. "Paul and the *agōnothetai* at Corinth: Engaging the Civic Values of Antiquity." Pages 271–326 in *The First Urban Churches 2: Roman Corinth*. Edited by James R. Harrison and Larry L. Welborn. WGRWSup 8. Atlanta: SBL Press, 2016.

———. *Paul and the Ancient Celebrity Circuit: The Cross and Moral Transformation*. WUNT 430. Tübingen: Mohr Siebeck, 2019.

———. *Paul and the Imperial Authorities at Thessalonica and Rome: A Study in the Conflict of Ideology*. WUNT 273. Tübingen: Mohr Siebeck, 2011.

———. "Paul and the Imperial Gospel at Thessaloniki." *JSNT* 25 (2002): 71–96.

———. *Paul's Language of Grace in Its Graeco-Roman Context*. WUNT 2/172. Tübingen: Mohr Siebeck, 2003.

Hendrix, Holland Lee. "Thessalonicians Honor Romans." PhD diss., Harvard University, 1984.

Hock, Ronald F. *The Social Context of Paul's Ministry: Tentmaking and Apostleship*. Philadelphia: Fortress, 1980.

Horsley, Greg H. R. "Appendix: The Politarchs." Pages 419–31 in *The Book of Acts in Its Graeco-Roman Setting*. Vol. 2. *The Book of Acts in Its First Century Setting*. Edited by David W. J. Gill and Conrad Gempf. Grand Rapids: Eerdmans, 1994.

———. "Dedications to the 'Most High God.'" *NewDocs* 1:25–29.

———. "Politarchs." *NewDocs* 2:34–35.

———. "The Politarchs in Macedonia." *MA* 7 (1994): 99–126.

Hullinger, Jerry M. "The Historical Background of Paul's Athletic Allusions." *BSac* 161 (2004): 343–59.

Janko, Richard. "The Derveni Papyrus ('Diagoras of Melos, Apopyrgizontes Logoi?'): A New Translation." *CP* 96 (2001): 1–32.

Jewett, Robert. "Tenement Churches and Communal Meals in the Early Church: The Implications of a Form-Critical Analysis of 2 Thess 3:10." *BR* 38 (1993): 23–43.

———. *The Thessalonian Correspondence: Pauline and Millenarian Piety.* Philadelphia: Fortress, 1986.
Johnson, Luke T. *The Acts of the Apostles.* SP 5. Collegeville, MN: Glazier, 1992.
Judge, Edwin A. "The Conflict of Educational Aims in the New Testament." Pages 693–708 in *The First Christians in the Roman World: Augustan and New Testament Essays.* Edited by James R. Harrison. WUNT 229. Tübingen: Mohr Siebeck, 2008.
Jung, UnChan. "Paul's Letter to Free(d) Casual Workers: Profiling the Thessalonians in Light of the Roman Economy." *JSNT* 42 (2020): 472–95.
Katsari, Constantina, and Stephen Mitchell. "The Roman Colonies of Greece and Asia Minor: Questions of State and Civic Identity." *Athenaum* 95 (2008): 219–47.
Keener, Craig S. *Acts: An Exegetical Commentary.* 4 vols. Grand Rapids: Baker Academic, 2012–2015.
Kloppenborg, John S. "ΦΙΛΑΔΕΛΦΙΑ, ΘΕΟΔΙΔΑΚΤΟΣ and the Dioscuri: Rhetorical Engagement in 1 Thessalonians 4:9–12." *NTS* 39 (1993): 265–89.
Koester, Helmut. "Archäologie und Paulus." Pages 393–404 in *Religious Propaganda and Missionary Competition in the New Testament World.* Edited by Lukas Borman, Kelly Del Tredici, and Angela Standhartinger. NovTSup 74. Leiden: Brill, 1994.
———. "Egyptian Religion in Thessalonike: Regulation for the Cult." Pages 133–50 in *From Roman to Early Christian Thessalonike: Studies in Religion and Archaeology.* Edited by Laura Nasrallah, Charalambos Bakirtzis, and Steven J. Friesen. HTS 64. Cambridge: Harvard University Press, 2010.
———. *Paul and His World: Interpreting the New Testament in Its Context.* Minneapolis: Fortress, 2007.
Koukouvou, Angeliki. "The Sarapieion: The Sanctuary of the Egyptian Gods Rises from the City's Ashes." Pages 104–11 in *Archaeology behind Battle Lines in Thessaloniki of the Turbulent Years 1912-1922.* Edited by Polyxeni Adam-Veleni and Angeliki Koukouvou. AMT 19. Thessaloniki: Ministry of Education and Religious Affairs, Culture and Sport, 2012.
Kouremenos, Theokritos, George M. Parássoglou, and Kyriakos Tsantsanoglou. *The Derveni Papyrus: Edited with Introduction and Commentary.* STCP 13. Florence: Casa Editrice Leo S. Olschki, 2006.

Kuhn, Karl Allen. *Luke, the Elite Evangelist*. PSN. Collegeville, MN: Glazier, 2010.

Lefebvre, Ludovic. "La diffusion du culte de Sarapis en Grèce continentale et dans les îles de l'Égée au IIIe siècle avant J.-C." *RHPR* 88 (2008): 451–67.

Levinskaya, Irina. *The Book of Acts in Its First Century Setting*. Vol. 5, *Diaspora Setting*. Grand Rapids: Eerdmans, 1996.

Lewis, Naphtali. *The Interpretation of Dreams and Portents in Antiquity*. Mundelein, IL: Bolchazy-Carducci, 1997.

Lifshitz, Baruch, and Jean Schiby. "Une synagogue Samaritaine à Thessalonique." *RB* 75 (1968): 368–78.

Llewelyn, Stephen R. "An Association of Samaritans in Delos." *NewDocs* 8:148–51.

Longenecker, Bruce W. "Exposing the Economic Middle: A Revised Economy Scale for the Study of Early Christianity." *JSNT* 31 (2009): 243–78.

Luciano, Franco. "Public Slaves in Rome and in the Cities of the Latin West: New Additions to the Epigraphic Corpus." 279–305 in *From Document to History: Epigraphic Insights into the Greco-Roman World*. Edited by Carlos Noreña and Nikolaos Papazarkadas. BSGRE. Leiden: Brill, 2019.

———. "The Servi Publici: Everybody's Slaves (SPES) Project." https://www.academia.edu/34504688/The_Servi_Publici_Everybody_s_Slaves_SPES_Project.

Maikidou-Poutrino, Dafni. "Women and Isis Lochia: Commemorations of Divine Protection in Roman Macedonia." *Arys* 16 (2018): 433–63.

Malherbe, Abraham J. *The Letters to the Thessalonians*. AB 32B. New York: Doubleday, 2000.

Marguerat, Daniel. "Le Judaïsme synagogal dans les Actes des Apôtres." Pages 177–200 in *Les Judaïsmes dans tous leurs états aux Ier–IIIe (Les Judéens des synagogues les Chrétiens et les rabbins): Actes du colloque de Lausanne 12–14 décembre 2012*. Edited by Claire Clivaz, Simon C. Mimouni, and Bernard Pouderon. Turnhout: Brepols, 2015.

Marshall, Jonathan. *Jesus, Patrons, and Benefactors: Roman Palestine and the Gospel of Luke*. WUNT 2/259. Tübingen: Mohr Siebeck, 2009.

Martin, Dale B. *Slavery as Salvation: The Metaphor of Slavery in Pauline Christianity*. New Haven: Yale University Press, 1990.

Masson, Charles. *Les deux épitres de Saint Paul aux Thessaloniciens*. Paris: Delachaux & Niestlé, 1957.

Mazurek, Lindsey A. "Globalizing the Sculptural Landscapes of the Sarapis and Isis Cults in Hellenistic and Roman Greece." PhD diss., Duke University, 2016.

Míguez, Néstor O. *The Practice of Hope: Ideology and the Intention in 1 Thessalonians*. PCC. Minneapolis: Fortress, 2012.

Murray, Timothy J. *Restricted Generosity in the New Testament*. WUNT 2/480. Tübingen: Mohr Siebeck, 2018.

Nasrallah, Laura Salah. *Archaeology and the Pauline Letters*. Oxford: Oxford University Press, 2019.

Neyrey, Jerome H. "Luke's Social Location of Paul: Cultural Anthropology and the Status of Paul in Acts." Pages 126–64 in *Fabrics of Discourse: Essays in Honor of Vernon K. Robbins*. Edited by David B. Gowler, L. Gregory Bloomquist, and Duane F. Watson. Harrisburg, PA: Trinity Press International, 2003.

Nigdelis, Pantelis M. "Synagoge(n) und Gemeinde der Juden in Thessaloniki: Fragen aufgrund einer neuen jüdischen Grabinschrift der Kaiserzeit." *ZPE* 102 (1994): 297–306.

Pachis, Panayotis. "The Cult of Mithras in Thessalonica." Pages 229–55 in *Studies in Mithraism*. Edited by John R. Hinnels. Roma: Erma di Bretscheider, 1994.

Panayotov, Alexander. "The Jews in the Balkan Provinces of the Roman Empire: An Epigraphic and Archaeological Survey." PhD diss., University of St Andrews, 2004.

Pfitzner, Victor C. *Paul and the Agon Motif: Traditional Athletic Imagery in the Pauline Literature*. Leiden: Brill, 1967.

Pillar, Edward. *Resurrection as Anti-imperial Gospel: 1 Thessalonians 1:9b–10*. Minneapolis: Fortress, 2013.

Pomeroy, Sarah B., Stanley M. Burstein, Walter Donlan, Jennifer Tolbert Roberts, David Tandy, and Georgia Tsouvala. *Ancient Greece: A Political, Social, and Colonial History*. Oxford: Oxford University Press, 1999.

Price, Derek J. de Solla. "Portable Sundials in Antiquity, Including an Account of a New Example from Aphrodisias." *Centaurus* 14 (1969): 242–66.

Punt, Jeremy. "The Accusation of 'World Disturbers' (Acts 17:6) in Socio-political Context." *VerbEccl* 37 (2016): a1595. http://dx.doi.org/10.4102/ve.v37i1.1595.

Richard, Earl J. *First and Second Thessalonians*. SP 11. Collegeville, MN: Glazier, 1995.

Rigaux, Béda. *Saint Paul: Les épitres aux Thessaloniciens*. Paris: Librairie Lecoffre/Gabalda, 1956.

Robert, Louis. *Les gladiateurs dans l'orient grec*. Amsterdam: Hakkert, 1971.

———. "Les inscriptions de Thessalonique." *RevPhil* 48 (1974): 180–246.

Rollens, Sarah E. "The God Came to Me in a Dream: Epiphanies in Voluntary Associations as a Context for Paul's Vision of Christ." *HTR* 111 (2018): 41–65.

Rouland, N. "A propos des *serui publici populi Romani*." *Chiron* 7 (1977): 261–78.

Rulmu, Callia. "Between Ambition and Quietism: The Socio-political Background of 1 Thessalonians 4:9–12." *Bib* 91 (2010): 393–417.

Russel, James R. "The Magi in the Derveni Papyrus." *NIBIJ* 1 (2001): 49–59.

Santamaría, Marco A., ed. *The Derveni Papyrus: Unearthing Ancient Mysteries*. PLB 36. Leiden: Brill, 2019.

Schueller, Matthew. "Public Entertainment Venues as Urban Network Actors in Roman Macedonia and Thrace." PhD diss., University of North Carolina, 2020.

Schuler, Carl. "The Macedonian Politarchs." *CP* 55 (1960): 90–100.

Shantz, Colleen. *Paul in Ecstasy: The Neurobiology of the Apostle's Life and Thought*. Cambridge: Cambridge University Press, 2009.

Skotheim, Mali A. "Greek Dramatic Festivals under the Roman Empire." Vol. 1. PhD diss., Princeton University, 2016.

Sokolowski, Franciszek. "Propagation of the Cult of Sarapis and Isis in Greece." *GRBS* 15 (1974): 441–48.

Stafford, Emma. "The People to the Goddess Livia: Attic Nemesis and the Roman Imperial Cult." *Kernos* 26 (2013): 205–38.

Steimle, Christopher. *Religion im römischen Thessaloniki. Sakraltopographie, Kult und Gesellschaft 168. Chr.–324 n. Chr.* STAC. Tübingen: Mohr Siebeck, 2008.

Stevenson, Gregory M. "Conceptual Background to Golden Crown Imagery in the Apocalypse of John (4:4, 10; 14:14)." *JBL* 114 (1995): 257–72.

Stiefel, Jennifer H. "A Rhetorical and Social Reading of Christians, Paul, and the Roman Empire in Acts 16–19." PhD diss., Union Theological Seminary, 2000.

Still, Todd D. *Conflict at Thessalonica: A Pauline Church and Its Neighbours*. JSNTSup 183. Sheffield: Sheffield Academic, 1999.

Talbert, Richard J. A. *Roman Portable Sundials: The Empire in Your Hands*. New York: Oxford University Press, 2017.

Tellbe, Mikael. *Paul between Synagogue and State: Christians, Jews, and Civic Authorities in 1 Thessalonians, Romans, and Philippians.* ConBNT 34. Stockholm: Almqvist & Wiksell, 2001.
"Thessaloniki, Portrait of Livia as Demeter." Livius.org. 3 April 2020. https://tinyurl.com/SBL4221b.
Tov, Emanuel. "Une inscription grecque d'origine samaritaine trouvée à Thessalonique." *RB* 81 (1974): 394–99.
Turner, Max, and David Mackinder. "Prophecy and Spiritual Gifts Then and Now." Pages 16–54 in *Christian Experience in Theology and Life.* Edited by I. Howard Marshall. Edinburgh: Rutherford House, 1988.
Tzanavari, Katerina. "The Worship of Gods and Heroes in Thessaloniki." Pages 177–262 in *Roman Thessaloniki.* Edited by Dēmētrios V. Gramenos. Thessaloniki: Thessaloniki Archaeological Museum, 2003.
Velenis, Giorgos, and Polyxeni Adam-Veleni. "Theatre – Stadium of Thessaloniki." Diazoma. https://tinyurl.com/SBL4221c.
Verhoef, Eduard. "Christians Reacted Differently to Non-Christian Cults." *HvST* 67 (2011), article 84. doi:10.4102/hts.v.6i1.804.
Vickers, Michael. "Hellenistic Thessaloniki." *JHS* 92 (1972): 156–70.
———. "The Theater-Stadium at Thessaloniki." *Byzantion* 41 (1971): 339–48.
Vos, Craig Steven de. *Church and Community Conflicts: The Relationships of the Thessalonian, Corinthian, and Philippian Churches with Their Wider Civic Communities.* SBLDS 168. Atlanta: Scholars Press, 1997.
Walsh, Robyn, and Laura Nasrallah. "Thessaloniki." In *Cities of Paul: Images and Interpretations from the Harvard New Testament and Archaeology Project.* CD-ROM. Minneapolis: Fortress, 2005.
Weaver, Paul R. C. *Familia Caesaris: A Social Study of the Emperor's Freedmen and Slaves.* Cambridge: Cambridge University Press, 1972.
Weima, Jeffrey A. D. "'Peace and Security' (1 Thess. 5.3): Prophetic Warning or Political Propaganda?" *NTS* 58 (2012): 331–59.
Weiß, Alexander. 2004. *Sklave der Stadt: Untersuchungen zur öffentlichen Sklaverei in den Städten des römischen Reiches.* Stuttgart: Steiner, 2004.
———. *Sociale Elite und Christentum: Studien zu ordo-Angehörigen unter den frühen Christen.* MillSt 52. Berlin: de Gruyter, 2015.
Welborn, Larry L. *Paul, the Fool of Christ: A Study of 1 Corinthians 1–4 in the Comic Philosophic Tradition.* JSNTSup 293. Edinburgh: T&T Clark, 2005.
———. "The Runaway Paul: A Character in the Fool's Speech." *HTR* 92 (1999): 420–35.

White, Joel R. "'Peace' and 'Security' (1 Thess. 5.3): Roman Ideology and Greek Aspiration." *NTS* 60 (2014): 499–510.

Wiedeman, Thomas. *Greek and Roman Slavery*. London: Routledge, 1981.

Wilson, Stephen. *The Means of Naming: A Social and Cultural History of Personal Naming in Western Europe*. London: UCL Press, 1998.

Winter, Bruce W. "'If a Man Does Not Wish to Work...': A Cultural and Historical Setting for 2 Thessalonians 3:6–16." *TynBul* 39 (1988): 303–15.

Witt, Rex. "The Egyptian Cults in Ancient Macedonia." Pages 324–33 in *Ancient Macedonia: Papers Read at the First International Symposium Held in Thessaloniki, 26–29 August 1968*. Edited by Basil Laourdas and Ch. Makaronas. Thessaloniki: Institute for Balkan Studies, 1970.

Wright, Michael T. "Greek and Roman Portable Sundials: An Ancient Essay in Approximation." *AHES* 55 (2000): 177–87.

Imperial Divine Honors in Julio-Claudian Thessalonica and the Thessalonian Correspondence

D. Clint Burnett

Most scholars agree that 1 Thessalonians attests to the mistreatment of first-century CE Thessalonian Christ-confessors at the hands of their compatriots (1 Thess 1:6; 2:14–16; 3:1–5, 7; cf. Acts 17:1–9). Those who accept 2 Thessalonians as authentic contend that this second letter to the nascent Thessalonian church evinces their continued social harassment (2 Thess 1:4–9).[1] Several scholars connect this suffering to imperial cultic activity in the city, arguing that the Christian *euangelion* (1 Thess 1:5; 2:2–4, 8, 9; 3:2; 2 Thess 1:8; 2:14) of *kyrios* Jesus (1 Thess 1:1, 3, 6, 8; 2:15, 19; 3:8, 11–13; 4:1–2, 6, 15–17; 5:2, 9, 12, 23, 27, 28; 2 Thess 1:1, 2, 7–9, 12; 2:1–2, 8, 13–14, 16; 3:1, 3–6, 12, 16, 18), his parousia and epiphany from heaven (1 Thess 2:19; 3:13; 4:13–18; 5:23; 2 Thess 1:7–8; 2:1, 8), and the establishment of God's *basileia* (1 Thess 2:12, 2 Thess 1:5) directly opposed Thessalonian imperial divine honors.[2] In a seminal article, Karl Paul Don-

---

1. I consider 2 Thessalonians to be authentic. For an epigraphic and archaeological proposal supporting this probability, see D. Clint Burnett, "'Seated in God's Temple': Illuminating 2 Thess 2:4 in Light of Inscriptions and Archaeology Related to Imperial Divine Honors," *LTQ* 48 (2018): 69–94. For a general defense of Pauline authorship, see Abraham J. Malherbe, *The Letters to the Thessalonians: A New Translation with Introduction and Commentary*, AB 32B (New York: Doubleday, 2000), 349–75. I interpret 1–2 Thessalonians as the product of Paul with Timothy and Silvanus as coauthors. For coauthorship of 1–2 Thessalonians, see Jerome Murphy-O'Connor, *Paul the Letter-Writer: His World, His Options, His Skills*, GNS 41 (Collegeville, MN: Liturgical Press, 1995), 16–20, 33–34; Karl P. Donfried, "Issues of Authorship in the Pauline Corpus: Rethinking the Relationship between 1 and 2 Thessalonians," in *2 Thessalonians and Pauline Eschatology: For Petr Pokorný on His 80th Birthday*, ed. Christopher M. Tuckett et al., ACEP 21 (Leuven: Peeters, 2013), 81–113.

2. Karl Paul Donfried, "The Cults of Thessalonica and the Thessalonian

fried traces the hostility that Christ-confessors faced to these aspects of the Christian kerygma, which, he claims, conflicted with imperial cults and ideology. Donfried locates the motivation for the denizens of Thessalonica's mistreatment of Christ-confessors to loyalty oaths to the princeps (which he identifies as "Caesar's decrees" in Acts 17:7) that were administered in Thessalonica and that called for the pursuit and physical harm of those guilty of sedition.[3]

The main goal of this essay is to explore what role, if any, Thessalonian imperial cults played in the social harassment of Christ-confessors. In the first part (sections 1 and 2) I present a more nuanced and up-to-date presentation of imperial cults in the city because current reconstructions are outdated, incomplete, and/or problematic. I examine evidence, some of which is heretofore unknown to many New Testament scholars, for Thessalonian imperial divine honors and demonstrate that the city did not establish cults for every Julio-Claudian princeps or family member.[4] Rather, Thessalonica voluntarily formed imperial cults for Julius Caesar,

---

Correspondence," *NTS* 31 (1985): 336–56; Donfried, *Paul, Thessalonica, and Early Christianity* (Grand Rapids: Eerdmans, 2002), 21–48; James R. Harrison, "Paul and the Imperial Gospel at Thessaloniki," *JSNT* 25 (2002): 71–96; Harrison, *Paul and the Imperial Authorities at Thessalonica and Rome*, WUNT 273 (Tübingen: Mohr Siebeck, 2011), 47–70; Bruce W. Winter, *Divine Honors for the Caesars: The First Christians' Responses* (Grand Rapids: Eerdmans, 2015), 250–55.

I use the phrases "imperial divine honors," "imperial cults," and "imperial cultic activity" instead of "imperial cult" to acknowledge the diversity of imperial cults and to indicate that nothing like a uniform "imperial cult" existed in the Principate. See Mary Beard, John North, and Simon Price, *Religions of Rome*, 2 vols. (Cambridge: Cambridge University Press, 1998), 1:318, 348. Imperial divine honors include temples/shrines, altars, priests, images, games, sacrifices, etc., established for the worship of Julio-Claudians. The worship of Roma is not evidence of imperial cultic activity. I use the terms *worship*, *veneration*, and *divine honor(s)* as synonyms and follow John M. G. Barclay ("Conflict in Thessalonica," *CBQ* 55 [1993]: 512–30) in defining the mistreatment of Thessalonian Christ-confessors as "social harassment."

3. Donfried, "Cults of Thessalonica," 336–56; see also Donfried, *Paul, Thessalonica*, 21–48.

4. Since Charles Edson's corpus of Thessalonian inscriptions (*Inscriptiones Thessalonicae et viciniae*, fasc. 1 of *Inscriptiones Macedoniae*, part 2 of *Inscriptiones Graecae X: Epiri, Macedoniae, Thraciae, Scythiae* [Berlin: de Gruyter, 1972], abbreviated *IG* 10.2.1), Pantelis M. Nigelis has recently published more epigraphs from the city (*Inscriptiones Thessalonicae et viciniae, Supplementum Primum* [Berlin: de Gruyter, 2017], abbreviated *IG* 10.2.1s).

Augustus, Livia, (probably) Claudius, and (probably) Nero, the purposes of which were to show appreciation for imperial benefaction and to court future munificence.[5] The trappings of these cults consisted of two, perhaps three, imperial temples/shrines, altars, sacrifices, priests, statues, and games. Although the inhabitants of Thessalonica *treated* Augustus, Livia, Claudius, and Nero like gods during their lifetimes, they *called* only Livia a god during her lifetime. The people of Thessalonica waited until the deaths of Julius Caesar and Augustus to acclaim them as gods, and they did not refer to any other Julio-Claudian as a god. Like most Greek cities during the Principate, Thessalonica did not isolate imperial cults from its traditional pagan religious (and political) system but incorporated them into it. By doing so, the city articulated the relationship between its gods and the Julio-Claudians: the Thessalonian gods welcomed the Julio-Claudians into their ranks and supported them as their earthly vice-regents, which legitimated and articulated the latter's rule in the city.

In the second part of the essay (section 3), I bring the above reconstruction to bear on the relationship between the social harassment of Thessalonian Christ-confessors and imperial cults in the city. In the process, I adjudicate the veracity of reconstructions like Donfried's, concluding that the evidence for Thessalonian imperial cultic activity does not support such proposals, which tend to isolate imperial cults as the source of mistreatment of Christ-confessors. To the contrary, the data suggest that the latter suffered for a more complex and nuanced reason. Given that imperial divine honors were incorporated into the city's traditional religious (and political) system, Christ-confessors were socially harassed because the people of Thessalonica interpreted their movement with its religious exclusivity as an attempt to overthrow two interconnected pillars of their society: religion and politics. Thus, by withdrawing from pagan cultic activity, including imperial cults, nascent Christianity threatened Thessalonica's safety, security, and "free" status that its gods maintained through Julio-Claudian rule. In short, Christ-confessors in the city suffered because their movement was deemed as jeopardizing Thessalonian social order.

---

5. For the reciprocal nature of Greco-Roman euergetism, see John M. G. Barclay, *Paul and the Gift* (Grand Rapids: Eerdmans, 2015), 32–35.

1. Thessalonian Imperial Divine Honors in Recent Scholarship

The seminal work on Thessalonian imperial divine honors is Holland-Hendrix's dissertation (1984) and the articles stemming from that project. He attempted to amass all available evidence for the veneration of Romans in Thessalonica from the second century BCE to the first century CE. Hendrix concludes that imperial divine honors originated in the city's Hellenistic cult of Roman benefactors, that Thessalonica called only Julius Caesar a god, and that the city built one imperial temple, which was dedicated to the cult of Julius Caesar and the noncultic honor of Augustus. He proposes that there is no evidence that the inhabitants of Thessalonica sacrificed directly to the Julio-Claudians. Rather, they sacrificed to the gods on the latter's behalf. Therefore, Hendrix argues that the concept of "imperial cult" obfuscates a proper understanding of Thessalonian imperial divine honors because Julio-Claudians were honored in the city for what they did, not for who or what they were.[6]

While most scholars rely on Hendrix, some use a more generalizing approach to Thessalonian imperial cults. In the process, they cite evidence outside the city to support their conclusions about imperial divine honors in the city. For example, Donfried and James R. Harrison, relying on Donfried, trace the suffering of Thessalonian Christ-confessors to imperial divine honors. They contend that the *euangelion* of *kyrios* Jesus and the coming *basileia* at the parousia conflicted with imperial royal ideology and aspects of imperial cults. In addition, both argue that Thessalonica's politarchs administered an imperial loyalty oath to the city's inhabitants, which motivated them to harm Christ-confessors physically. Donfried even proposes that some Christ-confessors suffered martyrdom (see 1 Thess 4:13–18).[7] Aside from using Hendrix's work

---

6. Holland Lee Hendrix, "Thessalonicans Honor Romans" (ThD diss., Harvard University, 1984), esp. 257–338; Hendrix, "Archaeology and Eschatology at Thessalonica," in *The Future of Early Christianity: Essays in Honor of Helmut Koester*, ed. Birger A. Pearson (Minneapolis: Fortress, 1991), 107–18; Hendrix, "Beyond 'Imperial Cult' and 'Cult of Magistrates,'" *SBL 1986 Seminar Papers*, ed. Kent Harold Richards, SBLSP 25 (Atlanta: Scholars Press, 1986), 301–8; Hendrix, "Thessalonica," *ABD* 6:523–27; Hendrix, "Thessalonike," in *Archaeological Resources for New Testament Studies: A Collection of Slides on Religion and Culture in Antiquity*, ed. Helmut Koester and Holland L. Hendrix, 2 vols. (Valley Forge, PA: Trinity Press International, 1994), 1:1–49.

7. Donfried, "Cults of Thessalonica," 342–46, 350; Donfried, *Paul, Thessalonica*, 31–46. Relying on the work of Adolf Deissmann (*Light from the Ancient East: The*

to establish that some imperial cultic activity occurred in Thessalonica, Donfried's and Harrison's evidence that *kyrios* and *euangelion* are "imperial" terms and that imperial loyalty oaths were taken in Thessalonica is from outside the city.

Such generalizing reconstructions are methodologically flawed because they assume, incorrectly, that a uniform "imperial cult" existed during the Principate. To the contrary, imperial cults differed from region to region, province to province, and even city to city.[8] Most cities and provinces in the Greek East established imperial divine honors to show appreciation for imperial benefaction and to court future beneficence. As G. W. Bowersock notes, "The honour was as much a means of securing favour in the future as it was an acknowledgment of favour already

---

New Testament Illustrated by Recently Discovered Texts of the Graeco-Roman World, trans. Lionel R. M. Strachan, 4th ed. [New York: Hodder & Stoughton, 1910; repr., Grand Rapids: Baker, 1978], 351–58), Donfried contends that *kyrios* was an imperial title from Augustus onward, despite the fact that he acknowledges that "the first verifiable inscription of the *Kyrios*-title in Greece dates to the time of Nero" ("Cults of Thessalonica," 344; *Paul, Thessalonica*, 34). Harrison concludes that Paul was so concerned about imperial cults and their effects on his converts that he interjected "heavily loaded Roman political terms" into the Thessalonian correspondence to discourage participation in them ("Paul and the Imperial Gospel," 82–92; *Paul and the Imperial Authorities*, 52–68).

8. Beard, North, and Price, *Religions of Rome*, 1:318, 348. For overviews of the different types of imperial cults, see Christian Habicht, "Die augusteische Zeit und das erste Jahrhundert nach Christi Geburt," in *Le culte des souverains dans l'Empire romain: Sept exposés suivis de discussions*, ed. Willem den Boer (Paris: Fondation Hardt, 1973), 41–88; Ittai Gradel, "Roman Apotheosis," in *Thesaurus Cultus et Rituum Antiquorum (ThesCRA)*, 9 vols. (Los Angeles: Getty, J. Paul Getty Museum), 2:186–99. For provincial, regional, and civic studies of imperial cultic activity, see S. R. F. Price, *Rituals and Power: The Roman Imperial Cult in Asia Minor* (Cambridge: Cambridge University Press, 1984); Duncan Fishwick, *The Imperial Cult in the Latin West: Studies on the Ruler Cult of the Western Provinces of the Roman Empire*, 3 vols., EPRO 108 (Leiden: Brill, 1987–2005); Ittai Gradel, *Emperor Worship and Roman Religion*, OCM (Oxford: Oxford University Press, 2002); Maria Kantiréa, *Les dieux et les dieux Augustes: Le cult impérial en Grèce sous les Julio-claudiens et les Flaviens; Études épigraphiques et archéologiques* (Paris: de Boccard, 2007); Monika Bernett, *Der Kaiserkult in Judäa unter den Herodiern und Römern: Untersuchungen zur politischen und religiösen Geschichte Judäas von 30 v. bis 66 n. Chr.*, WUNT 203 (Tübingen: Mohr Siebeck, 2007); Takashi Fujii, *Imperial Cult and Imperial Representation in Roman Cyprus*, Heidelberger althistorische Beiträge und epigraphische Studien 53 (Stuttgart: Steiner, 2013).

received."⁹ Manifestations of imperial divine honors in cities and provinces depended on local customs, the ethnicity of the leaders of a city or a province, and a community's status vis-à-vis Rome. In short, imperial cults, like Paul's letters, must be interpreted contextually.[10]

Thus, a better approach to Thessalonian imperial cultic activity is the contextualized one that Hendrix adopts. Any inquiry should begin with evidence from Thessalonica and look elsewhere if the evidence points in that direction. My agreement with Hendrix on method notwithstanding, two factors limit his work. First, discoveries since 1984 undermine his conclusions about (1) whom Thessalonica acclaimed as gods; (2) how many Julio-Claudian temples/shrines existed in the city; and (3) how the Julio-Claudians were worshiped. Second, Hendrix's refusal to call imperial divine honors a "cult" stems from an incorrect assumption about Greek religion, specifically that Greeks worshiped their gods because of their ontological statuses. Hence, he overlooks the pragmatic nature of Greek religion, which was founded on the principle of *do ut des*: Greeks sacrificed to the gods because the gods provided tangible benefaction.[11] This principle was operative in Thessalonica both with gods and Julio-Claudians.[12] In sum, this survey demonstrates that a more up-to-date and contextualized reconstruction of Thessalonian imperial cults is necessary before assessing the cults' relationship to embryonic Christianity in the city.

---

9. G. W. Bowersock, "The Imperial Cult: Perceptions and Persistence," in *Self-Definition in the Graeco-Roman World*, vol. 3 of *Jewish and Christian Self-Definition*, ed. Ben F. Meyer and E. P. Sanders (London: SCM, 1982), 171–82, here 171.

10. Beard, North, and Price conclude that imperial cults were so diverse because "they were located in very different contexts" (*Religions of Rome*, 1:348).

11. For Greek religion, see Simon Price, *Religions of the Ancient Greeks*, Key Themes in Ancient History (Cambridge: Cambridge University Press, 1999).

12. One Thessalonian inscription calls Isis and Sarapis "benefactor gods" ([Εἴσιδι κ]αὶ Σαράπιδι θεοῖς εὐεργέ|ταις, "for Isis and Sarapis, benefactor gods" [*IG* 10.2.1.90, ll. 1–2]) and another calls a first-century CE Julio-Claudian a benefactor ([— — — — — Καίσ]αρι [ν ε[ὐεργέ[τη — — —], "for benefactor Caesar" [*IG* 10.2.1.33, l. 3]). Hendrix leaves the impression (unintended, I think) that the motive for Thessalonian imperial cults—benefaction—is unique. Christian Habicht's conclusion for ruler cults in the Hellenistic period, however, is appropriate for those in the Principate: "A cult [of a ruler] is never justified by the importance of the recipient or by special qualities like ἀρετή, δικαιοσύνη, φιλανθρωπία, or σοφία, but rather always by very specific actions to the benefit of a city" (*Divine Honors for Mortal Men in Greek Cities: The Early Cases*, trans. John Noël Dillon [Ann Arbor: Michigan Classical Press, 2017], 161).

2. Thessalonian Imperial Divine Honors: The Evidence

Thessalonica decreed divine honors for Romans long before the Principate.[13] The earliest evidence dates to the aftermath of the Fourth Macedonian War (150–148 BCE). Since the Third Macedonian War (172–168 BCE), Rome had occupied the territory of the former kingdom of Macedon, which it had divided into four sectors, or *merides*. Around 150 BCE, a certain Andriscus claimed to be the rightful heir to the Macedonian throne. He mustered an army and attempted to expel Rome from the territory, inaugurating the Fourth Macedonian War. The Roman general Quintus Caecilius Metellus quelled the revolt, after which Macedonia was reorganized into a single province and Thessalonica became its capital.[14] To show appreciation for Metellus's victory, the city set up a public honorary statue of the general (148–146 BCE) with an inscription on its base, partly restored, acclaiming him Thessalonica's "savior and benefactor" (σω[τῆρα καὶ εὐεργέτην]) (*IG* 10.2.1.134, l. 3).[15] Hendrix concludes that the city did not establish a cult for Metellus because (1) the epigraph does not mention cult explicitly, (2) not all benefactors were venerated, and (3) a certain Thessalonian erected an honorary statue of Metellus at Olympia dedicated to Zeus.[16] While these observations are correct, Christian

---

13. Contra Gene L. Green (*The Letters to the Thessalonians*, PilNTC [Grand Rapids: Eerdmans, 2002], 39), there is no evidence that Thessalonica established a cult for any Macedonian king. Divine honors offered to Alexander the Great date to the third century CE and the revival of Hellenism in Macedonia. See Victoria Allamani-Souri, "The Imperial Cult," in *Roman Thessaloniki*, ed. D. V. Grammenos, trans. David Hardy, Thessaloniki Archaeological Museum Publication 1 (Thessaloniki: Archaeological Museum, 2003), 98–119, here 107–8.

14. D. Clint Burnett, "Imperial Loyalty Oaths, Caesar's Decrees, and Early Christianity in Thessalonica: Contextualizing Inscriptions," in *Studying the New Testament through Inscriptions: An Introduction* (Peabody, MA: Hendrickson, 2020), 97–120, here 110–12.

15. Κόιντον Καικέ[λιον Κοίντου Μέτελλον]| στρατηγὸν ἀ[νθύπατον Ῥωμαίων]| τὸν αὐτῆς σω[τῆρα καὶ εὐεργέτην]| ἡ π[όλις], "The city (set up this statue of) Quintus Caecilius Metellus son of Quintus, general, proconsul of the Romans, and its savior and benefactor." Contra Hendrix ("Thessalonicans Honor Romans," 20), who incorrectly translates Metellus's name as "Quintus Caeci[lius son of Quintus Metellus]." For public inscriptions and how they differ from private inscriptions, see Burnett, "Engraved for All Time: An Introduction to Inscriptions," in *Studying the New Testament*, 9–57, here 20–48.

16. Δάμων Νικάνορος Μακεδὼν ἀπὸ| Θεσσαλονίκης Κόϊντον Καικέλιον| Κοΐντου Μέτελλον, στρατηγὸν ὕπατον| Ῥωμαίων, Διὶ Ὀλυμπίωι|| ἀρετῆς ἕνεκεν καὶ

Habicht has shown that the hailing of king or general as "savior" in the Hellenistic period "always indicate[s] a cult for the person who receives [the title]."[17] This observation and the fact that Thessalonica formed a cult for Roman benefactors (see below) suggest that the city established a cult for Metellus, the trappings of which remain unknown.

A few years later, Thessalonica formed a cult for benefactors who were Roman citizens, the context of which must be the steady stream of Romans that frequented and those who resided in the provincial capital for governmental, military, and commercial purposes. Some of these Romans provided concrete benefactions to Thessalonica. To show appreciation and to court future euergetism, the city granted them divine honors. The cult is a unique Thessalonian manifestation of a broader Hellenistic practice that began in the second century BCE after Rome conquered the Greek East. At that time, Greek cities began to honor certain Romans as the source of munificence. Most such honors were not cultic, however, which makes the cult of Roman benefactors in Thessalonica singular.[18] The earliest evidence for this cult is a decree of gymnastic *neoi* (95 BCE) that honors a gymnasiarch named Paramonus because, among other things, he increased the sacrifices offered to the gods and the Roman benefactors (*IG* 10.2.1.4).[19] The epigraph attests that the cult was located in the gymnasium at that time, that sacrifices to Roman benefactors were customary (τὰς ἠθισμένας τειμάς, "the customary honors" [*IG* 10.2.1.4, l.

εὐνοίας ἧς ἔχων διατε|λεῖ εἴς τε αὐτὸν καὶ τὴν πατρίδα καὶ τοὺς λοιπούς| Μακεδόνας καὶ τοὺς ἄλλους Ἕλληνας, "Damon, son of Nicanor, a Macedonian from Thessalonica (set up this statue of) Quintus Caecilius Metellus son of Quintus, general and consul of the Romans for Olympian Zeus because of the virtue and goodwill that he has continuously for him, his home-city, the rest of the Macedonians, and the other Hellenes" (*IG* 10.2.1.1031 = *IvO* 325). Hendrix concludes, "His unusual acclamation as *sōtēr* ... probably acknowledged the distinctive service rendered by Metellus to the city ... rather than its recognition of the praetor as quasi-divine Hellenistic ruler" ("Thessalonicans Honor Romans," 20–25, 256–66; quotation from 259–60). Contra Hendrix ("Thessalonicans Honor Romans," 23), who again incorrectly translates Metellus's name as "Quintus Caecilius son of Quintus Metellus."

17. Habicht, *Divine Honors*, 99–115; quotation from 113.

18. Roman benefactors are mentioned in sixteen second- to first-century BCE inscriptions, most of which are noncultic honors. Thus, Andrew Erskine concludes, "This cult is at present not known to have existed anywhere but in Thessalonica" ("The Romans as Common Benefactors," *Historia* 43 [1994]: 70–87, here 80).

19. Hendrix, "Thessalonicans Honor Romans," 99–105.

10]), and that they were incorporated into the cult of the gymnastic gods (τοῖς τε θεοῖς καὶ Ῥωμαίοις εὐεργέταις, "for the gods and the Roman benefactors" [*IG* 10.2.1.4, ll. 10–11]). That the worship of Roman benefactors predates the decree is clear. By how much time is unknown. Nonetheless, this cult lasted into the second and perhaps third century CE and was incorporated into Thessalonian imperial cultic activity (*IG* 10.2.1.31, 32 [probably], 128, 133, 226), which is unusual because most Greek civic cults for Romans in the Principate focused on the living princeps and his family members (see below).[20]

When the Principate formed, the veneration of Romans in Thessalonica increased in terms of the number of individuals honored and the intensity of their cultic veneration.[21] Evidence indicates that the city established cults for Julius Caesar, Augustus, Livia, (probably) Claudius, and (probably) Nero.[22] The only evidence for Julius Caesar's cult is two coin series calling him θεός (*RPC* 1.1554–55).[23] These were minted not during

---

20. Simon Price, "Gods and Emperors: The Greek Language of the Roman Imperial Cult," *JHS* 104 (1984): 79–95, here 85.

21. While I heed Helmut Koester's warnings about "Biblical archaeology" and share his disapproval of some scholarly uses of archaeological materials in the interpretation of 1 Thessalonians, he is incorrect when he concludes that after the evidence for the cult of Roman benefactors there is "a period of three hundred years of silence with respect to the cult of the Roman emperors until the monuments from the time of the emperor Galerius" ("Archaeology and Paul in Thessalonike," in *Paul and His World: Interpreting the New Testament in Context* [Minneapolis: Fortress, 2007], 38–54, here 43).

22. There are no direct data attesting to the veneration of Tiberius and Gaius (Caligula) in Thessalonica. As a "free city," Thessalonica did not participate in the Macedonian provincial cult during the Julio-Claudian period. See Allamani-Souri, "Imperial Cult," 100–103. The city may have established a cult for Marc Antony after the battle of Philippi. See Emmanuel Voutyras, "Des honneurs divins pour Marc Antoine à Thessalonique?," in *More than Men, Less than Gods: Studies on Royal Cult and Imperial Worship; Proceedings of the International Colloquium Organized by the Belgian School at Athens (November 1–2, 2007)*, ed. Panagiotis P. Iossif, Andrzej S. Chankowski, and Catharine C. Lorber, StHell 51 (Leuven: Peeters, 2011), 457–73.

23. Sophia Kremydi-Sicilianou notes that Thessalonian coinage offers "direct evidence for divine honours" for Julio-Claudians ("'Belonging' to Rome, 'Remaining' Greek: Coinage and Identity in Roman Macedonia," in *Coinage and Identity in the Provinces*, ed. Christopher Howgego, Volker Heuchert, and Andrew Burnett [Oxford: Oxford University Press, 2005], 95–106, here 98). Because of Hendrix's influence ("Thessalonicans Honor Romans," 170–79, 316–17), Jeffrey A. D. Weima notes that the coins depicting Julius Caesar also have a bust of Augustus (*1–2 Thessalonians*,

his lifetime but during Octavian's/Augustus's reign (31 BCE–14 CE), which means that the former's cult was established postmortem.[24] Nothing is known of its trappings because (as I argue below) the temple that scholars conclude was dedicated to Julius Caesar belonged to Augustus. These two coin series evince that Thessalonica followed the political-religious developments of Rome in two ways. First, most Greek cities in the Julio-Claudian period minted coins depicting living, not deceased, Julio-Claudians, while coins picturing the deceased Julius Caesar are common in the Romanized western empire and colonies of Rome in the Greek East.[25] Second, Greek civic imperial cults focused mostly on living principes, while state imperial cults in Rome focused on deceased and officially deified principes known in Latin as *divi* (*divus* in the singular).[26] When *divus* was translated into Greek, the most common translation was *theos*.[27] By calling the deceased and deified dictator *theos*, the Thessalonian coinage reflects a conscious imitation of the state imperial cult of *Divus* Julius in Rome.

Most Thessalonian evidence for Julio-Claudian imperial divine honors relates to Augustus, the earliest of which is an official public inscription (27 BCE–14 CE) memorializing the construction of a heretofore unidentified

---

BECNT [Grand Rapids: Baker Academic, 2014], 19–20). Even though the title "son of god" is lacking on the coins, Weima argues that the association with Julius Caesar intimates it. He further contends that "son of god" is a divine title, which incorrectly imports later Christian theology into υἱὸς θεοῦ/*divi filius*.

24. These coins revolutionized post-168 BCE Thessalonian minting conventions, for Julius Caesar is the first nondeity or nonmythic person after 168 BCE to appear on the city's coinage and the first human to be called *theos*. See *BMC Macedonia*, 108–14, nos. 1–57. Hendrix notes only that Julius Caesar's bust is the first head of a Roman citizen to appear on Thessalonian coinage ("Thessalonicans Honor Romans," 170), thereby underestimating the significance of these coins.

25. See D. Clint Burnett, "Divine Titles for Julio-Claudian Imperials in Corinth," *CBQ* 82 (2020): 437–55; Burnett, "'God Highly Exalted Him': Phil 2:9–11, Ps 110:1, and Jesus's Share in God's Temple and Throne," in *Christ's Enthronement at God's Right Hand in Early Christianity and Its Greco-Roman Cultural Context*, BZNW 242 (Berlin: de Gruyter, 2021), 111–56; *RPC* 1.514–515 (Lugdunum), 517 (Vienna), 620 (Italy), 708 (Sicca), 759, 761 (Paterna), 771–772 (Hadrumetum), 785 (Lepti Minus), 799 (Achulla), 1116, 1132, 1134 (Corinth), 1283, 1286 (Dyme), 1650, 1653–1655 (Philippi), 2007, 2010 (Apamea), 2115, 2142 (Sinope), 5408, 5421 (Uncertain).

26. Habicht, "Die augusteische Zeit," 45–50; Gradel, "Roman Apotheosis," 192–93. Price comments, "The creation of a *divus* [in Rome] made little difference in the Greek world" ("Gods and Emperors," 85).

27. For the translation of *divus* into Greek, see Burnett, "Divine Titles," 448–49.

imperial temple. The epigraph names the project's patron, a Roman proconsul whose name is lost, the building's overseer, Sosonus, and its architect, Dionysus.[28]

> ... BOSA ... The proconsul ... made the temple of Caesar of quarried stone[29] in the time of the priest and president of imperial games for Imperator Caesar Augustus son of god ... -us son of Nicopolis priest of the gods. Do- ... son of ... -pus of Roma and the Roman benefactors. Nic- ... son of Paramonus. When Diogenes son of ... Cleon son of P-... Zopas son of Cal- ... Eulandrus son of ... Protogenes son of ... served as politarchs ... and supervised the work, Sosonus son of ... was treasurer of the city ... Dionysus son of ... was the architect. (*IG* 10.2.1.31)[30]

The two aspects of this epigraph that interest me are the references to the temple of Caesar and the priesthood and presidency of imperial games. Concerning the former, the main question is, to whom did the temple belong? Most scholars follow the conclusion of Charles Edson, the editor of *IG* 10.2.1, that the temple was dedicated to *theos* Julius Caesar because (1) the coins of *theos* Julius Caesar were probably minted to commemorate the temple's construction, and (2) A. D. Nock, the foremost specialist in the mid-twentieth century on imperial divine honors, assured Edson that the temple cannot belong to Augustus but "is surely a temple of Julius...."[31]

---

28. This epigraph, now lost, was found in 1874 in the rubble of the Golden Gate where it had been damaged by pickaxes.

29. Theodosia Stefanidou-Tiveriou argues that λατομίας means "quarried stone" ("Οἰκοδο-μή-ματα αὐτοκρατορικῆς λατρείας στὴ Θεσσαλονίκη: Ζητήματα τοπογραφίας καὶ τυπολογίας," *Saio Annuario* 87 [2009]: 613–31, here 615). Contra Hendrix, who proposes that it is the proper name Latomia ("Thessalonicans Honor Romans," 107).

30. [- - - -]ΒΟΣΑ[- - - - - - - - - -]|| ἀ[ν]θύπατος [- - - - - - -]|| λατομίας ἐπόησ[εν τὸν]|| Καίσαρος να[όν].|| ἐπὶ ἱερέως καὶ ἀγων[οθέτου · Αὐ]|τοκράτορος Καίσα[ρος · θεοῦ]|| υἱοῦ Σεβασ}βασ{το[ῦ · - - - - - - - -]||ως τοῦ Νεικοπόλ[εως · ἱερέως]|| δὲ τῶν θεῶν Δω[- - - - - τοῦ - - - -]||| που, Ῥώμης δὲ κ[αὶ Ῥωμαίων]|| εὐεργετῶν Νεικ[- - - - - - - -τοῦ]| Παραμόνου· ν.| πολειτα[ρχούντων]|| Διογένους το[ῦ - - - - - - - - -]||| Κλέωνος τοῦ Π[- - - - - - - -]|| Ζωπᾶ τοῦ Καλ[- - - - - - - - - -]|| Εὐλάνδρου τοῦ [- - - - - - -]|| Πρωτογένους τοῦ [- - - - - -]|| τοῦ καὶ προστα[τήσαντος]||| τοῦ ἔργου· ταμ[ίου τῆς πόλεως]| Σώσωνος τ[οῦ - - - - - - - - -]|| ἀρχιτεκ[τονοῦντος]| Διονυσίο[υ τοῦ - - - - - -].

31. Charles Edson, "Macedonia," *HSCP* 51 (1940): 126–36, here 132. Hendrix ("Thessalonicans Honor Romans," 106–9, 175–76, 292–99, 311), Allamani-Souri ("Imperial Cult," 103), Donfried ("Cults of Thessalonica," 345–46), Robert Jewett (*The*

Edson's conclusion is problematic for five reasons. First, it conflates the numismatic and epigraphic testimonies, which is methodologically unsound. It is more appropriate to interpret the inscription in light of itself. When this occurs, its most logical reading is that the temple is dedicated to the Caesar who is clearly mentioned in the epigraph, Caesar Augustus.[32] Second, no priests of *theos* Julius Caesar are attested in Thessalonian epigraphy.[33] Third, a newly published inscription (see below) refers to the priesthood and president of imperial games for Augustus, calling him Caesar and thus providing more evidence that Thessalonica called Augustus "Caesar" during his reign. Fourth, if Thessalonica mimicked *Divus* Caesar's state cult in Rome, as I argue, and if the temple in Thessalonica was dedicated to him, then the epigraph should reflect his divine status—as the Thessalonian coinage does—calling him *theos*, which it does not. Finally, Nock's flawed interpretation of the religiosity of imperial cultic honors influenced his, and thus Edson's, assessment of the temple. Nock worked with the assumption that imperial divine honors were not "real" cults, famously characterizing "ruler worship" as "an expression of gratitude which did not involve any theological implications ... [because acts of devotion to rulers] are all of the nature of homage and not of worship in the full sense, for worship implies the expectation of blessing to be mediated in a supernatural way."[34] Mary Beard, John North, and Simon Price note that such a conclusion is both incorrect and anachronistic because it foists a modern, Western, and above all Christianized interpretation of

---

Thessalonian Correspondence: Pauline Rhetoric and Millenarian Piety, FF [Philadelphia: Fortress, 1986], 124), and Weima (*1–2 Thessalonians*, 19) agree with Edson.

32. Christopher Steimle concludes that, if the *theos* Julius Caesar coinage did not exist, then there would be little doubt that the temple was Augustus's (*Religion im römischen Thessaloniki: Sakraltopographie, Kult und Gesellschaft 168 v. Chr.–324 n. Chr.*, STAC 47 [Tübingen: Mohr Siebeck, 2009], 51–52). Identifying the temple as Augustus's does not mean that Julius Caesar was not worshiped in it. It was commonplace for Greek cities to worship more than one Julio-Claudian in the same temple. See Burnett, "'Beside the Gods in Their Temples': Royal and Imperial Temple Sharing," in *Christ's Enthronement*.

33. Steimle, *Religion im römischen Thessaloniki*, 51. If the temple were dedicated to him, a reference to his priest in Thessalonian inscriptions is expected.

34. A. D. Nock, "Religious Developments from the Close of the Republic to the Death of Nero," in *CAH* 10:481–503, here 481.

religion onto antiquity.³⁵ For all these reasons, I contend that the temple of Caesar was dedicated to Augustus.

Some scholars have attempted to locate this temple and thus far there are two possibilities.³⁶ The first, which Hendrix suggests, is that the temple is near where *IG* 10.2.1.31 was found: in the rubble of the Golden Gate on the east side of the city.³⁷ This proposal assumes that *IG* 10.2.1.31 is dedicatory, which is unclear because the beginning of the epigraph is lost.³⁸ Thus, the epigraph's find-spot may not have any bearing on the temple's location. In addition, almost all imperial cultic data are from the opposite, western side of Thessalonica. The second hypothesis is that the temple of Caesar is the so-called Archaic temple, which is an Ionic temple found in 1936 on the west side of Thessalonica in Antigonidion Square. It was dubbed "Archaic" because *spolia*, some of which date to the fifth century BCE, were used in its construction.³⁹ During excavation, archaeologists found remains of marble statues of Hadrian (fig. 1) and the goddess Roma (fig. 2), which suggest that the building hosted imperial cultic activity, at least during Hadrian's reign. Unfortunately, the temple was re-covered in 1936 and its location was lost.⁴⁰ In 1999, Emmanuel Voutyras proposed that the Archaic temple's

---

35. Beard, North, and Price state, "If we seek to distinguish between cults [in the Roman world] that were (really) political and those that had a (genuine) spiritual dimension we are doing little more than engaging illicitly in Christian polemic against an alien religious system" (*Religions of Rome*, 1:359).

36. There is a remote possibility that the temple of Caesar Augustus is the so-called semicircular marble building that was discovered in 1950 on Stratigou Doubouiotis Street, on the west side of Thessalonica. This structure dates to the Principate, and two marble statues, one of Augustus and another (probably) of Claudius (discussed below), were found near it. The building's exact function, however, remains unknown, and the floor evidences no signs that statue bases had been placed on it. See Stefanidou-Tiveriou, "Οἰκοδομήματα," 616–19.

37. Hendrix, "Thessalonicans Honor Romans," 139.

38. Hendrix probably assumed that *IG* 10.2.1.31 refers to the dedication of the temple because Edson placed the epigraph in the dedication portion of *IG* 10.2.1. The beginning of the inscription is lost, making its exact categorization unclear: [- - - -] ΒΟΣΑ[- - - - - - - - -]. For dedicatory inscriptions, see Burnett, "Engraved for All Time," 20–23, 29–38, 42–43.

39. Some building material from this temple is housed at the Thessaloniki Archaeological Museum.

40. For the discovery and rediscovery of this temple, see Theodosia Stefanidou-Tiveriou, "Τα λατρευτικά αγάλματα του ναού του Διός και της Ρώμης στη Θεσσσαλονίκη," in Κλασική παράδοση και νεωτερικά στοιχεία στην πλαστική της

spolia are from a temple of Aphrodite in Thermi, which was transported to Thessalonica in the late first century BCE to house the joint cults of the goddess and *theos* Julius Caesar because he claimed descent from Venus/Aphrodite.[41] No Thessalonian evidence corroborates Voutyras's proposal, and more recent excavation of the Archaic temple undermines it. In 2000, the temple was rediscovered and further excavated. Excavators determined that it bears no signs of transportation because the temple's structural form remains unaltered. They suggest that the *spolia* used in the temple's construction are from local Thessalonian buildings.[42] Despite the improbability of Voutyras's hypothesis, the Archaic temple may be the temple of Caesar Augustus. During the 2000 excavation, archaeologists established that work occurred on the temple in the early Principate, which may align with the date of *IG* 10.2.1.31.[43] This possibility notwithstanding, a definitive conclusion cannot presently be reached.

Even if the Archaic temple is not the temple of Caesar Augustus, it housed imperial cultic activity in Hadrian's reign and probably in Nero's

---

ρωμαικής Ελλάδας, ed. Theodosia Stefanidou-Tiveriou, Paulina Karanastasē, and Dēmētrēs Damaskos (Thessaloniki: University Studio, 2012), 273–86. Stefanidou-Tiveriou suggests that Roma and Hadrian "were a cult couple inside the cella of the … temple" ("Art in the Roman Period, 168 BC–337 AD," in *Brill's Companion to Ancient Macedon: Studies in the Archaeology and History of Macedon, 650 BC–300 AD*, ed. Robert J. Lane Fox [Leiden: Brill, 2011], 563–84, here 571–72).

41. Using the paleography of mason's marks on the *spolia*, Emmanuel Voutyras dates this transportation of the temple to the early Principate ("Η λατρεία της Αφροδίτης στην περιοχή του Θερμαίου κόλπου," in Αρχαία Μακεδονία VI: Ανακοινώσεις κατά το Έκτο Διεθνές Συμπόσιο, Θεσσαλονίκη, 15–19 Οκτωβρίου / *Ancient Macedonia VI: Papers Read at the Sixth International Symposium Held in Thessaloniki, October 15–19, 1996*, 2 vols., Hidryma Meletōn Chersonēsou tou Haimou 272 [Thessaloniki: Hidryma Meletōn Chersonēsou tou Haimou, 1999], 2:1329–43). In 1992, Hendrix appears to have changed his position about the location of the temple, considering a form of this theory possible ("Thessalonica," 524).

42. Anastasia Tasia, Zoe Lola, and Omeros Peltekes, "Θεσσαλονίκη: Ο υστεροαρχαϊκός ναός," Το Αρχαιολογικό Έργο στη Μακεδονία και Θράκη 14 (2002): 227–46, esp. the English summary on 242–43. Further research seems to corroborate this hypothesis: see George Karadedos, "Ο 'περιπλανώμενος' υστεροαρχαϊκός ναός της Θεσσαλονίκης: Πρώτες εκτιμήσεις για την αρχιτεκτονική του," Το αρχαιολογικό έργο στη Μακεδονία και στη Θράκη 20 (2006): 319–31.

43. Tasia, Lola, and Peltekes,"Θεσσαλονίκη," 227–46. Allamani-Souri supports this identification but suggests that the temple was transported for the joint cult of Aphrodite and Julius Caesar ("Imperial Cult," 103–5).

as well. As noted, during the temple's initial excavation in 1936, statues of Hadrian and Roma were uncovered. In 2000, two more marble statues, one of Zeus Aigochus and another of a Julio-Claudian princeps that is probably Nero, were discovered.[44] This latter image is headless but depicts Nero in military garb, a decorated cuirass (fig. 3). While its style is not overtly cultic, the statue is made from the same material—marble—as the images of Hadrian, Zeus, and Roma, which are cultic. Provided that the identification of the statue as Nero is correct and that it was cultic, it is the only evidence for divine honors for him in the city.[45]

Depending on the identification of the temple of Caesar Augustus with the Archaic temple, a recently published inscription testifies to a second or perhaps third Julio-Claudian imperial temple/shrine near Thessalonica. The epigraph (12 BC–14 CE) indicates that a certain Thessalonian benefactress with Roman citizenship named Avia Posilla erected a temple/shrine to Augustus, among other objects of veneration, about fifteen kilometers southeast of the city in Loutras Sedes.[46] The temple/shrine was part of a larger complex with water installations whose construction was commemorated in a bilingual Greek and Latin inscription.

> Avia Posilla daughter of Aulus (set up) this temple, the baths, the cistern, and the stoas surrounding the basin from her own funds to Imperator Caesar Augustus son of god, Hercules, and the city.
> Avia Posilla daughter of Aulus (set up) this temple, the baths, the pool, and the portico around the pool from her own funds to Imperator Caesar Augustus *pontifex maximus divi filius*, Hercules, and the city of the Thessalonians. (*IG* 10.2.1s.1650)[47]

While nothing more is known of this complex, it demonstrates that Augustus's cult was embedded in that of other gods, one of whom is the

---

44. Tasia, Lola, and Peltekes, "Θεσσαλονίκη," 242, 244 fig. 5, 246 fig. 19. See Stefanidou-Tiveriou ("Art in the Roman Period," 571) for this identification.

45. Stefanidou-Tiveriou concludes that this statue was probably cultic and set up in the Archaic temple, which she concludes was transported to Thessalonica ("Art in the Roman Period," 571).

46. Avia Posilla also repaired a Thessalonian temple of Isis (*IG* 10.2.1s.1052).

47. Αὐτοκράτορι Καίσαρι θεοῦ υἱῶι| Σεβαστῶι καὶ Ἡρακλεῖ καὶ τῆι πόλει| Αὐία Αὔλου θυγάτηρ Πώσιλλα τὸν| ναὸν καὶ τὰ θερμὰ καὶ τὴν δεξαμενὴν|| καὶ τ]ὰ[ς περει]κειμέν[ας στοὰς τῶι ὕδατι ἐκ τοῦ ἰδίου.| v.| *Imp(eratori) · Caesari · divi · f(ilio) · Aug(usto) · pontif(ici) · max(imo)| et · Herculi et civitati Thessalonicensium| Avia A(uli) · f(ilia) · Posilla · aedem · aquas · piscinam · et| porticus · circa · piscinam de suo.*

personification of the city. Such an integration of Augustus's cult with that of the city's means that Avia Posilla and worshipers at the temple/shrine connected the safety and security of Thessalonica to the rule of Augustus and probably his successors. In addition, this inscription overturns Hendrix's conclusion that the inhabitants of Thessalonica did not sacrifice directly to Julio-Claudians.[48] Even though the epigraph does not record a sacrifice, it is safe to assume that Augustus's association with Hercules and the personification of Thessalonica was cultic.

In addition to temples, Thessalonica set up cultic images of Julio-Claudians. Along with the statue of Nero discussed above, images of Augustus and (probably) Claudius have been found on the west side of the city. The former was uncovered on Stratigou Doumbiotou Street in 1939.[49] It depicts a near naked Augustus in the guise of Zeus with his right hand—which once held a spear or scepter—raised (fig. 4).[50] This image resembles his Prima Porta statue in the Vatican Museum (fig. 5) but differs in one significant way: the Thessalonian image's half-nudity and posture stress Augustus's identification with Zeus and hence his divinity. This image probably functioned as a cultic image in the temple of Caesar Augustus.[51] When the statue was set up is unclear because its exact date is

---

48. Hendrix concludes that "there is nothing to suggest that citizens sacrificed to Augustus for anything (or, for that matter, out of gratuitous devotion). In fact, there is no direct evidence from the city of any sacrificial ritual directed to Romans" ("Beyond 'Imperial Cult'," 304).

49. The general location where the statues of Augustus and Claudius (see below) were found, near the Archaic temple, lends support to the theory that it is the temple of Caesar Augustus.

50. For Augustus's statue, see Paul Lemerle, "Chronique des fouilles et découvertes archéologiques en Grèce en 1939," *BCH* 63 (1939): 285–324, here 315; G. Despinis, T. Stefanidou-Tiveriou, and E. Voutyras, eds., Κατάλογος γλυπτών του Αρχαιολογικού Μουσείου Θεσσαλονίκης (Thessaloniki: Morphotiko Hidryma Ethnikes Trapezes, 2003), no. 244. Augustus's image was constructed of eight pieces, which Hendrix contends is evidence that it was made elsewhere and then imported to Thessalonica ("Thessalonicans Honor Romans," 50–54, 59–60). No evidence supports this claim. See G. Bakalakis, "Archäologische Gesellschaft zu Berlin 1972/73," *AA* 88 (1973): 671–84, here 675–77.

51. Christoph vom Brocke, *Thessaloniki, Stadt des Kassander und Gemeinde des Paulus: Eine frühe christliche Gemeinde in ihrer heidnischen Umwelt*, WUNT 2/125 (Tübingen: Mohr Siebeck, 2001), 59–60. Hendrix concludes that Augustus's statue was not in the temple of Caesar because the temple predates it ("Thessalonicans Honor Romans," 45–54, 59–60, 296). However, he overlooks that the image may have

unknown and proposals range from Augustus's reign to Claudius's.⁵² The probable statue of Claudius was discovered in 1957 on the same street, close to Augustus's image. How close the statue of Claudius was to that of Augustus remains unknown because neither statue was discovered in a scientific excavation and their exact find-spots went unrecorded. Claudius's statue is headless and depicts the princeps as half-naked and also in a Zeus-like posture (fig. 6).⁵³ Provided that the statue is of Claudius, it is cultic, dates to his reign, and is the only evidence for imperial cultic activity for him in the city.⁵⁴ This image was also probably erected in the temple of Caesar Augustus.

The most attested imperial cultic official in Thessalonian material culture served Augustus's cult and was known as "the priest and president of imperial games of Caesar Augustus son of god" (ἱερεύς καὶ ἀγωνοθέτης Καί σαρος θεοῦ υἱοῦ Σεβαστοῦ [*IG* 10.2.1.31, 32, 131, 132, 133; *IG* 10.2.1s.1059]). Because Hendrix concludes that the temple of Caesar Augustus was dedicated to *theos* Julius Caesar, he argues that this cultic official's duties were split. He served as priest in *theos* Julius Caesar's cult and as president of the games in honor of *theos* Julius Caesar and the noncultic honor of Augustus.⁵⁵ Besides the probable conclusion that the temple was not dedicated to *theos* Julius Caesar (see above), this proposal is unconvincing for two reasons. First, it overlooks the Greek grammar of almost all the aforementioned Thessalonian inscriptions, in which one preposition governs both genitives, ἐπὶ ἱερέως καὶ ἀγωνοθέτου (*IG* 10.2.1.31, 32, 131, 132, *IG* 10.2.1s.1059). Thus, one cultic official fulfilled two roles, both of which were for Augustus.⁵⁶ Second, newer evidence clearly connects this office with Augustus only. A recently published inscription (27 BCE–14 CE) on

---

been a replacement for an older statue of Augustus or even an addition to the temple's cultic assemblage.

52. Despinis, Stefanidou-Tiveriou, and Voutyras, Κατάλογος γλυπτών, no. 244.

53. For Claudius's statue, see Georges Daux, "Chronique des fouilles," *BCH* 82 (1958): 644–830, here 759; Despinis, Stefanidou-Tiveriou, and Voutyras, Κατάλογος γλυπτών, no. 245. Stefanidou-Tiveriou notes that, along with these statues, a marble hand was found, which she suggests may have been to a statue of Tiberius ("Art in the Roman Period," 570).

54. Stefanidou-Tiveriou proposes that the statue originally depicted Gaius but was altered after his death-("Art in the Roman Period," 570).

55. Hendrix, "Thessalonicans Honor Romans," 292–99, esp. 298–90.

56. Smyth 7661§b states, "A preposition is used with the first noun and omitted with the second when the two nouns … unite to form a complex." See also §1669.

a statue base found in Thessalonica's agora refers to this cultic official and omits any reference to *theos* Julius Caesar in the process: "The city and the Roman merchants (set up this statue of) Marcus Papius Maximus son of Marcus in the time of the priest and president of imperial games of Caesar Augustus son of god Nicolaus son of Demetrius also known as Clitomachus" (*IG* 10.2.1s.1059).[57]

The final data associated with the worship of Augustus provide evidence that the city called him a god after his death and official apotheosis in Rome in 14 CE. A recently published inscription (14–29 CE) discussed below hails the deceased Augustus as a god. In addition, coinage minted in Claudius's reign contains a bust of Augustus with the legend θεός Σεβαστός (*RPC* 1.1578–1580). These data evince that, as with the case of *theos* Julius Caesar, Thessalonica mimicked Augustus's postmortem state imperial cult in Rome, which acclaimed the deceased and officially deified Augustus a *divus*. Thus, *theos Sebastos* on these coins functions as the Greek translation of Augustus's new Latin title, *Divus* Augustus. In addition, these data contradict Hendrix's claim, which scholars often repeat, that Thessalonica hailed only Julius Caesar as *theos*.[58]

The final Julio-Claudian worshiped in Thessalonica was Livia, Augustus's wife. The evidence for her cult consists of one coin and one inscription. The coin was minted during Augustus's reign—and thus while Livia was alive—with a bust of her on the obverse and the legend θεά Λιβιά (*RPC* 1.1563).[59] Thus, based on current evidence, Livia is the only living Julio-Claudian that Thessalonica designated as such. The inscription in question postdates Augustus's death and Livia's adoption in the Julii clan in 14 CE (Tacitus, *Ann.* 1.8) but predates her death in 29 CE. It testifies that the city dedicated an object or building to her as a goddess and the wife of a god: "The city (dedicated this) to the goddess Julia Augusta, wife

---

57. [ἡ πόλις καὶ οἱ συμπρ[αγματευόμε|[νοι 'Ρωμαῖ]οι Μᾶρκον Πάπιον Μάρ||[κου υἱ]ὸν Μάξιμον, ἐπὶ ἱερέως| [κ]αὶ ἀγωνοθέτου Καίσαρος θεοῦ| υἱοῦ Σεβαστοῦ Νικολάου Δη|μητρίου τοῦ καὶ Κλιτομάχου.

58. Hendrix, "Thessalonicans Honor Romans," 170–88. Koester follows Hendrix and argues that while Julius Caesar is called a god, "neither Augustus nor any of his successors (with the exception of Nero) is ever designated in this way" ("Archaeology and Paul," 43). I have been unable to determine what evidence about Nero Koester has in mind.

59. It is possible that the coin reads θεοῦ Λιβιά (see *RPC* 1.1563), but Kremydi-Sicilianou contends that θεά Λιβιά is the better reading ("'Belonging' to Rome," 98).

of the god Caesar Augustus, and mother of Tiberius Caesar Augustus" (*IG* 10.2.1s.1060).[60]

While the circumstances surrounding the establishment of the cults of Livia, Claudius, and Nero are unclear, the circumstances are known for the cults of Julius Caesar and Augustus. After Caesar's assassination, Brutus and Cassius fled to Macedonia and sought refuge in Thessalonica. The city refused to admit them and Brutus threatened to pillage it (Plutarch, *Brut.* 46; cf. Appian, *Bell. civ.* 4.118). This threat never materialized because (mostly) Marc Antony and Octavian soon defeated Brutus and Cassius at the battle of Philippi (42 BCE).[61] In response to Thessalonica's fidelity to the Caesarian cause, Antony made it a "free city" (*civitas libera*), thereby granting Thessalonica autonomy and tax exemption.[62] The city cherished this benefaction, boasting of its new status in epigraphy (*IG* 10.2.1.6) and on coins (*RPC* 1.1551). It founded a cult of Eleutheria (*RPC* 1.1551) and erected a marble triumphal arch on the west side of the city, which was documented by European travelers before its destruction in 1877 (fig. 7).[63] After Actium, Thessalonica demonstrated quickly its fidelity to Octavian. Inscriptions mentioning Antony were defaced (*IG* 10.2.1.83, 109); the city minted coins depicting Nike on top of a prow (*RPC* 1.1556; cf. 1560), a reference to Actium; and Thessalonica probably rededicated the triumphal arch to Octavian only.[64] In light of such loyalty, Octavian reaffirmed Thessalonica's status as a "free city."[65] Afterward, the city experienced a time of heretofore unknown peace, security (see 1 Thess 5:3), and prosperity

---

60. [θεᾷ Ἰουλίᾳ Σεβαστῇ]| [γυναι]κὶ θεοῦ Σεβαστοῦ Καίσα[ρος]| [καὶ μ]ητρὶ Τιβερίου Καίσαρος| [Σε]βαστοῦ: ἡ πόλις. Θεά is reconstructed in the epigraph, which is plausible given that the city minted coins calling Livia a goddess while she was alive.

61. For the battle of Philippi, see Adrian Keith Goldsworthy, *Augustus: First Emperor of Rome* (New Haven: Yale University Press, 2014), 134–47.

62. Burnett, "Imperial Loyalty Oaths," 112–13.

63. Edward Daniel Clarke, *Travels in Various Countries of Europe, Asia, and Africa*, 11 vols. (London: Cadwell & Davies, 1816), 2:359. After Antony's bestowal of "free" status, the city also altered its calendar to reflect that its inhabitants were living in the Antonine era (*IG* 10.2.1.83, 109, 124) and minted coins advertising its concord with Rome (*RPC* 1.1553).

64. Burnett, "Imperial Loyalty Oaths," 113–15. The coins that Thessalonica minted depicting Octavian and *theos* Julius Caesar and the reference to Augustus's temple as Caesar's showcased that Augustus, not Antony, was the dictator's rightful heir.

65. For the proposal that "Caesar's decrees" (Acts 17:7) are letters reaffirming Thessalonica's status as a "free city," see Burnett, "Imperial Loyalty Oaths," 117–19.

that included an economic and construction boom.⁶⁶ Therefore, Hendrix is correct that Thessalonica established imperial cults to show appreciation for imperial benefaction and to court future munificence, at least with Augustus, but the same was probably the case for other Julio-Claudians.⁶⁷

To summarize, during the Julio-Claudian period, Thessalonica established cults for Julius Caesar, Augustus, Livia, (probably) Claudius, and (probably) Nero. Their trappings included sacrifices, games, priests, images, altars, and temples/shrines.⁶⁸ The evidence indicates that there were at least two, perhaps three, imperial temples/shrines, depending on whether the temple of Caesar Augustus is the Archaic temple. Julius Caesar's cult was postmortem, while the remaining cults were established during the lifetimes of Augustus, Livia, Claudius, and Nero. Augustus's cult lasted beyond his death and continued into the second and third centuries CE. Despite the establishment of imperial cults, Thessalonica was reluctant to call a living Julio-Claudian a god, except in the case of Livia. Most often the city waited until the death of a Julio-Claudian and the ruling of the senate in Rome before it acclaimed that person a god.⁶⁹

Thus, Thessalonian imperial cultic activity was a blending of Greek and Roman imperial cultic practices. The city's imperial cults resembled Greek practices in that grants of divine honors were established for Augustus, Livia, Claudius, and Nero while they were alive. On the other hand, the Roman influence is evident in that Thessalonica formed a postmortem cult for *theos* Julius Caesar and waited until the death of Augustus before hailing him as *theos*. To this end, in the city Greek *theos* functioned as a translation of the Latin *divus*. Thessalonian epigraphy provides a reason for the blending of Roman and Greek imperial cultic practices: Romans patronized imperial cults. The person who paid for the temple of Caesar Augustus was an unknown Roman proconsul, and the Roman citizen Avia Posilla constructed a building complex that included a temple/shrine dedicated to Augustus, Hercules, and Thessalonica, even memorializing her

---

66. Polyxeni Adam-Veleni, "Thessalonike: History and Town Planning," in Grammenos, *Roman Thessaloniki*, 143–62.

67. Hendrix, "Thessalonicans Honor Romans," 256–318.

68. Because imperial temples/shrines were erected in Thessalonica, imperial altars must have been set up as well, although concrete archaeological evidence for these is lacking.

69. There is no evidence that the city referred to Claudius or Nero as a god.

munificence in a bilingual Latin and Greek epigraph—a language combination rare in Julio-Claudian Thessalonica.[70]

3. Thessalonian Imperial Divine Honors and the Mistreatment of Christ-Confessors

I now turn to this essay's main goal of assessing the role that imperial cultic activity played in the social harassment of Thessalonian Christ-confessors. In light of the above reconstruction, there is little evidence to support the proposals of Donfried and Harrison. There is no evidence that *euangelion* and *kyrios* were "imperial" terms in Julio-Claudian Thessalonica.[71] For that matter, there is scant evidence that Julio-Claudians were known as *kyrioi* in the Greek East until the end of Nero's reign.[72] If these terms were not "imperial," then references to Jesus's parousia from heaven (1 Thess 1:10, 4:16, 2 Thess 1:7) may have been interpreted not as the visitation of a monarch but as the epiphany of a particular deity from heaven, which was quite common in the Greco-Roman world.[73] Nor is there any evidence that imperial loyalty oaths, which Donfried and Harrison identify as "Caesar's decrees" (Acts 17:7), were administered in Thessalonica. Elsewhere I have demonstrated that the total evidence for these oaths consists of eight inscriptions, all of which date between 31 BCE and 37 CE. These oaths were taken for three reasons: to acknowledge political transition in Rome, to show appreciation for imperial benefaction, and to curry favor with a newly crowned princeps. Moreover, they were taken at the behest of local officials, not principes, and thus cannot be Caesar's decrees.[74] In sum, the evidence for Thessalonian imperial divine honors evinces a more complex

---

70. The abiding Roman political and social presence in Thessalonica was due to its status as a provincial capital and its location on a seaport and the Via Egnatia. See Burnett, "Imperial Loyalty Oaths," 109–15.

71. It was not until after the first century CE that the reigning princeps was known as *kyrios* in Thessalonica (*IG* 10.2.1.1009). *Euangelion* never appears in association with the princeps in the city.

72. For *kyrios* in earliest Christianity and its relationship to Roman principes, see D. Clint Burnett, "Jesus, the Royal Lord: Inscriptions and Local Customs," in *Studying the New Testament*, 58–76.

73. See Georgia Petridou, *Divine Epiphany in Greek Literature and Culture* (Oxford: Oxford University Press, 2015).

74. See Burnett, "Imperial Loyalty Oaths," 97–120.

reason for the social harassment of Christ-confessors than a "Christ versus Caesar" paradigm.[75]

To the contrary, the above data indicate that divine honors for Romans, including Julio-Claudians, were most often integrated into the religious (and political) system of the city in that they were embedded into cults of traditional gods.[76] The cult of the Roman benefactors was wedded to the cult of the gymnastic gods. If the statue from the Archaic temple is Nero, his cult may have been embedded in that of Zeus Aigochus, Roma, or both (which clearly occurred for Hadrian during his reign). And Augustus's cult was incorporated into the cult of Roman benefactors as well as that of Hercules and the personification of Thessalonica. By establishing a temple/shrine in which Augustus and the personification of Thessalonica were venerated together, the city's success and well-being were linked to the princeps.

The reason why Thessalonica embedded Julio-Claudian imperial cults in its traditional religious (and political) system was to legitimate and articulate the relationship between the city's gods and the Julio-Claudians, which was one not of competition but of cooperation. Integrating imperial cults with traditional cults sanctioned Julio-Claudian hegemony and showcased that the gods partnered with the dynasty to ensure the prosperity of the city. In the process, Thessalonica's divine citizens demonstrated their approval of the Julio-Claudians by blessing the city with security and a robust economy and by welcoming some Julio-Claudians—Julius Caesar, Augustus, and Livia—into their ranks as gods, and others—Claudius and Nero—as somewhere between gods and humans. In this way, Thessalonian imperial cultic activity functioned as a concrete earthly demonstration of the city's celestial reality: the Julio-Claudians were earthly vice-regents of the gods and mediators of their blessings.[77]

---

75. Beard, North, and Price specifically warn against isolating imperial cults as a "competitor for Christianity" (*Religions of Rome*, 1:360). They also caution against interpreting imperial divine honors as solely political: "Ordinary inhabitants of the Roman empire *expected* that political power had a religious dimension. The opposite was also true: religious cults might quite properly have a political dimension" (359; emphasis theirs). Donfried acknowledges this integration of religion and politics in Thessalonica ("Cults of Thessalonica," 336; *Paul, Thessalonica*, 22), but by distinguishing between "religious" and "civic" cults or "imperial cults" he leaves the impression that religion and politics are not in fact integrated.

76. Beard, North, and Price, *Religions of Rome*, 1:360.

77. J. Rufus Fears concludes, "This concept of the ruler as the divinely endowed vicegerent of the gods was present at the very inception of ruler worship in Greece"

As Hendrix notes, the association of gods and Romans in cultic acts in Thessalonica "expressed a hierarchy of benefaction extending from the divine sphere into human affairs," which could demonstrate that the local gods were "responsible for the continued well-being of the city."[78] This perspective is clear from one of the only surviving literary sources from a Julio-Claudian citizen of Thessalonica, Antipater. In two of his epigrams, he prays that Hercules, among other gods, would make Gaius Caesar— Augustus's adoptive son—invincible (ἀνίκατος) (Greek Anthology 9.59) and calls Gaius, Zeus's child (Ζηνὸς τέκος) (Greek Anthology 9.297). In short, the integration of imperial and traditional cults in Thessalonica stabilized, structured, legitimated, and articulated the reality in which its denizens lived.[79]

Therefore, Thessalonian imperial cults contributed to the social harassment of Christ-confessors, but not in isolation from other cults in the city. Paul, Silvanus, and Timothy recognized this fact when they traced the suffering of their converts to their acceptance of the Christian *euangelion* (1 Thess 1:6) and their concomitant turning away from idols in general and not imperial cults in particular (1 Thess 1:9).[80] Given that imperial divine honors were often embedded in the cults of traditional gods and that the Julio-Claudians functioned as the earthly vice-regents of the gods, Christ-confessors were socially harassed because they had turned their backs on two aspects of ancient life that the inhabitants of Thessalonica deemed

---

("Ruler Worship," in *Civilization of the Ancient Mediterranean: Greece and Rome*, ed. Michael Grant and Rachel Kitzinger, 3 vols. [New York: Scribner, 1988], 2:1009–26, here 1020).

78. Hendrix, "Thessalonicans Honor Romans," 336–37.

79. For this purpose of religion in the Greek city, see Christine Sourvinou-Inwood, "What Is *Polis* Religion?," in *The Greek City: From Homer to Alexander*, ed. Oswyn Murray and Simon Price (Oxford: Clarendon, 1990), 295–322, here 295–307. For this purpose of imperial cults, see Price, *Rituals and Power*, 234–48. For two citizens of late first-century CE Thessalonica that are called φιλόπατρις ("lover of his home city") and φιλόκαισαρ ("friend/lover of Caesar"), see *IG* 10.2.1s.1062.

80. John M. G. Barclay is thus correct when he notes that Paul has the habit of "lumping [pagan gods] together into a single category" ("Paul, Roman Religion and the Emperor," in *Pauline Churches and Diaspora Jews* [Grand Rapids: Eerdmans, 2016], 345–62, here 355). Similarly, the author of the Acts of the Apostles attributes the mistreatment of nascent Christ-confessors to disregarding Caesar's decrees and turning the empire upside down (Acts 17:6–7), which has both political and religious implications. See Burnett, "Imperial Loyalty Oaths," 97–120.

proper, pious, and patriotic: the cults of the gods and the cults and reign of the Julio-Claudians. It was the neglect of these two, integrated pillars of Thessalonian society by nascent Christ-confessors that threatened the peace, stability, and "free" status of the city and motivated its inhabitants to socially harass them. The objective of such mistreatment was to convince their fellow compatriots to recant their new religious affiliation with its religious exclusivity and to restore them to the traditional fold of pagan religious (and political) activity.

4. Conclusion

This essay has probed the connection between Thessalonian imperial cults and the social harassment of Christ-confessors in the city. In the process, I have provided a more up-to-date and accurate presentation of imperial divine honors in Julio-Claudian Thessalonica that considers the latest material evidence, some of which has been unknown to New Testament scholars until now. This evidence suggests that imperial cults were not the sole reason for the mistreatment of Thessalonian Christ-confessors. Imperial cultic activity was often embedded in traditional cults of gods, and such integration served to legitimate and articulate the relationship between the gods of Thessalonica and the Julio-Claudians: the latter were earthly vice-regents of the gods and mediators of their blessings. By accepting the Christian *euangelion* and turning away from pagan cults in general, which included but were not limited to imperial cults, Thessalonian Christ-confessors were endangering the city's safety, success, and "free" status, which the gods maintained through their partnership with the Julio-Claudians; this accounts for the social harassment of the Thessalonians. In other words, Christ-confessors in the city suffered mistreatment because their compatriots considered their movement as threatening two integrated pillars of Thessalonian social order: religion and politics.

Bibliography

Adam-Veleni, Polyxeni. "Thessalonike: History and Town Planning." Pages 143–62 in *Roman Thessaloniki*. Edited by D. V. Grammenos. Translated by David Hardy. Thessaloniki Archaeological Museum Publication 1. Thessaloniki: Archaeological Museum, 2003.

Allamani-Souri, Victoria. "The Imperial Cult." Pages 98–119 in *Roman Thessaloniki*. Edited by D. V. Grammenos. Translated by David Hardy.

Thessaloniki Archaeological Museum Publication 1. Thessaloniki: Archaeological Museum, 2003.

Bakalakis, G. "Archäologische Gesellschaft zu Berlin 1972/73." *AA* 88 (1973): 671–84.

Barclay, John M. G. "Conflict in Thessalonica." *CBQ* 55 (1993): 512–30.

———. *Paul and the Gift*. Grand Rapids: Eerdmans, 2015.

———. *Pauline Churches and Diaspora Jews*. Grand Rapids: Eerdmans, 2016.

Beard, Mary, John North, and Simon Price. *Religions of Rome*. 2 vols. Cambridge: Cambridge University Press, 1998.

Bernett, Monika. *Der Kaiserkult in Judäa unter den Herodiern und Römern: Untersuchungen zur politischen und religiösen Geschichte Judäas von 30 v. bis 66 n. Chr.* WUNT 203. Tübingen: Mohr Siebeck, 2007.

Bowersock, G. W. "The Imperial Cult: Perceptions and Persistence." Pages 171–82 in *Self-Definition in the Graeco-Roman World*. Vol. 3 of *Jewish and Christian Self-Definition*. Edited by Ben F. Meyer and E. P. Sanders. London: SCM, 1982.

Brocke, Christoph vom. *Thessaloniki, Stadt des Kassander und Gemeinde des Paulus: Eine frühe christliche Gemeinde in ihrer heidnischen Umwelt*. WUNT 2/125. Tübingen: Mohr Siebeck, 2001.

Burnett, D. Clint. *Christ's Enthronement at God's Right Hand in Early Christianity and Its Greco-Roman Cultural Context*. BZNW 242. Berlin: de Gruyter, 2021.

———. "Divine Titles for Julio-Claudian Imperials in Corinth." *CBQ* 82 (2020): 437–55.

———. "'Seated in God's Temple': Illuminating 2 Thess 2:4 in Light of Inscriptions and Archaeology Related to Imperial Divine Honors." *LTQ* 48 (2018): 69–94.

———. *Studying the New Testament through Inscriptions: An Introduction*. Peabody, MA: Hendrickson, 2020.

Clarke, Edward Daniel. *Travels in Various Countries of Europe, Asia, and Africa*. 11 vols. London: Cadwell & Davies, 1816.

Daux, Georges. "Chronique des fouilles." *BCH* 82 (1958): 644–830.

Deissmann, Adolf. *Light from the Ancient East: The New Testament Illustrated by Recently Discovered Texts of the Graeco-Roman World*. Translated by Lionel R. M. Strachan. 4th ed. New York: Hodder & Stoughton, 1910. Reprint. Grand Rapids: Baker, 1978.

Despinis, G., T. Stefanidou-Tiveriou, and E. Voutyras, eds. Κατάλογος γλυπτῶν του Αρχαιολογικού Μουσείου Θεσσαλονίκης. Thessaloniki: Morphotiko Hidryma Ethnikes Trapezes, 2003.

Donfried, Karl P. "The Cults of Thessalonica and the Thessalonian Correspondence." *NTS* 31 (1985): 336–56.

———. "Issues of Authorship in the Pauline Corpus: Rethinking the Relationship between 1 and 2 Thessalonians." Pages 81–113 in *2 Thessalonians and Pauline Eschatology: For Petr Pokorný on His 80th Birthday*. Edited by Christopher M. Tuckett et al. ACEP 21. Leuven: Peeters, 2013.

———. *Paul, Thessalonica, and Early Christianity*. Grand Rapids: Eerdmans, 2002.

Edson, Charles. "Macedonia." *HSCP* 51 (1940): 126–36.

Erskine, Andrew. "The Romans as Common Benefactors." *Historia* 43 (1994): 70–87.

Fears, J. Rufus. "Ruler Worship." Pages 1009–26 in vol. 2 of *Civilization of the Ancient Mediterranean: Greece and Rome*. Edited by Michael Grant and Rachel Kitzinger. 3 vols. New York: Scribner, 1988.

Fishwick, Duncan. *The Imperial Cult in the Latin West: Studies on the Ruler Cult of the Western Provinces of the Roman Empire*. 3 vols. EPRO 108. Leiden: Brill, 1987–2005.

Fujii, Takashi. *Imperial Cult and Imperial Representation in Roman Cyprus*. Heidelberger althistorische Beiträge und epigraphische Studien 53. Stuttgart: Steiner, 2013.

Goldsworthy, Adrian Keith. *Augustus: First Emperor of Rome*. New Haven: Yale University Press, 2014.

Gradel, Ittai. *Emperor Worship and Roman Religion*. OCM. Oxford: Oxford University Press, 2002.

———. "Roman Apotheosis." Pages 186–99 in vol. 2 of *Thesaurus Cultus et Rituum Antiquorum (ThesCRA)*. 9 vols. Los Angeles: J. Paul Getty Museum, 2004.

Green, Gene L. *The Letters to the Thessalonians*. PilNTC. Grand Rapids: Eerdmans, 2002.

Habicht, Christian. "Die augusteische Zeit und das erste Jahrhundert nach Christi Geburt." Pages 41–88 in *Le culte des souverains dans l'Empire romain: Sept exposés suivis de discussions*. Edited by Willem den Boer. Paris: Fondation Hardt, 1973.

———. *Divine Honors for Mortal Men in Greek Cities: The Early Cases.* Translated by John Noël Dillon. Ann Arbor: Michigan Classical Press, 2017.

Harrison, James R. *Paul and the Imperial Authorities at Thessalonica and Rome.* WUNT 273. Tübingen: Mohr Siebeck, 2011.

———. "Paul and the Imperial Gospel at Thessaloniki." *JSNT* 25 (2002): 71–96.

Hendrix, Holland Lee. "Archaeology and Eschatology at Thessalonica." Pages 107–18 in *The Future of Early Christianity: Essays in Honor of Helmut Koester.* Edited by Birger A. Pearson. Minneapolis: Fortress, 1991.

———. "Beyond 'Imperial Cult' and 'Cult of Magistrates.'" Pages 301–8 in *SBL 1986 Seminar Papers.* SBLSP 25. Atlanta: Scholars Press, 1986.

———. "Thessalonica." *ABD* 6:523–27.

———. "Thessalonicans Honor Romans." ThD diss., Harvard University, 1984.

———. "Thessalonike." Pages 1–49 in vol. 1 of *Archaeological Resources for New Testament Studies: A Collection of Slides on Religion and Culture in Antiquity.* Edited by Helmut Koester and Holland L. Hendrix. 2 vols. ed. Valley Forge, PA: Trinity Press International, 1994.

Jewett, Robert. *The Thessalonian Correspondence: Pauline Rhetoric and Millenarian Piety.* FF. Philadelphia: Fortress, 1986.

Kantiréa, Maria. *Les dieux et les dieux Augustes: Le cult impérial en Grèce sous les Julio-claudiens et les Flaviens; Études épigraphiques et archéologiques.* Paris: de Boccard, 2007.

Karadedos, George. "Ο 'περιπλανώμενος' υστεροαρχαϊκός ναός της Θεσσαλονίκης: Πρώτες εκτιμήσεις για την αρχιτεκτονική του." Το αρχαιολογικό έργο στη Μακεδονία και στη Θράκη 20 (2006): 319–31.

Koester, Helmut. "Archaeology and Paul in Thessalonike." Pages 38–54 in *Paul and His World: Interpreting the New Testament in Context.* Minneapolis: Fortress, 2007.

Kremydi-Sicilianou, Sophia. "'Belonging' to Rome, 'Remaining' Greek: Coinage and Identity in Roman Macedonia." Pages 95–106 in *Coinage and Identity in the Provinces.* Edited by Christopher Howgego, Volker Heuchert, and Andrew Burnett. Oxford: Oxford University Press, 2005.

Lemerle, Paul. "Chronique des fouilles et découvertes archéologiques en Grèce en 1939." *BCH* 63 (1939): 285–324.

Malherbe, Abraham J. *The Letters to the Thessalonians: A New Translation with Introduction and Commentary.* AB 32B. New York: Doubleday, 2000.

Murphy-O'Connor, Jerome. *Paul the Letter-Writer: His World, His Options, His Skills.* GNS 41. Collegeville, MN: Liturgical Press, 1995.

Nock, A. D. "Religious Developments from the Close of the Republic to the Death of Nero." *CAH* 10:465–511.

Petridou, Georgia. *Divine Epiphany in Greek Literature and Culture.* Oxford: Oxford University Press, 2015.

Price, S. R. F. *Rituals and Power: The Roman Imperial Cult in Asia Minor.* Cambridge: Cambridge University Press, 1984.

Price, Simon. "Gods and Emperors: The Greek Language of the Roman Imperial Cult." *JHS* 104 (1984): 79–95.

———. *Religions of the Ancient Greeks.* Key Themes in Ancient History. Cambridge: Cambridge University Press, 1999.

Sourvinou-Inwood, Christine. "What Is *Polis* Religion?" Pages 295–322 in *The Greek City: From Homer to Alexander.* Edited by Oswyn Murray and Simon Price. Oxford: Clarendon, 1990.

Stefanidou-Tiveriou, Theodosia. "Art in the Roman Period, 168 BC–337 AD." Pages 563–84 in *Brill's Companion to Ancient Macedon: Studies in the Archaeology and History of Macedon, 650 BC–300 AD.* Edited by Robert J. Lane Fox. Leiden: Brill, 2011.

———. "Τα λατρευτικά αγάλματα του ναού του Διός και της Ρώμης στη Θεσσσαλονίκη." Pages 273–86 in Κλασική παράδοση και νεωτερικά στοιχεία στην πλαστική της ρωμαικής Ελλάδας. Edited by Theodosia Stefanidou-Tiveriou, Paulina Karanastasē, and Dēmētrēs Damaskos. Thessaloniki: University Studio, 2012.

———. "Οἰκοδο-μή-ματα αὐτοκρατορικῆς λατρείας στὴ Θεσσαλονίκη: Ζητήματα τοπογραφίας καὶ τυπολογίας." *Saio Annuario* 87 (2009): 613–31.

Steimle, Christopher. *Religion im römischen Thessaloniki: Sakraltopographie, Kult und Gesellschaft 168 v. Chr.–324 n. Chr.* STAC 47. Tübingen: Mohr Siebeck, 2009.

Tasia, Anastasia, Zoe Lola, and Omeros Peltekes. "Θεσσαλονίκη: Ο υστεροαρχαϊκός ναός." Το Αρχαιολογικό Έργο στη Μακεδονία και Θράκη 14 (2002): 227–46.

Voutyras, Emmanuel. "Des honneurs divins pour Marc Antoine à Thessalonique?" Pages 457–73 in *More Than Men, Less Than Gods: Studies on Royal Cult and Imperial Worship; Proceedings of the International*

Colloquium Organized by the Belgian School at Athens (November 1–2, 2007). Edited by Panagiotis P. Iossif, Andrzej S. Chankowski, and Catharine C. Lorber. StHell 51. Leuven: Peeters, 2011.

———. "Η λατρεία της Αφροδίτης στην περιοχή του Θερμαίου κόλπου." Pages 1329–43 in vol. 2 of Αρχαία Μακεδονία VI: Ανακοινώσεις κατά το Έκτο Διεθνές Συμπόσιο, Θεσσαλονίκη, 15–19 Οκτωβρίου / *Ancient Macedonia VI: Papers Read at the Sixth International Symposium Held in Thessaloniki, October 15–19, 1996*. 2 vols. Hidryma Meletōn Chersonēsou tou Haimou 272. Thessaloniki: Hidryma Meletōn Chersonēsou tou Haimou, 1999.

Weima, Jeffrey A. D. *1–2 Thessalonians*. BECNT. Grand Rapids: Baker Academic, 2014.

Winter, Bruce W. *Divine Honors for the Caesars: The First Christians' Responses*. Grand Rapids: Eerdmans, 2015.

A Return to "Peace and Security": The Parts and the Whole

Alan H. Cadwallader

In the debate about the level and nature of Paul's political teaching for Christ-groups in the Roman Empire, one small mound of words has gained mountainous attention in recent times—the reference to "peace and security" (εἰρήνη καὶ ἀσφάλεια) in 1 Thess 5:3. It is worth recalling that the interpretation of Paul's engagement with imperial ideology draws on a significant number of elements,[1] but this verse is treated as a prime piece. Jeff Weima provides a fulsome gathering of evidence designed to demonstrate that the phrase, presented as a quotation by Paul, was a discrete formulation of Roman imperial propaganda, circulating in Thessaloniki.[2] A fateful abbreviation of his argument, that it was "a fixed slogan of Roman political propaganda," may simply have joined a growing chorus of commentators from Ernst Bammel to Karl Galinsky.[3] But it became the tunneled target

---

1. See especially the work of James R. Harrison in this regard: *Paul and the Imperial Authorities at Thessalonica and Rome: A Study in the Conflict of Ideology*, WUNT 273 (Tübingen: Mohr Siebeck, 2011).
2. Jeffrey A. D. Weima, "'Peace and Security' (1 Thess 5.3): Prophetic Warning or Political Propaganda," *NTS* 58 (2012): 331–59. His main points are summarized in his commentary *1–2 Thessalonians*, BECNT (Grand Rapids: Baker, 2014), 347–51.
3. Weima, "Peace and Security," 355. See Ernst Bammel, "Ein Beitrag zur paulinischen Staatsanschauung," *TLZ* 85 (1960): 837–40; Bammel, "Romans 13," in *Jesus and the Politics of His Day*, ed. Bammel and C. F. D. Moule (Cambridge: Cambridge University Press, 1984), 375–78; Klaus Wengst, *Pax Romana and the Peace of Jesus Christ* (Philadelphia: Fortress, 1987), 19–25, 76–79; Holland L. Hendrix, "Archaeology and Eschatology at Thessalonica," in *The Future of Early Christianity: Essays in Honor of Helmut Koester*, ed. Birger A. Pearson (Minneapolis: Fortress, 1991), 112–14; Helmut Koester, "Imperial Ideology and Paul's Eschatology in I Thessalonians," in *Paul and Empire: Religion and Power in Roman Imperial Society*, ed. Richard A. Horsley (Har-

for rebuttal of both the amassed evidence and its implications for Paul as a counterimperial subversive (the extreme caricature of the argument).[4] Joel White, in a series of articles, first attempts to deconstruct any notion of a Roman slogan used by Paul and then, as a counterthesis, provides a conjoined, dichotomous pseudoslogan of Paul's own making.[5] Both take the context and inheritance of first-century Thessaloniki seriously, though with Weima accenting the Roman background and White the Hellenistic. A sophisticated attempt to bridge the divide by focusing on this background as the frame for the audience's reception is offered by Christoph Heilig.[6] My intention here is first to review some salient parts of the

---

risburg, PA: Trinity Press International, 1997), 158–66; Christoph vom Brocke, *Thessaloniki – Stadt des Kassander und Gemeinde des Paulus: Ein frühe christliche Gemeinde in ihren heidnischen Umwelt*, WUNT 2/125 (Tübingen: Mohr Siebeck, 2001), 167–85; James R. Harrison, "Paul and the Imperial Gospel at Thessaloniki," *JSNT* 25 (2002): 86–87; Ben Witherington III, *1 and 2 Thessalonians* (Grand Rapids: Eerdmans, 2006), 146–47; David Luckensmeyer, *The Eschatology of First Thessalonians* (Göttingen: Vandenhoeck & Ruprecht, 2011), 290–92; Karl Galinsky, "The Cult of the Roman Emperor: Uniter or Divider?," in *Rome and Religion: A Cross-Disciplinary Dialogue on the Imperial Cult*, ed. Jeffrey Brodd and Jonathan L. Reed, WGRWSup 5 (Atlanta: Society of Biblical Literature, 2011), 12; Nestor O. Míguez, *The Practice of Hope: Ideology and Intention in 1 Thessalonians* (Minneapolis: Fortress, 2012), 148–52; Murray J. Smith, "The Thessalonian Correspondence," in *All Things to All Cultures: Paul among Jews, Greeks and Romans*, ed. Mark Harding and Alanna Nobbs (Grand Rapids: Eerdmans, 2013), 294–95; Jeremy Gabrielson, *Paul's Non-violent Gospel: The Theological Politics of Peace in Paul's Life and Letters* (Cambridge: Clarke, 2014), 151–58.

4. Colin R. Nicholl, *From Hope to Despair in Thessalonica: Situating 1 and 2 Thessalonians* (Cambridge: Cambridge University Press, 2004), 53–54; Matthew F. Lowe, "'This Was Not an Ordinary Death.' Empire and Atonement in the Minor Pauline Epistles," in *Empire in the New Testament*, ed. Stanley E. Porter and Cynthia Long Westfall (Eugene, OR: Pickwick, 2011), 215–22; Nijay K. Gupta, *1–2 Thessalonians*, NCCS (Eugene, OR: Cascade, 2016), 104–5; J. Albert Harrill, "Paul and Empire: Studying Roman Identity after the Cultural Turn," *EC* 2 (2011): 281–311. Compare Michael F. Bird, "'One Who Will Arise to Rule over the Nations': Paul's Letter to the Romans and the Roman Empire," in *Jesus Is Lord, Caesar Is Not: Evaluating Empire in New Testament Studies*, ed. Scot McKnight and Joseph B. Modica (Downers Grove, IL: InterVarsity Press, 2013), 146–65.

5. Joel R. White, "Anti-imperial Subtexts in Paul: An Attempt at Building a Firmer Foundation," *Bib* 90 (2009): 305–33; White, "'Peace and Security' (1 Thess 5:3): Is It Really a Roman Slogan?," *NTS* 59 (2013): 382–95; White, "'Peace' and 'Security' (1 Thess 5.3): Roman Ideology and Greek Aspiration," *NTS* 60 (2014): 499–510.

6. Christoph Heilig, *Hidden Criticism? The Methodology and Plausibility of the Search for a Counter-imperial Subtext in Paul*, WUNT 2/392 (Tübingen: Mohr Siebeck, 2015).

arguments of Weima and White; second, to propose some new lines of investigation dealing with textual form, visual aesthetics, and the dynamics of cultural exchange in the early empire; third, to situate Paul within rather than outside his Roman context with respect to his purpose for introducing the phrase.

The Weima and White Positions

Weima has two objectives in his collation of materials. Weima assumes that the Greek, εἰρήνη καὶ ἀσφάλεια, is Paul's translation of the Latin *pax et securitas* or his quotation of an already prevalent Greek translation. This distinction remains undeveloped[7] but becomes important in White's response and my own suggestions. Weima is interested in showing how *pax* and *securitas* were in development as key categories of the Roman presence in the ancient world as discrete and as collated items. This processual approach allows him to bring together a trajectory of evidence spanning a period of four hundred years, from the inscription accompanying a magnus statue of pirate-crunching Pompey to that for territory stabilization of a legionary leader in Syria.[8] The ubiquity of this development is demonstrated by the broad category of evidence brought into the discussion: numismatics, monuments, epigraphy, and literature. He omits any dealings with the papyri but may have found tangential support in *BGU* 16.2657. This letter, dated to the fourteenth year of Augustus's reign, comes from the archive of the dioiketes, Athenodoros. It is a letter from a certain Semthoembe to two epistates, Petesuchos and Soteles. Although

---

7. Weima, "Peace and Security," 332 and n. 3; similarly, Laura Nasrallah, "Early Christian Interpretation in Image and Word: Canon, Sacred Text and the Mosaic of Moni Latomou," in *From Roman to Early Christian Thessalonike: Studies in Religion and Archaeology*, ed. Laura Nasrallah, Charalambos Bakirtzis, and Steven J. Friesen, HTS 64 (Cambridge: Harvard University Press, 2010), 386. Herman Hendrix had allowed that the Greek of 1 Thess 5:3 might reflect "Greek propagandistic responses to Roman beneficence" ("Archaeology and Eschatology," 114).

8. Weima deploys the description of "trajectory," particularly in relation to coins ("Peace and Security," 340–41) but it is clear that the sweep of evidence is covered by the term. The use of *trajectory* as a means of tracing a line of development goes back to James M. Robinson and Helmut Koester, *Trajectories through Early Christianity* (Philadelphia: Fortress, 1971). On the base of Pompey statue: ἀποκαθεστάκοτα δὲ [τὴν εἰρ]ήνην καὶ τὴν ἀσφάλειαν καὶ κατὰ γῆν καὶ θάλασσαν (SEG 46.1565); an honorific for M. Fl. Bonos ἄρξας ἡμ(ῶ)ν ... διὰ παντὸς εἰρηνεύεσθαι ἠσφαλίσατο (*OGI* 613).

fragmentary, it is clear that Semthoembe is seeking muscle to be present at a festival celebration ἵνα ἀσ-]φάλεια μεγάλη γένηται καὶ εἰρήν[η μένη] εἰς τὸν ἅπαντα χρόνον, "so that great security might be present and peace upheld for the whole time" (lines 16–18). This is not an imperial text, but it does demonstrate that the language of peace and security was already present early in Augustus's reign, in a context and for a purpose that Augustus would approve. It might well be argued that just as Paul was drawing on imperial values for his own (critical) objectives, so also (mimetically) was Semthoembe.

Weima acknowledges that *securitas* was later in development than *pax* and consequently is less pronounced in the evidence. But he affirms that the ground was laid for the conjunction of two key elements of imperial ideology and that a specific conjunction had in fact occurred before Paul wrote. The extant evidence for the pairing is, understandably, less than the distinct privileging of each item but does occur, for which readings in Velleius Paterculus and Plutarch and inscriptions on two related Praeneste altars become highly pertinent, supported by proximate occurrences of the terms in Josephus (Velleius Paterculus, *Hist. Rom.* 2.98.2; Plutarch, *Vit. Ant.* 40.4; *CIL* 14.2898, 2899; Josephus, *A.J.* 14.160, 247–248). The "sloganeering of the Roman state" is thereby, in Weima's judgment, soundly established.[9] The claim, according to Michael Gorman, is "now widely recognized."[10]

But not all have been convinced.[11] Two intertwining concerns shape Joel White's critique. First, he doubts whether there is sufficient evidence for an identifiable Roman slogan, *pax et securitas* or its Greek form, to be available to Paul.[12] Although White does not address the issue, given the purpose of his argument, the question of what makes for "an identifiable Roman slogan" is thereby raised. Second, he is concerned that the trajectory obfuscates the actual chronological appearance of elements (separately and together) in the phrase. Accordingly, he seeks to scour methodically through the evidence raised by Weima to demonstrate that

---

9. Weima, "Peace and Security," 358; Weima, *1–2 Thessalonians*, 351.

10. Michael J. Gorman, *Becoming the Gospel: Paul, Participation and Mission* (Grand Rapids: Eerdmans, 2015), 162.

11. Compare the earlier demurral of Abraham J. Malherbe, *The Letters to the Thessalonians*, AB 32B (New York: Doubleday, 2000), 303–4.

12. White, "Peace and Security," 384. His main lines of argument are summarized in "Roman Ideology and Greek Aspiration," 499–500.

it has been overinterpreted. The evidence for Weima's slogan is, he argues, not up to the load it is asked to bear. Significantly, as we shall see, he omits the monumental evidence from consideration, as much, I suspect, because Weima himself quickly shifts to the textual ingredients of the monuments (and, to some extent, coins) he mentions.[13]

He dismisses both the Pompey and the Syrian inscription as anachronistic: the fourth-century (CE) testimony, like the use of the third-century Corpus hermeticum,[14] is understandably suspect as direct evidence for the first century, though whether they might be reliant on an ancient formula is not considered. But the judgment on the Pompey inscription because it occurred more than a century before Paul, indeed, "long before the dawn of the Principate," and so cannot be counted as an instance of Roman imperial propaganda, is curious.[15] This fracturing of Weima's trajectory line requires also a fracturing of imperial Roman trajectories that were concerned, even in the so-called Augustan revolution, to accent continuities with the republic. In the Roman deference to antiquity, a "third of a century," which White regards as fatal,[16] would be barely the twitch of an eyelid. Pompey "the Great," for example, figures prominently in Plutarch's preoccupation with tracing Roman ascendancy, including Pompey's (sometimes equivocal) commitment to security (ἀσφάλεια; Plutarch, *Pomp.* 15.3, 55.4; see also 57.3; Plutarch, *Cic.* 35.1–2), even if his life ended, in Plutarch's assessment, tragically (*Pomp.* 76.6).[17] Alison Cooley has demonstrated how important Pompey and his renowned actions were as one counterpoint against which Augustus framed his most monumental piece of imperial propaganda, namely, the Res gestae divi Augusti.[18] That peace and security were already present in some measure in the late republic, as part of the presentation of Rome and its leaders, is at least a potential foundation for imperial improvisation on a received tradition. Certainly

---

13. The Ara Pacis is one notable exception but of little concern to White because it fails to mention or display *securitas*.
14. Corp. herm. 18.10: τοὺς τῆς κοινῆς ἀσφαλείας καὶ εἰρήνης πρυτάνεις.
15. White, "Peace and Security," 385–96, 391.
16. White, "Peace and Security," 395.
17. A quotation from the tragedian Sophocles become Pompey's last words (*Pomp.* 78.4). So profound was association that they are repeated a number of times (Appian, *Bell. civ.* 2.84; Dio Cassius, *Hist.* 42.4). Plutarch credits the mistakes of Pompey to family connections (*Comp. Ages. Pomp.* 1.3–4).
18. Alison E. Cooley, *Res Gestae Divi Augusti: Text, Translation and Commentary* (Cambridge: Cambridge University Press, 2009).

the Thessalonian coins featuring both the new emperor Tiberius and the past emperor Augustus show clearly the willingness to portray the present as anchored in the past.[19]

The Praeneste twin altars are reduced to separate examples of sycophantic adulation, even if "twin altars."[20] White claims, in reliance on a very general reference, that Salus and Victoria were also featured as part of the city's obsequiousness.[21] In fact, such inscriptions either do not appear (Salus) or bear no relation to the altars themselves (Victoria). Proximity does not equal derivation from or modulation of a simple template, White argues, and this governs Velleius Paterculus's summation of the end of a Thracian rebellion in circa 30 CE, of "security to Asia and peace to Macedonia." In any case, in an overreading of Alfred Kneppe, White asserts that *securitas* was a late developer as a corporate entity.[22] Kneppe actually recognizes the willingness of Augustus to incorporate Greek exempla into his model of government, including *securitas*, which was guaranteed and encapsulated in the person of the emperor—a clear template of how the individual and the corporate might be combined.[23] Velleius himself for a time served in Macedonia (*Hist. Rom.* 2.101.3) and would have been well-suited to recognize Hellenistic elements incorporated into Roman

---

19. *BMC Macedonia*, Thessalonica 117, §74. Some coins also combine Tiberius with Livia (§75). She frequently appeared on the reverse of coins as the personification of key virtues of the Roman state: *Pietas, Pax, Iustitia*, etc. (see *RPC* 1.25). Even Galba in 68–69 CE drew on Livia's past power for his present interests (*RIC* 1, Galba §§65–67).

20. In fact, in his summary rehearsal of his argument, he does not allow that those items of evidence where the words are closely connected include the Praeneste altars (White, "Roman Ideology and Greek Aspiration," 500).

21. White, "Peace and Security," 386. The work is Greg Rowe, *Princes and Political Cultures: The New Tiberian Senatorial Decrees* (Ann Arbor: University of Michigan Press, 2002), 117. Rowe simply claims that Pisan images of Augustus and Gaius as protectors and guardians mirrored other towns. He draws on Praeneste only for *pax* and *xecuritas*. See n. 37, which then cites Paul Zanker, *The Power of Images in the Age of Augustus* (Ann Arbor: University of Michigan Press, 1988), 307–8. Victoria (Augusta) occurs only in the calendrical *fasti* inscription (dated 4–10 CE) for April and August: *CIL* 1.2.1. See Christopher Francese and R. Scott Smith, *Ancient Rome: An Anthology of Sources* (Indianapolis: Hackett, 2014), 514.

22. White, "Peace and Security," 393, citing Alfred Kneppe, *Metus temporum: Zur Bedeutung von Angst in Politik und Gesellschaft der römischen Kaiserzeit des 1. Und 2. Jhdts n. Chr* (Stuttgart: Steiner, 1994), 233–34.

23. Kneppe, *Metus temporum*, 269.

administrative expositions and to provide them. We shall return to this consideration below.

Even if it be admitted, argues White, that peace and security were part of the terminology of Rome's imperial ideology, they cannot be held to be a slogan, especially given that such ideology generated a number of key terms among which peace and security were nongrouped participants. It is the specter of the slogan and the failure in synchronicity that arrests the muster of evidence.[24] In White's terms, the "literary context and the dating of texts" fail to support the thesis, even if, in his rigorous pursuit, some elements are jammed into the fit of his own refutation. Of course, by the time of Nero, when coins were clearly accenting *securitas*, the issue was probably academic. Those hearing Paul, now speaking only through his letters, were likely to have heard the slogan very clearly!

It is not as if White wishes to return the interpretation of 1 Thess 5:3 to a vacuum-sealed Jewish-Christian bubble immune to the prick of a Roman pilum, citing either prophetic texts or Jesus traditions as foundations.[25] While he thinks that looking back for the discovery of a Roman slogan does not satisfy the demands of chronological applicability, he yet turns to the Hellenistic period for his contribution to the meaning of the phrase in 1 Thess 5:3. He finds that it was rich in its use of ἀσφάλεια and in contexts expressing peace, though he wants to reserve peace to the *pax* of the Pax Romana. By examination of classical and Hellenistic authors, proxeny decrees, and even Philo and Josephus, he finds that ἀσφάλεια is a privileged Greek value. He might well have added the texts of treaties to his dossier, and perhaps noted that one fragmentary treaty inscription has been tentatively reconstructed with exactly Paul's phrase![26]

---

24. For White, persuasive evidence must fall between the establishment of the principate in 27 BCE and the writing of 1 Thessalonians, which he takes as 50 CE ("Roman Ideology and Greek Aspiration," 500).

25. The prophetic connections (Jer 6:14; Ezek 13:10, for example) still find their way into commentary: see Joseph Plevnik, *Paul and the Parousia: An Exegetical and Theological Investigation* (Peabody, MA: Hendrickson, 1997), 103–4; Earl J. Richard, *First and Second Thessalonians*, SP (Collegeville, MN: Liturgical Press, 1995), 250–51. Anthony C. Thiselton claims that the phrase "reminds us of Amos 5:18–20," an unfortunate, if revealing, use of the royal "we" for communal consent. See Thiselton, *1 and 2 Thessalonians through the Centuries* (Chichester: Wiley-Blackwell, 2013), 147.

26. Francis Piejko, "The Treaty between Antiochus III and Lysimachia: ca 196 B.C. (with Discussion of the Earlier Treaty with Philip V)," *Historia* 37 (1988): 154 (line a10). White only cites *IG* 7.4247 but notes this as one example among many

This may have qualified his assertion that the phrase becomes Paul's own construction that combines two leitmotifs of the two great cultures affecting Thessaloniki, Greek and Roman, "a pithy summation … one [term] with powerful connotations in Roman society (pax) and one strongly evocative of Greek conceptions of well-being (ἀσφάλεια)."[27] In the context of the letter, Paul is therefore addressing the common sensibilities of the Thessalonian populace from which the membership of the Christ-group is drawn, that is, Roman (merchants) and proud Greeks.[28] Of course, this constructs a dualism in Thessalonian society, one that the overwhelmingly Greek inscriptions, the demographic diversity intimated in onomastics, and, most of all, Rome's own blending of Greek values with its own agenda would challenge. As Emiliano Buis notes, "Roman diplomacy reproduced the vocabulary and content of the Hellenic tradition of treaty-signing,"[29] and, one should add, not just treaties.

Both Weima and White are revealed as textual critics, with the former only occasionally taking up the challenge to attend to the visual impact and purpose of Rome's imperial presence. Both understand the phrase to belong basically to the removal of fear and military conflict. Both treat Greek and Roman materials as discrete entities, Weima by neglect, White by hermetically sealing one from the other. Both understand Paul as standing apart from whatever it is that he is deploying in the phrase, a slogan that Paul either adopts or constructs. These are the matters that invite further consideration.

What Is a Slogan?

This is not the only time that slogans have entered New Testament interpretation. Larry Welborn some time ago bemoaned the lack of attention

---

("Roman Ideology and Greek Aspiration," 504). It may not be the most apt, given that ἀσφάλεια is but one of the list of benefits offered to a recognized benefactor; the full list has πολιτεία, ἀτέλεια, ἔγκτησις, ἀσυλία—all patently civic advantages. Compare SEG 50.542, 51.724, 51.1115, 57.521. But see SEG 36.552[1] for a "singular" example. For the use of ἀσφάλεια in treaties note SEG 59.1207.

27. White, "Roman Ideology and Greek Aspiration," 506–7.
28. White, "Roman Ideology and Greek Aspiration," 508.
29. Emiliano J. Buis, "Ancient Entanglements: The Influence of Greek Treaties in Roman 'International Law' under the Framework of Narrative Transculturation," in *Entanglements in Legal History: Conceptual Approaches*, ed. Thomas Duve (Frankfurt am Main: Max Planck Institute for European Legal History, 2014), 168.

to *form* in the statements of allegiance found in 1 Cor 1:12, 3:4.[30] No definitive outline of just what is the form of a slogan has emerged, and it was precisely at the level of form that his suggestion received criticism.[31] However, some features were able to be clarified by comparison with the canvassing graffiti found at Pompeii: the focus was personal, even if it was publicly painted; it declared allegiance and sought allegiance. Implicitly if not explicitly, they were oppositional, given that campaigns for electoral office were agonistic. Repeated elements were the name of the candidate, the office to which he aspired, the endorsing person or group, and a statement of support.[32] Welborn provides the example "Vatiam aed(ilem) Verus Innoces facit," "Verus Innoces backs Vatia for the office of festival organizer" (*CIL* 4.1080).

Further elements might be added to these insights. This public canvassing was not haphazard. Eeva-Maria Viitanen's Pompeii Project notes that 40 percent of the one thousand political messages surveyed from Pompeii were found on the walls of the homes of the wealthy—more than shops, taverns, and brothels.[33] She suggests that there may have been some (though far from complete) control over where and what political graffiti might be painted or incised, that a measure of literacy was assumed (which may explain the fewer examples at taverns), and that they indicate the interwoven yet hierarchical social networks operating at Pompeii.[34] A

---

30. Larry L. Welborn, "On the Discord in Corinth: 1 Corinthians 1–4 and Ancient Politics," *JBL* 106 (1987): 90.

31. Margaret M. Mitchell, *Paul and the Rhetoric of Reconciliation: An Exegetical Investigation of the Language and Composition of 1 Corinthians* (Louisville: Westminster John Knox, 1992), 83–86; similarly, Anthony Thiselton, *The First Epistle to the Corinthians*, NIGTC (Grand Rapids: Eerdmans, 2000), 121–22. See Welborn's rejoinder in his *Politics and Rhetoric in the Corinthian Epistles* (Macon, GA: Mercer University Press, 1997), 8–16.

32. Welborn, "On the Discord in Corinth," 92–93.

33. See Eeva-Maria Viitanen, Laura Nissinen, and Kalle Korhonen, "Street Activity, Dwellings and Wall Inscriptions in Ancient Pompeii: A Holistic Study of Neighbourhood Relations," in *Proceedings of the Twenty-Second Annual Theoretical Roman Archaeology Conference (TRAC 2012)*, ed. Annabel Bokern et al. (Oxford: Oxbow, 2012), 61–80.

34. The full study of the correlation of graffiti according to location has not been published at the time of writing. See Stephanie Pappas, "Pompeii 'Wall Posts' Reveal Ancient Social Networks," *Scientific American*, January 11, 2013, https://tinyurl.com/SBL4221d.

good example, though longer than the norm and unusually sensitive, is an endorsement for the office of *duovir*:

> L(ucium) Statium Receptum / IIvir(um) i(ure) d(icundo) o(ro) v(os) f(aciatis) vicini dig(num) / scr(ipsit) Aemilius Celer vic(ini) // invidiose / qui deles / ae[g]rotes
> His neighbours urge you to elect Lucius Statius Receptus duovir with judicial power; he is worthy. Aemilius Celer, a neighbor, wrote this. If you maliciously erase this, may you fall ill. (*CIL* 4.3775, from Regio I)

But, in 1 Thess 5:3, candidates or proposers are far from overt: Paul we know, but who are "they"? Rather, the focus of the slogan, whether adopted or constructed by Paul, is policy, not candidates: εἰρήνη καὶ ἀσφάλεια. Welborn thinks issues do not find their way into political sloganeering at Pompeii.[35] This is not thoroughgoing, however, as the following graffiti show:

> Lollium d(ignum) v(iis) a(edibus) s(acris) p(ublicis) o(ro) v(os) f(aciatis)
> I beg you to endorse Lollius, just the man for roads and public and sacred buildings. (*CIL* 4.7868)

Roads and infrastructure, it seems, are perennials. But endorsements might also be duplicitous, offering an appearance of support but perhaps delivering the opposite. So, for all the clear backing Lollius received,[36] he managed to score this ambiguous accolade:

> C(aium) Lollium / Fuscum IIvir(um) v(iis) a(edibus) s(acris) p(ublicis) p(rocurandis) / Asellinas(!) rogant(!) / nec sine Zmyrina
> Gaius Lollius Fuscus for duumvir, for maintaining the roads, the sacred and public buildings … Asellina's (girls) hanker after him … and Zmyrina wants in as well. (*CIL* 4.7863; translation informed by Plautus, *Aul.* 95–96)

Or more clearly, the aforementioned Vatia received this dubious endorsement:

> Vatiam aed(ilem) furunculi rog(ant)
> The petty crims want Vatia for festival organizer. (*CIL* 4.576)

---

35. Welborn, "On the Discord in Corinth," 92.
36. A run through volume 4 of *CIL* yields more than fifty endorsements for Lollius.

M(arcum) Cerrinium / Vatiam aed(ilem) o(rant) v(os) f(aciatis) seribibi / universi rogant / scr(ipsit) Florus cum Fructo
The late-night drunks implore you to elect Marcus Cerrinius Vatia as festival organizer. All of them want this. (And, in case you were wondering…) Fluff wrote this, aided and abetted by Fruity. (*CIL* 4.581)

These misdirections are slated in the literary texts. They are dubbed ὀνόματα εὐπρεπῆ, fine-sounding spin that delivers nothing or worse. This is probably how we ought understand the promise of εἰρήνη καὶ ἀσφάλεια given to Mark Anthony by King Phraates (Plutarch, *Ant.* 40.4), a wording that sounded appealing precisely because Mark Antony recognized it! His fault was to assume a truthful Parthian,[37] as the story goes on to reveal (Plutarch, *Ant.* 41.2–5).

Slogans are also the focus of a monograph by Sviatoslav Dmitriev that has as its focus the exalted position given to ἐλευθερία (as, for example, in IPriene 19.18–20).[38] He traces this as a slogan from Hellenistic to Roman times, especially noting how, from the time of Flaminius's oration in Greek to his audience at the games at Corinth (196 BCE), the Romans were adept at employing Greek political terms to serve their own "protectorate of the world," and a coin of Thessaloniki from 42–37 BCE clearly demonstrates just this: the obverse legend reads ἐλευθερία θεσσαλονικεων, surrounding probably the head of Octavia.[39] Dmitriev nowhere defines *slogan* but finds *freedom* constantly used in a variety of ways, both to secure the status quo and to justify aggressive advances. *Slogan* here does not endorse a person but is claimed by a person and is perceived as claimed by others. It has a distilled character, encapsulating a wider discourse, and it has an aggregating capacity of pulling together allegiances. At times, the slogan could be read as deceptively employed, as when Eumenes II expresses his annoyance at the fraudulence of the Rhodians' sloganeering of freedom and autonomy before the Roman senate: τὸ τῆς ἐλευθερίας ὄνομα καὶ αὐτονομίας (Polybius, *Hist.* 21.19.9). Significantly, as Francis Pielko points out, this was a reductionist formulation of the fourfold expression of freedoms for the citizens of a Greek polis: ἐλεύθεροι καὶ αὐτόνομοι καὶ

---

37. ἀληθής is frequently contrasted with εὐπρεπής: Euripides, *Tro.* 951; Herodotus, *Hist.* 3.72; Thucydides, *Hist.* 3.82.

38. Sviatoslav Dmitriev, *The Greek Slogan of Freedom and Early Roman Politics in Greece* (Oxford: Oxford University Press, 2011).

39. *RPC* 1.1551.

ἀφρούρητοι καὶ ἀφορολόγητοι ("freedom, autonomy, exemption from tax, absence of [externally imposed] garrisons").[40]

There is one particular illustration from Hellenistic times where it is clear that slogans were used, even if not the one proposed for 1 Thess 5:3. In Thucydides's study of the fracturing of familial loyalty at the heart of state conflict, opposing parties armed themselves with slogans that summed up what they stood for, what they were fighting for. This is the passage:

> οἱ γὰρ ἐν ταῖς πόλεσι προστάντες μετὰ ὀνόματος ἑκάτεροι εὐπρεποῦς, πλήθους τε ἰσονομίας πολιτικῆς καὶ ἀριστοκρατίας σώφρονος προτιμήσει, τὰ μὲν κοινὰ λόγῳ θεραπεύοντες ἆθλα ἐποιοῦντο
> The leaders in the cities on both sides contested for the commonwealth, which they pretended to be serving, by employing specious slogans: the one side, constitutional government with the equal sharing of power by all people; and the other side, government by the best men, which is responsible by reason of preferment.[41]

It is heuristically simple to dub this a combat between democracy and oligarchy, as does an ancient (probably Alexandrian) scholion on the passage.[42] What is important is that Thucydides provides slogans as the epitome of each side's program and commitment. The first slogan, for the democrats, is πλήθους ἰσονομίας πολιτικῆς, "the constitutional equality of the masses"; the second slogan, for the oligarchs, is ἀριστοκρατίας σώφρονος προτιμήσει, "responsible government by the best men acting rationally."[43] That Thucydides calls both slogans "fine-sounding" (εὐπρεποῦς) shows, first, that each had carried good connotations but, second, had become degraded—not unlike King Phraates's use of εἰρήνη καὶ ἀσφάλεια for Mark Antony.

The passage about conflicting groups armed by slogans had a life outside Thucydides's text. It is quoted by Dionysios of Halicarnassus, and it

---

40. Piejko, "Antiochus III and Lysimachia," 159; see, e.g., IIasos 2.

41. The expanded translation is from A. J. Graham and Gary Forsythe, "A New Slogan for Oligarchy in Thucydides III.82.8," *HSCP* 88 (1984): 45.

42. Karl Hude, *Scholia in Thucydidem ad optimos codices collata* (Leipzig: Teubner, 1927), 214.

43. I here follow the suggestion of Graham and Forsythe that there are two slogans of three words. Some commentators see the first slogan of three words, the second of two (Graham and Forsythe, "New Slogan"). The debate of democracy versus oligarchy is vibrant in Greek and Roman thought. See Plutarch, *Sept. sap. conv.* 11 (154d–f); Sallust, *Bell. Jug.* 41.5; Cicero, *Rep.* 1.31.

paraphrastically shapes the portrayal of the Cataline Wars by the Roman writer Sallust (Dionysius of Halicarnassus, *Thuc.* 33; Sallust, *Bell. Cat.* 38.3).[44] Key here is the recognition by Sallust that the respective parties of his historical analysis (of the period after 70 BCE) grouped around self-defining slogans:

> post illa tempora quicumque rem publicam agitavere, honestis nominibus, alii sicuti populi iura defenderent, pars quo senatus auctoritas maxima foret, bonum publicum simulantes pro sue quisque potential certabant. From that time, whoever disturbed the state under the guise of honorable slogans—some as though defending the rights of the people, others so that the senate's influence might be dominant—were, under pretense of the public good, in reality striving for their own ascendancy. (Rolfe)

The slogans are now reduced to two-word champions: *populi iura* and *senatus auctoritas*. Welborn notes this passage but as a demonstration of partisanship, overlooking the policy or issue-based slogans involved. Significantly, Sallust draws attention to the slogans with his use of *honestis nominibus*, his Latin equivalent for Thucydides's μετὰ ὀνόματος … εὐπροσώπου.

I have noted elsewhere the oppositional element at work in slogans, in the pericope over Caesar's coin in Mark 12:13–17.[45] The "things of Caesar" (τὰ Καίσαρος) was a pithy political slogan of the late republic indicating allegiance and support for Julius as against other groupings[46] and became indicative of a standard pro-imperial position. In Mark, the opposing side in the political contest is God, who also gains a slogan of allegiance (τὰ τοῦ θεοῦ).

This suggests that the phrase in 1 Thess 5:3 is likely to have an agonistic mirror and in fact the text delivers just that: ἡμέρα κυρίου, "the day of the Lord."[47] Paul proceeds to unpack the slogan, even though he tweaks the conceit of the Thessalonians that they already know all that they need to know (1 Thess 5:1–2). It is clear from 2 Thessalonians that "the day of

---

44. See Thomas F. Scanlon, *The Influence of Thucydides on Sallust* (Heidelberg: Winter, 1980), 82, 100.

45. Alan H. Cadwallader, "In Go(l)d We Trust: Literary and Economic Exchange in the Debate over Caesar's Coin (Mk 12:13-17)," *BibInt* 14 (2006): 486–507.

46. Josephus, *A.J.* 14.124 (τὰ Πομηίου … τὰ Καίσαρος); see also Plutarch, *Caes.* 34.2 (the side of Pompey against the cause of Caesar); *Cat. Min.* 58.1 (Cato versus Caesar).

47. The clash of slogans is hinted at by Thomas Neufeld, *Killing Enmity: Violence and the New Testament* (Grand Rapids: Baker, 2011), 137–38.

the Lord" remained a self-identifying encapsulation after Paul (2 Thess 2:2), though apparently it was still in need of clarification of what the slogan actually did encapsulate. Accordingly, it seems more likely that we have a clash of self-identifying slogans in 1 Thess 5:2–3 than a combined summation constructed by Paul, that is, εἰρήνη and ἀσφάλεια, the more especially given that the esteemed value of Hellenistic culture was ἐλευθερία, not ἀσφάλεια.

The slogan did not gain a formal definition or structural breakdown from the rhetoricians or grammarians, to my knowledge. But ancient writers knew it when they saw it, much as moderns do. What can be affirmed by this brief overview is that a slogan is public, is pithy in its construction, compresses larger discourses, is agonistic, serves to identify a group and an allegiance, and seeks to persuade an audience to its side (in terms of both grouping and ideology). As distillations of larger discourses, slogans can be broken up and expanded as need or preference requires. Further work on the form of a slogan is no doubt required, but I hope that this makes a partial contribution in response to Welborn's plea.

The Perception of a Slogan (Visual Aesthetics)

White argues that there is no reference anywhere to *pax et securitas* in the Latin, from which the Greek slogan could (presumably) derive.[48] In order to sustain the sweep of that assertion, he has to dismiss what he acknowledges are twin altars from Praeneste, a city approximately 38 km east of Rome on the Via Prenestina, a distance that the elderly Augustus sometimes took two days to complete (Suetonius, *Aug.* 81)[49] but which had been a strategic base for insurgency in former times (Plutarch, *Sull.* 29; Velleius Paterculus, *Hist. Rom.* 2.74). The history of its relationship with Rome in the early republic was fraught (Livy, *Urb. cond.* 6.22–28, 7.12, 42.1). Finally, after a bloody siege of the town by Sulla in 82 BCE that ended the first civil war, it had been turned into a Roman colony (Velleius Paterculus, *Hist. Rom.* 2.26–27; Plutarch, *Sull.* 32; *Praec. ger. rei publ.* 20 (816a); Florus, *Epit.* 2.9.21; Frontinus, *Strat.* 2.9.3; Appian, *Bell. civ.* 1.10.87–88; Valerius Maxi-

---

48. White, "Roman Ideology and Greek Aspiration," 500. Tacitus does come close if *salus* is introduced for stylistic variation: "illis Moesiae pacem, sibi salutem securitatemque Italiae cordi fuisse" (*Hist.* 3.53).

49. Compare, however, an army's march as a little more than two days in Livy, *Urb. cond.* 28.9 (during the war with Hannibal). Praeneste is given on the Peutinger Map.

mus, *Fact. dict.* 9.2.1).⁵⁰ The town became a favorite summer destination for the aristocracy of Rome, including Augustus and succeeding emperors (Suetonius, *Aug.* 72; Hist. Aug. 4.21; see also Horace, *Ep.* 2; *Carm.* 3.4; Martial, *Epigr.* 10.30; Statius, *Silv.* 4.12–19; Pliny, *Ep.* 5.45; Aulus Gellius, *Noct. att.* 11.3; Juvenal, *Sat.* 3.190–191, 14.86–88),⁵¹ as well as being patronized for oracles courtesy of Fortuna Primigenia (Cicero, *Div.* 2.41; Statius, *Silv.* 1.79–81; Strabo, *Geogr.* 5.11; Suetonius, *Tib.* 63.1; *Dom.* 8.2; Propertius, *Eleg.* 2.3), not to mention roses and nuts from its district (Naevius, *Com.* 22–26 in Macrobius, *Saturn.* 3.6; Pliny, *Nat.* 13.5, 21.16)! One of its famous sons, a freedman named Verrius Flaccus, was brought to Rome as teacher to Augustus's grandsons; he lived on into Tiberius's time and is responsible for the recording of the so-called Fasti Praenestini (Suetonius, *Gramm.* 17), significant portions of which have survived.⁵²

Significantly for our purposes, Polybius in the second century BCE provides the earliest mention of the legal option of *exilium*,⁵³ that is, the ability to go into exile from the city of Rome, as an alternative to an adverse judgment upon a serious crime. Praeneste was one of those cities with whom Rome had entered an arrangement by treaty to provide a city of refuge. Polybius's wording is striking:

ἔστι δ' ἀσφάλεια τοῖς φεύγουσιν ἔν τε τῇ Νεαπολιτῶν καὶ Πραινεστίνων, ἔτι δὲ Τιβουρίνων πόλει, καὶ ταῖς ἄλλαις, πρὸς ἃς ἔχουσιν ὅρκια

Security is provided for such exiles in the city of the Neapolitans, and of the Praenestians and the Tiburians, as well as some others, for which measure they have struck treaties. (*Hist.* 6.14.8–9)⁵⁴

The important word here is ἀσφάλεια. As mentioned previously, it is a key term found in a number of Hellenistic treaties (*IG* 2.1130, 1132, 1134;

---

50. It would later, under Tiberius, be granted the status of a *municipium* (Aulus Gellius, *Noct. att.* 16.13).

51. Compare also Cicero (*Leg.* 2.28), where he notes how the elite had aggregated significant landholdings in the district; see also Martial, *Epigr.* 4.64.

52. IItalia 13.2, 17, dated 6–9 CE, significant because it too, like the Priene calendar (*OGI* 458), marks a shift toward Augustan control of time.

53. Richard A. Bauman, *Crime and Punishment in Ancient Rome* (London: Routledge, 1996), 10–15; Daniel J. Gargola, *The Shape of the Roman Order: The Republic and Its Spaces* (Chapel Hill: University of North Carolina Press, 2017), 199.

54. My translation. It has been suggested that such an arrangement is akin to a treaty (SEG 60.601).

11.4.1050; see also SEG 60.985). Such treaties were generally placed on display in a central temple—in Praeneste's case, this would mean either the temple of Fortuna Primigenia, towering over the city, or the temple of Jupiter, at one end of the forum. For the Praenestians, Greek was an ancient inheritance. Not only was this included in the city's foundation story (Plutarch, *Parallela minora* 41 (316a–b); Propertius, *Eleg.* 2.3–4),[55] but it remained the butt of jokes in Latin comedy—even being called "barbarian," the height of insult to Greeks (Plautus, *Capt.* 880–887). Strabo, quite explicitly, states that Praeneste was called a "Greek city," formerly named "Polystephanos" (*Geogr.* 5.11; see also Pliny, *Ep.* 3.9). Even though we do not have the treaty itself between the Praenestians and Rome,[56] Polybius's language is highly suggestive of either familiarity with it or with the stereotyped language of Hellenistic formal alliances. This language, at least from the Praenestian side, was in Greek, just like the language of Rome's treaty with Knidos in 45 BCE, which, significantly, also uses ἀσφαλής (SEG 59.1207, ll. A9–10). Rome, it seems, from at least the second century BCE, was well-attuned to the dimensions of ἀσφάλεια.

Indeed, some Roman citizens were receiving proxenic honors, recorded in Greek. The terminology in the award from the town of Mondaia on the border of Thessaly and Macedonia (dated 175–159 BCE) for one Lucius Acutius is distinctly economic in its benefits. Acutius and his family are granted citizenship and have rights to own land and property (ἔγκτησις γῆς καὶ οἰκίας) in addition to asylum in times of war and peace; ἀσφάλεια falls between these two items, as one of the benefits the city conferred (SEG 56.648, ll. 12–13).[57] Other individuals, such as freeborn travelers (merchants, artists, athletes and the like), also could receive official grants of ἀσυλία and ἀσφάλεια as a safeguard on their movement and enterprise.[58] Little surprise that ἀσφάλεια, in mundane interactions, is the

---

55. Telegonos the son of Odysseus.

56. See Donald W. Baronowski, "Roman Treaties with Communities of Citizens," *ClQ* 38 (1988): 173.

57. Honors to Romans in Macedonia were frequent in the period from the time Macedonia became a Roman province in 148 BCE, but they understandably differed in their type. See also IThess 1.T8, T9. It should be acknowledged that ἀσφάλεια does not occur in all proxeny decrees. Indeed, the six or so key values may be combined in different ways and without always including all of them.

58. See Léopold Migeotte, "La mobilité des étrangers en temps de paix en Grèce ancienne," in *La mobilité des personnes en Méditerranée de l'antiquité à l'époque moderne*, ed. Claudia Moatti (Rome: École française de Rome, 2004), 615–48.

"security" or deposit required for a commercial transaction (*BGU* 4.1059, 4.1130, 8.1827; Arrian, *Epict. diss.* 2.13.7; Achilles Tatius, *Leuc. Clit.* 5.178.5; see also Plutarch, *Stoic. rep.* 8 [1061e]). Accordingly, ἀσφάλεια is about the safeguarding of material well-being—inevitably, that has an economic component. It is at this reductionist mercantile level that the link with *securitas* may be found, for the word is regularly used in Roman jurisprudence in the same sense of a deposit, surety, or guarantee.[59]

How important such a term became *in the Roman consciousness* is indicated from the writings of Cicero. He does use the word *securitas*, but as Kneppe indicates, followed by White, the context indicates an interior philosophical disposition to be cultivated, often related to *tranquillitas animi*. By contrast, Cicero laid hold of the Greek word ἀσφάλεια and applied it in the sense of the security that a town could provide.[60] Indeed, he was, according to Plutarch, praised by the citizens of Rome for the ἀσφάλεια (and σωτήρια) he had secured (Plutarch, *Cic.* 871.4–5). In this, Plutarch was merely reiterating Polybian usage from a century earlier.[61] Although there are various reasons behind Cicero deploying Greek in his writings, it suggests there may be a semantic edge in ἀσφάλεια that is not, at this point in time at least, found in *securitas*, which Cicero defines as an absence of disturbance (*vacuitas aegritudinis*), the mark of a trained sage (Cicero, *Tusc.* 5.22; see also *Off.* 1.69; *Fin.* 5.23; *Amic.* 45, 47).[62] Clearly, in the mind of this republican, *securitas* is a goal of an individual's philosophical training; ἀσφάλεια, for him, is much more societal and related to material needs, and it is this that shows out in the twin altars at Praeneste.

These altars have gained scarcely a footnote in reference to 1 Thess 5:3, usually no more than a citation of the inscription references. Weima and then White afford them a little more attention but both focus on

---

59. See Dig. 27.4.1, 34.3.5.2 (both from the time of Ulpian); see also O.Claud. 1.2. These both date to the second century but appear to reflect long-standing usage. The notion of a "security" is grounded in the fifth-century BCE Twelve Tables (Duodecim Tabularum), though there the term is *pignus* (6.1).

60. Cicero, *Att.* 418 (16.8).2, on the security that the city of Arpinum offers (*Arpinum ἀσφάλειαν habet is locus*). Compare also the use of a stock phrase, πρὸς τὸ ἀσφαλές (cf. Plutarch, *Phoc.* 4; Dio Cassius, *Hist.* 9), of a decision to move to a town or city for safety (Cicero, *Att.* 136 [7.13].2.

61. The Polybian usage is noted by Kneppe, *Metus temporum*, 225.

62. Cicero's use of αὐτάρκη, adopted from Zeno, is closer to his understanding (*Parad.* 16; cf. *Tusc.* 5.1). It should be remembered, however, that αὐτάρκεια was also the aspiration of a city (Aristotle, *Pol.* 1321b).

the inscriptions alone, Weima to argue that, by being twin altars, they proved a distilled conjunction of *pax et securitas*; White arguing that, because they were twin altars, the elements were, ipso facto, separated. However, the ability to recognize the altars as twins goes not to text but the visual aesthetics.[63]

Fig. 3.1. The altars to Augustan peace (front and rear) and security at Praeneste. Photographs by author.

The heavily molded carving of the altars is crucial here. It signals that the content of *pax* and, more especially, *securitas*, was being wrested away from personal mastery or militarist achievement, to the fecundity and plenty of the new Augustan age. Weima rightly understood the *Ara Pacis* in such terms but failed to see how important this is in its impact in sculpture, mosaics, and architecture at Praeneste in the Augustan period and beyond. Significantly, Nadia Agnoli, on whose art-historical appreciation of the altars I substantially rely in what follows, considers the altars to be a mimetic response to the stylistic text of the *Ara Pacis*, perhaps tied to the triumphant return of Augustus on 14 July 15 BCE after dealing with uprisings in Europe.[64]

---

63. At least John Crossan and Jonathan Reed provide a photograph, although it is given a misleading caption and compounded by reference to "*an* altar" (my emphasis). See Crossan and Reed, *In Search of Paul* (San Francisco: HarperSanFrancisco, 2004), 166, 167.

64. Nadia Agnoli, *Museo archeologico nazionale di Palestrina: le sculture*, XA (Rome: Bretschneider, 2003), 237–39.

The altars were originally found in Praeneste's forum,[65] and the reference to the decurions (the town senate) seems to confirm that this was probably their original location, possibly close to the temple of Jupiter that dominated the layout of this level of the organization of space. This connection of Augustan fertility with the benefaction of Jupiter is caught by Horace: "May our crops be nurtured with wholesome rains and Jupiter's breezes" (*Saec.* 31 [Zanker]; see also 73–74).

The inscriptions read:

> Paci August(i)/ sacrum / Decurion(es) Populusque / Coloniae Praenestin(ae).
> The Decurions and the People of the colony of Praenestina (erected) the altar to the Peace of Augustus.

> Securit(ati) Aug(usti) / sacrum / Decurion(es) Populusque / Coloniae Praenestin(ae)
> The Decurions and the People of the colony of Praenestina (erected) the altar to the Security of Augustus.

The inscription to *pax* is repeated "on the rear" but in slightly different arrangement of letters and abbreviations: "Paci August(i) / sacrum / decuriones populusque / coloniae Praenest(inae)." This duplication may indicate that the peace altar was positioned in the center of a double thoroughfare.

An inscription recording the building of the *aerarium*, the treasury, found in the same location (*CIL* 14.2975),[66] that is, near the temple of Jupiter, confirms that the forum was the location of both sacral and administrative objects, a spatial conjunction mirrored in the imagery of the altars.

I want to accent the visual impact of the altars in their position in the forum connected with the temple of Jupiter, but this does not preclude the aesthetics of the inscriptions themselves. They are carefully cut to accent the focus of honor in lettering that is both larger within each altar

---

65. Leonardo Cecconi, *Storia de Palestrina citta del prisco Lazio* (Ascoli: Ricci, 1756), 150.

66. "M(arcus) Anicius L(uci) f(ilius) Baaso M(arcus) Mersieius C(ai) f(ilius) aediles aerarium faciendum dederunt." "The aediles, Marcus Anicius Bassus, the son of Lucius, and Marcus Mercieuis, the son of Gaius, provided for the building of the Aerarium."

and symmetrical in relation to each other. Thus the *Paci Augusti* and the *Securitati Augusti* are both reduced to ten letters: PACIAUGUST and SECURITAUG. They are both neatly placed between the respective garlands and supported by the common SACRUM also within the garlands. It is not just the name *sacrum* that indicates the altar but the shape of the channels at the top, clearly fitted to receive the offerings that ritually expressed in response the very fecundity portrayed around the square stone.

The garlands and flowing ribbons and taenia are festooned with fruit and flowers and strung between the sacrificial bucrania on the corners. The fruit, all imagery of paradisal provision, includes pomegranates, pinecones, poppies, and ears of wheat, and is wreathed in burgeoning ties from the top loop on the horns of the bucrania down to the center bow.

The visual appeal that is made by the twinning of the motifs on the two altars is clearly intended to cause the two to be held together as a single program by the viewers and ritual participants. In terms of the phrase of our concern, the formal connective of καί was supplied *by the ones who beheld the altars*. In this sense, the intention of the stylistics was not merely to communicate the imperial agenda but to draw, indeed, compel, viewers to become an agent of the empire by making the conjunction themselves. That is, in the turning from right to left and left to right drawn by the identity of the visual dynamics, the viewer supplied the conjunction καί/ *et*. When Augustus died, the debt for peace and security owed to him and identified with him was made blatant by the addition of a single altar, in the same vein. Seneca would soon compound the *securitas* of the state with the *securitas* of the emperor's own person: "securitas securitate mutua paciscenda est" (*Clem*. 1.19.6).[67] But this was merely articulating what had been communicated visually already. All commentators recognize that the twin altars are drawn together by a third added later, that of Augustus, now declared in the inscription to be divine (*Divo Aug(usto) Sacrum*),[68] and surrounded by a cornucopia on each side. The design of the whole deliberately evokes the same fecundity as before but now compounded by the pairs of cornucopias that support the garlands on all four sides. If anything, the fruitfulness is multiplied in the festoons. Now the divine

---

67. "The cost of security is the mutuality of security," as applied to the mutuality of king and subjects largely in terms of the king's (read "emperor's") responsibility for the welfare of his citizens.

68. Zanker, *Power of Images*, 307; Agnoli, *Le sculture*, 243.

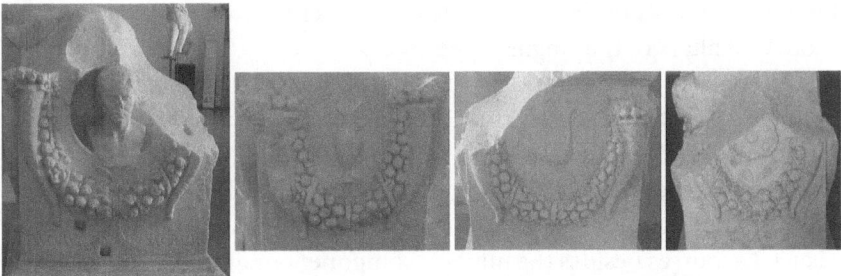

Fig. 3.2a–d. The four sides of the altar to the divine Augustus. Photographs by author.

Fig. 3.3. A prosperity panel from a nymphaeum at Praeneste. Photograph by author.

Augustus provides, as it were, the καί with the altar so positioned as to hold together the altar to *pax* and that to *securitas*.

The key here is that *pax* and *securitas* have become identified with the material benefits of the new regime. Everywhere this was the visual portrayal promoted by the Augustan propaganda machine. Within the forum at Praeneste, these altars were not the only visual testimony. One panel of an Augustan-period nymphaeum built (or remodeled) in the forum portrays the naturalistic scene of a sow feeding her young, again surrounded by other symbols of fecundity.⁶⁹ Beyond Praeneste, we find very similar models of altars of the Augustan period.⁷⁰

There is no question that violence underlay the foundation and maintenance of this settlement. After all, in a telling coin that portrays Pax and Nike at either side of Nero in quadriga, the figure of Mars lurks among the pillars of the triumphal arch beneath.⁷¹ But the "normalization" of the regime demanded a completely different set of literary and visual discourses besides the military component or even the rule of law. It had to be naturalized, conjuring not compulsion but desire, just as Seneca the Younger expounds (*Clem.* 1.19.5–9). There was nothing better than the elements of nature—its fecundity, fruitfulness, and provision—to be made the marks of Augustan rule.⁷² I would argue that the blending of Greek and Roman elements to be seen at Praeneste warrants the assertion that Rome borrowed from the materialistic well-being held by ἀσφάλεια for a development in the understanding of *securitas* far beyond what we see in its usage by Cicero. We too often forget how much time Octavian spent in the East and how, like Romans long before him, he had become well-acquainted in the association of ἀσφάλεια with friendship, alliance, well-being, … and, of course, stability.⁷³ Indeed, treaties (in Greek) were mounted in the Capitoline temple of Jupiter.⁷⁴

In this sense, Paul is not inventing a slogan. He is recognizing or at least tacitly acknowledging that the origins of the Roman *pax et securitas* actually lay in the East, in εἰρήνη καὶ ἀσφάλεια. The inherent dualism of White's formulation of Paul's invention cannot be sustained. This explains why Paul accents "a thief in the night" (1 Thess 5:2, 4). Even though New Testament commentators like to track Paul's words back to those of Jesus (Mattt 24:43 // Luke 12:39),⁷⁵ the nonmilitaristic content of the saying eludes their interpretation. In Greek and Roman uses of the compari-

---

69. Zanker, *Power of Images*, 177–78.

70. See, for example, the garlanded altar that displays *CIL* 6.244.

71. *RIC* 1.433.

72. See Shreyaa Bhatt, "The Augustan Principate and the Emergence of Biopolitics: A Comparative Historical Perspective," *FS* 22 (2017): 72–93.

73. See generally Buis, "Ancient Entanglements," 151–85.

74. As, for example, the treaty between Rome and Kibyra (*OGI* 762). It should be noted that the only known treaty in Latin between Rome and an eastern town is with Callatis, a colony of its mother city, Heraclea Pontica.

75. Richard, *First and Second Thessalonians*, 250; Luckensmeyer, *Eschatology of First Thessalonians*, 283–86.

son, it is clear that the attack is directed at possessions, the *nocturnus fur* / νυκτικλέπτης, for whom night is his chief weapon (see Phaedrus, *Fab. Aes.* 1.23; Virgil, *Georg.* 3.407; *Anth. Gr.* 11.176). Even the famous Twelve Tables of Roman Law specifically mentions the thief in the night (8.12; see Cicero, *Mil.* 3.9; see also Plato, *Leg.* 874B–C). Thieves breaking into houses are quite different from soldiers breaking down the gates and walls. Thieves evoke the loss of goods, a threat to economic well-being. But this neatly fits the semantics of ἀσφάλεια.

The Threat to Security

It might be objected that, even with some acknowledgment of the threat to property implied by the comparison with "a thief in the night," that the day of the Lord is far more violent. In this sense, it is more akin to the rigors of labor suddenly descending on a pregnant woman, though seeing this "natural" process equated with "sudden destruction" (αἰφνίδιος ... ὄλεθρος) might reflect Paul's domestic circumstances and experience.

However, Romans in the late republic and early principate were well-attuned to the vagaries of fortune, to the point where Good Fortune needed to be constantly patronized for fear that she might turn to Bad Fortune. The same applies to one god in the Greek pantheon, who had gained the epithet Asphaleios. Thessaloniki as a bay city had long esteemed Poseidon in relation to its sea traffic. Pantelis Nigdelis found the evidence for Poseidon somewhat scanty. However, a cultic association (συνήθεια) for Poseidon has come to light,[76] and a priest or other cultic official of Poseidon as well (*IG* 10.2.1s.1273).[77] One of Thessaloniki's late Hellenistic coins expresses the Poseidonic connection with sea trade.[78] Indeed, one of its poets, Philip of Thessalonica, in the first century (CE) wrote epigrams that expressed in text what was stamped as images on coins (*Anth. Gr.* 6.38, 90).

---

76. IThess 1:164–65 = *IG* 10.2.1s.1372 (later second century CE). This item should be added to the collection of John S. Kloppenborg and Richard S. Ascough, *Greco-Roman Associations: Texts, Translations, and Commentary I* (Berlin: de Gruyter, 2011).

77. Third century CE. One brief inscription, probably an epitaph, on the reverse of a stone also contains a framed relief of Poseidon on its front (*IG* 10.2.1s.1107; second century CE).

78. *ANS* 798–99. The coin with the reverse of a galley sometimes also shows a dolphin. The obverse also often adds a trident, a key identifier; see SNG Copenhagen 372; *BMC Macedonia*, 111.22.

The point is that Poseidon was called the Asphaleios, the Securer, precisely because he was the god of the negation of collapse. But if he could protect against falling, so too he could let it happen. In that sense he held a duality in his power,[79] and this explains why the god was also dubbed "Earth-shaker" (ἐννοσίγαιος; Homer, *Il.* 7.455; Plutarch, *Frag.* 106; Pausanias, *Hell. Per.* 9.29.1; Philostratus, *Imag.* 2.13–14; Hymn. hom. 22.4 [to Poseidon]; see also Archilochus, *Frag* 114; Plutarch, *Thes.* 34).

When Paul placed a slogan, "the day of the Lord," in contradiction to "peace and security" he was not merely seeking to form the self-identity and positioning of the Christ-followers in Thessaloniki. He was, in a very real sense, reminding these Thessalonians of an aspect of their own inheritance that had been swamped by the Roman ideological juggernaut. No security lasts in the face of the divine. The "peace and security" that any leader espouses or brings can only ever be temporary. Aristophanes's comedy *Peace* was factored on the fragility and liability of εἰρήνη. As Gordon Zerbe comments, "For Paul, the civic and political authorities have, at most, only a penultimate character, and that their reality has been fundamentally subverted."[80] The irony is that, rather than bringing a completely new idea to this fledgling Christ-group, Paul may have been reminding them of a long-held insight of Greek thought; and more so, doing it in a familiar inheritance of Greek and Roman politics, that is, by the placing of one slogan encapsulating a way of viewing reality against another.[81] Perhaps, then, his subversion is more complex than a simple alternate world governed by the "day of the Lord" rather than "peace and security."

Conclusion

This study began with the formative counterpoint between Weima and White on the contextual background of 1 Thess 5:3. The engagement with their evidence and interpretation has led to the argument that there is a subtle enticement to a viewer to connect the dots, as it were, in holding

---

79. Michael Dillon, *Politics of Security: Towards a Political Philosophy of Continental Thought* (London: Routledge, 1996), 124.

80. Gordon Zerbe, "The Politics of Paul: His Supposed Social Conservatism and the Impact of Postcolonial Readings," in *The Colonized Apostle: Paul through Postcolonial Eyes*, ed. Christopher Stanley (Minneapolis: Fortress, 2011), 68.

81. See the salutary remarks of Harrill, "Paul and Empire," 282–83.

together "peace and security," thereby becoming complicit in the promotion of imperial ideology. A criticism might be laid that an interpretation of evidence that relies mainly on material from Praeneste, just outside Rome, does not necessarily transfer to Thessaloniki. However, rather than εἰρήνη καὶ ἀσφάλεια being a translation of *pax et securitas*, I suggest that it is more accurate to suggest something like its opposite, that, especially in regard to ἀσφάλεια, the almost two centuries of direct Greek influence on Roman thought in Rome's provincial presence in Macedonia before Paul had actually encouraged Roman political thought to shift the semantics of *securitas* more in line with the Greek understanding of ἀσφάλεια. In other words, the Augustan settlement that cultivated a sense that the aspirations of an individual were (to be) in line with that of the state, most especially paraded by its leaders, saw *securitas* develop from an individual *tranquillitas* to a societal *fecunditas*. In so doing, the military upheavals that had wrought the regime change that established Augustus's imperial government became muted, even though Mars was never completely erased from the background.[82] In sound, agonistic Roman and Greek politicking, Paul mounts a counterslogan, but it is not a full-frontal militaristic alignment, as has sometimes been supposed for "the day of the Lord." Rather, in its use of an image of an attack on economic contentment—the "thief in the night"—Paul reminds his audience, formed as much in the ambiguity of Fortuna as the instability of Poseidon, that complacency and misplaced confidence can, like Atlantis, so easily go down (Plato, *Tim.* 25D; *Crit.* 113C–114; Plutarch, *Sol.* 31–32; Pliny, *Nat.* 2.90.205).[83]

Bibliography

Agnoli, Nadia. *Museo archeologico nazionale di Palestrina: le sculture*. XA. Rome: Bretschneider, 2003.

Ando, Clifford. *Imperial Ideology and Provincial Loyalty in the Roman Empire*. Berkeley: University of California Press, 2000.

Bammel, Ernst. "Ein Beitrag zur paulinischen Staatsanschauung." *TLZ* 85 (1960): 837–40.

---

82. See Clifford Ando, *Imperial Ideology and Provincial Loyalty in the Roman Empire* (Berkeley: University of California Press, 2000), xi–xiii.

83. Note the interpretation of Proclus that the story of Atlantis is a philosophical tale of the oppositions in the universe existing from of old (in Heraclitus, *All.* R92).

———. "Romans 13." Pages 365–83 in *Jesus and the Politics of His Day*. Edited by Ernst Bammel and C. F. D. Moule. Cambridge: Cambridge University Press, 1984.

Baronowski, Donald W. "Roman Treaties with Communities of Citizens." *ClQ* 38 (1988): 172–78.

Bauman, Richard A. *Crime and Punishment in Ancient Rome*. London: Routledge, 1996.

Bhatt, Shreyaa. "The Augustan Principate and the Emergence of Biopolitics: A Comparative Historical Perspective." *FS* 22 (2017): 72–93.

Bird, Michael F. "'One Who Will Arise to Rule over the Nations': Paul's Letter to the Romans and the Roman Empire." Pages 146–65 in *Jesus Is Lord, Caesar Is Not: Evaluating Empire in New Testament Studies*. Edited by Scot McKnight and Joseph B. Modica. Downers Grove, IL: InterVarsity Press, 2013.

Brocke, Christoph vom. *Thessaloniki – Stadt des Kassander und Gemeinde des Paulus: Ein frühe christliche Gemeinde in ihren heidnischen Umwelt*. WUNT 2/125. Tübingen: Mohr Siebeck, 2001.

Buis, Emiliano J. "Ancient Entanglements: The Influence of Greek Treaties in Roman 'International Law' under the Framework of Narrative Transculturation." Pages 151–85 in *Entanglements in Legal History: Conceptual Approaches*. Edited by Thomas Duve. Frankfurt am Main: Max Planck Institute for European Legal History, 2014.

Cadwallader, Alan H. "In Go(l)d We Trust: Literary and Economic Exchange in the Debate over Caesar's Coin (Mk 12:13-17)." *BibInt* 14 (2006): 486–507.

Cecconi, Leonardo. *Storia de Palestrina citta del prisco Lazio*. Ascoli: Ricci, 1756.

Cooley, Alison E. *Res Gestae Divi Augusti: Text, Translation and Commentary*. Cambridge: Cambridge University Press, 2009.

Crossan, John Dominic, and Jonathan L. Reed. *In Search of Paul*. San Francisco: HarperSanFrancisco, 2004.

Dillon, Michael. *Politics of Security: Towards a Political Philosophy of Continental Thought*. London: Routledge, 1996.

Dmitriev, Sviatoslav. *The Greek Slogan of Freedom and Early Roman Politics in Greece*. Oxford: Oxford University Press, 2011.

Francese, Christopher, and R. Scott Smith. *Ancient Rome: An Anthology of Sources*. Indianapolis: Hackett, 2014.

Gabrielson, Jeremy. *Paul's Non-violent Gospel: The Theological Politics of Peace in Paul's Life and Letters*. Cambridge: Clarke, 2014.

Galinsky, Karl. "The Cult of the Roman Emperor: Uniter or Divider?" Pages 1–21 in *Rome and Religion: A Cross-Disciplinary Dialogue on the Imperial Cult*. Edited by Jeffrey Brodd and Jonathan L. Reed. WGRW-Sup 5. Atlanta: Society of Biblical Literature, 2011.

Gargola, Daniel J. *The Shape of the Roman Order: The Republic and Its Spaces*. Chapel Hill: University of North Carolina Press, 2017.

Gorman, Michael J. *Becoming the Gospel: Paul, Participation and Mission*. Grand Rapids: Eerdmans, 2015.

Graham, A. J., and Gary Forsythe. "A New Slogan for Oligarchy in Thucydides III.82.8." *HSCP* 88 (1984): 25–45.

Gupta, Nijay K. *1–2 Thessalonians*. NCCS. Eugene, OR: Cascade, 2016.

Harrill, J. Albert. "Paul and Empire: Studying Roman Identity after the Cultural Turn." *EC* 2 (2011): 281–311.

Harrison, James R. *Paul and the Imperial Authorities at Thessalonica and Rome: A Study in the Conflict of Ideology*. WUNT 273. Tübingen: Mohr Siebeck, 2011.

———. "Paul and the Imperial Gospel at Thessaloniki." *JSNT* 25 (2002): 71–96.

Heilig, Christoph. *Hidden Criticism? The Methodology and Plausibility of the Search for a Counter-imperial Subtext in Paul*. WUNT 2/392. Tübingen: Mohr Siebeck, 2015.

Hendrix, Holland L. "Archaeology and Eschatology at Thessalonica." Pages 107–18 in *The Future of Early Christianity: Essays in Honor of Helmut Koester*. Edited by Birger A. Pearson. Minneapolis: Fortress, 1991.

Hude, Karl. *Scholia in Thucydidem ad optimos codices collate*. Leipzig: Teubner, 1927.

Kloppenborg, John S., and Richard S. Ascough. *Greco-Roman Associations: Texts, Translations, and Commentary I*. Berlin: de Gruyter, 2011.

Kneppe, Alfred. *Metus temporum: Zur Bedeutung von Angst in Politik und Gesellschaft der römischen Kaiserzeit des 1. Und 2. Jhdts n. Chr.* Stuttgart: Steiner, 1994.

Koester, Helmut. "Imperial Ideology and Paul's Eschatology in I Thessalonians." Pages 158–66 in *Paul and Empire: Religion and Power in Roman Imperial Society*. Edited by Richard A. Horsley. Harrisburg, PA: Trinity Press International, 1997.

Lowe, Matthew F. "'This Was Not an Ordinary Death.' Empire and Atonement in the Minor Pauline Epistles." Pages 197–220 in *Empire in the New Testament*. Edited by Stanley E. Porter and Cynthia Long Westfall. Eugene, OR: Pickwick, 2011.

Luckensmeyer, David. *The Eschatology of First Thessalonians*. Göttingen: Vandenhoeck & Ruprecht, 2011.

Malherbe, Abraham J. *The Letters to the Thessalonians*. AB 32B. New York: Doubleday, 2000.

Migeotte, Léopold. "La mobilité des étrangers en temps de paix en Grèce ancienne." Pages 615–48 in *La mobilité des personnes en Méditerranée de l'antiquité à l'époque modern*. Edited by Claudia Moatti. Rome: École française de Rome, 2004.

Míguez, Nestor O. *The Practice of Hope: Ideology and Intention in 1 Thessalonians*. Minneapolis: Fortress, 2012.

Mitchell, Margaret M. *Paul and the Rhetoric of Reconciliation: An Exegetical Investigation of the Language and Composition of 1 Corinthians*. Louisville: Westminster John Knox, 1992.

Nasrallah, Laura. "Early Christian Interpretation in Image and Word: Canon, Sacred Text and the Mosaic of Moni Latomou." Pages 361–95 in *From Roman to Early Christian Thessalonike: Studies in Religion and Archaeology*. Edited by Laura Nasrallah, Charalambos Bakirtzis, and Steven J. Friesen. HTS 64. Cambridge: Harvard University Press, 2010.

Neufeld, Thomas. *Killing Enmity: Violence and the New Testament*. Grand Rapids: Baker, 2011.

Nicholl, Colin R. *From Hope to Despair in Thessalonica: Situating 1 and 2 Thessalonians*. Cambridge: Cambridge University Press, 2004.

Pappas, Stephanie. "Pompeii 'Wall Posts' Reveal Ancient Social Networks." *Scientific American*, January 11, 2013. https://tinyurl.com/SBL4221d.

Piejko, Francis. "The Treaty between Antiochus III and Lysimachia: ca 196 B.C. (with Discussion of the Earlier Treaty with Philip V)." *Historia* 37 (1988): 151–65.

Plevnik, Joseph. *Paul and the Parousia: An Exegetical and Theological Investigation*. Peabody, MA: Hendrickson, 1997.

Richard, Earl J. *First and Second Thessalonians*. SP. Collegeville, MN: Liturgical Press, 1995.

Robinson, James M., and Helmut Koester. *Trajectories through Early Christianity*. Philadelphia: Fortress, 1971.

Rolfe, J. C., trans. *Sallust*. LCL. London: Heinemann, 1921.

Rowe, Greg. *Princes and Political Cultures: The New Tiberian Senatorial Decrees*. Ann Arbor: University of Michigan Press, 2002.

Scanlon, Thomas F. *The Influence of Thucydides on Sallust*. Heidelberg: Winter, 1980.

Smith, Murray J. "The Thessalonian Correspondence." Pages 269–301 in *All Things to All Cultures: Paul among Jews, Greeks and Romans*. Edited by Mark Harding and Alanna Nobbs. Grand Rapids: Eerdmans, 2013.

Thiselton, Anthony C. *1 and 2 Thessalonians through the Centuries*. Chichester: Wiley-Blackwell, 2013.

———. *The First Epistle to the Corinthians*. NIGTC. Grand Rapids: Eerdmans, 2000.

Viitanen, Eeva-Maria, Laura Nissinen, and Kalle Korhonen. "Street Activity, Dwellings and Wall Inscriptions in Ancient Pompeii: A Holistic Study of Neighbourhood Relations." Pages 61–80 in *Proceedings of the Twenty-Second Annual Theoretical Roman Archaeology Conference (TRAC 2012)*. Edited by Annabel Bokern, Marion Bolder-Boos, Stefan Krmnicek, Dominik Maschek, and Sven Page. Oxford: Oxbow, 2012.

Weima, Jeffrey A. D. *1–2 Thessalonians*. BECNT. Grand Rapids: Baker, 2014.

———. "'Peace and Security' (1 Thess 5.3): Prophetic Warning or Political Propaganda." *NTS* 58 (2012): 331–59.

Welborn, Larry L. "On the Discord in Corinth: 1 Corinthians 1–4 and Ancient Politics." *JBL* 106 (1987): 85–111.

———. *Politics and Rhetoric in the Corinthian Epistles*. Macon, GA: Mercer University Press, 1997.

Wengst, Klaus. *Pax Romana and the Peace of Jesus Christ*. Philadelphia: Fortress, 1987.

White, Joel R. "Anti-imperial Subtexts in Paul: An Attempt at Building a Firmer Foundation." *Bib* 90 (2009): 305–33.

———. "'Peace and Security' (1 Thess 5:3): Is It Really a Roman Slogan?" *NTS* 59 (2013): 382–95.

———. "'Peace' and 'Security' (1 Thess 5.3): Roman Ideology and Greek Aspiration." *NTS* 60 (2014): 499–510.

Witherington, Ben, III. *1 and 2 Thessalonians*. Grand Rapids: Eerdmans, 2006.

Zanker, Paul. *The Power of Images in the Age of Augustus*. Ann Arbor: University of Michigan Press, 1988.

Zerbe, Gordon. "The Politics of Paul: His Supposed Social Conservatism and the Impact of Postcolonial Readings." Pages 62–73 in *The Colonized Apostle: Paul through Postcolonial Eyes*. Edited by Christopher Stanley. Minneapolis: Fortress, 2011.

"Times and Seasons" or "Peace and Security"?
Paul and the Clash of Eschatologies in Thessalonica

Joel R. White

Introduction

There seems to have been some confusion in the church that Paul founded in Thessalonica about "the times and the seasons" (1 Thess 5:1: οἱ χρόνοι καὶ οἱ καιροί). This expression, a hendiadys with a fixed meaning in Jewish-apocalyptic thought, refers to God's prior determination and ordering of past and future events of significant salvation historical import.[1] Its biblical usage goes back to the OG and Theodotion versions of Daniel (see Dan 2:21, 4:37, 7:12), and Jewish believers in Jesus seem to have been familiar with the phrase. In Luke's account, Jesus refers to it in his answer to a question, posed by the disciples shortly before he is taken up into heaven, about the restoration of the kingdom of Israel: "It is not for you to know 'times or seasons,'" he is quoted as replying (Acts 1:6–7: οὐχ ὑμῶν ἐστιν γνῶναι χρόνους ἢ καιρούς). Questions regarding the authenticity of the scene as Luke describes it notwithstanding, there is nothing implausible per se about Jesus using this expression or his Palestinian audience understanding what he meant.

On the other hand, the fact that a largely gentile church in Thessalonica uses a quasi-technical Jewish-apocalyptic expression in a question they asked Timothy to convey to Paul, who was only in the city for a short time,[2] requires some explanation. According to Luke (see Acts 17:1–4),

---

1. See Stefan Schreiber, *Der erste Brief an die Thessalonicher*, ÖTK 13/1 (Gütersloh: Gütersloher Verlagshaus, 2014), 265.
2. See Ernest Best, *The First and Second Epistles to the Thessalonians*, BNTC (London: Black, 1986), 203–4; Robert Jewett, *The Thessalonian Correspondence: Pauline Rhetoric and Millenarian Piety* (Philadelphia: Fortress, 1986), 96; Joseph Plevnik,

the church was constituted around a handful of converts from the Jewish community, who were joined by many Godfearers: gentiles who were attracted to Jewish monotheism and ethics but did not become proselytes.³ This adequately explains the church's familiarity with the phrase.

Paul seems initially reticent to oblige the Thessalonians' desire for clarification on the subject. He somewhat disingenuously deflects the need to address the issue, or so it seems at first glance. It is, however, likely that Paul is employing paralepsis, that is, feigning a wish to pass over a topic he in fact intends to address.⁴ He reminds the Thessalonians that they had received adequate instruction concerning the "day of the Lord" (1 Thess 5:2), which in context can only refer to the parousia of Jesus,⁵ in spite of the fact that he only had the opportunity to instruct them for a short period. To Paul's mind their knowledge of this event was "precise and detailed" (ἀκριβῶς).⁶ From the point of view of the Thessalonians, however, some important questions had gone unanswered.

Paul and the Parousia: An Exegetical and Theological Study (Peabody, MA: Hendrickson, 1997), 99; Jeffrey A. D. Weima, *1–2 Thessalonians*, BECNT (Grand Rapids: Baker, 2014), 343–44. Contra Traugott Holtz, *Der erste Brief an die Thessalonicher*, EKKNT 13 (Benziger: Zürich; Neukirchen-Vluyn: Neukirchener Verlag, 1986), 210; Rudolph Hoppe, *Der erste Thessalonikerbrief: Kommentar* (Freiburg: Herder, 2016), 289. If Luke's "three Sabbath days" (Acts 17:2) are to be taken as consecutive, Paul may have been in Thessalonica for less than a month. This is not, however, a semantic necessity, and it seems more likely that one should think in terms of a couple of months, rather than a few weeks. In any case, Paul's stay was a comparatively short one (see Weima, *Thessalonians*, 26).

3. See Irina Levinskaya, *The Book of Acts in Its Diaspora Setting*, vol. 5 of *The Book of Acts in Its First Century Setting* (Grand Rapids: Eerdmans, 1996), 52–58. Despite sparse literary (and no definitive inscriptional) evidence for a Jewish community in first-century Thessalonica, there seems to be no compelling reason to doubt Luke's testimony on this point. See Christoph vom Brocke, *Thessaloniki – Stadt des Kassander und Gemeinde des Paulus: Eine frühe Gemeinde in ihrer heidnischen Umwelt*, WUNT 2/124 (Tübingen: Mohr Siebeck, 2001), 207–33. Indeed, the existence of such a community must be considered highly likely. See Rainer Riesner, *Die Frühzeit des Apostels Paulus: Studien zu Chronologie, Missionsstrategie und Theologie*, WUNT 71 (Tübingen: Mohr Siebeck, 1994), 304–8.

4. See BDF §495; Holtz, *Brief an die Thessalonicher*, 209.

5. See Colin R. Nicoll, *From Hope to Despair: Situating 1 and 2 Thessalonians*, SNTSMS 126 (Cambridge: Cambridge University Press, 2004), 51.

6. See Best, who argues that the term often carries this double nuance (*First and Second Epistles*, 205).

Paul should have expected as much, and perhaps he did, if his style stems from a conscious rhetorical strategy designed to counter the Thessalonians' "impatience with ambiguity."[7] There may, however, be a more prosaic explanation for the apparent breakdown in communication. We should not forget that most of the Thessalonian Christians were recent converts from paganism (1 Thess 1:9).[8] Paul's ideas were unfamiliar to them and—to borrow a metaphor from biochemistry—would not have easily found receptor cells to latch onto within a pagan worldview. After all, tropes such as "times and seasons" and "the day of the Lord" reflect decidedly Jewish conceptions of history.[9] Paul may well have thought that he had explained these concepts adequately, but that does not mean his audience understood them. On the contrary, it seems that, to put it in terms of modern speech-act theory, the illocutionary force of Paul's teaching was lost on the non-Jewish believers in the Thessalonian church. What their fellow believers from a Jewish background had to say about the matter only added to the confusion, and they were hoping that Paul would provide clarity.

This is not surprising when one considers that prior to their conversion only a few months earlier, these gentiles had inhabited an entirely different conceptual world, one characterized by Hellenistic modes of thought and expression. It is likely, for example, that the talk of "peace and security" (εἰρήνη καὶ ἀσφάλεια), to which Paul alludes in 1 Thess 5:3, stems from the quotidian pagan milieu out of which these early converts came. This assessment of the origin of the phrase cuts against the grain of much recent scholarship arguing that it was recognizable as an imperial slogan actively propagated by Rome throughout the empire.[10] Since my recent attempt to refute this reading is readily available,[11] I will not recapitulate my arguments here. Suffice it to say that I found no proof that "peace and security" was a recognizable slogan in the mid-first century CE.

---

7. Jewett, *Thessalonian Correspondence*, 97.

8. Jewett, *Thessalonian Correspondence*, 118–19.

9. See Plevnik, *Paul and the Parousia*, 315–19.

10. Ernst Bammel first proposed this thesis in "Ein Beitrag zur paulinischen Staatsanschauung," *TLZ* 85 (1960): 837–40. It quickly gained traction. Jeffrey A. D. Weima has offered the most thorough (and circumspect) defense of Bammel's thesis to date. See Weima, "'Peace and Security' (1 Thess 5.3): Prophetic Warning or Political Propaganda," *NTS* 58 (2012): 331–59, esp. 332.

11. See Joel White, "'Peace and Security' (1 Thess 5.3): Is It Really a Roman Slogan?," *NTS* 59 (2013): 382–95.

There is, however, ample evidence that these two terms had the quality of watchwords reflecting Roman political ideology and Greek societal aspirations, respectively.[12] Just as modern Europeans associate the rhetoric of unity with the European Union and talk of security with NATO, so these disparate terms seem to have differing pedigrees. Still, it was not Roman magistrates or even local Macedonian leaders who were talking about peace and security but the Thessalonian believers' nonelite friends and neighbors,[13] and the provenance of these terms was probably of little interest to them. In and around the shops and taverns where the common people gathered, the focus was on their daily lives. Roman merchants, who were numerous in Thessaloniki,[14] may have stressed the benefits the Pax Romana had brought them. The local Greek population, whose values and norms were influential in daily affairs,[15] may have expressed their concern for ongoing security, especially in the face of imperial policies designed to keep local populations in check by instilling fear in them through the threat of violence.[16]

That, however, was likely the extent of average Thessalonians' political interests, regardless of whether they looked favorably on Rome's maintenance of public order or askance at Rome's heavy hand in public life. Perhaps the upheavals caused by the slow demise of the Greek poleis in the leadup to Roman rule engendered a sense of angst in social memory and therefore a heightened desire for security among the common people. Perhaps this rendered them amenable to the tranquilizing effect of Roman peace propaganda. *They* did not know that and probably would not have cared, even if this sort of political or sociohistorical analysis could have been made available to them. They did not belong to scholarly elites in twentieth-century Western democracies attuned to the anti-imperial implications of Paul's arguments, but rather to the decidedly nonelite artisans and traders, or perhaps even to an unenviable cohort even lower on the social ladder—the free day laborers who lived from

---

12. See Joel White, "'Peace' and 'Security' (1 Thess 5.3): Roman Ideology and Greek Aspiration," *NTS* 60 (2014): 499–510.
13. White, "'Peace' and 'Security,'" 507–8.
14. See vom Brocke, *Thessaloniki*, 95–6.
15. Vom Brocke, *Thessaloniki*, 96–101.
16. See Alfred Kneppe, *Metus temporum: Zur Bedeutung von Angst in der Politik und Gesellschaft der römischen Kaiserzeit des 1. und 2. Jhdts. n. Chr.* (Stuttgart: Steiner, 1994), 233–34.

hand to mouth.[17] From where they stood, such concerns were high above their heads in terms of Maslow's hierarchy of needs. Average Thessalonians were probably simply eager to get on with their lives as best they could. Peace and security would have sounded good on the face of it.

In what follows I want to compare Paul's eschatological expectations and those of the Thessalonian believers against their respective pagan and Jewish backgrounds. At the outset, it is important to recognize the stark difference in terms of the information at our disposal for making such determinations. In the case of the gentile believers in Thessalonica, we are only able to describe in general terms what they (i.e., average mid-first-century Thessalonians) believed about the future based on epigraphic and literary sources. We are in a somewhat better position to describe general Jewish eschatological expectations, and in Paul's case we can analyze not only his views about the future generically (i.e., with reference to his Pharisaic background and association with the followers of Jesus) but also specifically his own relevant statements in his extant letters.

While we might wish for a more balanced picture, this situation may reflect the difference in perspective between Paul, Jewish believers, and gentile believers in Thessalonica. Even without the literary record Paul left behind, it would be a priori likely that he had given a great deal of thought to eschatological matters and operated from within a worldview that offered specific information about God's plan for the future. Jewish believers would have shared his general outlook. Conversely, if Hellenistic and Roman sources are any guide, believers from a pagan background would have had only vague and fluid conceptions of things to come. There, as we will see, lies the root of the problem.

Hellenistic Conceptions of Life after Death

One cannot properly speak of a Hellenistic or Roman eschatology, at least in the sense of *Heilsgeschichte*—a temporal progression of God's plan for creation toward an end goal that restores and/or moves beyond its concrete prelapsarian expression. This teleological component, so essential

---

17. See Néstor O. Míguez, *The Practice of Hope: Ideology and Intention in First Thessalonians*, PCC (Minneapolis: Fortress, 2012), 64; Jewett, *Thessalonian Correspondence*, 120–21; UnChan Jung, "Paul's Letter to Free(d) Casual Workers: Profiling the Thessalonians in Light of the Roman Economy," *JSNT* 42 (2020): 472–95, esp. 476–77, 485–88.

for making sense of early Jewish eschatology, is simply lacking in ancient pagan conceptions of the cosmos.[18] The latter's circular view of time and agonistic cosmogony allow only for what, in Christian terms, is often referred to as "individual eschatology."[19] Human beings live and die and may or may not continue to exist in some form and in some place, but the universe itself is not moving through time toward some ultimate goal.

Without a defining cosmic telos, conceptions of the fate of individuals remained characteristically diverse among ancient Greeks and Romans, and they had no authoritative scriptures to which they could appeal. Homer comes closest in the sense that his works were widely disseminated and hence his conceptualizations of postmortem states of existence widely known. For him the fate of the dead is a ghastly one, characterized by joyless, ghostlike existence (Homer, *Od.* 11.90–94, 204–224). There are a few exceptions, such as Hercules, who enjoys sensual pleasures such as food and female companionship at the banquet of the gods (11.601–604; though curiously his wraith still inhabits Hades), or Menelaus, who can look forward to good weather, at the very least, in Elysium (4.561–569). The great majority of the dead, however, are pitiable creatures, robbed of their wits, their strength, and all purpose. Even Achilles, whose fate is not quite as desperate, declares that he would gladly exchange all the glory and renown he had accrued for the life of a slave to landless man, if only he could return to the world of the living (11.486–492). An ancient Greek hero would have to be quite desperate to wish for that!

Virgil's description of Hades is dependent on Homer's and therefore in much the same vein,[20] but it is in some ways more pedestrian. For him, the realm of the dead is a sort of cosmic penitentiary, where punishments are meted out for those who have committed crimes of treachery, treason, and incest (Virgil, *Aen.* 6.526–627), but good souls enjoy chiliastic bliss in the Elysian Fields before crossing the river Lethe into oblivion, where they are recycled into new bodies (6.739–751).

---

18. James R. Harrison, *Paul and the Imperial Authorities at Thessalonica and Rome*, WUNT 273 (Tübingen: Mohr Siebeck, 2011), 97.

19. In what follows, I use the term *eschatology* with respect to gentile Thessalonians only in this limited sense.

20. Outi Lehtipuu, "The Imagery of the Lukan Afterworld in the Light of Some Roman and Greek Parallels," in *Zwischen den Reichen: Neues Testament und Römische Herrschaft*, ed. Michal Labahn and Jürgen Zangenberg, TANZ 36 (Tübingen: Francke, 2002), 133–46, esp. 136–37.

The philosophers were divided in their opinions on the fate of the dead. For Plato disembodied existence is the pinnacle of existence. He is optimistic that enlightened souls will eventually rise to the ether and live forever (*Phaedr.* 245e–247c). Pythagoras believed in reincarnation (Diogenes 8.1.14). The Epicureans did not believe that the soul continued to exist after death; the material of which the soul was composed dissolved at the moment of passing and returned to its elementary state (Diogenes 10.65–66). The Stoics shared this point of view, though the imperial Stoa held out the prospect that human souls did not immediately dissolve upon death but lived on until the next great cosmic conflagration (*ekpyrosis*).[21]

The differing conceptions of life after death among Greek and Roman elites demonstrate the lack of an overarching eschatology that shaped the beliefs of broad swaths of ancient society. Many, though by no means all, believed in Hades, the realm of the dead,[22] but there were myriad ideas about what "life" was like there. Were the dead happy or sad? Did they live forever? If so, did their mode of existence change? The answers to these questions are as diverse as the poets and philosophers who posed them.

If this was true of the literary and philosophical elites in ancient society, it must have been even more so for the pagans who had recently become Jesus-followers in Thessalonica. As we noted above, these were drawn, for the most part, from the nonelite artisans and traders. Their views on the afterlife would have been just as diverse as those of the elites and probably more tentative and somewhat vaguer. They had not read Homer (since they were not able to read, and even if they had been able to, they could not have afforded a book), though perhaps they had heard portions recited. They had not seen performances of Aeschylus's or Aristophanes's plays, though they might have known a few lines from them secondhand. Due to the harsh realities of ancient life, they had little time, energy, or even the inclination for such cultured pursuits.

While their views were certainly influenced by the literary and philosophical elites that shaped the Hellenistic age, that influence was indirect. It filtered down to street level in the courtyards of the insulae and the tav-

---

21. Stefan Schreiber, "Eine neue jenseits Hoffnung in Thessaloniki und ihre Probleme (1 Thess 4,13–18)," *Bib* 88 (2007): 326–50, esp. 341.

22. Schreiber, *Brief an die Thessalonicher*, 248.

erns where everyday Thessalonians took their meals.[23] Their talk would turn to those who recently died—a much more frequent topic of conversation than modern Westerners can conceive. The death of a child under the age of five, for instance, would have been a common event.[24] The loss of a baby due to malnutrition, a mother in childbirth, or a young man weakened by malaria or a bacterial infection would have been a regular (certainly monthly, perhaps weekly) occurrence among the urban poor.

Funerary epitaphs give us the best sense of what average people in the ancient world thought about death, and in a city such as Thessalonica the myriad associations insured that it was not merely the elite who enjoyed proper burials.[25] Tomb inscriptions from throughout the region reveal something of what the broad masses believed about the state of the dead. Some express resignation: "Why do we sigh for our dead sons, when not even the gods have power to protect their children from death?" (Anth. Gr. 7.8).[26] Some held out hope for future bliss: "If you seek Menander, you shall find him in the abode of Zeus or in the Islands of the Blest" (Anth. Gr. 7.370). Some express the conviction that impiety will not go unpunished: "Therefore he is bound by the dark Furies in the middle of Cocytus, with a dog-collar that chokes him round his neck" (Anth. Gr. 7.377). Stoic indifference in the face of death is a common theme: a certain Anakreon's death was apparently alcohol-related; his epitaph reminds others that they will end up in Hades even if they do not drink (Anth. Gr. 7.33). One sentiment—"non fui, fui, non sum, non curo" ("I was not, I was, I am not, I care not")—was so common that it was regularly reduced to the anagram n.f.f.n.s.n.c.[27] In light of these demonstrably variegated sentiments, gener-

---

23. Regarding daily life in the insulae, see Martin Ebner, *Die Stadt als Lebensraum der ersten Christen: Das Urchristentum in seiner Umwelt I*, GNT 1/1 (Göttingen: Vandenhoeck & Ruprecht, 2012), 81–85; Gudrun Gerlach, *Zu Tisch bei den alten Römern: Eine Kulturgeschichte des Essens und Trinkens* (Stuttgart: Theiss, 2001), 18–20, 30.

24. Nathan Pilkington estimates that the infant mortality rate in low-altitude densely populated areas of the Roman Empire such as Thessalonica would have been approximately 35 percent. See Pilkington, "Growing Up Roman: Infant Mortality and Reproductive Development," *JIH* 44 (2013): 1–35, esp. 33.

25. See Richard S. Ascough, "A Question of Death: Paul's Community-Building Language in 1 Thessalonians 4:13–18," *JBL* 123 (2004): 509–30, esp. 510–12.

26. Translations of the Anthologia Graeca are based on W. R. Paton, *The Greek Anthology*, 5 vols., LCL (London: Heinemann, 1916–1918), with slight modifications.

27. See N. T. Wright, *The Resurrection of the Son of God*, COQG 3 (Minneapolis: Fortress, 2003), 34.

alizations are difficult. Still, the great majority of pagan Greek and Roman epigraphs do not express a clear hope of an afterlife, and none of them look forward to anything like a final day, when the dead will be raised to life and receive their just reward.[28]

First-Century Jewish Eschatological Expectations

Jewish eschatological expectations at the time of Paul stand in stark contrast to those we find in pagan circles. The fate of individuals was not nearly as salient a concern; it was the progress of Israel's history toward "the day of the Lord" that fired the imaginations of the Old Testament prophets (Joel 1:15, 2:1-3, 3:18; Amos 9:11; Obad 1:15; Zeph 1:14-17; Mal 4:1-3). Jews in the first century looked forward to its coming, since it held the promise of the restoration of Israel's fortunes. Past exile in Assyria and Babylon and present Roman hegemony could not quell the hope that Israel's God would one day reign again in Zion.

The nation's fate weighed heavily on the minds of many, and there was a general sense that the Jewish people were still experiencing the Deuteronomic curse of exile. This thesis, associated especially with the work of N. T. Wright, has been the subject of protracted debate, but there is in fact a great deal of evidence that many Jews in Paul's day believed that Israel, as a whole, continued to live in a state of exile. In his Heidelberg dissertation of 1965, Odil Hannes Steck analyzes early Jewish prayers of repentance in the postexilic period and concluded that

> nirgends ist in diesen Gebeten das Gericht Gottes punktuell auf 722 und 587 beschränkt; das Gericht von 587 dauert vielmehr bis in die Gegenwart der Beter hinein an; der gegenwärtige Status Israels ist für diese Gebete das Sein unter dem seit (722 und) 587 währenden Gericht, dessen Andauer in seinen Auswirkungen, besonders der Zerstreuung Israels und der Fremdherrschaft im Verheißungslande, erfahren wird.[29]

---

28. See Schreiber, *Brief an die Thessalonicher*, 249; Wright, *Resurrection of the Son*, 32-38.

29. Odil Hannes Steck, *Israel und das gewaltsame Geschick der Propheten: Untersuchungen zur Überlieferung des deuteronomistischen Geschichtsbildes im AT, Spätjudentum und Urchristentum*, WMANT 23 (Neukirchen-Vluyn: Neukirchener Verlag, 1967), 122-23.

Wright builds on Steck's work and shows that this conception is widely attested in Second Temple literature.[30]

Fundamentally, Jewish convictions regarding Israel's ongoing exile derive from the undeniable fact that, although many (but by no means all) Judeans began to return from exile in Babylon in the latter part of the sixth century BCE, the northern tribes never came back from their earlier deportation at the hands of Assyria. The Jews of Paul's day did not accept this as a fait accompli, since Israel's great prophets had predicted that all the tribes would be restored to the land (see Isa 11:11–16, 49:5–6, 63:17; Jer 3:18; Ezek 48:30–35). Indeed, their return is a constant and recurring theme among various groups in the Second Temple period (see Sir 36:10–13, 48:10; Pss. Sol. 17.26–31; T. Benj. 9.2; T. Naph. 5.8; 4 Ezra 13.39–47; 2 Bar. 78.1–7; 1QM II, 2–3; III, 12–13), including the messianic movement that grew up around Jesus of Nazareth (see Matt 19:28; Luke 22:30; Acts 26:7; Jas 1:1).

Apart from the general sense that prophecies of restoration had not yet been fulfilled, there is a much more specific tradition, one whose influence on the eschatological expectations of Jews in the Second Temple period was pervasive and profound: the visions of the prophet Daniel. I have argued elsewhere that three Danielic motifs—the four kingdoms (Dan 2:31–45, 7:1–28, 8:1–27), the seventy year-weeks (9:20–27), and the abomination of desolation (9:27, 11:31, 12:11)—definitively shaped the eschatological outlook of most first-century Jews, including Paul,[31] so I will only review my conclusions here.

Daniel's four-kingdoms scheme, which is introduced in Dan 2 and further developed in Dan 7–8,[32] was understood by many Jews in the first century to identify the fourth kingdom with Rome (see T. Mos 10.7–8; Rev 13:1–3; 17:7–14; 4 Ezra 11.1–12.39; Josephus, *A.J.* 10.203–210, 269–276). This implies, of course, that they had a clear sense that they were living in

---

30. See especially Wright, *Paul and the Faithfulness of God*, COQG 4 (Minneapolis: Fortress, 2013), 139–63.

31. Joel White, "Anti-imperial Subtexts in Paul: An Attempt at Building a Firmer Foundation," *Bib* 90 (2009): 305–33, esp. 316–23.

32. The complex redaction history of Daniel need not detain us here. The book had already attained its canonical form by the time of its earliest traceable point in its reception history. See George W. E. Nickelsburg, *Jewish Literature between the Bible and the Mishnah*, 2nd ed. (Minneapolis: Fortress, 2005), 17. It was in this form that its impact on late Second Temple period Jews—our exclusive concern—was felt.

the penultimate period of salvation history, on the cusp of the next and final phase, that the coming kingdom of God would ring in.

The general understanding of salvation history implied by the four-kingdoms motif must have played an important role in generating the prophecy of the seventy year-weeks in Dan 9:20–27. The frame story in Dan 9:1–23 portrays Daniel reading Jeremiah's prophecy that the period of exile would last seventy years. In a classic prayer of repentance in the Deuteronomic vein, Daniel begs God to hasten its end, but Jeremiah's seventy years are clearly insufficient to incorporate not only Babylon but the reign of the other kingdoms that would follow. Thus, God sends the angel Gabriel to announce not a reprieve but rather an extension of the period of exile: Israel should expect to remain in exile not for seventy years, but for seventy weeks of years, that is, 490 years.

No other Old Testament prophecy captivated the imagination of Jews during the Second Temple period as much as this one. Indeed, many of them seem to have been interested to the point of obsession in figuring out when the protracted period of Israel's exile would end. As Roger Beckwith cogently states, "There is strong evidence to show that the Essenes, the Pharisees and the Zealots all thought that they could date, at least approximately, the time when the Son of David would come, and that in each case their calculations were based upon Daniel's prophecy of the seventy weeks (Dan 9:24–27), understood as seventy weeks of years."[33] There is no need to review all the evidence that Beckwith has amassed in support of his claim, but it is perhaps important for our purposes to note its concrete effect. First, it encouraged the widespread and tendentious periodization of history, since Daniel's 490 years neatly divide into ten Jubilee units of forty-nine years each (see, e.g., T. Levi 17.1–2; 4Q181 III; 11Q13 VI–VIII). Second, it led many Jews in the Second Temple period to expect that the end of exile promised by Gabriel was imminent. Three examples should suffice to prove this point:

1. The author of 4Q390 laments that "in the seventh jubilee of the devastation of the land they will forget the law, the festival, the sabbath and the covenant; and they will disobey everything and will do what is evil in my eyes ... and there will come the dominion of Belial upon them to deliver

---

33. Roger T. Beckwith, "The Year of the Messiah: Jewish and Early Christian Chronologies, and Their Eschatological Consequences," in *Calendar and Chronology, Jewish and Christian: Biblical, Intertestamental and Patristic Studies* (Leiden: Brill, 1996), 217.

them up to the sword for a week of years" (4Q390 I, 7-9; II, 3-4 [*DSSSE*]). This is a clear allusion to the period of hellenization under Antiochus Epiphanes IV leading up to the Maccabean revolt and the rededication of the temple in 164 BCE.[34] Allowing for some imprecision in dating depending on when the author placed this "week" within the seventh Jubilee of forty-nine years, his expectation would have been that Daniel's seventieth week would occur between 25 BCE and 20 CE.

2. The author of the Testament of Levi is even more precise. His focus is on the priesthood that corresponds to each of the jubilees. The "pollution" of the priesthood in the seventh jubilee (T. Levi 17.8) is a salient reference to the usurpation of Onias's high priesthood by Jason in 173 BCE during the reign of Antiochus Epiphanes IV.[35] The author further places the rededication of the temple in the fifth week of the seventh Jubilee period (T. Levi 17.10). Following this timetable, the author would have expected the seventieth week in the last decade BCE.

3. Mention should also be made of Seder Olam Rabbah, a rabbinic chronicle from the second century CE that also clearly derives its periodization of later Jewish history from Daniel's seventy weeks. It does so in a seemingly capricious manner, since the author is at pains to make the period from the beginning of the exile to the destruction of the temple last precisely 490 years (S. Olam Rab. 30). This is, objectively speaking, a fool's errand, of course, but it demonstrates the powerful hold Daniel's prophecy had on the imagination of Jews well into the early rabbinic era.

Finally, Daniel's "abomination of desolation" (Dan 9:27, 11:31, 12:11) played a major role in early Jewish expectations concerning the future course of Israel's history. Gabriel's revelation to Daniel concludes with the announcement that the temple sanctuary will be destroyed and be replaced by this enigmatic entity. It is closely associated in all three verses where it is mentioned with the cessation of sacrifice and the end—or at least the disruption—of the temple cult. Thus, it was only natural for the author of 1 Maccabees to see it fulfilled in the desecration of the temple by

---

34. See also Michael A. Knibb, "A Note on 4Q372 and 4Q390," in *The Scriptures and the Scrolls*, ed. Florentino García Martínez, Antonius Hilhorst, and Casper J. Labuschagne (Leiden: Brill, 1992), 164-77, esp. 175-76. According to Christoph Berner, the evidence allows only a general identification of events in the Hellenistic era. See Berner, *Jahre, Jahrwochen und Jubiläen. Heptadische Geschichtskonzeptionen im Antiken Judentum*, BZAW 363 (Berlin: de Gruyter, 2006), 415-16.

35. See Berner, *Jahre, Jahrwochen und Jubiläen*, 490-91.

Antiochus Epiphanes IV (1 Macc 1:54) and for Luke's Jesus to anticipate its fulfillment in the destruction of the temple in 70 CE (Luke 21:20–21).

These three Danielic motifs and their *Wirkungsgeschichte* in early Judaism combined to instill in many first-century Jews a pervasive sense that they were living at the very end of the present age and that the day on which "the Lord whom you seek will suddenly come to his temple" (Mal 3:1 NRSV), which would usher in the never-ending reign of God, was near at hand. This is confirmed by Josephus, who paints a picture of heightened expectation of the imminent advent of the Messiah beginning with the death of Herod and lasting through the First Jewish War (*A.J.* 17.269–284; 20.97–98, 169–171). The gospels round out this picture, portraying the crowds' reactions to the ministries of John the Baptist and Jesus of Nazareth against that same background (see, e.g., Mark 8:27–29; John 1:19–23).

Given this intense focus on the coming kingdom of God, it would not be surprising if early Jewish eschatological speculation proved to be more concerned with Israel's role in the grand scheme of things and less concerned with the fate of individuals. This seems, in fact, to be confirmed by the evidence from early Jewish funerary epigraphy.[36] On the one hand, it is interesting to note how hellenized Jewish epitaphs in this period are, even in Palestine. For instance, a representative epitaph from Beth She'arim (IBethShe'arim 127, early third century CE) makes use of the pagan formula θάρσει, οὐδεὶς ἀθάνατος, and proper nouns such as Ἅδης and Μοῖρα, with indifference to their pedigree.[37] On the other hand, many (though not all) epitaphs are sober, even jejune, in tone compared to the often forlorn pathos of pagan inscriptions. Typically, as in the case of epitaphs from Rome in the imperial period, they convey gratitude for a shared life (*CIJ* 123), describe the circumstances of death (*CIJ* 418), or express (usually measured) grief (*CIJ* 358). One from Jerusalem in the early imperial period (*CIJ* 1300) reads laconically: "This tomb was made for the bones of our fathers. Its length is two cubits. Do not open it above them."[38]

For our purposes, however, of greatest interest is the contrast between pagan and Jewish funerary epitaphs with regard to the fate of the dead. While the former express, as we saw above, intense interest in the fate of

---

36. See Pieter W. van der Horst, *Ancient Jewish Epitaphs: An Introductory Survey of a Millennium of Jewish Funerary Epigraphy (300 BCE–700 CE)*, CBET 2 (Kampen: Kok, 1991), 144–60.
37. Van der Horst, *Ancient Jewish Epitaphs*, 120–21, 150–51.
38. Van der Horst, *Ancient Jewish Epitaphs*, 153–54.

deceased loved ones and a range of emotions—despair, hope, guarded optimism, stoic bravado—about their well-being, the latter seem in comparison remarkably nonchalant.[39] This, however, should not be construed as indifference. They clearly wanted the best for their dearly departed, as certain stock phrases in funerary epitaphs such as the wish for "peaceful sleep" reveal (*CIJ* 358, 418, both from Rome in the imperial period). They simply seem less preoccupied with the fate of the dead than their pagan contemporaries. It seems fair to say that it was not nearly as prominent a concern for Jews as it was for pagans in the Hellenistic age, and it is perhaps not too much to say that both the Jewish focus on larger eschatological concerns (see above) combined with widespread certain belief in the resurrection (Dan 12:2–3; John 11:23–24) accounts for this.

Paul's Understanding of His Temporal Location within *Heilsgeschichte*

With this brief description of contrasting pagan and Jewish eschatological expectations in mind, we can begin to delineate the contours of Paul's eschatology, even if an exhaustive description is beyond our reach. While he certainly has plenty to say on the subject, he left behind no systematic summary of his eschatological positions, and all of his statements are tendentious in the sense that they respond to specific questions or difficulties that arose in specific situations. Thankfully, our interest lies solely with the temporal aspect of his eschatology, as described above, and on that subject Paul gives us enough clues to construct a sufficiently clear and coherent picture of his views.

Given Paul's Pharisaic Jewish background, it is a priori likely that he shared the common Second Temple understanding of salvation history described in the last section, especially Daniel's continuing exile paradigm.[40] There is certainly evidence at various points in his letters of prior and purposeful interaction with Daniel traditions.[41] The use to which Paul

---

39. Van der Horst, *Ancient Jewish Epitaphs*, 118: "In Beth She'arim there are very few inscriptions that indicate a belief in some form of afterlife."

40. See Wright, *Paul and the Faithfulness*, 158. "My case is not that all Jews throughout the period understood themselves to be living in a state of 'continuing exile', only that such an understanding was widespread, and was particularly likely to be true of zealous Pharisees."

41. I note this only in passing here, since I have dealt with this extensively elsewhere (see White, "Anti-imperial Subtexts," 325–33).

puts these traditions shows that the basic temporal structure of his eschatology remained essentially unchanged even after his conversion/calling. Of course, Paul's understanding of his location within *Heilsgeschichte* demanded modification. This was because he had become convinced, together with the earliest Christian communities, that the Messiah had come in the person of Jesus of Nazareth ... and gone away again! His coming did not bring about the immediate end of the present age, as most Jews expected. Rather, it ushered in an unforeseen interval of indeterminate duration before the return of the Messiah, which Paul eagerly awaited (Rom 8:23-25; 1 Cor 1:7; Phil 3:20).

Paul was able, however, to integrate this unexpected turn of events into his eschatology with impressive acumen and agility. The future he looked forward to was in essence the same one he had envisioned while still a Pharisee, and he still believed, in line with early Jewish expectations, that he was living in the penultimate period of salvation history. However, its character had changed because Messiah's reign had—unexpectedly—already begun. This only strengthened his conviction that he was standing on the cusp of one age, awaiting the imminent advent of the next and final one.

This becomes clear when we pay careful attention to the extensive metaleptical use Paul makes of a key Old Testament text—the so-called Song of Moses (Deut 32:1-43)—in Rom 9-11.[42] Paul's actualizing exegesis of this text—much like the Qumran community, Paul believed that prior revelation pointed to his age and mission—lies not so much on the surface of his discourse but behind it, which is why its import is often missed. Still, I am convinced that it is possible, though only with due care, to lay bare the assumptions that guided Paul's interpretation with a reasonable degree of confidence in our results.[43] It is to that task we now turn.

---

42. For a more detailed analysis see Joel R. White, "N. T. Wright's Narrative Approach," in *God and the Faithfulness of Paul: A Critical Examination of the Pauline Theology of N. T. Wright*, ed. Christoph Heilig, J. Thomas Hewitt, and Michael F. Bird, WUNT 2/413 (Tübingen: Mohr Siebeck, 2016), 181-204, esp. 199-201. Richard Hays defines metalepsis as "a diachronic trope ... [in which] a literary echo links the text in which it occurs to an earlier text, [and] the figurative effect of the echo can lie in the unstated or suppressed (transumed) points of resonance between the two texts." See Hays, *Echoes of Scripture in the Letters of Paul* (New Haven: Yale University Press, 1989), 20.

43. For a thorough discussion of the methodological parameters that must be heeded when attempting to reconstruct Paul's reading of OT texts, see Joel White, "Identifying Intertextual Exegesis in Paul. Methodological Considerations and a

Toward the middle of his discourse on God's faithfulness to Israel in Rom 9–11 Paul quotes a verse from the Song of Moses—"I will make you jealous of a people who are no people, and by means of a foolish nation I will arouse your anger" (Deut 32:21, my trans.)—in Rom 10:19. On the surface, this quotation facilitates Paul's argument that not only was the mission to the gentiles, in which he plays a crucial role, foreseen by Moses, but also the mechanism by which that mission would come about: the hardening of Israel.[44]

There is, however, much more going on below the surface. A careful analysis of Paul's discourse makes it clear that he does not have in mind simply the verse he quotes but rather the entire Song of Moses. Specifically, a comparison of Deut 32:1–43 with Rom 9–11 reveals that the former serves as a template for the latter, determining its narrative flow. The song can be divided thematically into the following sections:[45]

0. Prologue: Deut 32:1–3
1. Israel's election: Deut 32:4–9
2. Israel's salvation: Deut 32:10–14
3. Israel's rebellion against God: Deut 32:15–18
4. Israel's rejection by God: Deut 32:19–25
5. God's determination to have mercy on Israel: Deut 32:26–43

In Rom 9–11 Paul clearly follows the narrative trajectory of the song, even if he does not slavishly appropriate its content:

1. Israel's election (which always involved a chosen remnant): Rom 9:1–29
2. Israel's salvation (not yet accomplished): Rom 9:30–10:4

Test Case (1 Corinthians 6:5)," in *The Crucified Apostle: Essays on Peter and Paul*, ed. Todd A. Wilson and Paul R. House, WUNT 2/450 (Tübingen: Mohr Siebeck, 2017), 167–88. See also Timothy Berkley, *From a Broken Covenant to Circumcision of the Heart: Pauline Intertextual Exegesis in Romans 2:17–29*, SBLDS 175 (Atlanta: Society of Biblical Literature, 2000), 17–66.

44. On this point, see esp. Richard Bell, *Provoked to Jealousy: The Origin and Purpose of the Jealousy Motif in Romans 9–11*, WUNT 2/63 (Tübingen: Mohr Siebeck, 1994), 126–27.

45. I follow the outline provided by J. Gordon McConville, except that McConville further divides Deut 32:26–43 into two parts. See McConville, *Deuteronomy*, ApOTC 5 (Downers Grove, IL: InterVarsity Press, 2002), 451.

3. Israel's rebellion against God (in spite of hearing the message): Rom 10:5–21
4. Israel's rejection by God (except for the remnant): Rom 11:1–10
5. God's determination to have mercy on Israel: Rom 11:11–32

For our purposes, Paul's appropriation of the narrative substructure of the Song of Moses for the construction of his argument in Rom 9–11 is important because it confirms our assessment of his sense of temporal location within *Heilsgeschichte*. He and his compatriots presently find themselves in the penultimate phase of God's rejection of Israel. The final phase—the eschatological salvation of Israel—has not yet been inaugurated. The obvious question, since according to Paul's convictions the Messiah had come, is: Why not?

This is the question Paul addresses as he wraps up his discourse in Rom 9–11, and the Song of Moses and particularly Deut 32:21 clearly continue to shape his thinking. In Rom 11:25b–26 he maintains that "a hardening has come upon part of Israel, until the full number of the Gentiles has come in. And so all Israel will be saved" (NRSV). Thus, Paul positions the mission to the gentiles after the hardening of Israel (step 4 in the narrative progression outlined above) and before Israel's ultimate salvation (step 5). He characterizes this sequence as a "mystery," another term familiar to us from Jewish apocalyptic writings. It denotes an event that is determined by God in advance and perhaps even hinted at in Scripture but that only becomes clear in the light of later revelation.[46] In Paul's case, it was the coming of the Messiah Jesus and particularly his own direct calling by the risen Lord on the road to Damascus that allowed his mission to the gentiles to come into sharp focus.[47]

It is not apparent at first glance, however, where in the revelatory sequence of Rom 11:25b–25 the "mystery"—in the quasi-technical sense of the word described above—precisely lies for Paul. All three elements contained in it are clearly articulated in Old Testament texts with which Paul would have been very familiar: (1) the hardening of Israel (Deut 32:15–18; Isa 6:8–10), (2) the inclusion of the gentiles (Isa 2:2–4, 11:10, 19:19–25; Mic 4:1–4; Zeph 3:9–10; Zech 2:11, 8:20–23), and (3) the ulti-

---

46. See Douglas Moo, *The Epistle to the Romans*, NICNT (Grand Rapids: Eerdmans, 1996), 714.

47. See Seyoon Kim, "The 'Mystery' of Romans 11.25–26 Once More," *NTS* 43 (1997): 412–29.

mate salvation of Israel (among others, the texts quoted by Paul in Rom 11:26: Isa 59:20; Jer 31:33).

The locus of the mystery lies, it seems, not in any one of these elements per se, but rather, in all likelihood, in the timing of the inclusion of the gentiles. Jews in Paul's day had a variety of ideas about what God would do with the gentiles, ranging from their universal annihilation to their universal acceptance, but they seem to have shared a common conception that God would deal with them *after* he saved Israel. For those who believed that God would also save the gentiles, or at least some of them, they envisioned that this would happen in response to Israel's eschatological vindication.[48]

In contrast, Paul's reflection on the Song of Moses led him to the conclusion that the hardening of Israel (Rom 10:19) had unexpectedly opened up an unforeseen period between the salvation of the first part of Israel—the firstfruits offering of dough—and the inclusion the rest of the Jews—the whole lump (Rom 11:11).[49] Thus, for Paul, the mystery entailed his understanding that the mission to the gentiles, to which the Messiah had commissioned him, would be completed before the eschatological salvation of "all Israel" would be fully achieved.[50] That final stage of *Heilsgeschichte* had not yet been attained, and it will not be until "the fullness of the gentiles" has been incorporated. This, it would seem, explains the pervasive sense of urgency that characterizes Paul's missionary endeavors.

Acute *Naherwartung* in 1 Thessalonians?

As we turn our attention to 1 Thessalonians, we begin with a point of clarification. Based on the analysis above, it seems clear that when Paul wrote Romans, he believed that he inhabited the penultimate stage of *Heilsgeschichte* that would continue for some indeterminate amount of time. Most

---

48. See Terence L. Donaldson, *Paul and the Gentiles: Remapping the Apostle's Convictional World* (Minneapolis: Fortress, 1997), 51–78.

49. For an extensive analysis of this allusion, see Joel White, *Die Erstlingsgabe im Neuen Testament*, TANZ 45 (Tübingen: Francke, 2007), 70–109.

50. The exact identity of "all Israel" has been debated at length. I share James Scott's view that Paul would have conceived of this entity in line with OT and rabbinic usage as a group containing representatives of all tribes, rather than every individual Israelite or Jew. See Scott, "'And Then All Israel Will Be Saved' (Rom 11,26)," in *Restoration: Old Testament, Jewish, and Christian Perspectives*, ed. Scott, JSJSup 72 (Leiden: Brill, 2001), 496–515.

New Testament scholars assume, however, that his eschatological expectations were less well developed when he wrote 1 Thessalonians due to an "acute" *Naherwartung* that made more thoroughgoing theological reflection unnecessary.[51] Specifically, they assume on the basis 1 Thess 4:15-17, where Paul twice speaks in the first-person plural of "we who are alive" until the coming of the Lord, that he was convinced at that point, some six or seven years before wrote Romans, that the Messiah would return while he was still alive.[52] The years of ministry in the interim, however, caused him to ease up on his *Naherwartung*, so that he was no longer confident of Christ's imminent return by the time he wrote Romans.

Quite apart from the difficulties that beset all theories of a development in Paul's theology,[53] given the sparseness of his oeuvre and open questions about the chronological order of his letters, especially Galatians and Philippians, there is good reason to question the majority interpretation of 1 Thess 4:15-17. A close reading of Paul's teaching in 1 Thess 4:15-17 does not necessitate an assumption on his part that he would certainly be among the living when the Lord returned. It is true that, *if* it could be shown that Paul believed that, this would be one way to express it, and conversely, *if* Paul was certain that he would be dead when the parousia occurred, he could not have formulated his thought in this manner, but that by no means settles the matter. This is so because there is another option, generally overlooked, that better explains Paul's formulation, namely, that Paul

---

51. See, e.g., Udo Schnelle, *Einleitung in das Neue Testament*, 9th ed. (Göttingen: Vandenhoeck & Ruprecht, 2017), 70-72.

52. Schnelle, *Einleitung in das Neue Testament*. For other examples see Charles A. Wanamaker, *The Epistles to the Thessalonians: A Commentary on the Greek Text*, NIGTC (Grand Rapids: Eerdmans, 1990), 171-72; Abraham J. Malherbe, *The Letters to the Thessalonians: A New Translation with Introduction and Commentary*, AB 32 (New York: Doubleday, 2000), 270-71.

53. German scholars have debated the issue extensively. Wilfred Wiefel and Udo Schnelle argue for a clear development in Paul's theology between his earliest and latest letters, while Andreas Lindemann and Dieter Sänger doubt that it is possible to trace any development in Paul's thinking across his letters. See Wiefel, "Die Hauptrichtung des Wandels im eschatologischen Denken des Paulus," *TLZ* (1974): 65-81; Schnelle, *Wandlungen im paulinischen Denken*, SBS 137 (Stuttgart: Katholisches Bibelwerk, 1998), 37-41; Lindemann, "Paulus und die korinthische Eschatologie: Zur These von einer 'Entwicklung' im paulinischen Denken," *NTS* 37 (1991): 377-99; Sänger, "Die Adressaten des Galaterbriefs und das Problem einer Entwicklung in Paulus' theologischem Denken," in *Beiträge zur urchristlichen Theologiegeschichte*, ed. Wolfgang Kraus, BZNW 163 (Berlin: de Gruyter, 2009), 247-75.

could not say for sure whether he would be alive or dead at the coming of the Lord. This is, of course, exactly what 1 Thess 5:10 implies when the apostle expresses his hope, again in the first-person plural, that "whether we are awake or asleep we may live with him" (NRSV).

It seems reckless to overlook this statement when interpreting 1 Thess 4:15–17, but unfortunately many commentators do just that. This oversight facilitates the mistake they make with reference to 1 Thess 4:15–17: that of ignoring what Anthony Thiselton refers to as the "participant logic" of Paul's locution, by means of which the apostle endeavors to signal his solidarity with the Thessalonians.[54] It is this participation logic that prompts him to formulate his thought in the first-person plural, but since he does not know whether he will be alive or dead at the parousia, he has no choice but to group himself—provisionally, at least—with those who are now alive. He cannot say "we who will be dead" or even "you who are alive" without implying a conviction that he would already be dead when the Lord comes. Certainly, Paul could have used "spectator" logic and constructed his locution abstractly with "those who are alive" (and perhaps he would have done so, had he anticipated what Thiselton refers to as "the absurd amount of weight" commentators have placed on the phrase!),[55] but given that he wishes to use the first-person plural, there is no other way for him to succinctly articulate his thought.

Thus, when Paul says "we who are alive at the coming of the Lord" in 1 Thessalonians 4:15, 17 it could mean either that (1) he was convinced he would be alive at the parousia or (2) he did not know whether he would be alive or dead. If the latter conforms to his view, he would have no other option but to group himself with the living (since he cannot logically group himself with the dead, even provisionally). His formulation "whether we wake or sleep" in 1 Thess 5:10 indicates that option 2 is much more likely to be correct.

There is, then, no need to postulate that Paul's *Naherwartung* diminished between the composition of 1 Thessalonians and Romans. If anything, it seems to have intensified, as an objective reading of Rom 13:11–12 (i.e., one that does not presume a development in his thought) seems to indi-

---

54. Anthony Thiselton, *The First Epistle to the Corinthians*, NIGTC (Grand Rapids: Eerdmans, 2000), 581 n. 507: "While descriptive 'spectator' logic would offer an assertion, 'participant' logic must choose a standpoint in solidarity with the readers which invites them to take the possibility at issue seriously."

55. Thiselton, *First Epistle to the Corinthians*, 580–81.

cate. There, just as in 1 Thess 4:15–17, he employs participation logic, formulating his thought in the first-person plural, and notes that "salvation is nearer to us now than when we first believed." Paul clearly includes himself in this perspective: he actually experiences a sense of heightened *Naherwartung* due to the delay of the parousia. It seems therefore perfectly valid to use the information gleaned from Romans concerning the temporal aspect of Paul's eschatological expectations when interpreting Paul's understanding of "times and seasons" in 1 Thess 5:1, to which we now turn our attention.

"Times and Seasons" and "Peace and Security" (1 Thess 5:1–3)

Given Paul's Jewish and, more specifically, Pharisaic background, and in light of the palpable sense of urgency that he felt regarding the coming of the Lord, it comes as something of a surprise that his attitude with regard to speculation about "times and seasons" is so thoroughly negative. Within apocalyptic Judaism there was a veritable cottage industry devoted to working out the proper periodization of history (see 1 En. 93.1–10; 4 Ezra 12.8; 2 Bar. 14.1, 56.2),[56] and as we saw above, many of Paul's contemporaries (roughly speaking) were working overtime to determine when the extended Danielic exile would come to an end. Paul would certainly have been aware of these efforts; perhaps he had even indulged in such speculation himself before becoming a follower of Jesus. His eschatological presuppositions would have most likely been precisely the sort that would have led to heightened interest in determining when the parousia would occur.

Paul, however, will have none of it. On the contrary, in 1 Thess 5:2 he insists that the "day of the Lord" (ἡμερα κυρίου), which he equates with the parousia of Jesus,[57] will come like a "thief in the night." Paul's use of this latter term reflects his appropriation of Jesus tradition (Matt 24:43; Luke 12:39).[58] It therefore seems plausible that he derived his (for first-century

---

56. See Hoppe, *Thessalonikerbrief: Kommentar*, 290.
57. For an extensive discussion of these terms, their relationship to each other, and their traditio-historical roots, see Plevnik, *Paul and the Parousia*, 3–44.
58. See Holtz, *Brief an die Thessalonicher*, 213; Plevnik, *Paul and the Parousia*, 105; Seyoon Kim, "The Jesus Tradition in 1 Thess 4.11–5.13," *NTS* 48 (2002): 225–42, esp. 231; Schreiber, *Brief an die Thessalonicher*, 267. Contra Christopher M. Tuckett, "Synoptic Tradition in 1 Thessalonians?," in *The Thessalonian Correspondence*, ed.

Jews) atypical aversion to speculation concerning "times and seasons" from the same source (Mark 13:32 // Matt 24:36). If Jesus himself professed ignorance of and by implication insouciance regarding the "day and the hour" of his coming,[59] then it should concern Paul and his churches even less. The day of the Lord was imminent; it was enough to be sure of that. Determining its exact timing was the sort of speculation the apostle was at pains to discourage.

We have seen that Jews and gentiles had vastly different expectations regarding the age to come, as the former would have called it, or the afterlife, as the latter would likely have referred to it. Even the respective thought categories would have defied easy assimilation! It is against this background that I believe 1 Thess 5:1–3 can best be understood. It constitutes Paul's response to the clash of Jewish and pagan eschatologies in the nascent community of Jesus-followers in Thessalonica that surfaced only after Paul's brief stay in the city. It seems to have been sparked by gentile believers' unease regarding the fate of their deceased loved ones (1 Thess 4:13–18)—a typical pagan concern—and catalyzed by Jewish believers' unanswered questions regarding "times and seasons"—that phrase and the worldview it reflects are, as we saw above, thoroughly Jewish.

The Jewish followers of Jesus in Thessalonica were few, but their viewpoint was probably influential. Assuming they were captivated by the eschatological musings of their compatriots who left behind a literary record, they may well have indulged in characteristic early Jewish speculation concerning the promised end of extended Danielic exile and attempted on that basis to determine when they should await the return of the Messiah Jesus. They had clearly been instructed by Paul regarding the certainty of the parousia (1 Thess 5:2), and they knew that the apostle was eagerly looking forward to it (1 Thess 1:10). It would have seemed only natural to them to inquire as to its timing.

On the other hand, it was pagan Macedonians drawn mostly from the ranks of low-status subsistence-level artisans and traders who constituted the majority in the church. At the time of their conversion, their views on the fate of the dead would have ranged from nihilistic (the soul ceased to

---

Rob P. Collins, BETL 87 (Leuven: Peeters, 1990), 173–74; Hoppe, *Thessalonikerbrief: Kommentar*, 292–93.

59. It seems unlikely that early church would have placed a saying in Jesus's mouth *ex eventu* predicated on his ignorance of God's plan. See Francis J. Moloney, *The Gospel of Mark: A Commentary* (Peabody, MA: Hendrickson, 2002), 270 n. 266.

exist when the body died) to largely pessimistic (the dead lived on but in an unenviable state) to vaguely optimistic (the dead enjoyed at least some semblance of felicity), and these were in the main held tenuously. Clearly, they welcomed the gospel that Paul preached, and, of course, that would have included the proclamation of the resurrection of Jesus (1 Thess 4:14). There is, however no way of knowing whether these new believers had received instruction about the hope of the future resurrection of the dead.[60]

If they did, they certainly had not yet internalized it to the extent that it altered their worldview. All their lives they had heard that since life on earth had no telos, no overarching eschatological goal, a measure of peace and security was the best one could hope for. If they had attained that, they should enjoy it while it lasted. As for the dead, who really knew their fate? Whether or not they had ever heard of the Stoics or the Epicureans, the commoners in Thessalonica probably echoed their philosophies: "Don't worry about death since you can't do anything about it; simply accept it and concentrate on things that are in your power to change" (see Epictetus, *Ench.* 2). "Death doesn't concern the living, it is meaningless for us; do your best to ignore it and enjoy the present" (see Epicurus in Diogenes, 10.124–125).

Some of these average Thessalonians, however, had come to believe in the Messiah Jesus, and their lives suddenly and unexpectedly acquired an eschatological telos. Paul had held out the prospect of an endpoint to which their lives were progressing, the parousia, and they wanted to know what that meant for them personally and especially for their loved ones who had already died (1 Thess 4:13). The Jewish believers in the community could not or would not answer their questions to their satisfaction; they were too focused on the timing of the event and what it meant for Israel.

In this situation, Paul positions himself between the formerly noneschatological outlook of the gentile converts and the hypereschatological apocalyptic expectations of the Jewish believers in the Thessalonian church. In view of the imminent return of the Son of God (1 Thess 1:10), the gentile believers should no longer stake their hopes on peace and security in the present age. In light of the fact that the time of his coming was unknown, Jewish believers should free themselves from their misguided preoccupation with "times and seasons." The parousia was certain, and the

---

60. See Nicoll, *From Hope to Despair*, 35–38.

destiny of believers in Jesus was secure. That was all they needed to know in order to live circumspectly and confidently in the here and now.

Bibliography

Ascough, Richard S. "A Question of Death: Paul's Community-Building Language in 1 Thessalonians 4:13–18." *JBL* 123 (2004): 509–30.

Bammel, Ernst. "Ein Beitrag zur paulinischen Staatsanschauung." *TLZ* 85 (1960): 837–40.

Beckwith, Roger T. "The Year of the Messiah: Jewish and Early Christian Chronologies, and Their Eschatological Consequences." Pages 217–75 in *Calendar and Chronology, Jewish and Christian: Biblical, Intertestamental and Patristic Studies*. Leiden: Brill, 1996.

Bell, Richard. *Provoked to Jealousy: The Origin and Purpose of the Jealousy Motif in Romans 9–11*. WUNT 2/63. Tübingen: Mohr Siebeck, 1994.

Berkley, Timothy. *From a Broken Covenant to Circumcision of the Heart: Pauline Intertextual Exegesis in Romans 2:17–29*. SBLDS 175. Atlanta: Society of Biblical Literature, 2000.

Berner, Christoph. *Jahre, Jahrwochen und Jubiläen. Heptadische Geschichtskonzeptionen im Antiken Judentum*. BZAW 363. Berlin: de Gruyter, 2006.

Best, Ernest. *The First and Second Epistles to the Thessalonians*. BNTC. London: Black, 1986.

Brocke, Christoph vom. *Thessaloniki – Stadt des Kassander und Gemeinde des Paulus: Eine frühe Gemeinde in ihrer heidnischen Umwelt*. WUNT 2/124. Tübingen: Mohr Siebeck, 2001.

Donaldson, Terence L. *Paul and the Gentiles: Remapping the Apostle's Convictional World*. Minneapolis: Fortress, 1997.

Ebner, Martin. *Die Stadt als Lebensraum der ersten Christen: Das Urchristentum in seiner Umwelt I*. GNT 1/1. Göttingen: Vandenhoeck & Ruprecht, 2012.

Gerlach, Gudrun. *Zu Tisch bei den alten Römern: Eine Kulturgeschichte des Essens und Trinkens*. Stuttgart: Theiss, 2001.

Harrison, James R. *Paul and the Imperial Authorities at Thessalonica and Rome*. WUNT 273. Tübingen: Mohr Siebeck, 2011.

Hays, Richard. *Echoes of Scripture in the Letters of Paul*. New Haven: Yale University Press, 1989.

Holtz, Traugott. *Der erste Brief an die Thessalonicher*. EKKNT 13. Zürich: Benziger; Neukirchen-Vluyn: Neukirchener Verlag, 1986.

Hoppe, Rudolph. *Der erste Thessalonikerbrief: Kommentar*. Freiburg: Herder, 2016.
Horst, Pieter W. van der. *Ancient Jewish Epitaphs: An Introductory Survey of a Millennium of Jewish Funerary Epigraphy (300 BCE–700 CE)*. CBET 2. Kampen: Kok, 1991.
Jewett, Robert. *The Thessalonian Correspondence: Pauline Rhetoric and Millenarian Piety*. Philadelphia: Fortress, 1986.
Jung, UnChan. "Paul's Letter to Free(d) Casual Workers: Profiling the Thessalonians in Light of the Roman Economy." *JSNT* 42 (2020): 472–95.
Kim, Seyoon. "The Jesus Tradition in 1 Thess 4.11–5.13." *NTS* 48 (2002): 225–42.
———. "The 'Mystery' of Romans 11.25–26 Once More." *NTS* 43 (1997): 412–29.
Kneppe, Alfred. *Metus temporum: Zur Bedeutung von Angst in der Politik und Gesellschaft der römischen Kaiserzeit des 1. und 2. Jhdts. n. Chr.* Stuttgart: Steiner, 1994.
Knibb, Michael A. "A Note on 4Q372 and 4Q390." Pages 164–77 in *The Scriptures and the Scrolls*. Edited by Florentino García Martínez, Antonius Hilhorst, and Casper J. Labuschagne. Leiden: Brill, 1992.
Lehtipuu, Outi. "The Imagery of the Lukan Afterworld in the Light of Some Roman and Greek Parallels." Pages 133–46 in *Zwischen den Reichen: Neues Testament und Römische Herrschschaft*. Edited by Michal Labahn and Jürgen Zangenberg. TANZ 36. Tübingen: Francke, 2002.
Levinskaya, Irina. *The Book of Acts in Its Diaspora Setting*. Vol. 5 of *The Book of Acts in Its First Century Setting*. Grand Rapids: Eerdmans, 1996.
Lindemann, Andreas. "Paulus und die korinthische Eschatologie: Zur These von einer 'Entwicklung' im paulinischen Denken." *NTS* 37 (1991): 377–99.
Malherbe, Abraham J. *The Letters to the Thessalonians: A New Translation with Introduction and Commentary*. AB 32. New York: Doubleday, 2000.
McConville, J. Gordon. *Deuteronomy*. ApOTC 5. Downers Grove, IL: InterVarsity Press, 2002.
Míguez, Néstor O. *The Practice of Hope: Ideology and Intention in First Thessalonians*. PCC. Minneapolis: Fortress, 2012.
Moloney, Francis J. *The Gospel of Mark: A Commentary*. Peabody, MA: Hendrickson, 2002.

Moo, Douglas. *The Epistle to the Romans*. NICNT. Grand Rapids: Eerdmans, 1996.

Nickelsburg, George W. E. *Jewish Literature between the Bible and the Mishnah*. 2nd ed. Minneapolis: Fortress, 2005.

Nicoll, Colin R. *From Hope to Despair: Situating 1 and 2 Thessalonians*. SNTSMS 126. Cambridge: Cambridge University Press, 2004.

Paton, W. R., trans. *The Greek Anthology*. 5 vols. LCL. London: Heinemann, 1916–1918.

Pilkington, Nathan. "Growing Up Roman: Infant Mortality and Reproductive Development." *JIH* 44 (2013): 1–35.

Plevnik, Joseph. *Paul and the Parousia: An Exegetical and Theological Study*. Peabody, MA: Hendrickson, 1997.

Riesner, Rainer. *Die Frühzeit des Apostels Paulus: Studien zu Chronologie, Missionsstrategie und Theologie*. WUNT 71. Tübingen: Mohr Siebeck, 1994.

Sänger, Dieter. "Die Adressaten des Galaterbriefs und das Problem einer Entwicklung in Paulus' theologischem Denken." Pages 247–75 in *Beiträge zur urchristlichen Theologiegeschichte*. Edited by Wolfgang Kraus. BZNW 163. Berlin: de Gruyter, 2009.

Schnelle, Udo. *Einleitung in das Neue Testament*. 9th ed. Göttingen: Vandenhoeck & Ruprecht, 2017.

———. *Wandlungen im paulinischen Denken*. SBS 137. Stuttgart: Katholisches Bibelwerk, 1998.

Schreiber, Stefan. *Der erste Brief an die Thessalonicher*. ÖTK 13/1. Gütersloh: Gütersloher Verlagshaus, 2014.

———. "Eine neue jenseits Hoffnung in Thessaloniki und ihre Probleme (1 Thess 4,13–18)." *Bib* 88 (2007): 326–50.

Scott, James M. "'And Then All Israel Will Be Saved' (Rom 11,26)." Pages 496–515 in *Restoration: Old Testament, Jewish, and Christian Perspectives*. Edited by James M. Scott. JSJSup 72. Leiden: Brill, 2001.

Steck, Odil Hannes. *Israel und das gewaltsame Geschick der Propheten: Untersuchungen zur Überlieferung des deuteronomistischen Geschichtsbildes im AT, Spätjudentum und Urchristentum*. WMANT 23. Neukirchen-Vluyn: Neukirchener Verlag, 1967.

Thiselton, Anthony. *The First Epistle to the Corinthians*. NIGTC. Grand Rapids: Eerdmans, 2000.

Tuckett, Christopher M. "Synoptic Tradition in 1 Thessalonians?" Pages 160–82 in *The Thessalonian Correspondence*. Edited by Rob P. Collins. BETL 87. Leuven: Peeters, 1990.

Wanamaker, Charles A. *The Epistles to the Thessalonians: A Commentary on the Greek Text*. NIGTC. Grand Rapids: Eerdmans, 1990.

Weima, Jeffrey A. D. *1–2 Thessalonians*. BECNT. Grand Rapids: Baker, 2014.

———. "'Peace and Security' (1 Thess 5.3): Prophetic Warning or Political Propaganda." *NTS* 58 (2012): 331–59.

White, Joel. "Anti-imperial Subtexts in Paul: An Attempt at Building a Firmer Foundation." *Bib* 90 (2009): 305–33.

———. *Die Erstlingsgabe im Neuen Testament*. TANZ 45. Tübingen: Francke, 2007.

———. "Identifying Intertextual Exegesis in Paul. Methodological Considerations and a Test Case (1 Corinthians 6:5)." Pages 167–88 in *The Crucified Apostle: Essays on Peter and Paul*. Edited by Todd A. Wilson and Paul R. House. WUNT 2/450. Tübingen: Mohr Siebeck, 2017.

———. "N. T. Wright's Narrative Approach." Pages 181–204 in *God and the Faithfulness of Paul: A Critical Examination of the Pauline Theology of N. T. Wright*. Edited by Christoph Heilig, J. Thomas Hewitt, and Michael F. Bird. WUNT 2/413. Tübingen: Mohr Siebeck, 2016.

———. "'Peace and Security' (1 Thess 5.3): Is It Really a Roman Slogan?" *NTS* 59 (2013): 382–95.

———. "'Peace' and 'Security' (1 Thess 5.3): Roman Ideology and Greek Aspiration." *NTS* 60 (2014): 499–510.

Wiefel, Wilfred. "Die Hauptrichtung des Wandels im eschatologischen Denken des Paulus." *TLZ* (1974): 65–81.

Wright, N. T. *Paul and the Faithfulness of God*. COQG 4. Minneapolis: Fortress, 2013.

———. *The Resurrection of the Son of God*. COQG 3. Minneapolis: Fortress, 2003.

Infants, Orphans, Children, and Siblings: Strengthening the Familial Bonds of the *Ekklēsia* of the Thessalonians in God the Father and the Lord Jesus Christ

Rosemary Canavan

Introduction

From the beginning of the first letter to the Thessalonians, it is clear that Paul and his coworkers are addressing a specific community of people in a particular place and within the boundary of their common relationship to God and Jesus Christ. The focus in this essay is on illuminating the use of familial imagery, not only to define the community identity in the *ekklēsia* but also to reestablish the aesthetic and emotive depth of these familial relationships by rebuilding the community in wisdom. The framework for this study is undergirded with the understanding of the "wisdom rhetorolect" or the religious wisdom texture, defined as

> discourse that interprets the visible world by blending human experiences of geophysical, social, cultural and institutional human experiences with beliefs about God especially through parental and familial nurturing and caring modes of understanding. Wisdom is about doing good in the world, living faithfully, fruitfully and ethically. Its special rhetorical effect is to conceptualise the function of spaces, places, and people through practices characteristic of households and other teaching-learning environments.[1]

---

1. See the glossary in Roy R. Jeal, *Exploring Philemon: Freedom, Brotherhood and Partnership in the New Society* (Atlanta: SBL Press, 2015), xxviii.

The family portrait is constructed initially with God as Father (1 Thess 1:1, 3; 3:11, 13) and the Lord Jesus Christ as Son (1:10). What Paul and his companions are most concerned about are the familial bonds between them and the community members that hold them in the family portrait of their identity in God the Father and the Lord Jesus Christ.[2] This study will briefly look at God as Father and Jesus as Son and then move to the familial indicators that are the main focus of this essay: first "brothers and sisters" (ἀδελφοί) and then four images that are all introduced in the second chapter:

- 2:7a, infants (νήπιοι)
- 2:7b, wet nurse with her own children (τροφὸς θάλπῃ τὰ ἑαυτῆς τέκνα)
- 2:11, father with his own children (πατὴρ τέκνα ἑαυτοῦ)
- 2:17, orphans (ἀπορθανίζω, ἀπορφανισθέντες, participle and *hapax legomena*—used to refer to children orphaned from parents, or parents from children)

The text will be progressively worked through to illuminate these images. But before moving to this analysis, I will touch on the family in action in relation to Timothy's visit in chapter 3 and add a note on a final familial term, son (υἱός), twice mentioned in the plural.

The Family Portrait

The letter opens with the names of those addressing the community. This letter, carried, delivered, and then read in Thessaloniki, visually alerts the receivers to people they know: to Paul, Silvanus, and Timothy, who have previously been among them. They are now present again in the voice of the person reading the letter. As the names are uttered, so do the pictures of them rise in the minds of the hearers. Immediately they are transported to the prophetic words and deeds that called them to be the *ekklēsia* (community assembly) of

---

2. Pieter de Villiers affirms the use of familial terms by stating "He [Paul] opens the letter with a reference to God as Father, importing at this seminal point in his text benevolent familial terminology." See de Villiers, "Safe in the Family of God: Soteriological Perspectives in 1 Thessalonians," in *Salvation in the New Testament: Perspectives on Soteriology*, ed. Jan G. van der Watt (Atlanta: Society of Biblical Literature, 2005), 305–30.

the Thessalonians in God and the Lord Jesus Christ. Here I am engaging with the relationship between the text and the image, the rhetography as described by Vernon Robbins, "the graphic images people create in their minds as a result of the visual texture of a text."[3] Rhetography aligns easily with the use of ἔκφρασις known in the ancient progymnastic (*progymnasmata*) rhetoric exercises as vivid language that enlivens the imagination and which is defined as "descriptive language, bringing what is portrayed clearly [ἐναργος] before the sight."[4] This expressively graphic speech, ἔκφρασις, is only made clear through ἐναργεία, bringing before the eyes.[5]

The naming of this community locates them in a physical place and time, with a certain belonging affirmed with the particularity of "in God the Father and the Lord Jesus Christ" (1:1).[6] In both the Codex Sinaiticus and Codex Alexandrinus there is a repeat of this phrase following "Grace to you and peace," inserting "from God the/our Father and the Lord Jesus Christ." This formula of relationship is strengthened in 1:3: "remembering before our God and Father your work of faith and labor of love and steadfastness of hope in our Lord Jesus Christ." In 3:11 the relationship is again invoked with Timothy's return from Thessaloniki with good news of their faith: "Now may our God and Father himself and our Lord Jesus [Christ] direct our way to you."[7] In all of the repeats (1:2; 3:11, 13) this relationship is personalized with and qualified by "our."

From this opening the familial language of God as father sets the kinship of the members, a fictive kinship that crosses boundaries and allows freedom of relationships otherwise constrained by proprietaries of ethnicity, gender, and economic status. In these opening lines there is

---

3. Vernon Robbins, "Rhetography: A New Way of Seeing the Familiar Text," in *Words Well Spoken: George Kennedy's Rhetoric of the New Testament*, ed. C. Clifton Black and Duane F. Watson (Waco, TX: Baylor University Press, 2006), 368.

4. Aelius Theon, an Alexandrian sophist believed to be writing in the first century CE, provides this definition. See Harry O. Maier, *Picturing Paul in Empire* (London: Bloomsbury T&T Clark, 2013), 29. For the *progymnasmata* Maier refers to Leonardus Spengel, *Rhetores Graeci* (Leipzig: Teuber, 1894).

5. Maier, *Picturing Paul in Empire*, 30. This was ably demonstrated by Annette Weissenreider in a conference paper: "Images to See, Images to Hear? On the Limitation of Visual Art and Language as Ekprasis in Revelation 12 and 17" (paper presented at Annual Meeting of the Society of Biblical Literature, Baltimore, 23 November 2013).

6. Unless otherwise noted, Scripture translations follow the NRSV.

7. Some manuscripts include "Christ," notably Codex Sinaiticus (fourth century) and Codex Boernerianus (ninth century).

no perceived difference between Paul, Silvanus, and Timothy other than order. Paul is mentioned first and could by this position be seen to hold the leadership or authority position. None are described in relation to each other. From the beginning their collective identity is focused on God as Father. Their relational connection comes in the next verses.

The "we" of Paul, Silvanus, and Timothy makes a collegial and familial impression as the expression of thanks to God is uttered. The thanksgiving describes how they maintain their relationship in God: mentioning them in prayer and constantly remembering their work of faith, labor of love, and steadfastness of hope in the Lord Jesus Christ (1:2–3). Remembering (μνημενεύω) and remembrance (μνεία) feature four times in this letter (1:2, 3; 2:9; 3:6). They are integral to belonging to the family of the *ekklēsia*, as it makes them and their work present to each other and to God even when apart.[8] The identity of "you" is personalized as Paul and his associates address them in verse 4 as "brothers and sisters" (ἀδελφοί), "beloved by God" (ἀγαπάω), and "chosen" (ἐκλαγή). This introduction to the picture of them as brothers and sisters (ἀδελφοί) affirms the familial relationship and qualifies it further. Naturally, if the three companions address the community as brothers and sisters, then they too are brothers to each other and to the community. This abiding, emotive sibling relationship, appearing once in the opening, will be included four times in chapter 2 (2:1, 9, 14, 17), once in chapter 3 (3:7), four times in chapter 4 (4:1, 9, 10, 13), and seven times in the closing chapter (5:1, 4, 12, 14, 25, 26, 27). This repetition accentuates the claim Paul and his coworkers make on their identity and familial relationship. It is a means of shoring up their collective identity.

The study of inscriptions attests to some associations using the terminology of "brothers" and other familial terms. One such example is an inscription from an association of masons, having joint shares in a tomb, from around Cilicia in the mid-first century CE: "If any brother [ἀδελφός] should wish to sell his share, the remaining brothers shall buy it. If the brothers [οἱ ἀδελφοί] do not wish to buy the share, then let them take the aforementioned cash, and let them (all) withdraw from the association" (IKilikiaBM 2.201).[9]

---

8. Burke lists many more instances but adds instances of "as you know" as remembrance. See Trevor J. Burke, *Family Matters: A Socio-historical Study of Kinship Metaphors in 1 Thessalonians* (London: T&T Clark International, 2003), 143.

9. For this and further examples see Richard S. Ascough, *Paul's Macedonian Associations: The Social Context of Philippians and 1 Thessalonians*, WUNT 2/161 (Tübingen: Mohr Siebeck, 2003), 76–77, 90, 98.

More particularly, there are forty-four inscriptions, mostly funerary, from the imperial era identified in Thessaloniki, and these ratify thirty-nine associations.[10] Broadly, these can be classified into four categories—religious, professional, household, and associations of arena and theater devotees—but they cannot be considered mutually exclusive.[11] Of note is that the number of active associations was higher in Thessaloniki than in the surrounding cities of Macedonia and that the majority of them, twenty-four, were religious associations.[12] These may have offered a stronger backdrop for the context of the familial *ekklēsia*. Familial titles occurring in the associations include πατὴρ σπηλαίου ("father of the grotto": could also be rendered as "grave") and μήτηρ σπείρας ("guild mother").[13] In the inscriptions from the first century CE there are references to μήτηρ ("mother"), θυγατρός ("daughter"), πατρός ("father"), and υἱός ("son"), and these appear to be used in the usual way of identifying the relationship between members.[14] Indeed, the Thessalonians, particularly those from the middle and lower levels of society, sought membership in groups with which they had some solidarity by belief or profession so that they might as a collective identity be better able to participate as active citizens in the polis.[15] This contextual framework is helpful in understanding Paul's focus on the *ekklēsia* and familial bonds, but it is not the whole story. Paul is weaving the lineage of a new family.

As the words of the letter, read audibly, now refer to "our gospel" (εὐαγγέλιον) (1:5), the hearers can recall Paul, Silvanus, and Timothy among them and the power of their words as they delivered the good news

---

10. Pantelis M. Nigdelis, "Voluntary Associations in Roman Thessalonike: In Search of Identity and Supporting Cosmopolitan Society," in *From Roman to Early Christian Thessalonike: Studies in Religion and Archaeology*, ed. Laura Nasrallah, Charalambos Bakirtzis, and Steven J. Friesen, HTS 64 (Cambridge: Harvard University Press, 2010), 13–48.

11. Nigdelis, "Voluntary Associations," 14.

12. Nigdelis, "Voluntary Associations," 14, 20.

13. Nigdelis, "Voluntary Associations," 27, 29.

14. The first-century CE inscriptions: *IG* 10.2.1.16, 58, 68, 69, 70, 259, 679; Emmanuel Voutiras, "Berufs und Kultverein: Ein δοῦμος in Thessalonike," *ZPE* 90 (1992): 87; SEG 42.625. Also listed in the appendix to Nigdelis, "Voluntary Associations," 36–43.

15. Nigdelis concludes this function of membership of associations as integral to reintegration into the life of the city as an active citizen ("Voluntary Associations," 35–36).

that belongs to all of them.[16] Here the first instance of the phrase "as you know" (καθὼς οἴδατε) occurs, and it will be repeated eight times (2:1, 2, 5, 11; 3:3, 4; 4:2; 5:2), inviting the hearers to visualize their common experience and in doing so enjoin them in learning or relearning how they have come together.[17] Skillfully drawing on that memory, Paul and his coauthors remind the hearers that what they heard came to them "not in word only, but also in power and in the Holy Spirit and with full conviction" (1:5). The amplification of the authority of the gospel they received is delivered with the inclusion of the Holy Spirit, weaving God's action into the formation of this community and assuring them of their belief and confidence in the deliverers of the gospel. In 2:2, 8–9 this gospel is referred to as the "gospel of God," and in 2:4 the authors are "approved by God to be entrusted with the gospel." The good news, the gospel, comes from God and is for God's family, so that the members can own it as their gospel and proclaim and share it broadly, as will be affirmed in 1:6–7. In 3:2 Timothy is described as "our brother and co-worker of God in proclaiming the gospel of Christ."

With the power of the good news and the image of the proclaimers brought to mind, the we-you conversation introduces imitation as a means and demonstration of their learning and acceptance of the truth. It is a form of learning that sits easily within a family, where childhood imitation of parents and other family members is a prime mode of learning. Such an imitation of those of wisdom engages a discourse as described by the wisdom rhetorical dialect, encouraging the *ekklēsia* as a place of learning and wisdom. This will be affirmed in 4:1, where Paul exhorts the community thus: "Finally, brothers and sisters, we ask and urge you in the Lord Jesus that, as you received [παραλαμβάνω] from us how you ought to live/walk [περιπατέω] and to please God (as, in fact, you are doing), you should do so more and more." The sense of receiving how to live indicates some learning on behalf of the receivers. In 4:2 the members are reminded that what they received were instructions (παραγγελία) affirming the learning process. Further, in 4:9–10 Paul and his companions assert that there is no need to write to the brothers and sisters of how to love one another because they were taught by God (θεοδίδακτος). The compound adjective "taught by God" (θεοδίδακτος) makes its first and only appearance in the

---

16. NRSV translates this as "our message." I prefer "gospel" here, as the alternative lessens the impact of the rhetoric used here to persuade the Thessalonians and diminishes the imagery that is possible when recalling the experience of the hearers.

17. In some instances οἴδατε is used alone, but the effect is the same.

New Testament here.[18] The creativity of Paul in coining this word appears to follow a practice in Koine Greek of creating one compound word out of two as they appear in LXX, so here διδακτοὺς θεοῦ in Isa 54:13 (LXX) becomes Θεοδίδακτοι (1 Thess 4:9).[19] This learning is framed in a setting where the children have been taught to love by their father, who is God. This love they have shown throughout Macedonia.

Paul, Silvanus, and Timothy are inferred as imitators of Jesus. The Thessalonian believers are imitators of the three proclaimers and of "the Lord" (1 Thess 1:6). Jesus is depicted with authority and as prophetic. The affirmation of the Thessalonian believers is that they too have become prophetic, inspired by the Holy Spirit, in receiving the word with joy and becoming an example to all the believers in Macedonia and Achaia (1:7). Their example has been broadcast even further as the authors have made known their experience of the Thessalonian believers. Their practice of wisdom reveals their doing good in the world and blends this with their speech and action in the world as prophets.[20] Their imitation of their leaders and of the Lord is portrayed by their prophetic speech and action. This emanates from their lived experience in the *ekklēsia* as brothers and sisters.[21]

In 1:9–10 the narrative of their coming to belief names Jesus as "Son from heaven." This is the only instance where Jesus is referred to as "son" (υἱός) in the letter and further affirms the familial connections: the "you" are brothers and sisters of Paul, Silvanus, and Timothy, remembered to

---

18. For Θεοδίδακτοι as a Pauline neologism, see Stephen E. Witmer, "Θεοδίδακτοι in 1 Thessalonians 4:9: A Pauline Neologism," *NTS* 52 (2006): 239–50. This term appears at least seventy-seven times in the first five centuries, yet none of these is prior to 1 Thess 4:9 according to Witmer's online search of *Thesaurus Linguae Graecae* in 2004.

19. See Witmer, "Θεοδίδακτοι in 1 Thessalonians 4:9."

20. Vernon Robbins, *The Invention of Christian Discourse* (Blandford Forum: Deo, 2009), 1:xxiv.

21. In sociorhetorical terms this is described as prophetic belief, the goal of which is to "create a governed realm on earth where God's righteousness is enacted among all of God's people in the realm with the aid of God's specially transmitted word in the form of prophetic action and speech (thirdspace)." This is included in the definitions Vernon Robbins publishes in "P–Q," in Dictionary of Socio-rhetorical Terms, http://tinyurl.com/sBl7103i. See also Robbins, *Exploring the Texture of the Texts: A Guide to Socio-rhetorical Criticism* (Valley Forge, PA: Trinity Press International, 1996); Robbins, *Invention of Christian Discourse* 1:1.

"our God and Father" (1:3) and awaiting "his Son from heaven, whom he raised from the dead—Jesus" (1:10). The image of God's Son from heaven links the believers in the earthly realm with God's cosmos through the apocalyptic redemption possible through Jesus, the Son.[22] This God, who is Father to the *ekklēsia*, is also the initiator of salvation through Jesus, the Son, thus linking both familial and salvific terms.[23] In 1:10b Jesus is further defined as the one "who rescues us from the wrath that is coming." This is definitively affirmed in the closing chapter: "For God has destined us not for wrath but for obtaining salvation through our Lord Jesus Christ, who died for us" (5:9–10).

With 1 Thess 1 having set the scene, chapter 2 begins with Paul recalling their coming (εἴσοδος) or arrival into Thessaloniki. He cites the phrase "you know" (οἴδατε), continuing in the pattern of a familiarity between "you" and "us" and the common knowledge of their time together. Did he arrive with Silvanus and Timothy in the style of an orator?[24] Taking them back in memory and visual thought to their arrival in Thessaloniki, Paul implores that their coming was "not in vain" (οὐ κενή), resting his argument on the characteristics of that coming (εἴσοδος).[25] Reiterating "as you know" (καθὼς οἴδατε), Paul enjoins the Thessalonian believers to picture their acting despite their ill-treatment (ὑβρίζω) at Philippi and in the face of much opposition (ἐν πολλῷ ἀγῶνι) to speak boldly and proclaim the gospel of God (2:2). His use of speaking boldly (παρρησιάζομαι) begins his case for his original preaching in Thessaloniki consisting of frank and bold speech like that of a philosopher, thereby warding off any accusation that he was a flatterer using words of flattery (κολακεία, 2:5).[26] Itinerant philosophers had a need to distinguish themselves from charlatans and would

---

22. See also "Apocalytic Rhetorolect," in Robbins, *Invention of Christian Discourse* 1:xxi–ii.

23. De Villiers, "Safe in the Family," 305–30.

24. Bruce Winter recounts examples from Dio Chrysostom and Philostratus to secure that the entry was a planned event with invitations and hopeful of successful outcomes, especially of wealth and fame. For further details, see Winter, " Entries and Ethics of the Orators and Paul," *TynBul* 44 (1993): 57–60.

25. Donfried recommends "has not been found empty" as translation of οὐ κενή, connecting this to the concern regarding the character of Paul's labors in Thessaloniki. See Karl P. Donfried and Johannes Beutler, eds., *The Thessalonians Debate: Methodological Discord or Methodological Synthesis?* (Grand Rapids: Eerdmans, 2000), 47.

26. Dio Chrysostom (40–ca. 115 CE) contrasts flattery (κολακεία) with boldness of speech (παρρησιά; *4 Regn.* 4.15).

expect to arouse suspicion when entering a new location.²⁷ Abraham Malherbe makes a case for a similarity between Dio Chrysostom (ca. 40–115 CE), an orator who became a Cynic philosopher, and Paul, demonstrating the verbal and formal parallels between them.²⁸ These parallels include the terms "vain" (κενός), "ill-treatment" (ὑβρίζω), "struggle" or "opposition" (ἀγῶν), and "bold" speech (παρρησία).²⁹ These parallels do not mean that Chrysostom and Paul had the same meaning for them but rather open a way for understanding Paul, among other philosophers, making the distinction of the authenticity of their message.

Other allusions of such speech are evident in the Greek tragedy *Hippolytus* of Euripides (428 BCE), where the freedom of speech in Athens is idealized for Phaedra's husband and children: "that they may live in glorious Athens as free men, free of speech and flourishing" (*Hipp.* 422).³⁰

Isocrates speaks of faithful friends who should be given freedom of speech, having the good judgment to recognize artful flattery and true criticism: "Grant freedom of speech to those who have good judgement, in order that when you are in doubt you may have friends who will help you to decide. Distinguish between those who artfully flatter and those who loyally serve you" (*Nic.* [*Or.* 3] 2.28).³¹

This mention of their bold and frank speech (παρρησιά) visualizes them not only in their integrity but also exhibiting the qualities of the democracy of the city-state and aligning the *ekklēsia* family structure with the household (οἰκία) as the building block of the polis (Aristotle, *Pol.* 1253b). The synergy with the associations of Thessaloniki must be recalled here, where membership of associations gave those of the middle and lower strata the means to be active citizens.

Their integrity, fidelity, and gentleness were accompanied by their consistent affection and labor for the Thessalonians. Paul emphasizes the negative οὐ in order to reflect the fullness of their presence with the

---

27. On the basis of the situations described by Lucian of Samosata and other such writers, Abraham J. Malherbe proposes that "transient public speakers" would be suspect and that a "genuine philosophic missionary" would want to distance himself from such suspicion and this type of operator. See Malherbe, "'Gentle as a Nurse': The Cynic Background to 1 Thess II," *NovT* 12 (1970): 203–17.

28. Malherbe, "Gentle as a Nurse."

29. For the full explanation of the parallels, see Malherbe, "Gentle as a Nurse."

30. Trans. James Diggle, *Euripidis fabulae* (Oxford: Clarendon, 1984), 207–71.

31. Trans. Émile Brémond and Georges Mathieu, *Isocrate: Discours* (Paris: Les Belles Lettres, 1938), 97–111.

Thessalonians in what follows and then prepares them for words of encouragement.³² Their coming, indeed, was not like an orator building his own reputation and wealth but rather as the "kind of persons we proved to be among you for your sake" (1 Thess 1:5). In this manner Paul and his companions reframe the recalled memory, reestablishing the integrity of their relationships from what could have been distorted images of them and their visit.

Paul draws the audience into a visually drenched rhetorical argument. He builds familial and trusted ground, reasserting himself and his companions as innocent as infants and caring for them like a wet nurse (τροφός) with her own children.³³ Assuming that 1 Thessalonians is the earliest of Paul's writings, it is apparent that he finds the metaphor of a woman, in this case a wet nurse, most persuasive to his argument. In his later writings he continues to envision himself as a woman in labor (Gal 4:9) and again as wet nurse (1 Cor 3:1–2). An established figure in Greece and beyond is Kourotrophos, attested since circa the seventh century BCE and considered a manifestation of the mother and/or nursing principles.³⁴ Kourotrophos is a "multi-faced deity," either as a mother in the cult of Demeter, or nurturing children as Ge, or as a virgin rearing children, or as inspiring young men as Athena.³⁵ From the Hellenistic period there is an ephebic decree (79/78 BCE) that mentions an exit ceremony by the young people on the Acropolis in honor of Athena Polias, Kourotrophos, and Pandrose.³⁶ Standing *kourotrophoi* from the first century BCE located in the eastern cemetery of Thessaloniki (see fig. 5.1) indicate the association of this deity with the city prior to Paul's arrival. In the Roman period

---

32. Donfried, drawing on Stegemann, emphasizes that the point here is to emphasize the negative οὐ so as to show how full was their presence and to incorporate the hearers into the memory of their time together. See Donfried and Beutler, *Thessalonians Debate*, 47–48; Wolfgang Stegemann, "Anlass und Hintergrund der Abfassung von 1 Th 2, 1–12," in *Theologische Brosamen für Lothar Steiger*, ed. Gerhard Freund and Ekkehard Stegemann, DBAT (Heidelberg: Esprint, 1985), 397–416.

33. See also Frederick W. Weidmann, *Philippians, First and Second Thessalonians, and Philemon* (Louisville: Westminster John Knox, 2013), 116.

34. Theodora Hadzisteiou Price, *Kourotrophos: Cults and Representations of the Greek Nursing Deities* (Leiden: Brill, 1978), 2. See also Vinciane Pirenne-Delforge, "Qui est la Kourotrophos athénienne?," in *Naissance et petite enfance dans l'Antiquité*, ed. Véronique Dasen (Fribourg: Academic Press, 2004), 171–85.

35. Price, *Kourotrophos*, 2.

36. Pirenne-Delforge, "Qui est la Kourotrophos," 181.

Fig. 5.1a and b: Standing *kourotrophoi*, first century BCE, Thessaloniki eastern cemetery. Invoice No. MΘ 4810 (left) MΘ 4811 (right). The rights to these artefacts belong to the Greek State and the Ministry of Culture and Sports (Law 4858/2021). The artefacts are under the jurisdiction of the Archaeological Museum of Thessaloniki, Hellenic Ministry of Culture & Sports–Hellenic Organization of Cultural Resources Development.

Fig. 5.2. Kourotrophos, second half of fifth century BCE, Cypriot, limestone (12.7 x 10.5 x 7.6 cm). Accession number: 74.51.2512. Metropolitan Museum of Art, Cesnola Collection, purchased by subscription, 1874–1876.

all the documents date from the second century CE but continue to attest Kourotrophos with Demeter, Ge, and Athena in the sacrificial calendars.[37] The more private tribal and clan worship, along with the more intimate household rites, was fostered in the Greek religion.[38]

The nurse is also depicted on the hydria or water jug (fig. 5.3) in the image of a perfect family. Dated to 440–430 BCE, it reveals a domestic scene of a young father and mother with their baby boy being handed to the nurse. There is a loom in the background, attesting to the virtues of the woman as a good wife. This image prevails on grave reliefs, and this jug has a hole in the base, which would have rendered it useless for service in a household and more suitable for a tomb. The establishment of these early images lay the foundations for the metaphor used by Paul in a culture well attuned to family structure and the care of a nurse.

Fig. 5.3. Hydria (440–430 BCE) from Attica. Object number 1960.342 (34.6 x 24.6 cm; diameter with handles, 30.2 cm). Harvard Art Museums / Arthur M. Sackler Museum, bequest of David M. Robinson. Used with permission.

Among the credentials for a wet nurse is a cultural one that the wet nurse ought to be Greek or Greek-speaking.[39] This credential is connected to the need for the *paideia* process of education to begin from the earliest

---

37. Pirenne-Delforge, "Qui est la Kourotrophos," 184.

38. Price, *Kourotrophos*, 1.

39. Annette Bourland Huizenga, "On Choosing a Wet-Nurse: Physical, Cultural and Moral Credentials," in *The History of Religions School Today*, ed. Thomas R.

possible moment. Quintilian declares, "First of all, make sure the nurses speak properly.... These are the first people the child will hear, theirs are the words he will try to copy and pronounce.... So do not let the child become accustomed, even in infancy, to a type of speech which he will have to unlearn" (*Inst.* 1.5.4–5 [Russell]). So in describing himself as a wet nurse, Paul not only alludes to care and nourishment of the members of the *ekklēsia* but also to his engagement in the education of the family from the beginning.

This reading, which includes a wet nurse and infants, relies on a reconfiguration of the text from the way that it appears in the NRSV: "though we might have made demands as apostles of Christ. But we were gentle among you, like a nurse tenderly caring for her own children" (1 Thess 2:7).[40] Even though manuscript evidence supports "infants" (νήπιοι) as the more likely reading, "gentle" (ἤπιοι) has been adopted by commentaries in the English translation for ease of reading.[41] The rearrangement of the text allows the images of infants, wet nurse, and children to hold their meaning and amplify the familial ties that Paul is lavishly exploiting to make his point. As infants they are not deceptive but, in sharp contrast, display their innocence and vulnerability. With the introduction of God as witness (2:5b) there is a sense of judgment, a court scene, as Paul defends himself within this realm, his family community. He and his companions had not come demanding honor (2:6) or asserting their authority as apostles of Christ (2:7) but rather as family members in their most humble state, infants.

5a Οὔτε γάρ ποτε ἐν λόγῳ κολακείας ἐγενήθημεν,	For we never came with a word of flattery—
καθὼς οἴδατε,	as you know—
5b οὔτε ἐν προφάσει πλεονεξίας,	nor with a motive of greed—
θεὸς μάρτυς,	God is our witness—

Blanton IV, Robert Matthew Calhoun, and Clare K. Rothschild, ENTRAMT 340 (Tübingen: Mohr Siebeck, 2014), 241–52.

40. This configuration is drawn from Jeffrey Weima and Jennifer McNeel. See Weima, "'But We Became Infants among You': The Case for ΝΗΠΙΟΙ in I Thess. 2.7," *NTS* 46 (2000): 547–64; McNeel, *Paul as Infant and Nursing Mother: Metaphor, Rhetoric, and Identity in 1 Thessalonians 2:5–8*, ECL 12 (Atlanta: SBL Press, 2014), 43–47. The translation is mine.

41. McNeel, *Paul as Infant*, 35.

6 οὔτε ζητοῦντες ἐξ ἀνθρώπων δόξαν οὔτε ἀφ' ὑμῶν οὔτε ἀπ' ἄλλων,	nor were we demanding honor from people, neither from you nor from others—
7a δυνάμενοι ἐν βάρει εἶναι ὡς Χριστοῦ ἀπόστολοι.	even though we could have insisted on our importance as apostles of Christ—
7b ἀλλὰ ἐγενήθημεν νήπιοι ἐν μέσῳ ὑμῶν.	but we became infants among you.
7c Ὡς ἐὰν τροφὸς θάλπῃ τὰ ἑαυτῆς τέκνα,	Like a wet nurse caring for her own children,
8 οὕτως ὁμειρόμενοι ὑμῶν εὐδοκοῦμεν μεταδοῦναι ὑμῖν οὐ μόνον τὸ εὐαγγέλιον τοῦ θεοῦ ἀλλὰ καὶ τὰς ἑαυτῶν ψυχάς, διότι ἀγαπητοὶ ἡμῖν ἐγενήθητε.	so deeply do we care for you that we are determined to share with you not only the gospel of God but also our own selves, because you have become very dear to us.

Beginning the sentence with the phrase "like a wet nurse caring for her own children" exhibits a hyperbole of persuasion. Taking the part of a wet nurse with her own children exemplifies an intensity of desire to nourish and nurture, as well as to further affirm the relationship as true family, but not as a slave pressed into service, as may have been the case with a wet nurse with the children of others.[42] Even more, it exemplifies one who has been separated from the ones they would long to nourish. The participle ὁμειρόμενοι (1 Thess 2:8), not found anywhere else in the New Testament, does appear in grave inscriptions, often in situations of parents grieving for a lost child.[43] ὁμείρομαι ("to long for," "desire earnestly") also occurs in LXX Job 3:21, but in the sense of longing for death. More consistent with Paul's use is the example of a Lycaonian sepulchral inscription (*CIG*

---

42. The relationship of wet nurses with the children they nourished was often significant, especially when the wet nurse became the nanny and servant as the child grew. Epitaphs to wet nurses attest this. Here Paul takes it to another level. The distinction of nourishing is picked up in the reception of this text by Bede the Venerable: "[Paul] did not say 'mother.' Mothers are sometimes either more indulgent or less loving toward their children.... He called himself a nurse because he was nourishing them, and he called them his own children because he bore them." See Bede the Venerable, *Excerpts from the Works of St Augustine on the Letters of the Blessed Apostle Paul*, trans. David Hurst (Kalamazoo: Cistercian Publications, 1999); see also Anthony C. Thistleton, *1 and 2 Thessalonians through the Centuries* (Oxford: Wiley-Blackwell, 2011), 5.

43. Trevor J. Burke, "Pauline Paternity in 1 Thessalonians," *TynBul* 51 (2000): 59–80.

3.4000, fourth century CE) that describes grieving parents longing for their son, ὁμείρομενοι περὶ παιδός.[44] Furthermore, this word is considered borrowed from the language of the nursery.[45] The longing and desire of Paul and his companions to nurture, then, is also linked to the depth of affection indicated by a grieving parent. This is further affirmed in 1 Thess 2:17 with the expression "orphans," separated from them not by death but still with the sense of bereavement. Later, in 4:13, the issue of those who have died will be addressed, and Paul and his companions express that they would wish to spare them from such grief.

Continuing with the common memory of the Thessalonians as brothers and sisters, Paul remembers that "we worked night and day" (2:9), reiterating their good intentions and pulling their weight in the community, all for the cause of the gospel of God. Their labor among the Thessalonians will be recalled again in 5:12, with urging to keep this image of them. Again Paul is justifying his and his coworkers' integrity while at the same time holding before them the space of their lived reality together, where they can see themselves as witnesses, along with God. Paul and his companions describe their actions "like a father with his own children" (2:11), drawing a keen line to the sincerity of their relationships and thus their interdependent identity. In his exhortation to the Thessalonian believers in 2:12, Paul employs three participles ("urging," "encouraging," "pleading") that qualify how he conducts his paternity. In so doing, Paul sympathetically enables his converts to understand better the nature of their discipleship in Christ, which was taught and modeled by the apostle amid his own afflictions and trials (1:6–7, 2:1–2, 3:4, 4:1–2).[46] In this manner, Paul acts to resocialize the believers to their new way of life, similar to the way that a father instructed his children into the social constructs of life in the Greco-Roman world.

The elasticity of these metaphors allows Paul to be infant (2:7a), brother (2:1), mother (2:7b), father (2:11), and later orphan ("having been made orphan," 2:17) in this community and to redefine the family

---

44. MM, 447.

45. A further note on the entry ὁμειρόμενοι states: "The illustration of 1 Thess is peculiarly apt, if with Wohlenberg (in Zahn's *Kommentar ad 1*), we regard ὁμειρόμενοι there as a term of endearment ('ein edles Kosewort') borrowed from the language of the nursery" (MM, 447).

46. Charles A. Wanamaker, "'Like a Father Treats His Own Children': Paul and the Conversion of the Thessalonians," *JTSA* 92 (1995): 46–55; see also Burke, "Pauline Paternity in 1 Thessalonians," 70.

in God and the Lord Jesus Christ. In describing himself as being made orphan, Paul also invokes the Thessalonians as "brothers and sisters" (ἀδελφοί). The combination increases the force of his argument: "But we, brothers and sisters, having been orphaned from you for a short while, in person not by heart, more abundantly we hastened with much desire to see you face to face" (2:17). In using the participle and *hapax legomenon* ἀπορφανισθέντες to describe himself and his companions as "having been orphaned," Paul could be turning the tables on his previous metaphors of being the parent. He could be placing those whom he addresses as brothers and sisters in the position of parents, but the opposite seems clearer. In line with his previous metaphors, he and his companions are like parents orphaned from their children: cut off, longing to be in contact, grieving the loss of their presence.

The Family in Action: Timothy

Chapter 3 evidences the two-way relationship of these familial bonds as Paul sends Timothy to strengthen and encourage the community (1 Thess 3:2) and to hear news of the resilience of their faith (3:5). Unlike the opening lines of the letter where none of those named were further identified, Timothy is now described as τὸν ἀδελφὸν ἡμῶν καὶ συνεργὸν τοῦ θεοῦ ἐν τῷ εὐαγγελίῳ τοῦ Χριστοῦ, "our brother and co-worker of God in the gospel of Christ" (1 Thess 3:2). As "our brother" he is brother of Paul and Silvanus and also of the Thessalonians. Timothy is one of the family, and his status is cemented further as "coworker of God in the gospel of Christ." He is able to come in the place of Paul.

The resulting report from Timothy reveals a mutual longing to see each other (3:6) and a testimony that their faith also strengthens Paul and his companions (3:7). In 3:7 Paul addresses the community as brothers and sisters, emphasizing the mutuality of relationship as siblings, strengthening each other in faith, whether physically present to each other or apart.

Sons (υἱοί)

The introduction of sons (υἱοί) twice in one verse at 5:5, "for you are all children [υἱοί] of light and children [υἱοί] of the day; we are not of the night or of darkness," is interesting. There is the possibility of translating sons (υἱοί) inclusively as sons and daughters/children, as with brothers (ἀδελφοί), which is often rendered as "brothers and sisters." Yet in the family portrait arranged in the opening chapters there is no mention of the believers as sons or children of God. There is mention of children (τέκνα) in 2:7 in relation to Paul and his companions being like a wet nurse and her own children, and again in 2:11, where the same companions are likened to a father with his own children. Scholars have approached this aspect of Paul's sonship language here from a variety of differing perspectives.

Richard Ascough makes the controversial proposal that "the Thessalonian Jesus-group was composed at its inception primarily of males" and that "a pre-existing workers' association turned en masse to worshipping Jesus."[47] While this suggestion is possible, it cannot be substantiated conclusively and thus must be relegated to the realm of speculation. By contrast, in mapping Paul's family language, Reider Aasgaard observes that precisely because believers are not explicitly called God's children, being called children (sons, υἱοί) is not necessarily identical with being children of God,[48] although this could be inferred.

Another perspective is that "son of," an adjectival genitive, is considered a Semitic idiom, with the result that "sons of light/darkness" simply means that the people are "worthy of" or "associated with" light/darkness.[49] The term "sons of light" is common in the Qumran scrolls describing the members of the community (1QS I, 9; II, 16; III, 13, 24, 25; 1QM I, 9–11), in contrast to the "sons of darkness," who are the outsiders (1QS III, 25–27; see also 1QM XV, 9).[50] Paul uses these images in conjunction with the "day of the Lord" and effects the eschatology of their belonging in the Lord.

In sum, considering that the language of "sons" here is brought from a patriarchal period as a metaphor, it is reasonable to conclude that it is used in an inclusive way as "children." This coheres with the broader social reality revealed in Paul's letters, where women are included in the greetings, have specific ministry roles, and are clearly part of the fictive family portrait of the *ekklēsia*.

---

47. Richard Ascough, "Of Memories and Meals: Greco-Roman Associations and the Early Jesus-Group in Thessalonike," in Nasrallah, Bakirtzis, and Friesen, *From Roman to Early Christian Thessalonike*, 49–72.

48. Reidar Aasgaard, *"My Beloved Brothers and Sisters!": Christian Siblingship in Paul* (London: T&T Clark International, 2004), 121.

49. C. F. D. Moule, *An Idiom Book of New Testament Greek* (Cambridge: Cambridge University Press, 1953), 174–75.

50. See Abraham J. Malherbe, *The Letters to the Thessalonians: A New Translation with Introduction and Commentary*, AB 32B (New York: Doubleday, 2000), 294–95.

Fig. 5.4a. Grave Relief of Lucius Cornelius Neon. First century BCE, Thessaloniki. Invoice No. MΘ 10773.

Fig. 5.4b. Grave stela of Publius Popillius Maximus. Invoice No. MΘ 11037. The rights to the depicted monuments are under the jurisdiction of the Archaeological Museum of Thessaloniki. © Archaeological Museum of Thessaloniki, Hellenic Ministry of Culture & Sports–Hellenic Organization of Cultural Resources. See also Despinis et al, *Catalogue of Sculpture*, 140 (58), 143 (61). Corresponding inventory numbers of Museum and Catalogue: Inv. No.11037=140 (58); Inv, No.10773=143 (61).

Visual Texture and Intertexture

The examination of the text brings forth imagery well known to the hearers. It echoes their lived reality in their own families and their experience in the *ekklēsia*. Images of families are well attested in inscriptions and on funerary monuments, portraying the intimacy of relationship and the eternal bonds. In a grave relief for Lucius Cornelius Neon (fig. 5.4a), the couple holds hands. The woman's other hand is free from the cover of her mantle, as is shown, with the forefinger and little finger extended in the characteristic gesture of *mano cornuta*, acting like an amulet to ward off evil, in this case trying to avert the disaster of her loss.

A stylistically similar but free-standing grave stela (fig. 5.4b) of a banquet scene was widespread in the Hellenistic world and persisted in Thessaloniki throughout the Hellenistic period and the Roman Empire.[51] The seated woman, the grieving widow, also has her left hand in the *mano cornuta* gesture. Her right hand, holding her mantle, reveals her face tilted in endearment toward her husband. She holds his gaze.

One of the issues that needed attention for the Thessalonian believers was that of those who have died. These were likely members of their new family in God, so there was a question of whether they were still members and what would happen to them. Concern for the dead and specifically funerary arrangements was common in voluntary associations, as we have seen earlier.[52] Here the concern for the dead is another teaching moment for Paul in the *ekklēsia*. He links salvific terms with familial ones and reassures the believers not only that God will bring all those who have fallen asleep (κοιμάομαι) to him through Jesus (4:14) but that they will have priority. In this way not even the power of death can ostracize them as members of the family: "to be saved then means to be safe even in the face of death."[53]

The environment of voluntary associations, particularly the preponderance of religious associations, provides further synergy with the fictive kinship of the family portrait, where members have a new way of relating to one another. They have come together in a shared belief engaging in

---

51. Thea Stefanidou-Tiveriou, "Social Status and Family Origin in the Sarcophagi of Thessalonikē," in Nasrallah, Bakirtzis, and Friesen, *From Roman to Early Christian Thessalonike*, 151–88.

52. Ascough, "Of Memories and Meals," 56.

53. De Villiers, "Safe in the Family," 318.

activities together, both socializing and evangelizing, and in a collective identity in God and his Son Jesus.

Care and protective bonds also exist associated with the gods in the Greco-Roman pantheon. These are evidenced in the majority of religious associations in Thessaloniki and via Kourotrophos and an expression of collective identity.[54]

Analysis

From the beginning Paul's argumentation features visualization of the members of the *ekklēsia* in relation to God the Father and the Lord Jesus Christ (1:1). This is imaged further in a family portrait identifying the brothers and sisters (ἀδελφοί) as beloved of God, chosen, and remembered in prayer. The remembering/remembrance (μνεία/μνημονεύω) of each other, their work and their time together, and the recalling often "as you know" (καθὼς οἴδατε) heightens the sense of belonging and identity. The intensity of the argumentation for the connections of Paul, Silvanus, and Timothy with the brothers and sisters in Thessaloniki deliberately calls on the heart of family bonds, formed in love and ongoing care and existing with God the Father and Jesus the Son. The aesthetic texture of the care of Paul and his companions as father, mother, infants, and wet nurse is amplified. Paul is affirming and reframing the relationships in the *ekklēsia* and between the leadership and the *ekklēsia*. The instructions on how to walk/live (περιπατέω) are received in the *ekklēsia*, where the family gathers.

The context of Paul's forming of the familial bonds in the *ekklēsia* is one where there is a strong sense of building collective identity, as was the case in the voluntary associations at Thessaloniki. The activities of the voluntary associations often included the necessity of providing a decent funeral for loved ones. However, association activities were not limited to the provision of burial: they also operated for the sociability of members and the building of collective identity.[55] Paul and his confreres are shown to be actively engaged in such collective identity building, especially through recalling their shared experiences together, creating a new family, and defining the topos of *ekklēsia*, where they gather, learn, and

---

54. Nigdelis, "Voluntary Associations," 33.
55. Nigdelis, "Voluntary Associations," 33.

walk together in faith and love. Just as the associations gave the Thessalonians a place and means to be active citizens of the polis, the *ekklēsia* enabled the believers to enact their new citizenship with God.

Conclusion

Understanding this letter as the first of the letters of Paul and his companions, it stakes a significant claim on what will be understood as the topos of *ekklēsia* from this point onward. This letter marks out by its visual images of familial relationships in "God the Father and the Lord Jesus Christ" and Jesus, "Son from heaven," the wisdom space for the community. The argument situates the members and their teachers in aesthetically emotive family relationships of love and care for each other, maintaining all in God's care and in relationship with Jesus, Son of God, who rescues them from the wrath that is to come. The emerging discourse for this community in Thessaloniki is grounded in the reconfiguration of familial relationships that bind them together and describe their identity in the *ekklēsia*. Their identity is configured in the realm of God on earth, their own conceptualization and visualization of their role in God's world, and their ongoing lived reality in their religious life as familial members of the *ekklēsia*. The developments in later letters will build on this foundation of family care for each other and being the beloved of God: infants, orphans, children, parents, siblings, and a family that finds its wisdom and learning space on earth in the *ekklēsia*.

Bibliography

Aasgaard, Reidar. *"My Beloved Brothers and Sisters!": Christian Siblingship in Paul*. London: T&T Clark International, 2004.

Ascough, Richard S. "Of Memories and Meals: Greco-Roman Associations and the Early Jesus-Group in Thessalonike." Pages 49–72 in *From Roman to Early Christian Thessalonike: Studies in Religion and Archaeology*. Edited by Laura Nasrallah, Charalambos Bakirtzis, and Steven J. Friesen. HTS 64. Cambridge: Harvard University Press, 2010.

———. *Paul's Macedonian Associations: The Social Context of Philippians and 1 Thessalonians*. WUNT 2/161. Tübingen: Mohr Siebeck, 2003.

Bede the Venerable. *Excerpts from the Works of St Augustine on the Letters of the Blessed Apostle Paul*. Translated by David Hurst. Kalamazoo: Cistercian Publications, 1999.

Brémond, Émile, and Georges Mathieu. *Isocrate: Discours*. Paris: Les Belles Lettres, 1938.
Burke, Trevor J. *Family Matters: A Socio-historical Study of Kinship Metaphors in 1 Thessalonians*. London: T&T Clark International, 2003.
———. "Pauline Paternity in 1 Thessalonians." *TynBul* 51 (2000): 59–80.
Diggle, James. *Euripidis fabulae*. Oxford: Clarendon, 1984.
Donfried, Karl P., and Johannes Beutler, eds. *The Thessalonians Debate: Methodological Discord or Methodological Synthesis?* Grand Rapids: Eerdmans, 2000.
Huizenga, Annette Bourla. "On Choosing a Wet-Nurse: Physical, Cultural and Moral Credentials." Pages 241–52 in *The History of Religions School Today*. Edited by Thomas R. Blanton IV, Robert Matthew Calhoun, and Clare K. Rothschild. ENTRAMT 340. Tübingen: Mohr Siebeck, 2014.
Jeal, Roy R. *Exploring Philemon: Freedom, Brotherhood and Partnership in the New Society*. Atlanta: SBL Press, 2015.
Maier, Harry O. *Picturing Paul in Empire*. London: Bloomsbury T&T Clark, 2013.
Malherbe, Abraham J. "'Gentle as a Nurse': The Cynic Background to 1 Thess II." *NovT* 12 (1970): 203–17.
———. *The Letters to the Thessalonians: A New Translation with Introduction and Commentary*. AB 32B. New York: Doubleday, 2000.
McNeel, Jennifer Houston. *Paul as Infant and Nursing Mother: Metaphor, Rhetoric, and Identity in 1 Thessalonians 2:5–8*. ECL 12. Atlanta: SBL Press, 2014.
Moule, C. F. D. *An Idiom Book of New Testament Greek*. Cambridge: Cambridge University Press, 1953.
Nigdelis, Pantelis M. "Voluntary Associations in Roman Thessalonike: In Search of Identity and Supporting Cosmopolitan Society." Pages 13–48 in *From Roman to Early Christian Thessalonike: Studies in Religion and Archaeology*. Edited by Laura Nasrallah, Charalambos Bakirtzis, and Steven J. Friesen. HTS 64. Cambridge: Harvard University Press, 2010.
Pirenne-Delforge, Vinciane. "Qui est la Kourotrophos athénienne?" Pages 171–85 in *Naissance et petite enfance dans l'Antiquité*. Edited by Véronique Dasen. Fribourg: Academic Press, 2004.
Price, Theodora Hadzisteiou. *Kourotrophos: Cults and Representations of the Greek Nursing Deities*. Leiden: Brill, 1978.
Robbins, Vernon. *Exploring the Texture of the Texts: A Guide to Socio-rhetorical Criticism*. Valley Forge, PA: Trinity Press International, 1996.

———. *The Invention of Christian Discourse.* Vol. 1. Blandford Forum: Deo, 2009.

———. "Rhetography: A New Way of Seeing the Familiar Text." Pages 367–92 in *Words Well Spoken: George Kennedy's Rhetoric of the New Testament.* Edited by C. Clifton Black and Duane F. Watson. Waco, TX: Baylor University Press, 2006.

———. "P–Q." Dictionary of Socio-Rhetorical Terms. http://tinyurl.com/sBl7103i.

Russell, Donald A., trans. *Quintilian: The Orator's Education.* LCL. Cambridge: Harvard University Press, 2001.

Spengel, Leonardus. *Rhetores Graeci.* Leipzig: Teuber, 1894.

Stefanidou-Tiveriou, Thea. "Social Status and Family Origin in the Sarcophagi of Thessalonikē." Pages 151–88 in *From Roman to Early Christian Thessalonike: Studies in Religion and Archaeology.* Edited by Laura Nasrallah, Charalambos Bakirtzis, and Steven J. Friesen. HTS 64. Cambridge: Harvard University Press, 2010.

Stegemann, Wolfgang. "Anlass und Hintergrund der Abfassung von 1 Th 2, 1–12." Pages 397–416 in *Theologische Brosamen für Lothar Steiger.* Edited by Gerhard Freund and Ekkehard Stegemann. DBAT. Heidelberg: Esprint, 1985.

Thistleton, Anthony C. *1 and 2 Thessalonians through the Centuries.* Oxford: Wiley-Blackwell, 2011.

Villiers, Pieter G. R. de. "Safe in the Family of God: Soteriological Perspectives in 1 Thessalonians." Pages 305–30 in *Salvation in the New Testament: Perspectives on Soteriology.* Edited by Jan G. van der Watt. Atlanta: Society of Biblical Literature, 2005.

Voutiras, Emmanuel. "Berufs und Kultverein: Ein δοῦμος in Thessalonike." *ZPE* 90 (1992): 87–96.

Wanamaker, Charles A. "'Like a Father Treats His Own Children': Paul and the Conversion of the Thessalonians." *JTSA* 92 (1995): 46–55.

Weidmann, Frederick W. *Philippians, First and Second Thessalonians, and Philemon.* Louisville: Westminster John Knox, 2013.

Weima, Jeffrey. "'But We Became Infants among You': The Case for ΝΗΠΙΟΙ in I Thess. 2.7." *NTS* 46 (2000): 547–64.

Weissenreider, Annette. "Images to See, Images to Hear? On the Limitation of Visual Art and Language as Ekprasis in Revelation 12 and 17." Paper presented at Annual Meeting of the Society of Biblical Literature, Baltimore, 2013.

Winter, Bruce W. "Entries and Ethics of the Orators and Paul." *TynBul* 44 (1993): 57–60.
Witmer, Stephen E. "Θεοδίδακτοι in 1 Thessalonians 4:9: A Pauline Neologism." *NTS* 52 (2006): 239–50.

The Emergence and Development of Christianity in Thessalonica in the Postapostolic Age (Second through Sixth Centuries CE): An Epigraphic and Archaeological Perspective

Julien M. Ogereau

1. Introduction

Nestled on a sheltered recess of the Thermaic gulf, the city of Thessalonica commanded a strategic position in central Macedonia and the northern Aegean world. Thanks to the Via Egnatia and the Via Axia crossing nearby, it had a direct access to the fertile Axios-Haliacmon delta and its historic cities (Berea, Pella, and Edessa), as well as to territories further west, north, and east-southeast, namely, Upper Macedonia, the Axios Valley, Mygdonia, and Chalcidice. First established as the capital of the short-lived diocese of Macedonia by Constantine I (who also constructed or expanded its harbor), it was made the capital of the prefecture of eastern Illyricum after the death of Theodosius I in 395 CE and served as the seat of the papal vicariate of eastern Illyricum (in principle, at least) from the beginning of the fifth century until the eighth century.[1] As a result, Thessalonica grew into the main economic and cultural

---

For a more detailed treatment of this topic, see Julien M. Ogereau, *Early Christianity in Macedonia*, AJEC (Leiden: Brill, forthcoming), ch. 5. Figures 6.1–3, 7–15 are © Ephorate of Antiquities of Thessaloniki City, Hellenic Ministry of Culture & Sports–Hellenic Organization of Cultural Resources Development. Figures 6.4–6 are © Hellenic Ministry of Culture and Sports. Museum of Byzantine Culture, Thessaloniki; photograph by M. Skiadaresis. Figures 6.17–19, 21 are © Hellenic Ministry of Culture and Sports. Museum of Byzantine Culture, Thessaloniki; photo by J. M. Ogereau.

1. Theodosius's destiny is bound to the city. After Valens's defeat against the Goths at Hadrianopolis in 378 CE, Theodosius retreated to Thessalonica, where he was bap-

center of the province in the Roman imperial era and eventually became a metropolis of great political and ecclesiastical significance in the Balkan region in late antiquity.[2]

According to Acts 17:1–9 and 1 Thessalonians, Christianity reached Thessalonica in the late 40s or the early 50s CE thanks to the apostle Paul and his associates, who established the first Christ-believing communities at Thessalonica, Philippi, and Berea.[3] However, it would take almost two centuries for Christianity to come out of obscurity (in the epigraphic sources at least) and more than three centuries to impose itself in the region. As with the rest of the province, little is known of the development

---

tized by its bishop, A(s)cholius, following a severe illness in 380 CE; proclaimed an edict in support of Nicene Christianity in February of the same year (Cod. theod. 16.1.2, reiterated in Cod. theod. 16.2.25 and Cod. justin. 1.1.1; see also Cod. theod. 16.5.14 of 388 CE); and had seven thousand rioters massacred in the hippodrome in retaliation against the assassination of the Gothic *magister militum* of Illyricum in 390 CE. This earned him a reprimand from Ambrose of Milan; see Theodoret, *Hist. eccl.* 5.17–18; Sozomen, *Hist. eccl.* 7.25.1–8; Ambrose, *Ep.* 51. Thessalonica lost the *praefectus praetorio* when it was relocated to Sirmium for a brief interlude from 438 to 440/1 CE (Nov. const. 11).

2. For an overview of the history and topography of Thessalonica in the Roman imperial and late antique eras, see Julien M. Ogereau, "Thessaloniki I. (Stadtgeschichte)," *RAC* 32 (forthcoming), and the vast secondary literature therein referenced. See also Eugen Oberhummer, "Thessalonike," PW 6.A.2:143–63; Fanoula Papazoglou, *Les villes de Macédoine à l'époque romaine*, BCHSup 16 (Athens: École française d'Athènes, 1988), 189–212; Jean-Michel Spieser, *Thessalonique et ses monuments du IVe au VIe siècle: Contribution à l'étude d'une ville paléochrétienne* (Paris: De Boccard, 1984); Laura Nasrallah, Charalambos Bakirtzis, and Steven J. Friesen, eds., *From Roman to Early Christian Thessalonike: Studies in Religion and Archaeology*, HTS 64 (Cambridge: Harvard University Press, 2010).

3. This is the generally accepted date range. See, e.g., Helmut Koester, *History and Literature of Early Christianity*, 2nd ed. (Berlin: de Gruyter, 2000), 118–19; Rainer Riesner, *Paul's Early Period: Chronology, Mission Strategy, Theology*, trans. Douglas Stott (Grand Rapids: Eerdmans, 1994), 364. For others, such as John Knox and M. Jack Suggs, the Macedonian mission must have taken place in the early 40s CE. See Knox, *Chapters in a Life of Paul* (New York: Abingdon, 1950), 81–88; Suggs, "Concerning the Date of Paul's Macedonian Ministry," *NovT* 4 (1960): 60–68. For a historical discussion of Paul's activities in Thessalonica, see, e.g., Christoph vom Brocke, *Thessaloniki–Stadt des Kassander und Gemeinde des Paulus: Eine frühe christliche Gemeinde in ihrer heidnischen Umwelt*, WUNT 2/125 (Tübingen: Mohr Siebeck, 2001); Richard S. Ascough, *Paul's Macedonian Associations: The Social Context of Philippians and 1 Thessalonians*, WUNT 2/161 (Tübingen: Mohr Siebeck, 2003).

of the church in Thessalonica in the second and third centuries, the earliest epigraphic and archaeological material being usually dated between the end of the third century and the beginning of the fourth century (see §2 below).

Although modern Thessaloniki has far outgrown the ancient city, a few archaeological vestiges such as the Byzantine acropolis, the Romano-Byzantine city walls, the Antonine agora, and part of Galerius's palatial complex remain to this day visible and attest to its prestigious past as an imperial city.[4] Equally impressive are a number of extant ecclesiasti-

---

4. On the fortification of Thessalonica in general, see Spieser, *Thessalonique et ses monuments*, 25–80; Georgios M. Velenis, *Τα τείχη της Θεσσαλονίκης: Από τον Κάσσανδρο ως τον Ηράκλειο* (Thessaloniki: University Studio Press, 1998); Efthymios Rizos, "The Late-Antique Walls of Thessalonica and Their Place in the Development of Eastern Military Architecture," *JRA* 24 (2011): 450–68. On Galerius's imperial complex (including his triumphal arch), see, e.g., Hans P. Laubscher, *Der Reliefschmuck des Galeriusbogens in Thessaloniki*, AF 1 (Berlin: Mann, 1975); Spieser, *Thessalonique et ses monuments*, 97–123; Theodosia Stefanidou-Tiveriou, "Die Palastanlage des Galerius in Thessaloniki: Planung und Datierung," in *Diocletian, Tetrarchy and Diocletian's Palace on the Seventeen Hundredth Anniversary of Existence: Proceedings of the International Conference Held in Split from September 18th to 22nd 2005*, ed. Nenad Cambi, Josip Belamarić, and Tomislav Marasović (Split: Književni Krug, 2009), 389–410; Evangelia Hadjitryphonos, "The Palace of Galerius in Thessalonike: Its Place in the Modern City and an Account of the State of Research," in *Bruckneudorf und Gamzigrad: Spätantike Paläste und Großvillen im Donau-Balkan-Raum; Akten des Internationalen Kolloquiums in Bruckneudorf vom 15. bis 18. Oktober 2008*, ed. Gerda von Bülow and Heinrich Zabehlicky (Bonn: Habelt, 2011), 203–17; Fani Athanasiou et al., *Η αποκατάσταση των ερειπίων του Γαλεριανού συγκροτήματος στη Θεσσαλονίκη (1994–2014): Τεκμηρίωση και επεμβάσεις*, 2 vols. (Thessalonike: Ephoreia Archaioteton polis Thessalonikes, 2015); Aristoteles Mentzos, "Reflections on the Architectural History of the Tetrarchic Palace Complex at Thessalonikē," in Nasrallah, Bakirtzis, and Friesen, *From Roman to Early Christian Thessalonike*, 333–59. An "equilateral cross surrounded by rays" and "standing between two stylized plant ornaments" has been found in the apsidal wall of the palatial octagon. See Michael Vickers, "Observations on the Octagon at Thessaloniki," *JRS* 63 (1973): 114; see also figs. 17 and 44 in Athanasiou et al., *Γαλεριανού συγκροτήματος στη Θεσσαλονίκη*, 258–59. However, its significance and the function of the building itself, in particular its supposed conversion into a church, remain debated. See Vickers, "Observations on the Octagon," 114–20; Spieser, *Thessalonique et ses monuments*, 118 (with n. 237); Hjalmar Torp, "Thessalonique paléochrétienne: Une esquisse," in *Aspects of Late Antiquity and Early Byzantium: Papers Read at a Colloquium Held at the Swedish Research Institute in Istanbul 31 May–5 June 1992*, ed. Lennart Rydén and Jan Olof Rosenqvist (Uppsala: Swedish Council for Research in the Humanities and Social Sciences, 1993), 129 (with n.

cal buildings such as the Hagios Demetrios, the Hagios Georgios (a.k.a. the Rotunda), the Acheiropoietos, and the Hagia Sophia (see §5 below). These testify to the presence of a vibrant Christian community in Thessalonica, which progressively transformed the city's monumental landscape between the fourth and the seventh centuries.[5]

2. The Earliest Christian Inscriptions

The epigraphic evidence from Thessalonica constitutes by far the largest corpus of primary sources on Macedonian Christianity, with a total of about 160 inscriptions, which represents roughly a third of the overall Christian epigraphic material so far discovered in the region.[6] Much of the material is rather late, dating approximately between the fourth and sixth centuries, and quite fragmentary (particularly the gravestones of the humbler members of society), so that it fails to provide a complete picture of the development of Christianity in the city in the first few centuries.[7] The

---

80); Athanasiou et al., Γαλεριανού συγκροτήματος στη Θεσσαλονίκη, 227–326, 380–81; Mentzos, "Reflections on the Architectural History," 336–52.

5. See Torp, "Thessalonique paléochrétienne"; Slobodan Ćurčić, "Christianization of Thessalonikē: The Making of Christian 'Urban Iconography,'" in Nasrallah, Bakirtzis, and Friesen, *From Roman to Early Christian Thessalonike*, 213–44.

6. Most of the Christian inscriptions from Thessalonica have been published in IMakedChr and in *IG* 10.2.1 (1972) and 10.2.1s (2017), edited by Charles Edson and Pantelis M. Nigdelis. All have now been included in the online database Inscriptiones Christianae Graecae, which has been published in open-access on the repository of Edition Topoi at http://repository.edition-topoi.org/collection/ICG. Material such as brick stamps and early Byzantine graffiti were left out from Feissel's corpus (see IMakedChr, p. 16). On the graffiti discovered in a sixth- or seventh-century *hagiasma* (or funerary chamber) in the agora and on the walls of a cryptoporticus in the *odeon*, see Dēmētrios Pallas, *Les monuments paléochrétiens de Grèce découverts de 1959 à 1973* (Rome: Pontificio Istituto di Archeologia Christiana, 1977), 65–68, 75–76 (see ICG 3621; SEG 34.1682); Charalambos Bakirtzis, "Η αγορά της Θεσσαλονίκης στα παλαιοχριστιανικά χρόνια," in *Actes du Xe congrès international d'archéologie chrétienne, Thessalonique, 28 septembre–4 octobre 1980*, 2 vols. (Rome: Pontifico Istituto di Archeologia Cristiana, 1984), 2:14–17 (see *BE* [1987]: 438); Spieser, *Thessalonique et ses monuments*, 90; Torp, "Thessalonique paléochrétienne," 129–30; Pamela Bonnekoh, *Die figürlichen Malereien in Thessaloniki vom Ende des 4. bis zum 7. Jahrhundert: Neue Untersuchungen zur erhaltenen Malereiausstattung zweier Doppelgräber, der Agora und der Demetrios-Kirche* (Oberhausen: Athena, 2013), 207–75, 524.

7. Few are precisely dated by a consular or imperial date. See, e.g., ICG 3147–49 (IMakedChr 128–130 A), 3151–55 (IMakedChr 131–135).

earliest possible Christian evidence brings us to the end of the third century, when the first Christian epitaphs appear to have been carved. Hardly any of these can be surely identified as Christian, as they lack the stylistic and iconographic features that would later become distinctive of Macedonian Christian tombstones. Their simple formulary follows more or less the Greco-Roman standard of the time (ὁ δεῖνα τῷ δεῖνι μνήμης χάριν), and they present only very subtle iconographic or semantic hints that could indicate adherence to the Christian faith.

Among the earliest is the epitaph of Apollonios, the only attested presbyter at Thessalonica in this period: Ἀπολλώνιος | Ἀπολλωνίου | <π>ρεσβύτερος ("Apollonios, son of Apollonios, presbyter").[8] Neither the title πρεσβύτερος nor the palm branch (or *lulab*) adjacent to it can decisively identify Apollonios as Christian (or Jewish for that matter), but the fact that the terms ἱερεύς or ἀρχιερεύς (followed by the name of the divinity or cult in the genitive) predominates in non-Christian inscriptions, and that most *presbyteroi* in Macedonia are Christian, suggest that this *presbyteros*, one of three (so far) attested at Thessalonica, was indeed Christian.[9] Another that stands out is the now lost funerary altar of Epigone, which was inscribed with a rare exhortation to enjoy eternal life that somewhat echoes a dictum of Epicurean inspiration (ζῶν/ζῇ κτῶ χρῶ): Αἰ<ω>νία ζοῇ χρῶ | Μ(ᾶρκος) Καλ(πούρνιος) Νούλλων | καὶ Μεστρία Ἐπι|γόνῃ τῷ τέκνῳ | μνίας χάριν ("Enjoy eternal life! Marcus Calpurnius Noullon and Mestria to Epigone their child, in remembrance").[10] The epitaph of Euhemeros, at the bottom of which was carved a roughly shaped fish (a typically Christian symbol), is

---

8. ICG 3131 (IMakedChr 113; *IG* 10.2.1.431; second–third centuries CE). The forms of the *sigma* and *omega*, as well as the use of a patronymic (Ἀπολλωνίου) and of the nominative Ἀπολλώνιος (rather than the genitive), suggest a date earlier than the fourth century CE. For the *IJO* editors (*IJO* 1.Mac18), "the inscription is much more likely to be Jewish than Christian" given its early date.

9. See the presbyters Timothy (ICG 3157; IMakedChr 137) and Achillios (ICG 3156; IMakedChr 136) in n. 26 below. But see the unusual (Jewish) μελλοπρεσβύτερος in Berea (*IJO* 1.Mac8; fourth–fifth centuries CE), or the πρεσβυτεράρχης τῶν Ὀλυμπίων in IMaked 1.38 (Elimaea, third century CE).

10. ICG 3132 (IMakedChr 114; *IG* 10.2.1.459; second–third centuries CE). For the epicurean formula, see *IG* 12.9.1240 (Aidepsos, ca. first century CE); *TAM* 3.1.596 (Termessos, third century CE); IEph 2217 D (third century CE). See IMakedChr, p. 112; Erich Preuner, "ΖΩΝ ΚΤΩ ΧΡΩ," *JdI* 40 (1925): 40–41; Louis Robert, ed., *Inscriptions Grecques*, vol. 1 of *Collection Froehner* (Paris: Edition des bibliothèques nationales, 1936), 136–37, no. 90.

yet another classic example from the late third or the early fourth century that follows the standard Greco-Roman formulary: Ἰουλιανὸς | κὲ Μακεδὼν | Εὐημέρῳ | τῷ γλυκυ||τάτῳ ἀδελ|φῷ μνίας | χάριν ("Ioulianos and Makedon, to Euhemeros, their dearest brother, in remembrance").[11]

Fig. 6.1. ICG 3136 (IMaked-Chr 118): Epitaph of Euhemeros with fish (reproduced from Feissel, IMakedChr, pl. XXV).

While the absence of other characteristically Christian elements (such as a cross) invites caution when dealing with such inscriptions, doubt is no longer permitted for equally early epitaphs that employ distinctively Christian symbols and phraseology.[12] One famous example is the funerary plate Kalokairos set up for his parents, which sheds some important light on the emergence and development of the Christian epigraphic habit in Macedonia: Καλόκερος Μακεδό|νι κὲ Σωσιγενίᾳ τοῖς | γλυκυτάτοις γονεῦ|σιν τὸ

---

11. ICG 3136 (IMakedChr 118; *IG* 10.2.1.*931; Thessalonica, third–fourth centuries CE). Paleographic and stylistic features suggest a date in the late third or early fourth century CE.

12. On the criteria used to identify an inscription as Christian, see Cilliers Breytenbach and Julien M. Ogereau, "*Inscriptiones Christianae Graecae (ICG)* 1.0: An Online Database and Repository of Early Christian Greek Inscriptions from Asia Minor and Greece," *EC* 8 (2017): 415.

κοιμητήριον ἕως | ἀναστάσεως ("Kalokairos made for Makedon and Sosigenia, his dearest parents, this tomb until the resurrection").[13] It begins with the classic formula ὁ δεῖνα τῷ γλυκυτάτῳ δεῖνι but then replaces the standard μνείας χάριν at the end with an expression designating the tomb as the deceased's sleeping place until the resurrection (κοιμητήριον ἕως ἀναστάσεως). Likely deriving from the New Testament idea of the saints' repose prior to the resurrection, the term κοιμητήριον would be used more systematically as a heading on Christian tombstones in Macedonia, Attica, and the Corinthia in the fifth and sixth centuries (see, e.g., Matt 27:52; John 11:11–12; Acts 7:60, 13:36; 1 Cor 7:39; 11:30; 15:6, 18, 20, 51; 1 Thess 4:13–15; 2 Pet 3:4).[14]

The phrase ἕως ἀναστάσεως is rarer in inscriptions but appears on another well-known inscription from Thessalonica for a *procurator* of

Fig. 6.2. ICG 3137 (IMakedChr 119): Epitaph of Kalokairos for his parents with fish (reproduced from Feissel, IMakedChr, pl. XXV).

---

13. ICG 3137 (IMakedChr 119; ca. 300 CE). Feissel's commentary (IMakedChr, pp. 115–16) is particularly important. See also Franz J. Dölger, *Die Fisch-Denkmäler in der frühchristlichen Plastik Malerei und Kleinkunst*, vol. 5 of ΙΧΘΥΣ (Münster: Aschendorffsche Verlagsbuchhandlung, 1943), 710–14.

14. See also IMakedChr, pp. 116–17. On the origin, significance, and specific Christian usage of the term, see John S. Creaghan and Antony E. Raubitschek, "Early

imperial estates, which probably dates from the same period as Kalokairos's tombstone, if not slightly later, given the resemblance in style: Φλά(βιος) Κάλλιστος | ὁ <δ>ιασημ(ότατος) ἐπίτρο|πος χωρίων δε|σποτικῶν ἐποί||ησεν τὸ κοιμη|τήριον τοῦτο ἑαυ|τῷ καὶ τῇ συμβίῳ | ἑαυτοῦ ἅμα θυγατρὶ | ἕως ἀναστάσεως || μνήμης χάριν ("Flavius Kallistos, *vir perfectissimus*, *procurator* of imperial estates, made this tomb for himself and his wife, as well as his daughter, until the resurrection, in remembrance").[15] In this instance, the merging of the Greco-Roman standard formulary with Christian elements suggests that the Constantinian era inspired new developments in the Christian funerary formulary and illustrates how Christians began to feel more confident to identify themselves as such on their gravestones.

From the fourth century onward, more conspicuous Christian symbols, such as *chi-rho*s and crosses, indeed begin to be employed more frequently on epitaphs to affirm one's faith. The sarcophagi of Ailia Alexandra, on which she identifies herself as "being alive in Christ" (ζῶσα Χριστῷ), and that of Ioulios Ioulianos, on which a nicely carved *chi-rho* was likely used as an abbreviation for the adjective χριστιανός, are two early examples of this development.[16]

Christian Epitaphs from Athens," *Hesperia* 16 (1947): 5–6; Erkki Sironen, "Early Christian Inscriptions from the Corinthia and the Peloponnese," in *Identity and Authority in Emerging Christianities in Asia Minor and Greece*, ed. C. Breytenbach and Julien M. Ogereau, AJEC 103 (Leiden: Brill, 2018), 201–2; Éric Rebillard, "*Koimetérion* et *coemeterium*: tombe, tombe sainte, nécropole," *MEFR* 105 (1993): 975–1001.

15. ICG 3138 (IMakedChr 120; *IG* 10.2.1.351; ca. 325–350 CE). This epitaph can be dated more precisely to the second quarter of the fourth century on the basis of the formulary, the *nomen* Flavius, and the title διασημότατος (i.e., *perfectissimus*), which was commonly borne by imperial officials after Constantine. The expression ἕως ἀναστάσεως was not confined to Thessalonica or even Macedonia. For additional examples from Galatia, Phrygia, and Corinth, see ICG 3709 (IAnkyra 2.357; fourth century CE), ICG 1379–80 (SEG 31.1116, 1118), ICG 2583 (*IG* 4.2.3.1300; fourth century CE).

16. ICG 3134 (IMakedChr 116; *IG* 10.2.1.551; late third century CE): Αἰλία Ἀλεξάνδρα Αἰλίῳ Λύκῳ τῷ ἀνδρὶ μνήμης χάριν καὶ ἑαυτῇ ζῶσα Χ(ριστ)ῷ. "Ailia Alexandra to Ailius Lykos, her husband, in remembrance, and for herself, (being) alive in Christ."

ICG 3135 (IMakedChr 117; *IG* 10.2.1.607; ca. third century CE): Ἰούλ(ιον) Ἰουλιανὸν τὸν α[-]τατον χρ(ιστιανόν) οἱ ἀδελφοί. "To Ioulios Ioulianos, the most … (?) Christian, his brothers." The use of a *duo nomina* in the accusative (instead of the dative) indicates an early date.

The Emergence and Development of Christianity in Thessalonica   183

Fig. 6.3. ICG 3134 (IMakedChr 116): Sarcophagus of Ailius Lykos (reproduced from Feissel, IMakedChr, pl. XXIV).

Fig. 6.4. ICG 3135 (IMakedChr 117): Sarcophagus of Ioulios Ioulianos.

On a rare occasion, such as on the tombstone of the teacher and newly baptized (νεόφυτος) Eutychios (which concludes with an evasive threat of retribution against potential tomb desecrators), the epithet χριστιανός is even fully spelled out (twice by dittography).[17] Unsurprisingly, *chi-rho*s became more prevalent in the fourth century and were used indiscriminately by poorer members of the community, such as Kopryllos (whose name suggests he was rescued from a dung hill as a child), or by wealthier members, such as the couple Aurelia Eustorgia and Flavios, who were buried in a richly decorated vaulted tomb.[18] The couple was portrayed in fine attires on the back wall of their tomb, each holding a laurel branch, alongside two children (or servants?) standing on either side of a table (or altar?), and identified by an inscription painted in red ink within a delicate wreath in the *arcum soli*.[19]

This magnificent tomb, which provides the sole example of a Christian funerary portrait at Thessalonica, is one of several painted vaulted tombs discovered in the western and eastern necropoleis. These undoubtedly

---

17. ICG 3141 (IMakedChr 123; *IG* 10.2.1.397; fourth century CE): Κοιμητήριον Ἐὐτυ|χίου διδασκάλου χρη|στιανοῦ {χρηστειανοῦ} | νεοφωτείστου, ὅπου ||⁵ μή τις ἕταιρος τολμήσῃ | ἀνύξας ἄλλο σκήνω|μα ἀποθῆτε· ὁ γὰρ | τοῦτο τολμήσας οὐ|κ ἀγνοεῖ τὸν ἐπικεί||¹⁰μενον αὐτῷ κίνδυ|νον. "Tomb of Eutychios, a teacher (and) newly-baptised Christian. May no one else dare to open (this tomb) to lay another corpse here, for the one daring (to do so) does not ignore the danger s/he incurs." What the retribution might have consisted of is not articulated. Most often, it took the form of a fine, as exemplified by two other Thessalonian epitaphs: ICG 3218 and 3219 (IMakedChr 197 and 198).

18. ICG 3140 (IMakedChr 122; *IG* 10.2.1.*778; fourth century CE): (*Christogram*) Κοπρύλλου. "(Tomb) of Kopryllos."

19. ICG 3142 (IMakedChr 124; fourth century CE): + Φλαβί|ῳ |[–]| κὲ [Αὐρ] ηλ[ίᾳ]||| Εὐστοργίᾳ· | ὑγιένετε παρ[ο]|δῖτε (*Christogram*). "To Flavius ... (?) and Aurelia Eustorgia. Farewell, passer-by!" Another inscription was found painted above a female figure (the mother of Flavios or Eustorgia?) in the southeastern corner of the tomb (ICG 3142; IMakedChr 125): κὲ Αὐρηλίᾳ Πρόκλᾳ μητρὴ πάν|των. "and to Aurelia Prokla, mother of all." For a detailed description see Efterpi Marki, *Η νεκρόπολη της Θεσσαλονίκης στους υστερορωμαϊκούς και παλαιοχριστιανικούς χρόνους (μέσα του 3ου έως μέσα του 8ου αι. μ.Χ.)* (Athens: TAP, 2006), 138–39; Marki, "Die frühchristliche Grabmalerei in Thessaloniki," in *Frühchristliches Thessaloniki*, ed. Cilliers Breytenbach, STAC 44 (Tübingen: Mohr Siebeck, 2007), 58–60. The tomb could be as early as 300–320 CE (based on stylistic features), according to Stylianos Pelekanidis. See Pelekanidis, *Gli affreschi paleocristiani ed i piu antichi mosaici parietali di Salonicco* (Ravenna: Dante, 1963), 8–12; see also IMakedChr, p. 121; Marki, "Grabmalerei in Thessaloniki," 58–60; Bonnekoh, *Malereien in Thessaloniki*, 142, 146, 154.

The Emergence and Development of Christianity in Thessalonica 185

Figs. 6.5 and 6.6. ICG 3142 (IMakedChr 124): Vaulted tomb of Flavius and Aurelia Eustorgia.

belonged to prominent and affluent Christian families who could afford not only to buy or build the bulky monuments but also to decorate them in the latest artistic fashion with expensive pigments.[20] A handful of them, which have been dated to the fourth century and which can now be viewed at the Museum of Byzantine Culture of Thessaloniki, were adorned with large crimson Latin crosses or Christograms, as well as popular biblical (or apocryphal) scenes such as Noah in the ark, Abraham sacrificing Isaac, Daniel in the lions' den, the Good Shepherd, the raising of Lazarus, or even Thecla's martyrdom.[21]

Apart from Flavios and Eustorgia's tomb, however, none of these chambers included inscriptions (besides the legends of the scenes them-

---

20. About sixty-five such tombs have so far been unearthed (see Marki, "Grabmalerei in Thessaloniki," with photos, 140–80; Marki, Η νεκρόπολη της Θεσσαλονίκης, 120–204, with pls. 1–26, 59–68; Bonnekoh, *Malereien in Thessaloniki*, 13–206).

21. Marki dates twenty-nine tombs to the fourth century CE (Η νεκρόπολη της Θεσσαλονίκης, 137). The three most outstanding specimens are Tomb 15, found in the eastern necropolis at the theological faculty (ICG 3144—see n. 22 below; labeled Tomb 18 in Marki, "Grabmalerei in Thessaloniki," 61–62; and Gounaris); Tomb 49, excavated on Apolloniados St 18 (ICG 3145—see n. 22 below); and Tomb 52, discovered in the western necropolis on Demosthenous St. See Marki, Η νεκρόπολη της Θεσσαλονίκης, 130–37, 142–54; Bonnekoh, *Malereien in Thessaloniki*, 19–167 (on Tomb 52 on Demosthenous St); Georgios Gounaris, "Die Wandmalereien aus dem Grab Nr. 18 der theologischen Fakultät der Aristoteles-Universität Thessaloniki," in Breytenbach, *Frühchristliches Thessaloniki*, 79–89. Based on archaeological and numismatic evidence, as well as iconographic features, Marki, Gounaris, and Bonnekoh have generally dated these (with more or less precision) to the fourth century CE (Gounaris, "Wandmalereien aus dem Grab," 87–89; Bonnekoh, *Malereien in Thessaloniki*, 141–59). Also noteworthy are the large Christograms of Tombs 29 (fourth century CE; Marki, Η νεκρόπολη της Θεσσαλονίκης, 218, pls. 13–14) and 53 (Marki, Η νεκρόπολη της Θεσσαλονίκης, 223, pls. 19–20); the Latin crosses of Tombs 67, 87, 101, and 102 (fifth–eighth centuries CE; Marki, Η νεκρόπολη της Θεσσαλονίκης, 225, 228–30, pls. 25–26); and Tomb 89 (fourth century CE), which features Jesus as the good shepherd and a large red Christogram contained within a wreath held by two cupids (Marki, Η νεκρόπολη της Θεσσαλονίκης,, 229, pl. 6). See also Pelekanidis, *Gli affreschi paleocristiani*, 7–28; Stylianos Pelekanidis, *Studien zur frühchristlichen und byzantinischen Archäologie* (Thessaloniki: Institute for Balkan Studies, 1977), 75–96; Marki, "Grabmalerei in Thessaloniki," 61–63; Efterpi Marki, "Frühchristliche Darstellungen und Motive"; Gounaris, "Wandmalereien aus dem Grab"; Bonnekoh, *Malereien in Thessaloniki*, 19–206; Chrysanthi Mavropoulou-Tsioumi, "Susanna in einem frühchristlichen Grab von Thessaloniki," in Breytenbach, *Frühchristliches Thessaloniki*, 91–101.

selves) that could give us more information about the deceased or that could allow us to date them more precisely.[22] Nor have they delivered many inscribed grave goods (other than the usual clay or glass vessels, jewelries, and coins).[23] In this respect, the exhortation to "drink and live with the saints" (πίε ζήσης μετὰ τῶν ἁγίων), which was engraved on a glass flask found in a tomb in the eastern necropolis, offers us an all-too-rare glimpse into some of the funerary beliefs and practices of the Thessalonian Christians in this period.[24] Ironically, due to the dearth of epigraphic evidence, the people who were once among the most prominent are now probably those about whom we know the least.

3. Inscriptions Related to the Clergy

The clergy of Thessalonica are not particularly well documented, especially during the third and fourth centuries, a period for which we simply have (so far) no epigraphic evidence (except for the epitaph of the presbyter Apollonios mentioned above, if indeed he was Christian).[25] Not a single bishop, for instance, is attested in the epigraphic and archaeological record before the end of the sixth century, which defies belief for a city of this size and importance. And only a dozen inscriptions are known to us, which must represent a tiny fraction of the numerous ministers and attendants who served the Thessalonian church from the first century onward.

---

22. See, e.g., ICG 3144 (IMakedChr 126; SEG 44.559; fourth century CE): Ἡεισοῦ, "Jesus" (eastern wall); Δανιήλ, "Daniel" (west); Λάζαρ(ος)—Ἡεισοῦ, Ἀβραὰς θυσία—φωνή, "Lazarus, Jesus, Abraham's sacrifice—voice" (north); Νόερ, "Noah" (south). The legends were only partially published by Feissel but reedited in full by Gounaris ("Wandmalereien aus dem Grab") and Marki (Η νεκρόπολη της Θεσσαλονίκης, 130–37). See also ICG 3145 (IMakedChr 126 bis; SEG 32.653; fourth century CE) with similar scenes and legends, including Thecla's martyrdom; also Marki, Η νεκρόπολη της Θεσσαλονίκης, 142–45.

23. See under "Εὑρήματα" in each entry of Marki's catalogue (Η νεκρόπολη της Θεσσαλονίκης, 211–41, with pls. 68–69)—not all of these tombs are Christian. See also Efterpi Marki, "Die ersten christlichen Friedhöfe in Thessaloniki," in Breytenbach, Frühchristliches Thessaloniki, 51–52.

24. ICG 3146 (IMakedChr 127; fourth century CE): Ὑσύχι πίε [ζήσ]ης μετὰ [τῶν | ἁγί]ων πίε ζ[ήση]ς. "Hesychios, drink, [live] with [the] saints! Drink, [live]!" It was discovered as a single offering in a tomb in the eastern necropolis in 1966 (see pl. 69δ in Marki, Η νεκρόπολη της Θεσσαλονίκης).

25. See ICG 3131 (IMakedChr 113) in n. 8.

Among them are the fifth- or sixth-century presbyters Timothy and Achillios, the only two presbyters found at Thessalonica (Apollonios excepted), whose fragmentary epitaphs are characterized by their banality and minimal decoration.²⁶

Oddly enough, funerary inscriptions of deacons and lectors slightly outnumber those of presbyters and bishops (possibly because they existed in greater number). The longest of them, which can be precisely dated to the postconsulships of the Flavii Lampadios and Orestes in 532 CE, particularly stands out by its religious verbosity and contrasts with the brevity of Timothy and Achillios's epitaphs. Not content of being merely remembered as a "most devout" (θεοφιλέστατος) deacon, Andreas also felt the need to stress that he was "the *ex* night-watchman [νυκτοφύλαξ] of beloved memory of the venerable church" at which he officiated.²⁷ Other tombstones generally provide only scraps of information and simply identify deacons by their name, when they do, and sometimes by a generic epithet (e.g., εὐλαβέστατος). Based on their late formulary (κοιμητήριον διαφέροντα τοῦ δεινοῦ), one can hardly deduce anything more than that a Georgios, a Demetrios (who buried his grandparents in his tomb), a Ioannes (from an unknown village), and an Eleutherios served as deacons

---

26. ICG 3157 (IMakedChr 137; *IG* 10.2.1.675; fifth–sixth centuries CE): Ὧδε κῖτε Τιμόθεο|ς ὁ τὴν εὐλαβῆ μν|ήμην πρεσβύτερ|[ο]ς. "Here lies Timothy, the presbyter of revered memory."

ICG 3156 (IMakedChr 136; *IG* 10.2.1s.*1542; SEG 47.980; fifth–sixth centuries CE): + Μημόριν | τοῦ εὐλ(αβεστάτου) πρ(εσβυτέρου) | Ἀχιλλίου· | ὧδε κῖτε Α|ΦΟΡΟΥ. "Tomb of the most reverent presbyter, Achillios. Here lies … (?)." The SEG editors suggest δίφορον (i.e., δίσωμον) at the end.

27. ICG 3153 (IMakedChr 133; SEG 29.643; *IG* 10.2.1s.1519; 532 CE): [– ca. 8 –]ΙΣ μ(ετὰ) ὑ[π](ατείαν) Φλ(αβίου) ΙΟΥΣΤΙΝ [– ca. 15–|–ca. 5–ἀνε]παύσατο ὁ αὐτὸς θεοφιλ(έστατος) διάκο(νος) Ἀνδρέας |[μη(νὶ)–ca. 7 –]ε΄ ἰνδ(ικτίωνος) ι΄ ἡμ(έρᾳ) γ΄ δεὶς μ(ετὰ) τὴν ὑπ(ατείαν) Φλ(αβίων) Λαμπαδίου | [κ(αὶ) Ὀρέστου] τῶν μεγαλοπρ(επεστάτων) + Γέγονεν δὲ ὁ αὐτὸς [ὁ τὴν θεοφ]ιλῆ μνήμην ἀπὸ νυκτοφυλάκ(ων) τῆς εἰρημ(ένης) σεπτ(ῆς) ἐκκλ(ησίας). "Post-consulship of Flavius Justin/Justinian (?). The said Andreas, a most devout deacon, died on 5 (or 15? 25?) (month) in the 10th *indictio*, on the 3rd day (i.e., Tuesday), in the second post-consulship of Flavius Lampadios [and] Flavius [Orestos], *viri magnificentissimi*. He was also the ex night-watchman of beloved memory of the aforesaid venerable church." Note: the μετά in lines 1 and 3 is unusually abbreviated with the letter *mu* and a cross. The name of the church (see line 5) must have appeared on the now-lost top fragment. The ecclesiastical function of νυκτοφύλαξ seems unattested. See IMakedChr, p. 130; LSJ, s.v.; *PGL*.

or subdeacons at one of the local basilicas in the fifth and sixth centuries.²⁸ How many they were and what influence they held at Thessalonica is difficult, if not impossible, to say, although we might infer that, over time, they rose to a certain prominence. For in the ruins of the eastern city wall there emerged a plate dedicated to "the holiest deacons" (ἁγιώτατοι διάκονοι) of an unidentified church, an epithet that bishops (or churches), rather than deacons, would ordinarily bear.²⁹

The epigraphy of the fifth and sixth centuries brings to light lower-level clerics as well. It includes the two Andreas and Ioannes, whose damaged epitaphs tell us very little except that they were devout *lectores*.³⁰ It also

---

28. ICG 3159 (IMakedChr 139; *IG* 10.2.1.653; fifth–sixth centuries CE): [Κοιμ]ητήριον | διαφέροντα | Γεωργίου δια|κ[όνου -]. "Tomb belonging to Georgios, a deacon."
ICG 3150 (IMakedChr 130 B; *IG* 10.2.1.*780; sixth centuries CE): + Κυμητήριον διαφέ|ροντα τοῦ εὐλαβ(εστάτου) | διακόνου Δημητρίου | ΑΞΙ[... ἔν]θα κῖντε οἱ | πρὸς π[ατ]έραν πάποι. "Tomb belonging to the reverend deacon Demetrios ... where (his) paternal grand-parents lie."
ICG 3149 (IMakedChr 130 A; *IG* 10.2.1.*779; 469 CE?): Ἀνεπαύσατο [ὁ δεῖνα, ἰνδ(ικτίωνι) ζ'],| π(ρὸ) δ' νωνῶν Φεβ[ρουαρίων, ὑπατεία]| Ζήνων[ος κ]αὶ Μα[ρκιανοῦ], ὁμοίως καὶ |[. .]ΑΙΤΑ[.....]ΙC Παῦλος ὁ εὐλα||⁵[βὴς ......] τῇ αὐτῇ ἰνδικτ<ι>ῶν[ι | πρὸ ..] καλανδῶν Μαρτίων. "Has died [so and so, in the 7th *indictio*], on the 4th day before the nones of February (i.e., 2 February), [under the consulship] of Zenon and Markianos, as well as ... Paulos, the pious..., on the same *indictio*, ... [before] the calends of March."
ICG 3161 (IMakedChr 141; *IG* 10.2.1.*365; fifth–sixth centuries CE): [Κοιμητήριον μονό|σ]ωμω[ν δ]ιαφ[έρον | Ἰ]ωάννῃ [ὑ]ποδιακώ|νῳ τῆς ἐγθάδε ἁγί(ας) || τοῦ Θ(εο)ῦ ἐκ[κ]λησία[ς | ὁ]ρμού[μεν]ος ἀ[πὸ | κώ]μ[ης -]. "[Tomb] for one person belonging to Ioannes, sub-deacon of the holy church of God here, (and) originating from the village."
ICG 3160 (IMakedChr 140; *IG* 10.2.1.*790; sixth century CE): Κοιμητήριον δι|αφέροντα Ἐλευ|θερίου οἰποδι|κόνου, ἔνθα κα||τάκιτε Θεόδου|[λος -]. "Tomb belonging to Eleutherios, sub-deacon, where Theodoulos (or Theodoule?) lies."
29. ICG 3158 (IMakedChr 138; *IG* 10.2.1s.1501; fifth–sixth centuries CE): Μνημεῖον τῶν ἁγιωτάτων διακόνων | τῆς ἐκκλησίας ταύτης. "Memorial of the holiest deacons of this church." The stone, which had been reused in the city fortifications and is now lost, must have indicated the tomb where the deacons of one of the local churches were successively inhumed.
30. ICG 3162 (IMakedChr 142; *IG* 10.2.1.*793; sixth century CE): + Κυμητήριν δ[ιαφέρον]| Ἀνδρέου τοῦ τεοφ[ιλεστάτου]| ἀναγνόστου, οἱὴὸς [τοῦ τῆς ἀρίσ]|της {εμ} μνήμης Ἀρε[σίου/Ἀρειστείδου ?]. "Tomb belonging to Andreas, the most devout lector, son of Aresias (?) of excellent memory."
ICG 3633 (*IG* 10.2.1s.1497; SEG 52.642; fourth–sixth centuries CE): [Κοιμ]ητήριον ||[δίσω]μον δια|[φέρον] Ἀνδρέου τ||[οῦ εὐ]λαβεστάτου ||[ἀναγ]νόστου τῆς ἐν||[ταῦθ]α

features a doorkeeper (θυρωρός) named Kassianos, who must have served at a church or a martyrion dedicated to an unidentified saint, as well as, possibly, another *lector* named Demetrios who, as ἀποθηκάριος, managed a storehouse.[31] Although they must have played a significant role in the life of the church, and indeed could often serve as deaconesses, Christian women remain overall mostly invisible in the epigraphy of Thessalonica apart from two epitaphs of virgins—one of which is very fragmentary.[32] One would be hard pressed, however, to determine whether they belonged to a small monastic community, such as those attested at Berea and Edessa, or whether they simply died unmarried.[33] The latter seems more probable for the virgin Ioanna, since she was buried by her own parents after having passed away "by divine ordinance" (θεοῦ κελεύσει)—a rare enough expression in Macedonian inscriptions.[34]

ἁγιωτ(άτης) ἐκκλη|[σίας καὶ τ]οῦ υἱοῦ ... | ... ΥΙ [–] "Tomb for two people belonging to Andreas, the most reverent lector of the holiest church here, and son of... (?)." ICG 3163 (IMakedChr 143; *IG* 10.2.1.632; fifth–sixth centuries CE): ΕΒΣΑΛΙΤΟΥ[–]| τῇ αὐτοῦ [–]| IN Ἰωάννης ἀναγ<ν>ώ<σ>της. "and to his (wife?) ... Ioannes, lector."

31. ICG 3164 (IMakedChr 144; *IG* 10.2.1.360; fifth–sixth centuries CE): + + + | Μιμόριον | Κασιανοῦ θυ|ρωροῦ τοῦ ἁγί[ου–]. "Tomb of Kassianos, door-keeper of the holy... (?)." On the responsibilities of a θυρωρός, see Const. ap. 57.10.21.

ICG 3175 (IMakedChr 155; *IG* 10.2.1.*796; sixth century CE?): [Κο]ιμητήριον [διαφέρον Δημ|η]τρίου ἀνα{π}[γνώστου καὶ ἀ|πο]θηκαρίο[υ το|ῦ μ]ακαριω[τάτου]. "Tomb [belonging] to Demetrios, lector (?), [and] storehouse superintendent, (son of ?) of the blessed..." On the function of ἀποθηκάριος, see Louis Robert, *Opera minora selecta* (Amsterdam: Hakkert, 1969), 2:923–25.

32. ICG 3165 (IMakedChr 145; *IG* 10.2.1s.1524; fifth–sixth centuries CE): [–]|ας παρ|θένου | (staurogram) (staurogram) (staurogram). "[Tomb?] ... of a virgin."

ICG 3694 (*IG* 10.2.1s.*1533; fifth–sixth centuries CE): [μημ]όρι[ον]| Εὐγενίας | παρθένου. "Tomb of Eugenia, a virgin." On the role of women in the early church, see Ute E. Eisen, *Amtsträgerinnen im frühen Christentum: Epigraphische und literarische Studien* (Göttingen: Vandenhoeck & Ruprecht, 1996); Cilliers Breytenbach and Christiane Zimmermann, *Early Christianity in Lycaonia and Adjacent Areas: From Paul to Amphilochius of Iconium*, AJEC 101 (Leiden: Brill, 2018), 650–60.

33. See the inscription for the abbess Theodora, an "eternal virgin" (ἀειπάρθενος) and "mother of pious virgins" (μήτηρ παρθένων εὐσεβῶν) at Berea (ICG 3070; IMakedChr 60; fifth–sixth centuries CE), and the series of epitaphs of virgins at Edessa (ICG 3027–29, 3032; IMakedChr 20–22, 24; fifth–sixth centuries CE).

34. ICG 3155 (IMakedChr 135; *IG* 10.2.1.403; 535 CE): [– |.]Δ, θ(εο)ῦ δὲ κελεύσι ἀνεπαύσα[το | ἡ] γνησιωτάτη καὶ πολυπόθη[τος | ἡ]μον θυγάτηρ Ἰωάννα οὖσα πα[ρθ(ένος) | μη(νὶ)] Νοεμβρίου κα' ἡμ(έρᾳ) δ' ἰνδ(ικτίωνος) ιδ' vac |[ὑπ(ατείᾳ)]

As previously noted, bishops are not attested epigraphically before the end of the sixth century, which does not imply that they played no important role in the life of the church and of the city.³⁵ The seventh-century inscription commemorating the construction, or restoration, of the harbor fortification under the archbishop Eusebius is a case in point that illustrates the type of civic responsibilities bishops came to assume in late antiquity and early Byzantine times.³⁶ Identified as the archbishop of Thessalonica with whom Gregory the Great corresponded about various administrative matters between 597 and 603 CE, Eusebius also reportedly wrote to the emperor Maurice denying any knowledge of the whereabouts of St. Demetrios's relics.³⁷ In this respect, inscriptions effectively provide us with little information on the highest clerical office in Thessalonica and leave us primarily dependent on more or less reliable literary sources and traditions.³⁸ These shed light on notorious bishops such as Alexandros, who attended the Council of Nicaea in 325 CE and accompanied Constantine to Jerusalem, or A(s)cholius, who baptized Theodosius I in

---

Φλ(αβίου) Βιλισαρίου τοῦ μεγαλοπ[ρεπ(εστάτου)]. "And, by the command of God, has died our dearest and much regretted daughter Ioanna, a virgin (?), on 21 November, on the 4th day (i.e., Wednesday), in the 14th *indictio*, under the consulship of Flavius Belisarios, the *magnificentissimus*." For the restitution of the end of line 3 (οὖσα πα[ρθ(ένος)]) see *BE* (1987): 432. For other examples of the phrase κελεύσ(ε)ι Χριστοῦ, see IMakedChr, pp. 132–33.

35. The identification of bishop Andreas in a votive of the Acheiropoietos basilica is conjectural. See ICG 3114 (IMakedChr 102 B) below in n. 129.

36. ICG 3101 (IMakedChr 91; *IG* 10.2.1.46; ca. 600 CE): + Ἐπὶ τοῦ ἁγιω(τάτου) | ἀρχιεπισκό(που) | Εὐσεβ(ίου) ἐγέ[νετ]|ο PYM(–) ΛΥΤ(–). "Under the holiest archbishop Eusebios was made/restored... (?)." Line 4 remains unresolved (see Rizos, "Late-Antique Walls of Thessalonica," 455 n. 11).

37. For Eusebius's letters, see Philipp Jaffé, ed., *Regesta pontificum romanorum: Ab condita ecclesia ad annum post Christum natum MCXCVIII*² (Leipzig: Veit, 1885), nos. 1497, 1683, 1723, 1847, and 1921. On the topic of St. Demetrios's relics, see Miracula Sancti Demetrii §50–54, in Paul Lemerle, *Les plus anciens recueils des miracles de Saint Démétrius et la pénétration des Slaves dans les Balkans* (Paris: Éditions du Centre National de la Recherche Scientifique, 1979–1981), 1:87–90 (PG 116:1240–41); see also Lemerle, *Les plus anciens recueils* 2:27–28.

38. See esp. Louis Petit, "Les évêques de Thessalonique," *EO* 4.3 (1901): 136–45; 4.4 (1901): 212–21; Lemerle, *Les plus anciens recueils* 1:27–31. For the earliest (but not entirely trustworthy) list of bishops, see Michel Le Quien, *Oriens christianus, in quatuor patriarchatus digestus: Quo exhibentur ecclesiae, patriarchae, caeterique praesules totius Orientis* (Paris: Imprimerie royale, 1740), 2:27–66.

Thessalonica in 380 CE, participated in the council of Constantinople the following year, and corresponded with Basil the Great.[39] They also highlight the important role Thessalonica played in ecclesiastical and political developments in the late antique Balkans, revealing, for instance, that Innocent I extended (wittingly or unwittingly) patriarchal responsibilities to bishop Anysios and his successor, Rufus, in 402 and 412 CE, respectively.[40] As a result, Thessalonica would remain (in principle at least) the seat of the papal vicariate of eastern Illyricum until the eighth century (despite mounting pressure from the patriarchate of Constantinople from 421 CE onward).[41]

4. Inscriptions Related to the Laity

The remaining inscriptions, which comprise about 60 percent of the Christian epigraphic material at Thessalonica, were set up for the ordinary members of the community, most of whom were buried in the eastern and western *extra muros* necropoleis.[42] Among them were prominent figures

---

39. On Alexandros, see Socrates, *Hist. eccl.* 1.8.5, 1.13.12; Eusebius, *Vit. Const.* 4.43. On A(s)cholius, see Socrates, *Hist. eccl.* 5.6; Sozomen, *Hist. eccl.* 7.4; see also Basil, *Ep.* 154, 164, 165.

40. See Innocent I, *Ep.* 1 (PL 20:463–68) and 13 (PL 20:515–17), reproduced in Carlos da Silva-Tarouca, ed., *Epistularum romanorum Pontificum ad vicarios per Illyricum aliosque episcopos: Collectio thessalonicensis* (Rome: Pontificia Universitas Gregoriana, 1937), 20–22. See also Innocent I, *Ep.* 18 (PL 20:537–40); Geoffrey D. Dunn, "Innocent I and Anysius of Thessalonica," *Byzantion* 77 (2007): 124–48; Dunn, "Innocent I and Rufus of Thessalonica," *JÖB* 59 (2009): 51–64.

41. On the papal vicariate of eastern Illyricum, see esp. Dunn, "Innocent I and Anysius"; Dunn, "Innocent I and Rufus"; Geoffrey D. Dunn, "The Church of Rome as a Court of Appeal in the Early Fifth Century: The Evidence of Innocent I and the Illyrian Churches," *JEH* 64 (2013): 679–99. See also Louis Duchesne, "L'Illyricum ecclésiastique," *ByzZ* 1 (1892): 531–50; Stanley L. Greenslade, "The Illyrian Churches and the Vicariate of Thessalonica, 378–95," *JTS* 46 (1945): 17–30; Charles Pietri, "La géographie de l'Illyricum ecclésiastique et ses relations avec l'église de Rome (V–VIe siècles)," in *Villes et peuplement dans l'Illyricum protobyzantin: Actes du colloque organisé par l'École française de Rome (Rome, 12–14 Mai 1982)* (Rome: École française de Rome, 1984), 21–59.

42. The eastern cemetery appears to have been progressively abandoned around the seventh century CE (due to the Slavic incursions) and moved *intra muros*. On the earliest Christian cemeteries, see Marki, "Die ersten christlichen Friedhöfe in Thessaloniki"; Marki, Η νεκρόπολη της Θεσσαλονίκης. See also Paul Perdrizet, "Le

who held responsibilities in imperial offices or the army. A *clarissimus* and *comes* named Demetrios, for example, served as a *numerarius*, that is, a financial controller in the civil or military administration, and likely gained the honorary title of *comes* upon his retirement.[43] Others, such as the sixteen-year-old *notarius* and *vir clarissimus* Barbatio, one of the earliest attested Christians of senatorial status at Thessalonica, probably never held any official functions but owed his high status to his prestigious ancestry.[44]

Imperial officials of lower ranks are, however, better represented in the epigraphy of the fifth and sixth centuries. Among them are the two *eparchikoi* Martinos and Archetimos, who assisted the governor (ἔπαρχος) in a prefectural office in the early sixth century.[45] Others include an officer (ταξεώτης) named Demetrios, whose epitaph features a large footed cross, and the *palatinos* Bardion, likely a civil servant from the imperial treasury,

---

cimetière chrétien de Thessalonique," *MEFR* 19 (1899): 541–48; Kyriake Eleutheriadou, "Χριστιανικό κοιμητήριο στη Θεσσαλονίκη," *AEMT* 3 (1989): 271–82.

43. ICG 3152 (IMakedChr 132; *IG* 10.2.1.674; 519 CE): [+ Ὁ τ]ὴν λαμπρὰν καὶ ἀοίδιμ[ον]| μνήμην Δημήτριος ὁ λαμπρ[ότα]|τος κόμ(ης) κ(αὶ) ἀπὸ νουμεραρίων [ἐν|θ]α κεῖται, τελευτήσας μ[ηνὶ ||-]βρίου ς´ ἰνδ(ικτίωνος) γι ὑπ(ατεία) τοῦ δ[εσ|πό(του) ἡμ]ῶν Ἰουστίνου. "Here lies Demetrios, the *clarissimus comes* and *ex numerarius* of illustrious and notorious memory, who died on the 6th of the month of …bre, on the 13th *indictio*, under the consulship of our [Lord] Justinian."

44. ICG 3224 (IMakedChr 203; *IG* 10.2.1.331; fifth century CE?): + *Depositio Ba|rbationis | notari v(iri) c(larissimi) | Eutropi adv||ok(ati) in ann|is XVI + + +*. "Tomb of Barbatio, *notarius*, *vir clarissimus*, (son of) Eutropios, *advocatus*, (who died) at 16 years of age." This is one of only four Latin Christian epitaphs found at Thessalonica so far.

45. ICG 3154 (IMakedChr 134; *IG* 10.2.1.*804; 525–535 CE): + Κοιμητήριον δίσωμον [διαφέρον]| Μαρτίνῳ τῷ θαυμ(ασιωτάτῳ) ἐπα[ρχικῷ]| τῷ κατὰ τὸν τὴν ἐνδ[οξ(οτάτην) μνή]|μην ἀπ[ὸ ἐπ]άρχων Α/Λ[. ca. 6 .]||[5] νον, ἔγ[θα κατά]κιτε ἡ [. ca. 6 ..]|| ΠΑΣ[.. ca. 7 ..]ΗΤΗ[.. ca. 6 ..]|| ΠΑΡ[. ἀναπαυ]σαμέν[η . ca. 5 .]| κζ´ ἰν[δ(ικτίωνος) γ´ ὑπατε]ίᾳ Φλς [Φλς Φιλο]|ξένο[υ καὶ Π]ρόβου [τῶν λαμ]|||[10]προτάτων. + Ἀναπ[άη ὁ μα]||κάριος Ἀντωνῖνος τῇ [... ca. 6 ..]| ἰνδ(ικτίωνος) δι ὑπ(ατεία) Βελισαρίου λ[αμ(προτάτου)· ἔνθα]|| κατάκιτε. + "Tomb for two persons belonging to Martinos the admirable *eparchikos* (who served) the ex-prefect of most glorious memory, A/L(…) nos (?). Here lies…, having died on 27 (month), in the [3rd] *indictio*, under the consulship of Flavius Philoxenos [and] Flavius Probos, *viri clarissimi*. Has died the blessed Antoninos on the…, in the 14th *indictio*, under the consulship of Belisarios, *vir clarissimus*. [Here] he lies." The second epitaph for Antoninos was carved ten years after that of Martinos.

ICG 3677 (*IG* 10.2.1s.1512; SEG 52.640; fifth–sixth centuries CE): Κοιμητή|ριον Ἀρχε|τίμου, · ἐ|παρχικοῦ. "Tomb of Archetimos, *eparchikos*."

whose stela was decorated with a neatly carved Latin cross flanked by two birds.[46] We also know of a newly baptized subordinate of an ex-prefect, and of a *lector* (possibly) named Demetrios, who, as seen above in section 3, may have been a warehouse attendant (ἀποθηκάριος) or a manager of an imperial storehouse.[47]

Christian military personnel are also attested during this period. A certain Martyrios, for instance, held the functions of *stratelatianos*, an assistant of the *stratelates* (likely the *magister militum* of Illyricum), and of *curiosus*, a *magistrianus* responsible for inspecting the post system or patrolling the harbor.[48] A man named Petros operated as a courier (κούρσωρ) either in the army (as a lightly armed horseman) or in the civil administration.[49] Others, such as Maximianos from the *Ascarii iuniores*, or Leontianus from the *Atecotti* (*seniores*), served as elite soldiers in the *auxilia palatina*, special units in charge of escorting the emperor in Illyricum.[50]

This significant number of administrative and military staff represented in the local epigraphy is not surprising considering that Thessalonica

---

46. ICG 3169 (IMakedChr 149; *IG* 10.2.1.335; fifth–sixth centuries CE): + Κυμητήρια δ(ια)|φέρων Δημητρ(ίου) | ταξεώτου. + "Tombs belonging to Demetrios, an *officialis*." Note the plural κυμητήρια, which suggests Demetrios owned several tombs.
   ICG 3171 (IMakedChr 151; *IG* 10.2.1.*781; fifth–sixth centuries CE): (*avis*) + (*avis*) | Μημόριν Βαρδίωνος | παλατίνου. "Tomb of Bardion, *palatinos*."

47. ICG 3167 (IMakedChr 147; *IG* 10.2.1s.*1543; fifth–sixth centuries CE): + [Μημόρ]ιον |[νεοφ]ωτίστω |[. . .]ατίω ἀπὸ |[. . .]σώνων γε||⁵[νό]μενος τοῦ |[δ]εσπότου μου | Εὐθηρίω τοῦ ἀπὸ | ἐπάρχων· ἐν<θ>ά|<δ>ε κεῖτε.||¹⁰ (*staurogram*) MHPI. "Tomb of ...-atios (?), newly baptised, ex ...-son (?) of my master Eutherios, *ex-praefectus*. Here he lies." For the lector and warehouse attendant Demetrios, see ICG 3175 (IMakedChr 155) in n. 31.

48. ICG 3170 (IMakedChr 150; *IG* 10.2.1.*791, *799 A, *799 B; fifth–sixth centuries CE): + Μνημῖον διαφέρον | Μαρτυρίου στρα|τηλατιανοῦ | καὶ κουριού[σου]. "Memorial belonging to Martyrios, *stratelatianos* and *curiosus*."

49. ICG 3172 (IMakedChr 152; *IG* 10.2.1.*792; fifth–sixth centuries CE): Κυμητήριο|ν Πέτρου κού|ρσουρος, ἔνθα | κατάκιτε, ἀναπ||[. . .]ΙΟΟΕΙ[. . .]. "Tomb of Petros, *cursor*, where he lies..."

50. ICG 3173 (IMakedChr 153; *IG* 10.2.1.359; fifth century CE): Κυμητήριον μο|νόσωμον {σωμο|ν} ἔνθα κῖτε Μαξι|μιανὸς νομέρου || Ἀσκαρίον εἴνου|ρος. + "Tomb for one person where lies Maximianus of the *numerus* of the *Ascarii iuniores*."
   ICG 3226 (IMakedChr 205; *IG* 10.2.1s.*1493; fifth–sixth centuries CE): Mem(oria) ⁞ Leonti|ani ⁞ mil(itis) ⁞ de ⁞ n|um(ero) ⁞ Ate<c>u|t:torum. "Tomb of Leontianus, soldier of the numerus of the Atecotti."

was the imperial center of the province and suggests that Christianity had made significant forays in the Roman army. Yet the greater majority of the tombstones approximately dated to the fifth or sixth century, perhaps as many as 70 percent, were set up for and by ordinary Christians from the rank and file of Thessalonian society, who at times insisted that they paid for their own funerary expenses.[51]

Their epitaphs are usually made of white or gray marble and are simply decorated with one or two crosses or staurograms. They feature no elaborate formulary and generally follow, with small variances in spelling and syntax, the Christian formulary that, by the fifth century, was prevalent throughout mainland Greece, namely: κοιμητήριον/μεμόριον (μονόσωμον/δίσωμον) διαφέρον(τα) τοῦ δεῖνος ... ἐνθά(δε) (κατα)κεῖτε ("tomb belonging to so-and-so; here s/he lies").[52] The second part of the epitaph can sometimes differ slightly when someone other than the tomb owner(s)—most often a relative—was buried in it, in which case it is indicated with the following clause: ἐνθά(δε) (κατα)κεῖτε ὁ δεῖνα (ἀναπαυσάμενος/ἀνεπαύσατο + date of death). Few are dated, and when they are, they normally include the date of death (day and month), the indiction, and the consular year.[53]

---

51. See, e.g., ICG 3214 (IMakedChr 193; *IG* 10.2.1.*998; fourth–fifth centuries CE): [. Μα]κε|[δ]ονίου | καὶ Παρεγ|ορίου || ἐκ τῶν | ἐδίων. "(Tomb?) of Makedonios and Paregorios, (set up) at their own expenses."

ICG 3674 (*IG* 10.2.1s.1523; SEG 51.898; fourth–sixth centuries CE): Αὐριλι[-]|ἐποίησ[εν ἐκ τῶν ἰ]|δίων [ἐνθάδε]| κῖτα[ι–|| ἡ] μήτ[ηρ αὐτοῦ]. "Aurelios made (this tomb) at his own (expenses). Here lies his mother."

Most come from the eastern necropolis, on top of which the Hagios Demetrios hospital and the Aristotle University of Thessaloniki were later built, as well as from the western necropolis (a.k.a. the Vardar quarter). Their provenance was not always recorded scrupulously, but there seems to be little doubt that they were found in Thessalonica (see IMakedChr, pp. 12–14).

52. See Creaghan and Raubitschek, "Christian Epitaphs from Athens," 6–11; Erkki Sironen, *The Late Roman and Early Byzantine Inscriptions of Athens and Attica: An Edition with Appendices on Scripts, Sepulchral Formulae, and Occupations* (Helsinki: Hakapaino Oy, 1997), 384–400; Sironen, "Early Christian Inscriptions from the Corinthia," 201–2. The mention of the number of occupants (μονόσωμον/δίσωμον) is only occasionally included. See, e.g., ICG 3161 (IMakedChr 141), 3173 (IMakedChr 153), 3186 (IMakedChr 165), 3191 (IMakedChr 170).

53. The best examples are ICG 3149 (IMakedChr 130 A), 3151–3155 (IMakedChr 131–135). Not all include the consular year. See, e.g., ICG 3198 (IMakedChr 177; *IG* 10.2.1.*788; fifth–sixth centuries CE) and ICG 3199 (IMakedChr 178; *IG* 10.2.1.*794; fifth–sixth centuries CE).

The vocation of the deceased is only occasionally mentioned after his name; women's occupations are hardly, if ever, included. This contrasts quite starkly with the Christian epigraphic habit observed in Attica or the Corinthia, where one's profession is frequently recorded (as though it were an important social identifier).[54] However scarce this information may be, it is nonetheless valuable to help us sketch the social contours of the Christian community at Thessalonica in the fifth and sixth centuries, which must have comprised for a good part, perhaps the greater part, members from the lower levels of society, that is, the artisans and small-scale traders who usually populated the main urban centers in antiquity. Among them were the carpenter or joiner (λεπτουργός) Heliodoros, and a couple of clothes dealers (ἱματιοπράτης), perhaps a father and son.[55] The church must have also included members who had a higher level of education, such as the anonymous pedagogue who buried his son.[56] Not all exercised their skills freely, for some were simply domestic servants or slaves (οἰκέτης) in noble households. Such is the case of a Philoxenos who served a *comes* named Patrikios, and of Paramonos, the *oiketes* of the *clarissima* Tryphoniane who could afford to put up a long stela for a certain Demetrios (a relative?) for a little over four gold pieces.[57]

---

54. See Creaghan and Raubitschek, "Christian Epitaphs from Athens," 7–8; Sironen, *Inscriptions of Athens and Attica*, 121; Sironen, "Early Christian Inscriptions from the Corinthia," 203.

55. ICG 3177 (IMakedChr 156; *IG* 10.2.1.*787; fifth–sixth centuries CE): [Μημό]ριον Ἡλιοδώ|[ρου λε]πτουργοῦ|[καὶ Σω]σάννας. + "Tomb of Heliodoros, carpenter, and Sousanna (?)."

ICG 3178 (IMakedChr 157; *IG* 10.2.1.*795; sixth century CE): [Κοιμητήριον] διαφέροντα ‖[ca. 8-ἱμα]τιοπράτου καὶ ‖[τοῦ υἱοῦ (?) αὐτο]ῦ Δομνήγο[υ | ca. 10-κ]αὶ ἱμα[τιοπρά ‖ του -]. "[Tomb] belonging to … a clothes-dealer, and to [his son ?] Domninos … also a clothes-dealer."

56. ICG 3179 (IMakedChr 158; *IG* 10.2.1.374; sixth century CE): [Κοιμητή]ριον δια[φέρον-|-π]αιδαγω[γοῦ-| -] .γαμετη[- , ἔνθα | κεῖται] ὁ υἱὸς αὐ[τῶν-‖-μη(νὶ) Ἰο]υνίου θ' ἰ[νδ(ικτίωνος) ..]. "Tomb belonging to…, teacher, [and to his] wife (?), [where lies] their son…, on the 9th [of the month of] June, … *indictio*."

57. ICG 3181 (IMakedChr 160; *IG* 10.2.1.338; fifth–sixth centuries CE): Ἐνθά (*staurogram*) δε κα|τάκιτε | Φιλόξεν|ος οἰκέτης ‖ τοῦ κόμητος | Πατρικίου· ὃ ἠ|γόρασα παρὰ Βο|νοφατίου (*staurogram*). "Here lies Philoxenos, the household slave of the *comes* Patrikios. (Tomb) which I bought from Bonifatios."

ICG 3180 (IMakedChr 159; *IG* 10.2.1.*784; fifth century CE): + + | Μεμόριον Παρα|μόνου οἰκέτη|{ς} τῆς λαμπροτά|της Τρυφωνια‖⁵νῆς, ἀγορα|σθέντον χρ|υσίνων τεσσά|ρων καὶ γράμ|ματος· ἐνθά‖¹⁰δε κῖτε Δημή|τριος ἀναπαυ|σάμενος τῇ | πρὸ

Most of the Christian epitaphs from the period (fifth–sixth centuries CE) remain very basic. They mainly record the *praenomen* of the deceased without giving any further information about their vocations, social status, or involvement in the church, which leaves us with meager historical data to exploit. On their own, single names indeed tell us very little about the deceased other than, in some cases, their social or ethnic origin, family traditions of name-giving, and, at times, their religious background. Not much can be said, for instance, of the couple Alexandros and Antonina other than he was likely of Greek descent (with a typical Macedonian name) and she of Roman or Italian parentage.[58] The same goes for the Plo(u)tina (probably of Latin origin), who was interred in the single tomb of Kassandra (another classic Macedonian name), and for Alexandros and Tetradia (literally, "born-on-the-fourth-day"), who were both of Greek origin and in whose tomb were later buried the siblings Thalasios and Zenobia (their children?).[59] In other instances, names such as Ioannes and Apostolia could indicate a Christian parentage.[60] Theophoric names such as Theodoulos, Theodoras, Theodotes, Kyriakos, or Theophilos were also favorite classics, though not exclusively used by Christians.[61]

δεκαπέν|τε καλανδῶν ||¹⁵ Μαρτίων ἡμέ|ρᾳ Κρόνου. "Tomb of Paramonos, household slave of the *clarissima* Tryphoniane, bought for four gold pieces and a gram (i.e., a quarter of a coin). Here lies Demetrios, having died fifteen days before the calends of March, on the day of Kronos (i.e., on Saturday, 15 February)." The price of the tomb is relatively high, but see below (n. 86) that of Domesticus, who paid three and a half solidi (ICG 3225; IMakedChr 204).

58. ICG 3184 (IMakedChr 163; *IG* 10.2.1.*782; fifth–sixth centuries CE): ☩ Κυμητήρ[ιον]| δηαφέροντ[α]| Ἀλεξάνδρου | καὶ Ἀτονήνας. "Tomb belonging to Alexandros and Antonina."

59. ICG 3191 (IMakedChr 170; *IG* 10.2.1.353; fifth–sixth centuries CE): ☩ Μιμόριον | μονόσωμ|ον Κασσάν|δρας ἔνθα || κῖτε Πλου|τίνα. "Single tomb of Kassandra, where Plo(u)tina lies."

ICG 3185 (IMakedChr 164; *IG* 10.2.1s.1515; sixth century CE): (A) Κοιμ[ητήριον]| διαφέρ[ον Ἀλε]|ξάνδρου κ<α>ὶ | Τετραδίας (B) ['Εν]θάδε | κῖντε Ζη|νοβία καὶ Θα|λάσιος ἀδελ||φοί. "(A) Tomb belonging to Alexandros and Tetradia. (B) Here lie Zenobia and Thalasios, brother and sister." Inscriptions A and B were engraved at an interval by a different hand.

60. ICG 3188 (IMakedChr 167; *IG* 10.2.1.334; fifth–sixth centuries CE): Κυμητήριον | Ἰωάνου καὶ | τῆς συνβίου | αὐτοῦ Ἀποσ||στολίας. "Tomb of Ioannes and his wife Apostolia."

61. ICG 3192 (IMakedChr 171; *IG* 10.2.1.*364; fifth–sixth centuries CE): ☩ Μημόριον | ἔνθα κατά|κιτε Θεό|δουλος. "Tomb where Theodoulos lies."

Others were given more traditional Greek or Latin names, some of which had a strong mythological resonance as, for example, Nikon and Dionysia, Achillios, Nike, or Victoria.[62] Additional information about one's provenance can also sometimes be supplied by a specific reference to the village of origin, though it is rarely possible to locate those precisely. Such is the case of the Syrian Dorotheos from Adadega who buried his slave (δούλη) Theodora, of the anonymous Apamean man from the village of Thodea, or of the Basilis from Nitibis (or Nisibis).[63] Along with the three

---

ICG 3193 (IMakedChr 172; *IG* 10.2.1.333; fifth–sixth centuries CE): † Μημόριον Θεωδόρας· ἐν|θάδε κατάκειται. † † † "Tomb of Theodora, where she lies."

ICG 3194 (IMakedChr 173; *IG* 10.2.1.633; fifth–sixth centuries CE): Μημόριον Ἀβραμήου | καὶ τῆς συνβίου αὐ|τοῦ Θεωδότης. "Tomb of Abramios and his wife Theodote." Her husband's name, Abramios, is of Semitic origin but was commonly worn by Christians (see IMakedChr, p. 157).

ICG 3195 (IMakedChr 174; *IG* 10.2.1.*783; fifth–sixth centuries CE): Μημόριον Κυριακοῦ | κ(αὶ) Τρυφένας. "Tomb of Kyriakos and Tryphaina."

ICG 3684 (*IG* 10.2.1s.1505; fifth–sixth centuries CE): (*staurogram*) (*staurogram*) + Μημόριον | Θεοφίλου,| ἔνθα κῖτε || καὶ Μάρκελλα. "Tomb of Theophilos, where Markella also lies."

62. ICG 3675 (*IG* 10.2.1s.1520; SEG 51.899; fourth–sixth centuries CE): Νίκωνος | Διονυσίας | καὶ Ἰωάννου | κοιμητήριον. "(Tomb of) Nikon, Dionysia, and Ioannes."

ICG 3678 (*IG* 10.2.1s.1521; SEG 55.716; fourth–sixth centuries CE): Κυμητήριον, ἐν ᾧ ἀναπαυσά|μενοι ἀπόκινται οἱ μακαριώτα|τοι, Ἀχίλλιος μὲν μη(νὶ) Νοεμβρ(ίῳ) κα(ὶ) | Ἐλπιδία δὲ μη(νὶ) Φεβρ(ουαρίῳ) ιβ′ || α′. "Tomb in which were laid to rest the most blessed Achillios in the month of November, and Elpidia on 12 February, in the 1st (*indictio* ?)."

ICG 3680 (*IG* 10.2.1s.1496; SEG 58.655; fourth–sixth centuries CE): Κοιμητήριων δίσουμον | διαφέροντα Νίκις, ἔνθα | κατάκιτε ὠ ταύτης σύμ|βιο[ς] Σεκοῦνδος. "Tomb for two bodies belonging to Nike. Here lies her husband Secundus."

ICG 3683 (*IG* 10.2.1s.1504; fourth–sixth centuries CE): + Μημόριον | μονόσο|μων Βικτω|ρίας. "Single tomb of Victoria."

63. ICG 3182 (IMakedChr 161; *IG* 10.2.1.332; fifth century CE): (*staurogram*) Μιμόριν | Δωροθέου | κώ(μης) Αδαδηγων, | ἔνθα κεῖτε ἡ || δούλη αὐτοῦ | Θεοδώρα | (*staurogram*). "Tomb of Dorotheos, from the village of Adadega. Here lies his slave, Theodora."

ICG 3183 (IMakedChr 162; *IG* 10.2.1s.*1527; sixth century CE): [- |...] ὅρῳν | Ἀπαμέων | ἀπὸ κώμης | Θοδέων + +. "[Tomb of] ... (so and so) from the region of Apamea (Syria), from the village of Thodea."

ICG 3632 (*IG* 10.2.1s.*1532; SEG 52.641; fourth–sixth centuries CE): † † † Μημόριον δίσω|μον, ἔνθα κῖτε Βα|σιλις, κώμης Νιτί|βις. "Tomb for two people. Here lies Basilis, from the village of Nitibis."

other attested Sabbatis, these confirm the presence of Syrian Christians in Thessalonica in late antiquity.⁶⁴

Few of these epitaphs stand out of the ordinary by their specifically Christian decoration or iconography, apart from the following ones. Flavios and Demetrios's gravestones, for example, begin and end with the enigmatic ΧΜΓ symbol.⁶⁵ That of Dionysios and Zoson, on the other hand, features no fewer than five Latin crosses and two carefully executed Christograms on either side at the bottom.⁶⁶ The couple's proud Christian self-consciousness is hardly matched by anyone except perhaps Petros and Alexandra, whose crudely carved tombstone includes (at least) four crosses

---

64. ICG 3685 (*IG* 10.2.1s.1506; fourth–sixth centuries CE): † Κοιμητί|ριον διαφ(έ)|ρον Εὐφη|μίῳ καὶ Σ||[α]ββατί|δος. + "Tomb belonging to Euphemios and Sabbatis." See ICG 3189 (IMakedChr 168) and 3196 (IMakedChr 175) in nn. 69–70. On the Syrian community at Thessalonica, see Pantelis M. Nigdelis, "Habent sua fata lapides: Ξεχασμένες δημοσιεύσεις τοῦ Πέτρου Ν. Παπαγεωργίου γιὰ ἐπιγραφὲς τῆς Θεσσαλονίκης καὶ τῆς "Εδεσσας," *Tekmeria* 7 (2002): 95–104.

65. ICG 3186 (IMakedChr 165; *IG* 10.2.1s.*1534; fifth–sixth centuries CE): + Κοιμητήριον | δήσουμον | ἔνθα κῖται | Δημήτριος || υἱὸς Ἀνδρέου | καὶ Βερόης | ΧΜΓ. "Tomb for two persons. Here lies Demetrios, son of Andrea and Beroe. Christ born of Mary (?)."

ICG 3148 (IMakedChr 129; *IG* 10.2.1.350; 412 CE): ΧΜ[Γ | Ἀνεπαύσ]ατο Φλ(άβιος) Κα[- | -]ίου Αὐγ(ούστου) τ<ὸ> θ´ κ[αὶ -| -] Αὐγ [-]. "Christ born of Mary (?). Has died Flavius Ka ... (?), [under the consulships of Honorius] Augustus, (consul for) the 9th time, and [Theodosius] Augustus, [(consul for) the fifth time]."

The signum ΧΜΓ appears on two other inscriptions from Berea (ICG 3070; IMakedChr 60) and Edessa (ICG 3033; IMakedChr 25), as well as on numerous papyri, inscriptions, and amphorae, throughout the Greek East during the fourth–seventh centuries CE. Its significance remains debated and has been variously interpreted (even in antiquity) as the three names Χριστός, Μιχαήλ, Γαβριήλ, as the phrase Χριστὸν Μαρία γεννᾷ ("Mary begot Christ"), as the phrase Χριστὸς ἐκ Μαρίας γεννηθείς ("Christ born of Mary"), or even as an apotropaic isopsephism meaning θεὸς βοηθός ("God the helper"; ΧΜΓ = 643 = θ-ε-ὸ-ς-β-ο-η-θ-ό-ς). See the brief discussion in IMakedChr, pp. 43–44, 124–25; see also Henri Grégoire, "Épigraphie Chrétienne I: Les inscriptions hérétiques d'Asie Mineure," *Byzantion* 1 (1924): 700; Franz J. Dölger, *Das Fisch-Symbol in Frühchristlicher Zeit*, vol. 1 of ΙΧΘΥΣ (Münster: Aschendorffsche Verlagsbuchhandlung, 1928), 298–317; Jan-Olof Tjäder, "Christ, Our Lord, Born of the Virgin Mary (ΧΜΓ and VDN)," *Eranos* 68 (1970): 148–90; *NewDocs* 8:156–68.

66. ICG 3187 (IMakedChr 166; *IG* 10.2.1s.1503; fifth–sixth centuries CE): + Κυμητήριν +| Διονυσίου καὶ Ζώ|σωνος + ἔνθα κῖ|ται ὁ καλοκύμη||τος (*Christogram*) Διονύσις. + (*Christogram*) + "Tomb of Dionysios and Zoson. Here lies Dionysis, well asleep."

Fig. 6.7. ICG 3186 (IMakedChr 165): Epitaph of Demetrios with XMΓ signum (reproduced from Feissel, IMakedChr, pl. XXXIX).

Fig. 6.8. ICG 3187 (IMakedChr 166): Epitaph of Dionysios and Zoson with Christograms (reproduced from Feissel, IMakedChr, pl. XXXIX).

Fig. 6.9. ICG 3197 (IMakedChr 176): Epitaph of Euphrosynos (reproduced from Feissel, IMakedChr, pl. XLII).

The Emergence and Development of Christianity in Thessalonica 201

Fig. 6.10. ICG 3196 (IMakedChr 175): Epitaph of Sambatios and Maxima (reproduced from Feissel, IMakedChr, pl. XLII).

Fig. 6.11. ICG 3189 (IMakedChr 168): Epitaph of Demetrios and Sabbatis (reproduced from Feissel, IMakedChr, pl. XL).

at the top, and the *notarius* Barbatio mentioned earlier whose epitaph begins with one Latin cross and ends with three.[67] Markella's stela features three staurograms in the header, while that of Euphrosynos displays three Latin crosses at the top and, at the bottom, an odd shape with a cross at its center—either a breastplate (indicating that he was a soldier?) or a vase.[68] Just as unusual are the two (perhaps three) encircled and framed Christograms heading Sambatios's stela, and the small Latin cross standing over an angular base (perhaps a table or an altar) underneath Theodoros and Maria's epitaph.[69] Stranger still is the geometric pattern in the middle of Demetrios and Sabbatis's tombstone, which consists of a circle (a corona?), to which two *hedera* are connected at the end of two long stems.[70]

Animal figures are altogether rare. Fish are no longer represented, and birds are found on only two inscriptions, that of the *palatinos* Bardion mentioned earlier and that of (the little?) Chionis, at the top of which was engraved a small cantharus flanked by two peacocks and *hedera*.[71] The latter is a moving poetical epitaph drawing inspiration from metric funerary epigrams, in which the mother expresses her personal distress at the loss of her young: "For my salvation and my troubles, having received the words of God, Chionis she was called, a crown without blemish, (whom) I handed over to her own repose where toil ceases. And in my pain I received good offsprings, sons and a daughter of equal zeal, virgins."[72] This is by far

---

67. ICG 3190 (IMakedChr 169; *IG* 10.2.1.404; fifth–sixth centuries CE): + + + | + Κυμιτήριον | Π<έτρ>ου καὶ Ἀλεξά|δρας καὶ Ἀνδρέα | τοῦ υἱοῦ αὐτῶν. "Tomb of Petros and Alexandra, and Andrea their son." See ICG 3224 (IMakedChr 203) above in n. 44.

68. ICG 3672 (*IG* 10.2.1s.1507; SEG 42.627; fifth–sixth centuries CE): *(staurogram) (staurogram) (staurogram)* Μημόριον | Μαρκέλλας, | ἔνθα κῖτε ὁ || υἱὸς μοῦ Φωκᾶς. "Tomb of Markella. Here lies my son Phokas."

ICG 3197 (IMakedChr 176; *IG* 10.2.1.337; fifth–sixth centuries CE): + + +"Ενθάδε ἀναπαύ|εται Εὐφρόσυ|νος σύμβιος | Ἀμπελοχίας. "Here rests Euphrosynos, spouse of Ampelochia."

69. ICG 3196 (IMakedChr 175; *IG* 10.2.1.352; fifth–sixth centuries CE): ['E]νθα κατά|[κιν]τε Σαμβά|[τ]ις κὲ Μα|ξήμα. "Here lie Sambatios and Maxima."

ICG 3215 (IMakedChr 194; *IG* 10.2.1s.1511; fifth–sixth centuries CE): [– | . .]Π Θεω|δώρου κὲ | Μαρίας. + "(Tomb?) of Theodoros and Maria."

70. ICG 3189 (IMakedChr 168; *IG* 10.2.1.*785; fifth–sixth centuries CE): Κυμητήριον Δημη|τρίου καὶ Σαββατί|δος κὲ τῆς τούτω[ν]| θυγατρὸς Γλυκερία[ς]. "Tomb of Demetrios and Sabbatis and their daughter Glykeria."

71. See ICG 3171 (IMakedChr 151) in n. 46.

72. ICG 3200 (IMakedChr 179; *IG* 10.2.1s.1498; fourth–fifth centuries CE): *(avis-cantharus-avis)* Εἰς σωτερία|ν κὲ καμάτου|ς ἐμοὺς θεο<ῦ> λό|γους προσδεξα||⁵μένη

The Emergence and Development of Christianity in Thessalonica 203

Fig. 6.12. ICG 3171 (IMakedChr 151): Epitaph of Bardion with birds and a Latin cross (reproduced from Feissel, IMakedChr, pl. XXXIII).

Fig. 6.13. ICG 3200 (IMakedChr 179): Epitaph of Chionis with peacocks and a cantharus (reproduced from Feissel, IMakedChr, pl. XLIII).

Fig. 6.14. ICG 3201 (IMakedChr 180): Epitaph of Fortunatus with staurogram (reproduced from Feissel, IMakedChr, pl. XLIII).

one of the most touching and elaborate Christian epitaphs from Thessalonica, though perhaps not the most theologically evocative compared to Fortunatus's funerary plea to Jesus Christ, "the maker of all things by a single word," who grants "relief and forgiveness of sins."[73] The last clause is at least what Denis Feissel could read on a squeeze of the stone, for lines 7–8 were subsequently hammered out and replaced by a large staurogram flanked by an alpha and omega, a "common Christian symbol representing Jesus as the beginning and the end of all things."[74]

The rest of the Christian inscriptions from Thessalonica mainly consist of fragments of epitaphs, dedications, or invocations on pieces of architecture such as a baptismal font.[75] In most cases, one can only discern traces of a date, a cross, or the typical funerary formulary (not all of which can be identified with certainty as Christian), and at times, one can only tentatively reconstruct the name of the deceased.[76] All in all, not much historical insight can be gained from such stones other than that a Nikon, a Sambatis (?), an Antonina, or a Florentios identified themselves as Christians in the fifth or sixth century.[77] One will note among these fragments

---

Χιονὶς μὲν | ἐκαλέσθη, ἄσπιλος | στέφαν<ο>ς οὖσα κὲ | ταμίοις εἰδίοις | παρέδωκα λυσιπό||¹⁰νοις κὲ πόνῳ <ἐ>ν ἐμῷ | βλαστοὺς ἀγαθοὺς ἐ|γδέχομε{ν} υείους κὲ | θυγατέραν ὁμοιοζήλους | παρθένους.

73. ICG 3201 (IMakedChr 180; IG 10.2.1.*786; fourth–fifth centuries CE): Ἰ · (ησο) · ῦ · Χρ(ιστ)ὲ · ὁ | ποιήσας | ἑνὶ λόγου | τὰ πάντα,||⁵ δὸς ἄνεσ|ιν καὶ ἄφε|⟦σιν ἁ[μ]α-⟧|⟦[ρτιῶν]⟧| {το}⟧| τῷ δούλῳ ||¹⁰ σου Φορτου|νάτῳ. "Jesus Christ, who made all things through a single word, give relief and ⟦forgiveness of sins⟧ to your servant Fortunatus."

74. Sironen, "Early Christian Inscriptions from the Corinthia," 209.

75. E.g., ICG 3691 (IG 10.2.1s.*1490; fourth–sixth centuries CE): [– κύ]ριος ἐπὶ ὑδ[άτων –]. "The Lord upon the waters." See ICG 3692 (IG 10.2.1s.*1491; fifth–sixth centuries CE), ICG 3679 (IG 10.2.1s.1556; SEG 47.998; seventh–eighth centuries CE).

76. E.g., ICG 3147 (IMakedChr 128; IG 10.2.1.*776; 366 CE), ICG 3220 (IMakedChr 199; IG 10.2.1.959; fifth–sixth centuries CE), ICG 3690 (IG 10.2.1s.*1546; SEG 47.1012; sixth century CE), ICG 3203 (IMakedChr 182; IG 10.2.1.*797A, *800B; fifth–sixth centuries CE), ICG 3204 (IMakedChr 183; IG 10.2.1s.*1537; fifth–sixth centuries CE), ICG 3205 (IMakedChr 184; IG 10.2.1.*798; fifth–sixth centuries CE).

77. ICG 3206 (IMakedChr 185; IG 10.2.1s.*1535; fourth–fifth centuries CE): † Κοι[μητήριον]|| διαφ[έροντα]|| Νίκω[νος]. "Tomb belonging to Nikon."

ICG 3210 (IMakedChr 189; IG 10.2.1.398; fourth–fifth centuries CE): [Μημ]όριων [– | –] κὲ Σαμβ[ατ–| ἐνθά]δε κῖτε Φ[–]. "Tomb of ... (?) and Sambat ... (?), where F... (?) lies."

ICG 3212 (IMakedChr 191; IG 10.2.1.406; fifth–sixth centuries CE): [–] ΑΙΕΚΙΖΩΗ[– | –] κ(αὶ) ἡ σύμβιος [– | –] Ἀντωνίνα ἡ [– | –] κατὰ νοῦν λ[–] "and his wife ... Antonina."

the only Christian examples of funerary fines at Thessalonica, as well as, possibly, a rare Christian epigram (if indeed it was Christian).[78]

5. Christian Monumental Architecture

Just as in Philippi and Amphipolis, it was during the fifth and sixth centuries that a number of ecclesiastical buildings were constructed to accommodate the needs of a growing Christian population. Among the most notorious and imposing ones are the churches of Hagios Demetrios, the so-called Rotunda (a.k.a. Hagios Georgios), the Acheiropoietos, and the early Byzantine episcopal basilica of Hagia Sophia.[79] It is unlikely, however, that these were the first to be built. More modest edifices, such as the smaller ecclesiastical structures identified underneath the Hagios Demetrios and Hagia Sophia, are presumably earlier by a century or so. The cemeterial church and the adjacent cross-shaped martyrion found in the eastern necropolis underneath Third Septembre Street can be approximately dated to the late fourth century (thanks in part to a hoard of coins).[80] Likewise, the single-

---

ICG 3686 (*IG* 10.2.1s.1508; fifth–sixth centuries CE): + Κοιμητήριον μονό|[σ]ωμον, ἔνθα κῖται | Φλορέντις. "Single tomb where Florentios lies."

78. ICG 3218 (IMakedChr 197; *IG* 10.2.1s.*1525; fifth–sixth centuries CE): [- εἰ δέ τις τολ]μήσῃ ἀνοῖξε ἔτερ[ος-, δ]ώσει ταῖς ἁγιωτάτες [ἐκκλησίαις -]. "[And if someone] else dares to open…, he/she shall pay to the holiest [churches]."

ICG 3219 (IMakedChr 198; *IG* 10.2.1.*996; fifth–sixth centuries CE): [-Σ]ωζο|μένου ὁλο|κοτίνω<ν> δέ|κα. "of Sozomenos (?), ten coins."

ICG 3223 (IMakedChr 202; *IG* 10.2.1.*775; fifth–sixth centuries CE): [-]ΟΙ[- | -]ΟΝΟΜΟ[- | -]γ δὲ γυναι[- | -]ς κείνη πέλει [- || -] αἰαῖ τῆς πινυτῆς [- | -]ς ἀμβροσίοιο[- |-λέλ]οιπεν ἑῷ γλυκερῷ[- |-δόμ]ον ἡμιτελῆ[- | -]ΛΟΥ[-]. "And the woman … it was this one … Ha! What wisdom … immortal … she has left to her dear (husband)… a half-completed house."

79. Vestiges of a fifth- or sixth-century octagonal structure (ø ca. 22 m) have also been excavated near the golden gate, where St. Nestor, St. Demetrios's disciple in his *passio altera*, was allegedly martyred. It featured an octagonal baptistery and a martyrion, and was erected on a symmetrical axis to the Rotunda at the opposite end of the *via regia*. See Efterpi Marki, "Ένας άγνωστος οκταγωνικός ναός στη Θεσσαλονίκη," *Makedonika* 23 (1983): 117–33; see also Torp, "Thessalonique paléochrétienne," 127–28; Ćurčić, "Christianization of Thessalonikē," 224–26.

80. See Despoina Makropoulou, "Ο παλαιοχριστιανικός ναός έξω από τα ανατολικά τείχη της Θεσσαλονίκης," *Makedonika* 23 (1983): 25–46; Marki, *Η νεκρόπολη της Θεσσαλονίκης*, 79–83; Efterpi Marki, "Das kreuzförmige Martyrion und die christlichen Gräber an der Tritis-Septemvriou-Strasse in Thessaloniki," in Breytenbach,

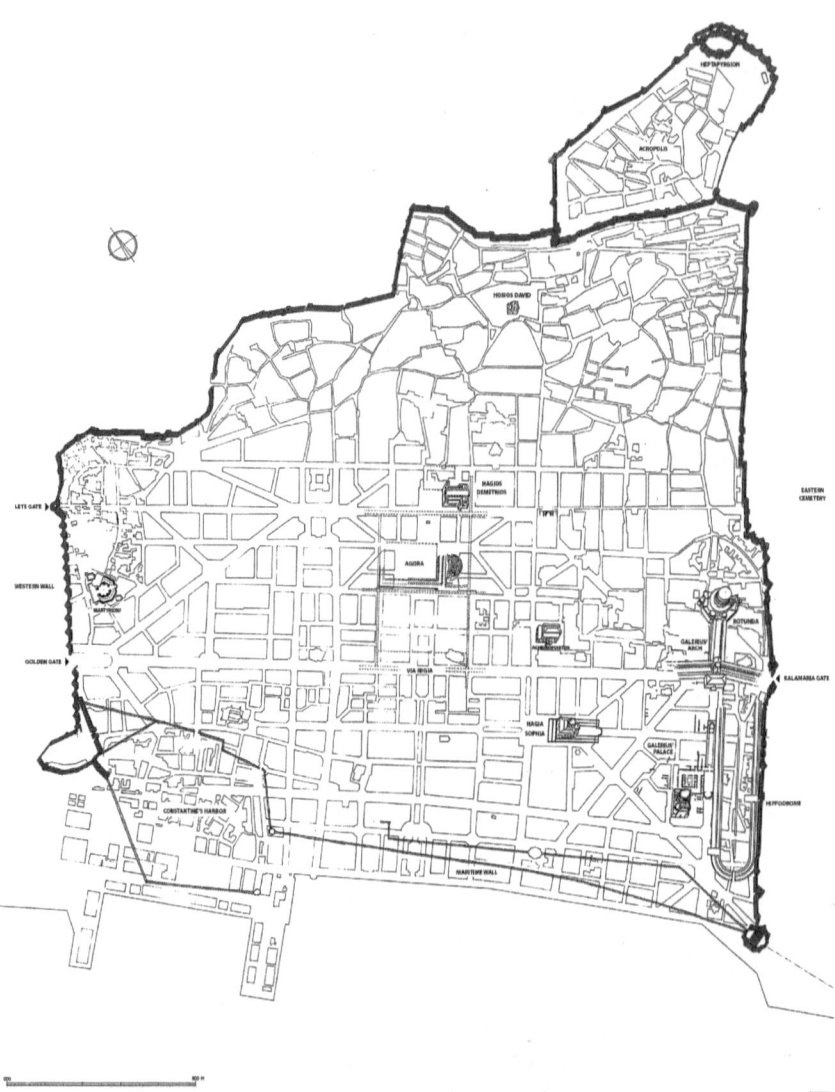

Fig. 6.15. Christian monuments of Thessalonica in late antiquity.

nave church located underneath the small mid-fifth-century, three-aisled basilica (13.5 x 16 m) discovered 100 m from the Kalamaria gate (a.k.a. Kassandreotiki gate), in Sintrivani Square, during rescue excavations in 2010 can be attributed to the same period given its basic architecture and floor plan, which resemble that of the basilica of Paul at Philippi.[81]

The cemeterial church, which features an apsidal crypt similar to that found in the episcopal basilica at Stobi, must have been a popular site for Christians wishing to be buried *ad sanctum*, for about seventy graves, including vaulted ones, were excavated in their immediate vicinity.[82] Likewise, eleven tombs (presumably reserved for bishops) were laid in the floor of the martyrion itself.[83] No funerary or votive inscription has been found, however, and only a small silver reliquary decorated with crosses and a monogram was discovered in the *enkainion* underneath the altar.[84] Incidentally, the same may be said of the other eight late antique martyria identified or suspected in the western and eastern necropoleis, which Efterpi Marki has connected, more or less persuasively, to various saints known from Byzantine hagiographical traditions.[85] None of them

---

Frühchristliches Thessaloniki, 11–41; Marki, "Die ersten christlichen Friedhöfe in Thessaloniki," 45 (with photos, pp. 121–36). Marki notes that there is no attested place of worship earlier than the fourth century CE ("Die ersten christlichen Friedhöfe in Thessaloniki," 44).

81. See Melina Paisidou, "ΜΕΤΡΟ Θεσσαλονίκης 2010: η παλαιοχριστιανική βασιλική στον σταθμό Σιντριβανιού," *AEMT* 24 (2010): 249–60.

82. See Caroline S. Snively, "Apsidal Crypts in Macedonia: Possible Places of Pilgrimage," in *Akten des XII. internationalen Kongresses für christliche Archäologie, Bonn, 22.–28. September 1991*, part 2, ed. Ernst Dassmann and Josef Engemann (Münster: Aschendorffsche Verlagsbuchhandlung, 1995), 1179–84.

83. Marki suggests the martyrion was dedicated to Alexandros of Pydna, but the literary evidence presented in favor of this interpretation is rather tenuous. See Marki, "Die ersten christlichen Friedhöfe in Thessaloniki," 45; Marki, *Η νεκρόπολη της Θεσσαλονίκης*, 81–83.

84. ICG 3620 (SEG 33.555; 380–450 CE): (*Christogram*) | Οὐ(γγίαι) δ΄ γρ(άμματα) ιδ΄. "4 unciae, 14 ounces (i.e. 127,306 g)." See Eutychia Kourkoutidou-Nikolaidou, "Το εγκαίνιο της βασιλικής στο ανατολικό νεκροταφείο της Θεσσαλονίκης," *AEC* (1983): 70–81; Makropoulou, "Ο παλαιοχριστιανικός ναός," 30.

85. See Marki, "Die ersten christlichen Friedhöfe in Thessaloniki," 45–50 (with plan pp. 114–15); Marki, *Η νεκρόπολη της Θεσσαλονίκης*, 69–99. With the help of Byzantine literary sources (mainly the tenth-century *Menologion* of Basil II), Marki has identified nine martyria in the eastern and western necropoleis: five outside the eastern walls, three beyond the western walls, and one to the north. Not all have

has yielded any epigraphic material, although one of them, the martyrion of an otherwise unknown martyr named Ioannes, which was presumably located by the entrance of the Hagios Demetrios hospital, might be mentioned in the epitaph of a certain Domesticus who was buried *ad sanctum* after paying three and a half solidi.[86]

5.1. Hagios Demetrios

Built around 500–525 CE over an earlier structure that may have contained the relics of the saint, the large cross-transept basilica dedicated to Demetrios (ca. 55 x 38 m), the patron saint of the city from the sixth century onward, remains to this day the most notorious and most frequently visited church of Thessalonica.[87] The first sanctuary is said to have been constructed in the fourth century near the public baths north of the agora, where Demetrios, a young military officer of senatorial descent (according

---

left archaeological traces. The western sanctuaries of Matrona and of Agape, Irene and Chione, are only mentioned in the Miracula Sancti Demetrii (§50, 107–108 in Lemerle, *Les plus anciens recueils* 1:87–90, 122–26; see PG 116:1240, 1277). Incidentally, the archbishop John of Thessalonica, who composed the miraculous account of St. Demetrios in the early seventh century, clearly explains that the Thessalonians secretly interred all their martyrs, so that, in his day, nobody knew their exact burial location except for St. Matrona. See Miracula Sancti Demetrii §50 in Lemerle, *Les plus anciens recueils* 1:87–90.

86. ICG 3225 (IMakedChr 204; *IG* 10.2.1.358; fifth–sixth centuries CE): *Domesti|cus posi|tus ād dō(mnum) | Ioāñ(nem) dat sol(idos) || tres et semis | pro memorium.* "Domesticus, laid next to the martyr Ioannes, gives three and a half solidi for the memorial." See also Elli S. Pelekanidou, "Νέα ευρήματα στο ανατολικό νεκροταφείο της Θεσσαλονίκης," *AEMT* 7 (1993): 379–81; Marki, "Die ersten christlichen Friedhöfe in Thessaloniki," 47; Marki, *Η νεκρόπολη της Θεσσαλονίκης*, 69–74. On the martyr Ioannes, see Hyppolite Delehaye, *Les origines du culte des martyrs*, 2nd rev. ed., SH 20 (Brussels: Société des Bollandistes, 1933), 231.

87. On the architecture and date of the basilica, see Georgios A. Soteriou and Maria G. Soteriou, *Η βασιλική του Αγίου Δημητρίου Θεσσαλονίκης* (Athens: H en Athenais Archaiologikes Etaireia, 1952); Paul Lemerle, "Saint Démétrius de Thessalonique et les problèmes du martyrion et du transept," *BCH* 77 (1953): 660–94 (with important critical remarks on earlier excavations); Spieser, *Thessalonique et ses monuments*, 165–214; Franz A. Bauer, *Eine Stadt und ihr Patron: Thessaloniki und der Heilige Demetrios* (Regensburg: Schnell und Steiner, 2013), 64–141. On the relics specifically, see James C. Skedros, *Saint Demetrios of Thessaloniki: Civic Patron and Divine Protector Fourth–Seventh Centuries CE*, HTS 47 (Harrisburg, PA: Trinity Press International, 1999), 56–60, 85–94.

to his *passio altera*), was allegedly martyred under Maximianus and secretly interred.[88] Restored in the seventh century after a fire damaged it the 620s CE, the sixth-century basilica attracted thousands of pilgrims seeking healing and protection from the saint throughout the Byzantine period.[89] When the cult actually started is not clear.[90] The *myron* located in the so-called crypt under the apse and transept of the sixth-century basilica is not mentioned in literary sources before 1040 CE.[91] However, both archaeological and literary evidence indicate that an hexagonal marble *ciborium* placed in the middle of the nave functioned as the saint's *oratorium* already by the sixth century.[92] Furthermore, two *ex-votos*, a fragmentary decree by

---

88. See *AASS, oct.* IV, pp. 50–209; PG 104:104–5 (summary by Photius of Constantinople); PG 116:1167–72 (*passio prima*); PG 116:1173–84 (*passio altera*); PG 116:1185–1324 (*passio tertia*); *BHG*, nos. 496–547. For a commented and annotated edition, see Lemerle, *Les plus anciens recueils*. See also Hyppolite Delehaye, *Les légendes grecques des saints militaires* (Paris: Picard, 1909), 103–9, 259–63; Soteriou and Soteriou, Ἁγίου Δημητρίου, 1–15, 35–63; Paul Lemerle, "La composition et la chronologie des deux premiers livres des *miracula S. Demetrii*," *ByzZ* 46 (1953): 349–61; Lemerle, *Les plus anciens recueils* 1:9–12.

89. See Charalambos Bakirtzis, "Late Antiquity and Christianity in Thessalonikē: Aspects of a Transformation," in Nasrallah, Bakirtzis, and Friesen, *From Roman to Early Christian Thessalonike*, 398–405; Bakirtzis, "Ὁ Ξενὼν τοῦ Ἁγίου Δημητρίου: Εἰκονογραφικὰ Ζητήματα," in *Medicine and Healing in the Ancient Mediterranean World*, ed. Demetrios Michaelides (Oxford: Oxbow, 2014), 308–19. On the history of the cult in late antiquity see Skedros, *Saint Demetrios*. For a well-documented and illustrated, diachronic survey, see Bauer, *Eine Stadt und ihr Patron*. On the date of its partial destruction and restoration, see Lemerle, *Les plus anciens recueils* 2:100; Spieser, *Thessalonique et ses monuments*, 165–67.

90. On the obscure origins and development of the cult, see, e.g., Delehaye, *Les légendes grecques*, 103–9; Lemerle, "Saint Démétrius," 671–73; Michael Vickers, "Sirmium or Thessaloniki? A Critical Examination of the St. Demetrius Legend," *ByzZ* 67 (1974): 337–50; Skedros, *Saint Demetrios*, 7–40; David Woods, "Thessalonica's Patron: Saint Demetrius or Emeterius?," *HTR* 93 (2000): 221–34; Jean-Michel Spieser, "Le culte de Saint Démétrius à Thessalonique," in *Des dieux civiques aux saints patrons (IVe-VIIe siècle)*, ed. Jean-Pierre Caillet et al. (Paris: Picard, 2015), 275–91.

91. Lemerle, "Saint Démétrius," 661–64; Charalambos Bakirtzis, "Pilgrimage to Thessalonike: The Tomb of St. Demetrios," *DOP* 56 (2002): 175–92; see also Soteriou and Soteriou, Ἁγίου Δημητρίου, 47–63; Bauer, *Eine Stadt und ihr Patron*, 143–83. The crypt was refurbished and fitted with a *myron* and a *ciborium* in the middle Byzantine period.

92. Lemerle, "Saint Démétrius," 665–73; Bakirtzis, "Pilgrimage to Thessalonike," 177–79; Spieser, "Le culte de Saint Démétrius," 283–85. The identification of the saint's tomb and relics remains a point of contention. Their location seems to have been kept secret by the local church authorities for fear that the relics might be transferred to Con-

Justinian mentioning the "revered house" (σεβάσμιος οἶκος) of Demetrios, and a 30-m mosaic frieze depicting the saint's miraculous agency across the northern inner aisle confirm the existence of a vibrant cult of St. Demetrios in Thessalonica in the sixth century.[93]

None of the original mosaic panels has been preserved, as they were all lost in the devastating fire of 1917, and only a handful of those copied or photographed a decade or so earlier can be confidently dated to the late fifth or mid-sixth century, that is, prior to the restoration of the basilica in the first half of the seventh century.[94] The focal point of the frieze is without a doubt Demetrios himself, who is represented throughout with a golden halo, wearing a chlamys and a *tablion*, and in the *orans* position or standing in front of an *aedicula* or pyramidal *ciborium* (the *locus sanctus* where the saint effectively was thought to "meet with" supplicants).[95]

---

stantinople. However, a small bottle that supposedly contained a few drops of the martyr's blood was found in a reliquary in the *enkainion* underneath the altar (see Soteriou and Soteriou, Ἁγίου Δημητρίου, 61–63; Spieser, *Thessalonique et ses monuments*, 89–96).

93. ICG 3104 (IMakedChr 94; SEG 47.995; *BE* [1987]: 432; sixth century CE): + Γρηγορίου μαγίστρου (?). "Of Gregorios magistros (?)."
ICG 3103 (IMakedChr 93; *IG* 10.2.1.66; fifth–sixth centuries CE): ᾽Εγὼ Βιταλιανὸς | δεκανὸς ἀνεθέμην | ὡρολόγιον τῷ ἁγίῳ μάρτυρι. "I, Vitalianos, *dekanos* (i.e., gravedigger?), dedicated this sundial to the holy martyr."
ICG 3091 (IMakedChr 81; *IG* 10.2.1.23; 538–565 CE): [- ᾽Ιουσ]τινιανὸς Ἀλαμανικὸς Γοτ[θικὸς-| -] νικητ(ὴς) τροπαιοῦχ(ος) ἀεισέβασ[τος |- μάρτυρο]ς Δημητρίου τοῦ κατὰ τ[- |-σ]εβασμίῳ οἴκῳ κατὰ τη[- ||⁵ -] προσευξόμενοι τῷ θ[(ε)ῷ-| -]πρακτων τῶν δ[-| -] πρᾶγμα ἐλαττω[- | -]ειναι αὐτὰς τ[- |-ἀν]ακωχῆς κα[- ||¹⁰ -]ιναι του[- | -]ιστ[-]. A staurogram replaces the *rho* in the martyr's name. The plate was found reused in the floor of the Hagios Demetrios.

94. See Charles Diehl and Marcel Le Tourneau, "Les mosaïques de Saint-Démétrius de Salonique," *MMFEP* 18 (1911): 225–48; Robin S. Cormack, "The Mosaic Decoration of S. Demetrios, Thessaloniki: A Re-examination in the Light of the Drawings of W. S. George," *ABSA* 64 (1969): 17–52; Charalambos Bakirtzis, Eutychia Kourkoutidou-Nikolaidou, and Chrysanthi Mavropoulou-Tsioumi, eds., *Mosaics of Thessaloniki: Fourth–Fourteenth Century* (Athens: Kapon, 2012), 131–79; Beat Brenk, "The Mosaics of Thessaloniki: The State of Research," in *The Mosaics of Thessaloniki Revisited: Papers from the 2014 Symposium at the Courtauld Institute of Art*, ed. Antony Eastmond and Myrto Hatzaki (Athens: Kapon, 2017), 19–21; Benjamin Fourlas, *Die Mosaiken der Acheiropoietos-Basilika in Thessaloniki: Eine vergleichende Analyse dekorativer Mosaiken des 5. und 6. Jahrhunderts*, 2 vols., MillSt 35 (Berlin: de Gruyter, 2012), 110–56. Feissel edited only the inscriptions predating the restoration.

95. On the importance of the *ciborium*, see Bakirtzis, "Pilgrimage to Thessalonike," 177–79; Spieser, "Le culte de Saint Démétrius," 283–85.

Accompanied by other saints (Pelagia, Matrona, and Alexandros) as well as donors portrayed in smaller medallions in the background, he effectively occupies the central stage on all spandrels (A, B, D, F), except for spandrels C and E, which depict, respectively, an enthroned Virgin Mary and Child (surrounded by attendant angels and saints, including Demetrios himself), and a standing Virgin.[96]

Although nothing is known of its original designer(s) and sponsor(s), the monumental artwork must have been meant as an act of gratitude toward Demetrios that commemorated his wonders (in this instance, the miraculous birth or healing of a little girl).[97] In effect, it represents a vivid illustration of the saint's attractive power and prominence in the popular imagination in late antique Thessalonica. As shown in the last spandrel (H), and as highlighted in the miracle account by the archbishop John, Demetrios continuously stood *orans* as the great intercessor of the city, ever ready to answer the people's petitions to heal and rescue them from impending dangers, be it foreign invaders or the plague.[98]

5.2. The Rotunda (a.k.a. Hagios Georgios)[99]

Saint or martyr veneration at Thessalonica was not solely restricted to Demetrios but also extended to other lesser-known saints such as those

---

96. ICG 3117 (IMakedChr 105; fifth–sixth centuries CE): (A) Ἡ ἀγ(ία) | Πελαγία, (B) Ἡ ἀγ(ία) | Ματρώνα. "(A) Saint Pelagia, (B) Saint Matrona."

ICG 3120 (IMakedChr 108; fifth–sixth centuries CE): (A) [Ὁ ἅγιος -]ος, (B) Ὁ ἅγι[ος Ἀλέξαν]δρος. "(A) Saint… (?), (B) Saint Alexandros (?)."

ICG 3116 (IMakedChr 104; fifth–sixth centuries CE; western end): Ὑπὲρ εὐ|χῆς οὗ | οἶδεν | ὁ Θ(εὸ)ς τὸ || ὄνο|μα. + "*Ex-voto* of the one whose name God knows."

ICG 3121 (IMakedChr 109; fifth–sixth centuries CE; eastern end): + Ὑπ[ὲρ ε]|ὐχῆ[ς ο]|ὗ οἶδ[εν]|| ὁ Θ(εὸ)ς [τὸ]||| ὄνο[μα] + "*Ex-voto* of the one whose name God knows."

97. The frieze concludes with a touching inscription on spandrel G, which records a family's petition to the saint for themselves and their daughter Maria. ICG 3119 (IMakedChr 107; fifth–sixth centuries CE): + Καὶ σύ, δέσποτά μο[υ]| ἅγιε Διμήτρι, βοήθι ἡμῖν | τοῖς δούλοις σου καὶ | τῇ δούλῃ σου Μαρί||ᾳ ἣν ἔδωκες + | ἡμῖν. + "And you, my Lord, Saint Demetrios, help us, your servants, and your servant Maria whom you gave to us." The anonymous parents likely sponsored, in part at least, the mosaic to show their appreciation to the saint. See Cormack, "Mosaic Decoration," 31–32; Charalambos Bakirtzis, "The Mosaics of the Basilica of St Demetrios," in Eastmond and Hatzaki, *Mosaics of Thessaloniki Revisited*, 98.

98. See Cormack, "Mosaic Decoration," 37–39.

99. On the original name of the church, see W. Eugene Kleinbauer, "The Origi-

already mentioned, as well as to the twenty male martyrs whose mosaic portraits adorned the walls of the cupola of the Rotunda.

Initially built as a temple of patron deities modeled on Rome's Pantheon that connected to Galerius's palace via a colonnaded street, the Rotunda was possibly converted into a Christian place of worship in the Theodosian era (at the earliest), with relics (of the martyrs displayed in the mosaics?) being placed under its altar and in two crypts adjacent to the apse.[100] Possibly dedicated to Christ, it was decorated with exquisite mosaics about the same time as its transformation or around the mid- to late fifth century, if not in the sixth century, and furnished with a sumptuous fan-shaped ambo with reliefs featuring the epiphany in the mid-sixth century.[101] Just as the basilica of Demetrios, the edifice has greatly suffered

---

nal Name and Function of Hagios Georgios at Thessaloniki," *CahA* 22 (1972): 55–60; Hjalmar Torp, *La rotonde palatine à Thessalonique: Architecture et mosaïques* (Athens: Kapon, 2018), 1:59–60.

100. The initial building was never completed and unlikely to have been intended as a mausoleum. See the latest discussion in Torp, *La rotonde palatine* 1:13–33 (and the rich bibliography therein). On the various proposed dates for the conversion, which ranges from the end of the fourth century to the sixth century, see the discussions and bibliographies in Torp, *La rotonde palatine* 1:35–68, 76–83; and Slobodan Ćurčić, *Some Observations and Questions regarding Early Christian Architecture in Thessaloniki* (Thessaloniki: Hypourgeio Politismou Ephoreia Byzantinon Archaioteton Thessalonikes, 2000), 14–15. Despite recent attempts by Ćurčić, as well as Bakirtzis and Mastora, to attribute this conversion to Constantine, definitive archaeological evidence supporting a pre-Theodosian date remains to be found (Ćurčić, *Early Christian Architecture in Thessaloniki*; Bakirtzis and Mastora, "Mosaics in the Rotunda"). See Charalambos Bakirtzis and Pelli Mastora, "Are the Mosaics in the Rotunda into (*sic*) Thessaloniki Linked to Its Conversion to a Christian Church?," *NB* 9 (2011): 33–45; Brenk, "Mosaics of Thessaloniki," 21–31; Jean-Michel Spieser, "À propos de trois livres récents sur des monuments de Thessalonique," *AT* 22 (2014): 303–5. On the relics, see Torp, *La rotonde palatine* 1:43–47, 59, 199–200, 211; W. Eugene Kleinbauer, "The Iconography and the Date of the Mosaics of the Rotunda of Hagios Georgios, Thessaloniki," *Viator* 3 (1972): 55 (with n. 108).

101. For a recent, detailed examination of the edifice and its mosaics (with an up-to-date bibliography), see the magisterial treatment by art historian Torp, *La rotonde palatine*. See also, e.g., André Grabar, "À propos des mosaïques de la coupole de Saint-Georges, à Salonique," *CahA* 17 (1967): 59–81; Spieser, *Thessalonique et ses monuments*, 113–64; Fourlas, *Acheiropoietos-Basilika*, 156–67, 177–95; Charalambos Bakirtzis, "Rotunda," in Bakirtzis, Kourkoutidou-Nikolaidou, and Mavropoulou-Tsioumi, *Mosaics of Thessaloniki*—with excellent photographic reproductions; Eastmond and Hatzaki, *Mosaics of Thessaloniki Revisited*. The date of the mosaics

The Emergence and Development of Christianity in Thessalonica 213

over the centuries, and only about a third of the original mosaic decoration has survived.[102] The central mosaic in the cupola medallion is now almost completely lost, but traces indicate that it must have represented a glorious Christ encircled by a starry band and a vegetal garland, a phoenix (a symbol of the resurrection), and four supporting angels.[103] Similarly, almost nothing (except the feet of floating figures) has been preserved of the intermediary zone between the medallion and the base of the dome, which is thought to have symbolized angels in the celestial realm.[104]

Fortunately, most of the panels around the base of the cupola have survived more or less intact (except for the one above the apse), along with thirteen of the twenty original mosaic inscriptions.[105] The 75-m circular ensemble can be divided into seven panels (I–VII), each of which contains two or three portraits, with a legend providing the name and occupation of the martyr (in the genitive), as well as the month in which he was presumably commemorated.[106] All of the figures are depicted without a nimbus,

---

remains disputed. For Torp, the conversion and decoration of the Rotunda were both undertaken by Theodosius I (*La rotonde palatine* 1:82–83, 445–89). Brenk, on the other hand, argues (among others) that they were likely completed in the second half of the fifth or sixth century based on historical, topographical, architectural, and iconographic grounds ("Mosaics of Thessaloniki," 30–31).

102. Torp, *La rotonde palatine* 1:71.

103. Still visible on the masonry in the *clipeus* are the preliminary drawing of a male figure, the upper part of a halo, a raised right hand, and the tip of a cross or scepter. See the detailed examination in Torp, who interprets the medallion mosaic as a theophanic vision of the victorious Christ *Sol* (*La rotonde palatine* 1:353–88). By contrast, Bakirtzis and Mastora argue that the central scene represents the *adventus* of Constantine in the form of *Sol invictus* ("Mosaics in the Rotunda," 39–40). For Grabar, Kleinbauer, and Nasrallah, the whole mosaic program of the Rotunda revolves around the parousia of Christ. See Grabar, "Saint-Georges"; Kleinbauer, "Rotunda"; Laura S. Nasrallah, "Empire and Apocalypse in Thessaloniki: Interpreting the Early Christian Rotunda," *JECS* 13 (2005): 465–508.

104. See Torp, *La rotonde palatine* 1:353–88 (esp. 354–57), 389–90. The original mosaics in the apse have also been lost. Those currently visible date from the ninth-tenth centuries CE. See Torp, *La rotonde palatine* 1:389–90.

105. Four inscriptions are lost, one was restituted (III.1), and one arbitrarily restored (V.1; see IMakedChr, p. 105).

106. The names in the genitive conform to the formula of the synaxaria and imply the word μνήμην (see IMakedChr, p. 109). For an exhaustive study of the martyrs, see chs. 6–11 in Torp, *La rotonde palatine* 1:161–351. See also Kleinbauer, "Rotunda," 44–62; Bakirtzis, "Rotunda," 62–114. *Note bene*: IMakedChr 110 and Bakirtzis retain a seven-panel division, while Torp follows an eight-panel division that is out of sync

Fig. 6.16. Cupola mosaic of the Rotunda. Reproduced with permission from C. Bakirtzis, E. Kourkoutidou-Nikolaidou, and C. Mavropoulou-Tsioumi, eds., *Mosaics of Thessaloniki*, 113, fig. 72.

wearing either a *chlamys* (if a soldier) or a *paenula* (if a cleric or a civilian), and standing *orans* in front of a golden *aedicula* or *frons scaenae* likely representing God's palace or temple in the heavenly Jerusalem.[107] Following Feissel's classification, and running clockwise when facing the apse, the

---

with that of Feissel and Bakirtzis (see Bakirtzis, "Rotunda, 64–65; Torp, *La rotonde palatine* 1:162). Panel I in Torp thus corresponds to panel II in Feissel and Bakirtzis. The panel above the apse (VII in Torp) was reconstituted by the painter Rossi in the late nineteenth century on the basis of the other panels and features neither martyr nor inscription (see Torp, *La rotonde palatine* 1:72–73).

107. The martyrs can be divided into two distinct groups: *chlamys*-wearing soldiers (seven in total) and *paenula*-wearing civilians, either laymen (six) or clerics (four), with the latter representing the minority. For a detailed examination of their portraiture, clothing, and possible identity, see chs. 6–7 in Torp, *La rotonde palatine* 1:162–220. On the architectural elements and their significance, see chs. 10–11 in Torp, *La rotonde palatine* 1:271–351. See also Grabar, "Saint-Georges," 69–76; Kleinbauer, "Rotunda," 58–62.

The Emergence and Development of Christianity in Thessalonica 215

Fig. 6.17. ICG 3123 (IMakedChr 110): panel II with the martyrs Onesiphoros and Porphyrios.

Fig. 6.18. ICG 3124 (IMakedChr 110): panel III with the martyrs Kosmas and Damianos.

Fig. 6.19. ICG 3128 (IMakedChr 110): panel VII with the martyrs Philippos, Therinos, and Damianos.

Fig. 6.20. Plan of the martyr mosaics in the Rotunda. Drawing by E. Dyggve; reproduced with permission from H. Torp, *La rotonde palatine*, 2:172–73, pl. XII.

martyrs consist of the soldier Leon (featured with a jeweled crown) and the flutist Philemon (I), the soldier Onesiphoros and a certain Porphyrios (II), the physician Damianos alongside Kosmas most likely (III), the presbyter Romanos and the soldier Eukarpion (IV), the presbyter Ananias and an unidentified ecclesiastic (Alexandros?) (V), the soldiers Basiliskos and Priskos (VI), and, finally, the soldier Therinos (also featured with a jeweled crown) flanked by the bishops Philippos and Kyrillos (VII).[108]

Of the twenty original portraits (fifteen of which have survived), only thirteen are thus known to us by name. Not all, however, can be identified with certainty or linked to a known martyr in hagiographical traditions. None of them originates from Thessalonica itself, and none appears to have been venerated there in subsequent centuries, or indeed to have become a major saint.[109] All come from the eastern part of the empire, and all seem to have been martyred during the Diocletian persecutions.[110] Even more remarkable, hardly any calendar month attributed to each martyr corresponds to his celebratory month(s) in the Roman *martyrologium* (except in the case

---

108. ICG 3122 (IMakedChr 110, I; sixth century CE): (1) Λέοντος | στρατ(ιώτου) | μηνὶ | Ἰουν(ίου), (2) (left) Φηλή|μονος | χοραύ|λου (right) μηνὶ | Μαρ|τ(ίου). "(1) Leon, soldier, in the month of June, (2) Philemon, chorus flutist, in the month of March."

ICG 3123 (IMakedChr 110, II; sixth century CE): (1) Ὀνησι|φόρου | στρ(ατιώτου) μηνὶ | Αὐγ(ούστου), (2) Πορ|φοιρίου | μηνὶ Αὐ|γ(ούστου). "(1) Onesiphoros, soldier, in the month of August, (2) Porphyrios, in the month of August."

ICG 3124 (IMakedChr 110, III; sixth century CE): (1) Κ[οσμᾶ | ἰατροῦ | μηνὶ Σεπ|τεμβρίου], (2) Δαμια|νοῦ ἰα|τροῦ μη|νὶ Σε|πτεμ(βρίου). "(1) K[osmas, physician, in the month of September], (2) Damianos, physician, in the month of September."

ICG 3125 (IMakedChr 110, IV; sixth century CE): (1) Ῥωμα|νοῦ | πρεσβ(υτέρου), (2) Εὐκαρ|πίωνος | στρατ(ιώτου) | μηνὶ Δε|κεμβρ(ίου). "(1) Romanos, presbyter, (2) Eukarpion, soldier, in the month of December."

ICG 3126 (IMakedChr 110, V; sixth century CE): (1) Ἀ[-]| Δ[-|-], (2), Ἀνανί|ου πρεσ|β(υτέρου) μηνὶ | Ἰανου|αρί(ου). "(2) Ananias, presbyter, in the month of January."

ICG 3127 (IMakedChr 110, VI; sixth century CE): (1) Βασιλί|σκου στρα(τιώτου) | μηνὶ Ἀπρι|λίου, (2) Πρίσκου | στρα(τιώτου) | μηνὶ | Ὀκτωβρί(ου). "(1) Basiliskos, soldier, in the month of April, (2) Priskos, soldier, in the month of October."

ICG 3128 (IMakedChr 110, VII; sixth century CE): (1) Φιλίπ|που ἐπι|σκ(όπου) μη|νὶ Ὀκτω||βρ(ίου), (2) Θερινοῦ | στρατ(ιώτου) | μηνὶ Ἰου|λ(ίου), (3) Κυρίλ|[λ]ου ἐπι|σκ(όπου) μην[ὶ | Ἰ]ουλ(ίου). "(1) Philippos, bishop, in the month of October, (2) Therinos, soldier, in the month of July, (3) Kyrillos, bishop, in the month of July."

109. See Brenk, "Mosaics of Thessaloniki," 31.

110. See Torp, *La rotonde palatine* 1:207, 211–13; Brenk, "Mosaics of Thessaloniki," 31.

of Damianos) or the synaxarion of Constantinople (except in the case of Ananias and Kyrillos).[111] Needless to say, these discrepancies have led to a variety of interpretations. According to Byzantinist Edmund Weigand, these could indicate that this ad hoc collection of martyrs was designed before the Eastern calendar was standardized.[112] For Hjalmar Torp, on the other hand, they reveal that the iconographic program of the Rotunda was primarily motivated by the ideological and sociopolitical agenda of the imperial house, rather than by liturgical or hagiographical considerations.[113]

The preponderance of soldiers is certainly striking, particularly the prominence placed on Leon and Therinos, who are both represented with a jeweled crown, while the blending of imperial and ecclesiastical iconographical motifs is altogether unique.[114] Judging from its spatial relation to the palatial complex, the Rotunda clearly belongs to an imperial context and must have therefore been intended as a palatine chapel for the imperial court, rather than as a church for the general population of Thessalonica.[115] According to Charalambos Bakirtzis and Pelli Mastora, the martyrs may in fact correspond to "specific persons in the Constantinian élite" who were present at "the triumphal *adventus* of Constantine the Great," and who must have been depicted in the dome medallion alongside the emperor's "tutelary deity Helios [represented by the phoenix] and the revealed Christ [represented by the cross]."[116] For W. Eugene Kleinbauer, on the other hand, the *orans* figures merely represent the founders of the Christian Rotunda or its financial sponsors.[117] Alternatively, Torp

---

111. See IMakedChr, pp. 106–10; Torp, *La rotonde palatine* 1:207–8.

112. Edmund Weigand, "Der Kalenderfries von Hagios Georgios in Thessalonike: Datierung, Ideen- und Kunstgeschichtliche Stellung," *ByzZ* 39 (1939): 116–45. But see Kleinbauer, "Rotunda," 74–78; Spieser, *Thessalonique et ses monuments*, 153–57; IMakedChr, pp. 109–10; Torp, *La rotonde palatine* 1:207–11.

113. Torp, *La rotonde palatine* 1:207–13, 467–89. On the political and theological implications of the Rotunda's iconographic program, see esp. chs. 15–16 in Torp, *La rotonde palatine* 1:445–89.

114. See Kleinbauer, "Rotunda," 63–68; Nasrallah, "Empire and Apocalypse in Thessaloniki"; Torp, *La rotonde palatine* 1:82, 209, 480.

115. See Aristoteles Mentzos, "Reflections of the Interpretation and Dating of the Rotunda of Thessaloniki," *Egnatia* 5 (1999–2000): 70; Bakirtzis and Mastora, "Mosaics in the Rotunda"; Bakirtzis, "Rotunda"; Torp, *La rotonde palatine* 1:480–81.

116. Bakirtzis, "Rotunda," 116; see also Bakirtzis and Mastora, "Mosaics in the Rotunda."

117. W. Eugene Kleinbauer, "The Orants in the Mosaic Decoration of the Rotunda

has argued, the martyrs may have functioned as heavenly protectors representing, and interceding for, the various dioceses of the Eastern empire from which they originated.[118]

Overall, the Rotunda remains somewhat of an enigma and will continue to generate much scholarly debate between archaeologists, art historians, and Byzantinists until thorough stratigraphic excavations and structural surveys of the building are finally conducted.[119] To this day, no real consensus has emerged as to the date of the building and its conversion. Similarly, no agreement exists as to the iconographic significance of this eclectic assemblage of Eastern martyrs, except that it is altogether exceptional and without any known parallel in terms of style or form in the whole Mediterranean world.[120] Most problematic is the fact that so little is known about the cult of these particular saints in late antiquity, apart from Kosmas and Damianos, two popular medical saints whose "veneration outside Syria is nowhere documented before the second third of the fifth century."[121] However one chooses to interpret the Rotunda's iconographic program, what is certain is that various martyrial cults blossomed in Thessalonica between the fourth and sixth centuries, encouraged in part by the imperial house itself.

5.3. The Hagia Sophia, Acheiropoietos, and Hosios David

Other impressive monuments from the late antique and early Byzantine eras include the Acheiropoietos basilica located north of the Via Regia and the Hagia Sophia on its opposite southern side, west of Galerius's imperial palace, which was erected on top of a massive five-aisled edi-

---

at Thessaloniki: Martyr Saints or Donors?," *CahA* 30 (1982): 25–45. But see Nasrallah's objections ("Empire and Apocalypse in Thessaloniki," 489).

118. Torp, *La rotonde palatine* 1:210–13, 480–81.

119. See Eastmond and Hatzaki, *Mosaics of Thessaloniki Revisited*, 15–17; Brenk, "Mosaics of Thessaloniki," 21–31; Nasrallah, "Empire and Apocalypse in Thessaloniki," 468–69. On the history of research, partial excavations, and restorations, see Torp, *La rotonde palatine* 1:69–86. Torp's magisterial two volumes should be followed in the near future by Bakirtzis and Mastora's study (as announced in their article "Mosaics in the Rotunda").

120. See Brenk, "Mosaics of Thessaloniki," 29–30; Hjalmar Torp, "Considerations on the Chronology of the Rotunda Mosaics," in Eastmond and Hatzaki, *Mosaics of Thessaloniki Revisited*, 35; Bakirtzis, "Rotunda," 116.

121. Brenk, "Mosaics of Thessaloniki," 29.

fice (ca. 120 x 50 m) in the fifth century.[122] Hagia Sophia is thought to have been dedicated to St. Mark initially, and the predecessor of the Hagia Sophia must have functioned as the first episcopal basilica given its size and the presence of a large quatrefoil baptistery to the south (which is now revered as the *hagiasma* of John the Baptist). Destroyed in the seventh century (perhaps after the quakes of the 620s CE), it was renovated in the iconoclastic period in the eighth century (hence its sparse decoration) and served as the metropolitan church of Thessalonica during the Byzantine era.[123] Despite its importance, no significant late antique inscription has so far been discovered in its vicinity, not even an *ex-voto* recording the name of a donor, as in, for example, the basilica of the Acheiropoietos.[124]

An imposing two-story building (ca. 51.9 x 30.8 m), the three-aisled structure was erected on the ruins of a bath complex in the second half of the fifth century (ca. 475 CE).[125] Known originally as the Church of the Virgin (to whom it was dedicated), it was renamed as the Acheiropoietos

---

122. The fifth-century basilica, the largest of its kind at Thessalonica, appears to have been constructed over a mid-fourth-century church, which itself had been built on top of a fourth-century Roman thermal complex and *nymphaeum*. See Ph. A. Drossoyianni, "θεσσαλονίκη: Αγία Σοφία," *AD* 18, B.2 (1963): 235–42; Aristoteles Mentzos, "Συμβολή στην έρευνα του αρχαιότερου ναού της Αγίας Σοφίας Θεσσαλονίκης," *Makedonika* 21 (1981): 201–21; Kalliopi Theoharidou, *The Architecture of Hagia Sophia, Thessaloniki: From Its Erection up to the Turkish Conquest* (Oxford: B.A.R., 1988), 9–13.

123. For a detailed survey of the history and architecture of the Hagia Sophia, see Theoharidou, *Hagia Sophia*; Chrysanthi Mavropoulou-Tsioumi, *Hagia Sophia: The Great Church of Thessaloniki* (Athens: Kapon, 2014), 4–9.

124. Besides the fragmentary epitaph ICG 3155 (IMakedChr 135), found reused in the floor of the apse, only a small inscribed piece of bronze decoration featuring vine foliage seems to have been discovered during the excavations of the Hagia Sophia basilica. See ICG 3111 (IMakedChr 100; fifth–sixth centuries CE): [– ἀ]νέθετο. + "[so and so...?] dedicated (this)." On the early Byzantine mosaic inscriptions, see Charalambos Bakirtzis, "Νεότερες παρατηρήσεις στην κτητορική επιγραφή του τρούλλου της Αγίας Σοφίας Θεσσαλονίκης," *Byzantina* 11 (1982): 165–80; Bakirtzis, Kourkoutidou-Nikolaidou, and Mavropoulou-Tsioumi, *Mosaics of Thessaloniki*, 241–95.

125. See Andreas Xyngopoulos, "Περί την Ἀχειροποίητον Θεσσαλονίκης," *Makedonika* 2 (1942–1952): 472–87; Charalambos Bakirtzis, "Ῥωμαϊκὸς λουτρῶν καὶ ἡ Ἀχειροποίητος τῆς Θεσσαλονίκης," in *Ἀφιέρωμα στην μνήμη Στυλιανού Πελεκανίδη* (Thessaloniki: Etaireia Makedonikon Spoudon, 1983), 311–29; Michael Vickers, "Fifth-Century Brickstamps from Thessaloniki," *ABSA* 68 (1973): 291–94 (esp. on the dating); W. Eugene Kleinbauer, "Remarks on the Building History of the Acheiropoietos Church at Thessaloniki," in *Actes du Xe congrès international d'archéologie chrétienne*, 241–57; Spieser, *Thessalonique et ses monuments*, 212 (on the dating); Bakirtzis,

("not-made-by-hands") after receiving a "miraculous" icon of the Virgin Hodegetria in the fourteenth century.[126] Decorated in luxurious Theodosian style, it featured large floor slabs of Proconesian marble (in the central aisle), delicately carved marble columns and capitals, and idyllic mosaics with floral motifs, birds, and crosses, in the intrados of the two central colonnades.[127] Several mosaic *ex-votos* have been discovered in its vicinity, including two on the soffits of the central and southern arches of the *tribelon* entrance.[128] While the first is anonymous, the second records the name of one of the main donors, the "humble Andreas."[129] First identified as the bishop of Thessalonica attested between 491–497 CE (so Cormack), Andreas may have simply been a presbyter (so Bakirtzis)—the title ἐπίσκοπος is missing—if he was not a noble layman who contributed financially to the edifice (so Ferrua and Février).[130] Whatever the case may have been, Andreas must have been connected to the foundation of the church since his dedication was prominently displayed on the intrados of the central arch of the tribelon.[131]

However, none of the preserved mosaics of the Acheiropoietos are as spectacular as that which adorned the apse wall of the chapel of

---

Kourkoutidou-Nikolaidou, and Mavropoulou-Tsioumi, *Mosaics of Thessaloniki*, 199–237; Fourlas, *Acheiropoietos-Basilika*.

126. Andreas Xyngopoulos, "Η λατρευτική εικών του ναού της Αχειροποιήτου Θεσσαλονίκης," *Hellenika* 13 (1954): 256–62.

127. For detailed study of these mosaics, see Fourlas, *Acheiropoietos-Basilika*, 30–109.

128. Beside ICG 3113 and 3114 (see n. 129 below), another late *ex-voto* inscription was found on the broken upper border of a chancel plate. See ICG 3108 (IMakedChr 98; *IG* 10.2.1.*281; sixth century CE): [Ὑπὲ]ρ εὐχῆς Δημητρίου. "*Ex-voto* of Demetrios."

129. ICG 3113 (IMakedChr 102 A; fifth century CE): + Ὑπὲρ ε[ὐχῆς οὗ ο]ἶδεν | + ὁ θεὸς τὸ ὄνομα. "*Ex-voto* of the one whose name God knows."
ICG 3114 (IMakedChr 102 B; fifth century CE): + Ὑπὲρ ε[ὐχῆ]ς |[Ἀ]νδρέου [τα]πινοῦ. + "*Ex-voto* of the humble Andreas."

130. See Cormack, "Mosaic Decoration," 51; Charalambos Bakirtzis, "Sur le donateur et la date des mosaïques d'Acheiropoietos à Thessalonique," in *Atti del IX congresso internazionale di archeologia Cristiana, Roma 21–27 settembre 1975*, 2 vols. (Rome: Pontificio Istituto di Archeologia Cristiana, 1978), 2:37–46; A. Ferrua and P.-A. Février in Bakirtzis, "Acheiropoietos à Thessalonique," 45. See also Denis Feissel and Jean-Michel Spieser, "Inventaires en vue d'un recueil des inscriptions historiques de Byzance: Les inscriptions de Thessalonique; Supplément," *TM* 7 (1979): 312, no. 6; Fourlas, *Acheiropoietos-Basilika*, 197–99.

131. See IMakedChr, p. 97.

Hosios David, the former catholicon of the nearby monastery of Latomos (wrongly) named after the famous dendrite.[132] Presumably founded and dedicated to the prophet Zacharias in the late fifth or early sixth century, it was decorated with a majestic mandorla mosaic of an enthroned beardless Christ.[133] Lost for centuries until its rediscovery by Andreas Xyngopoulos in 1927, the theophanic scene depicts a glorified, youthful Jesus seated on a rainbow arch with four rivers flowing at his feet and surrounded by representations of the four gospels, that is, four codices held by, respectively, a lion, a bull, an eagle, and an angel.[134] His right hand raised up, his left hand holds an open roll, on which can be read an adapted citation of Isa 25:9–10 (wherein Mount Zion, τὸ ὄρος, is replaced by the church, ὁ οἶκος): "Behold our God in whom we hope and rejoiced over our salvation, for he shall give rest to this house."[135] In addition, two bearded men feature to his right and left, one standing with a fearful and ecstatic look,

---

132. For a description of the building and its mosaics, see Andreas Xyngopoulos, "Τὸ καθολικόν τῆς Μονῆς Λατόμου ἐν Θεσσαλονίκῃ καὶ τὸ ἐν αὐτῷ ψηφιδωτόν," *AD* 12 (1929): 142–80; Efthymios N. Tsigaridas, Οἱ τοιχογραφίες τῆς μονῆς Λατόμου Θεσσαλονίκης καὶ ἡ βυζαντινή ζωγραφική τοῦ 12ου αἰώνα (Thessalonike: Etaireia Makedonikon Spoudon, 1986), 11–23; Tsigaridas, *Latomou Monastery: The Church of Hosios David* (Thessalonike: Institute for Balkans Studies, 1988); Bakirtzis, Kourkoutidou-Nikolaidou, and Mavropoulou-Tsioumi, *Mosaics of Thessaloniki*, 180–95. On the saint's life see *BHG*, no. 493; Alexander Vasiliev, "Life of David of Thessalonica," *Traditio* 4 (1946): 115–47; Raymond-Joseph Loenertz, "Saint David de Thessalonique: Sa vie, son culte, ses reliques, ses images," *RevEB* 11 (1953): 205–23.

133. See Xyngopoulos, "Μονῆς Λατόμου," 172, 179; Bakirtzis, Kourkoutidou-Nikolaidou, and Mavropoulou-Tsioumi, *Mosaics of Thessaloniki*, 194; Fourlas, *Acheiropoietos-Basilika*, 144–45 (with a detailed bibliography in n. 141). C. R. Morey rejects a date earlier than the seventh century CE. See Morey, "A Note on the Date of the Mosaic of Hosios David, Salonica," *Byzantion* 7 (1932): 339–46.

134. See Xyngopoulos, "Μονῆς Λατόμου," 142–43. On the symbolism of the mosaics, see Jean-Michel Spieser, "Remarques complémentaires sur la mosaïques de Osios David," in Διεθνές Συμπόσιο: Βυζαντινή Μακεδονία, 324–1430 μ.Χ, Θεσσαλονίκη 29–31 Οκτωβρίου 1992 (Thessaloniki: Etaireia Makedonikon Spoudon, 1995), 295–306; James Snyder, "The Meaning of the 'Maiestas Domini' in Hosios David," *Byzantion* 37 (1967): 143–52; Laura Nasrallah, "Early Christian Interpretation in Image and Word: Canon, Sacred Text, and the Mosaic of Moni Latomou," in Nasrallah, Bakirtzis, and Friesen, *From Roman to Early Christian Thessalonike*, 361–96; Nasrallah, "Ezekiel's Vision in Late Antiquity: The Case of the Mosaic of Moni Latomou, Thessaloniki," in Eastmond and Hatzaki, *Mosaics of Thessaloniki Revisited*, 77–89; Bakirtzis, Kourkoutidou-Nikolaidou, and Mavropoulou-Tsioumi, *Mosaics of Thessaloniki*, 188–95.

135. ICG 3115 (IMakedChr 103 B; fifth–sixth centuries CE): + Ἰδοὺ ὁ θ(εὸ)ς |

his hands raised to his face, the other calmly seated, almost contemplative, and holding an open codex, on which is written an acclamation likening Christ and the church to a "vivifying source welcoming (and) nourishing faithful souls."[136] The same acclamation is repeated once more on a band at the bottom of the mosaic and is completed by an anonymous *ex-voto* of a female donor who, having had her prayer answered, fulfilled her vow and had the mosaic made.[137]

While the two bearded men cannot be identified with certainty, they have generally been interpreted as the prophets Ezekiel, Habakkuk, Isaiah, or even as John of Patmos.[138] Whoever they might be, what is clear is that the acclamation on the open codex is not found anywhere else in biblical literature and that the identification of the church as a "vivifying, welcoming and nourishing source" (πηγὴ ζωτική, δεκτική, θρεπτική) is exceptional in inscriptions in Macedonia and beyond. Equally noteworthy are the iconographic allusions to Jewish-Christian texts such as Ezekiel and Revelation, and the unusual invitation to "behold God" (Ἰδοὺ ὁ θεὸς ἡμῶν).[139]

ἡμῶν ἐ|φ' ᾧ ἐλπίζο|μεν κ(αὶ) ἠγαλ||λιώμεθα | ἐπὶ τῇ σω|τηρίᾳ ἡ|μῶν ὅτι ἀ|νάπαυσιν || δώσει ἐπὶ | τὸν οἶκον | τοῦτον.

136. ICG 3115 (IMakedChr 103 C; fifth–sixth centuries CE): (left) + Πη|γὴ ζω|τική, δε|κτ<ικ>ή, θρεπτική (right) ψυ|χῶν πι|στοῦν | ὁ <π> παν|έν<τι>μος | οἶ<κ>ος ο|<ὗτ>ος. + "Vivifying source, welcoming, nourishing the faithful souls, (such is) this venerable house."

137. ICG 3115 (IMakedChr 103 A; fifth–sixth centuries CE): + Πηγὴ ζ<ω>τική, δεκτική, θρεπτική ψυχῶν πιστῶν ὁ πανέντιμος οἶκος οὗτος. Εὐξαμένη ἐπέτυχα καὶ ἐπιτυχοῦσα ἐπλήροσα. + | Ὑπὲρ εὐχῆς ἧς οἶδεν ὁ θεὸς τὸ ὄνομα. "Vivifying source, welcoming, nourishing the faithful souls, (such is) this venerable house. Having made a vow, my wish was granted, and, being (thus) granted, I fulfilled (my vow). *Ex-voto* of the one whose name God knows." The donor is unlikely to have been Theodora, the daughter of emperor Maximianus, as the ninth- or tenth-century legendary narrative by the abbot Ignatios recounts (on which see Vasiliev, "David of Thessalonica," 137–40). See also Xyngopoulos, "Μονῆς Λατόμου," 172–78.

138. See Xyngopoulos, "Μονῆς Λατόμου," 158–59; Tsigaridas, *Latomou Monastery*, 36–50; Rotraut Wisskirchen, "Zum Apsismosaik der Kirche Hosios David/ Thessalonike," in *Stimuli: Exegese und ihre Hermeneutik in Antike und Christentum; Festschrift für Ernst Dassmann*, ed. Georg Schöllgen and Clemens Scholten (Münster: Aschendorff, 1996), 588–92; Bakirtzis, Kourkoutidou-Nikolaidou, and Mavropoulou-Tsioumi, *Mosaics of Thessaloniki*, 190–94. For Snyder and Matthias Exner, the figure seated to the right represents John of Patmos. See Snyder, "Hosios David," 151; Exner, "Das fischreiche Gläserne Meer vor dem Thron Christi: Bemerkungen zum Apsismosaik von Hosios David in Thessaloniki," *MJBK* 67 (2016): 7–14.

139. See Nasrallah, "Mosaic of Moni Latomou"; Nasrallah, "Ezekiel's Vision."

Fig. 6.21. Mandorla mosaic of Hosios David.

Whoever sponsored this magnificent art work, she was obviously deeply attached to this "venerable house" (ὁ πανέντιμος οἶκος) and displayed great artistic and theological sensitivity.

5.4. Monumental Patronage

A final question that these magnificent edifices raise is who actually sponsored their construction. In the case of the Rotunda, the sheer size of the building, its integration into the palatial complex, and its 2,000 m² of magnificent mosaic decoration undoubtedly point to the imperial house (despite the absence of explicit literary or epigraphic evidence).[140] Similarly, the architectural and ornamental correspondence between the Acheiropoietos and ecclesiastical buildings at Constantinople strongly suggests an imperial impetus behind the monumentalization (as well as fortification) of Thessalonica between the fifth and sixth centuries and the

---

140. See esp. Torp, *La rotonde palatine* 1:52, 467–89. See also Fourlas, *Acheiropoietos-Basilika*, 175 (with the bibliography referenced in n. 277). On the material and construction technique of the mosaics, see ch. 14 in Torp, *La rotonde palatine* 1:409–43.

direct involvement of workshops from Constantinople.[141] Still, the emperors may not have been solely responsible for this construction boom. High imperial officials such as the praetorian prefect of Illyricum, bishops, and wealthy individuals or families must have also played a role in the emergence of Christian art and architecture in late antique Thessalonica—the first two groups certainly contributed to its fortification.[142] Besides those found in the basilica of Hagios Demetrios, the Acheiropoietos, and the Hagia Sophia, the series of late monogrammatic *ex-votos* discovered in the eastern wall provide plenty of evidence that affluent individuals were willing and able to participate financially in the foundation and embellishment of places of worship.[143] This in turn implies that, just as in Italy or in other Eastern provinces, the church had made significant forays in the upper echelons of Macedonian society and in the imperial administration by the end of the fourth century.

---

141. See Spieser, *Thessalonique et ses monuments*, 123; Torp, "Thessalonique paléochrétienne," 125–26, 131–32; Spieser, *La rotonde palatine* 1:467–89; Ćurčić, "Christianization of Thessalonikē," 213–22; B. Killerich in Eastmond and Hatzaki, *Mosaics of Thessaloniki Revisited*, 49. For the rampart dedication by Theodosius II, see ICG 3098 (IMakedChr 88; *IG* 10.2.1.42; ante 450 CE): Θευδόσιος σκη<π>τοῦ[χος | ἄν]αξ τόδε τεῖ<χος> ἔτε<υξ>εν (?). "Theodosios, scepter-bearing Lord, built this wall." On the fortification of Thessalonica in general, see Spieser, *Thessalonique et ses monuments*, 25–80; Velenis, *Τα τείχη της Θεσσαλονίκης*; Rizos, "Late-Antique Walls of Thessalonica."

142. See the following two building inscriptions by Hormisdas, likely the praetorian prefect of the East in 450 CE (who may well have been the praetorian prefect of Illyricum previously), and by the consul Paulus in 512 CE. See also ICG 3101 (IMakedChr 91), mentioned above in n. 36.

ICG 3099 (IMakedChr 89; *IG* 10.2.1.43; ante 450 CE): τεί[χ]εσιν ἀρ[ρή]κτοις Ὁρμίσδας ἐξετέλεσσε τήνδε πόλ[ι]ν [–]ΕΤΙ[–]ΣΕ[–]ΝΚΑΟΛΡ[–]. "With unbreakable walls, Hormisdas completed this city … (?)."

ICG 3100 (IMakedChr 90; *IG* 10.2.1.280; ca. 512 CE): Παύλου τοῦ Βιβιανοῦ. "(Work) of Paul, son of Vivianus."

143. See ICG 3108, 3111, 3113, 3114, 3116, 3121 (IMakedChr 98, 100, 102 A–B, 104, 109) mentioned above in nn. 128, 124, 129, 96. See also the series ICG 3105 (IMakedChr 95; *SEG* 47.964; *BE* [1987]: 432; post-525 CE), ICG 3106 (IMakedChr 96; *SEG* 47.965; *BE* [1987]: 432; post-525 CE), ICG 3107 (IMakedChr 97; *SEG* 47.966; *BE* [1987]: 432; post-525 CE).

6. Summary

While the beginnings of Christianity in Thessalonica are traditionally connected to the ministry of the apostle Paul, it is only in the Constantinian age that Christianity started to gather momentum and in the Theodosian age that it imposed itself as the dominant religion. Christians indeed remain conspicuously absent in the epigraphy and archaeology of the second and third centuries, begin to identify themselves as such on their epitaphs from the late third or the early fourth century, and pervade the funerary epigraphy of the fifth and sixth centuries. The same may be said of ecclesiastical architecture. Though the earliest buildings date to the fourth century, it was in the fifth century that a vast monumental program sponsored in great part by the imperial house and Christian elites transformed the entire city landscape. Taken together, the epigraphic and archaeological evidence vividly illustrate how Thessalonica flourished as a center of religious and artistic life in late antiquity, drawing richly from both Eastern and Western influences. Having safely navigated the turbulent waters of the fifth and sixth centuries, Thessalonica thus eventually emerged from late antiquity as one of the leading cities of the Byzantine world.

Bibliography

Ascough, Richard S. *Paul's Macedonian Associations: The Social Context of Philippians and 1 Thessalonians*. WUNT 2/161. Tübingen: Mohr Siebeck, 2003.

Athanasiou, Fani, Venetia Malama, Maria Miza, and Maria Sarantidou. *Η αποκατάσταση των ερειπίων του Γαλεριανού συγκροτήματος στη Θεσσαλονίκη (1994–2014): Τεκμηρίωση και επεμβάσεις*. 2 vols. Thessalonike: Ephoreia Archaioteton polis Thessalonikes, 2015.

Bakirtzis, Charalambos. "Η αγορα της Θεσσαλονίκης στα παλαιοχριστιανικά χρόνια." Pages 5–19 in vol. 2 of *Actes du Xe congrès international d'archéologie chrétienne, Thessalonique, 28 septembre–4 octobre 1980*. 2 vols. Rome: Pontifico Istituto di Archeologia Cristiana, 1984.

———. "Late Antiquity and Christianity in Thessalonikē: Aspects of a Transformation." Pages 397–426 in *From Roman to Early Christian Thessalonike: Studies in Religion and Archaeology*. Edited by Laura Nasrallah, Charalambos Bakirtzis, and Steven J. Friesen. HTS 64. Cambridge: Harvard University Press, 2010.

---. "The Mosaics of the Basilica of St Demetrios." Pages 91–101 in *The Mosaics of Thessaloniki Revisited: Papers from the 2014 Symposium at the Courtauld Institute of Art*. Edited by Antony Eastmond and Myrto Hatzaki. Athens: Kapon, 2017.

---. "Νεότερες παρατηρήσεις στην κτητορική επιγραφή του τρούλλου της Αγίας Σοφίας Θεσσαλονίκης." *Byzantina* 11 (1982): 165–80.

---. "Ὁ Ξενὼν τοῦ Ἁγίου Δημητρίου: Εἰκονογραφικὰ Ζητήματα." Pages 308–19 in *Medicine and Healing in the Ancient Mediterranean World*. Edited by Demetrios Michaelides. Oxford: Oxbow, 2014.

---. "Pilgrimage to Thessalonike: The Tomb of St. Demetrios." *DOP* 56 (2002): 175–92.

---. "Rotunda." Pages 51–117 in *Mosaics of Thessaloniki: Fourth–Fourteenth Century*. Edited by Charalambos Bakirtzis, Eftychia Kourkoutidou-Nikolaidou, and Chrysanthi Mavropoulou-Tsioumi. Athens: Kapon, 2012.

---. "Ρωμαϊκὸς λουτρὼν καὶ ἡ Ἀχειροποίητος τῆς Θεσσαλονίκης." Pages 311–29 in *Αφιέρωμα στην μνήμη Στυλιανού Πελεκανίδη*. Thessaloniki: Etaireia Makedonikon Spoudon, 1983.

---. "Sur le donateur et la date des mosaïques d'Acheiropoietos à Thessalonique." Pages 37–46 in vol. 2 of *Atti del IX congresso internazionale di archeologia Cristiana, Roma 21–27 settembre 1975*. 2 vols. Rome: Pontificio Istituto di Archeologia Cristiana, 1978.

Bakirtzis, Charalambos, Eutychia Kourkoutidou-Nikolaidou, and Chrysanthi Mavropoulou-Tsioumi, eds. *Mosaics of Thessaloniki: Fourth–Fourteenth Century*. Athens: Kapon, 2012.

Bakirtzis, Charalambos, and Pelli Mastora. "Are the Mosaics in the Rotunda into (*sic*) Thessaloniki Linked to Its Conversion to a Christian Church?" *NB* 9 (2011): 33–45.

Bauer, Franz A. *Eine Stadt und ihr Patron: Thessaloniki und der Heilige Demetrios*. Regensburg: Schnell und Steiner, 2013.

Bonnekoh, Pamela. *Die figürlichen Malereien in Thessaloniki vom Ende des 4. bis zum 7. Jahrhundert: Neue Untersuchungen zur erhaltenen Malereiausstattung zweier Doppelgräber, der Agora und der Demetrios-Kirche*. Oberhausen: Athena, 2013.

Brenk, Beat. "The Mosaics of Thessaloniki: The State of Research." Pages 19–33 in *The Mosaics of Thessaloniki Revisited: Papers from the 2014 Symposium at the Courtauld Institute of Art*. Edited by Antony Eastmond and Myrto Hatzaki. Athens: Kapon, 2017.

Breytenbach, Cilliers, and Julien M. Ogereau. "*Inscriptiones Christianae Graecae (ICG)* 1.0: An Online Database and Repository of Early Christian Greek Inscriptions from Asia Minor and Greece." *EC* 8 (2017): 409–19.

Breytenbach, Cilliers, and Christiane Zimmermann. *Early Christianity in Lycaonia and Adjacent Areas: From Paul to Amphilochius of Iconium.* AJEC 101. Leiden: Brill, 2018.

Brocke, Christoph vom. *Thessaloniki–Stadt des Kassander und Gemeinde des Paulus: Eine frühe christliche Gemeinde in ihrer heidnischen Umwelt.* WUNT 2/125. Tübingen: Mohr Siebeck, 2001.

Cormack, Robin S. "The Mosaic Decoration of S. Demetrios, Thessaloniki: A Re-examination in the Light of the Drawings of W. S. George." *ABSA* 64 (1969): 17–52.

Creaghan, John S., and Antony E. Raubitschek. "Early Christian Epitaphs from Athens." *Hesperia* 16 (1947): 1–52.

Ćurčić, Slobodan. "Christianization of Thessalonikē: The Making of Christian 'Urban Iconography.'" Pages 213–44 in *From Roman to Early Christian Thessalonike: Studies in Religion and Archaeology.* Edited by Laura Nasrallah, Charalambos Bakirtzis, and Steven J. Friesen. HTS 64. Cambridge: Harvard University Press, 2010.

———. *Some Observations and Questions regarding Early Christian Architecture in Thessaloniki.* Thessaloniki: Hypourgeio Politismou Ephoreia Byzantinon Archaioteton Thessalonikes, 2000.

Delehaye, Hyppolite. *Les légendes grecques des saints militaires.* Paris: Picard, 1909.

———. *Les origines du culte des martyrs.* 2nd rev. ed. SH 20. Brussels: Société des Bollandistes, 1933.

Diehl, Charles, and Marcel Le Tourneau. "Les mosaïques de Saint-Démétrius de Salonique." *MMFEP* 18 (1911): 225–48.

Dölger, Franz J. *Das Fisch-Symbol in Frühchristlicher Zeit.* Vol. 1 of ΙΧΘΥΣ. Münster: Aschendorffsche Verlagsbuchhandlung, 1928.

———. *Die Fisch-Denkmäler in der frühchristlichen Plastik Malerei und Kleinkunst.* Vol. 5 of ΙΧΘΥΣ. Münster: Aschendorffsche Verlagsbuchhandlung, 1943.

Drossoyianni, Ph. A. "Θεσσαλονίκη: Αγία Σοφία." *AD* 18, B.2 (1963): 235–42.

Duchesne, Louis. "L'Illyricum ecclésiastique." *ByzZ* 1 (1892): 531–50.

Dunn, Geoffrey D. "The Church of Rome as a Court of Appeal in the Early Fifth Century: The Evidence of Innocent I and the Illyrian Churches." *JEH* 64 (2013): 679–99.

———. "Innocent I and Anysius of Thessalonica." *Byzantion* 77 (2007): 124–48.

———. "Innocent I and Rufus of Thessalonica." *JÖB* 59 (2009): 51–64.

Eastmond, Antony, and Myrto Hatzaki, eds. *The Mosaics of Thessaloniki Revisited: Papers from the 2014 Symposium at the Courtauld Institute of Art*. Athens: Kapon, 2017.

Eisen, Ute E. *Amtsträgerinnen im frühen Christentum: Epigraphische und literarische Studien*. Göttingen: Vandenhoeck & Ruprecht, 1996.

Eleutheriadou, Kyriake. "Χριστιανικό κοιμητήριο στη Θεσσαλονίκη." *AEMT* 3 (1989): 271–82.

Exner, Matthias. "Das fischreiche Gläserne Meer vor dem Thron Christi: Bemerkungen zum Apsismosaik von Hosios David in Thessaloniki." *MJBK* 67 (2016): 7–14.

Feissel, Denis, and Jean-Michel Spieser. "Inventaires en vue d'un recueil des inscriptions historiques de Byzance: Les inscriptions de Thessalonique; Supplément." *TM* 7 (1979): 303–46.

Fourlas, Benjamin. *Die Mosaiken der Acheiropoietos-Basilika in Thessaloniki: Eine vergleichende Analyse dekorativer Mosaiken des 5. und 6. Jahrhunderts*. 2 vols. MillSt 35. Berlin: de Gruyter, 2012.

Grabar, André. "A propos des mosaïques de la coupole de Saint-Georges, à Salonique." *CahA* 17 (1967): 59–81.

Greenslade, Stanley L. "The Illyrian Churches and the Vicariate of Thessalonica, 378–95." *JTS* 46 (1945): 17–30.

Grégoire, Henri. "Épigraphie Chrétienne I: Les inscriptions hérétiques d'Asie Mineure." *Byzantion* 1 (1924): 695–716.

Gounaris, Georgios. "Die Wandmalereien aus dem Grab Nr. 18 der theologischen Fakultät der Aristoteles-Universität Thessaloniki." Pages 79–89 in *Frühchristliches Thessaloniki*. Edited by Cilliers Breytenbach. STAC 44. Tübingen: Mohr Siebeck, 2007.

Hadjitryphonos, Evangelia. "The Palace of Galerius in Thessalonike: Its Place in the Modern City and an Account of the State of Research." Pages 203–17 in *Bruckneudorf und Gamzigrad: Spätantike Paläste und Großvillen im Donau-Balkan-Raum; Akten des Internationalen Kolloquiums in Bruckneudorf vom 15. bis 18. Oktober 2008*. Edited by Gerda von Bülow and Heinrich Zabehlicky. Bonn: Habelt, 2011.

Jaffé, Philipp, ed. *Regesta pontificum romanorum: Ab condita ecclesia ad annum post Christum natum MCXCVIII*². Leipzig: Veit, 1885.

Kleinbauer, W. Eugene. "The Iconography and the Date of the Mosaics of the Rotunda of Hagios Georgios, Thessaloniki." *Viator* 3 (1972): 27–107.

——. "The Original Name and Function of Hagios Georgios at Thessaloniki." *CahA* 22 (1972): 55–60.

——. "The Orants in the Mosaic Decoration of the Rotunda at Thessaloniki: Martyr Saints or Donors?" *CahA* 30 (1982): 25–45.

——. "Remarks on the Building History of the Acheiropoietos Church at Thessaloniki." Pages 241–57 in vol. 2 of *Actes du Xe congrès international d'archéologie chrétienne, Thessalonique, 28 septembre–4 octobre 1980*. 2 vols. Rome: Pontifico Istituto di Archeologia Cristiana, 1984.

Knox, John. *Chapters in a Life of Paul*. New York: Abingdon, 1950.

Koester, Helmut. *History and Literature of Early Christianity*. 2nd ed. Berlin: de Gruyter, 2000.

Kourkoutidou-Nikolaidou, Eutychia. "Το εγκαίνιο της βασιλικής στο ανατολικό νεκροταφείο της Θεσσαλονίκης." *AEC* (1983): 70–81.

Laubscher, Hans P. *Der Reliefschmuck des Galeriusbogens in Thessaloniki*. AF 1. Berlin: Mann, 1975.

Le Quien, Michel. *Oriens christianus, in quatuor patriarchatus digestus: quo exhibentur ecclesiae, patriarchae, caeterique praesules totius Orientis*. 3 vols. Paris: Imprimerie royale, 1740.

Lemerle, Paul. "La composition et la chronologie des deux premiers livres des *miracula S. Demetrii*." *ByzZ* 46 (1953): 349–61.

——. *Les plus anciens recueils des miracles de Saint Démétrius et la pénétration des Slaves dans les Balkans*. 2 vols. Paris: Éditions du Centre National de la Recherche Scientifique, 1979–1981.

——. "Saint Démétrius de Thessalonique et les problèmes du martyrion et du transept." *BCH* 77 (1953): 660–94.

Loenertz, Raymond-Joseph. "Saint David de Thessalonique: Sa vie, son culte, ses reliques, ses images." *RevEB* 11 (1953): 205–23.

Makropoulou, Despoina. "Ο παλαιοχριστιανικός ναός έξω από τα ανατολικά τείχη της Θεσσαλονίκης." *Makedonika* 23 (1983): 25–46.

Marki, Efterpi. "Ένας άγνωστος οκταγωνικός ναός στη Θεσσαλονίκη." *Makedonika* 23 (1983): 117–33.

——. *Η νεκρόπολη της Θεσσαλονίκης στους υστερορωμαϊκούς και παλαιοχριστιανικούς χρόνους (μέσα του 3ου έως μέσα του 8ου αι. μ.Χ.)*. Athens: TAP, 2006.

———. "Die ersten christlichen Friedhöfe in Thessaloniki." Pages 43–53 in *Frühchristliches Thessaloniki*. Edited by Cilliers Breytenbach. STAC 44. Tübingen: Mohr Siebeck, 2007.

———. "Die frühchristliche Grabmalerei in Thessaloniki." Pages 55–63 in *Frühchristliches Thessaloniki*. Edited by Cilliers Breytenbach. STAC 44. Tübingen: Mohr Siebeck, 2007.

———. "Frühchristliche Darstellungen und Motive, die die weltliche Malerei nachahmen, in einem Doppelgrab der Westnekropole von Thessaloniki." Pages 65–78 in *Frühchristliches Thessaloniki*. Edited by Cilliers Breytenbach. STAC 44. Tübingen: Mohr Siebeck, 2007.

———. "Das kreuzförmige Martyrion und die christlichen Gräber an der Tritis-Septemvriou-Strasse in Thessaloniki." Pages 11–41 in *Frühchristliches Thessaloniki*. Edited by Cilliers Breytenbach. STAC 44. Tübingen: Mohr Siebeck, 2007.

Mavropoulou-Tsioumi, Chrysanthi. "Susanna in einem frühchristlichen Grab von Thessaloniki." Pages 91–101 in *Frühchristliches Thessaloniki*. Edited by Cilliers Breytenbach. STAC 44. Tübingen: Mohr Siebeck, 2007.

———. *Hagia Sophia: The Great Church of Thessaloniki*. Athens: Kapon, 2014.

Mentzos, Aristoteles. "Reflections of the Interpretation and Dating of the Rotunda of Thessaloniki." *Egnatia* 5 (1999–2000): 57–80.

———. "Συμβολή στην έρευνα του αρχαιότερου ναού της Αγίας Σοφίας Θεσσαλονίκης." *Makedonika* 21 (1981): 201–21.

———. "Reflections on the Architectural History of the Tetrarchic Palace Complex at Thessalonikē." Pages 333–59 in *From Roman to Early Christian Thessalonikē: Studies in Religion and Archaeology*. Edited by Laura Nasrallah, Charalambos Bakirtzis, and Steven J. Friesen. HTS 64. Cambridge: Harvard University Press, 2010.

Morey, C. R. "A Note on the Date of the Mosaic of Hosios David, Salonica." *Byzantion* 7 (1932): 339–46.

Nasrallah, Laura. "Early Christian Interpretation in Image and Word: Canon, Sacred Text, and the Mosaic of Moni Latomou." Pages 361–96 in *From Roman to Early Christian Thessalonike: Studies in Religion and Archaeology*. Edited by Laura Nasrallah, Charalambos Bakirtzis, and Steven J. Friesen. HTS 64. Cambridge: Harvard University Press, 2010.

———. "Empire and Apocalypse in Thessaloniki: Interpreting the Early Christian Rotunda." *JECS* 13 (2005): 465–508.

———. "Ezekiel's Vision in Late Antiquity: The Case of the Mosaic of Moni Latomou, Thessaloniki." Pages 77–89 in *The Mosaics of Thessaloniki Revisited: Papers from the 2014 Symposium at the Courtauld Institute of Art*. Edited by Antony Eastmond and Myrto Hatzaki. Athens: Kapon, 2017.

Nasrallah, Laura, Charalambos Bakirtzis, and Steven J. Friesen, eds. *From Roman to Early Christian Thessalonikē: Studies in Religion and Archaeology*. HTS 64. Cambridge: Harvard University Press, 2010.

Nigdelis, Pantelis M. "Habent sua fata lapides: Ξεχασμένες δημοσιεύσεις τοῦ Πέτρου Ν. Παπαγεωργίου γιὰ ἐπιγραφὲς τῆς Θεσσαλονίκης καὶ τῆς Ἐδέσσας." *Tekmeria* 7 (2002): 85–106.

Oberhummer, Eugen. "Thessalonike." PW 6.A.2:143–63.

Ogereau, Julien M. *Early Christianity in Macedonia*. AJEC. Leiden: Brill, forthcoming.

———. Thessaloniki I. (Stadtgeschichte)." *RAC* 32, forthcoming.

Paisidou, Melina. "ΜΕΤΡΟ Θεσσαλονίκης 2010: η παλαιοχριστιανική βασιλική στον σταθμό Σιντριβανιού." *AEMT* 24 (2010): 249–60.

Pallas, Dēmētrios. *Les monuments paléochrétiens de Grèce découverts de 1959 à 1973*. Rome: Pontificio Istituto di Archeologia Christiana, 1977.

Papazoglou, Fanoula. *Les villes de Macédoine à l'époque romaine*. BCHSup 16. Athens: École française d'Athènes, 1988.

Pelekanidis, Stylianos. *Gli affreschi paleocristiani ed i piu antichi mosaici parietali di Salonicco*. Ravenna: Dante, 1963.

———. *Studien zur frühchristlichen und byzantinischen Archäologie*. Thessaloniki: Institute for Balkan Studies, 1977.

Pelekanidou, Elli S. "Νέα ευρήματα στο ανατολικό νεκροταφείο της Θεσσαλονίκης." *AEMT* 7 (1993): 373–87.

Perdrizet, Paul. "Le cimetière chrétien de Thessalonique." *MEFR* 19 (1899): 541–48.

Petit, Louis. "Les évêques de Thessalonique." *EO* 4.3 (1901): 136–45; 4.4 (1901): 212–21.

Pietri, Charles. "La géographie de l'Illyricum ecclésiastique et ses relations avec l'église de Rome (V–VIe siècles)." Pages 21–59 in *Villes et peuplement dans l'Illyricum protobyzantin: Actes du colloque organisé par l'École française de Rome (Rome, 12–14 Mai 1982)*. Rome: École française de Rome, 1984.

Preuner, Erich. "ΖΩΝ ΚΤΩ ΧΡΩ." *JdI* 40 (1925): 39–41.

Rebillard, Éric. "*Koimetérion* et *coemeterium*: tombe, tombe sainte, nécropole." *MEFR* 105 (1993): 975–1001.

Riesner, Rainer. *Paul's Early Period: Chronology, Mission Strategy, Theology*. Translated by Douglas Stott. Grand Rapids: Eerdmans, 1994.

Rizos, Efthymios. "The Late-Antique Walls of Thessalonica and Their Place in the Development of Eastern Military Architecture." *JRA* 24 (2011): 450–68.

Robert, Louis, ed. *Inscriptions Grecques*. Vol. 1 of *Collection Froehner*. Paris: Edition des bibliothèques nationales, 1936.

———. *Opera minora selecta*. Vol. 2. Amsterdam: Hakkert, 1969.

Silva-Tarouca, Carlos da, ed. *Epistularum romanorum Pontificum ad vicarios per Illyricum aliosque episcopos: Collectio thessalonicensis*. Rome: Pontificia Universitas Gregoriana, 1937.

Sironen, Erkki. "Early Christian Inscriptions from the Corinthia and the Peloponnese." Pages 201–16 in *Identity and Authority in Emerging Christianities in Asia Minor and Greece*. Edited by Cilliers Breytenbach and Julien M. Ogereau. AJEC 103. Leiden: Brill, 2018.

———. *The Late Roman and Early Byzantine Inscriptions of Athens and Attica: An Edition with Appendices on Scripts, Sepulchral Formulae, and Occupations*. Helsinki: Hakapaino Oy, 1997.

Skedros, James C. *Saint Demetrios of Thessaloniki: Civic Patron and Divine Protector Fourth–Seventh Centuries CE*. HTS 47. Harrisburg, PA: Trinity Press International, 1999.

Snively, Caroline S. "Apsidal Crypts in Macedonia: Possible Places of Pilgrimage." Pages 1179–84 in *Akten des XII. internationalen Kongresses für christliche Archäologie, Bonn, 22.–28. September 1991*. Part 2. Edited by Ernst Dassmann and Josef Engemann. Münster: Aschendorffsche Verlagsbuchhandlung, 1995.

Snyder, James. "The Meaning of the 'Maiestas Domini' in Hosios David." *Byzantion* 37 (1967): 143–52.

Soteriou, Georgios A., and Maria G. Soteriou. *Η βασιλική του Αγίου Δημητρίου Θεσσαλονίκης*. Athens: H en Athenais Archaiologikes Etaireia, 1952.

Spieser, Jean-Michel. "Le culte de Saint Démétrius à Thessalonique." Pages 275–91 in *Des dieux civiques aux saints patrons (IVe–VIIe siècle)*. Edited by Jean-Pierre Caillet, Sylvain Destephen, Bruno Dumézil, and Hervé Inglebert. Paris: Picard, 2015.

———. "À propos de trois livres récents sur des monuments de Thessalonique." *AT* 22 (2014): 297–306.

———. "Remarques complémentaires sur la mosaïques de Osios David." Pages 295–306 in *Διεθνές Συμπόσιο: Βυζαντινή Μακεδονία, 324–1430* μ.Χ, Θεσσαλονίκη 29–31 Οκτωβρίου 1992. Thessaloniki: Etaireia Makedonikon Spoudon, 1995.

———. *Thessalonique et ses monuments du IVe au VIe siècle: Contribution à l'étude d'une ville paléochrétienne*. Paris: De Boccard, 1984.

Stefanidou-Tiveriou, Theodosia. "Die Palastanlage des Galerius in Thessaloniki: Planung und Datierung." Pages 389–410 in *Diocletian, Tetrarchy and Diocletian's Palace on the Seventeen Hundredth Anniversary of Existence: Proceedings of the International Conference Held in Split from September 18th to 22nd 2005*. Edited by Nenad Cambi, Josip Belamarić, and Tomislav Marasović. Split: Književni Krug, 2009.

Suggs, M. Jack. "Concerning the Date of Paul's Macedonian Ministry." *NovT* 4 (1960): 60–68.

Theoharidou, Kalliopi. *The Architecture of Hagia Sophia, Thessaloniki: From Its Erection up to the Turkish Conquest*. Oxford: B.A.R., 1988.

Tjäder, Jan-Olof. "Christ, Our Lord, Born of the Virgin Mary (XMΓ and VDN)." *Eranos* 68 (1970): 148–90.

Torp, Hjalmar. "Considerations on the Chronology of the Rotunda Mosaics." Pages 35–47 in *The Mosaics of Thessaloniki Revisited: Papers from the 2014 Symposium at the Courtauld Institute of Art*. Edited by Antony Eastmond and Myrto Hatzaki. Athens: Kapon, 2017.

———. *La rotonde palatine à Thessalonique: Architecture et mosaïques*. 2 vols. Athens: Kapon, 2018.

———. "Thessalonique paléochrétienne: Une esquisse." Pages 113–32 in *Aspects of Late Antiquity and Early Byzantium: Papers Read at a Colloquium Held at the Swedish Research Institute in Istanbul 31 May–5 June 1992*. Edited by Lennart Rydén and Jan Olof Rosenqvist. Uppsala: Swedish Council for Research in the Humanities and Social Sciences, 1993.

Tsigaridas, Efthymios N. *Latomou Monastery: The Church of Hosios David*. Thessalonike: Institute for Balkans Studies, 1988.

———. Οι τοιχογραφίες της μονής Λατόμου Θεσσαλονίκης και η βυζαντινή ζωγραφική του 12ου αιώνα. Thessalonike: Etaireia Makedonikon Spoudon, 1986.

Vasiliev, Alexander. "Life of David of Thessalonica." *Traditio* 4 (1946): 115–47.

Velenis, Georgios M. Τα τείχη της Θεσσαλονίκης: Από τον Κάσσανδρο ώς τον Ηράκλειο. Thessaloniki: University Studio Press, 1998.

Vickers, Michael. "Fifth-Century Brickstamps from Thessaloniki." *ABSA* 68 (1973): 285–94.

———. "Observations on the Octagon at Thessaloniki." *JRS* 63 (1973): 111-20.

———. "Sirmium or Thessaloniki? A Critical Examination of the St. Demetrius Legend." *ByzZ* 67 (1974): 337-50.

Weigand, Edmund. "Der Kalenderfries von Hagios Georgios in Thessalonike: Datierung, Ideen- und Kunstgeschichtliche Stellung." *ByzZ* 39 (1939): 116-45.

Wisskirchen, Rotraut. "Zum Apsismosaik der Kirche Hosios David/Thessalonike." Pages 582-94 in *Stimuli: Exegese und ihre Hermeneutik in Antike und Christentum; Festschrift für Ernst Dassmann*. Edited by Georg Schöllgen and Clemens Scholten. JACSup 23. Münster: Aschendorff, 1996.

Woods, David. "Thessalonica's Patron: Saint Demetrius or Emeterius?" *HTR* 93 (2000): 221-34.

Xyngopoulos, Andreas. "Ἡ λατρευτική εικών του ναού της Ἀχειροποιήτου Θεσσαλονίκης." *Hellenika* 13 (1954): 256-62.

———. "Περί την Ἀχειροποίητον Θεσσαλονίκης." *Makedonika* 2 (1942-1952): 472-87.

———. "Το καθολικόν της Μονής Λατόμου εν Θεσσαλονίκη και το εν αυτῷ ψηφιδωτόν." *AD* 12 (1929): 142-80.

"Sounding Forth":
Reading the Thessalonians as God's Musical Instrument

Isaac T. Soon

1. Introduction: Hearing Echoes

In his letter to the Roman assemblies, Paul flatters the communities there by mentioning their reputation of faith among the whole world (Rom 1:8). This note of praise from the apostle to the gentiles is a rare accolade brandished only by one other Pauline community, the one in Thessalonica. In 1 Thess 1:8, Paul describes how "the word of the Lord sounded forth" (ἀφ' ὑμῶν γὰρ ἐξήχηται ὁ λόγος τοῦ κυρίου) from the *ekklēsia* to all of Macedonia and Achaia.[1] While Paul's language in Rom 1:8 is merely that of a report, his depiction of the promulgation of faith from Thessalonica is metaphorically evocative. In particular, Paul's language arouses melodious and sonic overtones.

This essay argues that Paul's description of the Thessalonians' faith as "sounding forth" (ἐξήχηται) can be understood as a musical metaphor in the context of ancient Mediterranean musical culture. Literary and archaeological sources demonstrate how music was an everyday part of the life of the citizens of Thessalonica. The focus on the sound of the Thessalonians

---

1. This essay does not deal with the issue of whether Paul's words in 1 Thess 1:8 suggest that the Thessalonians were involved in "missionary" work. On this see Nikolaus Walter, Eckart Reinmuth, and Peter Lampe, *Die Briefe an die Philipper, Thessalonicher und an Philemon*, NTD 8/2 (Göttingen: Vandenhoeck & Ruprecht, 1998), 120–21; Richard S. Ascough, "Redescribing the Thessalonians' 'Mission' in Light of Graeco-Roman Associations," *NTS* 60 (2014): 61–82; Charles A. Wanamaker, *The Epistles to the Thessalonians: A Commentary on the Greek Text*, NIGTC (Grand Rapids: Eerdmans, 1990), 83; James Ware, "The Thessalonians as a Missionary Congregation: 1Thessalonians 1, 5–8," *ZNW* 83 (1992): 126–31.

as mere noise and not as also melody overlooks the sensorial quality of Paul's words in 1 Thess 1:8. This is not the only way that ἐξήχηται can be interpreted, but in the musical context of ancient Thessalonian material evidence, it is a viable one.

2. More Than Just a Clang: The Lexical Semantics of ἐξηχέω

Most commentators focus on the *extent* of the sound made by the Thessalonians, implied in 1 Thess 1:8, namely, that it "rang out."[2] Only a few are concerned with the quality and character of the sound itself. Following J. B. Lightfoot and Sir 40:13, a number of scholars suggest that it alludes to the sound of a thunderclap.[3] Others suggest that it refers to the sound of a trumpet.[4] The interpretation of Paul's language as a trumpet blast has ancient moorings in the homilies of John Chrysostom, who said that the sounding out of the Thessalonians is as if "every nearby place is filled of the resounding of a blaring trumpet" (ὥσπερ σάλπιγγος λαμπρὸν ἠχούσης ὁ πλησίον ἅπας πληροῦται τόπος; *Hom. 1 Thess* 2 [PG 62:399]).[5] Chrysostom had a penchant for music metaphors, especially involving the *salpinx*. He calls Paul "the heavenly trumpet" (*Hom. 2 Cor 11:1* 1 [PG 51:301]).[6]

---

2. Günter Haufe, *Der Erste Brief des Paulus an die Thessalonicher*, THKNT 12/1 (Leipzig: Evangelische Verlagsanstalt, 1999), 28; Jeffrey A. D. Weima, *1–2 Thessalonians*, BECNT (Grand Rapids: Baker Academic, 2014), 105; Hermann Olshausen, *Die Briefe Pauli an die Galater, Ephesier, Kolosser und Thessalonicher* (Königsberg: August Wilhelm Unzer, 1844), 432; Rinaldo Fabris, *1–2 Tessalonicesi* (Milano: Figlie di san paolo, 2014), 72.

3. J. B. Lightfoot, *Notes on Epistles of St. Paul from Unpublished Commentaries* (London: Macmillan, 1895), 15; Ben Witherington III, *1 and 2 Thessalonians: A Socio-rhetorical Commentary* (Grand Rapids: Eerdmans, 2006), 73.

4. F. F. Bruce, *1 and 2 Thessalonians*, WBC 45 (Dallas: Word, 1982), 17; Leon Morris, *1 and 2 Thessalonians: An Introduction and Commentary*, TNTC 13 (Downers Grove, IL: InterVarsity Press, 1984), 47; Gene L. Green, *The Letters to the Thessalonians*, PNTC (Grand Rapids: Eerdmans, 2002), 101; Laurie Ruth Wheeler, "Divine Communication in the Letters of Paul: 1 Thessalonians as Source" (PhD diss., Durham University, 2016), 209; Abraham J. Malherbe, *The Letters to the Thessalonians: A New Translation with Introduction and Commentary*, AB 32B (New Haven: Yale University Press, 2000), 117; G. K. Beale, *1–2 Thessalonians*, IVPNTC (Downers Grove, IL: InterVarsity Press, 2003), 59.

5. Unless otherwise indicated translations of ancient texts are mine.

6. See Margaret M. Mitchell, *The Heavenly Trumpet: John Chrysostom and the Art of Pauline Interpretation*, HUT 40 (Tübingen: Mohr Siebeck, 2000), 1, 76.

But his suggestion that such a sound has its origin with a musical instrument deserves consideration, especially since the *salpinx*—a commanding instrument often used in war—was often compared to the human voice.⁷

Still, many recent interpreters deny that the verb ἐξήχηται is linked "necessarily to any particular sound or musical instrument."⁸ Jeffrey Weima argues that "the focus is not on the identity of the sound but on its expanding character."⁹ It is possible, however, that the scholarly emphasis on the extent of the sound is not a result of the focus of the text but on the semantic ambiguity in the verb itself.¹⁰ Additionally—and more to the point of this essay—the quality of the sound made by the Thessalonians is not a tangential matter. Surely Paul does not envision the Lord's word reverberating outward as a racket or din haranguing the other cities of the Aegean? Is it a distasteful sound or, as Gottlieb Lünemann (echoing Chrysostom) noted over 160 years ago, is it "like the sound of a resounding instrument" ("gleichsam wie der Ton eines weithin schallenden Instruments")?¹¹

The restricted interpretation of ἐξηχέω is partly due to lexicographic limitations. The three primary passages used to argue that ἐξηχέω envisions merely the traveling of sound outward and not necessarily a melodic or musical sense also happen to be some of the few passages cited by nineteenth-century commentators, which likely made their way into earlier editions of what is now the BDAG lexicon, and then were fed back

---

7. Carolyn Susan Bowyer, "Echoes of the *Salpinx*: The Trumpet in Ancient Greek Culture" (MPhil diss., Royal Hollway, University of London, 2016), 251–52.

8. Ernest Best, *The First and Second Epistles to the Thessalonians*, BNTC (London: Continuum, 1986), 80–81; Traugott Holtz, *Der Erste Brief an die Thessalonicher*, EKKNT 13 (Zürich: Benziger; Neukirchener Verlag, 1986), 52 n. 136; Weima, *1–2 Thessalonians*, 105; Wanamaker, *Epistles to the Thessalonians*, 83; James Everett Frame, *A Critical and Exegetical Commentary on the Epistles of St. Paul to the Thessalonians*, ICC (New York: Scribner's Sons, 1912), 85–86; Ascough, "Redescribing the Thessalonians' 'Mission,'" 76.

9. Weima, *1–2 Thessalonians*, 105.

10. Scholars tend to focus on what aspects of the text they are most interested in. Gordon Fee, for example, argues that Paul's concern is not the specific geographic locations where the word has gone out (an issue of concern among German interpreters of the text) but on the content of the word itself. See Fee, *The First and Second Letters to the Thessalonians*, NICNT (Grand Rapids: Eerdmans, 2009), 43.

11. Gottlieb Lünemann, *Die Briefe an die Thessalonicher*, KEK (Göttingen: Vandenhoeck & Ruprecht, 1859), 31.

into more recent commentaries: 3 Macc 3:2, Sir 40:13, and LXX Joel 3:14.[12] Lightfoot cites Pollux's *Onomasticon*; Ernst von Dobschütz conjectures that there may be a connection between 1 Thess 1:8 and Ps 19:4, although he does not know what it might be; and Gene Green mentions Philo (*Flacc.* 39)—a passage also found in BDAG—but no interpreters seem to depart much from these examples.[13] In all of these passages, the sound mentioned is characterized as "noise," whether thunder, shouting, or an ill-report.

However, in various places, Philo of Alexandria connects the verb not just to sound in general but to a musical sound. In *Her.* 15 he uses a metaphor about the "whole instrument of the mind" (ὅλου δὴ τοῦ διανοίας ὀργάνου), which "sounds according to the harmony of the fourth/fifth or octave" (κατὰ τὴν διὰ πασῶν ἢ δὶς διὰ πασῶν συμφωνίαν ἐξηχοῦντος).[14] Elsewhere, Philo uses ἐξηχέω to describe the communal singing of hymns by the Therapeutai during symposia (*Contempl.* 81).[15]

Significant for our study is Philo's use of the verb to describe God's announcement of his law at Sinai, which blends both vocal and musical qualities. In his exposition of how God communicated the Decalogue, Philo explains how God "spoke" to Israel, arguing that it was an "invisible sound" (ἦχος ἀόρατος) whose character transcended the melodious and harmonic nature of human voices and "like air through a trumpet it sounded forth, so great an articulated sound" (καθάπερ πνεῦμα διὰ σάλπιγγος φωνὴν τοσαύτην ἔναρθρον ἐξήχησεν, *Decal.* 33). Philo describes this event in the exact same way in his treatise on the special laws as "a voice of a trumpet sounded from heaven" (ἀπ' οὐρανοῦ φωνὴ σάλπιγγος ἐξήχησεν, *Spec.* 2.189). Further on, in his *De decalogo*

---

12. 3 Macc 3:2: Frame, *Critical and Exegetical Commentary*, 84; Green, *Letters to the Thessalonians*, 101; Sir 40:13: Lightfoot, *Notes on Epistles of St. Paul*, 15; Lünemann, *Die Briefe an die Thessalonicher*, 31; Frame, *Critical and Exegetical Commentary*, 85; Olshausen, *Die Briefe Pauli*, 432; Green, *Letters to the Thessalonians*, 101; Malherbe, *Letters to the Thessalonians*, 117; Joel 3:14 LXX: Lünemann, *Die Briefe an die Thessalonicher*, 31; Ernst von Dobschütz, *Die Thessalonicher-Briefe*, KEK (Göttingen: Vandenhoeck & Ruprecht, 1974), 75; Olshausen, *Die Briefe Pauli*, 432; Frame, *Critical and Exegetical Commentary*, 85.

13. Lightfoot, *Notes on Epistles of St. Paul*, 15; von Dobschütz, *Die Thessalonicher-Briefe*, 75.

14. On the expression διὰ πασῶν συμφωνίαν, see Pseudo-Plutarch, *Mus.* 23 (1139C).

15. On the musicality of the Therapeutai, see the extensive comments of Joan E. Taylor and David M. Hay, *Philo of Alexandria: On the Contemplative Life. Introduction, Translation, and Commentary*, PACS 7 (Leiden: Brill), 321–24.

46, he uses ἐξηχέω again to describe the voice that "sounded forth" from the fire from heaven, a sound that he says "they seemed more likely to see than to hear" (ὡς ὁρᾶν αὐτὰ μᾶλλον ἢ ἀκούειν δοκεῖν). Philo references the strange language in Exod 20:18 (LXX) of the people "seeing the voice" (ὁ λαὸς ἑώρα τὴν φωνὴν) and "the sound of the trumpet" (τὴν φωνὴν τῆς σάλπιγγος).[16] Philo's reference to the sound as of a trumpet likely stems from the latter part of Exod 20:18. The association between ἐξηχέω and the sound of a σάλπιγξ in both Philo and John Chrysostom makes one wonder whether Chrysostom knew some of the passages from Philo mentioned above.[17]

Nevertheless, given Philo's use of the verb to denote musicality or melody—especially in scenes of divine revelation—there is the possibility that Paul was aware of this semantic use and had intended it for 1 Thess 1:8. Regardless of authorial intention, however, Paul's Thessalonian readers could have independently interpreted Paul's words as a musical metaphor, especially given the role of music in the city itself. It is to this musical culture that we now turn.

3. Music from the Material: The Melodious in the Everyday Life of Thessalonica

The place where Paul's Thessalonian community would have most obviously encountered music and the sounds of music was in the city's theater-stadium. There are ruins in the city today near the Roman Forum of an *odeum* (a theater), which had been converted from a city *bouleuteriom*, but it was built and renovated much later than the first century, possibly the second or third century CE.[18] Since at least the nineteenth century, scholars were aware that there had been a theater-stadium-like-structure in the city. In Greek extracts from the Bollandists' work Acta Sanctorum, there are anonymous accounts of the martyrdom of Saint Demetrios of Thessaloniki, which describe how in the early fourth century there was a "theater" in the city "called 'the Stadium'" (θέατρον τὸ

---

16. The Hebrew is no less ambiguous: וכל־העם ראים את־הקולת ... ואת קול השפר.
17. On the reception of Philo among the early fathers, see David T. Runia, *Philo and the Church Fathers: A Collection of Papers*, VCSup 32 (Leiden: Brill, 1995).
18. Matthew Schueller, "Public Entertainment Venues as Urban Network Actors in Roman Macedonia and Thrace" (PhD diss., University of North Carolina at Chapel Hill, 2020), 223.

καλούμενον στάδιον).¹⁹ However, because, Thessaloniki has been continually inhabited since antiquity, so many ancient ruins lie under layers of city construction or have been destroyed by new developments. Up until the 1980s, no structure was known. But in the late 1980s, archaeologists discovered a section of what they think is the *sphendona* of a larger theater-stadium structure, judged to be at least 100 m wide.[20] Rather than an amphitheater, which is rare in the cities of the Eastern empire, archaeologists argue that the structure is a theater-stadium where one end is concave (e.g., the Panathenaic Stadium in Athens).[21] This kind of structure allowed for more flexible use, from celebrations to parades, theater shows, and sporting events.[22] We know that the theater-stadium was around at least since in the first century CE because of Flavian numismatic evidence from the lowest layers of the *sphendona*.[23] Hampered by municipal delays, the structure remains covered by sand and debris at 6 Apellou Street in modern-day Thessaloniki.

Ancient literary and epigraphic sources attest to gladiatorial shows, games, and even musical festivals in the city (e.g., Pseudo-Lucian, *Asin.* 49–50; *IG* 10.2.1.38).[24] At such events as the Pythian Games mentioned in *IG* 10.2.1.38 (held undoubtedly in Thessalonica's theater-stadium), professional musicians would showcase their abilities in front of the city. Musicians and singers such as the *kithara* (lyre) players, *kithara* singers (C lines 11–12), or trumpeters (C line 1) displayed desirable cultural values such as "professional skill, natural talent, courage, and determination."[25] *Kithara* were stringed instruments that used a soundbox to amplify the sound of a plectrum against strings. Unfortunately, no *kithara* has survived from antiquity, so all we possess today are reconstructions.[26]

---

19. See the study by Γιώργος Βελένης and Πολυξένη Αδάμ-Βελένη, "Το θέατρο-στάδιο της Θεσσαλονίκης," in *Αρχαία θέατρα της Μακεδονίας*, ed. Πολυξένη Αδάμ Βελένη, ΑΘ 83 (Αθήνα: Διαζωμα, 2012), 159–72.

20. Βελένης and Αδάμ-Βελένη, "Το θέατρο-στάδιο της Θεσσαλονίκης," 159.

21. Βελένης and Αδάμ-Βελένη, "Το θέατρο-στάδιο της Θεσσαλονίκης," 160.

22. Βελένης and Αδάμ-Βελένη, "Το θέατρο-στάδιο της Θεσσαλονίκης," 163.

23. Schueller, "Public Entertainment Venues," 223.

24. Albert Tougard, *De l'Histoire Profane dans les Actes Grecs Des Bollandistes: Extraits Grecs, Traduction Française, Notes, avec les Fragments Laissés par les Bollandistes, Volumes 12–101* (Paris: Didot, 1874), 9.

25. Schueller, "Public Entertainment Venues," 233–34.

26. Chrēstos Terzēs, "Musical Instruments of Greek and Roman Antiquity," in *A Companion to Ancient Greek and Roman Music*, ed. Tosca A. C. Lynch and Eleonora

Music was also an important part of religious rituals and sacrifice in ancient Thessalonica. The only ancient papyrus ever to be found in Greece and the oldest papyrus in all of Europe also happens to come from a funeral pyre in the Thessaloniki region, found in the winter of 1962. The Derveni Papyrus, dating to about the late fourth century BCE (but containing a text that is possibly from the century before), contains an allegorical commentary on a Dionysiac mystery cult poem ascribed to the legendary poet Orpheus.[27] Although fragmented, one of the initial columns talks about possibly offering up hymns or incantations "adapted to music" to dead souls (αρμ]οστο[υ]ς τῆι μους[ι]κῆι).[28] At these rituals, and at other community events such as city processions, performances, or symposia, popular instruments such as the *aulos* would have been played and heard.[29] At the Archaeological Museum of Thessalonica, there is a fourth-century BCE twin bone *aulos* from Makrygialos, Pieria, a city just to the southwest across the Thermaic Gulf. Ancient *auloi* were versatile flute-like instruments that took advantage of dual flutes to create di-chords.[30]

Rocconi (Hoboken, NJ: Wiley & Sons, 2020), 214–16. Although images of various type of *kithara* can be found on ancient iconography, it is generally held that such representations should not be considered precise or even accurate depictions of the real thing (Terzēs, "Musical Instruments," 213).

27. On the study of this text see Richard Janko, "The Derveni Papyrus ('Diagoras of Melos, Apopyrgizontes Logoi?'): A New Translation," *CP* 96 (2001): 1–32; Theokritos Kouremenos, George M. Parássoglou, and Kyriakos Tsantsanoglou, eds., *The Derveni Papyrus*, STCP (Florence: Olschki, 2006); Richard Janko, "Reconstructing (Again) the Opening of the Derveni Papyri," *ZPE* 166 (2008): 37–51; André Laks and Glenn W. Most, eds, *Studies on the Derveni Papyrus* (Oxford: Clarendon, 1997).

28. Transcription by Kyriakos Tsantsanoglou, "The First Columns of the Derveni Papyrus and Their Religious Significance," in Laks and Most, *Studies on the Derveni Papyrus*, 93. The text does not name the souls explicitly but calls them Erinyes, which specialists on the Derveni Papyrus have understood to be the souls of the dead and not necessarily vengeful spirits. See Tsantsanoglou, "First Columns of the Derveni Papyrus," 104–5; Gábor Betegh, *The Derveni Papyrus: Cosmology, Theology and Interpretation* (Cambridge: Cambridge University Press, 2004), 85; see also Kouremenos, Parássoglou, and Tsantsanoglou, *Derveni Papyrus*, 145.

29. On the presence of music in ancient Macedonia see Triantafyllia Giannou, "Theater and Music in Classical and Hellenistic Macedonia," *Logeion* 6 (2016): 30–92.

30. For the various types of *auloi*, see the fragment of Aristoxenus in Fritz Wehrli, *Die Schule des Aristoteles*, vol. 2 of *Aristoxenos*, (Basel: Schwabe, 1967), 34. On the types of musical expression that an *aulos* could have, see Pollux, *Onom.* 4.71–73, in *Julii Polucus. Onomasticon Cum Annotationibus Interpretum*, ed. Guilielmus Dindorfius (Lipsiae: Libraria Kuehniana, 1824), 201. See also Terzēs, "Musical Instruments," 219–20.

Paul's Thessalonian community would have been quite familiar with the sounds of such instruments, of the music in the processionals of the city streets, and of the music at the public games, festivals, and events they had attended in the past. Of course, singing would have been also a regular part of their own assemblies and meetings (e.g., 1 Cor 14:26; see also Eph 5:19; Jas 5:13; Acts 16:25). This was known even among pagans, as Pliny the Younger notes in his letter to Trajan (*Ep.* 10.96) that some former Christians reported they would sing a hymn to Christ early in the morning. The "sounding forth" of early Christian communities like the ones in Thessalonica was not simply a clanging noise or resounding gong, the sound of a thunderclap or of a shouting crowd. The noise in their everyday lives often had melody and harmony. Given the possible lexical semantics of ἐξηχέω as shown by its use in Philo of Alexandria as well as the ancient cultural life of Thessalonica, with music infused into public and private situations, we might also understand Paul's words as suggestive of musicality.

This connection can be demonstrated further by the association between revelation and musicality. In 1 Thess 1:8, ἐξηχέω is directly associated with the Old Testament prophetic expression "word of the Lord" (ὁ λόγος τοῦ κυρίου). Although it is often understood as merely representing Paul's own particular brand of εὐαγγέλιον, the syntactical synonymity between the expressions ὁ λόγος τοῦ κυρίου and ἡ πίστις ὑμῶν suggests that it is the faith of the Thessalonians and their reception of Paul's gospel that is going out to all places like a prophetic utterance.[31] As we already saw above, for Philo the divine revelation from Sinai had a musical quality to it. Socrates in Plato's *Phaedo* shares about how he came to compose a certain hymn to the god Apollo and how during the festival to Apollo (the Pyanopsia) he was compelled in a dream to "make music" (*Phaed.* 603–61b). In a fragment by Strabo (C333 F18), the prophet and sorcerer Orpheus—the same of the Derveni Papyrus above—was said to initially

---

31. On the synonymity of the two expressions see Malherbe, *Letters to the Thessalonians*, 116. For an overview of how the "word of the Lord" functions in Paul, see Michael W. Pahl, *Discerning the "Word of the Lord": The Word of the Lord in 1 Thessalonians 4:1*, LNTS 389 (London: Bloomsbury, 2009), esp. 30–31, 168. Pahl interprets both 1 Thess 1:8 and 4:15 as a reference to Paul's gospel (see 1 Cor 15:1-11). While I agree that both retain the prophetic overtones from the LXX and pertain to Paul's larger message, I think both include something situation-specific such as the faith of the Thessalonians or a divine oracle giving insight into the order of eschatological events.

live by both "music and divination."³² In Plutarch's *De defectu oraculorum* 15, Cleombrutus speaks about how oracles are dependent on *daimonioi* who help the oracles speak "like musical instruments" (καθάπερ ὄργανα; see also *Def. orac.* 38, 50; *Pyth. orac.* 6).

Paul himself draws an analogy between divine revelation and musicality in 1 Cor 14:6–7. Arguing that speaking in tongues must be accompanied by other types of spiritual gifts (i.e., revelation, knowledge, prophecy, teaching), Paul draws an analogy between communal divinatory practices and musical instruments: "Likewise, those instruments that produce a lifeless sound, whether *aulos* or *kithara*, if they do not make a distinction among tones, how can what is played by the *aulos* or *kithara* be known?" (ὅμως τὰ ἄψυχα φωνὴν διδόντα, εἴτε αὐλὸς εἴτε κιθάρα, ἐὰν διαστολὴν τοῖς φθόγγοις μὴ δῷ, πῶς γνωσθήσεται τὸ αὐλούμενον ἢ τὸ κιθαριζόμενον; NA²⁸). The metaphor implies that for the intelligibility of divine revelation itself among the community there must be a level of harmony between different "players," not mere noise. Where divine revelation is concerned, the sounds that produces it must work together to produce *music*. For "the word of the Lord" to "sound forth" from Thessalonica southward through Macedonia and down into Achaia, we should expect a level of musical prosody. In other words, when these latter areas heard about the Thessalonians, Paul does not characterize the testimony merely as a sound that traveled across the peninsula but as a glorious symphony of divine revelation and faith.

4. Conclusion

In the same way that John Chrysostom envisions Paul the apostle as God's instrument of gospel proclamation, so too can we read Paul as valorizing the Thessalonian congregation as God's instrument, harking the beautiful melodies of divine revelation, faith, and Jesus Christ in 1 Thess 1:8. From another perspective—that of ὁ λόγος τοῦ κυρίου as a reference to Paul's gospel—we might think of the Thessalonians like an ancient *odeum* or theater-stadium, "sounding forth" Paul's message and allowing the good news about Jesus of Nazareth to be heard by other listeners.

The material evidence from Thessalonica helps us to understand Paul's words with our ears, not forgetting the sense-perceptual contexts of his

---

32. Daniel Ogden, *Magic, Witchcraft, and Ghosts in the Greek and Roman Worlds: A Sourcebook* (Oxford: Oxford University Press, 2002), 24.

ancient readers. The sonic aesthetics of Paul's metaphorical language are enriched by the objects and spaces of ancient life. It is easy to reduce the decipherment of Paul's words to mere lexical semantics, forgetting all the while that there is an uncontrollable *affectual* aspect to his words that stimulates his readers depending on their own embodied experiences. The human imagination is a requirement for us as interpreters today even as it was required for Paul's readers, who did not merely read his letters quietly in their heads but who encountered his words also as vibrations moving through air.

Bibliography

Ascough, Richard S. "Redescribing the Thessalonians' 'Mission' in Light of Graeco-Roman Associations." *NTS* 60 (2014): 61–82.

Beale, Gregory K. *1–2 Thessalonians*. IVPNTC. Downers Grove, IL: InterVarsity Press, 2003.

Βελένης, Γιώργος, and Πολυξένη Αδάμ-Βελένη. "Το θέατρο-στάδιο της Θεσσαλονίκης." Pages 159–72 in *Αρχαία θέατρα της Μακεδονίας*. Edited by Πολυξένη Αδάμ. Βελένη. ΑΘ 83. Αθήνα: Διάζωμα, 2012.

Best, Ernest. *The First and Second Epistles to the Thessalonians*. BNTC. London: Continuum, 1986.

Betegh, Gábor. *The Derveni Papyrus: Cosmology, Theology and Interpretation*. Cambridge: Cambridge University Press, 2004.

Bowyer, Carolyn Susan. "Echoes of the *Salpinx*: The Trumpet in Ancient Greek Culture." MPhil diss., Royal Hollway, University of London, 2016.

Bruce, F. F. *1 and 2 Thessalonians*. WBC 45. Dallas: Word, 1982.

Dindorfius, Guilielmus, ed. *Julii Polucus. Onomasticon Cum Annotationibus Interpretum*. Lipsiae: Libraria Kuehniana, 1824.

Dobschütz, Ernst von. *Die Thessalonicher-Briefe*. KEK. Göttingen: Vanderhoeck & Ruprecht, 1974.

Fabris, Rinaldo. *1–2 Tessalonicesi*. Milano: Figlie di san paolo, 2014.

Fee, Gordon D. *The First and Second Letters to the Thessalonians*. NICNT. Grand Rapids: Eerdmans, 2009.

Frame, James Everett. *A Critical and Exegetical Commentary on the Epistles of St. Paul to the Thessalonians*. ICC. New York: Scribner's Sons, 1912.

Giannou, Triantafyllia. "Theater and Music in Classical and Hellenistic Macedonia." *Logeion* 6 (2016): 30–92.

Green, Gene L. *The Letters to the Thessalonians*. PNTC. Grand Rapids: Eerdmans, 2002.
Haufe, Günter. *Der Erste Brief des Paulus an die Thessalonicher*. THKNT 12/1. Leipzig: Evangelische Verlagsanstalt, 1999.
Holtz, Traugott. *Der Erste Brief an die Thessalonicher*. EKKNT 13. Zürich: Benziger; Neukirchener Verlag, 1986.
Janko, Richard. "The Derveni Papyrus ('Diagoras of Melos, Apopyrgizontes Logoi?'): A New Translation." *CP* 96 (2001): 1–32.
———. "Reconstructing (Again) the Opening of the Derveni Papyri." *ZPE* 166 (2008): 37–51.
Kouremenos, Theokritos, George M. Parássoglou, and Kyriakos Tsantsanoglou, eds. *The Derveni Papyrus*. STCP. Florence: Olschki, 2006.
Laks, André, and Glenn W. Most, eds. *Studies on the Derveni Papyrus*. Oxford: Clarendon, 1997.
Lightfoot, J. B. *Notes on Epistles of St. Paul from Unpublished Commentaries*. London: Macmillan, 1895.
Lünemann, Gottlieb. *Die Briefe an die Thessalonicher*. KEK. Göttingen: Vandenhoeck & Ruprecht, 1859.
Malherbe, Abraham J. *The Letters to the Thessalonians: A New Translation with Introduction and Commentary*. AB 32B. New Haven: Yale University Press, 2000.
Mitchell, Margaret M. *The Heavenly Trumpet: John Chrysostom and the Art of Pauline Interpretation*. HUT 40. Tübingen: Mohr Siebeck, 2000.
Morris, Leon. *1 and 2 Thessalonians: An Introduction and Commentary*. TNTC 13. Downers Grover, IL: InterVarsity, 1984.
Ogden, Daniel. *Magic, Witchcraft, and Ghosts in the Greek and Roman Worlds: A Sourcebook*. Oxford: Oxford University Press, 2002.
Olshausen, Hermann. *Die Briefe Pauli an die Galater, Ephesier, Kolosser und Thessalonicher*. Königsberg: August Wilhelm Unzer, 1844.
Pahl, Michael W. *Discerning the "Word of the Lord": The Word of the Lord in 1 Thessalonians 4:1*. LNTS 389. London: Bloosmbury, 2009.
Runia, David T. *Philo and the Church Fathers: A Collection of Papers*. VCSup 32. Leiden: Brill, 1995.
Schueller, Matthew. "Public Entertainment Venues as Urban Network Actors in Roman Macedonia and Thrace." PhD diss., University of North Carolina at Chapel Hill, 2020.
Taylor, Joan E., and David M. Hay. *Philo of Alexandria: On the Contemplative Life; Introduction, Translation, and Commentary*. PACS 7. Leiden: Brill, 2020.

Terzēs, Chrēstos. "Musical Instruments of Greek and Roman Antiquity." Pages 213–27 in *A Companion to Ancient Greek and Roman Music*. Edited by Tosca A.C. Lynch and Eleonora Rocconi. Hoboken, NJ: Wiley & Sons, 2020.

Tougard, Albert. *De l'Histoire Profane dans les Actes Grecs Des Bollandistes: Extraits Grecs, Traduction Française, Notes, avec les Fragments Laissés par les Bollandistes, Volumes 12–101*. Paris: Didot, 1874.

Tsantsanoglou, Kyriakos. "The First Columns of the Derveni Papyrus and Their Religious Significance." Pages 93–128 in *Studies on the Derveni Papyrus*. Edited by André Laks and Glenn W. Most. Oxford: Clarendon, 1997.

Walter, Nikolaus, Eckart Reinmuth, and Peter Lampe. *Die Briefe an die Philipper, Thessalonicher und an Philemon*. NTD 8/2. Göttingen: Vandenhoeck &Ruprecht, 1998.

Wanamaker, Charles A. *The Epistles to the Thessalonians: A Commentary on the Greek Text*. NIGTC. Grand Rapids: Eerdmans, 1990.

Ware, James. "The Thessalonians as a Missionary Congregation: 1 Thessalonians 1, 5–8." *ZNW* 83 (1992): 126–31.

Wehrli, Fritz. *Aristoxenos*. Vol. 2 of *Die Schule Des Aristoteles*. Basel: Schwabe, 1967.

Weima, Jeffrey A. D. *1–2 Thessalonians*. BECNT. Grand Rapids: Baker Academic, 2014.

Wheeler, Laurie Ruth. "Divine Communication in the Letters of Paul: 1 Thessalonians as Source." PhD diss., Durham University, 2016.

Witherington, Ben, III. *1 and 2 Thessalonians: A Socio-rhetorical Commentary*. Grand Rapids: Eerdmans, 2006.

Paul, the Jews, and the Thessalonians: New Observations on 1 Thessalonians 2:14–16

Angela Standhartinger

First Thessalonians 2:14–16 contains the harshest anti-Jewish polemics in the entire New Testament. Of course, Acts's Peter also blames the Judeans among his Jerusalem audience for having killed Jesus of Nazareth. But Peter adds—historically more correct—"by the hand of lawless people" (διὰ χειρὸς ἀνόμων, Acts 2:23). Acts's Paul is even more accurate: "The residents of Jerusalem, together with their leaders … demanded to Pilate that he be executed" (Acts 13:27–28; see also 3:13–14).[1] On the contrary, 1 Thess 2:14 accuses all Jews of Judea, and in verses 15–16 not only Judeans but Jews as a people, *ethnos*, or race of having "killed the Lord." Moreover, nowhere else in the New Testament are Judeans and Jews blamed for being "opponents of all human beings" (πᾶσιν ἀνθρώποις ἐναντίοι). Nowhere else is it said that "God's wrath has reached them (and only them) until the end."

Today this text is part of Paul's letter to the newly founded community of Christ believers at Thessaloniki. Most scholars agree that 1 Thessalonians is the oldest surviving letter of Paul, Silvanus, and Timothy, written around the year 50 CE from Corinth to Thessaloniki. The puzzling question about 1 Thess 2:14–16 is: Why does such a strong anti-Jewish polemic appear in a letter written by three Jews, well known for their proud awareness of their ancestors and fellow people, Israel's law, and God's faithfulness to his people? In the following, I will review answers to this question. My first point gathers observations of those interpreters who argue that this text, or even the whole letter, was not

---

1. Peter's speeches include a more vague, shorter form; his accusations use the biblical phrase from Deuteronomy, "hung him upon a tree" (Deut 21:22–23, 26:26, Gen 40:19, Esth 5:14, etc.). His targets are either the Sanhedrin or an unspecified group (Acts 4:10, 5:30, 10:39). Unless otherwise indicated, all biblical translations are mine.

written by Paul. Second, I will look at arguments that have been raised in order to defend Pauline authorship of this passage. While no one, so far as I know, ignores the strong anti-Jewish stance, or is willing to agree with the text's anti-Jewish bias, there is a strong hesitation to exclude this text as a later gloss added to the text. While I can only speculate about reasons for those hesitations, I will, third, add some observations regarding the original context in which this text emerged.

1. 1 Thessalonians 2:13–16 Not Written by Paul

In 1854, Ferdinand Christian Baur was the first to argue that 1 Thess 2:14–16 has a "thoroughly un-Pauline stamp."[2] Nowhere does the apostle hold up the Jewish Christians as a pattern for gentile Christians. Nowhere else does Paul use a polemic so external and vague that the enmity of the Jews toward the gospel is characterized solely in terms of that well-known charge that the gentiles assigned them of *odium generis humanis*. Un-Pauline for Baur was also the expression κωλυόντων ἡμᾶς τοῖς ἔθνεσιν λαλῆσαι ἵνα σωθῶσιν ("by hindering us from speaking to the gentiles so that they may be saved"), which reminded him of Acts 14:1; 16:6, 32; 18:9.[3] Finally, the phrase ἔφθασεν δὲ ἐπ' αὐτοὺς ἡ ὀργὴ εἰς τέλος ("but God's wrath has overtaken them at last") suggested to Baur, very naturally, "the punishment that came upon them in the destruction of Jerusalem."[4] Baur concluded that not only this text but the whole letter was written at a much later period when the church was no longer engaged in conflict with Jewish Christ-believers—as Paul was—but with Judaism itself.[5] The later author's source was Acts's account about Paul and Silas's stay at Thessaloniki, where the success in the synagogue of the city among devout gentiles and promi-

---

2. Ferdinand C. Baur, *Paul, the Apostle of Jesus Christ*, trans. Eduard Zeller (London: Williams and Norgate, 1887), 2:87.

3. Acts 14:1: καὶ λαλῆσαι οὕτως ὥστε πιστεῦσαι Ἰουδαίων τε καὶ Ἑλλήνων πολὺ πλῆθος (they spoke with the result that a very large number of both Jews and Greeks came to believe, NRSV). Acts 16:6: κωλυθέντες ὑπὸ τοῦ ἁγίου πνεύματος λαλῆσαι τὸν λόγον ἐν τῇ Ἀσίᾳ (the Holy Spirit vetoed proclamation of the message in Asia, NRSV). Acts 16:32: καὶ ἐλάλησαν αὐτῷ τὸν λόγον τοῦ κυρίου (They spoke the word of the Lord to him, NRSV). Acts 18:9: Εἶπεν δὲ ὁ κύριος ἐν νυκτὶ δι' ὁράματος τῷ Παύλῳ· μὴ φοβοῦ, ἀλλὰ λάλει καὶ μὴ σιωπήσῃς (One night the Lord said to Paul in a vision, "Do not be afraid, but speak and do not be silent," NRSV).

4. Baur, *Paul* 2:88.

5. Baur, *Paul* 2:320.

nent women provoked jealousy from "the Judeans/Jews," who created the disturbance that led to Paul's departure from the city (Acts 17:5–8).

However, most interpreters found Baur's contestation of the authenticity of 1 Thessalonians unsatisfactory. Direct influence of Acts 17:1–9 on 1 Thessalonians cannot be demonstrated.[6] On the contrary, the two accounts of events in Thessaloniki obviously contradict each other. First Thessalonians 1:9 refers to members of the community as former non-Jews, not as affiliated with the (still unattested) synagogue of the city (cf. Acts 17:1–4). The Thessalonians of the letter are poor (cf. 2 Cor 8:2). They could not support the missionary team financially. Paul depended on money from Philippi and on his own work (Phil 4:15; 1 Thess 2:9). The Thessalonians of Acts include women from the first families of the city, thereby benefactors of the synagogue, and Paul's host, Jason, is a well-off citizen who can pay a security to the officials to avoid imprisonment (Acts 17:4, 9). In 1 Thessalonians, Jesus is a heavenly savior, not an earthly monarch, as in Acts (see 1 Thess 1:10, 4:16–18; Acts 17:7).[7] Whatever sources Luke used for his Thessaloniki account, they obviously presuppose a social setting of the community different from that reflected in the first letter to the Thessalonians.

While the discussions of the nineteenth century were almost forgotten in the twentieth,[8] some doubts about the authenticity of the passage made it into the apparatus of the Greek New Testament. Until the twenty-seventh edition of Nestle-Aland, the critical apparatus mentioned some Vulgate manuscripts that omit verse 16c: "but God's wrath has overtaken them at last." One example of these unspecified manuscripts is a Latin codex called the Ripoll Bible (MS Vat. lat. 5729) from the early eleventh-century Catalan monastery Ripoll, an illustrated manuscript with some Jewish influences on its illustrations.[9] Unfortunately, the twenty-eighth

---

6. Pace N. H. Taylor, "Who Persecuted the Thessalonian Christians?," *HTS* 58 (2002): 784–801.

7. See Richard Pervo, *Acts: A Commentary*, Hermeneia (Minneapolis: Fortress, 2009), 418.

8. See Karl Clemen, *Die Einheitlichkeit der paulinischen Briefe an der Hand der bisher mit Bezug auf sie aufgestellten Interpolations- und Compilationshypothesen* (Göttingen: Vandenhoeck & Ruprecht, 1894); Raymond F. Collins, "Apropos the Integrity of 1 Thess," *ETL* 65 (1979): 67–106.

9. MS Vat. lat. 5729, folio 452r. The facsimile of the Ripoll Bible can be seen online at Digivatlib, http://digi.vatlib.it/view/MSS_Vat.lat.5729. See Anreina Contessa, "Noah's Ark and the Ark of the Covenant in Spanish and Sephardic Medieval Manuscripts," in *Between Judaism and Christianity: Art Historical Essays in Honor of*

edition of Nestle-Aland omits this information, as well as the names of those modern scholars who proposed a conjecture, such as Hippolyte Rodrigues and Albrecht Ritschl.[10]

In 1971, Birger Pearson argued that 1 Thess 2:13–16 is a post-70 interpolation.[11] His arguments are the following:

1. The aorist ἔφθασεν "must be taken as referring to an event that is now past." Εἰς τέλος in verse 16c means "until the end," "finally," or "completely" and underscores that God's wrath is an event that already occurred.[12] The most logical referent is the destruction of Jerusalem in 70 CE.
2. With Baur, Pearson argues that the phrase καὶ πᾶσιν ἀνθρώποις ἐναντίων, "opponents of all human beings," is the accusation of misanthropy against the Jews, "widespread in the Greco-Roman world."[13] With the identification of *odium generis humanis*, Baur referred to Tacitus (*Ann.* 15.44.4), notably a post-70 CE author.
3. The charge of killing the prophets is a reflection of a Jewish tradition widespread in the New Testament.[14] But it is only in early Christian literature that "it becomes standard to interpret the death of Jesus in connection with the murder of the prophets." Most problematic is the charge of killing the Lord Jesus. Instead, Paul attributes the killing of Jesus to the demonic "rulers of this age" (1 Cor 2:8).
4. It is impossible to ascribe to the Jew Paul (see Gal 2:15) a passage that is diametrically opposed to Rom 9–11.

Elisheva (Elisabeth) Revel-Neher, ed. Katrin Kogman-Appel and Mati Meyer, MedMed 81 (Leiden: Brill, 2009), 172–89.

10. There has been some discussion on who was the first scholar in modern times to propose the conjecture regarding this sentence, mentioned until NA[27]. See Tjitze Baarda, "1 Thess 2:14–16. Rodrigues in Nestle Aland," *NedTT* 39 (1985): 186–93.

11. Birger A. Pearson, "1 Thessalonians 2:13–16: A Deutero-Pauline Interpolation," *HTR* 64 (1971): 81.

12. Pearson, "1 Thessalonians 2:13–16," 81–83. Some manuscripts (B, D*, Ψ, 0278, and the two minuscules 104 and 1505) read the perfect ἔφθακεν. However, with εἰς τέλος the meaning points to the same finality and must have at least some visible beginning in the present time.

13. Pearson, "1 Thessalonians 2:13–16," 83.

14. See 1 Kgs 19:10 = Rom 11:3; Neh 9:26; 2 Chr 36:15–16; Josephus, *Ant.* 10.38–39; Mark 12:1–12 // Matt 21:33–45; Matt 23:29–39 // Luke 11:49–51; 13:34–35; Acts 7:52. See below.

5. We have no information about Jewish persecutions of Christ believers in first-century Judea, nor can the tribulation mentioned in 1 Thess 1:6 and 3:3 be identified as a systematic persecution by "compatriots" in Thessaloniki.
6. The use of μιμηταί is not consistent with Paul's usage elsewhere.
7. Verse 13 introduces a second thanksgiving period that does not fit the normal letter form of Paul. Therefore, Pearson starts in verse 13 and speculates that the interpolator used the word of the first thanksgiving period in 1 Thess 1:1–10.

While Pearson initially convinced many, since 1990 most interpreters seem to argue against an interpolation hypothesis.[15] The exception is Marlene Crüsemann, who revived the hypothesis in line with Baur's view that the whole of 1 Thessalonians is a post-Pauline pseudepigraphic letter. Her argumentation is twofold. On the one hand, 1 Thess 2:14–16 cannot have been written before 70 CE and thus not by Paul. On the other hand, it is documented in all manuscripts and cannot be seen as a later addition.[16] I will come back to the second argument below (see 3.1).

2. 1 Thessalonians 2:14–16 as Written by Paul

Those who argue that 2:14–16 is an integral part of Paul's letter to the Thessalonians take a principled, critical stance against interpolation theo-

---

15. For a list of those who were initially convinced, see, e.g., Todd D. Still, *Conflict at Thessalonica: A Pauline Church and Its Neighbours*, JSNTSup 183 (Sheffield: Sheffield Academic, 1999), 24–25 n. 2. Daryl Schmidt adds stylistic observations. See Schmidt, "1 Thess 2:13–16: Linguistic Evidence for an Interpretation," *JBL* 102 (1983): 269–79. For the history of scholarship, see Carol J. Schlueter, *Filling Up the Measure: Polemical Hyperbole in 1 Thessalonians 2.14–16*, JSNTSup 98 (Sheffield: JSOT Press, 1994).

16. Marlene Crüsemann, *Die pseudepigraphen Briefe an die Gemeinde in Thessaloniki. Studien zu ihrer Abfassung und zur jüdisch-christlichen Sozialgeschichte*, BWANT 191 (Stuttgart: Kohlhammer, 2010), 46, 76, 285. Crüsemann argues further that the passage is "fest verankert im Kontext," yet without very strong evidence (47). As she herself notices, ὀργή is used differently in 1 Thess 1:10 and 2:16; that there are other provinces mentioned in 1 Thess 1:7–8 and 4:10 is no argument for the originality of "Judea" in 2:14, especially since Macedonia is the province, Thessaloniki the capital, and Achaia its neighboring province. That the missionaries want to please God and that the Thessalonians should please God (ἀρέσκω θεῷ, 2:4; 4:10; see Gal 1:10, 1 Cor 7:32, etc.) is not evidence that the criticism of the Judeans in general for displeasing God (1 Thess 2:15) belongs to the same level of argumentation.

ries, without attention to manuscript data. Moreover, they argue that the verses "fit sufficiently well in their present epistolary context."[17] First Thessalonians 2:13–16 forms an *inclusio* with 1:2–10 and resumes the terms: εὐχαριστέω; λόγος (1:2–5, 2:13); μιμηταί (1:6, 2:14); and ὀργή (1:10, 2:16).[18] With these verses Paul tries to explain to the Thessalonians the cause of their suffering and to offer them comfort (see 1 Thess 3:4–7).[19]

While I agree that 2:13 resumes the thanksgiving period and extends the thanksgiving in 1 Thessalonians to 3:13, the repetition of words is not an argument in itself. On the contrary, some of the terms denote different concepts. According to 1:10, people await ὀργή as ἐρχόμενη, God's wrath coming over the world in the near future (see 5:9), while in 2:16 God's wrath has already reached at least some Jews/Judeans in some form.[20] Interpreters seek concrete historical circumstances that might situate Paul's "rhetorical hyperbole" and "emotional outbreak."[21]

- Some argue that Paul's charge is not directed against "*the* Jews, but against *those* Jews whom he specified," namely, the Judeans and the other groups specified by their works named in the list of deeds.[22]
- For some, the text refers to a concrete historical persecution during the 40s in Judea, in the aftermath of the death of Herod Agrippa I in 43/44, the famine in Judea under Claudius, or the expulsion of the Jews from Rome.[23]

---

17. See Still, *Conflict at Thessalonica*, 31; Charles A. Wanamaker, *The Epistles to the Thessalonians: A Commentary on the Greek Text*, NIGTC (Grand Rapids: Eerdmans, 1990).

18. Didier Pollefeyt and David J. Bolton, "Paul, Deicide, and the Wrath of God: Towards a Hermeneutical Reading of 1 Thess 2:14–16," in *Paul's Jewish Matrix*, ed. Thomas G. Casey and Justin Taylor (Rome: Gregorian & Biblical Press, 2011), 238.

19. David Luckensmeyer, *The Eschatology of First Thessalonians*, NTOA 71 (Göttingen: Vandenhoeck & Ruprecht, 2009), 117–72.

20. See Crüsemann, who also observes that the notion of the future wrath (ὀργή) in 1 Thess 1:10 contradicts the wrath that has already occurred in 1 Thess 2:16 (*Die pseudepigraphen Briefe*, 73–75). For further contradictions, see below.

21. Schlueter, *Filling Up the Measure*; Markus A. Bockmuehl, "1 Thessalonians 2:14–16 and the Church in Jerusalem," *TynBul* 52 (2001): 1; Michael A. Rydelnik, "Was Paul Anti-Semitic? Revisiting 1 Thessalonians 2:14–16," *BSac* 165 (2008): 62–63.

22. Frank Gillard, "The Problem of the Anti-Semitic Comma between 1 Thessalonians 2.14 and 15," *NTS* 35 (1989): 498.

23. Bockmuehl detects a persecution of the Jerusalem church that took place in the eighth year of Claudius's reign (48/49 CE), proposed by sixth-century chroni-

- For some, only those Judeans/Jews are blamed who hindered the missionaries "from speaking to the Gentiles so that they may be saved" (2:16a). Thus, the text address the issue of the completion of the mission.[24]
- Some interpret the aorist ἔφθασεν as prophetic or ingressive: "finally the wrath will come" or "is going to come," and so on. Others find a gnomic aorist: "always the wrath will come finally." Thus, God's wrath would come "only" temporarily and does not refer to a final punishment.[25]

However, these arguments have not proven convincing to all interpreters, for good reasons. Misanthropy is a stereotypical charge against ethnic groups—not only the Judeans/Jews—in antiquity.[26] Moreover, at the end of 2:15, the text shifts from the past to the present tense (ἐκδιωξάντων ... ἀρεσκόντων). The reproach is no longer restricted to Judeans in Judea and/or those who are responsible for hindering Paul from speaking to the gentiles but is opened up to all Jews, who at the same time are collectively charged with being opposed to the Christian preaching of salvation.[27]

---

cler Malalas of Antioch ("1 Thessalonians 2:14–16"). For a list of further proposals see Luckensmeyer, *Eschatology of First Thessalonians*, 153. Recently Sarah E. Rollens describes the passage as an invented tradition that attaches the Thessalonians to the identity of the *ekklēsia* in Jerusalem and the biblical prophets. See Rollens, "Inventing Tradition in Thessalonica: The Appropriation of the Past in 1 Thessalonians 2:14–16," *BTB* 46 (2016): 123–32. However, how Paul could "invent" a tradition that blames his own people?

24. Torsten Jantsch, *"Gott alles in allem" (1 Kor 15,28): Studien zum Gottesverständnis des Paulus im 1. Thessalonicherbrief und in der korinthischen Korrespondenz*, WMANT 129 (Neukirchen-Vluyn: Neukirchener Verlag, 2011), 131–32.

25. In favor of a gnomic aorist is Ekkehard W. Stegemann, "Zur antijüdischen Polemik in 1 Thess 2,14–16," in *Paulus und die Welt: Aufsätze*, ed. Christina Tuor and Peter Wick (Zürich: Theologischer Verlag Zürich, 2005), 59–72. For further proposals see Rydelnik, "Was Paul Anti-Semitic?," 66–67.

26. George H. van Kooten, "Broadening the New Perspective on Paul: Paul and the Ethnological Debate of His Time—the Criticism of Jewish and Pagan Ancestral Customs (1 Thess 2:13–16)," in *Abraham, the Nations, and the Hagarites: Jewish, Christian, and Islamic Perspectives on Kinship with Abraham*, ed. Martin Goodman, George H. van Kooten, and Jacques T. A. G. M. van Ruiten, TBN 13 (Leiden: Brill, 2010), 319–44.

27. John M. Barclay, "Hostility to the Jews as Cultural Construct: Egyptian, Hellenistic, and Early Christian Paradigms," in *Josephus und das Neue Testament. Wechselseitige*

Whatever happened during the 40s in Judea and elsewhere—our information is limited for these years—the major crises, described by Christian apologetics of the second to the fifth century as the final coming of God's wrath, occurred during the destruction of the Jerusalem temple in 70 CE, or even during the devastation of Judea after the second or third Jewish-Roman war in 135 CE. The charge of hindering Christian mission is only one in the list and, besides employing typically Lukan language,[28] represents only one aspect of the apostle who wanted to become "a Jew for the Jews" (1 Cor 9:20) and who fights for table fellowship between Jews and gentiles elsewhere. First Thessalonians 2:14–16 is neither an instance of prophetic speech nor a proverb but a list of deeds culminating in a final result (εἰς τέλος). Therefore, naturally, the aorist ἔφθασεν refers to an event that has already "arrived." In contrast to Rom 9:22–24 and 11:25–30, 1 Thess 2:14–16 does not say "that God's covenantal faithfulness is greater than his wrath."[29]

But how could three Jewish authors—Paul, Silvanus, and Timothy—accuse their fellow Jews in this way? Many current interpreters detect a combination of typical anti-Jewish polemic, such as "godless" and "opposed to all people" in 2:15, with general accusations of "killing the prophets" and "filling up the measure of sins."[30] For these interpreters, texts such as Mark 12:1–9, Matt 23:29–38, and Acts 7:52 document the fact that early Christian discourse developed "a common set of tropes in which the Christian experience of 'persecution' from Judean/Jewish sources was linked to the history of Israel's rejection of prophets, the death of Jesus and the mission to the Gentiles."[31] We have to examine this tradition in greater detail.

Wahrnehmungen. II. Internationales Symposium zum Corpus Judaeo-Hellenisticum, 25.–28. Mai 2006, Greifswald, ed. Christfried Böttrich, Jens Herzer, and Torsten Reiprich, WUNT 209 (Tübingen: Mohr Siebeck, 2007), 382–83.

28. See n. 3.

29. See Pollefyt and Bolton, "Paul, Deicide, and the Wrath," 256.

30. Odil Hannes Steck, *Israel und das gewaltsame Geschick der Propheten* (Neukirchen-Vluyn: Neukirchner Verlag, 1967), 274–79; Barclay, "Hostility to the Jews," 379–80; Rudolf Hoppe, "Der Topos der Prophetenverfolgung bei Paulus," *NTS* 50 (2004): 535–49; Stefan Schreiber, *Der erste Brief an die Thessalonicher*, ÖTK 13.1 (Gütersloh: Gütersloher Verlagshaus, 2014), 152–56; et al.

31. Barclay, "Hostility to the Jews," 382.

3. The Original Context of 1 Thessalonians 2:14–16

The three main arguments in defense of Pauline authorship of 1 Thessalonians 2:14–16 are (1) lack of manuscript evidence, (2) a quotation of Jewish and Early Christian topoi, and (3) Pauline language.

3.1. Material Evidence for 1 Thessalonians 2:14–16

The first argument raised by almost all scholars is that there is no manuscript without 1 Thess 2:14–16. However, there is also no manuscript that documents 1 Thess 2:14–16 before Sinaiticus and Vaticanus in the fourth century CE. All three papyri containing some portions of 1 Thessalonians have a lacuna in these verses. P^{30} (= P.Oxy. 1598), originally dated to the third or fourth century, consists of two consecutive leaves of a papyrus codex, containing 1 Thess 4:12–5:28 and 2 Thess 1:1–2 with considerable lacunae. P^{46} (Chester Beatty Papyrus), late second or early third century, is preserved only at 1 Thess 1:1, 8–10; 2:1–3; 5:5–9, 23–28. P^{65} (PSI 14.1373), from the third century CE, is a one-page papyrus containing some fragments, 1 Thess 1:3–2:1; 2:6–13, the last verse only in three letters. Yet it is not possible to tell whether these manuscripts originally contained 2:14–16. The first author of the Greek-speaking world who clearly knew 1 Thess 2:14–15 and attributes it to Paul is Origen (185–254 CE). In his commentary on Matt 13:57, Origen claims that the prophet, who "is not without honor except in his own country," must be the Savior, referring to Acts 7:52 and to Paul's statements in 1 Thess 2:14–15 (*Comm. ser. Matt* 10.18). Commenting on Matt 22:1–14, the parable of the wedding banquet, Origen compares the anger of the king with the anger of the apostle about the Jews when he says, "God's wrath has overtaken them at last" (1 Thess 2:16). For Origen, Jesus's parable predicts the destruction of Jerusalem and the Jewish people (*Comm. ser. Matt.* 17.15). In the Latin-speaking world, the first to evince knowledge of these verses is Tertullian (150–220 CE), who blames Marcion for being inconsistent when he reads "who both killed the Lord, and their own prophets" in 2:15.[32] In Tertullian's polemic against Marcion's conception of two gods, there

---

32. The reading of ἀποκτεινάντων Ἰησοῦν καὶ τοὺς ἰδίους προφήτας is documented also by D¹, K, L, Ψ, minuscules 104, 365, 630, 1241, 1501, 2464; MT, sy. It is clearly in line with later theology. It is hard to tell how it appeared in Tertullian's manuscript of the collection of Paul's epistles used by the Marcionite church of his time.

would have been nothing to complain about if the Jews, who "put to death Christ, the preacher of a different god," also "had slaughtered the prophets of their own God" (Tertullian, *Marc.* 5.15.2).[33] However, it is difficult to tell how Marcion's text originally read. A second witness to Marcion's *Apostolos*, Adamantius's *Dialogue*, does not read "their own prophets."[34] It must remain an open question whether and in what form Marcion's text included 1 Thess 2:15. If so, then Marcion's edition from the mid-second century would be the earliest witness to our text.

3.2. 1 Thessalonians 2:14–16 in the Context of Jewish and Early Christian Tradition

As many have noted, the Bible and Jewish literature lament over kings and other members of the Jerusalem elite who killed prophets so as not to have to listen to them (see Neh 9:26; 2 Chr 36:15–16; Josephus, *A.J.* 10.37–39; et al.). The Sayings Source (Q 11:49–51; 13:34–35) as well as the parable of the tenants (Mark 12:1–9 par.) cite this tradition. However, nowhere is the accusation of killing the prophets directed against "the Jews" of a specific region or province, or even as a people. In fact, the Sayings Source Q and the parable of the tenants charge Jerusalem, its political elite, and "the Pharisees." Another tradition declares that the sins of some people have reached a full measure. However, in Jewish literature, this is said about other nations (Gen 15:16 = Jub 14:16; Dan 8:23; 2 Macc 6:14). In only a few instances is such a statement made about Israel in order to explain why God has forsaken his city and temple (LAB 26.13).[35] However, in every case "the punishments were designed not to destroy but to discipline our people" (2 Macc 16:12). Only the Testament of Levi declares, "However, the Lord's wrath has come upon them finally"[36] The context of T. Levi 6

---

33. Translated by Ernest Evans, *Tertullian Adversus Marcionem*, vol. 2, *Books 4 and 5* (Oxford: Clarendon, 1972), 605.

34. See Ulrich Schmid, *Marcion und sein Apostolos. Rekonstruktion und historische Einordnung der marcionitischen Paulusbriefausgabe*, ANTF 25 (Berlin: de Gruyter, 1995), 214.

35. Rainer Stuhlmann, *Das eschatologische Maß im Neuen Testament*, FRLANT 132 (Göttingen: Vandenhoeck & Ruprecht, 1983), 103–4.

36. T. Levi 6.11: ἔφθασε δὲ ἡ ὀργὴ κυρίου ἐπ' αὐτοὺς εἰς τέλος. Many highlight T. Levi 6.8–11 for several conceptual parallels to 1 Thess 2:14–16. See Jeffrey S. Lamp, "Is Paul Anti-Jewish? Testament of Levi 6 in the Interpretation of 1 Thessalonians 2:13–16," *CBQ* 65 (2003): 408–27; Barclay, "Hostility to the Jews," 279–80. The provenance

is an extensive debate in Jewish-Hellenistic literature on Shechem's rape of Jacob's daughter Dinah in Gen 34. How could it be justified, or at least explained, that Jacob's sons Simeon and Levi killed the recently circumcised people of Shechem?[37] The Testament of Levi excuses Levi not only by extending the list of misdeeds that proves the fault of the people of Shechem but also by transforming him into an instrument of God's wrath. Notably, the people of Shechem are dead when Levi tells this to his children on his deathbed.[38]

For a combination of the topoi "killing of prophets" and "measure of sins" with the charge of "killing the Lord Jesus" and hindering Christian mission, many interpreters point to Matt 23:29–38 and Acts 7:52.[39] In Matthew, the charge of killing the prophets is turned against "this generation," which is furthermore prompted to "fill up the measure of your ancestors." However, Matthew's charge is not directed against the "Jews," nor even Judeans, but rather against the Pharisees, the most eminent and unopposed teaching authority of this community of Christ-believers, according to Matt 23:2–3. While many commentators explain the incitement to fill up the measure of their fathers as filling up the sins of their ancestors,[40] this is not stated here (but see, e.g., Barn. 5.11; Gos. Pet. 5.17). On the contrary, in Matt 23:29–30, the measure of the fathers more easily refers to the double standard involved in building tombs for the prophets after killing them.[41]

---

of Testament of the Twelve Patriarchs is debated, but most recently David A. deSilva raises a number of convincing arguments against the hyper-Christianization of the Testaments in modern scholarship. See deSilva, "The Testaments of the Twelve Patriarchs as Witnesses to Pre-Christian Judaism: A Re-assessment," *JSP* 22.4 (2013): 21–68.

37. On this context, see Angela Standhartinger, "'Um zu sehen die Töchter des Landes.' Die Perspektive Dinas in der jüdisch-hellenistischen Diskussion um Gen 34," in *Religious Propaganda and Missionary Competition in the New Testament World: Essays Honoring Dieter Georgi*, ed. Lukas Bormann, Kelly Del Tredici, and Angela Standhartinger, NovTSup 74 (Leiden: Brill, 1994), 89–116.

38. This seems to have been overlooked by Lamp, who argues for close structural and thematic similarities ("Is Paul Anti-Jewish?").

39. See Barclay, "Hostility to the Jews," 381–82 et al.

40. See William D. Davies and Dale C. Allison, *The Gospel according to Saint Matthew* (Edinburgh: T&T Clark, 2000), 3:306; Ulrich Luz, *Das Evangelium nach Matthäus. 3. Teilband: Mt 18–25*, EKKNT 1/3 (Zürich: Benziger, 1997), 344–45 et al.

41. There is a strong tradition for commentaries on Matthew to refer to 1 Thess 2:14–16 and vice versa. Differences are often overlooked (see Crüsemann, *Die pseudepigraphen Briefe*, 57–58).

Matthew 23 does not reproach the Pharisees for having killed the Lord Jesus. Closer in this respect to 1 Thess 2:15 is Acts 7:52. The speech of Luke's arch-martyr Stephen culminates in the reproach:

> Which of the prophets did your forebears neglect to persecute? They murdered those who foretold the coming of the righteous one. Now that he has come, you betrayed and murdered him.[42]

Here the "killing of the prophets" stands in line with the "killing of the righteous one." While Jesus and the subsequent victim Stephen stand in the background, the reproach is not explicitly framed in terms of "killing of the Lord Jesus." However, this is first time this specifically Christian apologetic notion appears, that is, the notion that the prophets were killed in order to suppress their predictions of the advent of the Messiah.[43]

While Acts comes close to 1 Thess 2:14–16, the first author who directly reproaches the Jews, and his Jewish interlocutor Trypho, with the charge "you have slain Christ" (τὸν Χριστὸν ἀποκτείναντες), is Justin Martyr in the middle of the second century (*Dial.* 133.6).[44] Justin is also the first to combine the charges "killing of prophets" and "killing of the Lord Jesus":

> For you have murdered the Just One, and his prophets before him; now you spurn those who hope in him, and in him who sent him, namely, almighty God, the Creator of all things; to the upmost of your power you dishonor and curse in your synagogues all those who believe in Christ. (*Dial.* 16.4; see also *Dial.* 93.4, 95.4, 136.2–3; Clement, *Strom.* 6.5.127)

Justin combines this charge with the notion that Judea and Jerusalem lay in ruins after the war of 135 CE.

> Indeed the custom of circumcising the flesh, handed down from Abraham, was given to you as a distinguishing mark, to set you off from other nations and from us Christians. The purpose of this was that you and

---

42. Trans. Pervo, *Acts*.
43. See Pervo, *Acts*, 192 (1 Clem. 17.1; Pol. *Phil.* 6.3; Ign. *Phld.* 5.2).
44. Translations follow Thomas B. Falls, *St. Justin Martyr Dialogue with Trypho* (Washington, DC: Catholic University of America Press, 2003). Already Martin Dibelius found the parallel in Justin, *Dial.* 6.4. See Dibelius, *An die Thessalonicher I.II. An die Philippe*, 3rd ed., HNT (Tübingen: Mohr Siebeck, 1937), 11.

only you might suffer the afflictions that are now justly yours; that only your land be desolate, and your cities ruined by fire; that the fruits of your land be eaten by strangers before your very eyes; that not one of you be permitted to enter Jerusalem. (*Dial.* 16.2)

In my view, neither Matt 23 nor Acts 7:52 but only Justin Martyr's extensive collection of anti-Judean and anti-Jewish reproaches is the ancestor, or at least provides the context, of 1 Thess 2:14–16.⁴⁵

3.3. The Language of 1 Thessalonians 2:14–16

Some argue that 1 Thess 2:14–16 contains Pauline language throughout.⁴⁶ As I have shown above, the notion of ὀργή (wrath) in 1 Thess 2:16 differs from the idea in 1 Thess 1:10 and 5:9 that wrath is coming. Strikingly, older interpreters argued that because the language is un-Pauline throughout, the passage must be a quotation from an early Christian tradition.⁴⁷ The notion of μιμητής differs as well. "Imitation" does not mean copying but describes a creative act of emulation and appropriation.⁴⁸ In 1 Thess 1:6, the Thessalonians had become imitators of their missionaries, Paul, Silvanus, and Timothy, because their preaching and fame had spread already to Macedonia and Achaia and even to "every place"; they thus became even more successful than their own missionaries (1 Thess 1:6–8). In other words, the Thessalonians have remodeled their missionaries in a creative way. On the contrary, becoming a μιμητής in 2:14 means

---

45. For recent authors in this line of interpretation, see Rainer Kampling, "Eine auslegungsgeschichtliche Skizze zu 1 Thess 2,14–16," in *Im Angesicht Israels. Studien zum historischen und theologischen Verhältnis von Kirche und Israel*, ed. Matthias Blum, SBB 47 (Stuttgart: Katholisches Bibelwerk, 2002), 153–81.

46. But see n. 15 above.

47. To the opposite, European interpreters of the twentieth century argued that, because the language throughout is un-Pauline, Paul must be quoting an early Christian tradition. See Steck, *Israel und das gewaltsame*, 274–75; see also Reinier Schippers, "The Pre-synoptic Tradition in 1 Thessalonians II 13–16," *NovT* 8 (1966): 223–34.

48. Jo-Ann A. Brant, "The Place of *Mimēsis* in Paul's Thought," *SR* 22 (1993): 285–300. For the concept of *mimesis*—a concept that does not mean imitation in a modern sense but reinvention of a given subject or model—see Helmut Flashar, "Die klassizistische Theorie der Mimesis," in *Le Classicisme à Rome aux Iers Siècles avant et après J.-C. Neuf Exposés suivis de Discussions* (Vandoeuvres-Genève: Fondation Hardt, 1979), 79–112; Stephen Halliwell, *The Aesthetics of Mimesis: Ancient Texts and Modern Problems* (Princeton: Princeton University Press, 2002).

passively enduring similar sufferings as others. This notion of imitation is known by second-century Christian writers and appears in Christian martyr theology (see Pol. *Phil.* 8.2; Ign. *Eph.* 10.3; Ign. *Rom.* 6.3; Ps.-Clem. Hom. 11.20.5).

The other odd term is συμφυλέται, usually translated as "compatriots." However, a φυλή is actually a subunit of citizens in a given city.[49] For Thessaloniki, four *phylai* are documented, named Antigonis, Askepias, Dionysias, and Gnaias.[50]

> Inherited membership of a *phyle* was as a rule a prerequisite for participation in full citizenship. Based on a roughly equally large number of citizens…, the *phylai* made a substantial contribution to the political, administrative, cultural and military organisation of the *pólis*.[51]

In a letter to a city called Naryka, Hadrian named the existence of *phylai* as an important sign of holding the right to be a polis.[52] Another meaning of the term φυλή is "tribe," as it is used for the twelve tribes of Israel in the LXX or some tribes of Arabs elsewhere.[53] Both meanings cause problems in this context. Either the author of the text supposes the addressees to be among the city's elite structured in *phylai*,[54] or he speaks of the Thessalo-

---

49. Luckensmeyer argues for a specific local, not an ethnic sense of the term, but the term is used all over the Roman-Hellenistic world (*Eschatology of First Thessalonians*, 136–40).

50. Ursula Kunnert, *Bürger unter sich. Phylen in den Städten des kaiserzeitlichen Ostens* (Basel: Schwabe, 2012), 49–51.

51. Bernhard Smarczyk (Cologne) and Hans Lohmann (Bochum), "Phyle," in *Brill's New Pauly* (electronic version).

52. SEG 51.641, l. 14: φυλαὶ Ἑλληνικαί. For a translation of this passage, see Kunnert, *Bürger unter sich. Phylen*, 1. The term συμφυλέτης is attested only three times independently from 1 Thess 2:14. A Hellenistic inscription from Lesbos documents an honorary degree of the *phyle* of Aiolis for its φυλάρχης (chief officer of a *phyle*) Aristophanes. Among other honors, he is provided with a female sheep to sacrifice to Athena "for the health and safety of the *symphyletai*" (ὑπὲρ ὑγιείας [κ]αὶ σωτηρία[ς] τῶν συμφυλετῶν; IG 12.2.505, ll. 17–18). A first-century commentary on the *Iliad* uses συμφυλέτης for military groups originally formed by parts of a citizen's body (Aristonicus, *De signis Iliadis*, on *Il.* 4.307). The Christian apologetic writer Hermias († 341 CE) uses συμφυλέτης for the school of the Pythagoreans (Hermias, *Irr. gent. phil.* 16.2).

53. Fritz Gschnitzer, "Phylarchos," *PWSup* 11 (1968): 1070–72.

54. For this position, see Christoph vom Brocke, *Thessaloniki-Stadt des Kassander*

nians as a tribe. None of this is likely for the time of Paul. Second-century apologists might place themselves and other Christians, correctly or not, among a city's elite.

4. Conclusion

Why would such a strong anti-Jewish polemic as 1 Thess 2 has in verses 14–16 appear in a letter written by three Jews? My answer to this puzzling question is: because someone in the aftermath of the 135 CE Jewish-Roman war added it to the letter. Tertullian and Origen and perhaps Marcion are our first witnesses to the text. First Thessalonians 2:14–16 is a full-blown collection of anti-Jewish charges raised by Justin, Clement, and later Christian apologists. If at all, the text only superficially remodels Pauline language. Its sociohistorical and theological premises are from the second or even later centuries, not from the first.

But why did someone place the sentence between 1 Thess 2:13 and 2:17, two verses that run smoothly after each other by recapitulating the initial thanksgiving and moving on to the missionaries' eager desire to visit Thessaloniki again?[55] My suggestion is: because 1 Thessalonians differs from almost all other letters attributed to Paul—Romans, 1 and 2 Corinthians, Galatians, Philippians, Colossians, Ephesians, and even 1 Timothy and Titus—by virtue of their complete silence on Israel, Hebrews, Judeans, and Jews. A later interpolator filled this supposed "lack" by adding a set of charges that had become standard by his or her time. Whoever he or she had in mind by the *sympheletai*, the main point was to expand on the suffering of Christians inflicted by Judeans and Jews. As with Justin Martyr and later apologists, so for this interpolator, God had forsaken his own people. For Paul, the author of Rom 11, God obviously had not forsaken Israel.[56]

---

und Gemeinde des Paulus. Eine frühe christliche Gemeinde in ihrer heidnischen Umwelt, WUNT 2/125 (Tübingen: Mohr Siebeck, 2002), 162–66.

55. The two verses praise the community for their theological understanding, which the missionaries are proud of. Therefore, they emphasize their eager desire to visit the Thessalonians again.

56. On the dangerous memory and politics of reading of 1 Thess 2:14–16 see Melanie Johnson-DeBaufre, "A Monument to Suffering: 1 Thessalonians 2:14–6, Dangerous Memory, and Christian Identity," *JECH* 1 (2011): 91–118.

Bibliography

Baarda, Tjitze. "1 Thess 2:14–16. Rodrigues in Nestle Aland." *NedTT* 39 (1985): 186–93.

Barclay, John M. "Hostility to the Jews as Cultural Construct: Egyptian, Hellenistic, and Early Christian Paradigms." Pages 365–85 in *Josephus und das Neue Testament. Wechselseitige Wahrnehmungen. II. Internationales Symposium zum Corpus Judaeo-Hellenisticum, 25.–28. Mai 2006, Greifswald*. Edited by Christfried Böttrich, Jens Herzer, and Torsten Reiprich. WUNT 209. Tübingen: Mohr Siebeck, 2007.

Baur, Ferdinand C. *Paul, the Apostle of Jesus Christ*. 2 vols. Translated by Eduard Zeller. London: Williams & Norgate, 1887.

Bockmuehl, Markus A. "1 Thessalonians 2:14–16 and the Church in Jerusalem." *TynBul* 52 (2001): 1–31.

Brant, Jo-Ann A. "The Place of *Mimēsis* in Paul's Thought." *SR* 22 (1993): 285–300.

Brocke, Christoph vom. *Thessaloniki-Stadt des Kassander und Gemeinde des Paulus. Eine frühe christliche Gemeinde in ihrer heidnischen Umwelt*. WUNT 2/125. Tübingen: Mohr Siebeck, 2002.

Clemen, Karl. *Die Einheitlichkeit der paulinischen Briefe an der Hand der bisher mit Bezug auf sie aufgestellten Interpolations- und Compilationshypothesen*. Göttingen: Vandenhoeck & Ruprecht, 1894.

Collins, Raymond F. "Apropos the Integrity of 1 Thess." *ETL* 65 (1979): 67–106.

Contessa, Anreina. "Noah's Ark and the Ark of the Covenant in Spanish and Sephardic Medieval Manuscripts." Pages 172–89 in *Between Judaism and Christianity: Art Historical Essays in Honor of Elisheva (Elisabeth) Revel-Neher*. Edited by Katrin Kogman-Appel and Mati Meyer. MedMed 81. Leiden: Brill, 2009.

Crüsemann, Marlene. *Die pseudepigraphen Briefe an die Gemeinde in Thessaloniki. Studien zu ihrer Abfassung und zur jüdisch-christlichen Sozialgeschichte*. BWANT 191. Stuttgart: Kohlhammer, 2010.

Davies, William D., and Dale C. Allison. *The Gospel according to Saint Matthew*. 3 vols. Edinburgh: T&T Clark, 2000.

deSilva, David A. "The Testaments of the Twelve Patriarchs as Witnesses to Pre-Christian Judaism: A Re-assessment." *JSP* 22.4 (2013): 21–68.

Dibelius, Martin. *An die Thessalonicher I.II. An die Philippe*. 3rd ed. HNT. Tübingen: Mohr Siebeck, 1937.

Evans, Ernest. *Tertullian Adversus Marcionem*. Vol. 2, *Books 4 and 5*. Oxford: Clarendon, 1972.

Falls, Thomas B. *St. Justin Martyr: Dialogue with Trypho*. Washington, DC: Catholic University of America Press, 2003.

Flashar, Helmut. "Die klassizistische Theorie der Mimesis." Pages 79–112 in *Le Classicisme à Rome aux Iers Siècles avant et après J.-C. Neuf Exposés suivis de Discussions*. Vandoeuvres-Genève: Fondation Hardt, 1979.

Gillard, Frank. "The Problem of the Anti-Semitic Comma between 1 Thessalonians 2.14 and 15." *NTS* 35 (1989): 481–502.

Gschnitzer, Fritz. "Phylarchos." *PWSup* 11 (1968): 1067–90.

Halliwell, Stephen. *The Aesthetics of Mimesis: Ancient Texts and Modern Problems*. Princeton: Princeton University Press, 2002.

Hoppe, Rudolf. "Der Topos der Prophetenverfolgung bei Paulus." *NTS* 50 (2004): 535–49.

Jantsch, Torsten. *"Gott alles in allem" (1 Kor 15,28): Studien zum Gottesverständnis des Paulus im 1. Thessalonicherbrief und in der korinthischen Korrespondenz*. WMANT 129. Neukirchen-Vluyn: Neukirchener Verlag, 2011.

Johnson-DeBaufre, Melanie. "A Monument to Suffering: 1 Thessalonians 2:14–6, Dangerous Memory, and Christian Identity." *JECH* 1 (2011): 91–118.

Kampling, Rainer. "Eine auslegungsgeschichtliche Skizze zu 1 Thess 2,14–16." Pages 153–81 in *Im Angesicht Israels. Studien zum historischen und theologischen Verhältnis von Kirche und Israel*. Edited by Matthias Blum. SBB 47. Stuttgart: Katholisches Bibelwerk, 2002.

Kooten, George H. van. "Broadening the New Perspective on Paul: Paul and the Ethnological Debate of His Time—the Criticism of Jewish and Pagan Ancestral Customs (1 Thess 2:13–16)." Pages 319–44 in *Abraham, the Nations, and the Hagarites: Jewish, Christian, and Islamic Perspectives on Kinship with Abraham*. Edited by Martin Goodman, George H. van Kooten, and Jacques T. A G. M. van Ruiten. TBN 13. Leiden: Brill, 2010.

Kunnert, Ursula. *Bürger unter sich. Phylen in den Städten des kaiserzeitlichen Ostens*. Basel: Schwabe, 2012.

Lamp, Jeffrey S. "Is Paul Anti-Jewish? Testament of Levi 6 in the Interpretation of 1 Thessalonians 2:13–16." *CBQ* 65 (2003): 408–27.

Luckensmeyer, David. *The Eschatology of First Thessalonians*. NTOA 71. Göttingen: Vandenhoeck & Ruprecht, 2009.

Luz, Ulrich. *Das Evangelium nach Matthäus. 3. Teilband: Mt 18–25*. EKKNT 1/3. Zürich: Benziger, 1997.

Pearson, Birger A. "1 Thessalonians 2:13–16: A Deutero-Pauline Interpolation." *HTR* 64 (1971): 79–94.

Pervo, Richard. *Acts: A Commentary*. Hermeneia. Minneapolis: Fortress, 2009.

Pollefeyt, Didier, and David J. Bolton. "Paul, Deicide, and the Wrath of God: Towards a Hermeneutical Reading of 1 Thess 2:14–16." Pages 229–57 in *Paul's Jewish Matrix*. Edited by Thomas G. Casey and Justin Taylor. Rome: Gregorian & Biblical Press, 2011.

Rollens, Sarah E. "Inventing Tradition in Thessalonica: The Appropriation of the Past in 1 Thessalonians 2:14–16." *BTB* 46 (2016): 123–32.

Rydelnik, Michael A. "Was Paul Anti-Semitic? Revisiting 1 Thessalonians 2:14–16." *BSac* 165 (2008): 58–67.

Schippers, Reinier. "The Pre-synoptic Tradition in 1 Thessalonians II 13–16." *NovT* 8 (1966): 223–34.

Schlueter, Carol J. *Filling Up the Measure: Polemical Hyperbole in 1 Thessalonians 2.14–16*. JSNTSup 98. Sheffield: JSOT Press, 1994.

Schmid, Ulrich. *Marcion und sein Apostolos: Rekonstruktion und historische Einordnung der marcionitischen Paulusbriefausgabe*. ANTF 25. Berlin: de Gruyter, 1995.

Schmidt, Daryl. "1 Thess 2:13–16: Linguistic Evidence for an Interpretation." *JBL* 102 (1983): 269–79.

Schreiber, Stefan. *Der erste Brief an die Thessalonicher*. ÖTK 13.1. Gütersloh: Gütersloher Verlagshaus, 2014.

Smarczyk, Bernhard, and Hans Lohmann. "Phyle." *Brill's New Pauly Online*. https://brill.cpm/view/package/bnpo.

Standhartinger, Angela. "'Um zu sehen die Töchter des Landes.' Die Perspektive Dinas in der jüdisch-hellenistischen Diskussion um Gen 34." Pages 89–116 in *Religious Propaganda and Missionary Competition in the New Testament World: Essays Honoring Dieter Georgi*. Edited by Lukas Bormann, Kelly Del Tredici, and Angela Standhartinger. NovTSup 74. Leiden: Brill, 1994.

Steck, Odil Hannes. *Israel und das gewaltsame Geschick der Propheten*. Neukirchen-Vluyn: Neukirchner Verlag, 1967.

Stegemann, Ekkehard W. "Zur antijüdischen Polemik in 1 Thess 2,14–16." Pages 59–72 in *Paulus und die Welt: Aufsätze*. Edited by Christina Tuor and Peter Wick. Zürich: Theologischer Verlag Zürich, 2005.

Still, Todd D. *Conflict at Thessalonica: A Pauline Church and Its Neighbours*. JSNTSup 183. Sheffield: Sheffield Academic, 1999.
Stuhlmann, Rainer. *Das eschatologische Maß im Neuen Testament*. FRLANT 132. Göttingen: Vandenhoeck & Ruprecht, 1983.
Taylor, Nicholas H. "Who Persecuted the Thessalonian Christians?" *HTR* 58 (2002): 784–801.
Wanamaker, Charles A. *The Epistles to the Thessalonians: A Commentary on the Greek Text*. NIGTC. Grand Rapids: Eerdmans, 1990.

Gentle Philosopher, Rhetorician, or Selfless Benefactor? Paul's Apostolic Image and Ethos in 1 Thessalonians 2:1-12

James R. Harrison

The rhetorical genre and the conceptual background on which Paul draws in 1 Thess 2:1-12 for his apostolic self-presentation has remained a hotly contested area of scholarship ever since the decisive contribution of Abraham J. Malherbe in 1970.[1] Previous to Malherbe, most scholars "mirror-read" the rhetorical form of *apologia* from Paul's antithetical statements in 1 Thess 2:1-2, 3-4, 5-7b, 7c-8.[2] But, abandoning the consensus,

---

1. See Abraham J. Malherbe, "'Gentle as a Nurse': The Cynic Background to 1 Thessalonians 2," in *Paul and the Popular Philosophers* (Minneapolis: Fortress, 1989), 39-45. Martin Dibelius anticipates Malherbe to some extent when, in commenting on 1 Thess 2:6, he says that, in analogous ways, Paul appeals to "das Ideal des Philosophen," citing Epictetus (Arrian, *Epict. diss.* 3.22.13) as evidence. See Dibelius, *Die Briefe des Apostels Paulus an die Thessalonicher I II and die Philipper* (Tübingen: Mohr Siebeck, 1911), 7.

2. For a summary of scholarship positing that Paul's antithetical statements in 1 Thess 2 point to an *apologia*, see Karl P. Donfried, "The Epistolary and Rhetorical Context of 1 Thess 2:1-10," in *Paul, Thessalonica, and Early Christianity* (London: Continuum T&T Clark, 2002), 163-64. For other scholars supporting the proposal of an *apologia*, see also James E. Frame, *Epistles of St Paul to the Thessalonians*, ICC (Edinburgh: T&T Clark, 1912), 94; Denys E. H. Whiteley, *Thessalonians in the Revised Standard Version*, NCB (Oxford: Oxford University Press, 1969), 40; F. F. Bruce, *1 and 2 Thessalonians*, WBC 45 (Waco, TX: Word, 1982), 27-28; Leon Morris, *The First and Second Epistles to the Thessalonians*, rev. ed. (Grand Rapids: Eerdmans, 1991), 57; Simon Légasse, *Les épîtres de Paul aux Thessaloniciens*, LD 7 (Paris: Cerf, 1999), 108-9; Todd D. Still, *Conflict at Thessalonica: A Pauline Church and Its Neighbours*, LNTS 183 (Sheffield: Sheffield Academic, 1999), 143-48; Gregory K. Beale, *1-2 Thessalonians* (Downers Grove, IL: InterVarsity Press, 2003), 69-71; Gordon D. Fee, *The First and Second Letters to the Thessalonians*, NICNT (Grand Rapids: Eerdmans, 2009), 55-56.

Malherbe situated the pericope within the social milieu of the wandering Cynic philosophers, proposing that the apostle depicted himself as the "gentle philosopher" in engaging with his converts (Plutarch, *Adul. am.* 28 [69b–c]), as opposed to the "harsh philosopher" who famously excoriated his students for their moral failings. Paul's genre of self-presentation, therefore, was not an *apologia* whereby the apostle distinguished himself from the contemporary peripatetic hucksters who exploited their audience city by city to their own advantage (Dio Chrysostom, *Alex.* 7–10; Lucian, *Peregr.* 13).[3] Referring to Dio Chrysostom's portrayal of the ideal Cynic (*Alex.* 11–12; see also *In cont.* 10),[4] Malherbe suggests instead that Paul employed Cynic commonplaces in his self-presentation, but with the important qualification that the apostle understood the common terminology in theologically different ways from the famous peripatetic orator from Prusa.[5] In sum, Malherbe's contribution was strikingly original, paradigm shifting,[6] and exegetically fruitful in its careful contextualization of

---

Worthy of note, however, long before Malherbe's 1970 article, is Béda Rigaux, who espoused a nonapologetic understanding of 1 Thess 2:1–12: "on valorisera les assertions de l'âpotre non comme des réponses à des accusations, mais comme autant de motifs d'encouragement, de force, d' union, de persévérance et de consolation." See Rigaux, *Saint Paul: Les épitres aux Thessaloniciens* (Paris: Librairie Lecoffre, 1956), 62. On mirror-reading, Stanley K. Stowers comments regarding the paraenesis of 1 Thessalonians 2:1–10: "When one understands 1 Thessalonians as a paraenetic letter rather than a mirror, with a reverse image, it reads quite differently." See Stowers, *Letter Writing in Greco-Roman Antiquity* (Philadelphia: Westminster, 1986), 26. For the structure of the antitheses, see Fee, *First and Second Letters*, 66. For their rhetorical context in the popular philosophers, see Abraham J. Malherbe, *The Letters to the Thessalonians: A New Translation with Introduction and Commentary*, AB 32B (New York: Doubleday, 2000), 154–56.

3. Malherbe, "Gentle as a Nurse," 38–39. As Malherbe writes, Paul's rhetorical contrasts were not provoked by "specific statements that had been made about him personally" (48). Additionally, note Abraham J. Malherbe, *Paul and the Thessalonians* (Minneapolis: Fortress, 1987), 8–12, 48, 54–55, 74–75; Malherbe, *Letters to the Thessalonians*, 81–86, 133–63.

4. Malherbe, "Gentle as a Nurse," 45–48.

5. Malherbe, "Gentle as a Nurse," 48.

6. For some examples of scholars agreeing with Malherbe's paraenetic evaluation of 1 Thess 2:1–12, see George Lyons, *Pauline Autobiography: Toward a New Understanding*, SBLDS 73 (Atlanta: Scholars Press, 1985), 185; Charles A. Wanamaker, *Commentary on 1 and 2 Thessalonians*, NIGTC (Grand Rapids: Eerdmans, 1990), 91; Earl J. Richard, *First and Second Thessalonians*, SP 11 (Collegeville, MN: Glazier, 1995), 88–89; Beverly R. Gaventa, *First and Second Thessalonians*, IBC (Louisville: John

Paul's rhetorical strategy. It provided Pauline scholarship with an intriguing pastoral portrait of a more culturally adaptive, more philosophically attuned, and less confrontational apostle than often had been the case in the past.

This essay, however, agrees with the return of some scholars recently to the category of *apologia* in interpreting 1 Thess 2:1–12. Malherbe, I will argue, has not sufficiently considered the polemic underlying Dio Chrysostom's evidence and its possible relevance for Paul's pastoral situation. This calls into question Malherbe's argument that *apologia* is an inappropriate designation for our pericope, a conclusion he comes to on the basis that Dio Chrysostom was not responding to specific charges against himself.[7] I will argue that Paul employs a variety of rhetorical genres more suggestive of the "mixed" letter-type in our pericope, with a view to addressing the reputational damage incurred by his hasty exit from Thessalonica (see Acts 17:5–10) and by the invidious comparisons, whether explicitly aired or internally perceived by some Thessalonians, drawn between the apostle and the wandering preachers. Paul's distinctive rhetorical contribution in 1 Thess 2:1–10 was to differentiate himself from the negative reputation of the Cynic mission by employing the positive epigraphic language of honor and benefaction to establish the credibility of his apostolic ἦθος.

The forementioned "hasty exit" scenario, presented more fully below, is dependent on the historicity of the portrait of Paul's ministry in Acts 17. Needless to say, it is vulnerable to criticism from those scholars who reject the historicity of Acts 17:1–10. Tellingly, it might be very legitimately argued that because there is no explicit mention of a hasty exit in the primary document of 1 Thessalonians, the entire hypothesis has been imported into the text from an alien secondary source, the book of Acts. However, this is to overlook the reputational damage that a full epistolary avowal by Paul of his hasty exit from Thessalonica might have had in the familiar world of wandering Cynic preachers: it would provide further fuel for the critics of the apostle's brief ministry in the city. Thus, in a preemptive rhetorical response, Paul depicts himself as a selfless benefactor, drawing extensively from the terminology of the honorific inscriptions. Nevertheless, he concedes that he had experienced "strong opposition" while he was

---

Knox, 1998), 25–26; Traugott Holtz, "On the Background of 1 Thessalonians 2:1–12," in *The Thessalonians Debate: Methodological Discord or Methodological Synthesis?*, ed. Karl P. Donfried and Johannes Beutler (Grand Rapids: Eerdmans, 2000), 71–72.

7. Malherbe, "Gentle as a Nurse," 48.

at Thessalonica (1 Thess 2:2b), with the result that he was subsequently "orphaned" from his converts by being "separated" from them (2:17). Paul, I argue, is recasting circumspectly the historical traditions underlying his hasty exit from the city in more positive terms. Notwithstanding, this does not lead the apostle to deny surreptitiously his rejection by various Thessalonian opponents. This resulted, as he admits, in his painful separation from his converts by an unspecified event. We have to allow the apostle the rhetorical freedom to respond to his opponents as he sees fit, city by city, epistle by epistle.

1. Scholarship on 1 Thessalonians 2:1–12 after Malherbe: Unresolved Tensions

Although Malherbe's contribution has been seminal, little has been resolved in the subsequent scholarly debate regarding the occasion, milieu, rhetorical intent, and genre of the pericope. Karl Donfried, to cite a prominent example, argues that the pericope is an expression of epideictic or consolatory rhetoric, being neither apologetic nor polemical in intention, and, in the process, dismisses the suggestion that epistolary conventions might throw rhetorical light on the passage.[8] In Donfried's view, the *narratio* recounts the friendship between the apostle and his converts, thereby

---

8. Donfried, "Epistolary and Rhetorical Context," 166–70. However, scholarship had identified the epistolary convention of thanksgiving in 1 Thessalonians long before Malherbe and Donfried. See Paul Schubert, *Form and Function of the Pauline Thanksgivings*, BZNW 20 (Berlin: Töpelmann, 1939), 43–82. But, in my opinion, Paul's Thessalonian εὐχαριστῶ-periods (1 Thess 1:2–5, 2:13) frame our pericope (2:1–12) rather than define its overall function rhetorically. On gratitude in our pericope, see Jan Lambrecht, "Thanksgivings in 1 Thessalonians," in Donfried and Beutler, *Thessalonians Debate*, 135–62; Michael R. Whitenton, "Figuring Joy: Gratitude as Medicine in 1 Thessalonians 2:1–20," *PRSt* 39 (2012): 15–23. Nevertheless, other epistolary tropes and paraenesis appear in our pericope. Note in this regard (1) Paul's reminding the addressees of what is already known and not new information (1 Thess 2:2 [οἴδατε], 5 [οἴδατε], 9 [μνημονεύετε], 11 [οἴδατε]; see 1:5; 3:4, 6; 4:1, 9, 10; 5:1, 11; Pliny, *Ep.* 8.24), and (2) the appearance of the "unity in friendship" topos (1 Thess 2:8). On the unity-in-friendship topos, see Johannes Schoon-Janssen, "On the Use of Ancient Epistolography in 1 Thessalonians," in Donfried and Beutler, *Thessalonians Debate*, 187–88. Charles A. Wanamaker also attempts to integrate epistolary and rhetorical perspectives in 1 Thessalonians. See Wanamaker, "Epistolary vs. Rhetorical Analysis: Is a Synthesis Possible?," in Donfried and Beutler, *Thessalonians Debate*, 255–86.

distinguishing Paul's gospel and ethos from its false counterparts.⁹ Furthermore, eschatological indicators such as Paul's Spirit-filled (1 Thess 1:6, 8; 2:13; 4:15) and prophetic word (5:19–21) move the apostle away from the world of itinerant Cynic preachers to the more predictable milieu of Jewish mystical apocalypticism.¹⁰ Here we see a polarization within Pauline scholarship that still bubbles below the interpretative surface: the valorization of Paul's Jewish background as an explanatory tool over against Paul's hermeneutical engagement, as the apostle to the gentiles, with the diverse religious, philosophical, social, and political currents of the Greco-Roman world.¹¹ Surely Paul operates on each front with consummate skill and pastoral caution? But even where Malherbe's Cynic hypothesis has been accepted, not all scholars have been fully persuaded by its explanatory power. Bruce Winter, while conceding the importance of the ancient moralists for a proper understanding of our pericope, nevertheless argues that the apostle distanced himself from the pompous entries (εἴσοδος: 1 Thess 1:9, 2:1) of itinerant philosophers into cities and their self-aggrandizing rhetoric (see 1 Cor 2:1–5).¹²

Another approach has been to highlight (what is purported to be) the paraenetic and exemplary rhetoric of the pericope. Frank Hughes helpfully probes the rhetorical relationship between the *exordium* of the letter (1 Thess 1:1–10) and its subsequent *narratio* (2:1–3:10).¹³ The exemplary paradigms invoked in the *exordium* (προοίμιον)—specifically, the Thessalonian imitation of their suffering Lord, apostle, and missionary coworkers (1 Thess 1:6: ὑμεῖς μιμηταὶ ἡμῶν ἐγενήθητε) and, conversely,

---

9. Donfried, "Epistolary and Rhetorical Context," 170–88.
10. Donfried, "Epistolary and Rhetorical Context," 191.
11. See Abraham J. Malherbe, "Paul: Hellenistic Philosopher or Christian Pastor?," in *Paul and the Popular Philosophers*, 67–88.
12. Bruce W. Winter, "The Entries and Ethics of Orators and Paul (1 Thessalonians 2:1–12)," *TynBul* 44 (1993): 71–90.
13. Frank W. Hughes, "The Rhetoric of 1 Thessalonians," in *The Thessalonian Correspondence*, ed. Rob F. Collins, BETL 87 (Leuven: Leuven University Press; Peeters, 1990), 94–116. More fully, see Hughes, "The Rhetoric of Letters," in Donfried and Beutler, *Thessalonians Debate*, 194–240. For a slightly different construction on where the *narratio* commences (i.e., 1 Thess 1:6–3:13), see Robert Jewett, *The Thessalonian Correspondence: Pauline Rhetoric and Millenarian Piety* (Philadelphia: Fortress, 1986), 71–76. For differing scholarly attempts to identify rhetorical structure in 1 Thess 1–3, see Mark D. Roberts, "Images of Paul and the Thessalonians" (PhD diss., Harvard University, 1992), 96.

the example that the faithfulness of the Thessalonians provided to believers in Macedonia and Achaia (1:7: ἡ πίστις ὑμῶν ἡ πρὸς τὸν θεόν)—are said to be reinforced in the *narratio* (διήγησις). There Paul "uses himself and the Thessalonians' own experience as *exempla* (παραδείγματα) of honour."[14] This is implemented, Hughes posits, within an overall framework of epideictic rhetoric, best exemplified by funeral and consolatory speeches, though it is carried out with important distinctives in 1 Thessalonians.[15] Again, in this rhetorical construction of the *narratio* of our pericope and the wider epistle, which Hughes argues arises from but is not bound by the classical rhetorical handbooks (i.e., Aristotle, Quintilian, Cicero, Menander Rhetor),[16] there is no need to assume that Paul is mounting an *apologia*.

However, whether it is correct to identify Paul's rhetorical intent as providing an exemplum in 1 Thess 2:1–12 remains a moot point. The language of exemplarity and imitation is absent from the pericope, as Gene Green notes.[17] Retrieving the suggestion of Ernst von Dobschütz from early last century,[18] Green posits that is more likely that Paul is explaining

---

14. Hughes, "Rhetoric of 1 Thessalonians," 101. As Hughes elaborates, "Paul uses the *narratio* to show the consistency of his past behaviour with his present behaviour, and to show its consistency with the Thessalonians' past righteous behaviour already mentioned in the *exordium*, 1,3.6–10 ... so as to show that he has the ἦθος of an honourable man" (101–2).

15. Hughes, "Rhetoric of 1 Thessalonians," 107. On 1 Thess 1:6–2:16 as a consolatory laudation, see Abraham Smith, *Comfort One Another: Reconstructing the Rhetoric and Audience of 1 Thessalonians* (Louisville: Westminster John Knox, 1995), 76–80; see also Juan Chapa, "Consolatory Patterns? 1 Thess 4:13–18; 5:11," in Collins, *Thessalonian Correspondence*, 220–28. On the genre of funeral oration and 1 Thessalonians, see Jae-Kyung Cho, "The Rhetorical Approach to 1 Thessalonians in Light of Funeral Oration" (PhD diss., Asbury Theological Seminary, 2013).

16. Hughes, "Rhetoric of 1 Thessalonians," 99. Hughes observes: "Rhetorical criticism should not be made into a new form of form-critical strait jacket into which letters should be forced. Scholars reading letters of Cicero and Demosthenes have no doubts that these writers could and would consciously use rhetorical strategies in order to accomplish their purposes. If Paul used many of the same strategies in his letters (albeit for different purposes than Greek and Roman orators), we are equally justified in identifying the Apostle as a rhetorical writer" (108–9).

17. Gene L. Green, *The Letters to the Thessalonians*, PNTC (Grand Rapids: Eerdmans, 2002), 113.

18. Ernst von Dobschütz, *Die Thessalonicherbrief*, KEK 10 (Göttingen: Vandenhoeck & Ruprecht, 1909), 106–7.

why he did not return to Thessalonica (1 Thess 2:17–20) and what he did through his coworkers to rectify his pastoral severance from his converts, caused by his untimely exit from the city (3:1–5). Following Green's lead, the apostle's personal circumstances provide an important clue for understanding the intensity of his rhetoric in our pericope. Paul's apostolic ἦθος had been placed at risk though circumstances beyond his control, and his reputation, in his view at least, had to be upheld before God (1 Thess 2:4–5a, 10a) and his converts (2:10).[19] Malherbe is certainly correct in pointing to the Cynic mission as valuable comparanda for Paul's rhetoric by virtue of its common vocabulary and antithetical constructions in Dio Chrysostom (*Ad Alexandrinos*). But the evidence of Dio Chrysostom and Seneca also throws important light, overlooked by Malherbe, on the reputation of peripatetic missionaries in eastern Mediterranean cities and, concomitantly, how that might inform us about the apologetic type of rhetoric Paul employs in the pericope.

Cynic preachers were vulnerable to popular criticism. Dio Chrysostom excoriates the "harsh" Cynics for the damage they do to the credibility of true philosophers by virtue of their self-serving and parasitic behavior while they were present in the city:

> These Cynics, posting themselves at street corners, in alley-ways, and at temple gates, pass around the hat and play upon the credulity of lads and sailors and crowds of that sort, stringing together rough jokes and much tittle-tattle, and that low badinage that smacks of the market place. Accordingly, they achieve no good at all, but rather the worst possible harm, *for they accustom thoughtless people to deride philosophers in general*, just as one might accustom lads to scorn their teachers, and, when they ought to knock the insolence out of their hearers, these Cynics merely increase it. (*Alex.* 9)[20]

---

19. On ἦθος construction at Thessalonica, see Smith, *Comfort One Another*, 32–40; Edgar Krentz, "1 Thessalonians: Rhetorical Flourishes and Formal Constraints," in Donfried and Beutler, *Thessalonians Debate*, 308–10. Seyoon Kim notes that Paul repeatedly calls on his readers (1 Thess 2:1, 2, 5, 9, 10, 11) and God (1 Thess 2:5, 10) as witnesses in establishing his character in our pericope. See Kim, "Paul's Entry (εἴσοδος) and the Thessalonians' Faith (1 Thessalonians 1–3)," *NTS* 51 (2005): 533.

20. Unless otherwise noted, translations of Dio Chrysostom follow James W. Cohoon and H. Lamar Crosby, trans., *Dio Chrysostom, Discourses 31–36*, LCL (Cambridge: Harvard University Press, 1940).

Furthermore, Dio Chrysostom highlights the entry of the harsh Cynics into the city, their sparing use of frankness to little pastoral effect, and also their hasty exit either from the city or a disorderly mob, as case may be, when the pressure was really on:

> They merely utter a phrase or two, and, then, after berating rather than enlightening you, *they make a hurried exit*, anxious lest before they have finished you may raise an outcry and send them packing, behaving in very truth quite like men who in winter muster up courage for a brief and hurried voyage out to sea. But to find a man who in plain terms and without guile [ἀδόλως] speaks his mind with frankness [παρρησιαζόμεν], and neither [μήτε] for the sake of reputation [μήτε δόξης] nor [μήτ'] for gain makes false pretensions, but [ἀλλ'] out of good will and concern for his fellow man, stands ready, if need be, to submit to ridicule and the disorder of the mob—to find such a man as that is not easy, but [ἀλλ'] rather the good fortune of a very lucky city, so great is the dearth of noble, independent souls and such the abundance of toadies [κολάκων], mountebanks, and sophists. (*Alex.* 11)[21]

Scholars have highlighted several terminological overlaps in this passage between Dio Chrysostom's criticism of the Cynics and the style of ministry that Paul avoids in 1 Thess 2:1–12, as well as the presence of antitheses (μήτε, ἀλλά).[22] But how would Paul's exit from Thessalonica been have viewed by his converts? And against what cultural grid might they have made their moral assessment, given the brevity of the apostle's stay in Thessalonica?

---

21. Interesting examples from the inscriptions throw further light on Dio Chrysostom's terminology additional to the Cynic resonances. An inscription (*IG* 7.7.53, ll. 29–31; 232 CE) speaks of the people of Arkesine honoring their dead benefactor, Aur(elius) Octabios, as a hero and with a gold crown during his funeral rites, "seeing that neither by money nor by flattery [κολακείᾳ] nor by supplicatory prayer nor by tears will a man of destiny be able at any time to transgress (his) limit (of life)." ἀδόλως ("without guile") appears regularly in the inscriptions with ἁπλόως ("openly"), ἀβλαβέως ("without harming": *TAM* 2.1183), ἀπροφασίστως ("without evasion"), and δικαίως ("justly": SEG 35:59 [Caria]). On ἁπλόως, see Angelos Chaniotis, *Die Verträge zwischen kretischen Poleis in der hellenistischen Zeit* (Stuttgart: Steiner, 1996), §60B (Rhodes); IC IV 186 (Crete). On ἀπροφασίστως see Malcolm Errington, "Antiochos III., Zeuxis und Euromos," *EA* 8 (1986): 1–7.

22. ἀδόλως (Dio Chrysostom, *Alex.* 11); ἐν δόλῳ (1 Thess 2:3b). παρρησιαζόμεν (Dio Chrysostom, *Alex.* 11); ἐπαρρησιασάμεθα (1 Thess 2:2b). δόξης (Dio Chrysostom, *Alex.* 11); δόξαν (1 Thess 2:6b, 12b). κολάκων (Dio Chrysostom, *Alex.* 11); κολακείας (1 Thess 2:5a).

Cultural bias against the itinerant missionary figures of the Greek East would surely come into play in this context.[23] Insinuations about the inconstancy of Paul's pastoral care at Thessalonica may have arisen if believers were tempted to draw unflattering comparisons between the apostle's mission and that of the Cynic philosophers (1 Thess 2:3, 6–7). Some may have alleged that the apostle was irresponsible (indeed, cowardly?) in allowing himself to be pressured by his fellow believers to exit from Thessalonica (2:17–18; see Acts 17:1–9), simply because, to borrow Dio Chrysostom's words, he was facing "the disorder of the mob" (*Alex.* 11). As a result, the Thessalonian believers were exposed to further trials and persecutions without the presence of their apostle (1 Thess 3:3–5; see also 1:6, 2:14). Such perceptions would potentially hamper the progress of the gospel in the city by virtue of a Thessalonian loss of confidence in the personal commitment of their apostle. Thus, in counterpoint, Paul places a strong emphasis on his own sufferings and persecutions for the gospel and their paradigmatic value for his converts (1 Thess 1:6; 2:2; 3:4, 7). In conclusion, an inelegantly handled exit either from a city or from an agitated crowd could deleteriously affect itinerant preachers as much as extravagant entries could enhance their reputation.

Furthermore, itinerant preachers who were contemporary with Paul "attempted to maintain their image before the public" by disassociating themselves from "disreputable figures."[24] Dio Chrysostom carefully steered a course between public disrepute and an honorable reputation as a philosopher. While admitting that his outward appearance approached that of the Cynic beggars (*1 Regn.* 9, 50; *Exil.* 10–13; *1 Tars.* 14; *2 Tars.* 2; *Cel. Phryg.* 2; *Borysth.* 17; *De habitu*), he nevertheless avoided their more questionable aims and methods, appealing instead to the venerable examples of Socrates (*Exil.* 6, 14, 16, 29–31) and Diogenes (*Tyr.* 60; *Virt.* 1, 5, 16; *Isthm.* 2; *De servis* passim) as sources of honor.[25] So great was the concern of some itinerant preachers about their public reputation that they feared that if they differentiated themselves too much from routine conformity to social conventions, then the exemplum that they set forth

---

23. See Claude Coulot on the challenges facing Thessalonian Christians from the traveling preachers of the Greco-Roman world. Coulot, "Paul à Thessalonique (1Th 2:1–12)," *NTS* 52 (2006): 384–85.

24. Walter L. Liefeld, "The Wandering Preacher as a Social Figure in the Roman Empire" (PhD diss., Columbia University, 1967), 285.

25. Liefeld, "Wandering Preacher," 46–51, 285.

would be vitiated by the demeanor and disreputable reputation of the other wandering preachers. Seneca sums up the dilemma for the peripatetic philosopher thus:

> I warn you, however, not to act after the fashion of those who desire to be conspicuous rather than to improve, by doing things which will rouse comment as regards your dress or general way of living. Repellent attire, unkempt hair, slovenly beard ... and any other perverted forms of self-display, are to be avoided. The mere name of philosophy, however quietly pursued, is an object of sufficient scorn; and what would happen if we should begin to separate ourselves from the customs of our fellow-men. Inwardly, we ought to be different in all respects, but our exterior should conform to society. Do not wear too fine, nor yet too frowzy, a toga.... Let us try to maintain a higher standard of life than that of the multitude, but not a contrary standard; otherwise we shall frighten away and repel the very persons whom we are trying to improve. We also bring it about that they are unwilling to imitate us in anything, because they are afraid lest they might be compelled to imitate us in everything. (*Ep.* 5.1–3 [Gummere])[26]

The problem with Malherbe's Cynic hypothesis for interpreting 1 Thess 2:1–12 is not the paradigm itself but rather that he has abstracted its expression from Paul's social and historical context, preferring to concentrate on the apostle's rhetoric instead. Malherbe has paid insufficient attention to the fact that this rhetoric was articulated in local urban contexts where the Cynics, along with other missionary preachers, mutually positioned themselves against each other in a completion for status, honor, and public recognition, characterized rhetorically by heated rivalry and stinging polemic. Why would we assume that somehow the situation was different for Paul, when he adopts similar rhetoric in delineating his apostolic self-understanding? The content of the polemic was understood from the perspective of Paul's gospel (τὸ εὐαγγέλιον τοῦ θεοῦ: 1 Thess 2:2, 8, 9), but the rivalry among competing missionary preachers, including the early Christians, was an ever-present reality. In particular, the blurring between philosopher, wonderworkers, mendicants, divine personages, and prophets during the first and second century CE in the eastern Mediterranean basin meant that each "took on each other's characteristics."[27] Walter

---

26. Cited in Liefeld, "Wandering Preacher," 287.
27. Liefeld, "Wandering Preacher," 302.

Liefeld spells out the public consequences of this for the Greco-Roman wandering missionary movement:

> Naturally those who sensed that they were considered inferior and socially unacceptable tried to present themselves in a respectable role, such as that of a philosophic missionary. At the same time, those who were genuine philosophic or religious moralists were forced to take measures to avoid being confused with the lower types. Unless they could, like most rabbis, travel among sympathetic communities where they could lecture within a legitimate school or sanctuary, they were unavoidably exposed to public scepticism.[28]

It could be argued, as Robert Jewett does,[29] that Paul's exhortation of the Thessalonians (1 Thess 5:12–13) to respect their local leaders was necessitated by some type of internal division in the house churches. This, Jewett proposes, provoked Paul's rhetorical avowal that his ministry had not been in vain (1 Thess 2:1) and that it was powerful "not only in word but also in power" (1 Thess 1:5). Certainly the force of 1 Thess 1:5 in a thanksgiving context raises a serious question whether the verse has polemical intention. But popular perceptions could also carry the day in terms of the evaluation of leaders, as the evidence of Dio Chrysostom and Seneca clearly indicates. So we do not need to resort to speculations about internal divisions to appreciate why Paul differentiated his mission from that of his Cynic contemporaries in coming to grips with lingering concerns or insinuations about his extended absence from Thessalonica.

However, the main problem with the scenario outlined above, in the view of many New Testament scholars, is that "Paul nowhere implies that the team is under attack for its integrity or for its absence."[30] There is no explicit evidence, Gary Shogren observes, that Paul is trying to protect his "tottering reputation."[31] Furthermore, the positive statements Paul makes about the faith, hope, and love of the Thessalonians (1 Thess 1:3, 3:6, 4:9–10; see also 2:19–20) undermine the idea that the apostle is under attack, and they stand in sharp contrast to the savage tone of other epistles where

---

28. Liefeld, "Wandering Preacher," 302–3.
29. Jewett, *Thessalonian Correspondence*, 102–4.
30. Gary S. Shogren, *1 and 2 Thessalonians: Exegetical Commentary on the New Testament* (Grand Rapids: Zondervan, 2012), 81.
31. Shogren, *1 and 2 Thessalonians*, 26.

he is under genuine attack (e.g., Gal 1:6; 2 Cor 11:4, 12:20–21).[32] So where does this leave us?

In several publications, however, Jeffrey Weima points to several unusual dimensions of Paul's rhetoric that help us to identify the pericope as an *apologia*.[33] Weima notes the following features: (1) the unusually defensive polemic of 1 Thess 1:5 in what is ostensibly a thanksgiving, (2) the frequency of the antithetical statements ("not *x* but *y*") throughout the epistle (1 Thess 1:5, 8; 2:17; 4:7, 8; 5:6, 9, 15), (3) the unusual emphasis on God as his witness (2:5, 10; see also Rom 1:9; 2 Cor 1:23; Phil 1:8) and God's examination of Paul (1 Thess 2:4); (4) Paul's repeated claims of the Thessalonian direct knowledge of his ministry ethos in the city (οἴδατε),[34] and (5) the tight nexus between our pericope and the subsequent detailed exposition of his absence from the suffering Thessalonians (2:17–3:10).

Additionally, Seyoon Kim spotlights Paul's fear that the tempter would cast doubt on his apostolic ἦθος by calling into question his integrity and εἴσοδος (1 Thess 3:5), which, to the absolute joy of Paul (3:7–8), was subsequently vindicated by the arrival of the good news about the Thessalonian believers longing for Paul's parousia (3:6).[35] The rhetorical complexity of what Paul is engaging in is again underscored by the fact that the motifs of longing for and the parousia of an absent friend are both epistolary topoi.[36] Kim rightly points to Paul's desperation over the absence of news (3:1a: "when we could bear it no longer"; 3:5a: "when I could bear it no longer").

While the specifics behind the satanic temptation are kept silent by Paul,[37] the threat is nonetheless very real and is not just a matter of Paul's

---

32. Judith L. Hill, "Establishing the Church in Thessalonica" (PhD diss., Duke University, 1990), 86–89.

33. Jeffrey A. D. Weima, "An Apology for the Apologetic Function of 1 Thessalonians 2:1–12," *JSNT* 68 (1997): 73–99; Weima, *1–2 Thessalonians*, BECNT (Grand Rapids: Baker Academic, 2014), 122–25; Weima, *Paul the Ancient Letter Writer: An Introduction to Epistolary Analysis* (Grand Rapids: Baker Academic, 2016), 109–13.

34. See n. 8 above.

35. Kim, "Paul's Entry (εἴσοδος)," 526.

36. On parousia and the expression of "longing" as epistolary conventions, see David E. Aune, *The New Testament in Its Literary Environment* (Cambridge: Clarke, 1987), 172; Stowers, *Letter Writing in Greco-Roman Antiquity*, s.v. "Index of Selected Epistolary Commonplaces": "Longing for or to be with a loved one," "Present in Spirit … through absent in body."

37. Possibilities might include whether Paul's converts would persevere under persecution (1 Thess 3:3, 10; see 1:6b, 2:14), Thessalonian disquiet over Paul's per-

rhetorical construction of his apostolic persona. Malherbe's discussion of Dio Chrysostom does not sufficiently take into account the polemic against the harsh Cynics and their abrupt exits from difficult situations: this makes his contention that there is no apologetic element in our pericope unlikely.[38] Paul's polemic in 1 Thess 2:1–12 more likely addresses the perception that the apostle had acted like the harsh Cynics, not only exiting the city but also exposing his converts to further danger, instead of courageously facing a difficult and dangerous situation in the city. Little wonder that Paul highlights that he had repeatedly tried to return to the city only to be blocked by Satan (1 Thess 2:18) and that he, like the Thessalonians, had experienced additional persecutions subsequent to his exit from Thessalonica (3:7; see also 3:1b; Acts 17:10–14, 18:1–17).[39] *Apologia*, therefore, best represents the rhetorical strategy that Paul undertakes in response to these unwarranted perceptions.[40]

Finally, identifying what type of rhetoric is being used in 1 Thessalonians and its appropriate context is also a matter of contention among New Testament scholars.[41] The options of deliberative (advice-giving), epideictic (praising and blaming), and protreptic rhetoric (advocating the

---

ceived lack of credibility in not returning to the city after his exit (2:17–18), or the impact of external pressures from Greco-Roman missionary preachers on the Christian mission at Thessalonica.

38. Roberts argues that our pericope "is not directly apologetic, formed in response to specific criticism or opponents ... but it does reflect the general spirit of competition between the many proclaimers of 'truth' in the Graeco-Roman world" (*Images of Paul*, 126). However, an *apologia*, I would argue, can be general in its critique as much as it can be specifically targeted, depending on whether the author is working broad-canvas or pointillist. This point is overlooked by those who deny the genre of *apologia* for 1 Thess 2:1–12.

39. Weima, *1–2 Thessalonians*, 222–23; contra Malherbe, *Letters to the Thessalonians*, 202.

40. Timothy A. Brookins opts for a compromise position, positing that "Paul was responding to *specific* charges without necessarily responding to a specific group of *opponents*." See Brookins, *First and Second Thessalonians*, Paideia (Grand Rapids: Baker Academic, 2021), 41.

41. Gaventa writes perceptively: "The debate about the purpose of 1 Thessalonians involves several highly technical and complex questions, such as the nature of ancient epistolary theory, the extent to which rhetorical practice obtained in letter writing, the extent to which any rhetorical artefact ever offered a 'pure' example of a rhetorical genre, and the sorts of evidence that should be regarded as relevant for understanding rhetorical practice" (*First and Second Thessalonians*, 6).

true way of philosophy and morality) have all been canvassed for 1 Thessalonians in terms of the rhetorical handbooks on speech-making.[42] We should remember that Paul's epistles were read out aloud (1 Thess 5:27), so Paul is likely to have adapted rhetorical categories appropriate to speeches in his letters.[43] Epistolary rhetorical categories (paraenetic [Pseudo-Libanius, *Epist.* 5]; paracletic [Pseudo-Libanius, *Epist.* 7, 54; see 1 Thess 2:3, 12: 4:1, 10, 18; 5:11]) have also been proposed, and we have already noted the frequency of their topoi in the letter.[44] The Jewish dimensions of rhetorical convention, as Philip Kern observes,[45] including the synagogal sermon, should also be considered in this context. For our purposes, however, we will only refer to Paul's Jewish-Christian apocalypticism and his LXX intertextual echoes.

Given this rich blend of genres, we have to ask whether an exemplary or epideictic rhetoric accounts for the subtlety of Paul's self-presentation, or whether, as I have argued, its complexity has been provoked by apologetic needs related to Paul's exit and its negative perception in a Greco-Roman missionary context. If the latter is the case, then the "mixed" letter-type in antiquity would have been the appropriate rhetorical choice for the apostle in mounting a comprehensive *apologia* for his defense (Pseudo-Libanius, *Epist.* 4: μικτή). As Pseudo-Libanius describes the genre, "The mixed style [μικτή] is that which we compose from many styles" (*Epist.* 45; see also Pseudo-Dionysius, *Rhet.* 276).[46] Since the "mixed" style best accounts for the wide range of rhetorical genres proposed for 1 Thess 2:1–12, it should not surprise us that semantic domains drawn from the eulogistic inscrip-

---

42. On 1 Thessalonians as deliberative, see George A. Kennedy, *New Testament Interpretation through Rhetorical Criticism* (Chapel Hill: University of North Carolina Press, 1984), 142.

43. See the comprehensive defense of this position by Ben Witherington III, "'Almost Thou Persuadest Me...': The Importance of Greco-Roman Rhetoric for the Understanding of the Text and Context of the NT," *JETS* 58 (2015): 63–88; contra Philip H. Kern, *Rhetoric and Galatians: Assessing an Approach to Paul's Epistle*, SNTSMS 101 (Cambridge: Cambridge University Press, 1998).

44. Roberts, *Images of Paul*, 87–90. See nn. 9, 39 above.

45. Kern, *Rhetoric and Galatians*, 243. On synagogal sermons, see William R. Stegner, "The Ancient Jewish Synagogue Homily," in *Greco-Roman Literature and the New Testament*, ed. David E. Aune, SBLSBS 21 (Atlanta: Scholars Press, 1988), 51–69; James R. Harrison, *Paul's Language of Grace in Its Graeco-Roman Context*, WUNT 2/172 (Tübingen: Mohr Siebeck, 2003), 151–57.

46. Pseudo-Libanius's example of the "mixed" genre is found in *Epist.* 92.

tions also underlie the pericope: the world of honor and benefaction looms large, though Paul redefines these in light of the LXX and the gospel of the crucified and risen Christ.

In the second half of the essay, I will argue that in contrast to Paul's dependence on Cynic motifs, aired almost exclusively in the negative antitheses (1 Thess 2:1 [οὐ], 3a/3b [οὐκ, οὐδέ], 4b [οὐχ], 5a/5b [οὔτε, οὔτε], 6a/6b [οὔτε, οὔτε]), the apostle frequently employs terminology from the epigraphic domains of honor and benefaction in the positive antitheses (2:2 [ἀλλά], 4a/4c [ἀλλά, ἀλλά], 7b–8 [ἀλλά]). This culminates in the graphic vignette of his selfless munificence as the nurse of the Thessalonians (2:7b), drawn equally from epigraphic honorific and LXX domains, and his self-portrait as their paternal benefactor (2:9–12). It is significant that Paul draws from the contemporary polemic against the harsh Cynics in the negative antitheses. However, the positive antitheses and the vignettes of the apostle's Thessalonian ministry are characterized by honorific and benefaction language, though elements of polyvalence are also present in the form of LXX intertextual echoes, and, in one instance, Cynic resonances appear. In sum, Malherbe's contention that Paul presents himself as the gentle philosopher may be implied by the negative antitheses, but, more concretely, Paul's language is drawn from semantic domains other than the world of the Cynics in the positive antitheses. That Paul so heavily draws on honorific and benefaction language in his self-presentation is another important piece of evidence supporting the contention that the apostle is engaged in an *apologia* for his apostolic honor and selfless ministry in 1 Thess 2:1–12.

2. The Selfless Benefactor Who Honors God:
Paul Sets the Record Straight

2.1. The Divinely Approved and Entrusted Apostle: Resonances of Honor and Benefaction (1 Thess 2:4)

After depicting the ministry of contemporary itinerant preachers in 1 Thess 2:4, employing rhetorical elements from the Cynic world critical of the harsh philosopher, Paul presents himself and his coworkers in verse 4 as divinely approved and entrusted missionaries in order to distance himself from unwarranted insinuations about his unfaithfulness to his gospel and converts. Two key words that are central to his self-defense are the passive participle δεδοκιμάσαμεθα and the complimentary passive infinitive πιστευθῆναι, each of which acquires considerable gravitas by virtue of their mutual attachment to the phrase ὑπὸ τοῦ θεοῦ, underscoring the apostolic mission's "investiture by God."[47] In an epigraphic context, cognates of the former word capture elements of personal honor through divine and human endorsement, whereas cognates of the latter the word highlight the apostle's role of benefactor in bringing the gospel to the Thessalonians.

In the case of the inscriptional perfect participle δεδοκιμασμένος, two examples are particularly instructive. In an honorific decree (41 CE) for a *libertus* of Augustus Claudius, the recipient, Tyrannus, is eulogized thus:

> Since Tiberius Claudius Tyrannus, *libertus* of Augustus, our citizen, a ma[n] approved [δεδοκιμασαμένος] by the divine judgements of the Augusti [τοῖς θείοις κριτηρίοις τῶν Σεβαστῶν], both for his skill of a doctor and propriety of character, (who), being suitably at hand for his country, has carried out his stay with all solemnity in regard to himself, having contributed h[u]manely to all citizens. (IMagnMai 113)

Not only is this decree fascinating because its avowal of a plurality of leadership so late in the Julio-Claudian principate, but the unique phrase τοῖς θείοις κριτηρίοις τῶν Σεβαστῶν only appears in this sole Magnesian inscription in the entire Greek epigraphic corpus.[48] The reference to the "divine judgements of the Augusti" is intriguing, creating an aura of a legal endorsement of Tyrannus,[49] an official approval that is conveyed by a divine legitimating authority in the rhetoric employed. A divine examination and endorsement of Tyrannus is clearly implied in this case, as opposed to a merely expedient approval of Tyrannus because of his medical skills and trusted character.

In another inscription from Thyatira, Aurelius Hermogenes is honored by the council of the Lydian city. But, significantly, Hermogenes's approval stems not only from the reputation accrued through his voluntary service

---

47. Richard, *First and Second Thessalonians*, 80.

48. Based on a search of the Packard Humanities Institute Greek Inscriptions program at http://www.inscriptions.packhum.org. For literary examples, Greco-Roman and Jewish, see Green, *Letters to the Thessalonians*, 120. See also Rigaux, *Saint Paul: Les épitres aux Thessaloniciens*, 409, on the epigraphic and papyrological use of δοκιμάζω and cognates. On the Judio-Claudian principate, see James R. Harrison, "Diplomacy over Tiberius' Succession," *New Docs* 10:64–75, and the literature there cited.

49. On the judicial nuances of τὸ κριτήριον, see LSJ, s.v. "κριτέος," III.

of the city via the civic *cursus honorum* but also from the personal disposition in which it was carried out: "The best and Augustus-loving council honoured Aurelius Hermogenes, the third (son) of Barcha, with the erection of a statue, a man approved [δεδοκιμασαμένος] in magistracies and liturgies arising from both himself and his race in (personal) habit and dignity" (*TAM* 5.2.953).

The judicial element of Tyrannus's endorsement by the Augusti, noted above, finds resonances with Paul's emphasis on God testing the hearts (1 Thess 2:4b: δοκιμάζοντι τὰς καρδίας ἡμῶν) of those entrusted with his gospel (2:4a: δεδοκιμάσαμεθα). As we have seen, the disposition of the entrusted benefactor was also important in the honorific inscriptions where only human approval was involved. For Paul, however, everything in terms of character and entrustment flows from divine approval, as opposed to pleasing men via the ancient honor system (1 Thess 2:4b: ἀνθρώποις ἀρέσκοντες). The conceptual worlds are vastly different: God's examination of human hearts (1 Thess 2:4b) flows from Paul's eschatological gospel (see Rom 2:16), already emphasized earlier (1 Thess 1:9) and later in what follows (2:19–20). Moreover, behind Paul's thought lies the Old Testament tradition of the divine examination of human hearts (Deut 8:2; 1 Sam 16:7; 1 Chr 29:17; 2 Chr 32:31; Eccl 3:18; Pss 7:9, 11:4–5, 26:2, 139:23; Prov 17:3; Job 17:18; Jer 11:20 [LXX: δοκιμάζων νεγροὺς καὶ καρδίας], 12:3, 17:10), as well as Jesus's prophetic discernment of what was in a person's heart (διαλογίσμος: Luke 2:35, 5:22, 6:8, 9:47).[50]

In contrast to the epigraphic emphasis on divine and human entrustment in honorific contexts, the appearance of πιστευθῆναι in 1 Thess 2:4 (see also Gal 2:4: πεπίστευμαι τὸ εὐαγγέλιον) exhibits strong resonances with the world of benefaction. This is evident in a fragmentary inscription from late republican Aphrodisias.[51] The decree not only details an extraordinary range of magistracies (*stephanephoros*, gymnasiarch, priesthood of

---

50. Jeffrey A. D. Weima, "1–2 Thessalonians," in *Commentary on the New Testament Use of the Old Testament*, ed. Gregory K. Beale and Donald A. Carson (Grand Rapids: Baker Academic, 2007), 873; Collin Bullard, *Jesus and the Thoughts of Many Hearts: Implicit Christology and Jesus in the Gospel of Luke*, LNTS 530 (London: Bloomsbury T&T Clark, 2015).

51. Joyce Reynolds, *Aphrodisias and Rome: Documents from the Excavation of the Theatre at Aphrodisias Conducted by Professor Kenan T. Erim, Together with Some Related Texts*, JRSM 1 (London: Society for the Promotion of Roman Studies, 1982), §30.

Rome, *agoranomos*, military offices) held by a local benefactor of the city but also recounts the dangers to which he submitted in delivering the city from external military threat.[52] What is significant for our purposes is that he has carefully discharged his duty in guarding the forts entrusted to him by the city and thereby has personally vindicated their trust in him for the benefit of the country's common interest. The terminological interplay of faith (πίστεις) entrusted with faith vindicated (ἐμπιστευθέντα) in the case of this benefactor is striking:

> …] saviour and benefactor, having saved his country from many dangers and great dangers, having fought bravely in all the wars which beset his country, having guarded the forts entrusted (τὰ ἐμπιστευθέντα ὀχυρώματα) to him by the city and preserved faith (πίστεις) to the common interest (?) in the most difficult circumstances, having filled all the magistracies with integrity (καθαρῶς) and justice (δικα[ί]ως), and to the advantage of the city, having been *stephanephoros* and gymnasiarch, in which offices he was magnificently generous, having held the priesthood of Rome, having been *agoranomos* at a time of most serious famine and provided corn at a fair price at his own expense, [having held] offices in the wars […

But, whereas our unnamed Aphrodisian benefactor vindicated the human trust placed in him, Paul focuses on his divine entrustment, faithfully preaching the gospel of God in the knowledge that he and his coworkers continuously live under God's "scrutiny and approval."[53]

2.2. Household Images of Apostolic Honor and Benefaction: τροφός and πατήρ (1 Thess 2:7, 11)

2.2.1. The τροφός Image

In rebutting the insinuation that he had abandoned the Thessalonian believers to their own fate by his exit from the city, Paul counters with two positive images, respectively drawn from the world of honor and beneficence, that highlight the integrity of his apostolic persona: namely, τροφός

---

52. On the "endangered" benefactor, see Frederick W. Danker, *Benefactor: Epigraphic Study of a Graeco-Roman and New Testament Semantic Field* (St. Louis: Clayton, 1982), 417–35.

53. Shogren, *1 and 2 Thessalonians*, 94.

("nurse": 1 Thess 2:7) and πατήρ ("father": 2:11).⁵⁴ In the case of τροφός,⁵⁵ the text perhaps most pertinent to Paul's rhetoric in 1 Thess 2:7 is Plutarch's employment of the "nurse" simile to describe the pedagogical method of gentle philosopher, as opposed to the sharp moral rebukes of the harsh philosopher. The two competing approaches to ancient pyschagogy are set out thus:

> But for a man who is sick it is intolerable, nay, an aggravation of the sickness to be told, "See what comes of your intemperance, your soft living, your gluttony and wenching." "Heavens, man, what a time to talk of that! I am writing my will, the doctors are preparing for me a dose of castor or scrammony, and you admonish and lecture me!" Under such conditions, then, the very circumstances in which the unfortunate find themselves leave no room for frank speaking [παρρησίαν] and sententious saws, but they do require gentle usage and help. When children fall down, the nurses [αἱ τίτθαι] do not rush up to them to berate them, but they take them up, wash them, and straighten their clothes, and, after this is done, they then rebuke and punish them. (Plutarch, *Adul. am.* 28 [69c–d] [Babbitt])

Whereas the harsh philosopher steers potential converts towards philosophy and away from their life of ethical error by means of his biting censure, the gentle philosopher models himself on the nurse who initially restores "immature infants," morally speaking, to spiritual stability through sensitive care and help, before addressing their more intractable character traits by frank and targeted speech. If Cynic resonances underlie Paul's choice of simile at this juncture, then the apostle is rhetorically contrasting the dishonorable style of ministry characteristic of his Greco-Roman competitors—the so-called toadies, mountebanks, and sophists of the negative antitheses—with the honorable persona of the gentle philosopher (1 Thess

---

54. See also Rosemary Canavan's essay in this volume, which also discusses the τροφός image.

55. Gaventa writes: "The use of nurses, wet nurses, or lactating nurses in particular, was widespread in the Graeco-Roman world.… The nurse was not only a common but a beloved figure, as is clear in literary references and from the number of inscriptions in which adults honour those who nursed them" (*First and Second Thessalonians*, 27). For full discussion of the literary evidence undergirding the nurse image, though with no reference to the epigraphic and visual evidence, see Jennifer Houston McNeel, *Paul as Infant and Nursing Mother: Metaphor, Rhetoric, and Identity in 1 Thessalonians 2:5–8*, ECL 12 (Atlanta: SBL Press, 2014).

2:7b) in the positive antitheses. This carefully cultivated image was chosen by Paul to express the true nature of apostolic ministry that the Thessalonians had experienced under his care when he was present in the city and which continued in the present through his heartfelt solicitude for his converts (2:17), notwithstanding his current absence.

But Paul's imagery, I would argue, is polyvalent in this instance, and we have to be open to the possibility that Paul would have also been exposed in his travels to inscriptions honoring nurses or even visual imagery of nurses on clay vessels of various kinds.[56] First, while normally little is said about the nurse on inscriptions other than the identification of the name and family, there is occasionally an epithet revealing the genuine affection and high esteem held for the nurse (τροφός χρηστή ["kindly nurse"]: *IG* 2.2.12563) or the privileged place that the nurse had in the life of the household (τροφός καὶ νάννη ["nurse and maternal aunt"]: SEG 12.231). The prized place of the nurse in family life is underscored.

Second, the visual evidence depicting nurses also adds an important dimension to the epigraphic evidence above. One prominent example will suffice. The role of the nurse in protecting a child from an unspecified threat is seen in a painting present on the extant fragments of a large, slender-proportioned, three-handled water jar (hydria-*kalpis*) from Athens.[57] In a scene depicting the famous farewell of Amphiaraos to his wife and child, Amphiaraos stands equipped for the deadly expedition against Thebes, resolutely grasping a spear in his left hand. Amphiaraos looks intently at (what is now only a small fragment of) the head of Eriphyle, his deceitful wife, who is situated to his left.[58] Both of them are probably holding clasped hands, but since the rest of the painting cannot be restored, this remains conjecture. But, significantly, a nurse stands in full-frontal view to the right, extending her right hand, while securely clasping on her left arm the child Amphilochos, the son of Amphiaraos

---

56. For inscriptions honoring the τροφός, see *IG* 2.2.5592; 2.2.12563; SEG 12.231; SEG 47.1075; CIRB 421; *IG* 12s.1013; KFF 48; Preuner, Hermes 55, 1920, 184–87; IEph 6.2269A.

57. Lacey D. Caskey and John D. Beazley, *Attic Vase Paintings in the Museum of Fine Arts, Pt. 1, Plates 1–33 Text nos. 1–65* (London: Oxford University Press for Museum of Fine Arts, Boston, 1931–1963), pl. 27.

58. Caskey and Beazley write: "The names of Amphiaraos and Eriphyle are inscribed above their heads in letters carelessly drawn and so faint as to be nearly illegible: A[ΜΦ]ΙΑΡΗΟΣ or A[ΜΦ]ΙΑΡΑΟΣ (not A[ΜΦ]ΙΑΡΕΟΣ) … and [ΕΡΙ] ΦΥΛΗ" (*Attic Vase Paintings*, pl. 27).

and Eriphyle. A strong sense of imminent threat is captured by the wide-open eyes of all the figures in the scene, with the child's fear graphically expressed by his hand clasping his nurse's shoulder. The serious danger posed is symbolically conveyed by the fillet tied to the child's head, from which hangs a cord over his right shoulder, and which, significantly, has three protective amulets attached to it. The nurse, therefore, is a pivotal figure in the scene, protecting and preserving the future generation of the family, symbolized by the child, from what would be betrayal and calamity for the father at Thebes.

How do these background materials—literary, epigraphic, and visual—contribute to our rhetorical understanding of Paul's aims in 1 Thess 2:7? We have seen that in terms of the Cynic understanding of the τροφός image, scholars are justified in pointing out that Paul contrasts his apostolic pastoral style with the maligned paradigm of the harsh philosopher, preferring instead to depict himself as the gentle philosopher in handling his converts.[59] But Malherbe does not consider the epigraphic and visual evidence in his interpretative construct, thereby missing out on the epigraphic and visual evidence nuances of the τροφός as a kind, deeply valued, and honored member of the household, who was responsible for the care of the children as well as assuming a protective role in ensuring a safe future for the upcoming generation.[60] In sum, Paul traded on the polyvalent dimension of the image, though we must not discount the strong possibility that LXX intertextual echoes also determine his choice of a feminine image in 1 Thess 2:7 (Num 11:12; Isa 66:13; see also 1QH^a XV, 23–25; possibly 1QH^a XVII, 29B–36), which is later joined with a male household image in 2:11.[61] Paul's τροφός image, therefore, is subtle, capturing philosophical, epigraphic, and LXX resonances of language, projecting

---

59. Beverly R. Gaventa rejects Malherbe's proposal of Paul as the gentle philosopher, arguing that Paul "draws upon a well-known figure in the ancient world." See Gaventa, *Our Mother Saint Paul* (Louisville: Westminster John Knox, 2007), 24. But, if 1 Thess 2:1–12 is an apologia against invidious comparisons of Paul, locally drawn, with peripatetic missionaries (which Gaventa denies), then Malherbe's possibility of an implied contrast with the gentle philosopher remains open.

60. We will not touch on the vexed textual issue of whether we should translate ἤπιοι ("gentle") or νήπιοι ("infants") in 1 Thess 2:7 (see Shogren, *1 and 2 Thessalonians*, 99–103; Weima, *1–2 Thessalonians*, 180–87).

61. Gaventa, *First and Second Thessalonians*, 28, 31–34; Gaventa, *Our Mother Saint Paul*, 22–25. For discussion of the Jewish evidence, see Houston, *Paul as Infant*, 99–121.

a powerful portrait of relentless care, and countering the slur that the apostle had orphaned the Thessalonians by his exit.

2.2.2. The πατήρ Image

In terms of the father image in 1 Thess 2:11 (ὡς πατήρ), there is epigraphic evidence of paternal imagery being used of benefactors in antiquity. Two important examples from the eastern Mediterranean basin are discussed below, but we should also remember the use of "father" for military figures who deliver their dependents or legions, for the imperial rulers as saviors of the Roman state, and for benefactors and leaders in associations (including synagogues), among other examples.[62] First, a remarkable inscription

---

62. On military figures as fathers: An elogium of the southeast exedra of the Augustan forum eulogizes Q. Fabius Cunctator (consul, 209 BCE) for his preservation of the besieged army of Minucius by bringing them military help when dictator of Rome: "(As) Dictator, to the master of the horse, Minucius, whose imperium with the people with the dictator's had equated, and to (his) shattered army, he did bring help, and on that account by the army of Minucius he was called 'father.'" For full translation, see Edwin A. Judge, "The Eulogistic Inscriptions of the Augustan Forum: Augustus on Roman History," in *The First Christians in the Roman World: Augustan and New Testament Essays*, ed. James R. Harrison, WUNT 229 (Tübingen: Mohr Siebeck, 2008), 179 B11.

On imperial rulers as fathers: The ubiquitous term of the Roman imperial inscriptions for the ruler, πατὴρ πατρίδος, is used most famously in Res gest. divi Aug. 35.1 ("the senate and equestrian order and people of Rome all together hailed me as father of the fatherland [πατέρα πατρίδος; [p]atr[rem p]atriae]"). Alison E. Cooley comments that *pater patriae* was used of leading Romans who had rescued Rome from enemies such as the Gauls (Camillus: Livy, *Urb. cond.* 5.49.7), the Cimbri (Marius: Cicero, *Rab. Post.* 10.27), and Catiline (Cicero: Cicero, *Pis.* 3.6). See Cooley, *Res Gestae Divi Augusti: Text, Translation, and Commentary* (Cambridge: Cambridge University Press, 2009), 273; see also John Scheid, *Res Gestae Divi Augusti: Hauts faits du divin Auguste* (Paris: Les Belles Lettres, 2007), 92–93. Caesar, too, was called "father" (Cassius Dio, *Hist.* 44.4.4; Suetonius, *Jul.* 85). Note, too, the link of Augustus as "savior" and "father" in Horace, *Saec.* 3.24.25–32; see also Ovid, *Trist.* 2.574. Additionally, as far as Augustus, see Ovid, *Fast.* 2.127–128; Suetonius, *Aug.* 58.1–2; Cassius Dio, *Hist.* 55.10.10. In terms of the occurrence of πατὴρ πατρίδος in an imperial context at Thessalonica, there is only one extant use of the phrase in an inscription honoring a Roman ruler, namely, Antoninus Pius (*IG* 10.2.1.15; ca. 143–161 CE), though the phrase is restored: "Τ(ίτος) · Αἴλιος Ἀδριανὸς Ἀντωνῖ]νος Σεβαστός, ἀρχιερεὺ[ς μέγιστος], / [δημαρχικῆς ἐξουσίας τὸ .' αὐτο]κράτωρ τὸ β ὕπατος τὸ [.' πατὴρ πατρίδος] / [Θεσσαλονεικέων τοῖς ἄρχουσι καὶ] τῆι βουλῆι καὶ τ[ῶι δήμωι χαίρειν]." On benefactors and leaders in associations

of Olbia, datable to the late republic or early principate, describes the benefactor Theokles as follows:

> by his moderation [διὰ τὸ μέτριον αὐτο], and his affection [φιλόστοργον] in regard to his country, and his hospitality [φιλόξενον] towards all the Greeks, he has surpassed all his ancestors [νεικῆσαι μὲν τοὺς προγόνους τοὺς ἑαυτοῦ], ... having administered public affairs with all concord [πᾶσαν ὁμόνοιαν], becoming as a brother [ὡς ἀδελφός] to the men of his own age, as a son [ὡς υἱός] to the more aged, as a father [ὡς πατήρ] to the more young, adorned with all merit [πάσῃ ἀρετῇ]. (*CIG* 2.2059, ll. 16–18, 28–30)[63]

The breadth of fictive familial relationships envisaged in this inscription (ἀδελφός, υἱός, πατήρ) helps us to see how Paul, as an apostolic benefactor of his converts, articulated relationships of the founding fatherhood, corporate brotherhood, and divine sonship within the body of Christ, with a view to maintaining unity and concord among his fellow believers.[64] We need not be naive about the purported selflessness of Theokles's motivations here: like most elites in antiquity, his aim was to surpass victoriously (νεικῆσαι) the glory of his ancestors.

Second, in an honorific decree for Kallimachos (March 39 CE), the governor of the Egyptian Thebaid, the fatherly role of Kallimachos in

---

as fathers, see, for example, Richard S. Ascough, Philip A. Harland, and John S. Kloppenborg, *Associations in the Greco-Roman World: A Sourcebook* (Waco, TX: Baylor University Press, 2012), §§41, 314, 322. For full discussion and epigraphic sources, see Philip A. Harland, "Familial Dimension of Group Identity (II): 'Mother' and 'Father' in Associations and Synagogues of the Greek World," *JSJ* 38 (2007): 57–79. Note, too, the inscriptional evidence touching on the spiritual use of πατήρ in the Greco-Roman mithraic cults. On this, see Pedro Gutierrez, *La paternité spirituelle selon Saint Paul* (Paris: Librairie Lecoffre, 1968), 60–62.

63. Wesley P. Clark comments regarding this inscription: "Occasionally a bit of genuine feeling shines out from the records which are for the most part quite matter of fact, revealing a sort of game between givers and recipients, the latter voting honours, thanks, crowns, and the like in order to induce the former to continue their good works or to increase them and to move others to do likewise." See Clark, "Benefactions and Endowments in Greek Antiquity" (PhD diss., Chicago University, 1928), 261.

64. On the rhetorical importance of "concord" (ὁμόνοια) in deliberative speeches, see Margaret M. Mitchell, *Paul and the Rhetoric of Reconciliation: An Exegetical Investigation of the Language and Composition of 1 Corinthians* (Louisville: Westminster John Knox, 1992), 60–64.

delivering Thebes from the threat of famine is underscored. Although the word πατήρ is restored in the inscription, the language of "fatherhood" is nevertheless implied by the reference to the "fatherland" (οἰκείας πατρίδος) and "legitimate children" (τέκνων γνησίων):

> And indeed, [he displayed] his goodness of heart, and in beneficence those who excel in generosity [---]. And further, now [---] [--- the] severe famine caused by crop-failure like none hitherto recorded, and when the city had almost been crushed by [need], having devoted himself wholeheartedly, voluntarily contributed to the salvation of each of the local inhabitants. Having laboured as [a father on behalf of] his own fatherland [οἰκείας πατρίδος] and his legitimate children [τέκνων γνησίων], with the good will of the gods, in continuous abundance of [food] he maintained nearly everyone; and [he kept them] unaware of the circumstance from which he furnished the abundance. (*OGI* 194, ll. 10–14)[65]

Again, what light does this epigraphic evidence throw on Paul's use of πατήρ in 1 Thess 2:11? The fictive familial relationships depicted in the Olbia decree throw light on Paul's depiction of the family relationships within the body of Christ: but the restriction of a benefactor's fatherly care to the legitimate children of his fatherland in the case of Kallimachos at Thebes constricts Paul's multiethnic vision of apostolic care in his house churches. But, as noted, there are again LXX intertextual echoes of Old Testament depictions of fatherly care (e.g., Ps 103:13) that should not be discounted, as well as its appearance in 1QH VII, 20b–22.[66] What is significant, however, is how Paul adumbrates the nature of his paternal care by means of the three participles employed subsequently in 1 Thess 2:12 (παρακαλοῦντες, παραμυθούμενοι, μαρτυρόμενοι), two of which, as we will see, are used in honorific and benefaction contexts in the eulogistic inscriptions.

---

65. Trans. Stanley M. Burstein, ed. and trans., *The Hellenistic Age from the Battle of Ipsos to the Death of Kleopatra VII* (Cambridge: Cambridge University Press, 1985), §111.

66. Shogren, *1 and 2 Thessalonians*, 107; Gutierrez, *La paternité spirituelle selon Saint Paul*, 38. For a full discussion of paternity in the OT evidence, see Gutierrez, *La paternité spirituelle selon Saint Paul*, 15–38; for a full discussion of the metaphor πατήρ in antiquity, see 15–83.

2.3. The Paradox of a Laboring Benefactor: Paul's Refusal to Be a Burden (1 Thess 2:9)

At the outset of 1 Thess 2:9 Paul speaks of the labor and hardships of himself and his coworkers at Thessalonica as they worked "night and day" (νυκτὸς καὶ ἡμέρας: see 1 Thess 3:10; 2 Thess 3:8; 1 Tim 5:5; 2 Tim 1:3) so that they might not be a financial burden to the Thessalonian church. The phrase νυκτὸς καὶ ἡμέρας appears repeatedly in a series of thanksgiving and priestly dedications at Panamara, of which we cite only one inscription as representative of the rest. Two priests, Publius Aelius Hekatomnos and Apphias Trphaina Drakontis, are eulogized thus:

> [having performed all] (rituals) towards the god piou[sly and always generously towards their dependents, but a]lso restoring the meals and sacrificing for all who were want[ing (to honour the gods) without hindrance, they offered willingly the rites of sacrifices], and they acted as gymnasiarchs [both in regards to the succession to the crown and (during) the ten days of the Panamareia] throughout the entire night and day (νυκτὸς καὶ ἡμέρας), [having assigned the oil without hindrance for the fortune and vigour of local residents and] foreigners and (their) wives, [and also having] pla[ced salve].... (IStratonikeia 245)[67]

Another word Paul employs in 1 Thess 2:9 that is found in epigraphic benefaction contexts is ἐπιβαρῆσαί and its cognates. In a letter of Octavian to Stephanos (39/38 BCE), the Aphrodisian freedman of the triumvir and future ruler of Rome, C. Julius Zoilos, is considered by Octavian to be worthy of a reward for his services:

> Caesar to Stephanus, greetings. You know my affection for (? that I am beholden to) my friend Zoilos. I have freed his native city and recommended it to Antonius. Since Antonius is absent, take care that no burden [ἐπιβάρησις] falls upon them. This one city I have taken out of all Asia. I wish these people to be protected as my own townsmen [ὡς ἐμοὺς πολείτας]. I shall be watching to see that you carry out my recommendation to the full.[68]

---

67. For further examples of honorific inscriptions from Panamara employing νυκτὸς καὶ ἡμέρας, see IStratonikeia 203, 205, 244, 246, 247, 311, 312, 345. Additionally, *TAM* 5.2.1055; *OGI* 740; IFayum 3:152.

68. Reynolds, *Aphrodisias and Rome*, §10. On Zoilos as freedman of Octavian, see Reynolds, *Aphrodisias and Rome*, §36. On the career of Zoilos, see Reynolds, *Aphrodisias*

Joyce Reynolds highlights the versatility of meaning as far as the "burdens" (ἐπιβαρῆσαί and cognates) mentioned in the inscriptions. She notes that in *IG* 12.5.860, lines 9 and 32 (ἐπιβαρηθῆναι, ἐπιβαρήσεις: Tenos, first century BCE), the reference is to the "burden of debts," whereas the verb in *SIG* 807, line 15 (ἐπιβεβαρῆσθαι: Magnesia ad Meandrum, first century CE), denotes "an authoritative personality."[69] In the context of Octavian's letter, therefore, Reynolds suggests that ἐπιβάρησις must refer to "any kind of burdensome infliction."[70] It is especially worth observing that this refusal to impose unfairly on the Aphrodisians stems from the special relationship that they had with Octavian, probably commencing after the Pact of Brundisiam (40 BCE) and originating from Julius Caesar's prior benefactions to the goddess of Aphrodisias.[71] The language of citizenship (ὡς ἐμοὺς πολείτας) is not only "unexpected," as Reynolds rightly notes,[72] but also illustrates the bonds of clientage and friendship forged between eastern Mediterranean cities—embracing their gods, people, and rulers—and the various members of the Second Triumvirate at Rome (43–33 CE). That the Aphrodisians are Octavian's personal citizens (ἐμούς) indicates that either the Aphrodisians had conferred citizenship on Octavian as an honor,[73] for which there is no proof, or more likely, fictive bonds of citizenship are being articulated here, expressing the intimacy and warmth that Octavian feels toward a city previously honored by his father.

Last, the appearance of the passive participle of ἐπιβαρέω in an honorific inscription from Ramnous (83/82 BCE) is also instructive.[74] The text states that Zenophon Antiochus, the honorand, made it clear he would provide the public services in the temple of Ramnous at his own cost, elaborating that he would sacrifice to the gods in the specified times and longer. More-

---

and Rome, appendix 5: C. Julius Zoilos, §§33–40; Roland R. R. Smith, *Aphrodisias I: The Monument of C. Julius Zoilos* (Manz am Rhein: von Zabern, 1993), 4–13.

69. Reynolds, *Aphrodisias and Rome*, 98.
70. Reynolds, *Aphrodisias and Rome*, 98.
71. Reynolds, *Aphrodisias and Rome*, 98, §§8, 12.
72. Reynolds, *Aphrodisias and Rome*, 99. Reynolds suggests a legitimate parallel with Antony's letter to Hyrcanus in Josephus, *A.J.* 14.308 (ἴδιον ἥγημαι).
73. Reynolds, *Aphrodisias and Rome*, 99.
74. Vasileios Ch. Petrakos, *Ho dēmos tou Ramnountos: Synopsē tōn anaskaphōn kai tōn ereunōn (1813–1998), II. Hoi epigraphes* (Athens: Hē en Athēnais Archaiologikē Hetaireia, 1999), §179. See also *IG* 10.2.3.31 (ἐ[πιβαρεῖν]: Scythia Minor, mid-first century CE); *IG* 12.5.860 (ἐπιβαρηθῆναι, ἐπιβαρήσεις, ἐπιβαροῦντας: Tenos, first century BCE).

over, "having been pressed heavily upon by some people" (ἐπιβαρούμενος ὑπό τινων), Antiochus would also work at providing "beyond the precise proportion" (παρὰ τὸ καθῆκον), encouraging (παρακαλεῖ) the presiding council, in undertaking piety toward the gods, to take proper heed of him in their decisions. Consequently, just before our inscription breaks off due to damage, the council ratifies the role of Antiochus in sponsoring the appropriate liturgies to the gods in Ramnous.

We have seen that epigraphic terminology, used of benefactors refusing to impose on their dependents and providing beneficence "night and day," provides an appropriate context for Paul's refusal to burden his dependents financially (1 Thess 2:9; see also 2 Thess 3:8; 1 Cor 4:12; 2 Cor 11:9, 12:16a; Acts 20:34). But what is shocking, in contrast to elite benefactors whose substantial reserves allow them a life of leisure, is that Paul, an elite individual before his conversion, now works with his hands in the socially despised trades (1 Thess 4:11).[75]

2.4. Affirming the Irreproachable Conduct of the Apostolic Benefactor and His Coworkers (1 Thess 2:10)

In 1 Thess 2:10 the apostle sets out a triad of three adverbs that are intended to establish his impeccable behavior as an apostle when he was present with the Thessalonians: ὁσίως ("devoutly"), δικαίως ("righteously"), and ἀμέμπτως ("blamelessly"). What is intriguing is that the honorific inscriptions similarly employ adverbial doublets or triplets in conveniently characterizing the ethos of benefactors, with overlaps of terminology present. In the case of the doublets the following combinations appear: ὁσίως καὶ δικαίως (*IG* 2.2.1340; 5.1.139, 516; IByzantion S24: *IG* 2s.141; SEG 32.825; *IG* 7.6.2.592; 7.7.234; IMylasa 101), ὁσίως καὶ εὐσεβῶς (FD 3.1.152), εὐσεβῶς καὶ ὁσίως (FD 3.1.362+4.354; FD 3.2.33; Syll² 672), ὁσίως καὶ ἐνδόξως (FD 3.1.451; Syll² 534, 534B), καλῶς καὶ ὁσίως (FD 3.3.383), δικαίως καὶ ὁσίως (FD 3.4.132), and σεμνῶς καὶ ὁσίως (*IG* 12.3.910). Further, in the case the triplets, these combinations can be found: ὁσίως καὶ εὐαγῶς καὶ μεγαλοψύχως (*IG* 5.1.583), καλῶς καὶ δικαίως καὶ ὁσίως (FD 3.4.133), and ὁσίως καὶ δικαίως καὶ φιλαγάθως (SEG 32.825). In employing a triad of adverbs in such an honorific context, Paul was following the epigraphic rhetorical conventions of his day.

---

75. See Ronald F. Hock, *The Social Context of Paul's Ministry: Tentmaking and Apostleship* (Philadelphia: Fortress, 1980), passim.

Last, although ἀμέμπτως does not appear in the epigraphic adverbial doublets or triplets discussed above, the word nevertheless is employed eulogistically of benefactors. A Thessalonian inscription, for example, speaks of Terentianos Asklepiakos as "having served as a gymnasiarch blamelessly (ἀμέμπτως)" and, at his own expense, yearly providing oil en masse for the anointing of athletes at the various games and, presumably, in the gymnasium itself (*IG* 10.2.1.215; 244/245 CE).[76] The adverb ἀμέμπτως is also used in honorific contexts for a secretary at Delphi (FD 3.1.465; 119 CE: καλῶς καὶ ἀμέμπτως), a magistrate at Nicopolis ad Istrum (IGBulg 5.5217 = SEG 37.621; see also *IG* 12.7.372), a gymnasiarch at Apollonia (IGBulg 1.2.390; second–first centuries BCE: τελίως καὶ ἀμέμπτως), a priest at Scythia Minor (*IG* 10.2.2.96; second–third centuries CE: ἁγνῶς καὶ ἀμέμπτως), and, amid several other offices accruing to the individual, an ambassador to the Augusti (IStratonikeia 1205).

Thus, in establishing his personal integrity by means of ἀμέμπτως, Paul has astutely chosen a word that would have registered with a Greco-Roman audience familiar with the local icons of civic virtue in their cities. But, although Paul is drawing from the epigraphic rhetorical conventions in using the adverbial triads, the words in their LXX context express the right relationship of the apostolic mission with God and, correspondingly, their rightness toward their disciples at Thessalonica.[77] More specifically, Pedro Gutierrez argues that ὁσίως and δικαίως are employed ethically for what is just before the eyes of God and before men.[78] Moreover, Gutierrez notes that ἄμεμπτος occurs in LXX Job 1:2 and 8:2 alongside δίκαιος and θεοσεβής, used "to describe the perfection of Job, a perfection which in the last resort is only able to be judged by God."[79] Thus the word is employed elsewhere in 1 Thess 3:13 and 5:23 (see also Phil 2:15) for "the characteristic that Christians must exhibit during the advent of their Saviour."[80] Once again we are seeing the polyvalent nature of Paul's terminology, spanning the world of accrued civic virtue through the disposal of beneficence, while providing the opportunity for the Thessalonians to engage the God of Israel though Paul's apostolic gospel. Ultimately, Paul's ethics are

---

76. Tombstones at Thessalonica also speak of the deceased living ἀμέμπτως ("blamelessly"): *IG* 10.2.1.623, 692. IGBulg 3.2.1741: καλῶς καὶ ἀμέμπτως.

77. Shogren, *1 and 2 Thessalonians*, 107.

78. Gutierrez, *La paternité spirituelle selon Saint Paul*, 104.

79. Gutierrez, *La paternité spirituelle selon Saint Paul*, 106.

80. Gutierrez, *La paternité spirituelle selon Saint Paul*, 106.

determined by the radical consequences of the in-breaking of the future kingdom in the crucified and risen Christ. The Spirit brings conformity to the image of the risen Christ in believers (Rom 7:6; 8:3–5, 11–12, 29; Gal 5:5–6, 16–26; 6:7–8), and the consequent imperative of holiness, expressed in peripatetic language in our pericope (1 Thess 2:22b: εἰς τὸ περιπατεῖν ὑμᾶς), is necessitated in 1 Thessalonians by God's call of believers into his eschatological kingdom and glory (2:12b; see 1:9b–10, 3:13, 4:7–8, 5:23).

2.5. The Exhortation and Encouragement of the Benefactor: Establishing Cultic Decisions Worthy of the God (1 Thess 2:12)

In 1 Thess 2:12 Paul prefaces his pastoral admonition to the Thessalonians regarding their continuing engagement with God under their current difficult circumstances with two virtually synonymous participles—παρακαλοῦντες and παραμυθούμενοι—and μαρτυρόμενοι. However, in the case of παραμυθέομαι, the honorific inscriptions employ its cognates primarily not in honorific or benefaction contexts but rather in contexts where consolation is being offered relatives in funerary inscriptions.[81] But what about the two other participles that Paul employs in conjunction with παραμυθούμενοι? Are they more promising candidates?

First, in terms of παρακαλέω, we have already noticed above how the benefactor Zenophon Antiochus encouraged (παρακαλεῖ) the presiding council to undertake piety toward the gods and to heed his own readiness to help with the sacrifices required.[82] However, sometimes in the honorific inscriptions it is underscored that no encouragement was required to elicit the generosity of a benefactor. In an inscription from Kamiros in Rhodes (225 CE), several benefactors gave money freely without any encouragement (ἄνευ παρακλήσιο[ς]) to furnish colonnades and their coverings, as well as providing honors for the gods.[83] The demos of Knidos, too, encourages visiting judges and others from Magnesia for their legal work in the city by returning honors and worthy thanks to them (IMagnMai 15a; 221–220 BCE: τᾶι [π]αρακήσει αὐτοῦ). Last, in a fragmentary honorific

---

81. παραμύθιον: IG 2.2.12794, 3754; 4.2.1.83, 84; ILindos 2.441. Thessalonica: 10.2.1.173: παραμυθίαν. παραμυθησομένη: IG 12.5.328. παραμυθήσασθαι: 9.7.54, 394, 399, 400. παραμυθία: IIasos 123; IMylasa 411.

82. See n. 74 above.

83. Mario Segre and Giovanni Pugliese Carratelli, "Tituli Camirenses," *ASAtene* 27–29 (1949–1951): 141–318, no. 158.

decree eulogizing a gymnasiarch, there is the telling fragmentary phrase " be[ing] a summons to [παράκλησιν] (the provision) of ca[re] of their own (citizens?)" (IMylasa 419).

In sum, both sides of the reciprocity rituals of encouragement are explored in this selection from the honorific inscriptions, focusing not only on the benefactor's encouragement of his dependents through his beneficence but also on the encouragement of the benefactor either by the council's appropriate return of honor itself or by other significant players in the reciprocity transaction who encourage the council to act commensurately.[84] While consolatory rhetorical traditions are rightly identified elsewhere in 1 Thessalonians,[85] this is not the case in this instance. Rather, as the human benefactor of the Thessalonians, the apostle encourages his converts to walk worthily of the infinite generosity of the divine Benefactor (1 Thess 2:12). An understanding of the benefaction context of Paul's paracletic terminology works better semantically here than the consolatory traditions elsewhere.[86]

Second, as far as μαρτύρομαι, testimonials regarding the integrity and honor of benefactors are regularly invoked in the eulogistic inscriptions. An Aphrodisian inscription of the Roman ruler Hadrian to the people of Smyrna will suffice to establish the benefaction context of Paul's testimony language. In the imperial letter the generous Aphrodisian benefactor, Tiberius Julianos Attalos, a resident of Smyrna, is granted exemption from civic liturgies in the city temple due to the Aphrodisian testimonials of esteem, sent in support of their prestigious citizen, and also because of the Roman-conferred freedom of Aphrodisian citizens from obligations within Asia. The Aphrodisian testimony secures the benefactor's exemption from liturgy:

> Imperator Caesar Trajanus to the Smyrnaeotes. I wish no one from the free cities to be forced into (performing) your liturgy, and especially no one from Aphrodisias, since that city has been removed from the *formula provinciae* so that it is not liable either to the common liturgies of

---

84. E.g., *IG* 2.2.1043; SEG 22:111, 25:134: παρακαλοῦσιν.
85. See n. 15 above.
86. Contra Gutierrez, who argues that the prophetic consolation of Israel had become, in Paul's thought, "the consolation of the Father, who had sent his Son Jesus Christ, in whom he manifests his love for mankind" (*La paternité spirituelle selon Saint Paul*, 111).

Asia or to others. I release Tiberius Julianos Attalos from (performance of a liturgy in) the temple in Smyrna; (he is) a man who has the highest testimonials [μάλιστα μαρτυρούμενον] from his own city; and I have written about these matters to Julius Balbus, my friend and the proconsul.[87]

But what about Paul's language of walking "worthily of God" (1 Thess 2:12: ἀξίως τοῦ θεοῦ)? The honorific inscriptions from Delphi in particular emphasize the importance of cultic sacrifices and games being held in a manner that would honor the god. The people of Athens are eulogized for holding the games of Pythian Apollo "magnificently and worthily of the god (ἀ[ξ]ίως τοῦ τε θεοῦ)" (*SIG* 711K).[88] Athanadas, a kitharodist, is praised by the people at Delphi, for being a distinguished person in hosting the two days of games worthily of the god (ἀξίως τοῦ θεο[ῦ]).[89] Alkidamos Euphanous, an Athenian citizen, is eulogized for being reverently and piously disposed toward the god and the city, instancing his "leading a tripod on a chariot worthily of the god [ἀξίως τοῦ τε θεοῦ] of your people and of us," undoubtedly in some type of religious procession (FD 3.2.33; 128 BCE).[90] Probably the tripod was intended to recall publicly the prophetic role of the priestess of Apollo at Delphi, who, sitting on a tripod, delivered the oracles to inquirers at the site.[91] Thus games, cultic sacrifices, and various processions in honor of the god were carried out with reverence and piety in order to enhance the reputation of the local god.

---

87. Reynolds, *Aphrodisias and Rome*, §14. For other Aphrodisian examples, see IAph 12.105: "Similarly the Council and the People and the Gerousia also honoured with the finest and fitting honours Antonia Flaviane, daughter of L(ucius) Antonius Flavianus, the wife of Potitianos, a loving wife and a loving mother, who lived in a well-ordered way, so that everyone bears witness (μαρτυρεῖσθα[ι]) to her temperance." IAph 12.920: "for these reasons both on many other occasions and now praising the man and bearing witness (μαρτυροῦντες) to him we have sent resolutions to the appointed emperors, considering that (these would be) the greatest and appropriate returns to him for his goodwill towards us."

88. See also Megaris: *IG* 7.219 [ἀξίως τοῦ θ[εοῦ]]; *SIG* 737.

89. Georges Daux, "Inscriptions de Delphes inédites ou revues," *BCH* 73 (1949): 276, §27; see FD 3.2.248.

90. See also FD 2.2.248; 3.2.250; 3.2.92; 3.3.218, 226, 349; 3.4.22, 24; IDelph 4.65, 95.

91. See Joseph Fontenrose, *The Delphic Oracle: Its Responses and Operations with a Catalogue of Responses* (Berkeley: University of California Press, 1978) s.v. "General Index, tripod." For Delphic oracular responses referring to the tripod, see Fontenrose, *Delphic Oracle*, Q17, 76, 123; L93, 96, 109, 176; D34.

Local benefactors and members of the celebrity circuit associated with the ancient games were crucial in this process of the civic magnification of divine honor at the sanctuary of Delphi.

Notwithstanding the rich terminological overlaps here with Paul, the Delphic inscriptions make it plain that the city was preoccupied with correct cult, processional culture, and the games in honor of Apollo. Provided these foci are maintained, the community performs its obeisance worthily of the god, the inscriptions aver. Paul, however, speaks of walking worthily of God (1 Thess 2:12: ἀξίως τοῦ θεοῦ), reflecting the balanced lifestyle required of believers who respect the tension between the imperative and the indicative in their Christian discipleship.[92] Furthermore, in regard to Old Testament intertextual echoes, Gutierrez argues that these three participles describe a pedagogic activity, drawing on LXX wisdom traditions that spoke of children being an honor to their father (Prov 17:6; Sir 3:2), which Paul reconfigures in terms of his converts learning to walk worthily of God in light of the gospel teaching from their wise apostolic father (1 Thess 2:12b).[93] Although this is a different context from the eastern Mediterranean honor and benefaction motifs that I have outlined above, a sharp polarization of the Jewish and Greco-Roman contexts here is unwise in such a rhetorically complex pericope. Rather, the apostle to the gentiles grafts his Thessalonian converts theologically into the vine of Israel, while simultaneously helping them to appreciate his apostolic role as the faithful benefactor of the honorific inscriptions, as opposed to being a peripatetic huckster who had hurriedly exited from the city.

3. Rebutting the Slur of a Hurried Exit (1 Thess 2:19–20): The Honorific Crowns of Believers and the Outcry over Demosthenes's Departure from Chaeronea

My contention has been that Paul, in employing the epigraphic language of honor and benefaction in the positive antitheses, is presenting himself as a selfless benefactor who has honored God, over against the slur that he had pastorally orphaned the Thessalonians in leaving the city unexpectedly (1 Thess 2:14, 17–19). If this suggestion has merit, why does Paul bring his *apologia* to a resounding eschatological and judicial conclusion

---

92. Traugott Holtz, *Die Erste Brief an Die Thessalonicher*, EKKNT 13 (Zürich: Benziger; Neukirchener Verlag, 1986), 91.

93. Gutierrez, *La paternité spirituelle selon Saint Paul*, 107–15; see also 28–38.

Gentle Philosopher, Rhetorician, or Selfless Benefactor?

with the reference to the Thessalonians being his hope (ἐλπίς), joy (χαρά), and crown of boasting (ἡ στέφανος τοῦ καυχήσις) at the parousia of Christ as Judge and Lord? Is there a further benefaction lens through which we can view Paul's rhetorical strategy here? Paul gives the issue special rhetorical emphasis by the use of two pointed questions in verse 19, with the second question ("[Is it] not in fact you?") interrupting the first question, setting up the expectation that the answer will be affirmative by means of the negative οὐχί.[94] Why is Paul so confident rhetorically that the Thessalonians will be persuaded about the genuineness of his motivations in wanting to return to them, notwithstanding Satan's blockages?[95] What rhetorical traction is there for Paul in a benefaction context here?

The departure of a benefactor in ignominy from a city was a famous rhetorical topos used against one's opponents ever since Demosthenes's famous speech *De corona*.[96] The speech is, among other things, the tirade of an unrequited benefactor who had been denied the honor of a golden crown—proposed by Ctesiphon in 336 BCE and opposed in court by Aeschines in 330 BCE—for his benefits to Athens. After the defeat of Athens at Chaeronea in 338 BCE by Philip II, Demosthenes had been elected the commissioner for the repair of walls. However, the ten talents entrusted for the task proved to be insufficient, and Demosthenes topped up the shortfall with a further three talents from his own funds. In the speech, Demosthenes, after demanding the honor of a crown for reciprocation of his efforts as a benefactor of Athens at that time, vaunts his ethical superiority over against the attack of Aeschines, countering his opponent's slurs with series of negative and positive antitheses that savagely denigrated the character of his adversary while adeptly counterpointing with a positive presentation of his own unsullied integrity:

> And now, Aeschines, I beg you to examine in contrast, quietly and without acrimony, the incidents of our respective careers.... You were an usher, I a pupil; you were an acolyte, I a candidate; you were clerk-

---

94. For the reasons for this translation, see Weima, *1–2 Thessalonians*, 203–4.

95. Légasse writes: "Les versets 19 et 20 ... fournissent aux destinataires les raisons profondes de ce qui vient d'être dit: on va savoir ce qui a motivé l'Apôtre et ses collaborateures à tout faire pour revenir à Thessalonique et revoir la communauté qu'ils avaient fondée" (*Les épîtres de Paul aux Thessaloniciens*, 171). On the blockages of Satan, see Shogren, *1 and 2 Thessalonians*, 132–34.

96. What follows draws partially on an extended discussion of 2 Cor 10–13 in Harrison, *Paul's Language of Grace*, 332–40.

at-the-table, I addressed the House; you were cat-called, I hissed; you have ever served our enemies, I have served my country. Much I pass by; but on this very day, I am on proof for the honour of a crown, and acknowledged to be guiltless; you have already the reputation of an informer, and the question at hazard for you is, whether you are still to continue in that trade, or be stopped for ever by getting less than your quota of votes. And that is the good fortune enjoyed by you, who denounce the shabbiness of mine! (Demosthenes, *Cor.* 265–266 [Vince and Vince])

We also possess Aeschines's invaluable speech *Against Ctesiphon*. The evidence of Aeschines allows us to hear the other side of the debate over Demosthenes's crowning. Aeschines's rhetorical tactics largely duplicate those of Demosthenes. But, importantly for our purposes, Aeschines latches onto the fact although Demosthenes was briefly present at the battle of Chaeronea in 338 BCE, the so-called benefactor returned so quickly to organize the defenses of Athens that he could be justifiably be said to have run away in cowardice:

But you are a rich man, you serve as a choregus—to your own lusts. In a word, the king's gold stays with Demosthenes, the dangers, fellow citizens, with you.… Now let us compare what is taking place to-day. A politician, the man who is responsible for all our disasters, *deserted his post in the field, and then ran away from the city*: this man is calling for a crown, and he thinks he must be proclaimed. Away with the fellow, the curse of all Hellas! Nay, rather, seize and punish him, the pirate of politics, who sails on his craft of words over the sea of state. (Aeschines, *Ctes.* 240, 250)[97]

Dinarchus, the fourth-century Carthaginian orator resident at Athens (ca. 360–ca. 290 BCE), also wrote a famous speech against Demosthenes, where he made the same point more expansively:

Is it fitting that … you are ordering others to take the field *when you yourself deserted the battle-line*? … For when (Demosthenes) heard that Philip was intending to invade our land after the battle of Chaeronea he appointed himself envoy *in order that he might escape from the city*.… In a nutshell he is this sort of man: in the battle line he is a stay-at-home, among those who remain at home he is an envoy, and

---

97. Trans. Charles D. Adams, *The Speeches of Aeschines* (London: Heinemann, 1919).

among envoys he is a runaway. (Dinarchus, *Dem.* 71, 80–82; see also 12–13)[98]

Here we see graphically displayed, amid the heated rhetoric of self-defense and accusation between the various contesting parties at Athens, how the decisions of benefactors, in the exigencies of national crisis, to leave the battlefield or their beleaguered cities could easily be misunderstood, misinterpreted, or deliberately maligned.[99] It allows us to see how Paul's own exit as an endangered benefactor at Thessalonica might have been perceived or portrayed by some. But, like Demosthenes, Paul may well have been tempted to claim personal vindication over his critics at Thessalonica, who were drawing invidious comparisons between his mission and the quick exits of the traveling Cynic preachers. What type of vindicatory crown could he, as the benefactor of the Thessalonian church, claim or be expected to claim, given this famous rhetorical precedent of impugned coronal honor known throughout the Greek world?

Certainly Paul asserted that all believers would receive an eschatological crown at the judgment day for their perseverance in faith and for a life lived worthily of God (1 Cor 9:24–25; Phil 4:1; 1 Thess 2:19; see also 2 Tim 4:8), including himself as their founding apostle.[100] But how could the apostle encourage the Thessalonians to persevere and claim that his own actions were honorable without sounding self-serving and self-justifying? To be sure, Earl Richard correctly observes, "A Hellenistic reader would have readily understood Paul's claim that his good reputation derived from the fruits of his labour."[101] However, in the transaction of coronal honor in this instance, Paul unconventionally gives a group (the Thessalonian believers), not a virtuous individual, the honorific crown, though there were rare exceptions to the individualistic emphasis of coronal rituals in antiquity.[102]

---

98. Demosthenes, of course, denies the charge (*Cor.* 173, 197). For a translation of Dinarchus's *Against Demosthenes*, see Ian Worthington, *Greek Orators II: Dinarchus and Hyperides* (Warminster: Aris & Philips, 1999).

99. For further rhetorical examples of the motif, see Harrison, *Paul's Language of Grace*, 337 n. 165.

100. On crowning, see James R. Harrison, "'The Fading Crown': Divine Honour and the Early Christians," *JTS* 54 (2003): 493–529; Janelle Peters, "Crowns in 1 Thessalonians, Philippians, and 1 Corinthians," *Bib* 96 (2015): 67–84.

101. Richard, *First and Second Thessalonians*, 138.

102. Sometimes the *demos* of a city (e.g., Stratonikeia) crowns another city (e.g.,

Furthermore, as Charles Masson notes,[103] although the Thessalonians were not the only group of believers to whom Paul accorded this coronal honor (Phil 1:4: χαρὰ καὶ στέφανός), he acknowledges Thessalonian priority in esteem without any reservation because they had continued to confess their faith under considerable suffering.

Importantly, the description of the crown itself, ἡ στέφανος καυχήσεως, initially fits snugly into the culture of self-advertisement in antiquity, with most commentators referring to the likelihood of a games context (1 Cor 9:25), though we should not necessarily rule out the honorific rituals associated with ancient benefactors. The boasting referent is appropriate to both contexts. But the coronal description is also directly borrowed from the LXX and, with the consideration of a doxological appellation, from Second Temple Judaism more widely (Ezek 16:12, 23:42; Prov 16:31 [17:6]; cf. "crown of glory": 1QS IV, 7; T. Benj. 4.1; Ascen. Isa. 9.10; Bar 15.8).[104] It is unwise to polarize the Greco-Roman context against the Jewish context here:[105] rather, the imagery is polyvalent. Paul's gentile audience at Thessalonica (1 Thess 1:9) would certainly have responded to the Greco-Roman agonistic, civic, and benefaction contexts of coronal boasting, including the resonances with Demosthenes's famous claim for honor, outlined above. But Paul nevertheless took very seriously the LXX perspective that the only legitimate human boasting is boasting in the Lord (1 Chr 16:10, 25; Jer 4:2, 9:23; Pss 34:2, 20:7, 44:8, 105:3; cf. Rom 2:17, 15:17; 1 Cor 1:31; 2 Cor 10:17; Gal 6:14; Phil 1:26, 3:3). Consequently, instead of confining coronal honor to his own achievements, as did the self-vindicating Demosthenes, Paul chooses the unusual strategy in antiquity of transfer-

---

Assos: IAssos 8), or the demos of a city (e.g., Chios) crowns a league (e.g., the Aitolian League). On the latter, see Stephen G. Miller, *Arete: Greek Sports from Ancient Sources* (Berkeley: University of California Press, 1991), §132. See also Demosthenes, *Cor.* 92–93.

103. Charles Masson, *Les deux épîtres de Saint Paul aux Thessaloniciens*, CNT 11A (Paris: Delachaux & Niestlé, 1957), 37.

104. Légasse, *Les épîtres de Paul aux Thessaloniciens*, 170.

105. E.g., Weima: "Paul's use of the expression 'crown of boasting,' however, does not likely stem from these OT and Jewish texts … but from the Hellenistic athletic contexts where the victor received a wreath" (*1–2 Thessalonians*, 203); Richard: "Paul employs *stephanos kauchêsôs* with its LXX meaning, whereby the first term designates the culminating sign of his achievement (a community of believers) and the second underscores his justifiable pride in the Lord's presence" (*First and Second Thessalonians*, 134).

ring crowning to a community and then postponing it to the eschaton: the faithful Thessalonians are his crown, his glory, his joy at the parousia, experienced in a *mutual* sharing of the allocation of divine honor. The oscillation between the vindication of Paul's impugned honor and the celebration of Thessalonian δόξα and χαρά (1 Thess 2:20: see also 2:19a), where ὑμεῖς ("for you") is in the emphatic position in the Greek sentence (2:20a),[106] is delicately poised. But the glory and joy include the apostle as well (1 Thess 2:20: ἡ δόξα ἡμῶν καὶ ἡ χαρά; 2:19: ἡμῶν ἐλπίς ἢ χαρά). Ultimately, the oscillation of honor between Paul and the Thessalonians is subsumed under the transformation of eschatological glory, with the intense rejoicing of believers together (χαρά, 2x: 1 Thess 2:19a, 20b) occurring at the return of the risen and reigning Lord (2:19b; 2 Thess 1:5–10; 2:1, 8).[107] A daring rhetorical strategy that was likely to unravel is now brought to completion in a breathtaking tapestry for all believers to see: in the mutual honoring of the Thessalonians and Paul at the eschaton, the full revelation of the unrivaled glory of Christ's eternal kingdom had begun.

4. Conclusion

I have argued that, while Malherbe rightly locates Paul's rhetoric in 1 Thess 2:1–12 in the world of the Cynic mission, he is incorrect in refusing to allow that the apostle was engaged in specific *apologia* against misrepresentations of his ministry at Thessalonica, as opposed to the pericope merely being a general case of paraenetic and exemplary rhetoric. Not only has the challenge offered by Weima to the consensus emanating from Malherbe's contribution been convincing in this regard, but I have argued that Malherbe overlooked elements of a personal *apologia* against the harsh Cynics in the evidence of Dio Chrysostom, on which his case heavily relies. Particularly important in this regard was the hasty exits of the harsh Cynics when the pressure was on from the cities they had visited. Needless to say, their exits were reminiscent too of Paul's hurried exit from Thessalonica, as well as the much earlier controversy aroused over

---

106. Malherbe, *Letters to the Thessalonians*, 186; Ben Witherington III, *1 and 2 Thessalonians: A Socio-rhetorical Commentary* (Grand Rapids: Eerdmans, 2006), 91.

107. Linda M. Bridges points to the accumulation of emotive words in 1 Thess 2:17–20, by which the apostle reveals his deep care for the Thessalonian believers, as well as the broken syntax in verse 19, indicating "an extremely excited speaker." See Bridges, *1 and 2 Thessalonians*, SHBC (Macon, GA: Smyth & Helwys, 2008), 77.

Demosthenes's claim for coronal honor upon his exit from Chaeronea in 338 BCE. We are dealing here not only with the negative perception of some Thessalonians regarding the (alleged) disreputable conclusion to Paul's ministry among them, but also with how long-standing rhetorical conventions insinuated that those orators and individuals of high social status who had hastily exited from difficult situations were in reality individuals without honor. Perception is everything, and Paul had to address these slurs, exacerbated not only by his absence but also by Satan's temptations at work within the church to bring about disunity. Even unvoiced apprehensions about the continuing care of apostle for the Thessalonians had to be addressed if he was to retrieve the situation pastorally for the sake of the further advancement of the gospel.

Thus Paul's *apologia*, carried out primarily in the positive antitheses (1 Thess 2:2, 4a, 4c, 7b–8) but ranging more widely throughout our pericope, draws on the language of the eulogistic inscriptions, depicting the apostle as the selfless benefactor who honors God. Malherbe's contention that Paul presents himself as the gentle philosopher may have some rhetorical traction on the basis of the τροφός image in 1 Thess 2:7, but even this claim is open to challenge on the basis of the honorific inscriptional and visual evidence. But even more fundamentally, as the LXX and Second Temple Judaism evidence outlined above shows, Paul draws on the faith of Israel to show his Thessalonian converts that he, like them, had been ushered by grace into the cruciform service of their glorious Lord, the risen Messiah. Paradoxically, the experience of the shame of the cross in their sufferings for Christ had become an unsurpassed honor for both the apostle and his converts. This exploration of 1 Thess 2:1–12 is not meant to be a criticism of our "gentle philosopher" and giant in New Testament scholarship, Abraham Malherbe, but rather represents an inadequate homage to the brilliance and incisiveness of his contribution to our exegetical discipline.

Bibliography

Adams, Charles D., trans. *The Speeches of Aeschines*. London: Heinemann, 1919.

Ascough, Richard S., Philip A. Harland, and John S. Kloppenborg. *Associations in the Greco-Roman World: A Sourcebook*. Waco, TX: Baylor University Press, 2012.

Aune, David E. *The New Testament in Its Literary Environment*. Cambridge: Clarke, 1987.
Babbitt, Frank Cole, trans. *Plutarch, Moralia, Volume I: The Education of Children; How the Young Man Should Study Poetry; On Listening to Lectures; How to Tell a Flatterer from a Friend; How a Man May Become Aware of His Progress in Virtue*. LCL. Cambridge: Harvard University Press, 1927.
Beale, Gregory K. *1–2 Thessalonians*. Downers Grove, IL: InterVarsity Press, 2003.
Bridges, Linda M. *1 and 2 Thessalonians*. SHBC. Macon, GA: Smyth & Helwys, 2008.
Brookins, Timothy A. *First and Second Thessalonians*. Paideia. Grand Rapids: Baker Academic, 2021.
Bruce, F. F. *1 and 2 Thessalonians*. WBC 45. Waco, TX: Word, 1982.
Bullard, Collin. *Jesus and the Thoughts of Many Hearts: Implicit Christology and Jesus in the Gospel of Luke*. LNTS 530. London and New York: Bloomsbury/T&T Clark, 2015.
Burstein, Stanley M., ed. and trans. *The Hellenistic Age from the Battle of Ipsos to the Death of Kleopatra VII*. Cambridge: Cambridge University Press, 1985.
Caskey, Lacey D., and John D. Beazley. *Attic Vase Paintings in the Museum of Fine Arts, Pt. 1 Plates 1–33 Text nos. 1–65*. London: Oxford University Press for Museum of Fine Arts, Boston, 1931–1963.
Chaniotis, Angelos. *Die Verträge zwischen kretischen Poleis in der hellenistischen Zeit*. Stuttgart: Steiner, 1996.
Chapa, Juan. "Consolatory Patterns? 1 Thess 4:13–18; 5:11." Pages 220–28 in *The Thessalonian Correspondence*. Edited by Rob F. Collins. BETL 87. Leuven: Leuven University Press/Peeters, 1990.
Cho, Jae-Kyung. "The Rhetorical Approach to 1 Thessalonians in Light of Funeral Oration." PhD diss., Asbury Theological Seminary, 2013.
Clark, Wesley P. "Benefactions and Endowments in Greek Antiquity." PhD diss., Chicago University, 1928.
Cohoon, James W., and H. Lamar Crosby, trans. *Dio Chrysostom, Discourses 31–36*. LCL. Cambridge: Harvard University Press, 1940.
Cooley, Alison E. *Res Gestae Divi Augusti: Text, Translation, and Commentary*. Cambridge: Cambridge University Press, 2009.
Coulot, Claude. "Paul à Thessalonique (1Th 2:1–12)." *NTS* 52 (2006): 377–93.

Danker, Frederick W. *Benefactor: Epigraphic Study of a Graeco-Roman and New Testament Semantic Field*. St. Louis: Clayton, 1982.

Daux, Georges. "Inscriptions de Delphes inédites ou revues." *BCH* 73 (1949): 248-93.

Dibelius, Martin. *Die Briefe des Apostels Paulus an die Thessalonicher I II and die Philipper*. Tübingen: Mohr Siebeck, 1911.

Dobschütz, Ernst von. *Die Thessalonicherbrief*. KEK 10. Göttingen: Vandenhoeck & Ruprecht, 1909.

Donfried, Karl P. "The Epistolary and Rhetorical Context of 1 Thess 2:1-10." Pages 163-94 in *Paul, Thessalonica, and Early Christianity*. London: Continuum T&T Clark, 2002.

Errington, Malcolm. "Antiochos III., Zeuxis und Euromos." *EA* 8 (1986): 1-7.

Fee, Gordon D. *The First and Second Letters to the Thessalonians*. NICNT. Grand Rapids: Eerdmans, 2009.

Fontenrose, Joseph. *The Delphic Oracle: Its Responses and Operations with a Catalogue of Responses*. Berkeley: University of California Press, 1978.

Frame, James E. *Epistles of St Paul to the Thessalonians*. ICC. Edinburgh: T&T Clark, 1912.

Gaventa, Beverly R. *First and Second Thessalonians*. IBC. Louisville: John Knox, 1998.

———. *Our Mother Saint Paul*. Louisville: Westminster John Knox, 2007.

Green, Gene L. *The Letters to the Thessalonians*. PNTC. Grand Rapids: Eerdmans, 2002.

Gummere, Richard M., trans. *Seneca, Epistles*. Vol. 1, *Epistles 1-65*. LCL. Cambridge: Harvard University Press, 1917.

Gutierrez, Pedro. *La paternité spirituelle selon Saint Paul*. Paris: Librairie Lecoffre, 1968.

Harland, Philip A. "Familial Dimension of Group Identity (II): 'Mother' and 'Father' in Associations and Synagogues of the Greek World." *JSJ* 38 (2007): 57-79.

Harrison, James R. "Diplomacy over Tiberius' Succession." *NewDocs* 10:64-75.

———. "'The Fading Crown': Divine Honour and the Early Christians." *JTS* 54 (2003): 493-529.

———. *Paul's Language of Grace in Its Graeco-Roman Context*. WUNT 2/172. Tübingen: Mohr Siebeck, 2003.

Hill, Judith L. "Establishing the Church in Thessalonica." PhD diss., Duke University, 1990.
Hock, Ronald F. *The Social Context of Paul's Ministry: Tentmaking and Apostleship*. Philadelphia: Fortress, 1980.
Holtz, Traugott. *Die Erste Brief an Die Thessalonicher*. EKKNT 13. Zürich: Benziger; Neukirchener Verlag, 1986.
———. "On the Background of 1 Thessalonians 2:1–12." Pages 69–80 in *The Thessalonians Debate: Methodological Discord or Methodological Synthesis?* Edited by Karl P. Donfried and Johannes Beutler. Grand Rapids: Eerdmans, 2000.
Hughes, Frank W. "The Rhetoric of 1 Thessalonians." Pages 94–116 in *The Thessalonian Correspondence*. Edited by Rob F. Collins. BETL 87. Leuven: Leuven University Press; Peeters, 1990.
———. "The Rhetoric of Letters." Pages 194–240 in *The Thessalonians Debate: Methodological Discord or Methodological Synthesis?* Edited by Karl P. Donfried and Johannes Beutler. Grand Rapids: Eerdmans, 2000.
Jewett, Robert. *The Thessalonian Correspondence: Pauline Rhetoric and Millenarian Piety*. Philadelphia: Fortress, 1986.
Judge, Edwin A. "The Eulogistic Inscriptions of the Augustan Forum: Augustus on Roman History." Pages 165–81 in *The First Christians in the Roman World: Augustan and New Testament Essays*. Edited by James R. Harrison. WUNT 229. Tübingen: Mohr Siebeck, 2008.
Kennedy, George A. *New Testament Interpretation through Rhetorical Criticism*. Chapel Hill: University of North Carolina Press, 1984.
Kern, Philip H. *Rhetoric and Galatians: Assessing an Approach to Paul's Epistle*. SNTSMS 101. Cambridge: Cambridge University Press, 1998.
Kim, Seyoon. "Paul's Entry (εἴσοδος) and the Thessalonians' Faith (1 Thessalonians 1–3)." *NTS* 51 (2005): 519–42.
Krentz, Edgar. "1 Thessalonians: Rhetorical Flourishes and Formal Constraints." Pages in 287–318 in *The Thessalonians Debate: Methodological Discord or Methodological Synthesis?* Edited by Karl P. Donfried and Johannes Beutler. Grand Rapids: Eerdmans, 2000.
Lambrecht, Jan. "Thanksgivings in 1 Thessalonians." Pages 135–62 in *The Thessalonians Debate: Methodological Discord or Methodological Synthesis?* Edited by Karl P. Donfried and Johannes Beutler. Grand Rapids: Eerdmans, 2000.
Légasse, Simon. *Les épîtres de Paul aux Thessaloniciens*. LD 7. Paris: Cerf, 1999.

Liefeld, Walter L. "The Wandering Preacher as a Social Figure in the Roman Empire." PhD diss., Columbia University, 1967.

Lyons, George. *Pauline Autobiography: Toward a New Understanding*. SBLDS 73. Atlanta: Scholars Press, 1985.

Malherbe, Abraham J. "'Gentle as a Nurse': The Cynic Background to 1 Thessalonians 2." Pages 35–48 in *Paul and the Popular Philosophers*. Minneapolis: Fortress, 1989.

———. *The Letters to the Thessalonians: A New Translation with Introduction and Commentary*. AB 32B. New York: Doubleday, 2000.

———. *Paul and the Thessalonians*. Minneapolis: Fortress, 1987.

———. "Paul: Hellenistic Philosopher or Christian Pastor?" Pages 67–88 in *Paul and the Popular Philosophers*. Minneapolis: Fortress, 1989.

Masson, Charles. *Les deux épîtres de Saint Paul aux Thessaloniciens*. CNT 11A. Paris: Delachaux & Niestlé, 1957.

McNeel, Jennifer Houston. *Paul as Infant and Nursing Mother: Metaphor, Rhetoric, and Identity in 1 Thessalonians 2:5–8*. ECL 12. Atlanta: SBL Press, 2014.

Miller, Stephen G. *Arete: Greek Sports from Ancient Sources*. Berkeley: University of California Press, 1991.

Mitchell, Margaret M. *Paul and the Rhetoric of Reconciliation: An Exegetical Investigation of the Language and Composition of 1 Corinthians*. Louisville: Westminster John Knox, 1992.

Morris, Leon. *The First and Second Epistles to the Thessalonians*. Rev. ed. Grand Rapids: Eerdmans, 1991.

Peters, Janelle. "Crowns in 1 Thessalonians, Philippians, and 1 Corinthians." *Bib* 96 (2015): 67–84.

Petrakos, Vasileios C. *Ho dēmos tou Ramnountos: Synopsē tōn anaskaphōn kai tōn ereunōn (1813–1998), II. Hoi epigraphes*. Athens: Hē en Athēnais Archaiologikē Hetaireia, 1999.

Reynolds, Joyce. *Aphrodisias and Rome: Documents from the Excavation of the Theatre at Aphrodisias Conducted by Professor Kenan T. Erim, Together with Some Related Texts*. JRSM 1. London: Society for the Promotion of Roman Studies, 1982.

Richard, Earl J. *First and Second Thessalonians*. SP 11. Collegeville, MN: Glazier, 1995.

Rigaux, Béda. *Saint Paul: Les épitres aux Thessaloniciens*. Paris: Librairie Lecoffre, 1956.

Roberts, Mark D. "Images of Paul and the Thessalonians." PhD diss., Harvard University, 1992.

Scheid, John. *Res Gestae Divi Augusti: Hauts faits du divin Auguste*. Paris: Les Belles Lettres, 2007.

Schoon-Janssen, Johannes. "On the Use of Ancient Epistolography in 1 Thessalonians." Pages 179–93 in *The Thessalonians Debate: Methodological Discord or Methodological Synthesis?* Edited by Karl P. Donfried and Johannes Beutler. Grand Rapids: Eerdmans, 2000.

Schubert, Paul. *Form and Function of the Pauline Thanksgivings*. BZNW 20. Berlin: Töpelmann, 1939.

Segre, Mario, and Giovanni Pugliese Carratelli. "Tituli Camirenses." *ASAtene* 27–29 (1949–1951): 141–318.

Shogren, Gary S. *1 and 2 Thessalonians: Exegetical Commentary on the New Testament*. Grand Rapids: Zondervan, 2012.

Smith, Abraham. *Comfort One Another: Reconstructing the Rhetoric and Audience of 1 Thessalonians*. Louisville: Westminster John Knox, 1995.

Smith, Roland R. R. *Aphrodisias I: The Monument of C. Julius Zoilos*. Manz am Rhein: von Zabern, 1993.

Stegner, William R. "The Ancient. Jewish Synagogue Homily." Pages 51–69 in *Greco-Roman Literature and the New Testament*. Edited by David E. Aune. SBLSBS 21. Atlanta: Scholars Press, 1988.

Still, Todd D. *Conflict at Thessalonica: A Pauline Church and Its Neighbours*. LNTS 183. Sheffield: Sheffield Academic, 1999.

Stowers, Stanley K. *Letter Writing in Greco-Roman Antiquity*. Philadelphia: Westminster, 1986.

Vince, Charles A., and James H. Vince, trans. *Demosthenes, Orations, Volume II: Orations 18–19; De Corona, De Falsa Legatione*. Cambridge: Harvard University Press, 1926.

Wanamaker, Charles A. *Commentary on 1 and 2 Thessalonians*. NIGTC. Grand Rapids: Eerdmans, 1990.

———. "Epistolary vs. Rhetorical Analysis: Is a Synthesis Possible?" Pages 255–86 in *The Thessalonians Debate: Methodological Discord or Methodological Synthesis?* Edited by Karl P. Donfried and Johannes Beutler. Grand Rapids: Eerdmans, 2000.

Weima, Jeffrey A. D. "1–2 Thessalonians." Pages 871–89 in *Commentary on the New Testament Use of the Old Testament*. Edited by Gregory K. Beale and Donald A. Carson. Grand Rapids: Baker Academic, 2007.

———. *1–2 Thessalonians*. BECNT. Grand Rapids: Baker Academic, 2014.

———. "An Apology for the Apologetic Function of 1 Thessalonians 2:1–12." *JSNT* 68 (1997): 73–99.

———. *Paul the Ancient Letter Writer: An Introduction to Epistolary Analysis.* Grand Rapids: Baker Academic, 2016.
Whiteley, Denys E. H. *Thessalonians in the Revised Standard Version.* NCB. Oxford: Oxford University Press, 1969.
Whitenton, Michael R. "Figuring Joy: Gratitude as Medicine in 1 Thessalonians 2:1–20." *PRSt* 39 (2012): 15–23.
Winter, Bruce W. "The Entries and Ethics of Orators and Paul (1 Thessalonians 2:1–12)." *TynBul* 44 (1993): 71–90.
Witherington, Ben, III. *1 and 2 Thessalonians: A Socio-rhetorical Commentary.* Grand Rapids: Eerdmans, 2006.
———. "'Almost Thou Persuadest Me …': The Importance of Greco-Roman Rhetoric for the Understanding of the Text and Context of the NT." *JETS* 58 (2015): 63–88.
Worthington, Ian. *Greek Orators II: Dinarchus and Hyperides.* Warminster: Aris & Philips, 1999.

Roman Provincial Coinage and Paul at Thessalonica

Michael P. Theophilos

1. Introduction

New Testament commentators have often overlooked the relevance of numismatic evidence for their interpretive task.[1] Ancient coinage, however, preserves a microcosm of language, culture, and otherwise inaccessible insight into significant aspects of Greco-Roman thought. One consideration in employing numismatic data in the interpretive task is the extent to which the ancients noticed, examined, or even understood the inscriptions and iconography on the coins they handled daily. Literary evidence suggests that people did in fact pay attention to coinage and were aware, to some extent, of the images, symbols, inscriptions and their meanings. In addition to Jesus's appeal to his audience's awareness of the imagery on a denarius (Matt 22:17b–21; see Matt 22:15–22; Mark 12:13–17; Luke 20:20–26), three further examples should suffice in establishing the plausibility of this working assumption:

1. The Stoic philosopher Epictetus, writing toward the end of the first century or beginning of the second century CE, notes, τοὺς χαρακτῆρας, οὓς ἔχων ἐν τῇ διανοίᾳ ἐλήλυθεν, οἵους καὶ ἐπὶ τῶν νομισμάτων ζητοῦντες, ἂν μὲν εὕρωμεν, δοκιμάζομεν, ἂν δὲ μὴ εὕρωμεν, ῥιπτοῦμεν. τίνος ἔχει τὸν χαρακτῆρα τοῦτο τὸ τετράσσαρον; Τραιανοῦ; φέρε. Νέρωνος; ῥῖψον ἔξω, ἀδόκιμόν ἐστιν, σαπρόν ("the imprints which he brought with him in his mind, such as we look for also upon coins, and, if we find them, we accept the coins, but if we do not find them, we throw the coins away. 'Whose imprint does this sestertius bear? Trajan's? Give it to me. Nero's?

---

1. See discussion and examples in Richard Oster, "Numismatic Windows into the Social World of Early Christianity," *JBL* 101 (1982): 195–223.

Throw it out, it will not pass, it is rotten'"; Epictetus, *Diatr.* 4.5.16–17 [Oldfather]).[2]

2. Dio Cassius (*Hist.* 47.25.3) offers a description and interpretation Brutus's famous Ides of March coin, Βροῦτος μὲν ταῦτά τε ἔπρασσεν, καὶ ἐς τὰ νομίσματα ἃ ἐκόπτετο εἰκόνα τε αὐτοῦ καὶ πιλίον ξιφίδιά τε δύο ἐνετύπου, δηλῶν ἐκ τε τούτου καὶ διὰ τῶν γραμμάτων ὅτι τὴν πατρίδα μετὰ τοῦ Κασσίου ἠλευθερωκὼς εἴη ("In addition to these activities Brutus stamped upon the coins which were being minted his own likeness and a cap and two daggers, indicating by this and by the inscription that he and Cassius had liberated the fatherland" [Cary and Foster]).

3. Suetonius (*Nero* 6.25) highlights the intentionality in the design of an imperial coin of Nero, "Sacras coronas in cubiculis circum lectos posuit, item statuas suas citharoedico habitu, qua nota etiam nummum percussit" ("He placed the sacred crowns in his bedchambers around his couches, as well as statues representing him in the guise of a lyre-player; and he had a coin too struck with the same device" [Rolfe]). Not coincidentally, the obverse of *RIC* 1, Nero 380, together with several other Neronian examples, depicts Nero as Apollo Citharoedus, laureate and advancing right in flowing robes, playing a lyre held in his left hand.[3]

While numismatic iconography may have been the most noticeable feature on a coin, the inscription also played an important role in communicating the overall message.[4] This current study seeks to demonstrate that Roman provincial coinage significantly aides in contextualizing Paul at

---

2. An important distinction is to be acknowledged between Roman coins and their Greek predecessors. Although "designs on Greek coins typically remained unchanged for decades or even centuries, varying only in style or detail over time," Roman coinage exhibited both continuity and discontinuity in its iconography stamped on coinage. See Jonathan Williams, "Religion and Roman Coins," in *A Companion to Roman Religion*, ed. Jörg Rüpke (Oxford: Blackwell, 2007), 143. It is true that, as Meshorer says, "it was the usual practice in the ancient world to imitate existing types that were current locally, in order to secure greater confidence in and prestige for a new coin minted by a recently established authority," but it is also apparent that Roman coinage was much more dynamic and adaptable to new images and environments. See Ya'akov Meshorer, *Jewish Coins of the Second Temple Period* (Tel-Aviv: Am Hassefer, 1967), 58.

3. RIC 1, Nero 73–82, 121–23, 205–12, 380–81, 384–85, 414–17, 451–55.

4. Michael H. Crawford, "Roman Imperial Coin Types and the Formation of Public Opinion," in *Studies in Numismatic Method Presented to Philip Grierson*, ed. Christopher Brooke et al. (Cambridge: Cambridge University Press, 1983), 54–57; Christopher Howgego, *Ancient History from Coins* (London: Routledge, 1995), 75.

Thessalonica within the matrix of the Roman political world. Issues to be addressed include Thessalonica's (1) divine honors for Caesar and Octavian (including the language and iconography of crowning), (2) favored political relationship with Rome, and (3) religious identity shaped by the city's past.

2. Thessalonian Coinage

The first autonomous coins to be struck at Thessalonica occurred approximately a decade after the defeat of Perseus at the battle of Pydna (168 BCE). Livy and other ancient authors inform us that Macedonia was divided into four administrative regions (Livy, *Urb. cond.* 45.18.3–7, 29.5–11; Diodorus Siculus, *Bib. hist.* 31.8.7–8; Strabo, *Geogr.* 7.47),[5] presumably to increase dependence on Rome, which prohibited trade between the regions and controlled the profitable mines and forests (see Livy). Thessalonica was capital of the second region. Almost all the coinage of this period is struck in the name of the first region. SNG Ash 3300 (fig. 10.1) is a silver tetradrachm from the first region minted in Amphipolis during the period 167–149 BCE. The obverse depicts a diademed draped bust of Artemis facing right with a bow and quiver on her shoulder at the base of a Macedonian shield. The reverse depicts a club separating the inscription ΜΑΚΕΔΟΝΩΝ ΠΡΩΤΗΣ with monogram above and Ν below, all within an oak wreath. In the outer field is a thunderbolt. Only limited numbers of tetradrachms are attested from the second region, and no known coinage during the period from the third and fourth regions. AMNG 3.2.41 is a silver tetradrachm from the second region minted in Thessalonica during the period 167–149 BCE. The obverse and reverse are similar to that of the first region example previously mentioned, except that the inscription reads ΜΑΚΕΔΟΝΩΝ ΔΕΥΤΕΡΑΣ, has a different monogram, and excludes the Ν mintmark below.

The region divisions were dissolved in 148 BCE, when the territory became a Roman province. Although silver coinage was not minted for another half century, governors issued a variety of bronze coinage. Silver coinage resumed again in 93 BCE, and the most widespread issue was by

---

5. The first was east of the Strymon with its capital at Amphipolis; the second was between the Strymon and Axios, with its capital at Thessalonica; the third between the Axios and Peneos, with its capital at Pella; and the fourth included most of Upper Macedonia, with its capital at Heraclea Lynci.

Fig. 10.1. SNG Ash 3300 type. Image courtesy of Nomos AG, nomos 9, lot 97. Used with permission.

the quaestor Aesillas. SNG Ash 3301 is a silver tetradrachm of Aesillas Quaestor (ca. 95–65 BCE) with, on the obverse, the diademed head of Alexander the Great facing right with the horn of Ammon, with inscription below ΜΑΚΕΔΟΝΩΝ below and Θ behind. The reverse inscribes AESILLAS Q in two lines above a money chest, club, and chair, all within a wreath.

Recent studies of Thessalonian coinage have resolved several key problems associated with their interpretation, although some residual ambiguities persist. The Roman coinage of Thessalonica can be divided into three broad periods: republic, triumviral, and imperial. The influence of Rome is clearly visible on the republic coinage of Thessalonica. SNG Cop 369 is an assarius of Thessalonica from 187–168/7 BCE. On the obverse it depicts the laureate head of Janus, with a value mark of I above. The reverse has ΘΕΣΣΑΛΟΝΙΚΗΣ below the Dioscuri on horses rearing left and right with a grain ear in exergue.[6] In relation to the triumviral period, Michael Grant introduced a curious identification of the bronzes of Q HORTENSI PROCOS, PRAEF COLON DEDVC to Macedonia, but later studies, including the monumental Roman Provincial Coinage

---

6. See Semis of Thessalonica (half an as), which depict on the obverse the laureate head of Zeus, right, and on the reverse have ΘΕΣΣΑΛΟΝΙΚΗΣ (top and bottom) with a bull charging, right, with monograms, below (Moushmov 6594). See Nikola Moushmov, *Ancient Coins of the Balkan Peninsula*, trans. Denista Genkova, Dave Surber, and Slavei Theodore Slaveev (Sofia: K&K, 1912).

project, confirm that this series was minted for Dium or Cassandrea.⁷ Ioannis Touratsoglou has produced an extensive catalogue and discussion of Macedonian coins in the imperial period and reattributes several coins that had previously been dated to an earlier period by Hugo Gaebler.⁸ It is hoped that the current discussion will aid in nuancing the often uncritical use of numismatic evidence in relation to the Pauline circumstances at Thessalonica.

3. Case Studies

3.1. Divine Honors for Caesar

The accusation by the Thessalonian mob against Paul, Silas, and their host Jason to the city's authorities in Acts 17:6 was that they were τὴν οἰκουμένην ἀναστατώσαντες ("turning the world upside down," NRSV), and had now come to Thessalonica to do the same. In particular, they are accused of acting "contrary to the δογμάτων Καίσαρος (decrees of Caesar), saying that there is another βασιλέα (king), Jesus" (Acts 17:7). Similar themes are found throughout the Thessalonian correspondence through the usage of key terminology such as παρουσία (1 Thess 4:15), ἐπιφάνεια (2 Thess 2:8), ἀπάντησις (1 Thess 4:17), εἰρήνη καὶ ἀσφάλεια (1 Thess 5:3), and ἐλπίδα σωτηρίας (1 Thess 5:8). Jeffrey Weima highlights the significance of these matters for the Thessalonians by noting that the inhabitants would be especially concerned about these charges due to the "memory still fresh in their mind of the loss of their senatorial status under Tiberius and its recovery just six years earlier under Claudius."⁹

As has been explored by several commentators, most eruditely James Harrison,¹⁰ the imperial cult at Thessalonica shaped the city. One avenue

---

7. *RPC* 1.297. See Michael Grant, *From Imperium to Auctoritas* (Cambridge: Cambridge University Press, 1946), 33.

8. Ioannis Touratsoglou, *Die Münzstätte von Thessaloniki in der römischen Kaiserzeit: 32/31 v. Chr. bis 268 n. Chr.* (Berlin: de Gruyter, 1988); Hugo Gaebler, *Die antiken Münzen von Makedonia und Paionia, Die antiken Münzen Nord-Griechenlands* (Berlin: de Gruyter, 1935), 3:26.

9. Jeffrey A. D. Weima, *1–2 Thessalonians* (Grand Rapids: Baker Academic, 2014), 7.

10. James R. Harrison, *Paul and the Imperial Authorities at Thessalonica and Rome: A Study in the Conflict of Ideology*, WUNT 273 (Tübingen: Mohr Siebeck, 2011), 55–56; Harrison, "Paul and the Imperial Gospel at Thessaloniki," *JSNT* 25 (2002): 71–96; Harrison, "'The Fading Crown': Divine Honour and the Early Christians," *JTS* 54 (2003):

to further explore this imperial emphasis is through the numismatic record. *RPC* 1.1554 (fig. 10.2) is a leaded bronze minted in Thessalonica and is often appealed to in regard to divine honors worn by deified Caesar. However, the provincial coinage of Augustus at Thessalonica poses several problems. *RPC* 1.1554 has the letter Δ under the head of Augustus, which Gaebler claims stands for the number 4 (asses).[11] The weakness of this proposal is that the E on the triumvir coinage such as the leaded bronze *RPC* 1.1552 refers to year 5 (which is accepted by Gaebler). The obverse has ΑΓΩΝΟΘΕΣΙΑ with the head of Agonothesia facing right and the alphabetic numeral E referring to year 5, which corresponds to 37 BCE. The reverse has ANT KAI in a wreath. A strong case can then be made by analogy that the Δ on *RPC* 1.1554 should also refer to a date.[12]

RPC 1.1555 (fig. 10.3) omits several features including the date and wreath on Caesar's head on the obverse. On the reverse the inscription has the lunate *sigma* rather than the four-bar *sigma*,[13] and it is 30 percent lighter (7.33 g vs 10.34 g). Touratsoglou argues on the basis of style, epigraphy, and weight that *RPC* 1.1555 was issued during the reign of Domitian.[14] Christopher Howgego, however, notes that several of the countermarks on these coins "are otherwise found on only Augustan coins of Amphipolis, and has questioned so late a date."[15] Despite that fact that the lunate *sigma* is found on the coinage of Tiberius, a more telling critique against Touratsoglou's later date is that a portrait of Julius Caesar would be highly unusual on provincial coinage after the Julio-Claudian period.

RPC 1.5421 (fig. 10.4) is a 7.13-g bronze issue with the bare head of Caesar facing right on the obverse with ΘΕΟΣ in the left field. The reverse depicts the bare head of Augustus facing right with ΣΕΒΑΣΤΟΣ in right field and ΘΕ in left field. This is assigned to Thessalonica by Barclay Head in *BMC* 5.61,[16] presumably on the basis of the general similarity with *RPC*

493–529; Harrison, "Paul and Empire II: Negotiating the Seduction of Imperial 'Peace and Security' in Galatians, Thessalonians and Philippians," in *An Introduction to Empire in the New Testament*, ed. Adam Winn, RBS 84 (Atlanta: SBL Press, 2015), 165–84.

11. Gaebler, *Die antiken Münzen Nord-Griechenlands* 3.2:125.
12. Touratsoglou, *Münzstätte von Thessaloniki*, 25.
13. Contra *RPC* 1.1554.
14. Touratsoglou, *Münzstätte von Thessaloniki*, 42–43.
15. Christopher J. Howgego, *Greek Imperial Countermarks: Studies in the Provincial Coinage of the Roman Empire* (London: Royal Numismatic Society, 1985), 702, 705.
16. Barclay V. Head, *Catalogue of Greek Coins in the British Museum: Attica, Megaris, Aegina* (London: British Museum, 1888), 5.115.

1.1554 and 1.1555. This is disputed by Touratsoglou on the basis of style and axis orientation (6 o'clock).[17] The authors of *Roman Provincial Coinage* follow Touratsoglou, listing this type as "Uncertain Mint." However, CNG 75.2007.798,[18] die-linked to a coin bearing the ethnic of Thessalonica *RPC* 1.5421 and as having been issued by that city, is contemporaneous with *RPC* 1.1555. The coinage of Thessalonica canonically includes the ethnic, and a closer examination of the coin suggests that the original ethnic may have been altered to accommodate the new legend. One possible explanation could be that the dies were reused shortly after the deification of Augustus in 14 CE, with the reverse ethnic removed and the new legend put in its place, with coins commemorating the new divus being struck. ΘΕ is an otherwise unknown abbreviation for ΘΕΟΥ, and an otherwise unnecessary one, given the plentiful amount of space on the die. It is possible, although not certain, that the dies were reworked to accommodate the deification of Augustus, although questions still remain over the peculiar use of the abbreviation ΘΕ for ΘΕΟΥ.

RPC 1.1563 is also relevant for the imperial cult at Thessalonica. It depicts a bust of Livia facing right with the inscription ΘΕΑ/ΘΕΟΥ ΛΙΒΙΑ. The reverse has a horse galloping right and ΘΕΣΣΑΛΟΝΙΚ. This seems to be a lifetime issue of Augustus, despite the honorific ΘΕΑ/ΘΕΟΥ, because it uses Livia rather than Sebaste, which is normal after 14 CE. The use of ΘΕΟΥ on one die, apparently referring to Augustus, is surprising (possibly a mistake for ΘΕΑ, as most examples).[19] Although no other coins minted in Thessalonica ascribe divinity to Augustus during his lifetime, a parallel issue from Larissa does exist under the Thessalian League (a loose confederacy of city states in northern Greece) where Augustus is referred to as ΘΕΟΣ and Livia is referred to as ΛΙΒΙΑ rather than ΣΕΒΑΣΤΕ.[20] *RPC* 1.1427 has, on the obverse, ΘΕΟΣ ΚΑΙΣΑΡ ΘΕΣΣΑΛ ΙΤΑ with bare head facing right. The reverse has ΗΡΑ ΛΕΙΟΥΛΙΑ ΠΕΤ (monogram) with the head of Livia. The ΙΤΑ and ΠΕΤ refer to the magistrates Italos and Petraios. The Thessalian League produced silver and

---

17. Touratsoglou, *Münzstätte von Thessaloniki*, 43 n. 69. Touratsoglou further argues that *RPC* 1.5421 should be associated with *RPC* 1.5420 based on similar obverse inscription; however, the style is not similar and hence doubt remains.
18. Classical Numismatics Group Auction 75, 23 May 2007, lot 798.
19. Touratsoglou, *Münzstätte von Thessaloniki*, 28 n. 12.
20. *RPC* 1.1427, 1.298.

Fig. 10.2. *RPC* 1.1554. Image courtesy of Nomos AG, obolos 9, lot 285. Used with permission.

Fig. 10.3. *RPC* 1.1555. Image courtesy of Nomos AG, obolos 16, lot 962. Used with permission.

Fig. 10.4. *RPC* 1.5421. Image courtesy of Nomos AG, obolos 16, lot 962. Used with permission.

bronze coinage in the second and first centuries BCE.[21] Edgar Rogers dates the coinage mentioning Petraios to 48–27 BCE,[22] and this is affirmed by Andrew Burnett, Michel Amandry, and Ian Carradice.[23] Enhancing this divine portrayal of Augustus is a marble statue discovered in the serapeum of Thessalonica that depicts the emperor in a divine posture.[24] Holland Hendrix concludes that Thessalonica displayed a "distinctive sensitivity to propaganda about Roman rule."[25]

The manner in which the above numismatic evidence informs our reading of Paul at Thessalonica is primarily twofold. First is the prominence of the imperial cult in Thessalonica and the way in which the visual culture and ideology of the city was shaped by the iconography on coinage. This, of course, is corroborated by many other forms of evidence, such as an inscription (*IG* 10.2.1.31) attesting to a Thessalonian temple to Caesar during the time of Augustus. As far as the numismatic contribution goes, we have at least three examples and several subtypes that attest to the prominence of the imperial cult at Thessalonica.[26] Second, specific mention of the στέφανος (1 Thess 2:19) is illuminated by our above discussion. In Paul's defense of his present absence from Thessalonica (1 Thess 2:17–3:10) he assures his readers of his genuine desire to see τὸ πρόσωπον ὑμῶν ("your face," 1 Thess 2:17). In 2:19 he refers to a στέφανος (crown) καυχήσεως ("of boasting") directly in relation to the Thessalonian community themselves, ἢ οὐχὶ καὶ ὑμεῖς; ("Is it not you?"). We are told that this crown consists of the recipients themselves "in the presence of our Lord Jesus at his coming" (1 Thess 2:19b). The symbolic στέφανος could seek to recall (1) the civic crown (*corona civica*), which consisted of a wreath of

---

21. Bruno Helly, "Le groupe des monnaies fédérales thessaliennes avec Athéna 'aux pompons,'" *RN* 6 (1966): 7–32; Edgar Rogers, *The Copper Coinage of Thessaly* (London: Spink & Son, 1932).

22. Rogers, *Copper Coinage of Thessaly*, 20.

23. *RPC* 1.280.

24. Holland Lee Hendrix, "Archaeology and Eschatology at Thessalonica," in *The Future of Early Christianity: Essays in Honor of Helmut Koester*, ed. Birger A. Pearson (Minneapolis: Fortress, 1991), 116–17. There is no consensus on whether the marble statue was an import into Thessalonica or a local production. Hendrix and others have generally dated the statue to the time of Claudius and have noted that the Thessalonians had great interest in supporting and strengthening imperial propaganda.

25. Hendrix, "Archaeology and Eschatology," 117–18.

26. On the prominence of the cult of Caesar in the provinces, see Stefan Weinstock, *Divus Julius* (Oxford: Oxford University Press, 1971), 401–10.

oak leaves granted by the senate in recognition of saving the life of a fellow Roman citizen in battle, or (2) a laurel wreath awarded to a victor in an athletic contest.[27] In Harrison's definitive study noted above, "The Fading Crown: Divine Honour and the Early Christians," he argues persuasively that "the postponement of crowning would have been puzzling in a culture that prized the prompt reciprocation of honour."[28] This is reinforced by the clear evidence on the coins.[29]

3.2. Thessalonica's Favored Political Relationship with Rome

Three coins attest to Thessalonica's favored political relationship with Rome. First, as a reward for lending its support to the Second Triumvirate after the death of Julius Caesar, the city was granted "free status" in 42 BCE by Marcus Antoninus (Mark Antony).[30] This is evidenced in *RPC* 1.1551 (fig. 10.5), an issue of coinage under Antony in 37 BCE that on the obverse has ΘΕΣΣΑΛΟΝΙΚΕΩΝ ΕΛΕΥΘΕΡΙΑΣ with a bust of Eleutheria facing to the right. The reverse depicts Nike advancing left with a wreath and palm, accompanied by the standard catalogue of names and titles, Μ ΑΝΤ ΑΥΤ Γ ΚΑΙ ΑΥΤ. This series elevates Antony and Octavian and celebrates the defeat of Brutus and the subsequent freedom it afforded. Pliny states the following, "On the Macedonian coast of the gulf are the town of Chalastra and, farther in, Pylorus, Lete, and at the centre of the curve of the coast the *free city of Saloniki*" (*Nat.* 4.17 [Rackham]). Further attestation of Thessalonica's free status is evidenced in *IG* 10.2.1.6. Hendrix notes that this freedom was "granted only to people and cities which had displayed remarkable loyalty

---

27. William E. Raffety, "Crown," *ISBE* 1:831–32. Res gest. divi Aug. 34 states, "In my sixth and seventh consulships, after I had extinguished civil wars.... For this service of mine I was named Augustus by decree of the senate, and the door-posts of my house were publicly wreathed with bay leaves and a civic crown was fixed over my door and a golden shield was set in the Curia Julia, which, as attested by the inscription thereon, was given me by the senate and people of Rome on account of my courage, clemency, justice and piety." Translated by Peter A. Brunt and John M. Moore, *Res Gestae Divi Augusti: The Achievements of Divine Augustus* (Oxford: Oxford University Press, 1983), 35–37. See also Cassius Dio, *Hist.* 53.16.4.

28. Harrison, "Fading Crown," 527.

29. Konrad Kraft, "Der goldene Kranz Caesars und der Kampf um die Entlarvung des 'Tyrannen,'" *JRS* 3/4 (1952–1953): 7–97.

30. Charles A. Wanamaker, *The Epistles to the Thessalonians: A Commentary on the Greek Text* (Grand Rapids: Eerdmans, 1990), 3.

to the interests of the Roman people."[31] Benefits of this free status included (1) the right to mint both local and imperial coinage (although the latter did not occur until 298 CE under Diocletian), (2) freedom from military occupation, (3) tax concessions, (4) exemption from being a Roman colony and therefore not subject to the Ius Italicum (legal institution), and (5) not being responsible for the resettlement of discharged Roman soldiers, as was the case in Philippi and elsewhere.[32] "This naturally left the local ruling elite in control of the city with its traditional institutions intact."[33]

Fig. 10.5. *RPC* 1.1551. Image courtesy of Nomos AG, obolos 9, lot 688. Used with permission.

Second, numismatic evidence also supports the concept of an eager embrace of the imperial cult. Antony's defeat of Brutus in 42 BCE was commemorated as the dawn of a new age, including celebratory games.[34]

---

31. Holland Lee Hendrix, "Thessalonicians Honor Romans" (ThD diss., Harvard University, 1984), 245.
32. See Robert Jewett, *The Thessalonian Correspondence: Pauline Rhetoric and Millenarian Piety* (Philadelphia: Fortress, 1986), 123; Frank Frost Abbott, *A History and Description of Roman Political Institutions* (Boston: Ginn, 1911), 90–91; Gene L. Green, *The Letters to the Thessalonians* (Grand Rapids: Eerdmans, 2002), 18–20.
33. Wanamaker, *Epistles to the Thessalonians*, 3; Green, *Letters to the Thessalonians*, 19. On the politarchs see Greg H. R. Horsley, "The Politarchs," in *The Book of Acts in Its Greco-Roman Setting*, vol. 2 of *The Book of Acts in Its First Century Setting*, ed. David W. J. Gill and Conrad Gempf (Grand Rapids: Eerdmans, 1994), 419–31.
34. Richard A. Horsley, *Paul and the Roman Imperial Order* (New York: Trinity Press International, 2004), 57.

RPC 1.1552 is a bronze issue under M Antony and Octavian in 37 BCE. The obverse reads ΑΓΩΝΟΘΕΣΙΑ with the head of Agonothesia facing right (with E denoting year 5). The reverse has ANT KAI in a wreath. The *agonothete* was the judge of the public games, and *RPC* 1.1552 suggests "the Thessalonians were actively cultivating the patronage of the emperor and imperial figures in seeking political leverage."[35]

Toward the end of the first century BCE, a temple was built in Thessalonica in honor of Caesar, and a priesthood was established to service the temple. An important collection of inscriptions from Thessalonica includes *Inscriptiones Thessalonicae* 31 (*IG* 10.2.1), which refers to "the temple of Caesar," the "priest and agōnothetēs of Imperator Caesar Augustus son [of god]," and the "priest of the gods ... and priest of Roma and the Roman benefactors."[36] Hendrix's analysis of this and other inscriptions from Thessalonica (*IT* 32, 132, 133) suggests that officials, such as the *agonothete*, who were connected with the imperial cult were generally superior over other priesthoods, and "in every extant instance in which the 'priest and agonothete of the Imperator' is mentioned, he is listed first in what appears to be a strict observance of protocol. The Imperator's priest and agonothete assumes priority, the priest of 'the gods' is cited next, followed by the priest of Roma and Roman benefactors."[37] Especially significant is *IT* 133, a dedication to a renovation to the gymnasium where priest and *agonothete* are listed first.[38]

Third, Thessalonica's favored relationship with Rome is celebrated in the Homonoia between Thessalonica and Rome. The Homonoia established between Thessalonica and the triumvirs is "one of the earliest attested instances of such Homonoia between two cities."[39] *RPC* 1.1553 is an issue in 37 BCE by M Antony and Octavian. The obverse reads ΟΜΟΝΟΙΑ with a bust of Homonoia facing right, while the reverse has ΘΕΣΣΑΛΟΝ ΡΩΜ with a horse galloping, right. Pieter Franke and Dietrich Klose convincingly argue that there is no "overall explanation for all the 'alliance' coinages, but that they are a single manifestation of many different sets of circumstances (rivalry between cities, political or religious links, bound-

---

35. Horsley, *Paul and the Roman Imperial Order*, 57.
36. Cited in Weima, *1–2 Thessalonians*, 35.
37. Hendrix, "Thessalonicians Honor Romans," 312.
38. Hendrix, "Thessalonicians Honor Romans," 312 n. 1.
39. *RPC* 1.297.

ary disputes)."⁴⁰ Examples in the Julio-Claudian period indicate that alliance coinages had not yet been standardized.⁴¹ For instance, the word OMONOIA does not always occur; rather, two cities can simply be listed, joined by καί, or even have a variant of OMONOIA, OMHPOΣ⁴²—which may refer to the person responsible for the issue rather than the relationship per se, but still the phraseology is not standardized. Nonetheless, in regard to the coinage of Thessalonica, the composite picture is one of the aristocracy's imperial indebtedness, political commitment, and ideological allegiance to Rome.

Other avenues for applying numismatic data to New Testament Thessalonica and Thessalonian correspondence have been suggested by commentators. A wide range of scholars over the last half century, including Ernst Bammel, Karl Donfried, Klaus Wengst, Helmut Koester, and Hendrix have argued that the phrase εἰρήνη καὶ ἀσφάλεια ("peace and security," 1 Thess 5:3) offers a critique of a Roman imperial slogan of the Pax Romana.⁴³ The relevant terminology occurs frequently, not only on the coinage of the period⁴⁴ but also in epigraphic materials. Todd Still highlights, among other inscriptions, *IT* 32 (noted above) and *IT* 33, which consist of a selection of decrees of the city issued in conjunction

---

40. *RPC* 1.48; Peter R. Franke, "Zu den Homonoia-Münzen Kleinasiens," in *Stuttgarter Kolloquium zur Historischen Geographie des Altertums I, 1980*, ed. Eckart Olshausen (Bonn: Habelt, 1987), 81–102; Dietrich O. A. Klose, *Die Münzprägung von Smyrna in der römischen Kaiserzeit* (Berlin: de Gruyter, 1987), 44–63.

41. Such as *RPC* 1.1553 (Thessalonica and Rome), *RPC* 1.2143 (Amisus and Rome stand facing), *RPC* 1.2988 (Pergamum and Sardis under Augustus), *RPC* 1.5445 (Hypaepa and Sardis under Tiberius), *RPC* 1.5446 (Hypaepa and Sardis), *RPC* 1.2912 (Laodicea and Smyrna under Claudius), *RPC* 1.2928 (Laodicea and Smyrna under Nero).

42. *RPC* 1.1553 and 1.2143; *RPC* 1.2912; *RPC* 1.2928, respectively.

43. Ernst Bammel, "Ein Beitrag zur paulinischen Staatsanschauung," *TLZ* 85 (1960): 837–40; Karl P. Donfried, "The Cults of Thessalonica and the Thessalonian Correspondence," *NTS* 31 (1985): 341; Klaus Wengst, *Pax Romana and the Peace of Jesus Christ* (Philadelphia: Fortress, 1987), 19–21, 77–79; Helmut Koester, "From Paul's Eschatology to the Apocalyptic Schemata of 2 Thessalonians," in *The Thessalonian Correspondence*, ed. Rob F. Collins (Leuven: Leuven University Press, 1990), 449–50; Hendrix, "Archaeology and Eschatology," 107–18. See also Todd D. Still, *Conflict at Thessalonica: A Pauline Church and Its Neighbours* (Sheffield: Sheffield Academic, 1999), 260–67. Still summarizes recent scholarship on the "peace and security" phrase.

44. Hendrix, "Archaeology and Eschatology," 115.

with a specific Roman group, and *IT* 4, where Roma and Roman benefactors become part of the city cult of the gods.⁴⁵ An inscription at Ilium (SEG 46.1565; 62 BCE) honors Pompey for liberating the inhabitants of Alexandria Troas, ἀπό τε τῶν βαρβαρικῶν πολέμων [καῖ τῶν π]ιρατικῶν κινδύνων ἀποκαθεστάκοτα δὲ [τὴν εἰρ]ήνην καὶ τὴν ἀσφάλειαν καὶ κατὰ γῆν καὶ κατὰ θάλασσαν ("from wars with the Barbarians and the dangers from pirates, having restored peace and security on the land and the sea.").⁴⁶ Furthermore, as *IT* 31 evidences, a temple was built at some point between 26 BCE and 14 CE in honor of Augustus. This evidence strongly suggests that the political overtones in the phrase εἰρήνη καὶ ἀσφάλεια are clearly in the foreground in 1 Thess 5:3. Harrison strengthens this proposal by drawing attention to the Jewish Psalms of Solomon 8.8, which refers to Rome's occupation by Pompey as follows: "He entered in peace [μετ' εἰρήνης] as a father enters his son's house; he set his feet securely [μετὰ ἀσφαλείας]."⁴⁷ In light of this, Hendrix's conclusion is certainly justified when he states, "Thessalonica's interests increasingly were influenced by Romans and by regard for the Roman emperor."⁴⁸

More recently the debate has been reignited with the robust interchange between Jeffrey Weima and Joel White.⁴⁹ Weima presents a fresh articulation of the argument in support of the phrase εἰρήνη καὶ ἀσφάλεια (1 Thess 5:3) as deriving from a critique of a Roman imperial slogan. White takes issue with the identification of the Thessalonian phrase with a slogan per se and questions the role of *securitas* in the imperial equation. It is not that White denies Roman imperial political ideology, but he contends there is only limited evidence that the two terms circulated as a slogan. The contribution of numismatics at this point would be to simply point out the frequency with which both terms are used on the imperial coinage of the first century. Harrison sums up the numismatic evidence

---

45. Still, *Conflict at Thessalonica*, 263.
46. Peter Oakes, "Re-mapping the Universe: Paul and the Emperor in 1 Thessalonians and Philippians," *JSNT* 27 (2005): 317–18.
47. Harrison, *Paul and the Imperial Authorities*, 61 n. 64.
48. Hendrix, "Archaeology and Eschatology," 115.
49. Jeffrey A. D. Weima, "'Peace and Security' (1 Thess 5.3): Prophetic Warning or Political Propaganda?," *NTS* 58 (2012): 331–59; Joel R. White, "'Peace and Security' (1 Thessalonians 5.3): Is it Really a Slogan?," *NTS* 59 (2013): 382–85; White, "'Peace' and 'Security' (1 Thess 5.3): Roman Ideology and Greek Aspiration," *NTS* 60 (2014): 499–510.

perfectly in stating that "both Latin words [*pax* and *securitas*] appear individually on the imperial coinage with monotonous regularity."[50]

Particularly compelling examples include *RIC*, Claudius 61 (aureus), and *RIC*, Claudius 62 (denarius), newly issued by Claudius in 51–52 CE, the probable year of Paul's arrival to Thessalonica.[51] The obverse depicts the laureate head of Claudius facing right with the inscription TI CLAUD CAESAR AUG P M TR P XI IMP PP COS V. The reverse has PACI AUGUSTAE with a depiction of a winged Pax-Nemesis advancing right, with left hand holding a caduceus pointing down at a snake, and with the right hand holding out a fold of drapery below chin. Slightly less common but strongly attested is the legend SECURITAS, although more common on the coins from Nero onward. What is particularly striking on the coins of Claudius, however, and which has thus far not been alluded to or drawn on in this discussion are the coinage issues with a conceptually related term to *securitas*, namely, *servator*.

The Oxford Latin Dictionary gives three senses for *servator*: (1) a savior, preserver; (2) an observer, one who keeps watch or guard; and (3) one who observes or maintains (a rule of conduct); if offers five senses for *securitas*: (1) freedom from anxiety or care; (2) complacent negligence; (3) freedom from danger, safety, security; (4) the personification of public and political security; and (5) security for a payment of debt.[52] There has been a long-established scholarly tradition of interest in Latin synonyms and especially nuances between related lexemes. From Marcus Terentius Varro's (116–27 BCE) nascent attempts, to Isidore of Seville's (560–636 CE) encyclopedic projects, to the sophisticated discipline in modern lexicography, scholarly interest in Latin lexicology in this area has not waned.[53] Jean-Baptiste Gardin Dumesnil's *Synonymes Latins et*

---

50. Harrison, *Paul and the Imperial Authorities*, 61.

51. This was the eighth time the reverse type was issued by Claudius during his reign (previously as *RIC* Claudius 9, 10, in 41–41 CE; *RIC* Claudius 21, 22, in 43–44 CE; *RIC* Claudius 27, 28, in 44 CE; *RIC* Claudius 38, 39, in 46–47 CE; *RIC* Claudius 46, 47, in 49–50 CE; *RIC* Claudius 51, 52, 57, 58, in 50–51 CE).

52. *Oxford Latin Dictionary* (Oxford: Clarendon, 1968), 1745, 1722.

53. Georg Goetz, "Differentiae scriptores," PW 5:481–84; Georg Goetz, "Glossographie," PW 7:1433–66. For a summary of the field of Latin glossaries see Peter Schmidt, "Differentiarum Scriptores," *DNP* 3:558–59. For a modern survey of the field of Latin lexicography see Alfred Breitenbach, "Lexikon II (lateinisch)," *RAC* 23:1–29. The standard Latin text of Isidore's *Etymologiae* is Wallace M. Lindsay, *Isidori Hispalensis episcope etymologiarum sive originum libri XX*, 2 vols. (Oxford: Clarendon,

Leurs Significations (1777) contains over 7,000 words in 2,541 domains of synonyms.[54] Domain 2230 consists of *servator, conservator, liberator,* and *soter*.[55] Although Dumesnil does not list *securitas*, the more comprehensive work of Ludwig Döderlein does list the term under domain 77, together with *tutus* and *incuriosus*.[56] Franz Wagner's *Lexicon Latinum Universae Phraseologiae Corpus Congestum* (1878) associates both terms via function when he notes of *servator* "usus: Urbis, capitis mei servator et custos."[57]

When considering related lexemes or synonyms, several of the above lexicographers (Dumesnil, Döderlin, Pompa) can, at times, be accused of drawing too fine a distinction between certain terminology. The difference in words is not always related to morphology but often more strongly correlated to register, style, genre, and author. It is thus with a more porous exchange in *meaning* that certain terminology on the record of Latin coinage of Claudius could illuminate a further dimension of the Greek phrase.

RIC Claudius 5 (aureus), and 6 (denarius) were issued in 41–42 CE and had inscribed on the obverse TI CLAUD CAESAR AUG P M TR P (Tiberius Claudius Caesar Augustus Pontifex Maximus Tribunicia Potestate [Tiberius Claudius Caesar, August, Greatest Pontiff invested with the Tribunician Power]). The reverse has lettering over four lines within an oak wreath, EX S C OB CIVES SERVATOS (Ex Senatus Consulto Ob Cives Servatos [by Decree of the Senate for Having Saved the Citizens]). As Duncan Fishwick notes, "the concept of the *princeps* as *servator* is central in Augustan ideology" and is replicated by Claudius on his coinage during his reign for the purposes of typological association.[58] *RIC* Claudius 15 (aureus) and 16 (denarius; see fig. 10.6) were also issued in 41–42 CE, with similar obverse (TI CLAUD CAESAR AUG GERM P M) and reverse (EX S C OB CIVES SERVATOS in three

---

1911). For an English translation, see Stephen A. Barney et al., *The "Etymologies" of Isidore of Seville* (Cambridge: Cambridge University Press, 2006).

54. M. Jean-Baptiste Gardin Dumesnil, *Latin Synonyms with Their Different Significations: And Examples Taken from the Best Latin Authors*, trans. J. M. Gosset (London: Richard Taylor, 1888).

55. Dumesnil, *Latin Synonyms*, 511.

56. Ludwig Döderlein, *Lateinische Synonyme und Etymologieen: Dritter Theil* (Leipzig: Vogel, 1829), 3:120.

57. Franz Wagner, *Lexicon Latinum Universae Phraseologiae Corpus Congestum*, trans. Augustin Borgnet (Ridgwood, NJ: Gregg, 1878), 642.

58. Duncan Fishwick, *The Imperial Cult in the Latin West* (Leiden: Brill, 1993), 108.

lines within an oak wreath) inscriptions. The obverse of *RIC* Claudius 96 (Sestertius; see fig. 10.7) depicts the laureate head of Claudius facing right with the inscription TI CLAVDIVS CAESAR AVG P M TR P IMP. The reverse has lettering over four lines within an oak wreath, EX S C OB CIVES SERVATOS (Ex Senatus Consulto Ob Cives Servatos [by Decree of the Senate for Having Saved the Citizens]). This is not to suggest that the meanings of *securitas* and *servatos* are synonymous but that they share significant semantic overlap in their linguistic senses. This could potentially be one dimension of the phrase εἰρήνη καὶ ἀσφάλεια ("peace and security") in 1 Thess 5:3 hitherto neglected. The chronological time frame in regard to Paul's visit to Thessalonica, during the reign of Claudius, enhances the probability.

Fig. 10.6. *RIC* Claudius 16. Image courtesy of Nomos AG, obolos 15, lot 768. Used with permission.

Fig. 10.7. *RIC* Claudius 96. Image courtesy of Nomos AG, obolos 9, lot 167. Used with permission.

3.3. Thessalonica's Religious Identity Shaped by the City's Past

There were a number of coexisting and competing cults at Thessalonica, including Dionysus, Egyptian cults primarily focused on Serapis and Isis but also with interest in Osiris and Anubis, and of course the above-discussed imperial cult. The cult of Kabeiros, however, was perhaps the most prominent[59] and was regularly represented on coinage. It was not indigenous to the Macedonian area but imported from Samothrace.[60] Macedonians were interested in Samothracian gods from at least the time of Phillip II onward, as Plutarch indicates: "and we are told that Philip, after being initiated into the mysteries of Samothrace at the same time with Olympias, he himself being still a youth…" (*Alex.* 2 [Perrin]). Other early evidence is cited by Charles Edson,[61] which includes reference to Antigona of Pella, who was captured by the Persian fleet in 333 BCE en route from Macedonia to Samothrace to partake in mysteries, further strengthening the cultic association between the two locations. *IG* 12.8.195 connects the Macedonians with Samothracian gods by providing a list of visitors from Macedonia who participated in ΜΥΣΤΑΙ ΕΥΣΕΒΕΙΣ ("pious mysteries") dated securely to Augustus's reign. These and other factors suggest that, at the latest by Augustus's time, there was considerable interest in Samothracian gods in Thessalonica. Edson concludes that by Augustus "members of the city's upper classes were showing interest in the cult of the Samothracian gods."[62]

Koester rightly notes the limitation of our knowledge of the Kabeiros cult at Thessalonica, as opposed to the specificity elsewhere in the empire, such as the single god in Thessalonica rather than twin gods in Samothrace, which were conflated with the Dioscuri twins Castor and Polydeuces. Clement of Alexandria refers to the cult as pertaining to two brothers murdering and burying a third, to whom they set up a cult.[63] Robert Jewett

---

59. Contra Colin R. Nicholl, who claims that "the significance of the cult of Cabirus has been greatly overstated." See Nicholl, *From Hope to Despair in Thessalonica* (Cambridge: Cambridge University Press, 2004), 78 n. 110. Nicholl's conclusions are difficult to justify given the voluminous numismatic, inscriptional, monumental, and literary evidence for the cult at Thessalonica.

60. Charles Edson, "Cults of Thessalonica," *HTR* 41 (1948): 188–204.

61. Edson, "Cults of Thessalonica," 189 n. 3.

62. Edson, "Cults of Thessalonica," 190.

63. Clement of Alexandria, *The Absurdity and Impiety of the Heathen Mysteries and Fables about the Birth and Death of Their Gods* (ANF 2:177).

claims this is "structurally similar" to Paul's proclamation.[64] But we must not assume that an imposition of our knowledge from other locations is assumed for Kabeiros at Thessalonica. The date of arrival of the Kabeiros cult to Thessalonica is ambiguous, but it clearly has an established history even before the first century.[65] Weima notes that the cult was also well known in Larisa, the capital of nearby Thessaly, by 200 BCE,[66] but it is difficult to infer specific details about Thessalonica without further literary or archaeological evidence.

Donfried notes a series of pre-imperial Thessalonian coins with the helmeted head of Roma and suggests that they can be used to shed light on texts such as καὶ περικεφαλαίαν ἐλπίδα σωτηρίας ("and the hope of salvation as a helmet"; 1 Thess 5:8).[67] Donfried suggests that the laurel crown of Kabeiros or the rose crowns used in the commemoratory sacrifice of the cult of Dionysus would be the natural association for the recipients of the letter. But there are other possibilities and associations that may prove more viable avenues for accounting for the armor language in Thessalonians or other Pauline texts from the perspective of the writer, including Qumran literature, Isaiah, Jewish wisdom traditions,[68] or indeed the broader cultural milieu of the presence of Roman military throughout the Mediterranean world.

Kabeiros at Thessalonica primarily evidences itself in the coinage of the Flavian period (69 CE–96 CE). *RPC* 2.327 is a medium (20–23 mm) bronze coin that, on the obverse, depicts Kabeiros standing facing left, holding a *rhyton* (conical container for drinking or libation) and hammer, with an accompanying inscription ΚΑΒΕΙΡΟΣ. The reverse has ΘΕΣΣΑ/ΛΟΝΙΚΕ/ΩΝ in three lines, with a small eagle above, all of which is within an oak wreath. *RPC* 2.328 has a draped bust of Kabeiros facing right on the obverse. The reverse, like *RPC* 2.327, has ΘΕΣΣΑ/ΛΟΝΙΚΕ/

---

64. Jewett, *Thessalonian Correspondence*, 128.
65. Bengt Hemberg, *Die Kabiren* (Uppsala: Almqvist & Wiksell, 1950), 9.
66. Weima, *1–2 Thessalonians*, 16.
67. See discussion in Donfried, "Cults of Thessalonica," 341.
68. Wis 5:17–18: "The Lord will take his zeal as his whole armor, and will arm all creation to repel his enemies; he will put on righteousness as a breastplate, and wear impartial justice as a helmet" (NRSV). On the Qumran literature, see David Luckensmeyer, *The Eschatology of First Thessalonians* (Göttingen: Vandenhoeck & Ruprecht, 2009), 303. On Isaiah, see Jeffrey A. D. Weima, "1–2 Thessalonians," in *Commentary on the New Testament Use of the Old Testament*, ed. Gregory K. Beale and Donald A. Carson (Grand Rapids: Baker Academic, 2007), 882

ΩΝ in three lines, eagle above, all within an oak wreath. RPC 2.329 has on the obverse the draped bust of the city goddess facing right, with the inscription ΘΕΣΣΑΛΟΝΙΚΗ. The obverse depicts Kabeiros standing left, holding *rhyton* and hammer, with the inscription ΚΑΒΕΙΡΟΣ. RPC 2.330 has on the obverse the draped and turreted bust of the city goddess facing right, with the inscription ΘΕΣΣΑΛΟΝΙΚΕΩΝ. The obverse, similar to 329, depicts Kabeiros standing left, holding *rhyton* and hammer, with the inscription ΚΑΒΕΙΡΟΣ.

The regular depiction of Kabeiros carrying a hammer is significant. The hammer could refer to the city's pride in industry in general, that is, a celebration of hard work and labor built into the identity of the inhabitants. If so, then Paul's imperatives to work in 1 Thess 4:9–12 (esp. v. 11) builds rapport and rhetorically appeals to their shared common values (see also 1 Thess 2:9, "You remember our labor [κόπον] and toil [μόχθον], brothers and sisters; we worked [ἐργαζόμενοι] night and day, so that we might not burden any of you while we proclaimed to you the gospel of God" [NRSV]).

The image of the hammer might also refer more specifically to the industry of blacksmiths, which, as Acts 19 notes, was affected by the diminishing demand for idols, at least in Ephesus. Perhaps a similar dynamic arose in Thessalonica. Justin Hardin's argument, which takes the charges and judicial episode in Acts 17:1–10 as pertaining to Roman regulations of voluntary associations,[69] would more broadly allow this possibility. But the word ἐργαζόμενοι in 1 Thess 2:9 would certainly include manual labor, even if it was physically challenging κόπος (labor) and μόχθος (toil). Nonetheless, Paul maintains a positive association despite the generally negative attitude toward labor by Roman elites in antiquity,[70] which perhaps implies the lower-than-elite social status of Paul and his recipients. Either way, challenging the god of a city threatened the stability of the

---

69. Justin Hardin, "Decrees and Drachmas at Thessalonica: An Illegal Assembly in Jason's House (Acts 17.1–10a)," *NTS* 52 (2006): 29–49.

70. Ronald F. Hock, *The Social Context of Paul's Ministry: Tentmaking and Apostleship* (Philadelphia: Fortress, 1980), 36; Sandra R. Joshel, *Work, Identity, and Legal Status at Rome: A Study of the Occupational Inscriptions* (Norman: University of Oklahoma Press, 1992), 63–69; Ramsay MacMullen, *Roman Social Relations 50 B.C. to A.D. 284* (New Haven: Yale University Press, 1974), 114–16, 138–41; Richard S. Ascough, "The Thessalonian Christian Community as a Professional Voluntary Association," *JBL* 52 (2006): 311–28.

city both politically and ideologically. Paul's motivation for this emphasis on the continuance of normal working life is borne out of an apparent misunderstanding of the imminent return of Christ (1 Thess 4:15–17, 5:1–9; 2 Thess 2:1–3), which the Thessalonians appear to have interpreted as the suspension of their working lives. In light of the imagery on the numismatic record, this message would have certainly appealed to the inhabitants of the city.

4. Conclusion

This analysis has sought to illuminate aspects of the Thessalonian correspondence in light of the numismatic record. The above numismatic analysis sought to demonstrate (1) that the imperial cult at Thessalonica shaped the city (evidenced through, among other mediums, divine honors for Caesar on coins); (2) that Thessalonica enjoyed favored political relationship with Rome, and this subsequently brought appealing benefits for the inhabitants; and (3) that religious identity was shaped by the city's past, primarily through the embrace of the cult of Kabeiros. Taken together, the numismatic evidence supports the reconstruction of the Thessalonian aristocracy's "active cultivation of Roman power"[71] and simultaneously supports the view of Thessalonians functioning as resistance literature. This study also reminds us that "it is critical for us to realize how visible the Roman imperial ideology (as attested on the provincial coinage) would have been as a part of the everyday world of the Thessalonians when we read 1 Thessalonians."[72]

Bibliography

Abbott, Frank Frost. *A History and Description of Roman Political Institutions*. Boston: Ginn, 1911.

Ascough, Richard S. "The Thessalonian Christian Community as a Professional Voluntary Association." *JBL* 52 (2006): 311–28.

Bammel, Ernst. "Ein Beitrag zur paulinischen Staatsanschauung." *TLZ* 85 (1960): 837–40.

---

71. Horsley, *Paul and the Roman Imperial Order*, 58.
72. Horsley, *Paul and the Roman Imperial Order*, 58.

Barney, Stephen A., Wendy J. Lewis, Jennifer A. Beach, and Oliver Berghof. *The "Etymologies" of Isidore of Seville*. Cambridge: Cambridge University Press, 2006.

Breitenbach, Alfred. "Lexikon II (lateinisch)." *RAC* 23:1–29.

Brunt, Peter A., and John M. Moore. *Res Gestae Divi Augusti: The Achievements of Divine Augustus*. Oxford: Oxford University Press, 1983.

Cary, Earnest, and Herbert B. Foster, trans. *Dio Cassius, Roman History, Volume V: Books 46–50*. LCL. Cambridge: Harvard University Press, 1917.

Crawford, Michael H. "Roman Imperial Coin Types and the Formation of Public Opinion." Pages 47–64 in *Studies in Numismatic Method Presented to Philip Grierson*. Edited by Christopher Brooke, Bernard Stewart, John Pollard, and Terence Volk. Cambridge: Cambridge University Press, 1983.

Donfried, Karl P. "The Cults of Thessalonica and the Thessalonian Correspondence." *NTS* 31 (1985): 336–56.

Döderlein, Ludwig. *Lateinische Synonyme und Etymologieen: Dritter Theil*. 6 vols. Leipzig: Vogel, 1829.

Dumesnil, M. Jean-Baptiste Gardin. *Latin Synonyms with Their Different Significations: And Examples Taken from the Best Latin Authors*. Translated by J. M. Gosset. London: Taylor, 1888.

Edson, Charles. "Cults of Thessalonica." *HTR* 41 (1948): 188–204.

Fishwick, Duncan. *The Imperial Cult in the Latin West*. Leiden: Brill, 1993.

Franke, Peter R. "Zu den Homonoia-Münzen Kleinasiens." Pages 81–102 in *Stuttgarter Kolloquium zur Historische Geographie des Altertums I, 1980*. Edited by Eckart Olshausen. Bonn: Habelt, 1987.

Gaebler, Hugo. *Die antiken Münzen Nord-Griechenlands*. Vol. 3, part 2. Berlin: Reimer, 1935.

———. *Die antiken Münzen von Makedonia und Paionia, Die antiken Münzen Nord-Griechenlands*. Vol. 3. Berlin: de Gruyter, 1935.

Goetz, Georg. "Differentiae scriptores." *PW* 5:481–84.

———. "Glossographie." *PW* 7:1433–66.

Grant, Michael. *From Imperium to Auctoritas*. Cambridge: Cambridge University Press, 1946.

Green, Gene L. *The Letters to the Thessalonians*. Grand Rapids: Eerdmans, 2002.

Hardin, Justin. "Decrees and Drachmas at Thessalonica: An Illegal Assembly in Jason's House (Acts 17.1–10a)." *NTS* 52 (2006): 29–49.

Harrison, James R. "'The Fading Crown': Divine Honour and the Early Christians." *JTS* 54 (2003): 493–529.

———. "Paul and Empire II: Negotiating the Seduction of Imperial 'Peace and Security' in Galatians, Thessalonians and Philippians." Pages 165–84 in *An Introduction to Empire in the New Testament*. RBS 84. Edited by Adam Winn. Atlanta: SBL Press, 2015.

———. *Paul and the Imperial Authorities at Thessalonica and Rome: A Study in the Conflict of Ideology.* WUNT 273. Tübingen: Mohr Siebeck, 2011.

———. "Paul and the Imperial Gospel at Thessaloniki." *JSNT* 25 (2002): 71–96.

Head, Barclay V. *Catalogue of Greek Coins in the British Museum: Attica, Megaris, Aegina*. London: British Museum, 1888.

Helly, Bruno. "Le groupe des monnaies fédérales thessaliennes avec Athéna 'aux pompons.'" *RN* 6 (1966): 7–32.

Hemberg, Bengt. *Die Kabiren*. Uppsala: Almqvist & Wiksell, 1950.

Hendrix, Holland Lee. "Archaeology and Eschatology at Thessalonica." Pages 107–18 in *The Future of Early Christianity: Essays in Honor of Helmut Koester*. Edited by Birger A. Pearson. Minneapolis: Fortress, 1991.

———. "Thessalonicans Honor Romans." ThD diss., Harvard University, 1984.

Hock, Ronald F. *The Social Context of Paul's Ministry: Tentmaking and Apostleship*. Philadelphia: Fortress, 1980.

Horsley, Greg H. R. *Paul and the Roman Imperial Order*. New York: Trinity Press International, 2004.

———. "The Politarchs." Pages 419–31 in *The Book of Acts in Its Greco-Roman Setting*. Vol. 2 of *The Book of Acts in Its First Century Setting*. Edited by David W. J. Gill and Conrad Gempf. Grand Rapids: Eerdmans, 1994.

Howgego, Christopher J. *Ancient History from Coins*. London: Routledge, 1995.

———. *Greek Imperial Countermarks: Studies in the Provincial Coinage of the Roman Empire*. London: Royal Numismatic Society, 1985.

Jewett, Robert. *The Thessalonian Correspondence: Pauline Rhetoric and Millenarian Piety*. Philadelphia: Fortress, 1986.

Joshel, Sandra R. *Work, Identity, and Legal Status at Rome: A Study of the Occupational Inscriptions*. Norman: University of Oklahoma Press, 1992.

Klose, Dietrich O. A. *Die Münzprägung von Smyrna in der römischen Kaiserzeit*. Berlin: de Gruyter, 1987.

Koester, Helmut. "From Paul's Eschatology to the Apocalyptic Schemata of 2 Thessalonians." Pages 441–58 in *The Thessalonian Correspondence*. Edited by Rob F. Collins. Leuven: Leuven University Press, 1990.

Kraft, Konrad. "Der goldene Kranz Caesars und der Kampf um die Entlarvung des 'Tyrannen.'" *JRS* 3/4 (1952–1953): 7–97.

Lindsay, Wallace M. *Isidori Hispalensis episcope etymologiarum sive originum libri XX*. 2 vols. Oxford: Clarendon, 1911.

Luckensmeyer, David. *The Eschatology of First Thessalonians*. Göttingen: Vandenhoeck & Ruprecht, 2009.

MacMullen, Ramsay. *Roman Social Relations 50 B.C. to A.D. 284*. New Haven: Yale University Press, 1974.

Meshorer, Ya'akov. *Jewish Coins of the Second Temple Period*. Tel Aviv: Am Hassefer, 1967.

Moushmov, Nikola. *Ancient Coins of the Balkan Peninsula*. Translated by Denista Genkova, Dave Surber, and Slavei Theodore Slaveev. Sofia: K&K, 1912.

Nicholl, Colin R. *From Hope to Despair in Thessalonica*. Cambridge: Cambridge University Press, 2004.

Oakes, Peter. "Re-mapping the Universe: Paul and the Emperor in 1 Thessalonians and Philippians." *JSNT* 27 (2005): 301–22.

Oldfather, William A., trans. *Epictetus: Discourses, Books 3–4; Fragments; The Encheiridion*. LCL. Cambridge: Harvard University Press, 1928.

Oster, Richard. "Numismatic Windows into the Social World of Early Christianity." *JBL* 101 (1982): 195–223.

Perrin, Bernadotte, trans. *Plutarch. Lives, Volume VII: Demosthenes and Cicero; Alexander and Caesar*. LCL. Cambridge: Harvard University Press, 1919.

Rackham, Harris, trans. *Pliny, The Natural History, Volume II: Books 3–7*. LCL. Cambridge: Harvard University Press, 1942.

Raffety, William E. "Crown." *ISBE* 1:831–32.

Rogers, Edgar. *The Copper Coinage of Thessaly*. London: Spink & Son, 1932.

Rolfe, John C., trans. *Suetonius, Lives of the Caesars, Volume II: Claudius; Nero; Galba, Otho, and Vitellius; Vespasian; Titus, Domitian; Lives of Illustrious Men: Grammarians and Rhetoricians; Poets (Terence, Virgil, Horace, Tibullus, Persius, Lucan); Lives of Pliny the Elder and Passienus Crispus*. LCL. Cambridge: Harvard University Press, 1914.

Schmidt, Peter. "Differentiarum Scriptores." *DNP* 3:558–59.

Still, Todd D. *Conflict at Thessalonica: A Pauline Church and Its Neighbours*. Sheffield: Sheffield Academic, 1999.

Touratsoglou, Ioannis. *Die Münzstätte von Thessaloniki in der römischen Kaiserzeit: 32/31 v. Chr. bis 268 n. Chr.* Berlin: de Gruyter, 1988.

Wagner, Franz. *Lexicon Latinum Universae Phraseologiae Corpus Congestum*. Translated by Augustin Borgnet. Ridgewood, NJ: Gregg, 1878.

Wanamaker, Charles A. *The Epistles to the Thessalonians: A Commentary on the Greek Text*. Grand Rapids: Eerdmans, 1990.

Weima, Jeffrey A. D. "1–2 Thessalonians." Pages 871–90 in *Commentary on the New Testament Use of the Old Testament*. Edited by Gregory K. Beale and Donald A. Carson. Grand Rapids: Baker Academic, 2007.

———. *1–2 Thessalonians*. Grand Rapids: Baker Academic, 2014.

———. "'Peace and Security' (1 Thess 5.3): Prophetic Warning or Political Propaganda?" *NTS* 58 (2012): 331–59.

Weinstock, Stefan. *Divus Julius*. Oxford: Oxford University Press, 1971.

Wengst, Klaus. *Pax Romana and the Peace of Jesus Christ*. Philadelphia: Fortress, 1987.

White, Joel R. "'Peace and Security' (1 Thessalonians 5.3): Is it Really a Slogan?" *NTS* 59 (2013): 382–85.

———. "'Peace' and 'Security' (1 Thess 5.3): Roman Ideology and Greek Aspiration." *NTS* 60 (2014): 499–510.

Williams, Jonathan. "Religion and Roman Coins." Pages 143–63 in *A Companion to Roman Religion*. Edited by Jörg Rüpke. Oxford: Blackwell, 2007.

Contributors

D. Clint Burnett is an independent scholar (PhD Biblical Studies, Boston College) who specializes in the interpretation of early Christianity in light of the material culture of Greco-Roman cities. His recent publications include *Studying the New Testament through Inscriptions: An Introduction* (Hendrickson, 2020) and *Christ's Enthronement at God's Right Hand and Its Greco-Roman Cultural Context* (de Gruyter, 2021). He serves as a coeditor with James R. Harrison for *New Documents Illustrating the History of Early Christianity: Galatia*.

Alan H. Cadwallader is a Research Professor at the Australian Centre for Christianity and Culture at Charles Sturt University in Canberra. Recent monographs have been *Beyond the Word of a Woman* (ATF, 2008), *Fragments of Colossae* (ATF, 2015), and *The Politics of the Revised Version* (T&T Clark, 2019). He has edited a number of volumes on the interface of early Christianity, ancient culture, and contemporary issues: *Colossae in Space and Time* (Vandenhoeck & Ruprecht, 2011), *Pieces of Ease and Grace* (ATF, 2013), *Where the Wild Ox Roams* (Sheffield Phoenix, 2013), and *Stones, Bones and the Sacred* (SBL Press, 2016). He is currently completing an Earth Bible commentary on Mark's Gospel (T&T Clark, 2024) and a new monograph on Colossae and the Letters to the Colossians and Philemon (Vandenhoeck & Ruprecht, 2023). A new volume, *The Ancient Village and the Rise of Early Christianity* (T&T Clark, 2023), coedited with James R. Harrison, Angela Standhartinger, and L. L. Welborn, is also being finalized for publication.

Rosemary Canavan studied Theology at Flinders University and graduated from the doctoral program in 2011. She is a Senior Lecturer in Biblical Studies and was previously Academic Dean at Catholic Theological College, University of Divinity. Her doctoral thesis was published as *Clothing the Body of Christ at Colossae: A Visual Construction of Identity* (Mohr

Siebeck, 2012), and she is currently working on *Exploring 1 and 2 Thessalonians*, a commentary in the Rhetoric of Religious Antiquity series (SBL Press). She has also published a number of book sections and articles in relation to the Lycus Valley, clothing, numismatics, and epigraphy in the exploration of visual exegesis as an interpretive framework for biblical text in context.

James R. Harrison studied Ancient History at Macquarie University and graduated from the doctoral program in 1997. He is the Research Director at the Sydney College of Divinity. His recent monographs include *Paul and the Imperial Authorities at Thessalonica and Rome* (Mohr Siebeck, 2011), *Paul and the Ancient Celebrity Circuit* (Mohr Siebeck, 2019), and *Reading Romans with Roman Eyes* (Fortress, 2020). He is the chief editor of *New Documents Illustrating the History of Early Christianity* (vols. 11–16) and is editor of E. A. Judge, *The Conflict of Cultures: The Legacy of Paul's Thought Today* (Cascade, 2020). Along with Alan Cadwallader, Angela Standhartinger, and L. L. Welborn as coeditors, he is finalizing a new volume on *The Ancient Village and the Rise of Early Christianity* (T&T Clark, 2023).

Julien M. Ogereau (PhD, 2014) studied theology, New Testament, and early Christian studies at the Sydney College of Divinity and Macquarie University, Sydney. He is currently a researcher at the University of Vienna. His publications include *Paul's Koinonia with the Philippians* (Mohr Siebeck, 2014), *Authority and Identity in Emerging Christianities in Asia Minor and Greece*, coedited with C. Breytenbach (Brill, 2018), and *Early Christianity in Macedonia* (Brill, forthcoming).

Isaac T. Soon (PhD) studied New Testament and early Christianity at the University of Oxford and Durham University. He is Assistant Professor of Religious Studies (New Testament) at Crandall University. His first book, *A Disabled Apostle: Impairment and Disability in the Letters of Paul*, is forthcoming with Oxford University Press. He has published articles in the *Journal for the Study of the Pseudepigrapha*, *Novum Testamentum*, *Early Christianity*, *Vigiliae Christianae*, the *Journal of the Jesus Movement in Its Jewish Setting*, and the *Journal of Disability and Religion*.

Angela Standhartinger is Professor for New Testament Studies at the Philipps-University Marburg, Germany. Her research focuses on Pauline and deutero-Pauline letter writing, Jewish Hellenistic literature,

Greco-Roman meals and the origin of the Eucharist, and gender studies. Her most recent publications include *Der Philipperbrief* (Mohr Siebeck, 2021); "Greetings from Prison and Greetings from Caesar's House (Philippians 4.22): A Reconsideration of an Enigmatic Greek Expression in the Light of the Context and Setting of Philippians," *JSNT* 43.4 (2021): 468–84; and "'The Beloved Community' after Paul: Early Christianity in Philippi from the Second to the Forth Century," in *Philippi, from Colonia Augusta to Communitas Christiana*, ed. Steven J. Friesen, Michalis Lychounas, and Daniel N. Schowalter, NovT Sup 186 (Brill, 2021), 316–35.

Michael P. Theophilos is Associate Professor of Biblical Studies and Ancient Languages at the Australian Catholic University. His thirty-seven publications to date include three sole-authored books: *Numismatics and Greek Lexicography* (Bloomsbury, 2020); *The Abomination of Desolation in Matthew 24:15* (T&T Clark, 2012); and *Jesus as New Moses in Matthew 8–9* (Gorgias, 2011), with two monographs forthcoming: *A Lexicon of Greek Numismatic Inscriptions* (Brill); and *Matthean and Lukan Infancy Narratives* (Vandenhoeck & Ruprecht). He has been recipient of several prestigious national and international awards, including an Australian Government Citation for Outstanding Contributions to Student Learning. He is curator of papyrological materials at the Australian Institute of Archaeology and chair of the program unit in Numismatics and Biblical Interpretation at the Annual Meeting of the Society of Biblical Literature.

Joel R. White studied political science and theology at the University of Chicago, Gordon-Conwell Theological Seminary, and the University of Dortmund (Germany). He is Professor of New Testament at the Freie Theologische Hochschule Giessen, Germany. He published *Der Brief des Paulus an die Kolosser* in the series Historisch-Theologische Auslegung in 2018 and is currently working on a Philemon commentary in the same series.

Ancient Sources Index

Old Testament

Genesis
- 15:16 — 258
- 34 — 259
- 40:19 — 249

Exodus
- 20:18 LXX — 241

Numbers
- 6:22–27 — 45
- 11:12 — 289

Deuteronomy
- 8:2
- 21:22–23 — 249
- 26:26 — 249
- 32:1 — 139
- 32:1–3 — 138
- 32:1–43 — 137
- 32:4–9 — 138
- 32:10–14 — 138
- 32:15–18 — 138–39
- 32:19–25 — 138
- 32:21 — 138
- 32:26–43 — 138

1 Samuel
- 16:7 — 285

1 Chronicles
- 16:10 — 305
- 16:25 — 305
- 29:17 — 285

2 Chronicles
- 32:31 — 285
- 36:15–16 — 258

Nehemiah
- 9:26 — 258

Esther
- 5:14 — 249

Job
- 1:2 LXX — 296
- 3:21 LXX — 164
- 8:2 LXX — 296
- 17:18 — 285

Psalms
- 7:9 — 285
- 11:4–5 — 285
- 19:4 — 240
- 20:7 — 304
- 26:2 — 285
- 34:2 — 304
- 44:8 — 304
- 48:8 LXX — 45
- 48:11 LXX — 45
- 103:13 — 292
- 105:3 — 304
- 139:23 — 285

Proverbs
- 16:31 — 304
- 16:33 — 46
- 17:3 — 285
- 17:6 — 300, 304

Ecclesiastes		12:11	132, 134
3:18	285	Joel	
Isaiah		1:15	131
2:2–4	139	2:1–3	131
6:8–19	139	2:28–32 LXX	41
11:10	139	3:14	240
11:11–16	132	3:18	131
19:19–25	139		
49:5–6	132	Amos	
54:13 LXX	157	9:11	131
59:20	140		
63:17	132	Obadiah	
66:13	289	1:15	131
Jeremiah		Micah	
3:18	132	4:1–4	139
4:2	304		
9:23	304	Zephaniah	
11:20	285	1:14–17	131
12:3	285	3:9–10	139
17:10	285		
29:7	46	Zechariah	
31:33	140	2:11	139
		3:9–10	139
Ezekiel		8:20–23	139
16:12	304		
23:42	304	Malachi	
48:30–35	132	4:1–3	131

Deuterocanonical Books

Daniel			
2	123		
2:21	123	Wisdom of Solomon	
2:31–45	132	5:17–18	331
4:37	123		
7–8	123	Sirach	
7:1–28	132	3:2	300
7:12	123	36:10–13	132
8:21–27	132	40:13	238, 240
8:23	258	48:10	132
9:20–27	132–33		
9:24–27	133	Baruch	
9:27	132, 134	15:8	304
11:31	132, 134		
12:2	136		

Ancient Sources Index

1 Maccabees
   1:54   135

2 Maccabees
   6:14   258
   16:12   258

3 Maccabees
   3:2   240

Ancient Jewish Writings

1QH
   VII, 20b–22   292

1QH^a
   XV, 23–25   289
   XVII, 29B–36   289

1QM
   I, 9–11   167
   II, 2–3   132
   III, 12–13   132
   XV, 9   167

IQS
   I, 9   167
   II, 16   167
   III, 13   167
   III, 24   167
   III, 25   167
   III, 25–27   167
   I,V 7   304

4Q390   133
   I, 7–9   134
   II, 3–4   134

4Q181
   III   133

11Q13
   VI–VIII   133

Ascension of Isaiah
   9.10   304

2 Baruch
   14.1   143
   56.2   143
   78.1–7   132

1 Enoch
   93.1–10   143

4 Ezra
   11.1–12.39   132
   12.8   143
   13.39–47   132

Josephus, *Antiquitates judaicae*
   4.12   105
   10.37–39   258
   10.203–210   132
   10.269–276   132
   14.160   96
   14.247–248   96
   14.308   294
   17.269–284   135
   20.97–98   135
   20.169–171   135

Jubilees
   14.16   258

Liber antiquitatem biblicarum
   26.13   258

Philo, *De decalogo*
   33   240
   46   241–42

Philo, *De specialibus legibus*
   2.189   240

Philo, *De vita contemplativa*
   81   240

Philo, *In Flaccum*
39 240

Philo, *Quis rerum divinarum heres sit*
15 240

Psalms of Solomon
17.26–31 132
18.8 326

Seder Olam Rabbah
30 134

Testament of Benjamin
4.1 304
9.2 132

Testament of Levi
6 258–59
6.11 258
17.1–3 133
17.8 134

Testament of Naphtali
5.8 132

Testament of Moses
10.7–8 132

New Testament

Matthew
5:33–37 34
19:28 132
21:33–45 252
22:1–14 257
22:15–22 313
22:17b–21 313
23 260–61
23:2–3 259
23:29–30 259
23:29–38 256
23:29–39 .... 252, 259
24:3 143
24:36 144

24:43 114

Mark
8:27–29 135
12:1–9 .... 256, 258
12:1–12 252
12:13–17 .... 105, 313
13:32 144

Luke
1:41–42 43
1:67 43
2:25–32 43
2:35 285
5:22 285
6:8 285
6:30–36 29
7:1–9 48
7:1–10 29
8:3 29
9:47 285
11:49–51 .... 252, 258
12:13–21 29
12:39 .... 114, 143
13:34–35 .... 252, 258
20:20–26 313
21:20–21 135
22:24–25 29
22:26–28 29
22:30 132
24:47–48 42

John
1:19–23 135
11:11–12 181
11:23–24 136

Acts
1:1 28
1:8 42
1:22 42
2:11 43
2:16–21 41
2:17 40–42
2:17–18 42

2:18	40, 42	16:11	46
2:23	249	16:14–15	29
2:33	42	16:19–39	38
3:13–14	249	16:25	244
4:10	249	16:32	250
4:31	43	17	271
5:30	249	17:1–4	123, 251
6:1–7	123	17:1–9	29, 47, 63, 176, 251, 277
7:52	252, 256, 259	17:1–10	37–38, 271, 332
7:55–56	42	17:2	28–29, 46–47, 124
7:60	181	17:4	251
8:29	42	17:5–8	251
8:39	42	17:5	28
9:3–5	42	17:5–10	47, 271
9:10	42	17:6	2, 15, 317
9:10–16	42	17:7	250, 317
9:12	42–43	17:8	2, 15
9:15–16	42	17:9	28, 251
10:3	42	17:10–14	271
10:3–6	42	17:34	29
10:9–23	42	17:52	260
10:10	42	18:1–7	281
10:10–23	42	18:9	42, 250
10:17	42	18:9–19	43
10:19	42	18:19	250
10:39	249	19	332
10:46	43	19:6	43
11:4–17	42	20:22–23	42
11:5	42	20:32–35	29
11:12	42	20:34	295
11:15	42	21:11	43
11:28–30	42	21:39	6
12:9	42	22:6–10	42
13:4–14	29	22:12–21	42
13:27–28	249	22:14–16	42
13:36	181	22:17	42
14:1	250	22:17–23	43
15:5	28	23:11	43
16:6	250	24:23	42
16:6	250	24:26–27	29
16:6–7	42	26:7	132
16:6–8	43	26:19	42
16:6–10	43	26:12–18	42
16:7–9	42	26:12–23	42
16:9–10	42–43	27:23–24	43

Ancient Sources Index

Romans
- 1:8 — 237
- 1:9 — 280
- 1:16 — 6
- 2:16 — 285
- 2:17 — 304
- 2:19–20 — 285
- 3:1–2 — 6
- 6:16 — 51
- 6:18 — 51
- 7:6 — 297
- 8:3–7 — 297
- 8:11–12 — 297
- 8:23–25 — 137
- 8:29 — 297
- 9–11 — 252, 137–39
- 9:1–5 — 6
- 9:1–29 — 138
- 9:22–24 — 256
- 9:30–10:4 — 138
- 10:5–21 — 139
- 10:19 — 138, 140
- 11 — 263
- 11:1–10 — 139
- 11:3 — 252
- 11:11 — 140
- 11:11–32 — 139
- 11:16–18 — 6
- 11:25–26 — 139
- 11:25–30 — 256
- 11:26 — 140
- 13:11–12 — 142
- 15:17 — 304
- 16:1–3, 23 — 28

1 Corinthians
- 1–4 — 38
- 1:7 — 137
- 1:12 — 101
- 1:26 — 27
- 1:26–29 — 49
- 1:31 — 304
- 2:1–5 — 273
- 2:8 — 151, 252
- 3:1–2 — 160
- 3:4 — 101
- 4:11 — 295
- 4:12 — 295
- 6:1–2 — 27–28
- 6:7 — 27–28
- 7:22 — 48
- 7:31 — 31
- 7:32 — 253
- 7:39 — 181
- 9:20 — 256
- 9:24–25 — 303
- 9:25 — 30–31, 304
- 11:17–22 — 28
- 11:30 — 181
- 14:6–7 — 245
- 14:26 — 244
- 15:6 — 181
- 15:18 — 181
- 15:20 — 181
- 15:51 — 181

2 Corinthians
- 1:23 — 280
- 8:2 — 27, 251
- 10:17 — 304
- 11:4 — 280
- 11:9 — 295
- 11:16–12:10 — 38
- 11:30–33 — 34, 38
- 11:31 — 34
- 12:1–4 — 43
- 12:16 — 295
- 12:20–21 — 280
- 12:21 — 43

Galatians
- 1:6 — 280
- 1:10 — 253
- 1:16 — 43
- 2:2 — 43
- 2:4 — 285
- 2:15 — 251
- 3:28 — 49
- 4:9 — 160
- 5:5–6 — 297

5:16–26 297
6:7–8 297
6:14 304

Ephesians
5:19 244

Philippians
1:4 304
1:8 280
1:26 304
1:30 36, 37
2:7–8 49
2:15 296
3:3 304
3:20 137
4:1 303
4:15 251

Colossians
2:1 36

1 Thessalonians
1–3 273
1:1 152–53, 170, 257
1:1–10 48, 253, 273
1:2 153
1:2–3 154
1:2–5 254
1:2–19 254
1:3 27, 152–53, 158, 279
1:3–2:1 257
1:4 154
1:5 156, 160, 272, 279–80
1:5–6 25
1:6 25, 27, 157, 252–54, 261, 273, 277, 280
1:6–7 18, 156, 165
1:6–8 261
1:6–2:16 274
1:6–3:13 273
1:7 157, 274
1:7–8 253
1:8 36, 237–38, 240–41, 244–45, 273, 280

1:8–10 257
1:9 125, 273, 304
1:9–10 25, 157, 197, 240
1:10 144–45, 152, 158, 251, 253–54, 261
1:14–16 27
2:1 154, 165, 256, 273, 275, 279, 283, 305
2:1–2 165, 269
2:1–3 257
2:1–10 271
2:1–12 269–72, 274, 276, 278, 281–83, 305–6
2:1–17 269
2:1–3:10 273
2:2 36–38, 156, 158, 272, 275–78, 306
2:2–5 272
2:3 282–83
2:3–4 269
2:3–12 38
2:4 17, 156, 253, 275, 280, 283, 285, 306
2:5 34, 158, 163, 256, 272, 275–76, 280, 283
2:5–7 269
2:5–10 305
2:6 17, 164, 269, 276, 283
2:6–7 277
2:6–13 257
2:7 152, 163–65, 167, 283, 286–89, 306
2:7–8 269, 283, 306
2:8 164, 272, 278, 298, 305
2:8–9 156
2:9 27, 154, 165, 251, 272, 275, 278, 293, 332
2:9–12 283
2:10 275, 295
2:11 27, 152, 165, 167, 256, 272, 275, 280, 286–87, 290, 292
2:12 17, 25, 165, 272, 276, 292, 297, 299–300
2:13 253–54, 263, 272–73
2:13–16 250, 252, 254
2:14 17, 48, 154, 253–54, 261–62, 277, 280, 300

1 Thessalonians (cont.)

2:14–15	18, 57
2:14–16	48, 249–50, 253, 256–58, 263
2:15	48, 253, 255–61
2:15–16	249
2:16	48, 252–55, 257, 261
2:17	38, 48, 152, 154, 165–66, 263, 272, 280, 321
2:17–18	277
2:17–19	300
2:17–20	275
2:17–3:10	280, 321
2:18	281, 288
2:19	18, 30–31, 303, 305, 321
2:19–20	18, 279, 300
2:20	305
2:22	297
3:1	278, 281
3:1–5	275
3:2	156, 166
3:3	252–53, 280
3:3–4	27, 156
3:3–5	277
3:4	25, 37, 165, 272, 277
3:4–7	254
3:5	166, 280
3:6	154, 166, 272, 279–80
3:7	37, 154, 166, 276–77, 281
3:7–8	280
3:8	295
3:10	280, 293
3:11	152–53
3:13	18, 152–54, 254, 272, 296–97
4:1	17, 156, 282
4:1–2	165
4:2	156
4:3	24
4:3–8	24
4:3–12	25
4:7	280
4:7–8	297
4:8	280
4:9	154, 157, 272
4:9–10	156, 279
4:9–12	24, 332
4:10	154, 253, 272, 282
4:11	27, 28, 332
4:11–12	27
4:12	27
4:12–5:28	257
4:13	145, 154, 165, 272
4:13–15	181
4.13–18	24, 144
4:14	145, 169
4:15	142, 244, 273,
4:15–17	141–43, 333
4:16–18	251
4:17	142, 317
4:18	282
4:19	157
5:1	123, 143, 154, 272
5:1–2	105
5:1–3	143–44
5:1–9	333
5:2	114, 124, 143–44, 156
5:2–3	106
5:3	24, 93, 99, 102, 104, 109, 116, 317, 325–26, 329
5:4	114, 154
5:4–11	25
5:5	166, 293
5:5–9	257
5:6	280
5:8	317, 331
5:9	261, 280
5:9–10	158
5:10	142
5:11	272, 282
5:12	154, 165, 297
5:12–13	279
5:12–23	18
5:13	18
5:14	28, 154
5:15	18, 280
5:19–21	273
5:23	18, 24, 296–97
5:23–28	257
5:25	154
5:26	154
5:27	154, 282

2 Thessalonians

1:1–2	257
1:3	293
1:4–5	18, 25
1:5	17
1:9–10	18
1:10	18
1:11	17
1:12	18
1:14	18
2:1–3	333
2:2	106
2:8	317
3:6–13	28
3:7	18
3:8	27, 293
3:9	18

1 Timothy

6:12	36

2 Timothy

4:7	36
4:8	303

James

1:1	132
5:13	244

2 Peter

3:4	181

Revelation

13:1–3	132
17:7–14	132

Early Christian Literature

Ambrose, *Epistulae*

51	176

Barnabas

5.11	259

Basil, *Epistulae*

154	192
164	192
165	192

1 Clement

17.1	260

Clement, *Stromata*

6.5.127	260

Codex justinianus

1.1.1	176

Codex theodosianus

16.1.2	176
16.2.25	176

Digesta

27.4.1	109
34.3.5.2	109

Eusebius, *Vita Constantini*

4.43	192

Gospel of Peter

5.17	259

Ignatius, *To the Ephesians*

10.3	262

Ignatius, *To the Philadelphians*

5.2	260

Ignatius, *To the Romans*

6.3	262

Innocent I, *Epistulae*

1	192
18	192

John Chrysostom, *Homilies on 2 Corinthians*

11.1 [PG 51:301]	238

John Chrysostom, *Homilies on 1 Thessalonians*
  2 [PG 62:399]   238

Justin Martyr, *Dialogue with Trypho*
  16.1   261
  93.4   260
  95.4   260
  133.6   260
  136.2–3   260

Novellae Constitutiones
  11   176

Origin, *Commentarium series in evangelium Matthaei*
  10:18   257
  17:15   257

Polycarp, *To the Philippians*
  6.3   260
  8.2   262

Pseudo-Clement, *Homilies*
  11.20.5   262

Socrates, *Historia ecclesiastica*
  1.8.5   192
  1.13.12   192
  2.20.7–11   127
  5.6   192

Sozomen, *Historia ecclesiastica*
  7.4   192
  7.25.1–8   176

Tertullian, *Adversus Marcionem*
  5.15.2   258

Theodoret, *Historia ecclesiastica*
  5.17–18   176

Greco-Roman Literature

Achilles Tatius, *Leucippe et Clitophon*
  5.178.5   109

Aeschines, *In Ctesiphonem*
  240   302
  250   302

Anthologia graeca
  6.38   115
  6.90   115
  7.8   130
  7.370   130
  7.377   130
  11.176   115

Appian, *Bellum civile*
  1.10.87–88   106

Archilochus, *Fragmenta*
  114   116

Arrian, *Epicteti dissertationes*
  2.13.7   109

Aristonicus, *De signis Iliadis*
  4.307   262

Aristotle, *Politica*
  1253b   159
  1321b   109

Aulus Gellius, *Noctes atticae*
  11.3   107
  16.13   107

Cicero, *De amicitia*
  45   109
  47   109

Cicero, *De divinatione*
  2.41   107

Ancient Sources Index

Cicero, *De finibus*
5.23 — 109

Cicero, *De legibus*
2.28 — 107

Cicero, *De officiis*
1.69 — 109

Cicero, *De republica*
1.31 — 104

Cicero, *Epistulae ad Atticum*
136 [7.13].2 — 109
418 [16.8].2 — 109

Cicero, *In Pisonem*
3.6 — 290

Cicero, *Paradoxa Stoicorum*
16 — 109

Cicero, *Pro Milone*
3.9 — 115

Cicero, *Pro Rabirio Postumo*
10.27 — 290

Cicero, *Pro Sulla*
6 — 8

Cicero, *Tusculanae disputationes*
5.1 — 109
5.22 — 109

Demosthenes, *De corona*
92–92 — 304
173 — 303
197 — 303
265–266 — 302

Dinarchus, *In Demosthenem*
12–13 — 303
71 — 303
80–82 — 303

Dio Cassius, *Historia romana*
9 — 109
47.25.3 — 314
53.16.4 — 322
55.10.10 — 290

Dio Chrysostom, *Ad Alexandrinos* 275
7–12 — 270
9 — 275
11 — 276–77
11–12 — 270

Dio Chrysostom, *Borysthenitica*
17 — 277

Dio Chrysostom, *Celaenis Phrygiae*
2 — 277

Dio Chrysostom, *De exilio*
6 — 277
14 — 277
16 — 277
10–13 — 277
29–31 — 277

Dio Chrysostom, *De habitu* — 277

Dio Chrysostom, *De regno 1*
9, 15 — 277

Dio Chrysostom, *De regno 4*
4.15 — 158

Dio Chrysostom, *De servis* — 277

Dio Chrysostom, *De tryrannide*
60 — 277

Dio Chrysostom, *De virtute*
1 — 277
5 — 277
17 — 277

Dio Chrysostom, *In contione*
10 — 270

Dio Chrysostom, *Isthmiaca*
2   277

Dio Chrysostom, *Tarsica prior*
14   277

Dio Chrysostom, *Tarsica altera*
2   277

Diodorus Siculus, *Bibliotheca historica*
31.8.7–8   315

Diogenes Laertius, *Lives and Opinions of Eminent Philosophers*
8.1.14   129
10.65–66   129
10.124–25   145

Dionysius of Halicarnassus, *De Thucydide*
33   105

Epictetus, *Diatribai (Dissertationes)*
2   145
4.5.16–17   314

Euripides, *Hippolytus*
422   159

Florus, *Epitome de T. Livio Bellorum omnium annorum DCC Libri duo*
2.9.21   106

Frontinus, *Strategemata*
2.9.3   106

Historia Augusta
4.21   107

Homer, *Iliad*
7.445   116

Homer, *Odyssey*
4.561–569   128
6.739–751   128
11.90–94   128
11.204–244   128
11.486–492   128
11.601–604   128

Homerici hymni
22.4   116

Horace, *Carmen saeculare*
3.24.25–32   290
31   111
73–74   111

Horace, *Carmina*
3.4   107

Horace, *Epistulae*
2   107

Isocrates, *Nicocles*
3.23   159

Juvenal, *Satirae*
3.190–191   107
14.86–88   107

Livy, *Ab urbe condita*
6.22–28   106
7.12   106
29.5–11   315
42.1   106
45.18.3–7   315

Lucian, *De morte Peregrini*
13   270

Macrobius, *Saturnaliorum Libri Septem*
3.6   107

Martial, *Epigrammata*
10.30   107

Menander Rhetor, *Treatise*
2.369.17–370.10   7

Ancient Sources Index

Naevius, *Comedies*
22–26   107

Ovid, *Fasti*
2.127–128   290

Ovid, *Tristia*
2.574   290

Pausanias, *Hellados Periegesis*
9.29.1   116
10.4.1   7

Petronius, *The Satyricon*
117   34

Phaedrus, *Fabularum Aesopiarum libri quinque*
123   115

Philostratus, *Imagines*
2.13–14   116

Plato, *Critias*
113C–114   117

Plato, *Leges*
874B–C   115

Plato, *Phaedrus*
245e–247c   129

Plato, *Timaeus*
25D   217

Plautus, *Aulularia*
95–96   102

Plautus, *Captivi*
880–887   108

Pliny the Elder, *Naturalis historiae*
2.19.205   117
4.17   322
4.36   1

5.30   7
13.5   107
21.16   107

Pliny the Younger, *Epistulae*
3.9   108
5.45   107
8.24   272
10.96   244

Plutarch, *Alexander*
2   40, 330

Plutarch, *Antonius*
40.4   96
41.2–5   103

Plutarch, *Brutus*
46.1   8

Plutarch, *Caesar*
34.2   105

Plutarch, *Cato Minor*
58.1   105

Plutarch, *Cicero*
35.1–2   97
871.4–5   109

Plutarch, *Phocion*
4   109

Plutarch, *Pompeius*
15.3   97
55.4   97
76.6   97

Plutarch, *Solon*
31–32   117

Plutarch, *Sulla*
22   106

Ancient Sources Index

Plutarch, *Theseus*
34 116

Plutarch, *De adulatore et amico*
28 (69b–c) 270
28 (69c–d) 287

Plutarch, *De defectu oraculorum*
15 245
38 245
50 245

Plutarch, *De Pythiae oraculis*
6 245

Plutarch, *De Stoicorum repugnantiis*
8 (1061e) 109

Plutarch, *Fragmenta*
106 116

Plutarch, *Parallela minora*
41 (316a–b) 108

Plutarch, *Praecepta gerendae rei publicae*
20 (816a) 106

Plutarch, *Septem sapientium convivium*
11 (154d–f) 104

Pollux, *Onomasticon*
4.71–73 243

Polybius, *The Histories*
6.14.8–9 107
21.19.9 203

Propertius, *Elegiae*
2.3 107
2.3–4 108

Pseudo-Dionysius, *Ars rhetorica*
276 282

Pseudo-Libanius, *Epistulae* 282

Pseudo-Lucian, *Asinus*
49–50 242

Quintilian, *Institutio oratoria*
1.5.4–5 163

Sallust, *Bellum catalinae*
38.3 105
17.3.47 8

Sallust, *Bellum jugurthinum*
41.5 104

Seneca, *De clementia*
1.19.5–9 114
1.19.6 112

Seneca, *Epistulae morales*
5.1–3 278
10.19 50
47.10 49
47.11 49
71.23 34

Statius, *Silvae*
1.79–81 107
4.12–19 107

Strabo, *Geographica*
5.11 107–8
7.47 315

Strabo (Fragment)
C333 F18 244

Suetonius, *De grammaticis*
17 107

Suetonius, *Vitae caesarum*
Aug. 58.1–2 290
Aug. 72 107
Aug. 81 106
Tib. 63.1 107
Cal. 15.3 12
Claud. 11.2 12

Nero 6.25	314	16.2657	95
Dom. 8.2	107		

BMC Macedonia
Tacitus, *Annales*
 Thessalonica 117, §74 98
 15.44.4 252

Burstein, *The Hellenistic Age*
Tacitus, *Historiae*
 §72 4
 3.53
 §111 292
 106

Chaniotis, *Die Verträge zwischen kretisch-*
Thucydides, *The History of the Pelopon-* *en Poleis*
nesian War §60B 276
 2.74 106
 3.82.8 104 Chester Beaty Papyrus
 p⁴⁶ 257
Twelve Tables of Roman Law
 8.12 115 *CIG*
 2.2059 291
Valerius Maximus, *Factorum ac dictorum* 3.4000 164–65
memorabilium libri IX
 9.2.1 106–7 *CIJ*
 123 135
Vellius Paterculus, *Historia romana* 358 135–36
 2.26–27 106 418 136
 9.98.2 96 1300
 135
Virgil, *Georgica*
 3.407 115 *CIL*
 1.2.98 98
 Inscriptions and Papyri 3.14507 6
 4.576 102
Ascough, Harland, and Kloppenborg, *As-* 4.581 103
sociations in the Greco-Roman World 4.1080 101
 §41 291 4.3775 102
 §52 41 4.7863 102
 §314 291 4.7868 102
 §322 291 6.244 114
 14.2898 96
BE 14.2899 96
 1987: 432 225 14.2975 111

BGU *CIRB*
 4.1059 109 421 288
 4.1130 109
 8.1827 109

Daux, "Inscriptions de Delphes"
§27 299

EA
17 (1991), 53–54, no. 3 217

FD
2.2.248 299
3.1.152 295
3.1.362+4.354 295
3.1.465 296
3.2.33 . . . . 295, 299
3.2.92 299
3.2.250 299
3.3.218 299
3.3.226 299
3.3.349 299
3.3.383 295
3.4.22 299
3.4.24 299
3.4.132 295
3.4.183 295

Fontenrose, *Delphic oracle*
Q17, 76, 123 299
L93, 96, 109, 176 299
D34 299

IAnkyra
2.357 182

1Aph
12.920 299

IAssos
8 304

IBethShe'arim
127 135

IByzantion
S24 295

IC
IV 186 276

ICG
1379–80 182
2583 182
3033 199
3070 199
3091 210
3098 224
3099 224
3100 224
3101 191
3104 210
3105 224
3106 224
3107 224
3108 . . . . 221, 224
3111 . . . . 220, 224
3113 . . . . 221, 224
3114 . . . . 191, 221, 224
3115 222–23
3116 . . . . 211, 224
3117 211
3119 211
3120 211
3121 . . . . 211, 224
3122 217
3123 217
3124 . . . . 215, 217
3125 217
3126 217
3127 217
3128 216–17
3131 . . . . 179, 187
3132 179–80
3134 182–83
3135 182–83
3137 181
3138 182
3140 184
3141 184
3142 184–85
3144 187
3145 187
3146 187
3147 204
3147 178

3148	178, 199	3201	203–4
3149	178, 189, 195	3203	204
3150	189	3204	204
3151–55	178, 195	3205	204
3152	193	3206	204
3154	193	3210	204
3155	190, 220	3212	204
3156	179	3214	195
3157	179	3215	202
3158	189	3218	184, 205
3159	189	3219	184, 205
3160	189	3220	204
3161	189, 195	3223	205
3162	189	3224	193, 202
3163	190	3225	197, 207–8
3164	190	3226	194
3165	190	3620	207
3169	194	3632	198
3170	194	3633	189
3171	194, 202–3	3672	202
3172	194	3674	195
3173	194–95	3675	198
3175	190, 194	3677	193
3177	196	3678	198
3179	196	3679	204
3180	196	3680	198
3181	196	3683	198
3183	198	3684	198
3184	197	3685	199
3185	197	3686	205
3186	195, 199–200	3690	204
3187	199–200	3691	204
3188	197	3692	204
3189	199, 201–2	3694	189
3190	202	3709	182
3191	195, 197		
3192	197	IDelph	
3193	198	4.65	299
3194	198	4.95	299
3195	198		
3196	199, 201–2	IEph	
3197	200, 202	1a 22	7
3198	195	1a 25	50
3199	195	2.403	9
3200	202–3	6.2217D	179

IEph (cont.)		10.2.1.32	14
6.2269A	288	10.2.1.33	14, 194
		10.2.1.34	10
IG		10.2.1.36	10
2s.141	295	10.2.1.37	20
2.1130	107	10.2.1.38	10, 36, 242
2.1132	107	10.2.1.42	224
2.1134	107	10.2.1.43	224
2.2.1043	298	10.2.1.46	191
2.2.1340	296	10.2.1.48	20–21, 26
2.2.12563	288	10.2.1.51	20
2.2.1.3754	297	10.2.1.53	20
2.2.5592	288	10.2.1.56	24
4.2.1.83	297	10.2.1.58	26, 155
4.2.3.1300	182	10.2.1.59	20, 24
5.1.139	295	10.2.1.61	10
5.1.516	295	10.2.1.62	23
5.1.583	295	10.2.1.64	20
6.1.2646	6	10.2.1.67	20, 40, 47
7.219	299	10.2.1.67–72	47
7.4247	99	10.2.1.68	26, 155
7.6.2.592	295	10.2.1.69	155
7.7.53	276	10.2.1.70	26, 155
7.7.234	276	10.2.1.72	47
9.7.54	297	10.2.1.73	20
9.7.394	297	10.2.1.75–80	20
9.7.399	297	10.2.1.75–123	20
9.7.400	297	10.2.1.77–80	20
10.2.1.1	3, 324	10.2.1.82	20, 40, 42
10.2.1.2	3	10.2.1.83	8
10.2.1.3	3, 16–17, 20	10.2.1.85	20
10.2.1.4	13, 14	10.2.1.87	20
10.2.1.5	2	10.2.1.88	20, 40
10.2.1.6	1, 7, 322	10.2.1.90	20
10.2.1.7	15	10.2.1.92–93	20
10.2.1.13	20	10.2.1.97	21
10.2.1.14	15	10.2.1.97–98	20
10.2.1.15	10, 20, 290	10.2.1.99	20, 40
10.2.1.16	20, 155	10.2.1.100	20, 22
10.2.1.19	10–11, 20	10.2.1.102	11
10.2.1.23	210	10.2.1.107	21
10.2.1.25	3	10.2.1.107–9	21
10.2.1.28	24	10.2.1.109	8
10.2.1.29	8	10.2.1.111	21
10.2.1.31	9–10, 14, 18, 321	10.2.1.114	20

10.2.1.120	40	10.2.1.333	198
10.2.1.126	15	10.2.1.334	197
10.2.1.130	10	10.2.1.337	202
10.2.1.131	10	10.2.1.338	196
10.2.1.133	14–15, 19	10.2.1.350	199
10.2.1.134	6	10.2.1.351	182
10.2.1.135	7, 15	10.2.1.353	197
10.2.1.137	15, 32	10.2.1.352	202
10.2.1.138	10	10.2.1.358	205, 208
10.2.1.138–39	11	10.2.1.359	194
10.2.1.141	11	10.2.1.*364	197
10.2.1.152	15	10.2.1.*365	189
10.2.1.154	15	10.2.1.374	196
10.2.1.155–56	15	10.2.1.397	184
10.2.1.160	15	10.2.1.398	204
10.2.1.162–63	15	10.2.1.403	50
10.2.1.163	15	10.2.1.406	204
10.2.1.164	7	10.2.1.431	179
10.2.1.165	10, 50	10.2.1.436	35
10.2.1.167	10, 50	10.2.1.459	179
10.2.1.173	297	10.2.1.476	50
10.2.1.175	30–31	10.2.1.506	26
10.2.1.177	150	10.2.1.541	30–31
10.2.1.199	23	10.2.1.550	34
10.2.1.206	26	10.2.1.551	182
10.2.1.215	216	10.2.1.607	182
10.2.1.221–22	20	10.2.1.623	296
10.2.1.231	50	10.2.1.633	198
10.2.1.244	20	10.2.1.653	189
10.2.1.254	20–21	10.2.1.674	193
10.2.1.254–59	20	10.2.1.679	155
10.2.1.255	26	10.1.1.692	296
10.2.1.257	23	10.2.1.701	48
10.2.1.259	24, 26, 155	10.2.1.739	31–32
10.2.1.260	26	10.2.1.*775	205
10.2.1.270	20	10.2.1.*776	204
10.2.1.275	19	10.2.1.*780	189
10.2.1.276	19	10.2.1.*781	194
10.2.1.278	19	10.2.1.*782	197
10.2.1.280	224	10.2.1.*783	198
10.2.1.*281	210	10.2.1.*784	196
10.2.1.292	26	10.2.1.*785	202
10.2.1.303	24	10.2.1.*786	204
10.2.1.306	24, 32		
10.2.1.331	193		

Ancient Sources Index

IG (cont.)

10.2.1.*787	196	10.2.1s.1074	10, 35
10.2.1.*788	195	10.2.1s.1074–75	7, 15
10.2.1.*790	189	10.2.1s.1075	10, 23, 35
10.2.1.*792	194	10.2.1s.1076	35
10.2.1.*793	189	10.2.1s.1107	115
10.2.1.*794	195	10.2.1s.1164	49
10.2.1.*795	196	10.2.1s.1192	33
10.2.1.*797A	204	10.2.1s.1198	48
10.2.1.*798	204	10.2.1s.1206	48
10.2.1.*799A	194	10.2.1s.1217	23
10.2.1.*799B	194	10.2.1s.1255	16
10.2.1.*800B	204	10.2.1s.1263	32
10.2.1.*804	193	10.2.1s.1287	32
10.2.1.821	20	10.2.1s.1273	115
10.2.1.971	21	10.2.1s.1299	48
10.2.1.*931	180	10.2.1s.1363	16
10.2.1.933	19	10.2.1s.1368	21
10.2.1.959	204	10.2.1s.1372	115
10.2.1.*996	205	10.2.1s.1386	36
10.2.1.998	195	10.2.1s.1392	51
10.2.1.1023	6	10.2.1s.1396	51
10.2.1.1031	6	10.2.1s.1472	16
10.2.2.96	296	10.2.1s.*1490	204
10.2.3.31	294	10.2.1s.*1491	204
11.4.1050	108	10.2.1s.*1493	194
12.2.505	262	10.2.1s.1496	198
12.3.910	295	10.2.1s.1498	202
12.5.338	297	10.2.1s.1501	189
12.5.860	294	10.2.1s.1503	199
12.7.372	296	10.2.1s.1504	198
12.8.195	330	10.2.1s.1505	198
12.8.381B	11	10.2.1s.1506	199
12.9.1240	179	10.2.1s.1507	202
10.2.1s.1042	16	10.2.1s.1508	205
10.2.1s.1045	16–17	10.2.1s.1511	202
10.2.1s.1047	15	10.2.1s.1512	193
10.2.1s.1054	47	10.2.1s.1515	197
10.2.1s.1058	24	10.2.1s.1516	26, 32
10.2.1s.1059	15	10.2.1s.1520	198
10.2.1s.1060	10, 18	10.2.1s.1521	198
10.2.1s.1063	15	10.2.1s.1523	195
10.2.1s.1072	35	10.2.1s.*1525	205
10.2.1s.1073	10	10.2.1s.1527	26
10.2.1s.1073–75	35	10.2.1s.1532	26
		10.2.1s.*1532	198

Ancient Sources Index

10.2.1s.*1533	190	IMakedChr	
10.2.1s.*1534	199	25	199
10.2.1s.*1535	204	60	199
10.2.1s.*1537	204	81	210
10.2.1s.*1543	194	88	224
10.2.1s.*1546	204	89	224
10.2.1s.1556	204	90	224
10.2.1s.1579	16	91	191
12s.1013	288	94	210
		95	224
IGBulg		96	224
1.2.390	296	97	224
3.2.1741	296	98	221, 224
5.5217	296	100	220, 224
		102A	221, 224
IIasos		102B	191, 221, 224
2	104	103A	223
123	297	103B	222
		103C	223
IItalia		104	211, 224
13.2, 17	107	105	211
		107	211
IJO 1		108	211
13–18	44	109	211, 224
Mac13	44–45	110	215–16
Mac 13	45	110, I	217
Mac 15	45–46	110, II	217
Mac 16	46	110, III	217
Mac17	45	110, IV	217
Mac 18	46, 179	110, V	217
		110, VI	217
IKilikiaBM		110, VII	217
2.201	154	113	179, 187
		114	179–80
IKorinthMeritt		116	182–83
§19	11	117	182–83
		119	181
ILindos		120	182
2.441	297	122	184
		123	184
IMagnMai		124	184–85
15a	297	125	184
113	284	126	187
		126 bis	187
		127	187

IG (cont.)		177		195
128	204	178		195
128–130A	178	179		202–3
129	199	180		203–4
130A	189, 195	182		204
130B	189	183		204
131–135	178, 195	184		204
132	193	185		204
134	193	189		204
135	190, 220	191		204
136	179	193		195
137	179	194		202
138	189	197		184, 205
139	189	198		184, 205
140	189	199		204
141	189, 195	202		205
142	189	203		193, 202
143	190	204		197, 207–8
144	190	205		194
145	190			
149	194	IMylasa		
150	194	101		295
151	194, 202–3	411		297
152	194	419		298
153	194–95			
155	190, 194	IPriene		
156	196	19.18–20		103
158	196			
159	196	ISmyrna		
160	196	67		379
162	198	440		246
163	197			
164	197	IStratonikeia		
165	195, 199–200	203		293
166	199–200	205		293
167	197	244		293
168	199, 201–2	245		293
169	202	246		293
170	195, 197	247		293
171	197	311		293
172	198	312		293
173	198	345		293
174	198	1205		296
175	199, 201–2			
176	200, 202			

IT

4	326
31	326
32	324–25
33	325
132	324
133	324

IThess

1.10A	32
1.10B	32
1.164–65	115
3.6	32
248	32

Kephalaio 3.7 16

T8	108
T9	108
T23	6
T25	6
T31	6
T39	6
T40	33, 37
T41	33
T50	31
T51	31
T59	8

Jaffé, *Regesta pontificum Romanorum*
§1497
§1683
§1723
§1847
§1921

Janko, "The Derveni Papyrus" 243

cols. I–IV	39
col. V	39
cols. VII–XIV	39
col. XX	39
cols. XXI–XXVI	39

Judge, "The Eulogistic Inscriptions"

179B11	290

KFF

48	288

Lemerle, *Les plus anciens recueils* 1
§50, 107–8	208

Miller, *Arete*
§132	304

MM
447	165

MRR
1.566	7

NewDocs 8 (1998)
8	47
156–68	188

NewDocs 3 (1986)
6	381

O.Claud.
1.2	109

OGI
194	292
613	95

Petrakos, *Ho dēmos tou Ramnountos*
§179	294

*PIR*¹
327	23
1501	12
1544–55	19
1563	11, 18
1564	12
1566	12
1567–71	12
1572	12
1573–75	12
1581–85	12
1587	12
1588	12

PIR¹ (cont.)
    1604–6A   12

Pirenne-Delforge, "Qui est la Kourotrophos,"
    181   160

Preuner, *Hermes* 55, 1920
    184–87   288

PSI
    14.1373   257

Res gest. divi Aug.
    34   322
    35.1   290

Reynolds, *Aphrodisias and Rome*
    §8   294
    §10   293
    §12   294
    §14   299
    §30   285–86
    §36   293

Robert, *Les gladiateurs dans l'orient grec*
    §12   32
    §13   31
    §14   32
    §34   33

Robert, *Opera Minores*
    3.1587, no. 53   11

Robert, *Inscriptions Grecques*
    §90   179

SEG
    12.231   288
    22.111   298
    25.134   298
    31.1116   182
    31.1118   182
    32.653   189
    32.825   295
    33.555   205
    35.59   276
    36.552[1]   100
    37.621   296
    42.625   26, 155
    42.627   202
    46.1565   95, 326
    47.964   224
    47.965   224
    47.995   210
    47.966   224
    47.998   204
    47.1012   204
    47.1075   288
    50.542   100
    51.641   262
    52.642   189
    51.724   100
    51.898   195
    51.899   198
    51.1115   100
    52.640   193
    55.716   198
    56.648   108
    57.521   100
    58.655   198
    59.1207   100, 108
    60.601   107
    60.985   108

Segre and Carratelli, "Tituli Camirenses"
    §158   297

SIG
    711K   299
    737   299
    807   294

Syll²
    534   295
    534B   295
    672   295

TAM
    2.1183   276

3.1.596	179	*RPC* 1	
5.2.953	285	25	98
		280	321
Coins		297	324
		298	11–12, 319
AMNG	315	1427	319
3.2.41		1551	8, 103, 322–23
		1552	318, 324
ANS		1553	324–25
798–99	115	1554	318–20
		1555	318–20
BMC		1563	319
5.61	318	2143	325
Macedonia 108–14, nos. 1–57	72	2912	325
Macedonia 111.22	115	2928	325
Macedonia, Thessalonica, 117, §74	98	5421	318–20

Head, *Greek Coins in the British Museum: Attica, Megaris, Aegina*

RPC 2

5.115	318	327	331
		328	331
		330	332

RIC 1

Claudius §§5–6	328	SNG Ashmolean	
Claudius §§9–10	327	3300	316
Claudius §§15–16	327	3301	316
Claudius §16	329		
Claudius §§21–22	327	SNG Copenhagen	
Claudius §§27–28	327	372	115
Claudius §§38–39	327		
Claudius §§46–47	327		
Claudius §§51–52	327		
Claudius §§57–58	327		
Claudius §§61–62	327		
Claudius §96	329		
Nero §§73–82	314		
Nero §§121–23	314		
Nero §§205–12	314		
Nero §380	314		
Nero §§380–81	314		
Nero §§384–85	314		
Nero §§414–17	314		
Nero §433	114		
Nero §§451–55	314		
Galba §§665–67	98		

Modern Authors Index

Aasgaard, Reidar 167, 171
Abbott, Frank Frost 323, 333
Adam-Velini, Polyxeni 2, 4, 19, 32, 35–36, 53, 82, 86–87, 242
Adams, Charles D. 302, 306
Agnoli, Nadia 110, 112, 117
Ahmadi, Amir 39, 53
Allamani-Souri, Victoria 69, 71, 73, 76
Allison, Dale C. 34, 43, 53, 259, 264
Amandry, Michel 11, 321
Ando, Clifford 117
Ascough, Richard S. 25–27, 41, 44, 53, 115, 119, 130, 146, 154, 165, 169, 171, 176, 226, 237, 239, 246, 291, 306, 332, 333
Athanasiou, Fani 177–78, 226
Aune, David E. 280, 282, 307, 311
Avadiah, Asher 44, 53
Baarda, Tjitze 252, 264
Babbitt, Frank Cole 287, 307
Bakalakis, G. 78, 87
Bakirtzis, Charalambos 4, 95, 120, 155, 169, 171–73, 176–78, 209–14, 218–23, 226–27, 231–32
Bammel, Ernst 93, 117–18, 125, 146, 325, 333
Barclay, John M. G. 24, 53, 64–65, 85, 87, 255–56, 258–59, 264
Barnett, Paul 43, 53
Barney, Stephen A. 328, 334
Baronowski, Donald W. 108, 118, 220
Barton, Carlin A. 34, 53
Bash, Anthony 16, 53
Bauer, Franz A. 208–9, 227
Bauman, Richard A. 107, 118

Baur, Ferdinand C. 250, 264
Beach, Jennifer A. 334
Beale, G. K. 238, 246, 269, 285, 307, 331, 337
Beard, Mary 64, 67–68, 75, 84, 87
Beazley, John D. 288, 307
Beckwith, Roger T. 133, 146
Behrmann, Ingrid 1, 54
Belamarić, Josip 177, 234
Belenes, Giorgos 242, 246
Bell, Richard 138, 146
Berghof, Oliver 334
Berkley, Timothy 138, 146
Berner, Christoph 134, 146
Bernett, Monika 67, 87
Best, Ernest 123–24, 146, 239, 246
Betegh, Gábor 39–40, 53, 243, 246
Beutler, Johannes 158, 160, 172, 271–73, 275, 309, 311
Bhatt, Shreyaa 114, 118
Bird, Michael F. 94, 118, 137, 149
Black, C. Clifton 153, 173
Blanton IV, Thomas R. 163, 172
Bloomquist, L. Gregory 7, 59
Blum, Matthias 261, 265
Bockmuehl, Markus A. 254–55, 264
Boer, Willem den 67, 88
Bokern, Annabel 101, 121
Bolder-Boos, Marion 121
Bolton, David J. 254, 256
Bonnekoh, Pamela 178, 184, 186, 227
Borgnet, Augustin 328, 337
Borman, Lukas 2, 259, 266
Böttrich, Christfried 256, 264
Bowersock, G. W. 68, 88

Bowyer, Carolyn Susan	239, 246	Chaniotis, Angelos	276, 307
Brändl, Martin	30, 53	Chankowski, Andrzej S.	71, 91
Brant, Jo-Ann A.	261, 264	Chapa, Juan	274, 307
Breitenbach, Alfred	327, 334	Cho, Jae-Kyung	274, 307
Brémond, Émile	159, 172	Clark, Wesley P.	291, 307
Brenk, Beat	210, 212, 217, 219, 227	Clarke, Edward Daniel	81, 87
Breytenbach, Cilliers	1, 54, 180, 182, 186–87, 190, 205, 207, 228–29, 231	Clemen, Karl	251, 264
		Clivaz, Claire	44, 58
Bridges, Linda M.	305, 307	Cohoon, James W.	275, 307
Briones, David E.	49, 54	Collins, Raymond F.	251, 264
Brocke, Christoph vom	2, 4, 23–24, 44, 47, 54, 78, 87, 94, 118, 124, 126, 146, 176, 227, 262–63, 264	Collins, Rob P.	144, 273, 307, 309, 325, 336
		Concannon, Cavan	3, 54
Brodd, Jeffrey	94, 119	Contessa, Anreina	251–52, 264
Broneer, Oscar	30, 54	Cooley, Alison E.	97, 118, 290, 307
Brooke, Christopher	314, 334	Cormack, Robin S.	210–11, 221, 227
Brookins, Timothy A.	28, 49, 54, 281, 307	Coulot, Claude	277, 307
		Crawford, Michael H.	314, 334
Bruce, F. F.	37, 41, 54, 238, 246, 270, 307	Creaghan, John S.	181, 195–96, 227
		Crosby, H. Lamar	275, 307
Brunt, Peter A.	322, 334	Crossan, John	110, 118
Buis, Emiliano J.	100, 114, 118	Crüsemann, Marlene	253–54, 259, 264
Bullard, Collin	285, 307	Ćurčić, Slobodan	178, 205, 212, 225, 227
Bülow, Gerda von	177, 229		
Burke, Trevor J.	154, 164–65, 172	Damaskos, Dēmētrēs	76, 90
Burnett, Andrew	11–12, 71	Danker, Frederick	286, 308
Burnett, D. Clint	63, 69, 72, 75, 81, 83, 85, 87	Dasen, Véronique	160, 172
		Dassmann, Ernst	207, 233
Burrell, Barbara	7, 54	Daux, Georges	79, 87, 299, 308
Burstein, Stanley M.	4, 54, 59, 292, 307	Davies, William D.	34, 54, 259, 264
Burton, Ernest DeWitt	15, 54	Deissmann, Adolf	66–67, 87
Cadwallader, Alan H.	31, 48, 54, 105, 118	Delehaye, Hyppolite	208–9, 227
		DeSilva, David A.	259, 264
Caillet, Jean-Pierre	209, 233	Despinis, G.	78–79, 88
Calhoun, Robert Matthew	163, 172	Destephen, Sylvain	233
Cambi, Nenad	177, 234	Dibelius, Martin	260, 264, 269, 308
Campbell, R. Alastair	46, 54	Diehl, Charles	210, 227
Canavan, Rosemary	51, 287	Diggle, James	159, 172
Carratelli, Giovanni Pugliese	297, 311	Dillon, John Noël	68, 89
Carson, Donald A.	285, 331, 337	Dillon, Michael	116, 118
Carter, Michael	33, 54	Dindorfius, Guilielmus	244, 246
Cary, Earnest	314, 334	Dmitriev, Sviatoslav	103, 118
Casey, Thomas G.	254, 266	Dobschütz, Ernst von	239, 246, 308
Caskey, Lacey D.	288, 307	Döderlein, Ludwig	328, 334
Cecconi, Leonardo	111, 118	Dodson, Joseph R.	49, 54, 274

Dölger, Franz J. 181, 227
Donaldson, Terence L. 140, 146
Donfried, Karl P. 24, 55, 63–64, 84, 88, 158, 160, 172, 269, 271–73, 275, 308–9, 311, 325, 331, 334
Donlan, Walter 59
Drossoyianni, Ph. A. 220, 227
Duchesne, Louis 192, 227
Dumesnil, M. Jean-Baptiste Gardin 328, 334
Dumézil, Bruno 233
Dunn, Geoffrey D. 192, 229
Duve, Thomas 100, 118
Eastmond, Antony 210, 212, 219, 225, 227, 232, 234
Ebner, Martin 130, 146
Eder, Walter 50, 55
Edson, Charles 20, 22, 55, 64, 73, 74, 88, 178, 330, 334
Eisen, Ute E. 190, 229
Eleutheriadou, Kyriake 193, 229
Engemann, Josef 207, 233
Errington, Malcolm 276, 308
Erskine, Andrew 70, 88
Evans, Ernest 258, 265
Exner, Matthias 223, 229
Fabris, Rinaldo 238, 246
Falls, Thomas B. 260, 265
Fears, J. Rufus 84–85, 88
Fee, Gordon 239, 246, 269–70, 308
Feissel, Denis 44, 55, 178, 180, 183, 187, 200–201, 203, 210, 221, 229
Ferrua, A. 221
Février, P.-A. 221
Flashar, Helmut 261, 265
Flexsenhar, Michael A., III 49, 51, 55
Fishwick, Duncan 67, 88, 328, 334
Fontenrose, Joseph 299, 308
Forbes, Christopher 43, 55
Forsythe, Gary 104, 119
Foster, Herbert B. 334
Fourlas, Benjamin 210, 221–22, 229
Frame, James Everett 239–40, 246, 269, 308
Francese, Christopher 98, 118, 227

Franke, Peter R. 325, 334
Freund, Gerhard 160, 173
Friesen, Steven J. 4, 7, 55, 95, 120, 155, 169, 171–73, 176–78, 209, 222, 226–27, 231–32
Fujii, Takashi 67, 88
Gabrielson, Jeremy 94, 118
Gaebler, Hugo 317–18, 334
Galinsky, Karl 94, 119
Gargola, Daniel J. 107, 119
Gaventa, Beverly 37, 55, 270–71, 281, 287, 289, 308
Gempf, Conrad 15, 56, 323, 335
Genkova, Denista 316, 336
Gerlach, Gudrun 130, 146
Giannou, Triantafyllia 243, 246
Gill, David W. J. 15, 29, 56, 323, 335
Gillard, Frank 254, 265
Goceva, Zlatozara 33–34, 55
Goetz, Georg 327, 334
Goldsworthy, Adrian Keith 81, 88
Gooder, Paula 43, 55
Goodman, Martin 255, 265
Goodrich, John K. 16, 55
Gorman, Michael J. 96, 119
Gosset, J. M. 328, 334
Gounaris, Georgios 186–87, 229
Gowler, David B. 7, 59
Grabar, André 212–13, 229
Gradel, Ittai 67, 72, 88
Graham, A. J. 104, 119
Gramenos, Dēmētrios V. 2, 5, 35, 53, 69, 86
Grant, Michael 85, 88, 317, 334
Green, Gene L. 69, 88, 238, 247, 274, 284, 308, 323, 334
Greenslade, Stanley L. 192, 229
Grégoire, Henri 199, 229
Grether, Gertrude 11, 55
Gschnitzer, Fritz 262, 265
Gummere, Richard M., 278, 308
Gupta, Nijay K. 94, 119
Gutierrez, Pedro 291–92, 296, 298, 300, 308
Habicht, Christian 67–68, 70, 72, 88–89

Haddad, Najeeb 24, 55
Hadjitryphonos, Evangelia 177, 229
Halliwell, Stephen 261, 265
Hanson, John S. 42, 55
Hardin, Justin K. 48, 55, 332, 334
Harding, Mark 94, 121
Hardy, David 69, 85
Harland, Philip A. 26–27, 41, 53, 291, 308
Harrill, Albert 94, 116
Harrison, James R. 10, 16–17, 24, 30–32, 34, 43, 51, 55–56, 64, 67, 80, 89, 93–94, 119, 127–28, 146, 282, 284, 290, 301, 303, 308–9, 317–18, 321–22, 326–27, 335
Hatzaki, Myrto 210, 212, 219, 225, 227, 232, 234
Haufe, Günter 238, 247
Hay, David M. 240, 247
Hays, Richard 137, 146
Head, Barclay V. 318, 335
Heilig, Christoph 94, 119, 137, 149
Helly, Bruno 321, 335
Hemberg, Bengt 331, 335
Hendrix, Holland Lee 5, 7–8, 10, 13–14, 19, 56, 66, 68–73, 75, 78–80, 82, 85, 88, 93, 119, 321, 323–24, 326, 335
Herzer, Jens 256, 264
Hewitt, J. Thomas 137, 149
Heuchert, Volker 71, 89
Hilhorst, Antonius 134, 147
Hill, Judith L. 280, 309
Hinnels, John R. 22, 55
Hock, Ronald F. 27, 56, 295, 309, 332, 335
Holtz, Traugott 124, 146, 239, 247, 271, 300, 309
Hoppe, Rudolph 124, 143, 147, 256, 265
Horsley, Greg H. R. 15, 47, 56, 323–24, 335
Horsley, Richard A. 93–94, 119, 323, 324
Horst, Pieter W. van der 135–36, 147
House, Paul R. 138, 149
Howgego, Christopher 71, 314, 318, 335
Hude, Karl 104, 119

Hughes, Frank W. 273–74, 309
Huizenga, Annette Bourland 162–62, 172
Hullinger, Jerry M. 30, 56,
Hurst, David 164, 171
Inglebert, Hervé 233
Iossif, Panagiotis P. 71, 91
Jaffé, Philipp 191, 230
Janko, Richard 39, 56, 243, 247
Jantsch, Torsten 255, 265
Jeal, Roy R. 151, 172
Jewett, Robert 23, 28, 56–57, 73–74, 89, 123, 125, 127, 147, 273, 279, 309, 323, 331, 335
Johnson-DeBaufre, Melanie 263, 265
Johnson, Luke T. 42, 57
Joshel, Sandra R. 332, 335
Judge, Edwin A. 34, 57, 290, 309
Jung, UnChan 27, 57, 127, 147
Kampling, Rainer 261, 265
Kantiréa, Maria 67, 89
Karadedos, George 76, 89
Karanastasē, Paulina 76, 90
Katsari, Constantina 10, 57
Keener, Craig S. 7, 42–43, 57
Kennedy, George A. 282, 309
Kern, Philip H. 282, 309
Kim, Seyoon 139, 143, 147, 275, 280, 309
Kitzinger, Rachel 85, 88
Kleinbauer, W. Eugene 211–13, 218–20, 227, 230
Kloppenborg, John S. 24, 26–27, 41, 53, 57, 115, 119, 291
Klose, Dietrich O. 324, 335
Kneppe, Alfred 98, 118, 126, 128, 147
Knibb, Michael A. 134, 147
Knox, John 176, 230
Koester, Hëlmut 2, 4, 24, 57, 66, 71, 80, 89, 93, 95, 119–20, 147, 176, 230, 325, 336
Kogman-Appel, Katrin 252, 264
Kooten, George H. van 255, 265
Korhonen, Kalle 101, 121
Koukouvou, Angeliki 4, 57

Kouremenos, Theokritos 38, 57, 243, 247
Kourkoutidou-Nikolaidou, Eutychia 207, 210, 212–13, 220–23, 227, 230
Kraft, Konrad 322, 336
Kraus, Wolfgang 141, 148
Kremydi-Sicilianou, Sophia 71, 80, 89
Krentz, Edgar 275, 309
Krmnicek, Stefan 121
Kuhn, Karl Allen 29, 58
Kunnert, Ursula 262, 265
Labahn, Michal 128, 147
Labuschagne, Casper J. 134, 147
Laks, André 243, 247
Lambrecht, Jan 272, 309
Lamp, Jeffrey S. 258–59
Lampe, Peter 237, 265
Lane Fox, Robert J. 76, 90
Laourdas, Basil 4, 62
Laubscher, Hans P. 177, 230
Lefebvre, Ludovic 5, 58
Légasse, Simon 269, 301, 304, 309
Lehtipuu, Outi 128, 147
Lemerle, Paul 78, 89, 191, 208–9, 230
Le Quien, Michel 191, 230
Le Tourneau, Marcel 210, 228
Levinskaya, Irina 44–47, 58, 124, 147
Lewis, Naphtali 42, 58
Lewis, Wendy J. 334
Liefeld, Walter L. 277–79, 310
Lifshitz, Baruch 45, 58
Lightfoot, J. B. 238, 240, 247
Lindemann, Andreas 141, 147
Lindsay, Wallace M. 327, 336
Llewelyn, Stephen R. 47, 58
Loenertz, Raymond-Joseph 222, 230
Lohmann, Hans 262, 266
Lola, Zoe 76, 77
Long, Cynthia 94, 119
Longenecker, Bruce W. 28, 58
Lorber, Catharine C. 71, 91
Lowe, Matthew F. 94, 119
Luciano, Franco 50, 58
Luckensmeyer, David 94, 114, 120, 254–55, 262, 265, 331, 336

Lünemann, Gottlieb 239–40, 247
Luz, Ulrich 259, 266
Lynch, Tosca A. C. 242, 248
Lyons, George 270, 310
Mackinder, David 42, 61
MacMullen, Ramsay 332, 336
Maier, Harry O. 153, 172
Maikidou-Poutrino, Dafni 20–21, 58
Makaronas, Ch. 4, 62
Makropoulou, Despoina 205, 207, 230
Malherbe, Abraham J. 37, 58, 63, 90, 96, 120, 141, 147, 159, 167, 172, 238, 240, 244, 247, 269, 270, 271–73, 281, 289, 305, 310
Marasović, Tomislav 177, 234
Marguerat, Daniel 44, 58
Marki, Efterpi 184, 186–87, 192, 205, 207–8, 230–31
Marshall, I. Howard 42, 58
Marshall, Jonathan 29, 58
Martin, Dale B. 50–51, 58
Martínez, Florentino García 134, 147
Maschek, Dominik 121
Masson, Charles 37, 58, 304, 310
Mastora, Pelli 212, 218, 227
Mathieu, Georges 159, 172
Matlock, R. Barry 3, 54
Mavropoulou-Tsioumi, Chrysanthi 186, 210, 212–13, 220–23, 227, 231
Mazurek, Lindsey A. 4, 59
McConville, J. Gordon 138, 147
McKnight, Scot 94, 118
McNeel, Jennifer 163, 172, 287, 310
Mentzos, Aristoteles 177, 231
Meshorer, Ya'akov 314, 336
Meyer, Ben F. 68, 87
Meyer, Mati 252, 264
Michaelides, Demetrios 209, 227
Migeotte, Léopold 108, 120
Míguez, Néstor O. 16, 27, 59, 94, 120, 127, 147
Mimouni, Simon C. 44, 58
Miller, Stephen G. 304, 310
Mitchell, Margaret M. 101, 120, 238, 247, 291

Mitchell, Stephen	10, 57,	Panayotov, Alexander	44, 47, 59
Moatti, Claudia	108, 120	Papazoglou, Fanoula	176, 232
Modica, Joseph B.	94, 118	Papazarkadas, Nikolaos	50, 58
Moloney, Francis J.	144, 147	Pappas, Stephanie	101, 120
Moo, Douglas	139, 148	Parássoglou, George M.	38, 243
Moore, John M.	322, 334	Paton, W. R.	130, 148
Morey, C. R.	222, 231	Pearson, Birger A.	89, 93, 119, 252, 266, 321, 335
Morris, Leon	238, 247, 269		
Most, Glenn W.	243, 247	Pelekanidis, Stylianos	184, 186, 232
Moule, C. F. D.	93, 118, 167, 172	Pelekanidou, Elli S.	208, 232
Moushmov, Nikola	316, 336	Peltekes, Omeros	76–77, 90
Murphy-O'Connor, Jerome	63, 90	Perdrizet, Paul	192–93, 232
Murray, Oswyn	85, 90	Perrin, Barnadotte	330, 336
Murray, Timothy J.	28, 59	Pervo, Richard	251, 260, 266
Nasrallah, Laura Salah	3–4, 20–22, 26, 40, 59, 61, 95, 120, 155, 169, 171–73, 176–78, 209, 213, 218–19, 222–23, 226–27, 231–32	Peters, Janelle	303, 310
		Petit, Louis	191, 232
		Petridou, Georgia	83, 90
		Petrakos, Vasileios Ch.	294, 310
Neufeld, Thomas	105, 120	Pfitzner, Victor C.	30, 59
Neyrey, Jerome H.	7, 59	Piejko, Francis	99, 104, 120–24,
Nicholl, Colin R.	94, 120, 124, 145, 148, 330, 336	Pietri, Charles	192, 232
		Pillar, Edward	5, 59
Nickelsburg, George W. E.	132, 148	Pilkington, Nathan	130, 148
Nigdelis, Pantelis M.	44, 46, 59, 64, 155, 170, 172, 178, 199, 232	Pirenne-Delforge, Vinciane	160, 162, 172
		Plevnik, Joseph	99, 120, 123, 125, 143, 148
Nissinen, Laura	101, 121		
Nobbs, Alanna	94, 121		
Nock, A. D.	74, 90	Pollard, John	334
Noreña, Carlos	50, 58	Pollefeyt, Didier	254, 256, 266
North, John	64, 67–68, 75, 84, 87	Pomeroy, Sarah B.	5, 59
Novenson, Matthew K.	3	Porter, Stanley E.	94, 119
Oakes, Peter	326, 336	Pouderon, Bernard	44, 58
Oberhummer, Eugen	176, 236	Preuner, Erich	179, 232
Ogden, Daniel	245, 247	Price, Derek J. de Solla	8, 59
Ogereau, Julien	1, 175–76, 180, 182, 228, 232	Price, Simon	64, 67–68, 71, 72, 75, 84–85, 87, 90
Oldfather, William A.	314, 336	Price, Theodora Hadzisteiou	160, 162, 172
Olshausen, Eckart	325, 334		
Olshausen, Hermann	238, 240, 247	Punt, Jeremy	48, 59
Oster, Richard	313, 336	Rackham, Harris	336
Pachis, Panayotis	22, 59	Raffety, William E.	322, 336
Page, Sven	121	Raubitschek, Antony E.	181, 195–96, 227
Pahl, Michael W.	244, 247		
Paisidou, Melina	207, 232	Rebillard, Éric	182, 232
Pallas, Dēmētrios	178, 232	Reed, Jonathan L.	94, 110, 119

Modern Authors Index

Reinmuth, Eckart 237, 248
Reiprich, Torsten 256, 264
Reynolds, Joyce 285, 293–94, 299
Richard, Earl J. 37, 59, 99, 114, 120, 270, 284, 303
Richards, Kent Harold 37, 59, 66
Riesner, Rainer 124, 148, 176, 233
Rigaux, Béda 37, 60, 270, 284
Ripollès, Pere Pau 11
Rizos, Efthymios 177, 191, 225, 233
Robbins, Vernon 153, 157, 158, 172–73
Robert, Louis 3, 19, 31–33, 60, 190, 233
Roberts, Jennifer Tolbert 59
Roberts, Mark D. 273, 281, 282
Robinson, James M. 95, 120
Rocconi, Eleonora 242–43, 248
Rogers, Edgar 321, 336
Rolfe, J. C. 105, 120, 336
Rollens, Sarah E. 41, 60, 255, 266
Rosenqvist, Jan Olof 177, 234
Rothschild, Clare K. 163, 172
Rouland, N. 50, 60
Rowe, Greg 98, 120
Ruiten, Jacques T. A. G. M. van 255, 265
Rulmu, Callia 1, 60
Runia, David T. 241, 247
Rüpke, Jörg 314
Russel, James R. 40, 60, 173
Rydelnik, Michael A. 254, 266
Rydén, Lennart 177, 234
Sampley, J. P. 31, 54
Sanders, E. P. 68, 87
Sänger, Dieter 141, 148
Santamaría, Marco A. 39, 60
Scanlon, Thomas F. 105, 120
Shantz, Colleen 43, 60
Scheid, John 290, 311
Schiby, Jean 45, 58
Schippers, Reinier 261, 266
Schlueter, Carol J. 253–54, 266
Schmid, Ulrich 258, 266
Schmidt, Daryl 153, 266
Schmidt, Peter 327, 336
Schnelle, Udo 141, 148
Schöllgen, Georg 223, 235
Scholten, Clemens 223, 235
Schoon-Janssen, Johannes 272, 311
Schreiber, Stefan 123, 129, 131, 143, 148, 256, 266
Schubert, Paul 272, 311
Schueller, Matthew 29, 31–32, 35, 36, 60, 241–42, 247
Schuler, Carl 15, 60
Scott, James M. 140, 148, 176
Segre, Mario 297, 311
Shogren, Gary S. 279, 286, 289, 292, 296, 301, 311
Silva-Tarouca, Carlos da 192, 233
Sironen, Erkki 182, 196, 233
Skedros, James C. 208, 233
Skotheim, Mali A. 35, 60
Slaveev, Slavei Theodore 316, 336
Smarczyk, Bernhard 262, 266
Smith, Abraham 274–75, 311
Smith, Murray J. 94, 121
Smith, Roland R. R. 294, 311
Smith, R. Scott 98, 118
Snively, Caroline S. 207, 233
Snyder, James 222–23, 233
Sokolowski, Franciszek 41, 60
Soteriou, Georgios A. 208, 210, 233
Soteriou, Maria G. 208, 210, 233
Sourvinou-Inwood, Christine 85, 90
Spengel, Leonardus 153, 173
Spieser, Jean-Michel 176, 178, 208–10, 212, 218, 220–22, 225, 229, 233–34
Stafford, Emma 11, 60
Standhartinger, Angela 2, 48, 259, 266
Stanley, Christopher 116, 121
Steck, Odil Hannes 131, 148, 256, 261, 266
Stefanidou-Tiveriou, Theodosia 73, 75–79, 88, 90, 169, 173, 234
Stegemann, Ekkehard 160, 173, 255, 266
Stegemann, Wolfgang 160, 173
Stegner, William R. 282, 311
Steimle, Christopher 2, 4, 9, 19, 60, 74, 90
Stewart, Bernard 334

Stiefel, Jennifer H. 48, 60
Still, Todd D. 48, 60, 253–54, 267, 269, 311, 325, 326, 337
Stowers, Stanley K. 270, 280, 311
Strachan, Lionel R. M. 67, 87
Stuhlmann, Rainer 258, 267
Suggs, M. Jack 176, 234
Surber, Dave 316, 336
Talbert, Richard J. A. 8, 60
Tandy, David 59
Tasia, Anastasia 76–77, 90
Taylor, Joan E. 240, 247
Taylor, Justin 266
Taylor, Nicholas H. 251, 267
Tellbe, Mikael 17, 61
Terzēs, Chrēstos 242–43, 248
Theoharidou, Kalliopi 220, 234
Thiselton, Anthony C. 99, 101, 121, 142, 148, 164, 173
Tjäder, Jan-Olof 199, 234
Torp, Hjalmar 177–78, 205, 212–13, 216–19, 224–25, 234
Tougard, Albert 242, 248
Touratsoglou, Ioannis 317–18, 337
Tov, Emmanuel 45, 61
Tredici, Kelly Del 2, 57, 259, 266
Tsantsanoglou, Kyriakos 38, 243, 248
Tsigaridas, Efthymios N. 222–23, 234
Tsouvala, Georgia 59
Tuckett, Christopher M. 63, 88, 143–44, 148
Tuor, Christina 255, 266
Turner, Max 42, 61
Tzanavari, Katerina 5, 19–24, 40, 61
Vasiliev, Alexander 222, 234
Velenis, Giorgos 33, 61, 225, 234
Verhoef, Eduard 23, 61
Vickers, Michael 2–3, 61, 177, 209, 220, 234–35
Viitanen, Eeva-Maria 101, 121
Villiers, Pieter de 152, 158, 169, 173
Vince, Charles A. 302, 311
Vince, James H. 302, 311
Volk, Terence 334
Vos, Craig Steven de 26, 61

Voutyras, Emmanuel 71, 76, 78–79, 88, 90–91, 155, 173
Wagner, Franz 328, 377
Walsh, Robyn 20–22, 26, 40, 61
Volk, Nikolaus 237
Wanamaker, Charles A. 141, 149, 165, 173, 237, 248, 267, 270, 272, 311, 322–23, 337
Ware, James 237, 248
Watson, Duane F. 7, 59, 153, 173
Watt, Jan G. van der 152, 173
Weaver, Paul R. C. 51, 61
Weidmann, Frederick W. 160, 173
Weigand, Edmund 218, 235
Weima, Jeffrey A. D. 24, 61, 71–72, 74, 91, 93, 95–96, 100, 121, 124–25, 149, 163, 173, 238–39, 248, 280–81, 285, 289, 301, 304, 311, 317, 324, 326, 331, 337
Weinstock, Stefan 321, 337
Weiß, Alexander 29, 50, 61
Weissenrieder, Annette 153, 173
Wehrli, Fritz 243, 248
Welborn, Larry L. 16, 38, 61, 101–2, 121
Wengst, Klaus 93, 121, 325, 337
Wheeler, Laurie Ruth 238, 248
White, Joel R. 24, 62, 95–100, 106, 121, 125–26, 132, 136–38, 140, 326, 337
Whiteley, Denys E. H. 269, 311
Whitenton, Michael R. 272, 311
Wick, Peter 255, 266
Wiedeman, Thomas 49, 62
Wiefel, Wilfred 141, 149
Williams, Jonathan 314, 337
Wilson, Stephen 50, 62
Wilson, Todd A. 138, 149
Winn, Adam 318, 335
Winter, Bruce W. 28, 62, 64, 91, 158, 174, 273, 311
Wisskirchen, Rotraut 223, 235
Witherington, Ben, III 94, 121, 238, 248, 282, 305, 311
Witmer, Stephen E. 157, 174
Witt, Rex 4, 62
Woods, Dave 209, 235
Worthington, Ian 303, 311

Wright, Michael T.	8, 62
Wright, N. T.	130, 132, 136, 149
Xyngopoulos, Andreas	220–23, 235
Zabehlicky, Heinrich	177, 229
Zangenberg, Jürgen	128, 147
Zanker, Paul	98, 114, 121
Zeller, Eduard	250
Zerbe, Gordon	116, 121
Zimmermann, Christiane	190, 228
Zoe, Lola	76, 90

www.ingramcontent.com/pod-product-compliance
Lightning Source LLC
Chambersburg PA
CBHW032147010526
44111CB00035B/1241